RAILROADS
IN THE

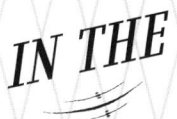

AFRICAN AMERICAN
EXPERIENCE

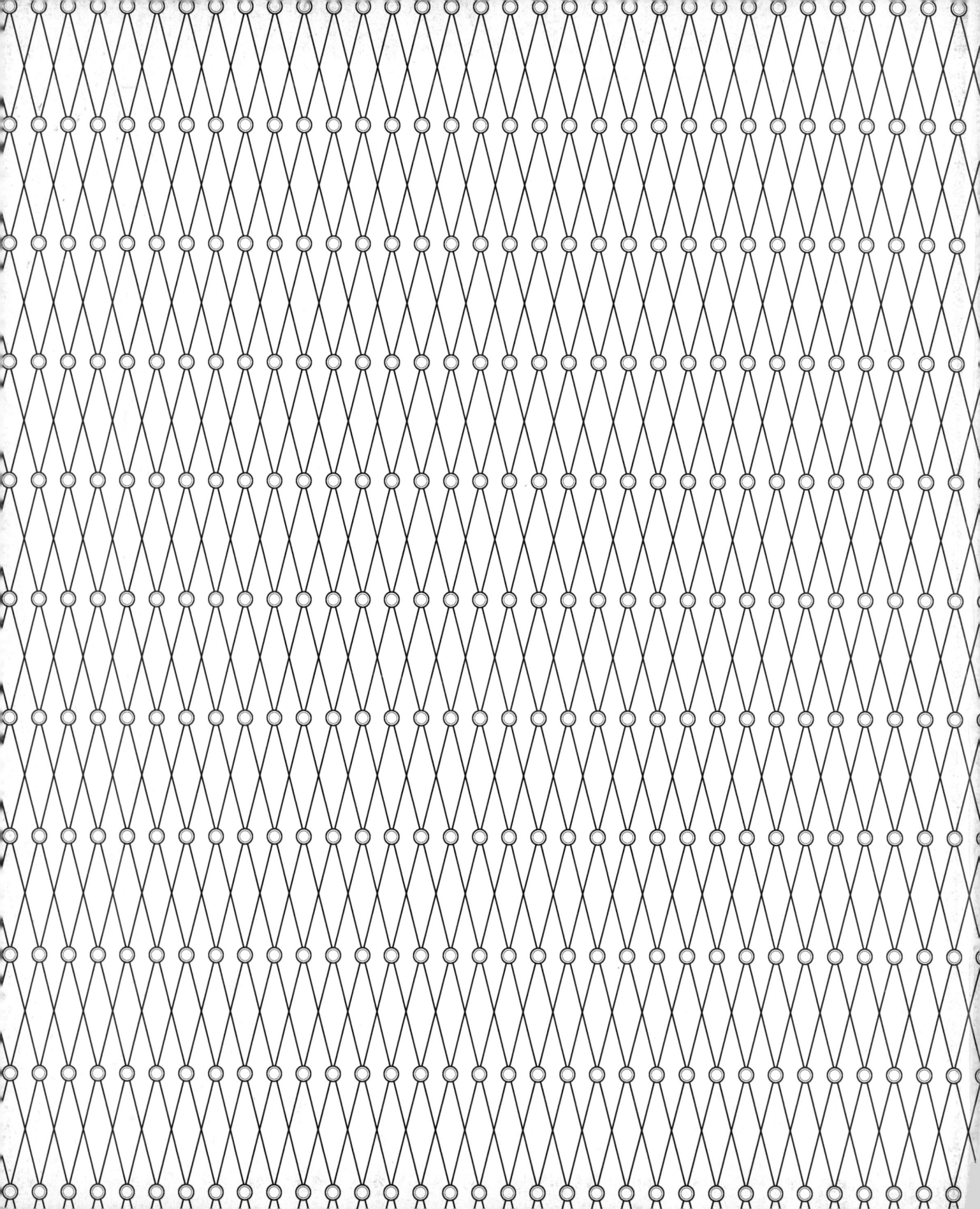

RAILROADS

IN THE

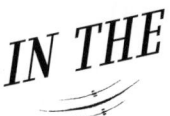

AFRICAN AMERICAN
EXPERIENCE

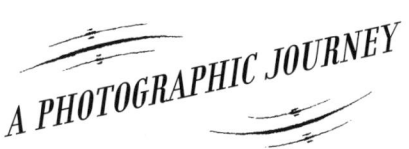

A PHOTOGRAPHIC JOURNEY

THEODORE KORNWEIBEL, JR.

○────────────○

THE JOHNS HOPKINS UNIVERSITY PRESS
Baltimore

The Johns Hopkins University Press
2715 North Charles Street
Baltimore, Maryland 21218-4363
www.press.jhu.edu

Library of Congress Cataloging-in-Publication Data

Kornweibel, Theodore.
  Railroads in the African American experience : a photographic journey /
  Theodore Kornweibel, Jr.
    p. cm.
  Includes bibliographical references and index.
  ISBN-13: 978-0-8018-9162-5 (hardcover : alk. paper)
  ISBN-10: 0-8018-9162-0 (hardcover : alk. paper)
  1. Railroads—United States—Employees. 2. African Americans
    Employment. 3. African Americans—Segregation. I. Title.
  HD8039.R12K67 2009
  331.6'396073—dc22   2008052305

A catalog record for this book is available from the British Library.

*Special discounts are available for bulk purchases of this book.
For more information, please contact Special Sales at 410-516-6936
or specialsales@press.jhu.edu.*

The Johns Hopkins University Press uses environmentally friendly book
materials, including recycled text paper that is composed of at least 30 percent
post-consumer waste, whenever possible. All of our book papers are acid-free,
and our jackets and covers are printed on paper with recycled content.

Book design by Kimberly Glyder Design

To Catherine, once again
To grandchildren Lilyann and Daniel
In memory of Margo Skinner

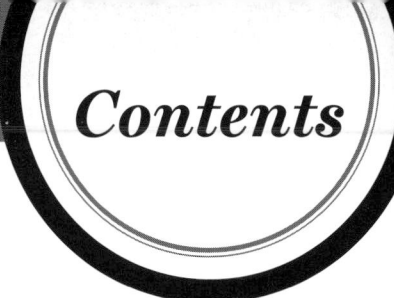

Contents

Preface

This book had serendipitous origins. I received a call from the Railroad Museum of Pennsylvania in 1993, asking if I could recommend anyone to give a talk on African Americans and the railroads. I knew of no one, and a library search revealed that no author had assayed the full sweep of blacks' railroad experiences. But the idea struck a chord in me because it linked two personal passions: African American history (my profession) and railroads (a hobby and lifelong fascination). As a child in the late 1940s and early 1950s I had devoured every railroad book in the public library, but blacks' roles in the industry had never been highlighted and only rarely even acknowledged. So despite the various parts of my background, I had never put the pieces together, although several times I had come close. While studying for my Ph.D. in African American Studies at Yale in the late 1960s, I had found diversion and (physical) therapy as a volunteer gandy dancer (track maintenance worker) on the Valley Railroad, which was rehabilitating an abandoned New York, New Haven & Hartford Railroad line for tourist-train service in eastern Connecticut. Upon completion of my degree, I took a job teaching Black Studies at Lafayette College, and once again brought balance to my life as a volunteer conductor and brakeman on another tourist line, the steam-powered New Hope & Ivyland Railroad, near Philadelphia. And when I moved to California in 1977 to teach African American Studies at San Diego State University, I soon discovered the Pacific Southwest Railway Museum in Campo, outside

San Diego, whose collection includes an ancient Jim Crow car; I have volunteered there for over two decades.

Fast forward to 1993 again. No authority on African American railroad history had surfaced, but I offered to prepare a talk and slide show, covering the basics, for the museum in Pennsylvania. The audience—rail fans and railroad historians, of both races—was more interested than I had expected. Soon I received invitations to repeat the presentation at the Virginia Museum of Transportation, North Carolina Transportation Museum, and California State Railroad Museum, some of the country's other great railroad museums. Everywhere, I encountered enthusiastic audiences. With my own appetite now whetted, I began my first formal research effort, compiling a census of surviving Jim Crow cars.[1]

The progress of research since then has been one eye-opener after another, as I plumbed the collections of nearly three dozen libraries, archives, and historical societies across the nation, particularly in the South. Combining a National Endowment for the Humanities Grant and sabbatical leave from San Diego State University, I was able to devote a full year to research. Then, as I began work on the manuscript, the slavery reparations movement tracked me down. Following the lawsuit filed by reparations crusader Deadria Farmer-Paellman, *USA Today's* business reporter wrote an in-depth article on railroad slavery, based largely on documentation I furnished him and quoting me.[2] Other newspapers picked up the story and I found myself invited to speak at a number of reparations conferences.[3] By then, numerous people, not only in the reparations movement, wanted to see my research, so I published "Railroads and Slavery" in the journal *Railroad History*.[4]

Railroad historians and "rail buffs" alike tend to be passionate about their subject. So, in retrospect, it wasn't surprising that "Railroads and Slavery" drew polarized reactions. Many readers were highly complimentary, but others were sharply critical. I was accused of writing a "gee, ain't it awful" story; failing to acknowledge the (allegedly equivalent) hardships of Irish and Chinese railroad builders; judging the past by present-day standards; and providing ammunition for the "enemy"(unscrupulous reparations activists out to extort money from someone's favorite line). One reader—a life member of the Railway and Locomotive Historical Society, which sponsors the journal—wrote to complain that my article wasn't "*directly* about railroads, railroad equipment, railroad people." I confess, I ignored the second criterion. But the entire article described the practices of specific antebellum southern railroads, with evidence gathered from their published annual reports. Was it possible that black firemen, brakemen, track laborers, and the like, weren't real "railroad people" because they were enslaved, or black? What prompted such negative reactions from a portion of the railroad history fraternity? In fact, I had uncovered unpleasant truths; challenged cherished stereotypes; confronted gender and racial biases; exposed hidden loyalties; and questioned some railroad historians' definitions of their field.

And one railroad, I was to learn, now viewed *me* as an enemy. I wanted to find photographs of Missouri Pacific Railroad employees, particularly since I frequently discuss them in this book. But when I contacted the Union Pacific Museum (the UP acquired the MoPac and its archives in 1982),

I received a phone call from its legal department informing me that, if I had any business with that company, I should address their attorneys. The reason? The UP is a defendant in the reparations lawsuit, and I'm apparently persona non grata because my research identifies a number of slave-using railroads that passed through numerous sales, mergers, and corporate identities over the course of a century and a half, and are today part of the Union Pacific system. Three years later, hoping that I might slip under their radar, I again inquired of the UP Museum regarding photographs, only to be more bluntly informed that I was not welcome there.

Despite the absence of MoPac photographs, I hope readers will find this book rich and informative. Admittedly, the African American railroad story is often not pretty. It's rife with racism. But this story comprises many fascinating chapters, a few of them well known (the Pullman porters; dining-car cooks and waiters), but others rarely, if ever, explored in depth. It enlarges the definition of "railroader" beyond the traditional notion of someone riding in a caboose or the cab of a locomotive. Indeed, black freight house truckers and station matrons, limited by racial barriers to humble and unskilled jobs, were as much railroaders as the engineers and conductors whose positions were reserved for Caucasians. Their pay envelopes came from the same source, and their skills and energies were all essential for the smooth functioning and profitable operation of the railroad.

The narrative that follows is often an inspiring story, unwrapping the resilience and spirit of resistance of black railroaders and their families. Some of the most powerful documentation is found in photographs that reveal dignity and courage under adversity. Discovering these photographs in historical societies and archives, as well as generously being loaned original images by several fine photographers and private collectors, plus finding some unique vintage photos on eBay, has been the most gratifying treasure hunt I have ever conducted.

There were other treasures to be unearthed, which I found as my research methodology unfolded. The social history of black railroading, aside from the experiences of Pullman porters and dining-car waiters and cooks, had been almost completely ignored. The reason was that scholars had neglected to make systematic use of the obituaries, retirement notices, and news items about black railroaders (and often their families) in railroad employee magazines. I studied eleven magazines in detail,[5] covering several decades, plus shorter spans of time for nine others. The *Missouri Pacific Lines Magazine* and the *Norfolk and Western Magazine* actually had separate "From Our Colored Employees" news columns that were written by workers from numerous shops, roundhouses, and freight houses. Other company magazines had extensive employee news columns organized by division and terminal, which included occasional items about black workers. Nearly all of these periodicals, at least up to the end of World War II, identified blacks as "colored" or with a "(c)". These monthly magazines are, by far, the richest surviving documentation on individual black railroaders, containing literally thousands of vignettes with extensive details about their personal lives and families beyond the workplace. These "snapshots," particularly those that were actually written by black railroaders or from copy supplied by them, invest this book with a unique depth and perspective. The black press proved to be an important source for other topics, notably employment discrimination and segregation. Most railroad corporate personnel records, whether for blacks or whites, were not preserved for posterity, but even had they not been discarded, they would reveal far less than is to be discovered in the company magazines.

It is my hope that this volume will unveil a rich heritage for blacks and a fascinating chapter in American (not just African American) history for readers of all hues. Nearly every African American has railroaders two, three, or four generations back, who helped build, maintain, or operate the country's most enduring transportation infrastructure. Yet the struggles and resilience of black railroaders over nearly two centuries are little remembered by their descendants and unknown to most others. In late 2006 I gave a tour of the Pacific Southwest Railway Museum's Jim Crow car (which I and a team of volunteers are currently restoring) and a preview of the contents of this book to 70 delegates attending the annual convention of the National Association of Black Storytellers in San Diego. These visitors were surprisingly unfamiliar with most of the African American railroad story. Few today recall the importance of railroaders to early civil rights activism, or the degree to which the black middle class was built on the foundation of railroad jobs. African Americans made greater contributions to railroading than to any other industry, but who remembers that today? The stories of Pullman porters and dining-car waiters have been popularized, but not those of slaves and convicts, freight truckers, station matrons, engine wipers, and many others. Hence the necessity for this book and these stories. Herein lie examples of hardship and heroism, exploitation and endurance, anger and artistry, revealing what was often a bittersweet encounter with railroads. Although the railroad industry remains viable today, the "railroad age" is a bygone era. All the more reason that the African American railroad heritage should not be forgotten.

A Note on Spelling

So that persons in the text may be understood in context,
I have not corrected idiosyncratic spelling or grammar. I have also not
modernized the spelling of "employe" or "employes," which was standard
usage at least up to 1950, including in the titles of company magazines.

Acknowledgments

It is with profound gratitude that I acknowledge the support, encouragement, and assistance of those who have helped bring this lengthy project to fruition. When I determined to seek grant support for a year off from teaching, devoted to research, I solicited letters of recommendation from the Smithsonian Institution's William Withuhn, my colleague Francis Stites, and the late Walter P. Gray III, then director of the California State Railroad Museum. They must have believed my topic was significant and they must have written eloquently, because I was blessed with a generous National Endowment for the Humanities fellowship plus smaller grants from the Pennsylvania Historical and Museum Commission, the Newberry Library, the Virginia Historical Society, and the Library Company of Philadelphia. I am much indebted to these individuals for writing on my behalf and to the institutions for providing the financial support that made my work possible.

I spent the 1999–2000 academic year conducting research, primarily in the Northeast, upper and lower South, and Southwest, visiting over three dozen libraries, archives, and historical societies. Everywhere I went, archivists and librarians were unfailingly helpful. I particularly want to thank Ellen Halteman, of the California State Railroad Museum, for truly extraordinary assistance. Although I can't begin to name the many others who aided me with great courtesy and professionalism, I hope they will see themselves in these acknowledgments. I am grateful to the staff of the following institutions for helping me while conducting on-site research: Alabama Department of Archives and History; Atlanta History Center; Baltimore & Ohio Railroad Museum; California State Railroad Museum; Chesapeake & Ohio Historical Society; Kheel Center for Labor-Management Documentation and Archives, Cornell University; Darlington (S.C.) Historical Commission; Special Collections Library, Duke University; Georgia Division of Archives and History; Georgia Historical Society; Hagley Museum and Library; Houston Public Library; John W. Barriger III National Railroad Library, St. Louis Mercantile Library; Kansas State Historical Society; Library of Congress; Minnesota Historical Society; Mississippi Department of Archives and History; National Archives, Fort Worth; National Archives, Suitland, Maryland; City Archives and Special Collections, New Orleans Public Library; Schomburg Center for Research in Black Culture, New York Public Library; Newberry Library; North Carolina Division of Archives and History; North Carolina Transportation Museum; Special Collections, Cline Library, Northern Arizona University; Pennsylvania State Archives, Pennsylvania Historical and Museum Commission; Special Collections Library, Pennsylvania State University; Railroad Museum of Pennsylvania; DeGolyer Library, Southern Methodist University; State Library and Archives of Florida; Special Collections Research Center, Syracuse University Libraries; Tennessee State Library and Archives; Howard-Tilton Memorial Library, Tulane University; United States Army Transportation Museum; Special Collections, Ekstrom Library, University of Louisville; Special Collections, University Libraries, University of Maryland; Wilson Library, University of North Carolina; University Archives, University of South Alabama Libraries; South Caroliniana Library, University of South Carolina; McCain Library and Archives, University of Southern Mississippi; Special Collections, University of Texas Libraries; Virginia Historical Society; Virginia Museum of Transportation; Library of Virginia; Special Collections, University Libraries, Virginia Tech University; Western Railway Museum; Wilmington Railroad Museum. I should add to this list Marvin Black of Raleigh, North Carolina, who generously opened his large collection of Southern Railway documents and memorabilia. Seth Bramson likewise allowed me to peruse items in his collection of Florida railroadiana.

Other librarians and archivists at the following institutions graciously responded to email, internet, and phone inquiries: Arkansas History Commission; Art Institute of Chicago; John Hay Library, Brown University Library; Carnegie Museum of Art; Historic Photograph Collection, Dallas Public Library; Durham (N.C.) County Library; Fort Lauderdale Historical Society; Historical Museum of Southern Florida; The History Center, Diboll, Texas; Donnelley and Lee Library, Lake Forest College; Lauren Rogers Museum of Art, Laurel, Mississippi; Michael Rosenfeld Galley, New York; Museum of African American Art, Los Angeles; Pack Memorial Library, Asheville, N.C.; The Phillips Collection; Smithsonian American Art Museum; Swannanoa Valley Museum, Black Mountain, N.C.; Thomaston-Upton Archives, Thomaston, Georgia; P. K. Younge Library of Florida History, University of Florida; Department of Archives and Special Collections, University of Mississippi Libraries; Western Historical Manuscript Collection,

University of Missouri and State Historical Society of Missouri; Western History Collections, University of Oklahoma Libraries; University of South Florida Library; Washington Memorial Library, Macon, Georgia.

Although I spent many nights in commercial lodgings while on research jaunts, it was a blessing to occasionally stay in the homes of friends and family: Martha and Gene Theriot, Marie and John Sanderson, Marion and David Brown, cousin Rhoda and David King, Judy and Chuck Wheaton, and beloved Aunt Margo Skinner, a great scholar who would have rejoiced to see this book in print. Richard and Gay Kornweibel, my gracious brother and sister-in-law, put me up many times while I was conducting research in Sacramento, loaning me a car as well. Betsy and John Mustol let me invite myself for Thanksgiving dinner on what would otherwise have been a very lonely day in western Virginia. Rick and Diane Gren and Bill and Linda Tiffan stored my car while I flew back home for all-too-brief visits. Others who provided hospitality were Dawn and Jerry Sheveland, Allisha and Doug Speed, Kevin and Ann McGhee, Karen Kornweibel, and my kinfolk at the Longacre Family Reunion in Barto, Pennsylvania. A most wonderful example of southern hospitality occurred in Jackson, Mississippi, over a Memorial Day weekend where a convivial crowd took over the motel where I was staying to hold their annual "Pig Out," barbequing a pig, cooking up barrels of spicy crawfish, and inviting me to share their food, drink, music, and merriment while forbidding me from paying a thing.

The manuscript went through many versions, and profited from the skillful critiques of several experts and colleagues. I owe enormous debts to Bill Diven, Chris Baer, Imre Quastler, Francis Stites, and Dan Cupper, who read the manuscript in its entirety and corrected errors, challenged weak assumptions, and in many ways made this a stronger, better book. Dan went further and, unbidden, researched century-old newspaper sources and unearthed many articles that enriched the narrative. Kyle Wyatt and Karen Kornweibel read portions of the manuscript and likewise offered many helpful suggestions. Johns Hopkins University Press's anonymous reader went through the entire manuscript twice, offering detailed suggestions and exposing poorly supported arguments. Although I rebelled against some blunt criticisms, the book is much stronger for his or her assessment. Despite everyone's best efforts, flaws inevitably remain, which are my responsibility alone.

Over the nearly decade and a half of research and writing, my path had been made easier by the assistance of many other individuals. Most I have never met in person. The Railway & Locomotive Historical Society's email discussion group is a marvelous forum for seeking information on the most arcane topics, and I have had many questions answered by persons knowledgeable on railroad technology, terminology, and practices. Other individuals, staff members of libraries and archives, have gone beyond their official duties to answer questions, track down documents, or verify information. A number of photographers and photograph collectors generously provided copies of wonderful images, some of which appear in this volume, others not, only because space and budget would not allow double the present content. I am also indebted to those who permitted me to interview them, usually by telephone. Their experiences filled in significant gaps in my own limited knowledge. Finally, some persons simply heard of my project and, unsolicited, sent me information, photos, and artifacts. Herewith is a list of all those individuals who I have not already thanked, alphabetically ordered because I cannot begin to quantify their assistance: Mark Aldrich, Michele Aldrich, Gregory P. Ames, Denny Anspach, Barney Barnier, Matthew C. Baumgarner, Kurt Bell, Pat Berkley, Antony Blackwell, Ed Bond, Stewart H. Bostic, David Bright, James R. Brown, Shirley Burman, Joe Cammalleri, Theola Campbell, Charles B. Castner, Daniel Chazin, Mac Connery, Earl and Michele Cook, Ray Cooney, Gene Cooper, Frank Corley, John B. Corns, Bob Cosgrove, Gordon S. Crowell, Lou Curtiss, Jeff Darter, Janet Davidson, Dick Dawson, Russ Davies, E. Davis, Buck Dean, John Decker, Tom DeFazio, Steve Delibert, John Denny, Henry Deutch, Thomas Dixon, Patrick C. Dorin, Larry Duffee, Marvin Dunn, George Eichelberger, Adrian Ettlinger, James R. Fair, Mallory Hope Ferrell, J. Barrett Fish, Bev Fitzpatrick, K. Forrest, Fred Gamst, Tom Garver, Rocky Gibbs, Susan Gillis, Jim Gillum, Larry Goolsby, Gene Green, Linda P. Gross, John Gruber, Lester Haines, John Hankey, Jim Harter, Herbert H. Harwood, Marv Havens, Sandy Hayes, Crew Heimer, John O. Hedrick, Donald R. Hensley, Jr., Neill Herring, Robert F. Hinely, Jr., Martha Hodes, Don Hofsommer, Stu Holmquist, Sadie Ann Hood, William F. Howes, Margo Howlett, Harold Hurwitz (The Boyer Corporation), Tom Irion, Muriel M. Jackson, Kenneth R. Janken, Warren Jones, Bob Kennell, Ken Kiegenbein, Tom King, Stan Kistler, Dave Knowles, Fritz N. Kuenzel, Bob Kutella, J. G. Lachaussee, J. Parker Lamb, Phil Lapsansky, John C. LaRue, Jr., Wes Leatherock, Eugene Lewis, Kent Loudon, Ginny Manor, C. K. Marsh, Jr., Steve Massengill, Tom Matoff, John McCall, Frank McGrane, Catherine McGrath, Clare V. McKanna, Jr., Tommy Meehan, Arthur Miller, Bernice Mistrot, Bart Nadeau, Scott Nelson, Rob Neufeld, Cheryl Oakes, Larry Occhiello, Richard Pennick, Joseph Piersen, Jerry Pitts, Nancy Pope, Robert J. Powers, David Price, Mark Priest, Jacki Pryor, Tony Reevy, Mark Reutter, Doug Riddell, Ted Rose, Joel Rosenbaum, Deirdre Routt, Eric Sager, Frank R. Scheer, Margaret Schmedding, Bill Schneider, Warren Scholl, Eric and Maribeth Schwandt, Philip J. Schwarz, Bradley A. Scott, Theodore Shrady, Tom Simpson, Richard Steinheimer, Joyce Y. Suber, Thomas T. Taber, John Teichmoeller, Russell Tedder, Abraham Thompson, Isaac Thompson, Charles Toombs, Barbara True, Peggy True, Allen Tuten, Charles Varnes, Harold K. Vollrath, Andrew Waldo, John Walker, Andrew L. Warren, Bob Webber, John H. White, Russell T. Wigginton, Jane Willis, Ray Wongus, Douglas Wornom, Ron Wright, Jim Wrinn, and Craig Zeni. My apologies to anyone whose name I have inadvertently missed.

I would be remiss in not acknowledging the support I received from San Diego State University. A sabbatical leave grant for 1999–2000, coupled with the NEH fellowship, made possible a full year's research. I was also the beneficiary of several smaller research grants that helped pay for travel and photocopying. The Interlibrary Loan office worked tirelessly to obtain obscure materials in timely fashion. I also wish to express appreciation to the staff of the Instructional Technology Service who helped me learn PhotoShop and assisted greatly in enhancing the images in this book: Rob Drake, Jim Edwards, Tom Farrington, Charles Hurley, Mark Pastor, Jon Rizzo, and Carol Tohsaku.

Finally, the support of friends and family is incalculable. Glen Scorgie, my faithful prayer partner and a fellow scholar, sympathized with my frustrations and helped me see things in better perspective. Sons Daniel and James endured a year of their teens with their father gone much of the time on research trips. That they do not appear to have suffered from my absences is due to the patient and sacrificial parenting of Catherine, my treasured wife for over 40 years. She has always believed in the significance of this book and has been a good listener and voice of sanity as I've unloaded stress and irritation. Although a previous volume was dedicated to her, she again deserves such recognition. And to God be the glory: He has blessed this endeavor bountifully and been my "refuge and strength."

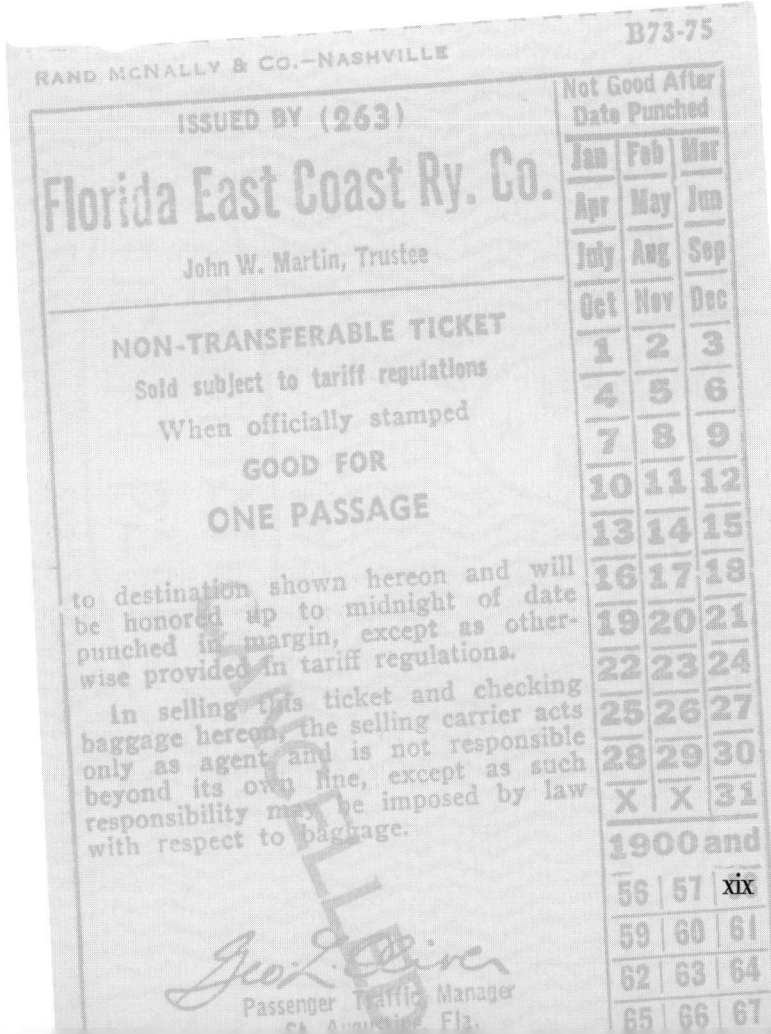

Abbreviations

ACL	Atlantic Coast Line
ACRT	Association of Colored Railway Trainmen
AFL	American Federation of Labor
AFL-CIO	American Federation of Labor–Congress of Industrial Organizations
AT&SF	Atchison, Topeka & Santa Fe
BDCCW	Brotherhood of Dining Car Cooks and Waiters
BLFE	Brotherhood of Locomotive Firemen and Enginemen
B&O	Baltimore & Ohio
B&OCT	Baltimore & Ohio Chicago Terminal
BRC	Brotherhood of Railway Clerks
BRT	Brotherhood of Railway Trainmen
BSCP	Brotherhood of Sleeping Car Porters
CCC	Civilian Conservation Corps
CN	Canadian National
CNJ	Central of New Jersey
C&NW	Chicago & North Western
C&O	Chesapeake & Ohio
C of G	Central of Georgia
CPR	Canadian Pacific Railway
CTA	Colored Trainmen of America
CV	Cumberland Valley
C&W	Cincinnati & Westwood
DCRFW	Dining Car and Railroad Food Workers
DL&W	Delaware, Lackawanna & Western
D&S	Durham & Southern
EEOC	Equal Employment Opportunity Commission
EMD	Electro-Motive Division
FEC	Florida East Coast
FEPC	Fair Employment Practice Committee
G&A	Greenwood & Augusta
GC&SF	Gulf, Colorado & Santa Fe
GM	Gainesville Midland
GM&O	Gulf, Mobile & Ohio
HRE	Hotel and Restaurant Employees
IARE	International Association of Railway Employees
IBRC	International Brotherhood of Red Caps
IC	Illinois Central
ICC	Interstate Commerce Commission
IGN	International-Great Northern
LCL	less than carload lot
L&N	Louisville & Nashville
M&PR	Mississippi & Pearl River

M&WP	Montgomery & West Point
MoPac	Missouri Pacific
MOW	maintenance of way
NAACP	National Association for the Advancement of Colored People
NAPE	National Alliance of Postal Employees
NCFHESE	National Council of Freight Handlers, Express and Station Employees
NCRR	North Carolina Railroad
NP	Northern Pacific
NS	Norfolk Southern
N&W	Norfolk & Western
NYC	New York Central
OSCP	Order of Sleeping Car Porters
PRR	Pennsylvania Railroad
R&B	rhythm and blues
R&D	Richmond & Danville
RF&P	Richmond, Fredericksburg & Potomac
R&G	Raleigh & Gaston
RIP	repair in place
RMA	Railway Mail Association
RMIBIA	Railway Men's International Benevolent Industrial Association
RMS	Railway Mail Service
R&P	Richmond & Petersburg
RPC	railway postal clerk
RPO	Railway Post Office
SAL	Seaboard Air Line
SP	Southern Pacific
SRR	Southern Railroad
UP	Union Pacific
USRA	U.S. Railroad Administration
VS&T	Vicksburg, Shreveport & Texas
WM	Western Maryland
WPA	Works Progress Administration
Y&MV	Yazoo & Mississippi Valley

Editor's Note

This volume consists of chronologically arranged illustrations interspersed
with thematic essays. The latter appear among the illustrations roughly where
an image or two will illustrate the subject of the essay. The number of images
separating the essays accordingly varies and, not surprisingly,
the more recent years are more generously illustrated.

RAILROADS

IN THE

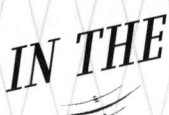

AFRICAN AMERICAN
EXPERIENCE

Prologue

Little did Rose know how cruelly her life would change when her owner, Frederick Nims, secured a contract in 1857 to build a section of the Charleston & Savannah Railroad. Nims, a Massachusetts-born, Andover-educated civil engineer, had come south two decades before to work on the Georgia Railroad, launching a career as a railroad surveyor and contractor. He eventually settled in Rock Hill, South Carolina, in the upcountry Piedmont region among its many Scots-Irish Presbyterians who had migrated down from Pennsylvania a century before. The backbone of the local economy was small-scale cotton farming. Most landowners possessed only a few slaves, although 40 percent of York County's population was black and enslaved. Rose was a domestic servant in the Nims household, almost certainly married, in her late 30s or early 40s, and with a husband and children also owned by Nims.[1] Working in the household, living in or near the bustling new town of Rock Hill—just recently connected to Charlotte, North Carolina, by railroad—could not have prepared her for life as a cook on a railroad construction gang in the swamps along the South Carolina seacoast.

Building the Charleston & Savannah Railroad was no simple task. It had to cross 13 rivers and innumerable streams and swamps in a region that was as much watershed as land. Large cotton and rice plantations, the latter dependent upon tidal surges, anchored the local economy. Nims arranged to use hired (rented) slaves, supplemented by Irish workers, to construct several miles of roadbed and 1,000 feet of trestle over the Ashepoo River. Although he brought some hired slaves from Rock Hill, his preference was local Ashepoo chattels. While the average summer high temperature was the same as in Rock Hill, around 90 degrees Fahrenheit, it was much more humid at the river, with malaria-spreading mosquitoes in abundance. Whereas Rose had dwelt in Nims's house, she would now live in a tent, and later in a rude cook shanty. She would know none of the male slaves whom Nims hired from local planters. How she would react to the Irish workers, and they to her, can only be conjectured. Certainly, as the only woman, she would be sexually vulnerable at the isolated construction site.[2]

Assuming Nims himself brought Rose to the Ashepoo, it was a tedious 3-day, 250-plus-mile journey. The Charlotte & South Carolina Railroad's southbound accommodation (passenger) train left Rock Hill at about 9:30 at night and took nearly 8 hours to traverse 83 miles, reaching Columbia, South Carolina, at a little after 5:00 a.m. Rose probably sat on a bench in a second-class, or "negro," car, otherwise in a baggage car. Nims rode in a first-class coach, but it hardly provided a luxurious ride or encouraged sleep. If there were no delays, breakdowns, or derailments and the train arrived on time, they boarded separate cars on a South Carolina Railroad train in Columbia at 6:00 a.m., transferred to a mainline train at Branchville soon after noon, and arrived in Charleston at 4 o'clock in the afternoon, completing this 130-mile portion of their journey at an average 13 miles per hour. The following day, they took a coach running on the old stagecoach road built in the 1720s between Charleston and Savannah, which the new railroad line roughly paralleled, finally reaching the construction camp, surely exhausted, after about 50 bumpy miles.[3]

Whereas Rose had recently prepared a variety of dishes for the Nims family (and herself) with both staples and fresh items from the local market and a kitchen garden, a much different task now awaited her. She was equipped with only a few basic cooking utensils and a week's supply of bacon, flour, coffee, sugar, corn meal, and grits, a typical high-carbohydrate, protein- and vitamin-deficient slave diet. As surviving documents make no mention of other cooks, it is assumed that Rose must have worked extremely hard, food preparation including building cooking fires and drawing water.

Rose cooked on the Ashepoo only until mid-July, when she and the other "upcountry black hands" were sent into a healthier inland region to cut crossties and 100,000 feet of the 10-inch-square timbers needed for the trestle. Only slaves acclimated to coastal regions, who had acquired immunities to tropical diseases, could be risked to work in the lowcountry during the malarial season, but Nims kept the Irish laborers on task. He was, after all, liable for the health and medical bills only of slaves. A sick Irishman was simply unpaid during his illness. Nonetheless, Nims, like contractors throughout the South, preferred slave labor. Other sections of the line were under contract to local planters who used their own bondsmen when they were not needed in the fields.[4] This practice, of amateur planter-contractors employing their superfluous slaves during slack agricultural periods to build portions of right of way, was widespread across the South.

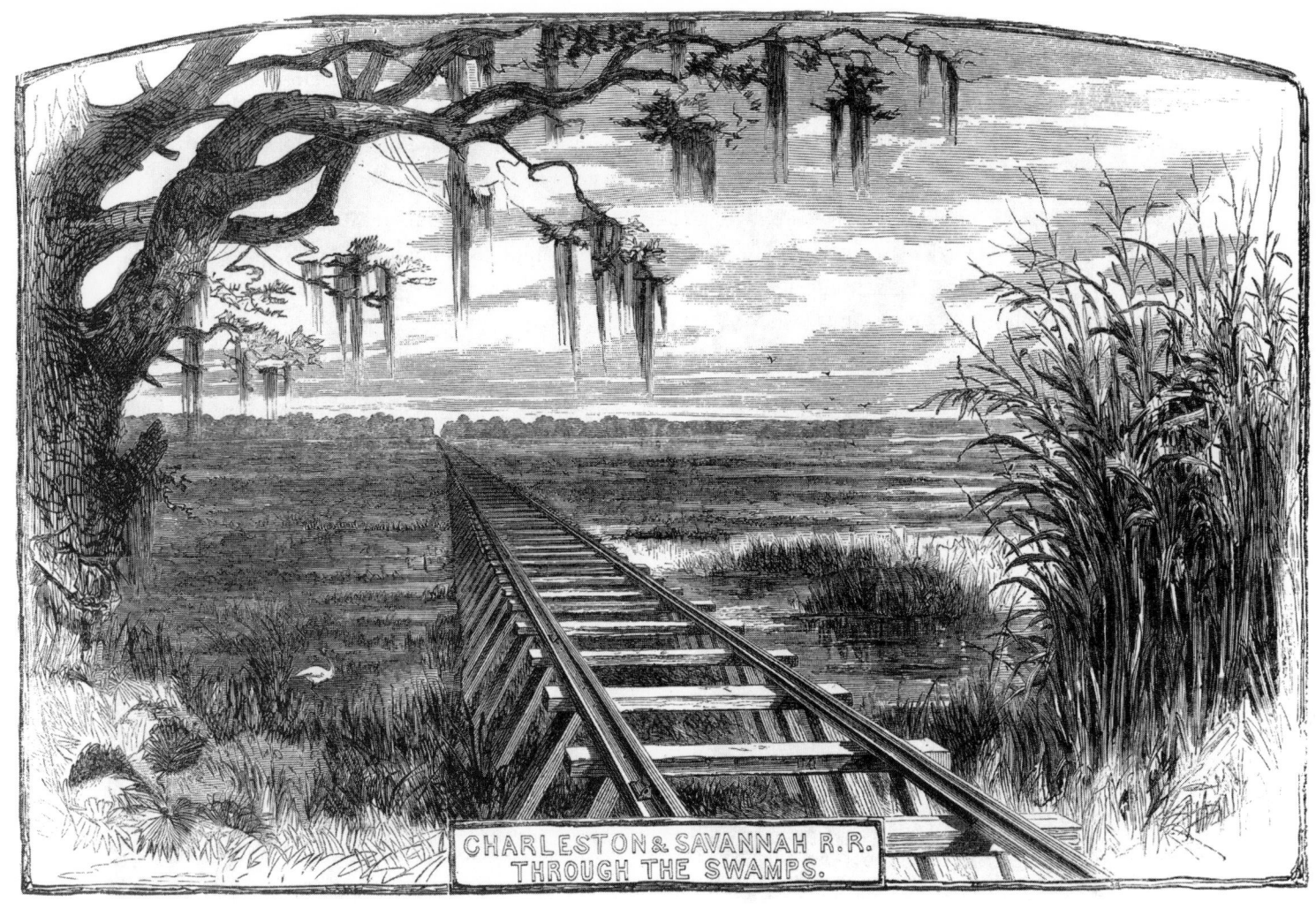

CHARLESTON & SAVANNAH R.R.
THROUGH THE SWAMPS.

*The African American railroad experience
began in slavery, and among the first female
railroaders were bondswomen like Rose, who
cooked for black slave and Irish construction
crews building roadbed and trestles for the
Charleston & Savannah Railroad across
South Carolina's Ashepoo River watershed in
the late 1850s. Theodore Kornweibel collection*

The health risks to the upcountry slaves were over by mid-fall, when they returned to the Ashepoo. Those for whom Rose cooked continued to grade, ditch, and build trestles into 1858 until work again came to a standstill in late June when nearly all the workers, except for "the acclimated negroes of this section," sickened from malaria. Nims himself became quite ill and longed to return home to recuperate but did not feel at liberty to do so "as long as I have a negro of my own here. They would get sick and die off." Rose and the other upcountry blacks eventually returned to Rock Hill to wait out the remainder of the malarial months. Not until late October did she return to the construction camp, now accompanied by some of Nims's own male slaves.[5] Rose's story vanishes from the historical record at this point.

Rose introduces us to many aspects of the African American railroad experience. Slaves were the primary railroad builders in the antebellum South, with women occasionally participating not only as cooks, but even as construction laborers. Railroads and railroad construction contractors sometimes owned slaves, but more often hired them from owners who had a surplus. After slavery, blacks continued to be the preferred muscle for southern railroad expansion, so much so that the states actively promoted their use through the infamous convict lease system. At the same time as Rose cooked for construction slaves on the Ashepoo, thousands of male slaves provided the backbone for repairing the South's trackage. After emancipation they continued to dominate southern maintenance of way forces, while in other parts of the nation they worked alongside men of European immigrant stock in integrated track gangs. Rose's contemporaries also included many enslaved firemen and brakemen, plus numerous others who supplied labor for roundhouses, freight houses, and passenger stations. These employment patterns, too, persisted after the end of slavery. With the growth of long-distance passenger service and amenities after the Civil War, many of Rose's male descendants found "cleaner" jobs (but worked just as hard) serving travelers as Pullman and coach porters and dining-car cooks and waiters, all in racially circumscribed roles. And in the twentieth century, during both world wars, Rose's granddaughters and great-granddaughters stepped into men's shoes to fill the labor gaps. Over the long sweep of the Industrial Revolution, railroads provided more jobs for African Americans, and supported more black families and community institutions, than any other business.

But the railroads' impact was always more than a matter of economics. They shaped the lives of generations of blacks. Like Rose, subsequent southern generations had to ride in segregated and usually inferior Jim Crow passenger cars. Many others, again like Rose, were separated for varying lengths of time from family and friends when railroad employment took them far from home. In a more positive sense, railroads provided the only practical means, for many decades, for blacks to migrate in search of new economic opportunities or for political or social freedoms. No wonder that railroads percolated into black culture and came to symbolize hopes and dreams as well as heartaches and disappointments. Rose could not rise above her status as an enslaved woman, and until passage of civil rights legislation in the 1960s, black railroaders—still overwhelmingly male—could advance no farther than had their railroading great-grandfathers.

Nonetheless, railroads were important to generations of African Americans, at the least offering the hope of escaping sharecropping and economic servitude. And a steady railroad job was a *good* job, one in which men and occasionally women, along with their families, took pride. But it didn't begin that way: it began with Rose and her enslaved compatriots.

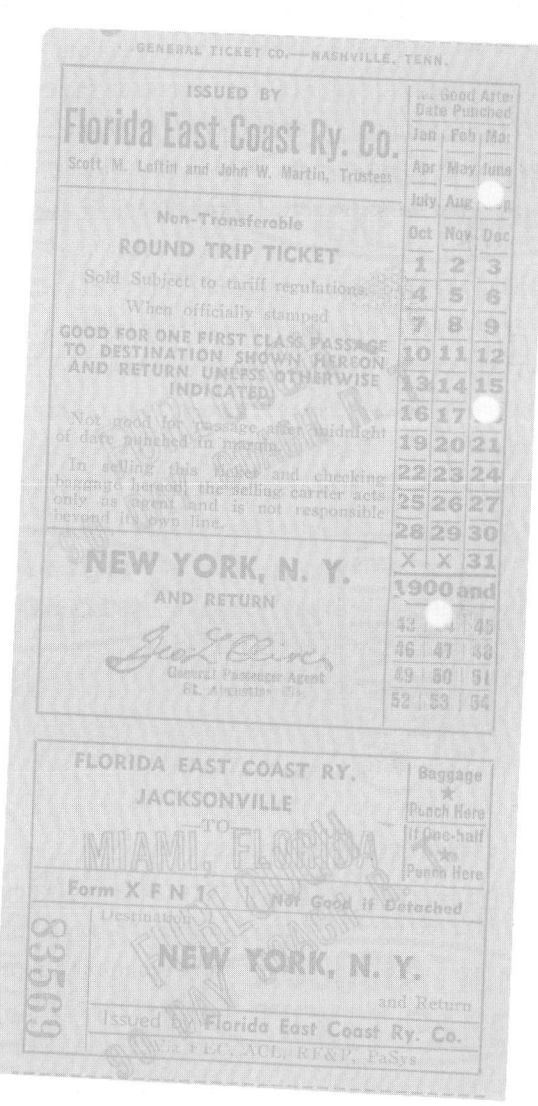

The Mobile & Girard Railroad began construction in 1854 with contractors being paid one-third in cash, one-third in stock, and one-third in five-year bonds. This contractors' offer of $180 hire two years later was a high price, reflecting a booming economy and relative scarcity of slaves. The line, built westward from Girard, Alabama, on the Alabama–Georgia line, only extended 52 miles by the Civil War and never reached Mobile, nearly 200 miles farther. Theodore Kornweibel collection

The South Carolina Railroad, like many other antebellum southern lines, used slaves in train operations. A slave fireman and a "train hand" (brakeman) were part of the crew of the first train pulled by the locomotive West Point in 1831. The car loaded with cotton was not freight; the bales were intended to shield the passengers in the coaches behind from exposure to a boiler explosion. Theodore Kornweibel collection

WANTED,

For the Year 1856, Fifty able-bodied

NEGRO MEN,

To lay Track on the Mobile and Girard Railroad.
Terms, $180 per annum, with good security.

Address PILLSBURY & BROTHER.
Columbus, Ga.

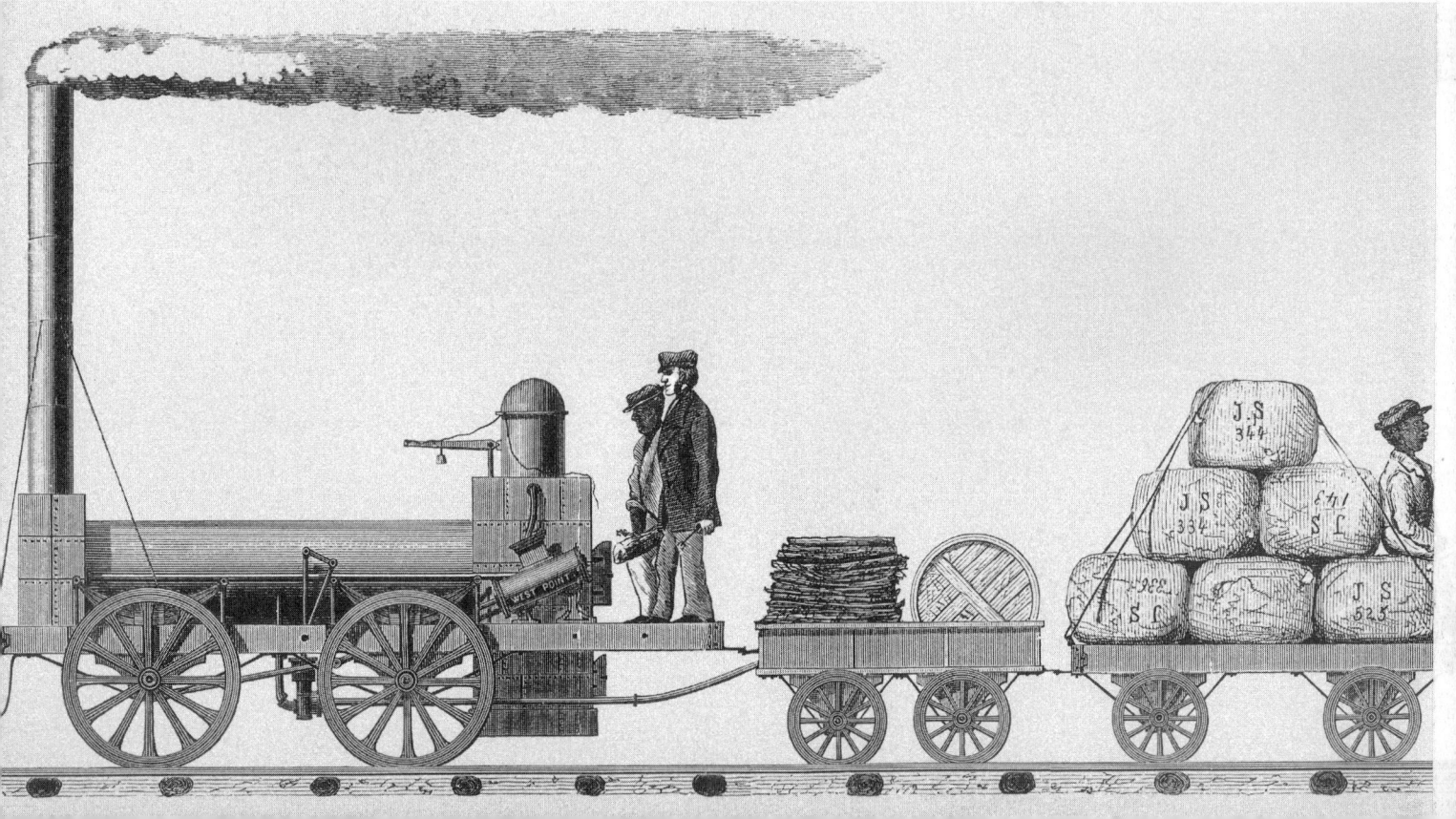

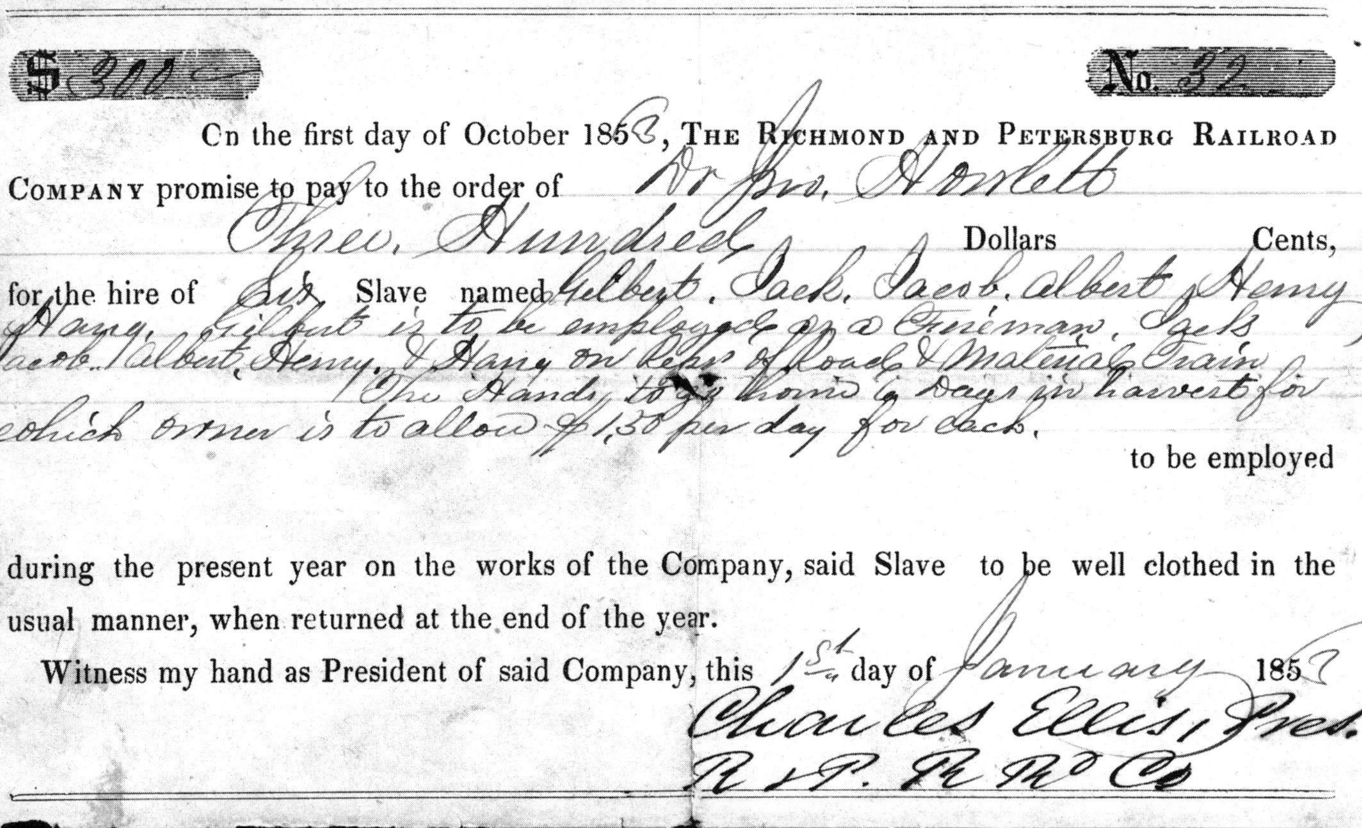

$ 300   No. 32

On the first day of October 185_, THE RICHMOND AND PETERSBURG RAILROAD
COMPANY promise to pay to the order of *Dr. Jno. Howlett*

Three Hundred Dollars Cents,

for the hire of *Six* Slave named *Gilbert, Jack, Jacob, Albert, Henry*
& Hany, Gilbert is to be employed as a Fireman. Jack
Jacob, Albert, Henry, & Hany on Road & Material Train
The Hands to go home 6 days in harvest for
which owner is to allow $1.50 per day for each.

to be employed

during the present year on the works of the Company, said Slave to be well clothed in the
usual manner, when returned at the end of the year.

Witness my hand as President of said Company, this *1st* day of *January* 185_

Charles Ellis, Pres.
R & P. R R Co

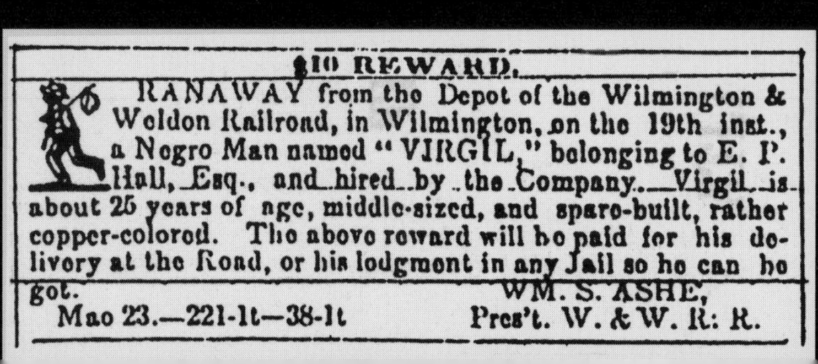

$10 REWARD.

RANAWAY from the Depot of the Wilmington &
Weldon Railroad, in Wilmington, on the 19th inst.,
a Negro Man named "VIRGIL," belonging to E. P.
Hall, Esq., and hired by the Company. Virgil is
about 25 years of age, middle-sized, and spare-built, rather
copper-colored. The above reward will be paid for his delivery at the Road, or his lodgment in any Jail so he can be
got.   WM. S. ASHE,
Mao 23.—221-1t—38-1t   Pres't. W. & W. R: R.

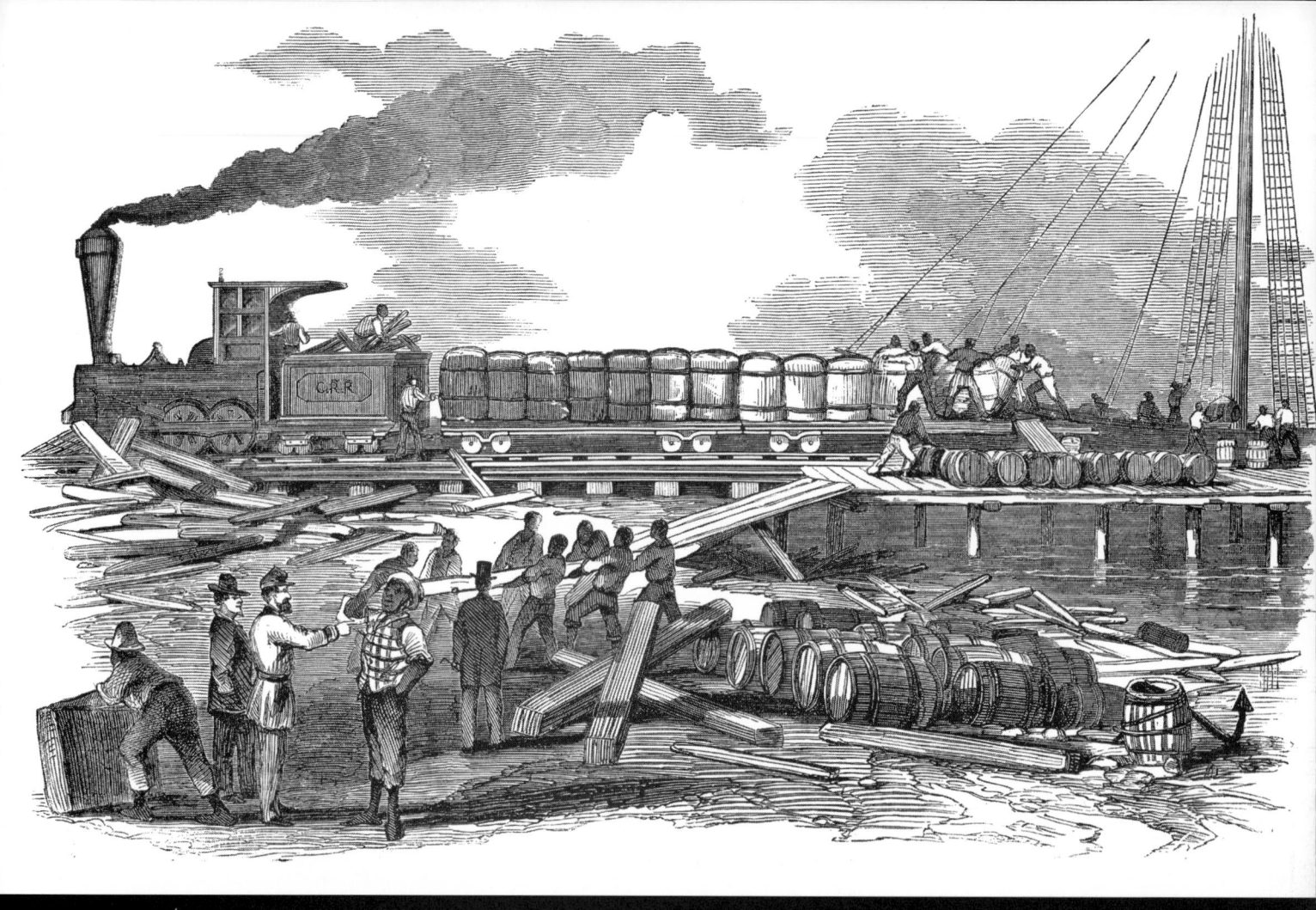

From the earliest railroad days, antebellum southern lines utilized slave "depot hands" to load and unload freight. In Union-occupied Fernandina, Florida, a Florida Railroad crew handles turpentine, cotton, and resin for shipment to New York in 1862, early in the Civil

Ingenious slaves used the railroads to flee from bondage. John Thompson, sold from Virginia to Alabama, escaped back to Virginia in 1857 by riding on the top of train cars at night and hiding during the day. Although he reunited with his family, he was caught and sold again. Eventually Thompson escaped to the North and secured his freedom. Theodore Kornweibel collection

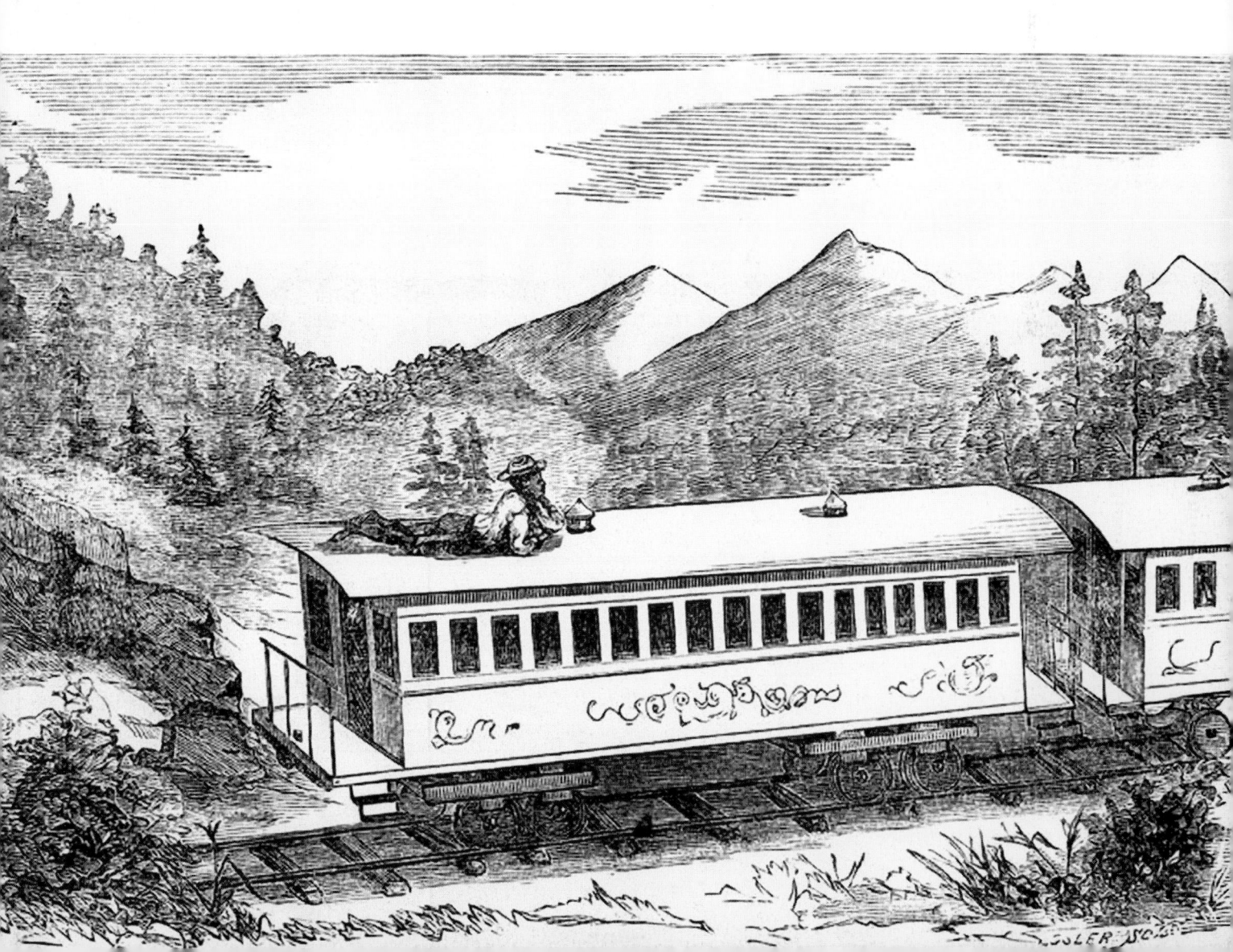

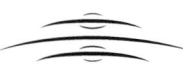

"NEGROES WILL DO MORE WORK"

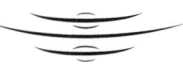

Slavery and the Dawn of Southern Railroading

In the summer of 1836, an advertisement ran in newspapers in Washington, D.C., Virginia, and North Carolina: "Wanted to hire. Any number of Able Bodied Men, for one, two, or three years. The Alabama, Florida & Georgia Rail Road Company engaged in the location and construction of a Rail-Road from Pensacola in West Florida, to Columbus, in Georgia (a distance of 200 miles) are desirous to hire for one, two, or three years as may be preferred by proprietors, as many as 4 or 500 able bodied negro men, from 18 to 40 or 45 years of age, to be employed in felling, cutting, and hewing timber, and in forming the excavations and embankments upon the route of said Rail Road."[1] This notice illustrates the main contours of the railroad slavery story. Slaves constructed most of the antebellum South's 8,784-mile (by 1861) rail network. They were frequently separated by time and distance from their families, forced to perform hard physical labor in climates where they were exposed to unfamiliar health perils. Enslaved African Americans also constituted the bulk of the workforce that maintained tracks and roadbed in good repair. Although they had no racial monopoly, large numbers of enslaved firemen, brakemen, and switchmen operated the South's trains. Slaves also loaded and unloaded freight cars. Railroads either purchased or, more commonly, hired (rented) slaves from individual owners, who profited handsomely from such transactions. By 1860, just before the Civil War, southern railroads worked nearly 15,000 slaves.

Railroad slavery was neither haphazard nor modest. In 1859, one-third of all southern lines employed 100 or more slaves, ranging from 1,200 at work building the Atlantic & Gulf Railroad in Georgia, to 500 building the Vicksburg, Shreveport & Texas Railroad, to 400 or more toiling on 7 other lines. In contrast, no single plantation was home to as many as 1,200 slaves, and 400 bondsmen were to be found on only a very few large estates. Perhaps the largest single concentration of enslaved railroaders was the 1,493 men and 425 boys at work constructing the North Carolina Railroad in 1852.[2]

Even the outbreak of Civil War did not diminish the use of slaves. New lines were rushed to completion to facilitate more efficient transport of soldiers and supplies. The Milledgeville Railroad, for example, pushed construction of its line from Macon to Sparta, Georgia, with a force of 1,000 hands using 210 mule-drawn carts.[3] Although the pace of new construction slackened, the necessity for slave labor increased as white men were absorbed into the Confederate army. And in areas of intense fighting, such as along the Richmond, Fredericksburg & Potomac Railroad in northern Virginia, both sides destroyed tracks and bridges, requiring larger than customary repair gangs. By the end of the war, some southern railroads were resorting to military-ordered impressments of slaves in order to keep operating.

The railroads' reliance on enslaved workers was not unusual. All other major southern industries—including canal and turnpike construction; coal, iron, gold, and lead mining; iron, tobacco, textile, and hemp manufacturing; lumbering; turpentine distilling; fisheries; and steamboat transportation—utilized slaves. Railroad slavery was unique, however, in that the vast majority of its bonded workers were hired, whereas other industries owned about four out of five of their enslaved laborers. In fact, the slave economy was flexible and elastic, just what the often capital-strapped new railroads needed.[4]

It was logical for southern railroads to use slaves from the start because unfree workers had already been used to build canals and levees. In the 1790s, more than three decades before the first railroads emerged, hundreds of slaves were purchased to dig South Carolina's 22-mile-long Santee Canal. Half of them were women. One Carolinian observed that "in ditching, particularly in canals, . . . a woman can do nearly as much work as a man." Santee Canal slaves were expected to haul 54 wheelbarrow-loads of earth daily during the excavation phase. The Dismal Swamp Canal also owned slaves in the early 1800s. In 1829, the state of Georgia owned 190 chattels for use on river and road projects. And in the final decade before the Civil War, the Cape Fear & Deep River Navigation Company purchased slaves of both sexes for work on its canal. Slave-hiring enterprises included the Potomac Canal (1780s); James River Canal (1790s–1800s); and Brunswick (Georgia) Canal (1830s).[5]

Mid-nineteenth-century railroad construction was extremely arduous. Steam shovels had not yet been invented, and few antebellum railroad builders used pile drivers. Black powder (gunpowder) was the only explosive available for hard rock blasting.[6] Tunneling and digging cuts through hills were accomplished mostly with hand drills, picks, shovels, and wheelbarrows, and by mule-

The Charleston & Savannah Railroad, like other antebellum southern lines, hired and occasionally owned female slaves. The differences in hiring rates indicate not only that the women worked as cooks for maintenance of way gangs rather than as section laborers, but also a high regional cost of prime male laborers and the greater safety risks of industrial versus agricultural slavery. Theodore Kornweibel collection

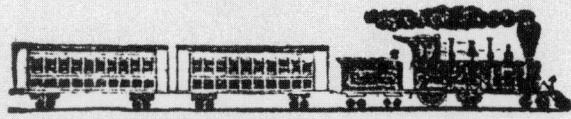

NOTICE.
OFFICE CHARLESTON AND SAVANNAH R. R.,
CHARLESTON, 2d December, 1859.

THIS COMPANY IS DESIROUS OF HIRING NEGRO HANDS, to work upon the repairs of their Road for the ensuing year, 1860.
 Will pay for Men from 150 to 180 dollars per annum; for Women, from 60 to 96 dollars per annum. Payments to be made quarterly, in April, July, October and January.
 Contracts can be made with James M. Rabb, Master Machinist, or the President in Charleston.
EDW. L. PARKER,
December 3   Sec'ry and Treasurer C. and S. R. R. Co.

drawn carts, plows, and scrapers. Construction was labor-intensive and technologically primitive. The first task was clearing brush and chopping down trees, followed by "grubbing" (removing boulders and stumps and excavating cuts). Finally, "graduation" (grading) involved leveling and filling the uneven ground so that crossties and rails could be laid on an even roadbed. Some contractors' gangs laid track, but it was also common for the railroads to use their own labor to complete the right of way. On the Charleston & Savannah Railroad, construction slaves were expected to excavate 12 cubic yards of sand, silt, and clay—about 14 tons—each day, whether in the cold of winter or the heat of summer.[7]

Railroad construction was not a task for the weak. Overseers, like those on plantations, supervised railroad slaves, often driving them strenuously. Contractor F. H. King, building part of the Charlotte & South Carolina Railroad, was unapologetic about the amount of labor he expected: "I go out there about half past five and get the niggers to work." This did not leave time to cook breakfast, so they ate cold food prepared the evening before. They were not fed again until 12:30 p.m., and then worked from 2 o'clock until sundown. This was at least a 14-hour workday during the summertime. No wonder that some of his laborers were, in King's words, "'damn' mean ones."[8]

Railroad building was also dangerous. Slaves were injured or killed in premature explosions and cave-ins, or in being struck by trains or handcars. They sickened and sometimes died from scarlet fever, cholera, and malaria, especially when contractors shifted them from one region—and disease environment—to another. It was a prudent contractor who vaccinated his hands against smallpox. The rigors of labor made it difficult for sick slaves to recover, particularly when returned

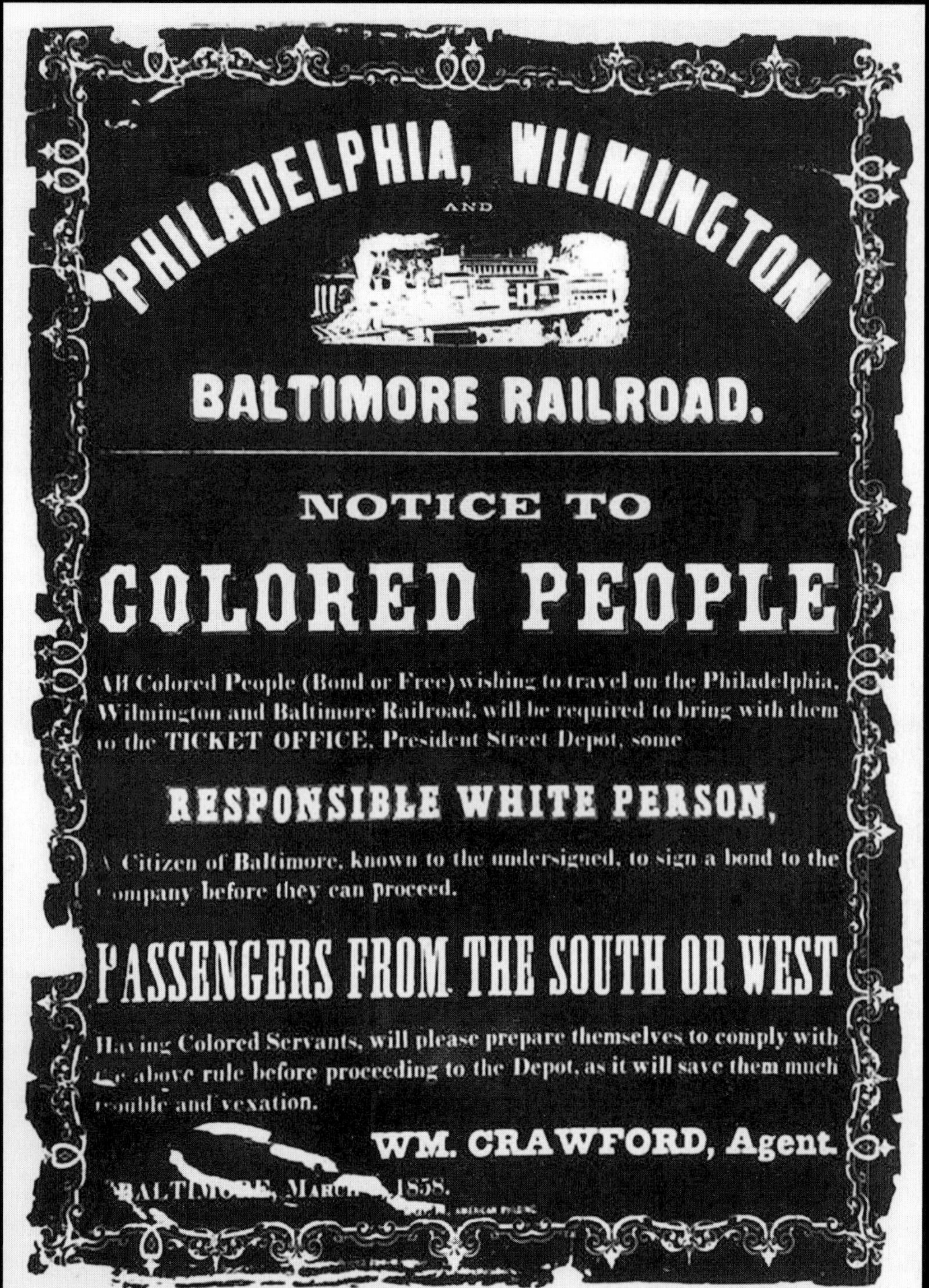
PHILADELPHIA, WILMINGTON
AND
BALTIMORE RAILROAD.

NOTICE TO
COLORED PEOPLE

All Colored People (Bond or Free) wishing to travel on the Philadelphia, Wilmington and Baltimore Railroad, will be required to bring with them to the TICKET OFFICE, President Street Depot, some

RESPONSIBLE WHITE PERSON,

A Citizen of Baltimore, known to the undersigned, to sign a bond to the Company before they can proceed.

PASSENGERS FROM THE SOUTH OR WEST

Having Colored Servants, will please prepare themselves to comply with the above rule before proceeding to the Depot, as it will save them much trouble and vexation.

WM. CRAWFORD, Agent.

BALTIMORE, MARCH [illegible], 1858.

to work too soon. When some conscienceless contractors sought to save money by scrimping on housing, slaves suffered from living in crude shanties or tents, or simply camping out in the open at the worksite. Mosquitoes prevented restful sleep in summer. Inadequate shelter in winter brought death from pneumonia and loss of limbs from frostbite. In one particularly egregious case, a contractor on the Atlantic & North Carolina Railroad kept slaves in "a square pen, made of pine poles, with large cracks, through which one might thrust his double fists, . . . [with] no shutter to the door." The roof did not shed water, and there was "no chimney and no floor, no bed clothing and no cooking utensils."[9]

Not surprisingly, some owners refused to hire out their property for railroad work.[10] Others did so, but took out insurance policies or insisted on contracts that excluded their slaves from the most dangerous tasks, like blasting. Lawsuits reveal that such agreements did not deter unscrupulous contractors or railroad managers from exposing hired slaves to risks. In one form of contract, owners received a greater-than-market payment for hiring out their slaves, while acknowledging that "all risks incurred, or liability to accidents . . . is compensated for and covered in the pay agreed upon."[11] In other cases, owners were willing to hire out their slaves for dangerous work but required the railroad or contractor to carry insurance on the full value of the slaves in case they should suffer permanent injury, die of disease or from an accident, or take advantage of lax supervision and run away.[12] Some owners who initially hired out their slaves subsequently abandoned the practice, one writing that "I shall not let my negroes work on the Rail Road any longer . . . for they don't take care of them and it is better to feed them and let them do nothing than to have them crippled up and no care taken of them."[13] And although neither southern nor northern white women would have been considered for labor of this nature, black women also toiled on southern railroad construction projects.

Mississippi slave owner Samuel Smith Downey hired out 27 of his slaves, including 11 women and children, to a contractor building the ill-fated Mississippi & Pearl River Railroad in 1836 northeast from Natchez toward Jackson. At least two slaves were elderly. In an unusual arrangement, Downey's agent, physician Joseph T. Hicks, accompanied the slaves. Although local residents reassured Hicks that "this is a very healthy section of the country," he predicted "we may calculate upon losing some of them in becoming acclimated."[14] Indeed, nearly every slave took sick during the next two years.

Working close to the Mississippi River proved to be unhealthy, and Downey's slaves suffered from a variety of illnesses. Lucy's child died suddenly of the croup. A dozen slaves had diarrhea at the same time. Abednigo fell painfully sick with rheumatism and a bladder stoppage, but was cured when Hicks bled him and gave him a cathartic. Old Uncle Lewis was also ill. Hicks complained that "it takes all my time to attend to them—we have been fortunate in not losing any of them. The hearse has been running regularly bearing bodies from the negroes market to the public cemetery" in Natchez.[15]

Summer brought still more illness to the slaves, including malaria, dysentery, and whooping cough. None of them recovered quickly. Washington's foot injury refused to heal. Old Granny was quite sick. (Why Downey even sent an elderly woman to a railroad construction site is inexplicable.) The heat was oppressive; it was "too warm for our hands to work all day without killing them." No wonder, reported Hicks, that "all our negroes seem to be dissatisfied." Another cause of demoralization was the crude shanties in which they lived, where "the mosquitoes torment them almost to death in the night time." The hapless slaves resisted as best they could. Ben ran away after a flogging. "John has done but very little work since he has been here, he seems to be clear of fever, looks well, eats hearty . . . but when he goes out to work he seems to think he cannot stand it." The disgusted contractor refused to pay for the days John was allegedly malingering.[16]

Hicks acknowledged the callousness of contractors. Although the hiring agreement called for "plenty of good and wholesome food," Hicks discovered that "the meat they use is very salty and a little spoiled." Since they only leased their laborers and had not invested large sums in their purchase, some were also heedless in seeking medical care. Hicks suggested that "if we had a part of the roads [i.e., if Downey or Hicks themselves became contractors] we could take better care of our negroes." But he revealed more pecuniary motives as well, reporting that "railroad business will be a first rate scheme to make money."[17]

Health conditions continued to be bad at the construction site. Malaria, afflicting men and women equally, was the most common fatal disease. Little Jack barely survived after battling it for 19 days. Mary, who had taken sick in May, was still not well in mid-August. But things were worse elsewhere on the line: "unacclimated hands" hired by other contractors died in droves.[18] Supposedly the sickly season was about over in early September, but Anderson and then Mary's child died. Old Uncle Lewis was again "very ill." Sophia was so sick that Hicks doubted she would recover. At one time, 15 of the slaves fell sick, several of them with chronic dysentery. The only good news was that Tabby had given birth to a healthy girl. Summing up the season, Hicks stated Downey's slaves would not have survived without "my unwearied attention while they were sick. I frequently have had to rise from my bed and go to the shantees at midnight and remain until morning."[19]

How much work these slaves actually performed during 1836 is uncertain, but their health risks were considerably higher than for those engaged in agriculture or urban industries.[20] Nonetheless, the following January, Downey leased his slaves to another contractor building the M&PR from the opposite end southwestward from Jackson. Again, Hicks accompanied them, reporting "the hands have enjoyed very good health" except for brief colds, principally because they now labored in the more healthful hill country away from swampy regions. They worked only into May, however, when all construction halted because of political turmoil in Jackson.[21]

Downey's slaves resumed work in 1838, this time hired directly to Hicks, who obtained a contract to grade 13 miles of the line. Romance bloomed, resulting in the marriage of Peter to Tamar, Lovelace to Sophia, and Tom to Martha. But ill health continued to plague the unfortunate slaves. Two mothers, Mary and Mirah, remained sickly after giving birth, although Hicks suspected that Mirah was malingering. Poor Joanna, on the other hand, was lingering, and was finally relieved of her earthly burdens, Hicks expending $10 for hearse, coffin, and grave. Despite this loss, he exulted, "I am doing a very fine business and making money faster than I ever expected to make it . . . I think I shall be rich enough to marry by the fall."[22] How hard the slaves had to toil to improve Hicks's marital prospects can be gauged from his remark that one could embark on a contract with merely the purchase of shovels, picks, wheelbarrows, carts, and mules.[23] No animal-drawn scrapers were considered to be necessary, although other contractors made use of them.

Exactly what labor the enslaved women performed is not revealed in Hicks's reports. Probably only one was a cook, and perhaps another was a laundress. (A single cook for a construction gang of 30 men was the recommended practice.)[24] One woman was a seamstress; Hicks bought shirts, shoes, and pants for the males, but purchased large quantities of cloth for the women's garments. So the other women likely cleared, grubbed, and graded alongside the men. This supposition is reinforced by the frequency of the women's illnesses.[25] And since infant- and child-care was a woman's responsibility, they, like their plantation sisters, probably toiled more hours than males on account of their after-work gendered domestic responsibilities. Older children were teamsters on the carts used to haul dirt from cuts to fills.

The fragmentary story of Downey's human property has an ironic conclusion. His slaves, along with other contractors' hired chattels and 106 blacks owned by the railroad itself, managed to complete only one-quarter (25 miles) of the Mississippi & Pearl River's intended line from Natchez through Jackson to Canton before the failure of its parent, the Mississippi Railroad and Banking Company, threw the road into inescapable debt in 1839. The line was ripped up and all its assets, from rails to slaves, were sold to satisfy creditors. Hicks repeatedly begged the bank to make good on his claim for $14,000, but was able to obtain a judgment for only partial payment.[26]

The majority of the South's antebellum railroads were built by contractors' laborers, sometimes owned, but more often hired. Some contractors were trained civil engineers, like Frederick Nims, whose workforce (including Rose, the cook) built a portion of the Charleston & Savannah

Railroad. Others, however, were local planters without technical expertise or construction experience who bid on short sections of a line, granted free rights of way across their land, and used their own slaves to do the work. As most new railways were hard pressed to raise capital for land, track, locomotives and rolling stock, and structures, they compensated contractors, where they could, only one-half or one-third in real money, paying the rest in the railroad's stocks and bonds.[27]

Contractors found native southern white laborers to be generally uninterested in railroad-building work. Irish and German immigrants were stereotyped as being prone to walk off the job and riot over pay disputes. So the vast majority of southern railroad construction laborers were enslaved. In Georgia by the 1840s, blacks performed all work except for masonry.[28] For multiple reasons, coerced labor was preferred. First, it was usually cheaper than white labor, although immigrants were sought when slave prices were high. Free blacks, who constituted only a very small proportion of the black population, were also employed, because they could be paid less than whites. Blacks, whether enslaved or free, could be driven harder and disciplined more effectively. And when low crop prices resulted in an abundance of slaves for hire, at lower than usual prices, railroads took advantage of the market. According to the New Orleans *Daily Crescent*, "negroes will probably do more work, and for one-fourth the cost, than double the number of hired [white] laborers." Ownership of slaves was believed to be even more desirable. *DeBow's Review* was of the opinion that "where the labor can be owned by the companies, . . . the grading, masonry, and mechanical work on railroads, . . . will be less than half the cost it would be under the system of contracts."[29]

Although contractors' hired bondsmen and local planters' slaves built most new lines, some railroads did purchase slaves for that purpose. When the Montgomery & West Point Railroad's construction stalled in 1844, the Alabama legislature granted a sizeable loan, $42,176 of which was used to purchase 84 slaves. They did not prove to be a tractable lot, the road's president admitted six years later: "With these negroes, for several years, the Company had great trouble. At one time as many as ten had run off. Some were found in Kentucky, some in Indiana, some in the mountains of Georgia, and two have never been heard from. But of this purchase there still remains a valuable force of 53 men, 7 women, and 11 children."[30] During the construction phase, children age 10 or older were used as cart drivers, while the most robust women cleared, grubbed, graded, and laid track alongside men. Other women cooked for the workforce. Their tasks were arduous: toting water, gathering firewood, keeping fires burning, preparing food with heavy utensils, and cleaning up. Once track laying was completed, the M&WP's female slaves were assigned to cook for section gangs. On occasion, cooks also nursed sick slaves.

Similar labor practices were followed on the Mobile & Great Northern Railroad as it built eastward from the bank of the Alabama River on the eve of the Civil War. Its 1861 annual report stated that "the Company force consists of 70 negro men, 11 women, 4 boys, 20 mules, 12 horses, 18 carts and 1 wagon." While the company recognized them as human laborers, slaves were also beasts of burden and implements. These 85 chattels constructed the first several miles of roadbed entirely through swamps. At first, they built an embankment for 3,000 feet, carting thousands of yards of earth from elsewhere. In one night, floodwaters washed away the result of weeks of labor. This necessitated totally new construction, with the slaves now cutting timber and building 1,500 feet of temporary trestles, which were later filled in with earth. Railroad officials acknowledged, "it was fortunate that we had a Company force to use upon this section, as no contractor would have willingly encountered the difficulties presented in executing the work." At least some of the women did such heavy labor, all 11 not being needed to cook for 74 others. Once the rest of the roadbed was cleared and graded by contractors, the company's slaves laid track along the entire 50-mile line.

Slave ownership was profitable for the Mobile & Great Northern. Hands (including the women and boys) averaged $336 of labor per year. Considering that the railroad paid an average $1,360 per slave, it recouped one-quarter of its investment in just one year. The road's chief engineer assured stockholders "the hands have been well clothed, fed and cared for, and have given but little trouble." Whether the slaves were "well fed" is debatable, as the railroad spent twice as much to feed a horse or mule as it did a slave. In fact, the total yearly cost per slave, for tools, quarters, provisions, clothing, medical services, superintendence, bedding, and incidentals, amounted to $170, $3 less than the cost of feed and harnesses for a single work animal.[31]

As soon as southern railroads began regular service, they established racial employment patterns that would last long after slavery. Railroad labor historian Eric Arnesen notes: "From its beginnings, the American railway labor force, with its multiple gradations of skill, prestige, and arduousness, was segmented along racial lines."[32] Conductors and engineers were white. Although a few southern railroad officials advocated the use of enslaved engineers because they could be hired for much less than white men's wages, no evidence exists that this practice was ever adopted. Firemen were drawn from both races, including a few free blacks. For whites, this was the stepping-stone to becoming an engineer. "Wood passers," either black or white, assisted firemen in stoking the firebox and replenishing the tender with cordwood at fuel stops. Brakemen (also known as train hands) and switchmen could also be either black or white. Black passenger brakemen were also expected to perform tasks that were later identified with those of porters, handling baggage and furnishing drinking water to travelers.[33]

Other enslaved black males worked as station hands, loading and unloading freight, pumping water, refueling locomotives, and performing general manual labor. Skilled slave blacksmiths and carpenters worked in railroad shops, although a majority of black shop workers were helpers or laborers. During the Civil War, Confederate armories and arsenals conscripted many skilled white railroad workers, leaving their lines dangerously short-staffed and necessitating a greater reliance on blacks.[34] After slavery, though, when white workers organized unions based upon their crafts, black railroaders lost their jobs in the skilled trades and were, for the most part, confined to the ranks of helpers and laborers.

A few railroads employed enslaved women as matrons at the largest stations, attending to the needs of white women passengers and keeping the premises clean. Several lines used maids, or "stewardesses," on their express passenger trains to wait on passengers and keep stoves lit. And a handful of women—perhaps wives of company-owned males—were seamstresses, making work clothes for male slaves.[35]

The greatest concentration of railroad-owned or -hired slaves occurred in maintenance of way (MOW) gangs that were supervised by white overseers. The right of way required constant repairs because many railroads were hastily built using shoddy or primitive materials. The first crossties were often not of hardwood, but simply cut from whatever trees were adjacent to the line. Much early trackage was un-ballasted and thus drained poorly, hastening the decay of ties and misalignment of track. So a large maintenance force was essential. Lines were divided into 5- to 12-mile sections, each under the supervision of an overseer (known in the North as a section master or section foreman). His qualifications were essentially the same as those for plantation overseers; one needed only experience "handling slaves."[36] Civil engineering expertise was not required. Under him was the requisite number of hands needed to maintain that stretch of track, usually about one man for every mile. The overseer assigned and supervised work and punished those who did not perform satisfactorily. Unless the section was close to a division point, the crew lived in shanties along its portion of track. Longer lines, like the South Carolina Railroad, also used "floating gangs" (later known as "extra gangs"), which bunked in decrepit passenger or freight cars parked on sidings wherever they were working. In addition to lining and re-spiking track, replacing, raising, and tamping ties, and clearing ditches, section gangs were responsible for keeping water tanks filled.[37]

Southern railroads assembled their slave forces during the hiring season that began on New Year's Day, the traditional date for negotiating transactions. Hiring bonds (contracts), specifying the monthly or yearly lease, were negotiated with each owner individually. The cost fluctuated from $100 to $125 per year in 1850 to as much as $200 in 1860. (Railroad construction projects could raise a region's normal hiring rate by as much as 20 percent.)[38] Larger railroads continued to obtain additional slaves throughout the year to fill specific needs, hiring from local owners by the day, week, or month. Bonds commonly specified the railroad was responsible for food, clothing, and medical care, while the owner was responsible for time lost if a slave ran away.

When southern railroad managers weighed the relative costs of hiring versus owning slaves, some concluded that ownership would be more profitable in the long run, particularly for skilled slaves like firemen or brakemen. But the idea was appealing for common laborers, too. The general superintendent of the South Carolina Railroad, recognizing the need for a stable MOW force, recommended in 1847 the purchase of 10 women and 75 men, each woman to cook for a 7- or 8-man section gang. For unrecorded reasons, this plan was not adopted, however, and the 82 slaves bought between 1848 and 1857 were all males.[39] A decade later, the president of the Raleigh & Gaston Railroad was similarly persuaded, urging the purchase of 4 men plus a female cook (and probably part-time track laborer) for each of its 8 sections. But he perceived an even greater value: "The increase [children] of the women would equal and probably excede any depreciation in value of the property [the slave herself]." The road did not implement this callous suggestion, probably for economic rather than moral reasons. Slave prices were high in the late 1850s, making it particularly costly to borrow funds for that purpose. Finally, in the middle of the Civil War, the R&G bought 47 slaves, but the record does not indicate whether any of them were women.[40]

It was much more common for railroads to hire slaves for MOW than to buy them, because they lacked the capital for such purchases. The Savannah, Albany & Gulf Railroad did so on a large scale, hiring 232 slaves in 1860–61, 26 of whom were women. The 200-mile-long road was divided into 21 sections, each the responsibility of a white overseer, 6 male slaves, and a female cook. The other 5 women cooked for bridge and ballast gangs.[41] Shorter lines likewise hired laborers. The South-Western Railroad advertised in Georgia newspapers in 1851 for the year-long hire of 40 slaves to be used in track repairs, one-fifth of them female cooks; 2 years later, having added trackage, the same line sought 60 men and 12 women for maintenance of the roadbed. And the tiny Upson County Railroad hired 8 slaves from local whites to keep up its 16 miles of tracks.[42]

The degree to which enslaved railroaders faced physical discipline depended upon their jobs. In general, construction and section laborers endured the worst. The Pensacola & Georgia and the Tallahassee railroads held no qualms about the use of severe punishment. According to their joint rulebook: "Overseers must not strike a negro with any other weapon than a switch, except in defense of their person. Where a negro requires correction, his hands must be tied by the overseer and he will whip him with an ordinary switch or strap not to exceed 39 lashes at one time nor more than 60 for one offense in one day, unless ordered to do so by the supervisor and in his presence."[43] Similar authority was granted to white overseers on the Memphis & Ohio Railroad: "Chastisement, if required, must be administered in moderation, and within the bounds of the law"—according to contemporary white notions of what constituted moderation—"which is not to exceed thirty-nine lashes." Presumably seeking to prevent injury to hired slaves whose owners would demand compensation, overseers were also forbidden to hit slaves with fists, clubs, or sticks.[44] Strict enforcement of such limits is doubtful.

Those put to less-regimented tasks had a somewhat easier lot. Whether working as blacksmiths or cooks, slaves of either sex were supervised less rigorously and had more autonomy. So long as the 26 female MOW cooks on the Savannah, Albany & Gulf exercised good stewardship of the supplies allotted to them, they were likely to remain unmolested by the whip. If a station matron or train maid was properly deferential toward whites and performed her assigned duties, she, too, did not live in daily fear of the lash. Slave firemen were not normally driven by fear, although engineers could punish them for inattention to duty. Likewise for brakemen. The Wilmington & Weldon Railroad's instructions to conductors made them responsible for train hands being "*constantly* on the *platforms* near the brakes—one between the two coaches and one between the second-class car and baggage car. They will be instructed to *lock both* brakes *as soon as possible:* to do so *promptly* . . . All Brake-men hereafter found away from their places without orders, when the train is in motion, must be punished properly" by the conductor.[45] White firemen and brakemen could merit discipline for poor job performance, but only slaves were subject to corporal punishment.

Granted that railroad construction work anywhere was characterized by extremely hard work under the direction of sometimes-abusive supervisors, the lot of construction slaves in the lower South was particularly difficult when compared to that of immigrant workers on northern railroads. As the New Orleans & Jackson Railroad built northward from that Louisiana metropolis, it encountered the "trembling prairies," miles and miles of swamps so soft that piles had to be driven down 35 feet before encountering a solid clay base. Workers faced alligators, snakes, and swarms of insects. A reporter for a Beaumont, Texas newspaper noted similar challenges in building the Texas & New Orleans Railroad: "For four miles, through very heavy timber, an embankment is thrown up, ranging from two to twelve feet, and twelve [feet] wide at the top; this is, however, interrupted by piling and trestle work at intervals along the line."[46] Laborers in the Deep South encountered diseases that were unknown in more northerly regions. The chief engineer of the Vicksburg, Shreveport & Texas reported in 1856: "There has been considerable sickness on the Line . . . Nearly all the negroes, . . . have been down with chills & fevers."[47] Toiling in the Gulf States during summer proved to be as physically taxing and dangerous as railroad labor got.

MOW work was fundamentally hazardous everywhere. Annual reports mentioned MOW slaves being injured or killed when they were struck or run over by hand cars and trains. Diligent supervision was not always possible. Although most section crews numbered fewer than 10 slaves plus an overseer, occasionally one overseer was responsible for as many as 30 slaves, divided into several gangs assigned to different parts of the line. Poor housing compromised the well being of section workers. And some MOW gangs were deployed in remote locations, far from medical help. Furthermore, southern whites tended to assume that sick slaves were malingering, and were not apt to quickly seek medical treatment. An overseer on the Spartanburg & Union Railroad admitted that he sent for a doctor "only when it was indispensably necessary."[48]

Locomotive firemen's duties were also dangerous and arduous, particularly during hot, humid weather. They had to continuously stoke the firebox, and if the engine ran out of fuel short of the next wood-yard, forage for brush or chop down a tree.[49] Derailments and boiler explosions were the occupational hazards to firemen and engineers. Injuries and fatalities due to poor track were likewise common.

Even more hazardous was the job of brakemen (train hands), the lowest-ranking workers on a train. Many railroads used slaves for this position. Their main tasks were helping to stop the train and coupling and uncoupling cars. Brakemen lost their lives by falling off the tops of moving, swaying freight cars, especially at night or in inclement weather, while manually applying brakes on each car. Even on passenger trains, they had to jump back and forth from car to car to apply brakes. Coupling with link and pins required the brakeman to attach an oval iron link with an iron pin in a pocket at the end of one car, stand between it and the other car, and be ready to drop another pin as the link entered the new car's pocket, while avoiding being crushed as the cars came together.

Switchmen performed the same coupling and uncoupling functions, but were stationed in yards and did not ride the trains. Because of the greater risks, railroads paid more to hire slave brakemen than they did for track laborers.

Despite such hazards, many slave owners welcomed the opportunity to hire out slaves to the railroads, particularly because it allowed them to maximize their investments by leasing slaves for outside work during slack periods at home. Most owners appear to have been satisfied with the level of care, and even discipline, that was given their hired chattels, one of them writing, "I found my boys vastly improved and in such a thriving condition" upon their return.[50] Railroads often found owners willing to hire out the same slaves over and over, evidence that they believed the remuneration and treatment to be satisfactory. The Richmond, Fredericksburg & Potomac, for example, secured between 75 and 100 slaves and free blacks annually in the late 1850s and into the Civil War, with many hiring bonds listing the same slaves year after year.[51]

By 1861, the South was interlaced with nearly 9,000 miles of track operated by more than 100 railroads, probably all of which used slave labor in some capacity. The Civil War brought hardships to many lines. Fluctuations in the supply of slaves, coupled with inflation, drove up hiring costs. By the middle of the war, railroads were often desperate for labor, hiring or purchasing slaves who would not have been considered earlier, including children, increased numbers of women, and sometimes entire families. The North Carolina Railroad found itself severely short-handed in 1863, having secured only 283 hires when 25 owners reneged on agreements to provide an additional 101 chattels. By the end of 1864, the line was in dire straits and agreed to purchase slaves for unprecedented sums payable in vastly depreciated Confederate currency. Healthy young males in their teens and 20s now cost $5,000 to $6,000 (3 times the prewar high price), while Lidia, age 20, who was described as "sound" and "healthy to date," cost $5,500. In December 1864, the NCRR purchased Margaret and her children Perry, Hal, Alonzo, Tom, and an infant for $20,000.[52] Surviving records do not identify what tasks they performed.

Many enslaved railroaders during the war were impressed (forcibly drafted) on orders of state legislatures acting at the behest of the Confederate government. They were a vital asset when it became necessary to complete or extend rail lines to better link the states and make it easier to move men and supplies. One such effort was closing the rail gap between Danville, Virginia, and Greensboro, North Carolina. In order to build this Piedmont Railroad, the Richmond & Danville Railroad purchased 71 new slaves, hired in excess of 800 others from Virginia owners, and made plans to hire still more. Confederate cavalrymen were detached to supervise the workers. When these slaves proved to be insufficient, the governor of North Carolina was urged to impress more, but he refused for political reasons. Across the South, planters were often resistant to labor drafts, and at times, force was applied in seizing slaves, even though owners were offered compensation. For their part, many slaves recognized that the war was being fought to preserve their chattel status. Some resisted being sent to dangerous railroad work, like hard rock blasting and roadbed grading, while others took advantage of unsettled conditions and sought their freedom. In North Carolina alone, hundreds of impressed slave railroaders fled, while many others were killed in trying. Overall, one in three bondsmen impressed for railroad work attempted to secure their liberty.[53]

As harsh as life was for slaves performing outdoor manual labor on construction gangs and section crews, others suffered even worse. Shortly before the Civil War, Virginia identified incarcerated slaves and free blacks as a source of revenue for the state. In 1858, the General Assembly passed "An Act providing for the employment of negro convicts on the public works," authorizing the lease of men and women to contractors engaged in building railroads and canals. This practice, later known as the convict lease, became common in the South after the Civil War.[54]

Contractors building the Covington & Ohio Railroad across the Appalachians into western Virginia negotiated directly with the governor for convict workers. In 1861, Robert F. and D. G. Bibb paid $175 apiece to obtain the labor of 25 free black and 18 enslaved "No. 1 Men," $95 apiece for 5 free black and 6 enslaved "No. 2 Men," and $50 or $25 apiece for 7 enslaved and 3 free black women. In short, they secured 64 convicts for slightly more than $11,000 for the year. This was far less than prevailing hiring rates. Among the female free black convicts was 24-year-old Martha Dixon. The Bibbs paid only $25 for her labor because she had an infant and could not work full-time. Of the 7 enslaved women, 2 had been teenagers when sentenced: Fanny, age 15; and Alberta, age 14. Sarah Ann, 17, had a child, so her labor, like that of Martha Dixon, was valued only at $25. Just how appalling this practice was is seen in the case of Judy, only 10 years old when she was sentenced in 1859. Now, at the age of 12, she was doomed to labor at a railroad construction site, alongside adult male convicts. As with the mothers, Judy's labor was obtained for only $25, probably because she was a "quarter-hand" in plantation parlance, too young and small to do a grown woman's labor.[55]

Another construction firm building a portion of the Covington & Ohio, Thomas Roper & Co., likewise secured convict labor from the state of Virginia in 1861: 1 female and 17 male free blacks; and 18 male and 4 female slaves. This contractor paid $5,447 for the right to their labor for the year. The 4 women were Mary, age 16 when sentenced in 1857; Mary Jane Mills, age 15 in 1858; Ellen, age 20 in 1858; and Narcissus, age 22 in 1860. All of them were leased at the rate of $50 per year.[56]

Contractors bore the expense of feeding, clothing, supervising, and guarding convicts.[57] It is doubtful that they expended anything beyond the bare minimum: unlike slave owners, they had not invested large sums in these chattels. If a convict died during the year, the hire was prorated accordingly. Even if one was permanently injured as a result of neglect, accident, or correction, the contractor incurred no penalty. The women who were not mothers or themselves children worked as long and as hard as the men, and were punished the same. As there is no evidence that they were housed or worked separately from the male convicts, their sexual vulnerability must be assumed.

Railroad slavery exacted a great toll on black families. For many construction and MOW laborers, domestic life was largely nonexistent. Most contractors employed only males, the rest using mostly men and a handful of women. The same was true for the railroads themselves. Thus thousands of men were separated from their wives who had to keep families together and endure the hardships of bondage without their mates. Although some males hired close to home, like those working on the 16-mile-long Upson County Railroad, probably visited their families often, many men, like the upper South slaves building the Alabama, Florida & Georgia in 1836, saw their kinfolk only from Christmas to the new hiring season in January.[58] In other words, many women were railroad widows for most of the year, a fact that made it essential that they build strong female-female relationships and lean on other women for emotional support. Some were literal widows, having lost mates to railroad accidents.

Still other enslaved women were widowed by the railroads' participation in the domestic slave trade. When the Montgomery & West Point obtained a loan from the state of Alabama to purchase slaves, it found the best deal not close to home, but in far-off Virginia. Three-quarters of the 84 purchases were males. Children of both sexes were included in the total. All but the children probably bid a last farewell to kin upon departure for Alabama. Other railroads purchased slaves in more local markets, so some of them may have been able to maintain family contact, at least on holidays. But if a railroad subsequently sold a slave, there was no guarantee he or she would remain in that region. Given the speculative nature of both railroading and slave ownership, and the displacement of hundreds of thousands of African Americans from the declining agricultural economies of the upper South into the expanding Deep South cotton belt, a considerable number of railroad-owned slaves were permanently separated from their families.

Southern railroads exacerbated this tragedy by offering financial incentives for transporting slaves and otherwise facilitating the interstate slave trade. Individual owners often sent slaves by train, entrusting them to the custody of a conductor or express agent, in which case they rode in a baggage car. The fare for "servants" was usually half price. Slave traders preferred trains, sometimes filling entire freight cars with 20 or more captives. At other times, they were transported in segregated "negro cars." Frederick Law Olmsted, traveling through the South in 1857, reported, "I have not been on or seen a railroad train, departing southward, that it did not convey a considerable number" of victims of the trade. In order to obtain the business of slave traders, railroads like the Virginia & Tennessee Railroad carried small children for free.[59] Weeping relatives gathered at depots to mourn their loved ones' going. Jacob Stroyer witnessed the departure of a large group, including his two sisters, on a South Carolina Railroad train, bound ultimately for Louisiana, which "was considered by the slaves a place of slaughter." By the time the unfortunates reached the station, a large crowd of blacks and whites had assembled. "Some were yelling and wringing their hands, while others were singing little hymns . . . for the consolation of those who were going away." Even after the train was out of sight, "we heard wailing and shrieks from those in the cars."[60]

A few enslaved male railroaders found modest opportunities to enhance the quality of their families' lives. Some railroads paid them for "extra work" such as cutting cordwood or crossties in their spare time. Others earned personal money by working on Sundays or during the Christmas holidays.[61] How many men used their earnings for the benefit of their families is uncertain, although some probably followed the example of plantation males who spent their occasional income gained from hunting, fishing, or personal gardens to purchase cooking utensils or articles of clothing for their wives.

Black railroaders did not always peacefully accept their bondage. Resistance was common. Corporate annual reports occasionally hinted at financial losses due to slaves running away. During the Civil War, hundreds of impressed slaves attempted escapes from railroad construction camps, while many others took advantage of unsettled conditions to flee by train from the border states of Missouri and Maryland. Some slaves malingered, working as little as they could get away with, including some of Samuel Smith Downey's bondsmen building the Mississippi & Pearl River. Attacking the railroad's profitability was a form of passive-aggressive resistance, just as it was on plantations. Olmsted observed an act of economic sabotage on the Richmond & Petersburg Railroad after his train was delayed by hotboxes caused by a want of oil in journal boxes housing the wheel axles. "I saw a negro oiling all the trucks [wheels] of the train; as he proceeded from one to the other, he did not give himself the trouble to elevate the outlet of his oiler, so that a stream of oil . . . was poured out upon the ground the whole length of the train."[62]

A dramatic form of resistance was outright refusing to work. In one instance, a group of hired slaves was unwilling to return to the construction site to begin the new work year in January, complaining that the contractor provided insufficient food, required them to cook their own meals, and only allowed time for clothes washing on Sunday, their day of rest. Whippings and other brutal discipline were also alleged. The railroad's hiring agent questioned each slave and convinced himself that the allegations were baseless, believing instead that they were conspiring to get out of work. If Charles, the ringleader, had indeed been "beaten with sticks, clubs, &c," as he claimed, "the scoundrel" had gotten what he deserved. In another striking example, slaves set fire to the railroad's storehouses, allowing their tools to burn while making off with personal "plunder."[63] The most extreme form of resistance was physically attacking or endangering a white superior. On one occasion, two maintenance of way slaves riding with their overseer on a hand-pump car spied an unanticipated train overtaking them and jumped off without warning the white man.[64] Most railroad slaves, of course, did not engage in overt resistance, and had to make the best of their lot while finding their own personal expressions of day-to-day resistance.

Slave labor was essential to antebellum southern railroading. Most whites strove to become independent landowning farmers, not industrial workers. The ability of the South to attract foreign immigrant labor was severely hampered by the existence of slavery, which depressed the wages of free workers. With railroad construction projects demanding hundreds of laborers at a time, slavery was *the* dependable source of manual labor. The slave economy usually included a surplus of bonded workers to be hired or sold to railroads. Whether for construction and maintenance, or sometimes operations, southern railroads could not do without enslaved black labor. Proof of this is seen in the fact that, after emancipation, former slaves continued to perform the same crucial roles in maintenance of way and construction, and remained an important percentage of firemen and brakemen.

Certainly, slaveholders had to weigh the risks. Railroad work was inherently more dangerous than agricultural labor.[65] But ultimately the elasticity of slavery worked to the benefit of both railroads and slave owners. An enslaved fireman could be made to do a brakeman's job; shop laborers could be redeployed as train hands; station hands could fuel locomotives. At the same time, owners could generate new income by hiring their slaves for that part of the year when they were not needed in agriculture, or negotiate profitable yearlong hires for truly surplus slaves.

Most railroad-employed slaves had family members who worked on plantations and farms. It remains to determine how their lives compared. First, railroad labor, particularly construction and maintenance of way, was physically more demanding than agricultural work. Clearing trees and boulders and grading was done with axes, picks, shovels, and wheelbarrows. Track laying was also done by hand, using much heavier tools than those employed in farming. The same was true for track repairs. Railroad slaves had to lift much heavier loads, particularly ties and rails.

Railroad slaves generally experienced more brutality than did their agricultural counterparts. While paternalism sometimes moderated the harshness of master-slave relationships on resident-owner plantations, such sentiments were absent in the railroad industry where no individual "owner" got to know "his" or "her" slaves personally. Many railroad slaves were worked in regimented gangs, ruled by white overseers and the whip. Worst off, of course, were convict laborers.

Working on a railroad was also more hazardous than agriculture. Plantations did not expose workers to injuries and deaths from blasting accidents, being run over by or crushed between trains, perishing in derailments and boiler explosions, or having one's feet crushed by falling rails or ties. Railroad work also subjected slaves to greater health risks. Contractors moved laborers from regions where they were acclimated into locales where they easily contracted new diseases. Their housing was generally more primitive and inadequate than on settled farms and plantations. And not only were they more likely to encounter spoiled or poorly prepared food, but their diet also was more deficient because, unlike plantation residents, they could not cultivate kitchen gardens or raise barnyard animals to supplement their rations.

Female railroad slaves faced a harder life than their plantation sisters, who could cushion the hardships of bondage through family life and the emotional and spiritual support derived from the community of women.[66] Women engaged in railroad construction experienced an overwhelmingly male environment. Cooks on section gangs lived exclusively among the company of black and white men. This greatly unbalanced ratio not only contributed to social and emotional isolation, but also to situations where they were at risk sexually. The fact that they lived and worked alongside black men was no guarantee of protection; enslaved mothers commonly warned their daughters against black, as well as white, rapists.[67]

Finally, railroad work wreaked more personal hardship on black families than did agricultural slavery. Hired slaves were often separated from their families for months at a time, causing heartache and loneliness to themselves and their spouses and children "back home." By tapping the interstate slave trade for the purchase of laborers, railroads severed family ties permanently. And enslaved women, usually working singly among groups of men, suffered particular isolation and vulnerabilities.

None of the southern railroads that operated as a corporate entity in 1861 exist today, but a part of their legacy persists. All of the antebellum lines were merged with, or absorbed by, others, a process that started soon after the Civil War. While the actual rails, ties, and trestles installed by slaves in the antebellum years were all replaced within a few decades, some of the rights of way cleared and graded by slave labor still remain in use by four of the five mega-systems that now dominate the railroad business. CSX Transportation, Norfolk Southern, Union Pacific, and Canadian National (which purchased Illinois Central) all operate lines that use antebellum rights of way, as do regional railroad Kansas City Southern and several short lines. CSX, NS, UP, and CN have all been sued, along with several financial institutions, insurance corporations, tobacco companies, and a textile firm, for slavery reparations. The consolidated cases seek financial compensation from the defendant companies, including the four railroads, for the damage done by their corporate ancestors that owned or hired slaves or provided services for slave owners. In one respect, of all the corporate defendants, the railroads are the most vulnerable. Not only is there more documentation on railroad slavery than for the other industries, there is more physical evidence—the actual property, the rights of way—carved out by slave laborers. The reparations lawsuit is currently stalled in a federal district court in Chicago.[68] The issue of reparations has clearly polarized public opinion, particularly along black-white lines. So the significance of the South's slavery-era railroads remains a controversial issue today.

Railroads meant progress to white southerners. But railroad construction, operation, and maintenance depended upon slaves. Thus, advancement rested on exploitation. For nearly four decades, from 1829 to the last gasp of the Confederacy, slavery deprived well over 100,000 African American railroaders of wages, family life, and personal health and safety. Finally, in 1865, blacks throughout the South could sing a new spiritual, "slavery chain done broke at last / gonna praise God 'till I die." Railroads had been an important link in that chain. Emancipation brought paid employment and greater opportunities for family stability. But race would continue to shape the structure of railroad employment for a century to come.

Railroads in the African American Experience

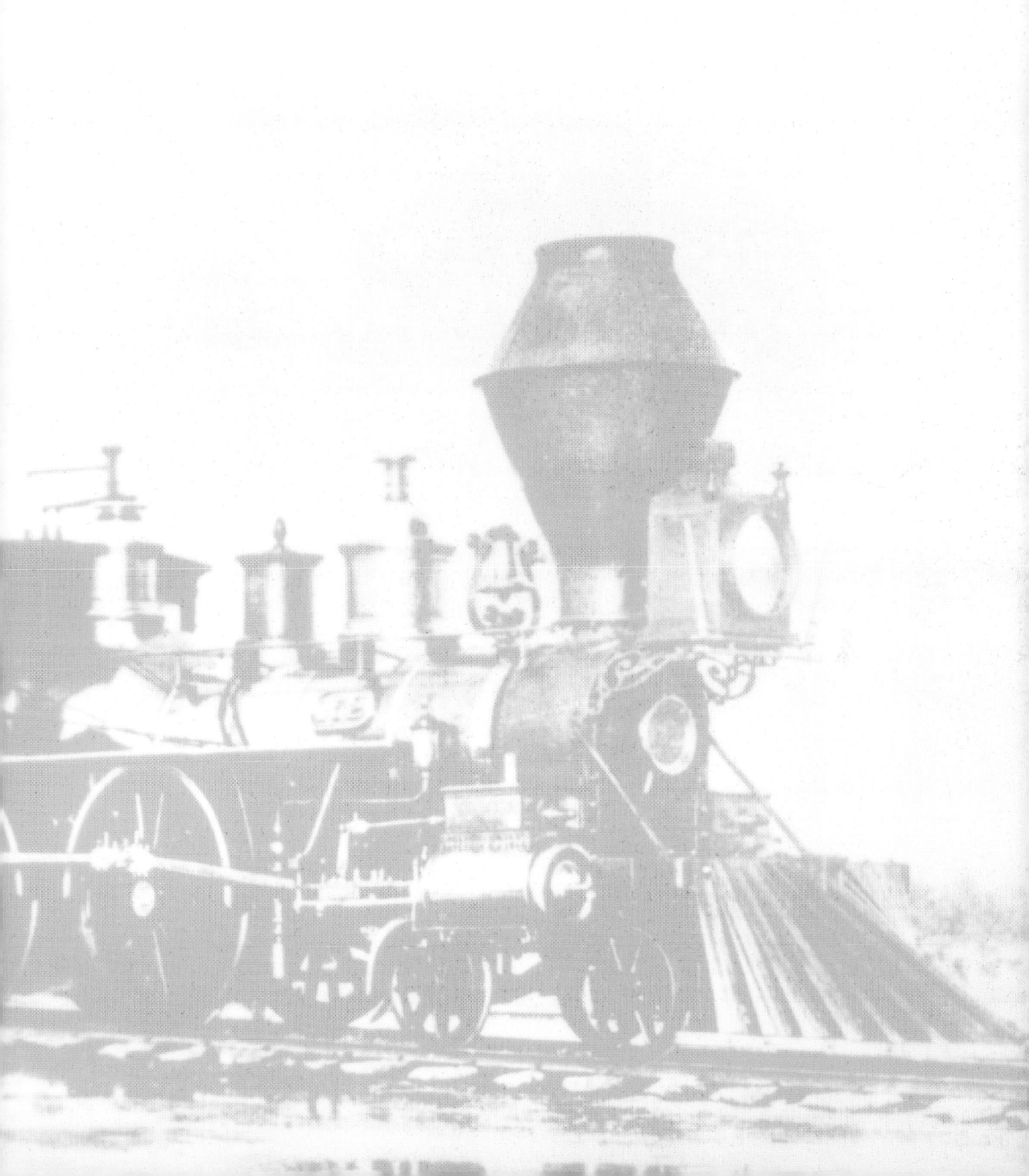

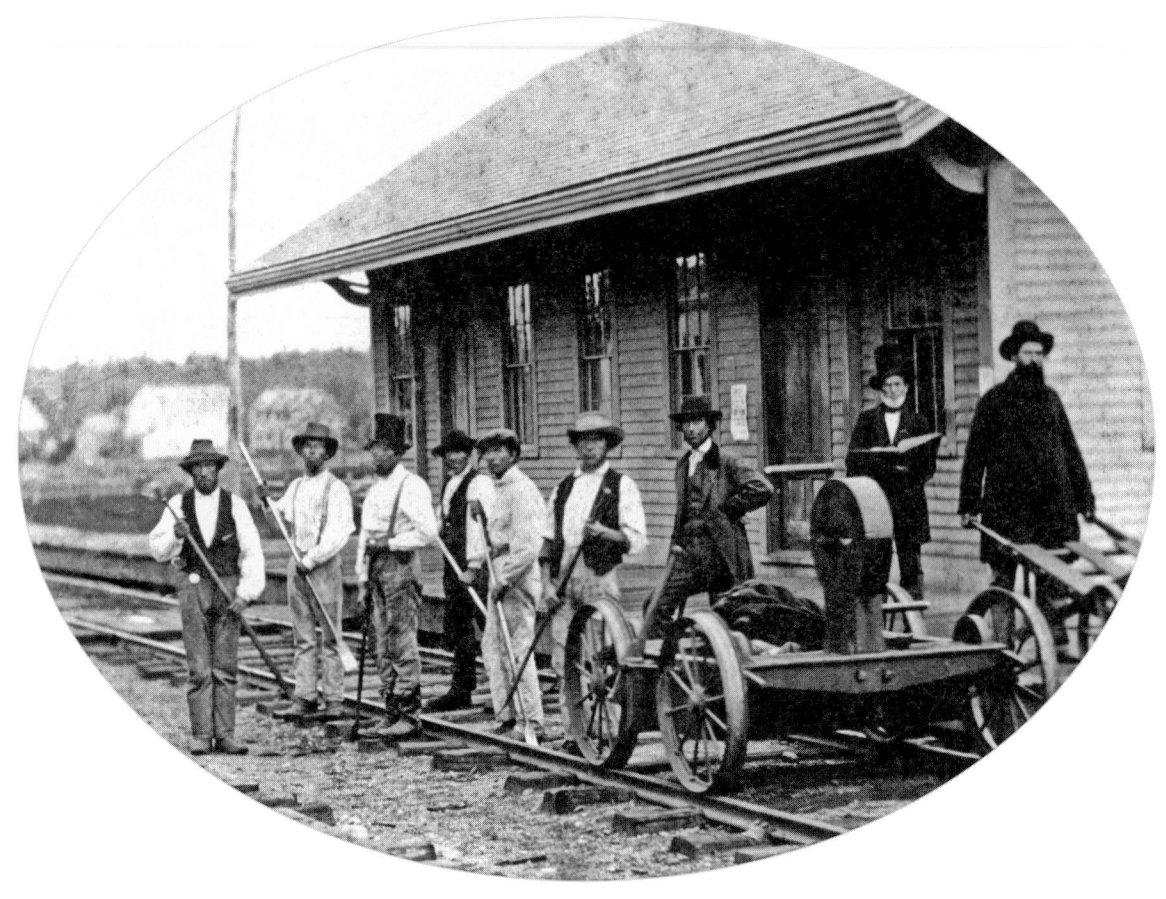

A very early photograph of a Civil War–era multiracial track gang, location unknown. Several of the laborers are holding ballast-tamping bars. Note their hand-cranked section car, with heavy flywheel and large tires. Eric Schwandt collection

(OPPOSITE) *As slaves fled to Union army lines early in the Civil War, they were deemed "contraband of war" and pressed into noncombat service, some for the U.S. Military Railroad. Part of the Union strategy was to destroy Confederate railroads. Here contraband laborers, also known as "pioneers," test a device for twisting rails so that they cannot possibly be straightened and used again. Andrew J. Russell photo, E. L. DeGolyer, Jr. Photograph Collection, DeGolyer Library, Southern Methodist University*

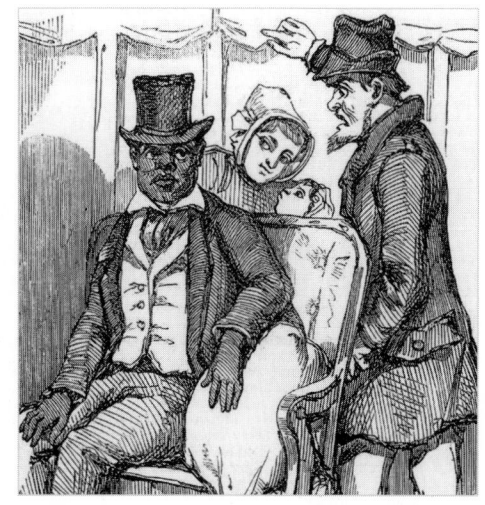

A London newspaper carried this illustration in 1856 with the caption, "Negro expulsion from railway car, Philadelphia." Whites in the antebellum North frequently objected, just as vehemently as in the South, to sitting with black passengers. Massachusetts was the only northern state where railroad segregation was abolished prior to the Civil War. Theodore Kornweibel collection

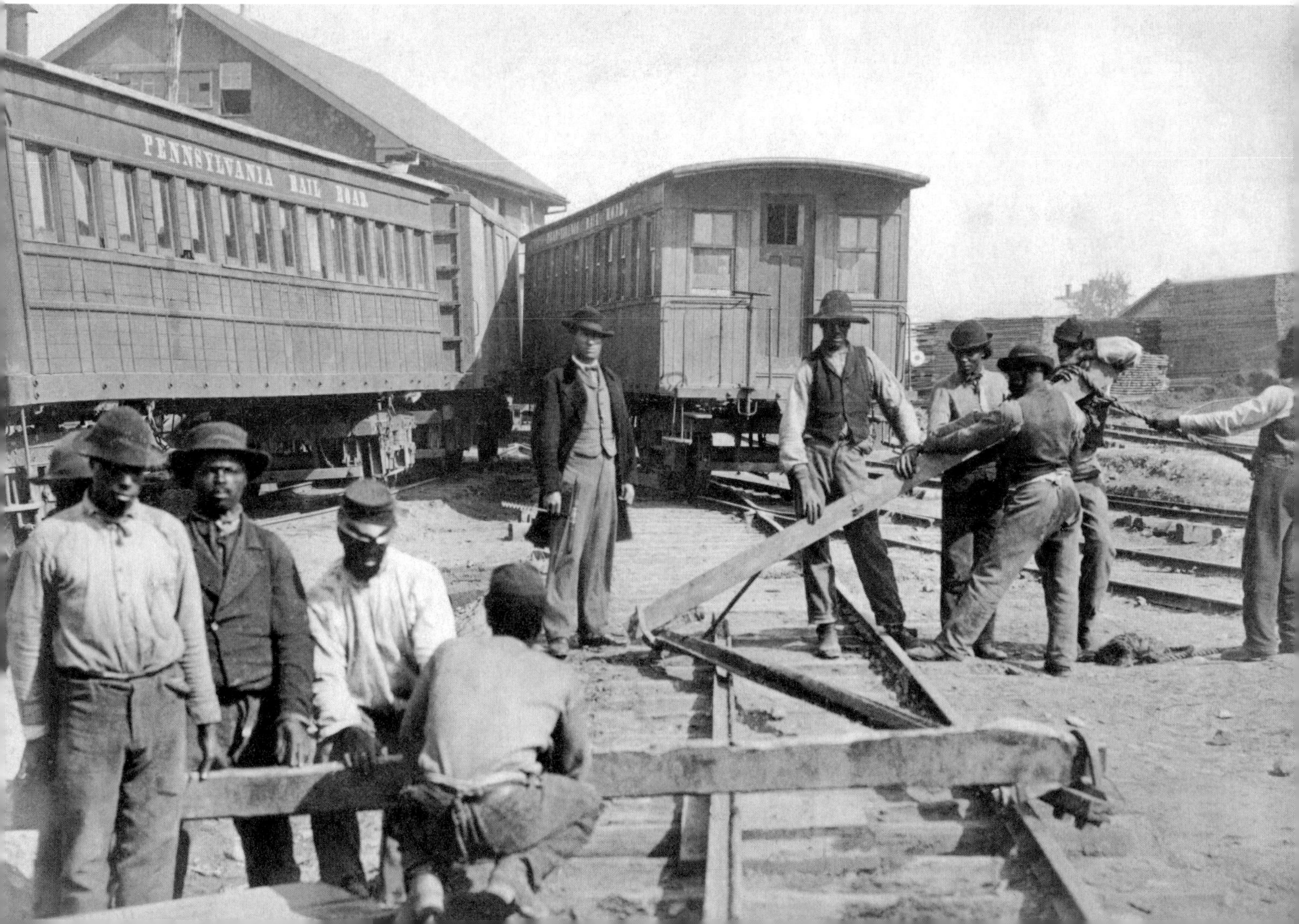

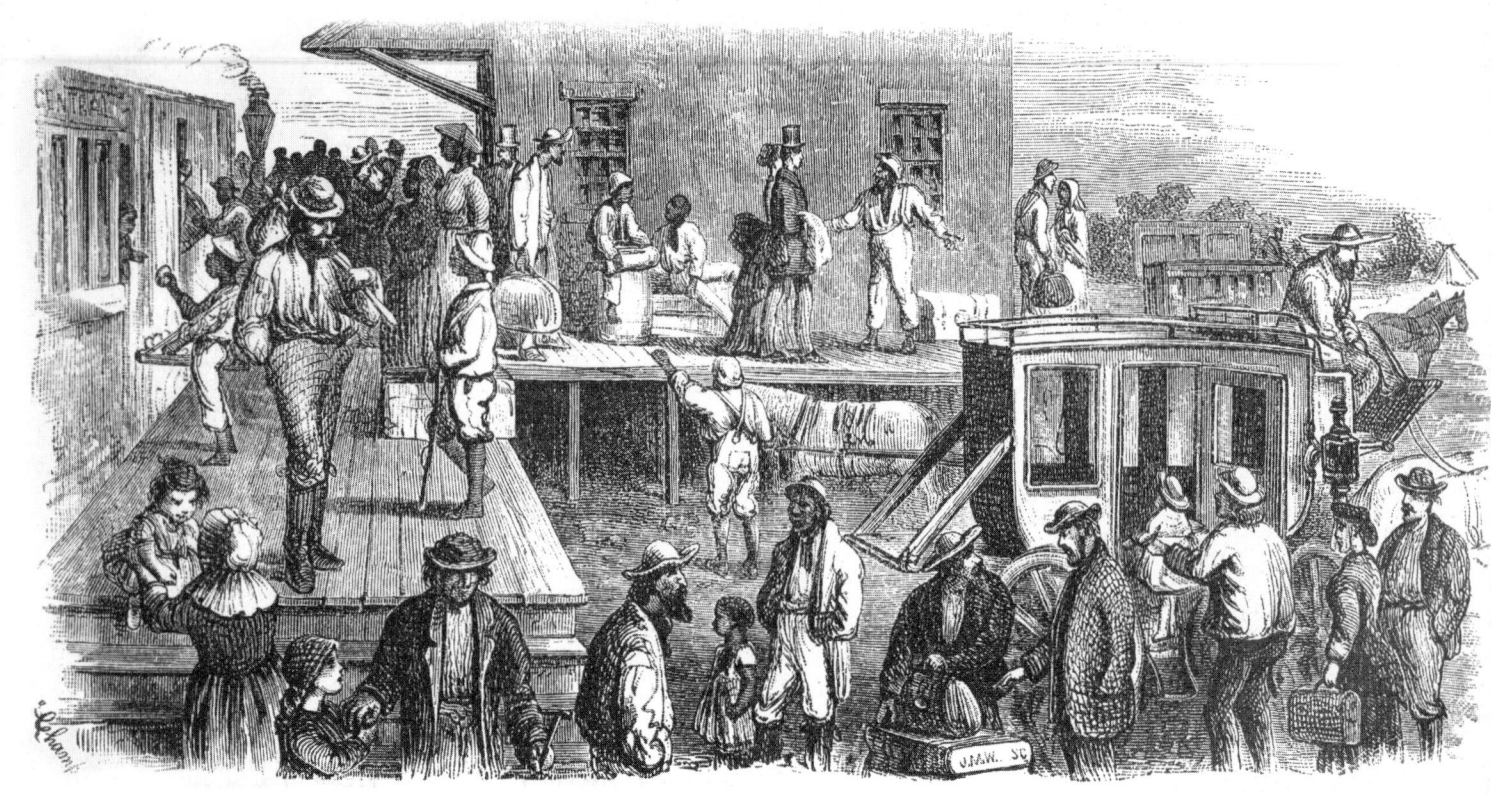

Railroads represented the freedom to move about and declare one's personal independence to many former slaves in the years immediately after emancipation. A visitor in the South in 1874 observed that "the railroad depots are everywhere crowded with negroes," some of whom were travelers, some of whom had come to see friends and family depart, and others who simply dreamed of better lives elsewhere. *Theodore Kornweibel collection*

(OPPOSITE) *George M. Pullman is credited with launching successful sleeping-car service. During the late nineteenth century he gradually bought up competitors or drove them out of business until, by 1900, the Pullman Company had an essential monopoly. From the beginning, Pullman staffed its cars with African American porters, believing them uniquely suited for providing white travelers an unparalleled quality of hospitality and personal service. Theodore Kornweibel collection*

Across the Continent in a Pullman Hotel Car of 1877

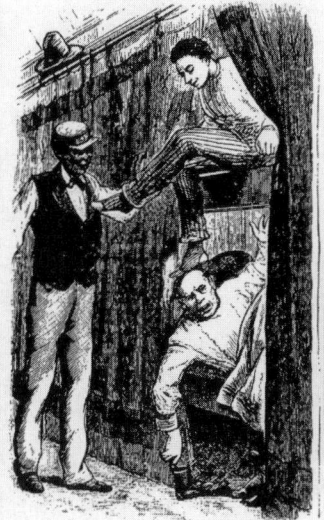

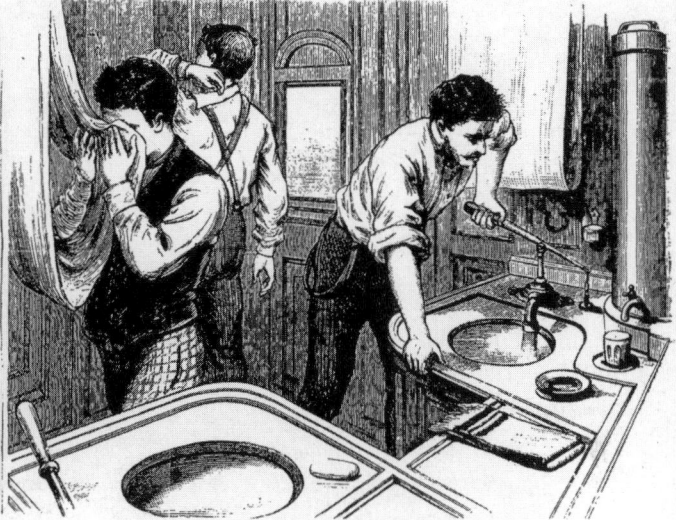

"MUST STEP SOMEWHERE"

PERFORMING THE MORNING ABLUTIONS

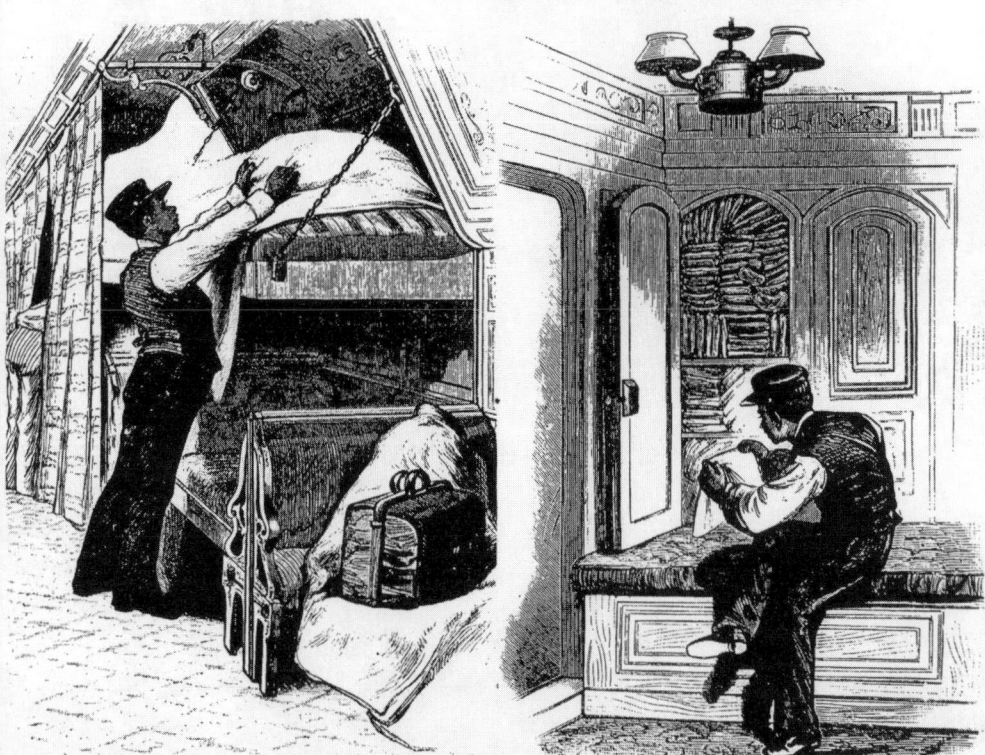

MAKING UP THE BERTHS

INSPECTING THE LINEN-CLOSET

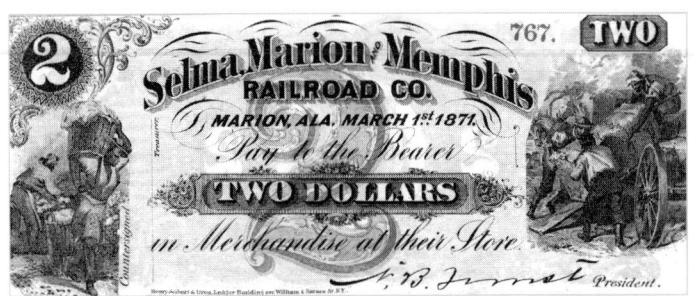

(ABOVE) *In the transition from slave to free black labor after the Civil War, southern railroads had to abandon the notion that they could completely control their workers. One form of manipulation that gradually died out was paying laborers in scrip redeemable at the company store, where they could expect to pay inflated prices. This Selma, Marion & Memphis Railroad note was signed by its president, former slave trader, plantation owner, and Confederate cavalry general Nathan Bedford Forrest, who after the war became the first Grand Wizard of the Ku Klux Klan. Norfolk Southern Railway Collection, Kenan Research Center at the Atlanta History Center*

(RIGHT) *Railroad excursions were popular social and recreational activities for blacks. Some offered entire trains where the humiliations of segregation could be avoided altogether. In other cases the lure was low fares and exciting attractions, like this Louisville & Nashville Railroad offer. Only 14 years after emancipation, the price, about 3 cents per mile, would still have been steep for many ex-slaves. Louisville & Nashville Railroad Records, University of Louisville Archives and Records Center*

COLORED FAIR, AND BALLOON ASCENSION

There will be a Grand Balloon Ascension at the Fair Grounds during the Colored Fair. The Ascension will take place about 2½ o'clock,

Friday, August 29th, 1879.

Arrangements have been made with the Louisville & Nashville & Great Southern R. R. to Shelby City or South Danville so that persons who wish to attend the Fair can do so at the following Excursion Rates to Danville and return, tickets good from 28th to September 1st:

RATES TO SHELBY CITY AND RETURN:

LEBANON $1.70   PENICKS $1.35   RILEYS $1.15
GRAVEL SWITCH 95c,   BRUMFIELD 70c,
MITCHELLSBURG 60c, PARKSVILLE, 40c, STANFORD 50c,
ALUM SPRINGS 15c,   RICHMOND JUNCT. 55c.
HALLS GAP 80c, CRAB ORCHARD $1.15   BRODHEAD $1.60
MT. VERNON $2.00   PINE HILL $2.35.
LIVINGSTON $2.65.

Fair two days, August 29th and 30th.

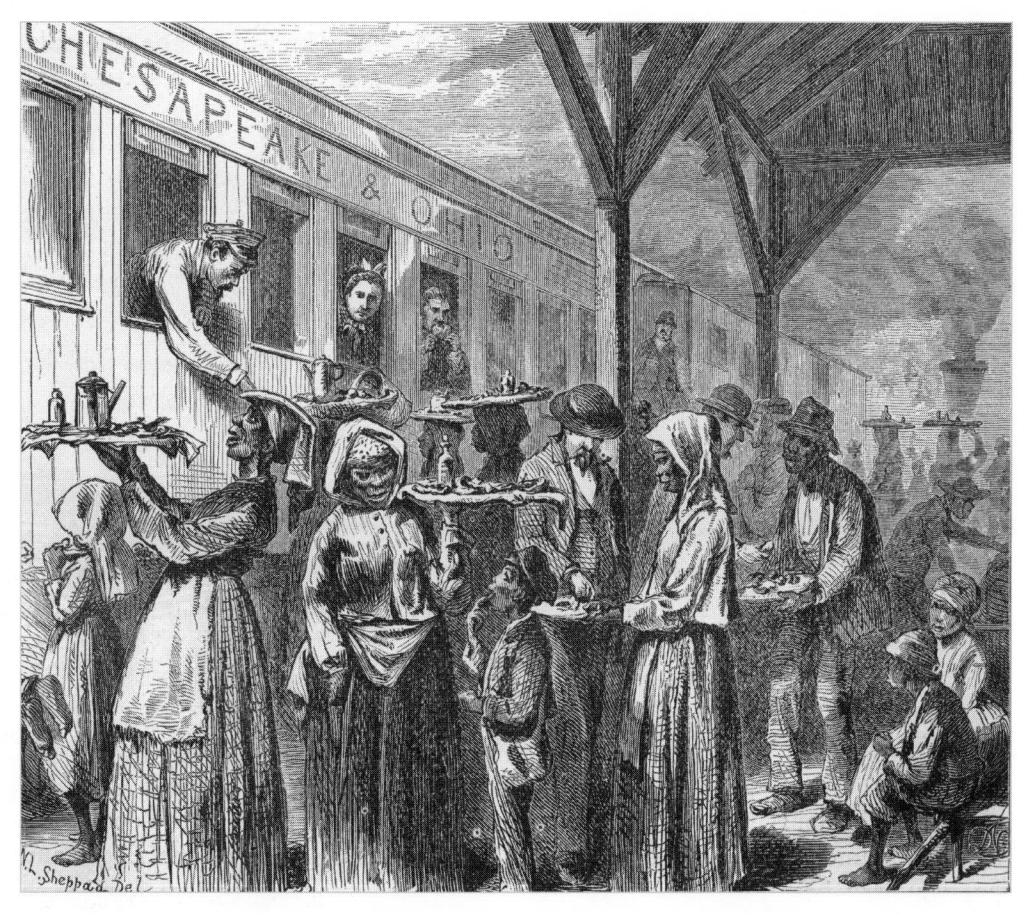

A traveler in 1875 observed that, at stations like Gordonsville, Virginia, where the Chesapeake & Ohio Railway's route from Newport News joined the main line from Washington to the west, formerly enslaved women served a vital function in the era before dining cars were common by peddling food to hungry passengers. Such entrepreneurship had been going on since slavery days. Theodore Kornweibel collection

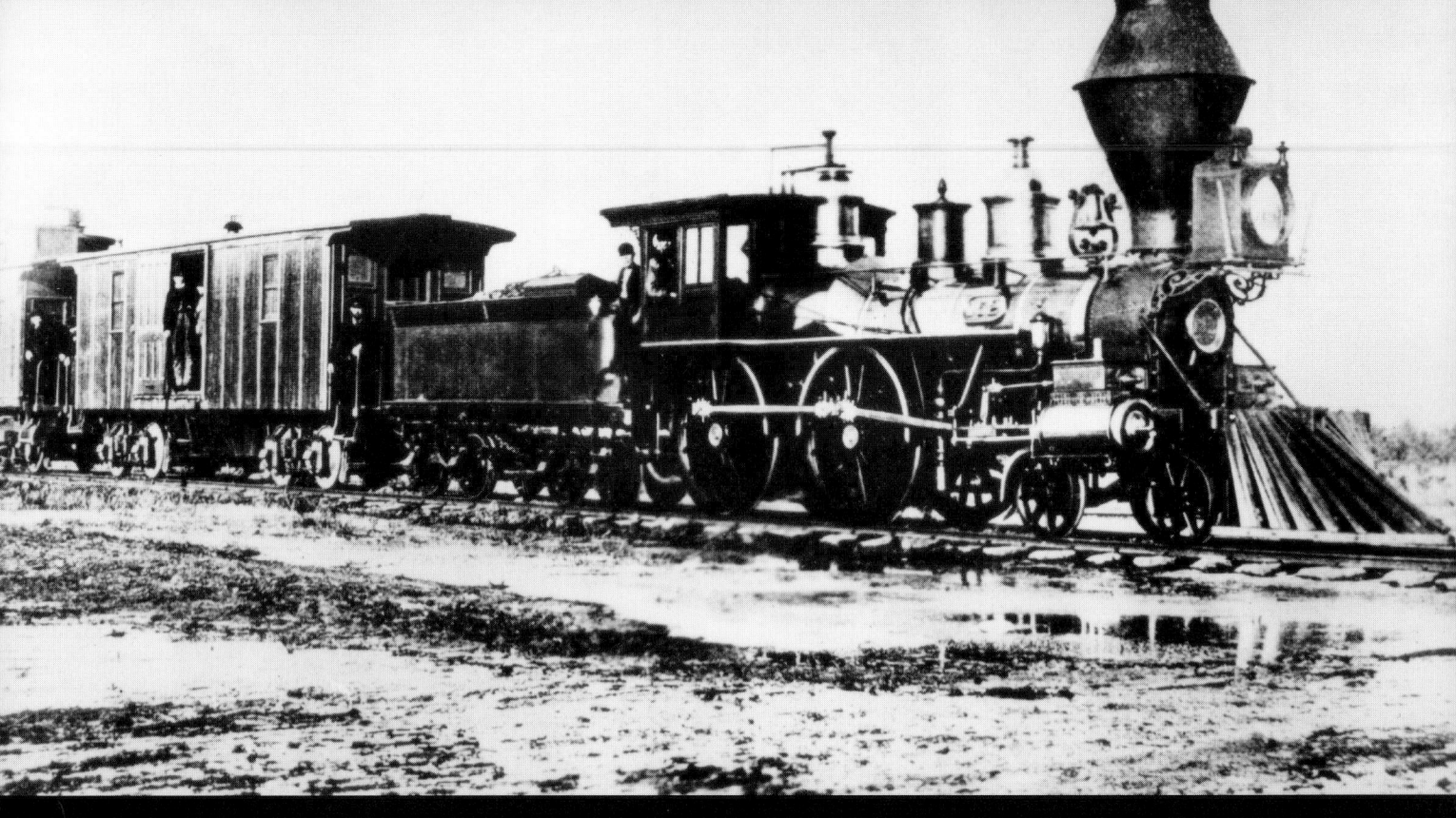

An Illinois Central Railroad passenger train in Chicago, 1856. Before the Civil War, whether in the North or South, black passengers were sometimes prohibited from occupying coaches and instead forced to ride in baggage cars like this one, directly behind the locomotive's tender. Even paying a lower fare, it was a demeaning experience. Courtesy California State Railroad Museum

Black prisoners building the Western North Carolina Railroad around 1880, under close supervision of armed guards in the employ of the construction contractor. Railroads and contractors throughout the South profited from the availability of nearly free convict labor in the late nineteenth century. The photo was one of a series of postcard scenes sold for popular enjoyment. Lindsey & Brown Collection, Rare Book, Manuscript, and Special Collections Library, Duke University

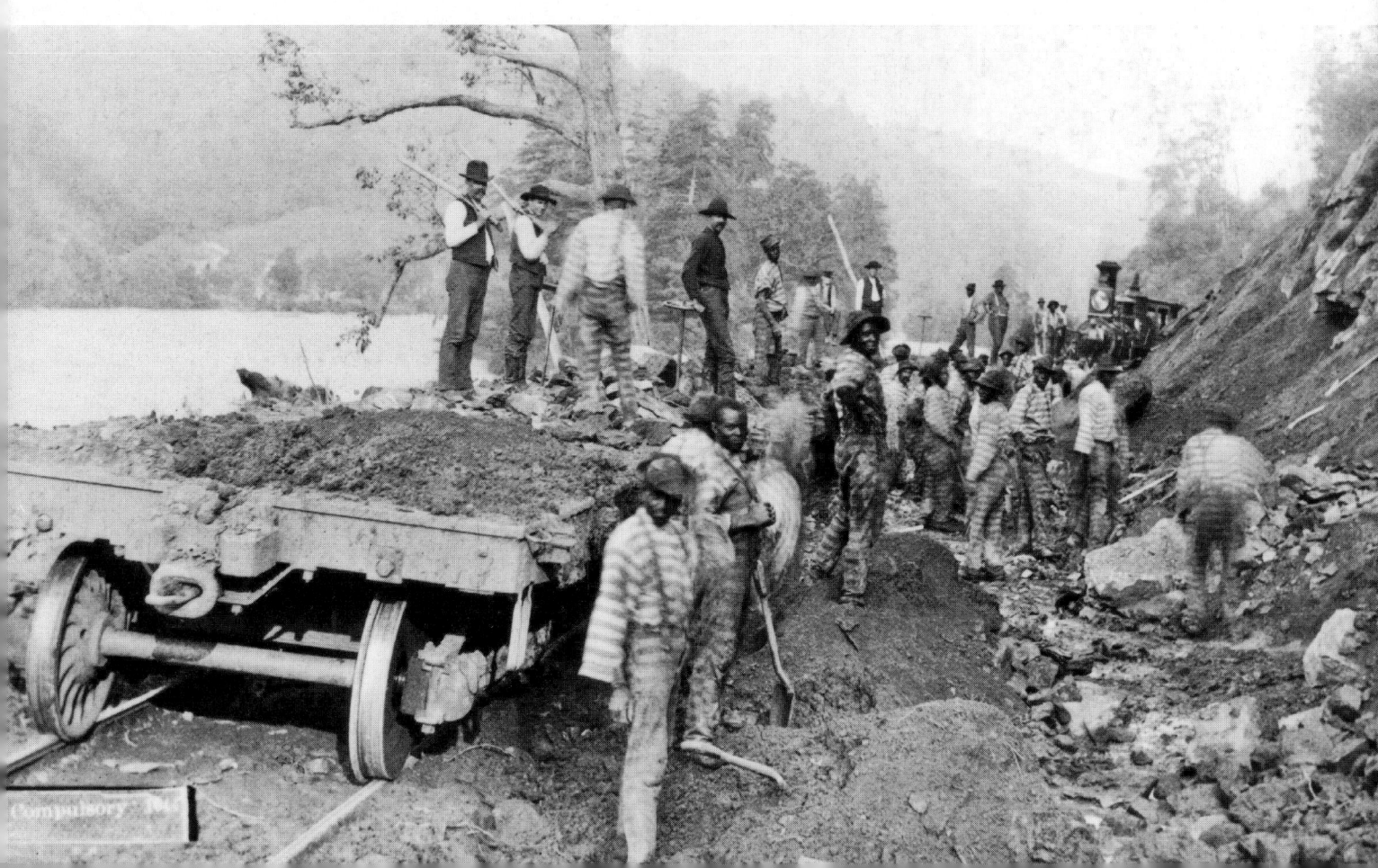

"WASN'T NO EQUIPMENT— IT WAS MANUAL LABOR"

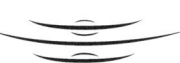

Construction and Track Laborers

James Dow was born into slavery in 1850. What he experienced in 15 years of bondage was never recorded. He subsequently worked on the Norfolk & Western Railway's main line in western Virginia as a section laborer—lining track, replacing ties, and spiking rails—day in and day out, in summer's humidity and winter's chill, for 50 years. How was it that he stood in the N&W president's office in 1930, wearing a suit and tie? Dow was there to receive a diamond pin rewarding his half-century's service to the railroad, and to be inducted into the Colored Division of the N&W Veterans Association, whose members had labored 25 or more years for the company. Dow had begun working for the railroad at the age of 18, 3 years after emancipation. Honored with him that day were 4 other black veterans, including 54-year employee Sandy Pryor, born into slavery in 1849, who joined the railroad in 1866 and finished his service in 1920 as a crossing watchman, and Frederick Matthews, who worked 52 years as a baggage porter, from 1865 to 1917, retiring at the age of 73.[1]

What explains these men's longevity with the railroad? Was it the company's loyalty to them, or a guarantee of job security, or the possibility of advancement to higher positions? None of these was promised to African American railroaders. Baggage porter Matthews neither expected nor received a promotion, because the next highest rung—baggage master—was reserved for whites. "Colored veterans" Josh Turpin and Stephen Fitzgerald, also recipients of diamond pins, risked their lives daily as brakemen without disability or life insurance or the hope of advancement to conductor. Turpin was still climbing on moving freight cars at the age of 69. Why did they do it? Despite the fact railroads had one of the most rigidly racist job ceilings, they offered some of the steadiest-paying jobs open to black males in the post–Civil War South, so long as those employees demonstrated an uncomplaining willingness to work and loyalty to the company. Many did so. Fortunate was the wife whose husband kept the family fed and housed on railroad pay. As a blues lyric expressed it, "When you marry, marry a railroad man / every Sunday, dollar in your hand."[2]

The Civil War dramatically expanded the need for black railroad workers. Both armies deliberately destroyed rolling stock, structures, and track. Hundreds of slaves who escaped to the Union army were conscripted into track gangs. Known as "pioneers," they rebuilt torn-up lines so that Federal troops and supplies could move by rail.[3] Confederate authorities impressed thousands of slaves to repair heavily used tracks and build new routes to close key gaps in the southern railway network.[4] After Appomattox, far greater numbers of laborers were needed to rebuild railroads shattered by four years of attacks, heavy traffic, and neglected maintenance. In Georgia, for example, thanks to General William T. Sherman's army, hundreds of miles of track had been ripped up and the Central of Georgia Railway and Macon & Western Railroad were virtually destroyed. With many farms and plantations also in ruins, plenty of former slaves were available for work. But for a short while, whites indulged the fantasy that blacks would die off without the care and supervision of owners, and dreamed of white or Asian workers providing the raw muscle for railroad construction and maintenance of way. Georgia's immediate postwar Democratic administration briefly barred ex-slaves from railroad work. But economics soon trumped politics, as railroads simply could not do without black workers. Once lines started to rebuild, they found themselves competing with agriculture for labor. Contributing to the Central of Georgia's frustration in obtaining and retaining the hundreds of laborers needed for track repairs was its determination to pay them skimpy wages.[5]

Formerly enslaved railroad workers were less tractable as freedmen, however. Whites claimed they were naturally shiftless, lacking ambition, and unwilling to work steadily for a living. This was a misperception. To ex-slaves, freedom meant the ability to choose one's employment and to walk away from abusive foremen. If railroad officials thought they could treat black workers the same as before, the freedmen disabused them of such notions. Certainly some were migratory or changed jobs frequently, but this was often a response to being limited to low-paying menial work with no opportunities for advancement.[6]

Through trial and error, blacks and whites negotiated the conventions of post-emancipation railroad employment. Most important, wages would be paid weekly. Only for a short while were rations, clothing, and medical attention part of one's compensation; railroads found they could attract sufficient workers without such inducements. Although the Muscogee Railroad found it necessary, in order "to secure suitable labor for the road, . . . to build . . . shanties to accommodate road hands and their families," spartan section houses for families were eventually provided only for permanently based track gangs. Some postwar maintenance of way crews, at least in Virginia, included ex-slaves and former Rebel soldiers working harmoniously side by side. But most section gangs replicated the prewar hierarchical pattern in which a white foreman supervised black laborers. Gone was the whip, except for use on convicts.[7]

One of the greatest motivations for seeking railroad work was avoiding sharecropping, the white South's new form of economic oppression.[8] When the freedmen's dream of gaining title to their own land didn't materialize, the options for supporting a family were few. No matter that railroad employment remained physically harder and more dangerous than farming: it paid cash wages. Many former enslaved railroaders remained on the job and were joined by thousands of other freedmen who had known only agriculture. The jobs most readily available to inexperienced blacks were on construction and MOW gangs.

Railroad construction boomed in the South during and after Reconstruction. Between 1865 and 1875, 35,000 black farmhands left South Carolina and Georgia for work in Louisiana, Arkansas, and Texas, one railroad alone employing 5,000 ex-slaves. Laborers in Louisiana earned as much as $1.75 a day (more than $500 a year), a princely sum when compared to the barely break-even remuneration of sharecropping. The Mississippi Central Railroad paid $20 per month, plus board, for able-bodied men in 1866. The pace of new construction kept accelerating into the 1880s, as hundreds of millions of dollars of northern and foreign capital was invested in nearly 200 new railroads.[9]

Although most black migration in response to railroad jobs was within the South in the decades immediately following emancipation, some men went west to work on the first transcontinental railroad. In the second half of the 1860s, 300 former slaves, including Union army veterans, toiled alongside tens of thousands of native-born whites and immigrants to build the Union Pacific Railroad from Omaha to Utah.[10] Once new lines were finished, modest numbers of African Americans secured employment on western railroads in maintenance of way work, as train porters and on dining cars, and in shops and yards. The Central Pacific Railroad operated its own sleeping cars between Sacramento and Ogden, with black porters in attendance.[11] As elsewhere in the nation, black railroaders only found jobs at the bottom. But cash wages and a lower incidence of racism toward them (Asians, Native Americans, and Mexicans were more often targets) overruled status considerations. Wyoming's black population growth shows the impact of the Union Pacific. More than half of the state's 1,250 black residents in 1930 lived in 6 towns astride the UP main line. Not surprisingly, of 536 gainfully employed black males in the state, 21 percent were railroad laborers, probably section hands. The next largest occupation—janitors—constituted only 10 percent of the male workforce.[12]

Individual towns all over the West reflected railroad opportunities. In Arizona, Winslow's black community was anchored by Atchison, Topeka & Santa Fe Railway coach porters. In the entire West, black railroaders were most numerous in Kansas, which had the highest black population in the West, aside from Oklahoma, as a result of the "Exodus" of tens of thousands from the Lower Mississippi Valley in 1879–80.[13] So powerful was the attraction of railroad work for African Americans that, by 1930, it was the largest category of nonagricultural employment in the state, utilizing 14 percent of the 16,760 black men performing nonfarm labor.[14] In towns like Topeka and Coffeyville, where railroads maintained shops and yards, black neighborhoods developed near the tracks, often becoming the cities' Tenderloin districts. On weekends, local laborers and section men back in town (including whites) frequented the saloons, gambling dens, and houses of prostitution that flourished with tacit civic permission. Males of both races who migrated from the South brought with them habits of responding to disputes or affronts to one's honor with violence. This propensity was fueled by the prevalence of alcohol and the sale of small, easily concealed, $3 revolvers. Homicides, interracial as well as black-on-black, reached high levels in such districts. Yet settlement patterns were not consistent, because job opportunities were not uniform. While the Santa Fe employed blacks in Topeka at the turn of the twentieth century, it hired none at all in Emporia, one of its Kansas division points, even though a considerable number of blacks lived in that town.[15]

Railroad employment provided blacks with cash wages, and sometimes steady incomes, but it did not always inspire a settled existence. A portion of railroaders—black as well as white—were "boomers" living an itinerant lifestyle, working until they felt like quitting or were fired, but eventually finding a new job on another railroad. Boomers were restless, wanting to see new places or escape one's dislikable surroundings. Not a few lost jobs because of alcohol. They tended to be more common in the lowest-paid categories, and among younger, single men.[16] So while railroading, particularly MOW jobs, introduced black populations into many areas of the West, not everyone stayed or settled down to become contributing members of a local community.

Most blacks, however, lacking the wherewithal to migrate long distances or the knowledge of opportunities elsewhere, remained in the South after slavery, so the black railroad experience was predominately southern for the rest of the nineteenth century. One thing changed, however: the technology of railroad building improved after the Civil War. The invention of dynamite and the widespread adoption of steam-driven pile drivers and shovels made construction safer and quicker. But brawn and muscle were still essential. Picks, shovels, and wheelbarrows had not been retired. Laying crossties and rails continued to be done by hand. It took a strong man to heft an 8-foot-by-6-inch-by-8-inch tie alone. Each yard of main line "iron" weighed 75 pounds in the early 1900s, making the then-standard 33-foot section of rail weigh 825 pounds. Track tools were similarly heavy: a jack weighed 50 pounds and a lining bar 20 pounds in the morning, and seemingly much more by the end of the day. Imagine the army of section men, mostly black, who changed 13,000 miles of southern 5-feet and 5-feet, 6-inches gauge track to 4-feet, 9-inches between the rails in just two days in 1886. The Charleston and Savannah Railway employed 359 men to change the gauge on 129 miles of main line and sidings (including 56 switches)—nearly 3 men per mile—all in a 7-hour day.[17]

Railroads in the African American Experience

Track work, whether one was white or black, was still hazardous. The worst accidents occurred when orders were not properly transmitted to engineers, conductors, and track foremen, resulting in speeding trains bearing down on workers and handcars. In addition, workers were run over, and sometimes killed, by handcars and push cars carrying tools and materials. Eye and facial injuries resulted from flying spikes. Feet were crushed, and toes cut off, when rails or ties were dropped, or a jack was lowered without warning. It was up to each person to work as safely as possible because an injury did not entitle one to paid time off.[18] And accidents aplenty still occurred in railroad construction, particularly from cave-ins and premature blasts. Blacks had no monopoly on construction jobs, even in the South, and economic hard times increased interracial employment friction. During the depression of 1896, immigrant Italian, Swedish, and Hungarian construction laborers attempted to drive black construction workers on the Kansas City, Pittsburg & Gulf Railway out of Polk County, Arkansas. Backed by sympathetic local whites, they raided the blacks' camp one night, killing three, wounding eight, and prompting others to flee for their lives.[19] But these were not the only perils. Some black construction laborers worked under a virtual death sentence.

From Reconstruction into the early 1900s, southern courts purposefully convicted large numbers of blacks—many for minor property crimes—and sentenced them to lengthy prison (not jail) terms to ensure that railroads and railroad construction companies, as well as mine and plantation owners, could obtain cheap labor from the state. This was the infamous convict lease system. Young blacks were literally railroaded directly from local courtrooms to convict work camps. Of 30 unfortunates sent to help build the state-owned Western North Carolina Railroad in January 1879, 24 were convicted of larceny. Robbery was an interpersonal crime, while larceny did not involve the actual presence of the victim, yet larceny sentences ranged as high as 15 years. In Georgia, 20 percent of black prisoners on railroad construction projects in 1870, who had been convicted of burglary, were serving life sentences.[20]

Although white prisoners were also put out to lease, the vast majority of leased convicts were black. A major purpose of this system was racial subordination, not the administration of justice. Like lynching at the turn of the century, it was employed to instill fear into African Americans who had not been sufficiently conditioned to passivity to whites by a life of outright slavery, and to reinforce the utter foolishness of challenging white supremacy. But convict leasing was driven by an additional motive: ensuring a plentiful supply of cheap, exploitable labor for first Republican and then New South Democratic economic interests. According to historian Edward Ayers, it "bridged the chasm between an agricultural slave economy and a society in the earliest stages of capitalist industrial development." Convicts supplied labor for railroad expansion without hampering the revival of agriculture, while at the same time reinforcing white supremacy. Thus social control and economic development were linked. Another historian, Alex Lichtenstein, connects the dots: the convict lease accommodated "the labor needs of an emerging class of industrialists without eroding the racial domination essential to planters."[21]

The emptying of prisons into the hands of private enterprises began in most states in the early days of Reconstruction, but it reached its apogee after white southern "Redeemer" Democrats brought Reconstruction to a close by recapturing political control of "their" states. During the slavery era, most state prisoners had been white, and they were not leased out. With the end of slavery, however, the complexion of the southern penal system changed dramatically. Blacks soon predominated, and by the late nineteenth century 90 percent of leased convicts were African Americans. Not only were cash-strapped states relieved of the cost of housing prisoners, the convict lease also served, for some states, as an important source of revenue. In Alabama, for example, for several years 6 to 10 percent of state funds derived from the practice.[22]

The contractors who leased convicts were generally politically connected, sometimes being the very politicians who shaped the system. While the cost of leasing varied from year to year and state to state, railroads obtained laborers at half or less of what they had paid slave owners to hire their bondsmen decades earlier. For a time, one large railroad contractor in Georgia got every one of its prisoners at no cost, with the state simply being relieved of the burden of guarding and caring for them. An official sent to inspect the railroad camps found inmates woefully overworked and brutally disciplined, and when it became public knowledge that sick prisoners were beaten to death simply because they could not do as much work as healthy convicts, white citizens petitioned the state to revoke its agreement with the contractor. Even after these revelations, a renewal agreement gave the same contractor every state prisoner for $50 per convict per year. The lease system resembled slavery, but without paternalism. It replicated slavery, but with an earlier death sentence.[23]

Despite the cheapness of convict labor, contractors and railroads did not use the savings to provide adequate care for the convicts. In state after state, investigators found foul living quarters, appalling sanitation, barbaric punishment, execrable rations, nonexistent medical care, and high death rates. In the first 12 years of the Georgia lease, more than 400 prisoners died. This was more than quadruple the number of penitentiary inmate deaths in the state's entire antebellum period. Alabama may have set the record for barbarity. Forty-one percent of all prisoners died in 1870, and although the mortality rate subsequently dropped, by 1883 convicts still, on average, survived for only 3 years. The following year an inspection of a camp for prisoners grading the Georgia Pacific Railroad in Walker County found 106 inmates in "two rough log houses, with a low roof, without a floor, and with no ventilation except through the cracks between the logs." Nearly 10 percent of the convicts died in the first three and a half months. Little care was provided for the sick, food was "rough and badly cooked," and "the privy system was simply buckets" that were not cleaned with disinfectants.[24]

The convict lease system practically guaranteed that sexual assaults would take place. Because states made no distinction between juvenile and adult offenders, boys were put to work alongside men and were frequently, if not invariably, raped by older inmates. At one point, one-quarter of all leased convicts in Mississippi were African American children and adolescents. Rarely were female prisoners segregated from males. In fact, some were literally chained to men and slept alongside them. In an environment in which inmates were brutalized, some convicts responded by brutalizing others. Although official state penal reports are understandably silent on the matter, women and children were obviously extremely vulnerable, and one may reasonably speculate that sexual assaults occurred.[25]

The southern railroad-building boom in the late 1860s, 1870s, and 1880s would not have been so successful without this form of state subsidy. Every former Confederate state engaged in convict leasing. The list of lines benefiting from the practice is long. In the 1870s, the Greenwood & Augusta Railroad started building its line with South Carolina convicts leased at $3 per month. (In comparison, the Macon & Western hired Georgia slaves in 1859 for $200 per annum.) The G&A took almost no heed of the welfare of its workers, who labored in chains and were underfed, poorly housed, and medically neglected. Almost half of the 265 prisoners died, the railroad admitting to the prevalence of scurvy and other "chronic illness." Some found death through brutal whipping or a guard's bullet. Railroads did not have to indemnify the state for inmate deaths, and if one died, more prisoners were usually available. Some made no cash payment for convict labor, instead indemnifying the state with the railroad's bonds. In another type of arrangement, lines like the Georgia & North Carolina Railroad obtained convicts from the North Carolina State Prison for no payment of any sort, only the requirement to assume all expenses in housing, feeding, and supervising them.[26] In some cases, payment was not required because the railroad or contractor had to assume responsibility not only for able-bodied convicts, but also for the elderly, infirm, sick, and insane as well.

While state prison reports reveal grim statistics concerning the convict lease, the testimony of eyewitnesses is unsurpassed. J. C. Powell commanded various Florida convict camps for 14 years and, for a time, the entire state lease system. He entitled his recollections *The American Siberia*, and the comparison was apt. Powell spared no detail in describing the abuse of prisoners under others' authority, although he painted a more benign picture where he was in command. When he first began work in 1876, 95 percent of the inmates were black, including quite a few women. By 1890, the number included considerably more whites, but only rarely a white woman.

One of the worst examples concerned convicts building a Plant System line through a trackless wilderness in central Florida under conditions that, in Powell's words, "stand unparalleled in criminal annals. Dozens of those who went into the tropical marshes and palmetto jungles . . . went to certain death. There was no provision made for either shelter or supplies. Rude huts were built of whatever material came to hand, and in the periods of heavy rain it was no unusual thing for the convicts to awake in the morning half submerged in mud and slime. The commissary department dwindled into nothing . . . there was no food at all. In this extremity, the convicts were driven to live as the wild beasts . . . to scour the woods for food. They dug up roots and cut the tops from 'cabbage' palmetto trees . . . It was not long before the camp was ravaged by every disease induced by starvation and exposure," including malaria, scurvy, pneumonia, and dysentery. The

A souvenir postcard showing black convicts building the Western North Carolina Railroad in the 1880s, lined up and waiting for a meal. Note the shackles on their feet. They are excavating a "cut" through the hill, largely by hand. It would have been brutal work for free workers, and was doubly so for convicts who died at alarming rates while "New South" entrepreneurs benefited enormously from state convict leases. Courtesy of the North Carolina State Archives

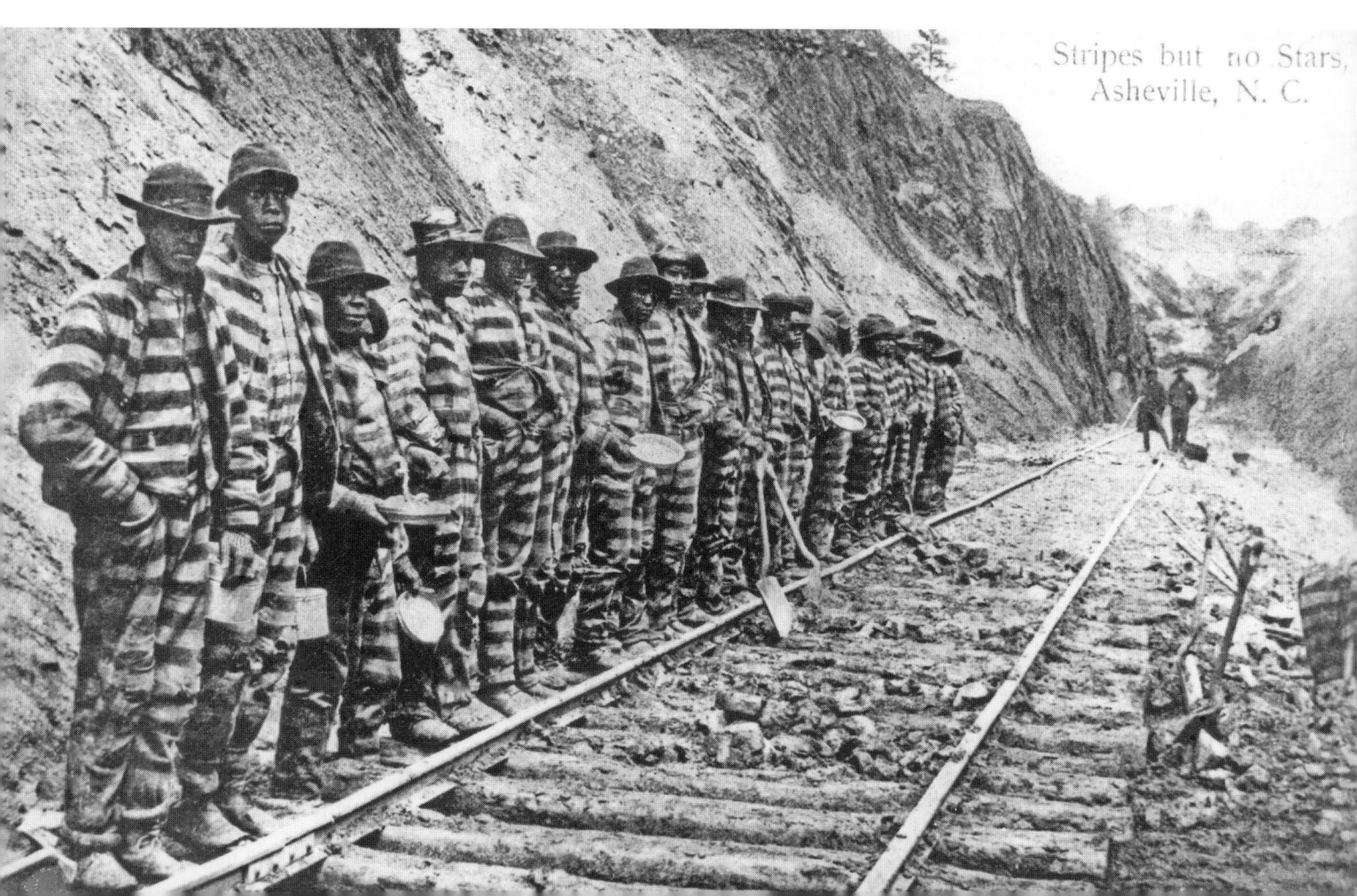

roadbed was "punctuated by grave-yards." Punishments were barbaric. "A negro convict was strung up . . . Whip-cords were fastened around his thumbs, the loose ends flung over a convenient limb and made taut until his toes swung clear of the ground . . . The captain had determined to make a salutary example, and he let the negro hang . . . His muscles knotted into cramps under the strain, his eyes started from his head, and sweat ran from his body in streams. An hour passed—then two. His shrieks had ceased and his struggles grown feeble, so they let him down and he fell to the ground like a log—dead."[27]

Powell professed to abhor such brutality, advocating instead the use of a "tough leather [strap] about a foot and a half long by three inches broad, and attached to a wooden handle." But corporal punishment was capricious: "There is no legal restriction, and never was, as to the number of blows, the frequency of punishment or by whom it shall be applied." Powell claimed to have allowed only wardens or captains in charge of camps to administer such whippings so as to keep discipline within what he regarded as reasonable limits.[28]

"Reasonable" discipline was an oxymoron. Powell unapologetically narrated the fate of convicts under his supervision who were building the Jacksonville & Waycross Short Line, 32 miles out from that Florida city. Although the railroad supposedly supplied "good and abundant" food and spared no expense in making the camp "first-class," a "prison horror . . . of the first magnitude" caused half the inmates to die in an epidemic of spinal meningitis brought upon by a sadistic officer. In the cold of winter, he prohibited the poor wretches from bathing in tubs inside their huts. Instead, he would "marshal the convicts in the yard, stark naked, and turn the hose upon them. The water was icy, a keen wind was often blowing, and the effect of such a bath was to chill the men to an almost paralyzing degree."[29]

Some of the most notorious abuses of the convict lease system occurred during construction of the Western North Carolina Railroad. In one 9-mile section, the steeply ascending line looped around itself eight times, clinging to cliffs and running through cuts blasted from the rock. Six bores, including the notorious Swannanoa Tunnel immortalized in folksong, were necessary to complete the line. Five hundred convicts were assigned to the work in 1877, with more added in subsequent years. Governor Zebulon B. Vance urged on the project, despite his knowledge of the appalling conditions under which prisoners labored. In one three-month period, they received only two days off, Sundays bringing no respite. Only 7 cents per day was spent to feed an inmate. A local white observer left this description: "The gorge swarmed with hundreds of wretched blacks in the striped yellow convict garb. After their supper was cooked (over open campfires) and eaten, they were driven into a row of prison [railroad] cars, where they were tightly boxed for the night, with no possible chance to obtain either air or light." The final toll was horrendous. At least 21 prisoners died in digging and blasting the Swannanoa Tunnel alone. Officially, 125 convicts perished, but the number was actually much higher, the warden of the state penitentiary subsequently reporting that survivors "were finally returned to the prison with shattered constitutions and their physical strength entirely gone, so that with the most skillful medical treatment and the best nursing, it was impossible for them to recuperate."[30]

The most famous railroad convict laborer was John Henry. Long assumed to be only a mythical figure, enshrined in legend and folklore, he has recently been shown by historian Scott Nelson to be a real person. New Jersey–born John William Henry, Virginia Penitentiary convict no. 497, may have been a Union army soldier who remained in the South after the Civil War to seek his fortune. Convicted of larceny and housebreaking in 1866 and sentenced to a 10-year term, he was one of hundreds, if not thousands, of black convicts who were leased to contractors building the Chesapeake & Ohio Railroad main line into West Virginia. He was a "steel drivin' man" (hammer man), pounding drill bits into rock so that explosives could be packed into the holes for detonation. The legend has him competing with a steam-powered drill while excavating the Big Bend Tunnel, but in fact he worked on the nearby Lewis Tunnel. (Indeed, steam drills were tried, but they proved to be unreliable.) More than 100 black convicts died, including John William Henry in 1871, before the Lewis bore was completed. His body was shipped back to the penitentiary in Richmond where it was buried, as the folksong has it, in a convict graveyard near the "white house." In fact, the main penitentiary building was plastered with lime, making it appear stark white.[31]

Tens of thousands of blacks suffered the convict lease system in the supposedly progressive New South. Railroads and railroad construction contractors benefited enormously from endlessly exploitable, rock-bottom-cheap laborers. As a white Mississippian later acknowledged, it was "the product of human rapacity, grafted upon the conditions that a defunct slavery had left behind it."[32] Only when the stench of abuses could no longer be hidden was the system "reformed," at the turn of the twentieth century, by using convicts on public works, like building roads. By then, the railroad construction boom was over. But keeping up track and roadbed was a never-ending requirement for all railroads, and in the South maintenance of way section gang workers were, like the leased convicts, overwhelmingly black. Two employment patterns emerged.

The first reflected the importance of regular work for cash wages to southern blacks. Many section men kept their jobs for decades, not because of any prospect of promotion to gang foreman or section master, not because of company loyalty to them, but because steady employment, even under grueling circumstances, was prized if one had a family to support and didn't want to take the risks associated with sharecropping. It was not uncommon to start as a water boy at a very young age. Theodore Haynes was a mere 9 years old when he began working for the Central of Georgia. Many others were in their early teens. Owen White was 17 when he began working on a Louisville & Nashville Railroad extra gang in 1926, toting water to the working-men and for the cook, keeping bunk car stoves supplied with coal, and tending fires in the cook's stove and that of the white foreman. To the young man, $30 a month, paid in silver dollars, plus board, was a fine wage. His family must have felt the same: not only was there one less mouth to feed, he sent home half of his earnings.[33]

Steady section men might stay on the same gang for years, developing a camaraderie that enabled them to respect one another and lighten their work as each man pulled his weight, sometimes literally. They often took pride in the neatness of their tool shed, or how evenly they kept the rock ballast "dressed" with uniform edges. They composed their own chants sung out by one of them, the caller, who synchronized and gave rhythm to carrying rails, driving spikes, lining track, and other repetitive tasks. The calls ranged from sacred to profane to nonsense:

If I could, I surely would / stand on the rock where Moses stood.

Susie, Susie don't you know / I can make your belly grow.

I wish my cow was blind / so I could push this track in line.[34]

"Preacher" Jones was a caller and water boy (although a grown man) on a Virginian Railway gang in West Virginia in the 1920s, who, because of his talent, performed little of the hardest track work. While others wielded their heavy lining bars, he launched into his chants. When he sang out "Ho," everyone leaned on his bar at once, and the rail moved. It was said that without Preacher's direction, the rail would not budge. Indeed, on many gangs, no rail moved, no tie was tamped, no spike was driven, without a call or chant.[35]

Section men were sometimes the railroads' best labor recruiters. When hard work, low wages, or high deductions reduced the number of "gandy dancers," Preacher Jones was given a pass on a passenger train to go home and round up new workers. In a week or so he would return with a fresh contingent. It was common practice for individuals to be periodically given passes to go home, and they could bring back as many friends as were willing to work, all riding on the same pass. Not all new recruits stayed for long, however. They either found better-paying jobs or became dissatisfied with pay as low as 1 cent after the company made deductions for tobacco, gloves, overalls, candy, and meals obtained on credit. Sometimes, the grub was no help in keeping them. Owen White remembered that, on his L&N extra gang, "we didn't have nothing but old side bacon and biscuits and molasses for breakfast. And we had beans and cornbread for dinner [the noon meal]. Beans and cornbread for supper at night."[36]

Southern whites only partially understood the character of career black section men. The Southern Railway's 1916 honor roll of 25-year veterans included 45 black MOW and bridge-and-building hands who had worked an average of 31 years each. They were described paternalistically as "the old-fashioned kind of negroes, sturdy, self-respecting and respectful men . . . of the kind with whom we all grew up and have associated, negroes who have our good-will and affection and who do their work well and cheerfully." "Self-respecting" best described men like Bob Cannon, who performed track work for 52 years, starting in 1864, or 4 others who toiled for more than 40 years, or the section men who worked for decades for Georgia's Upson County Railroad.[37] Although they were manual laborers on the bottom rung of the railroad status ladder, such career hands tended to be responsible family men, church and fraternal organization leaders, and members of the middle class. One retired track worker stressed that "those men who worked on the railroads [for decades] were the pride of the community." Their wives would not let them go out in public in clothing that was not starched and ironed because "that's a railroad man."[38]

Not all section men were steady workers, though. A second employment pattern reflected the careers of boomers (chronic ramblers), or those who were more interested in earning money by dice or card games, or men who were one step ahead of the law or spouses. Boomers were particularly common on extra gangs, large crews that worked six-day weeks, lived in camp cars, and were sent anywhere on a division for emergencies or special jobs. Maintaining the continuity of family life was difficult under such conditions. Boomers and extra-gang laborers were the ones more responsible for the drunkenness, gambling, stabbing, and shooting that characterized some section quarters and outfit cars at night and on the weekends. Owen White recalled fights in the mess car with combatants breaking up tin cups and pans to use as knives. Some battles may have begun as tests of strengths or informal wrestling or boxing matches, but then escalated under the influence of alcohol or goading from others. At times, this interpersonal violence grew to be so common that southern police didn't bother to investigate cuttings or murders. As Mississippi whites rationalized it, this "typical" African American behavior fell within the context of "negro law": blacks need be prosecuted only for offenses that directly affected the dominant white population, like property crimes (e.g., larceny) and interracial violence. Because black-on-black crime did not usually touch white interests, authorities tended to ignore it. Thus, some railroad camps got pretty violent, with white section foremen disinclined or unable to police them.[39]

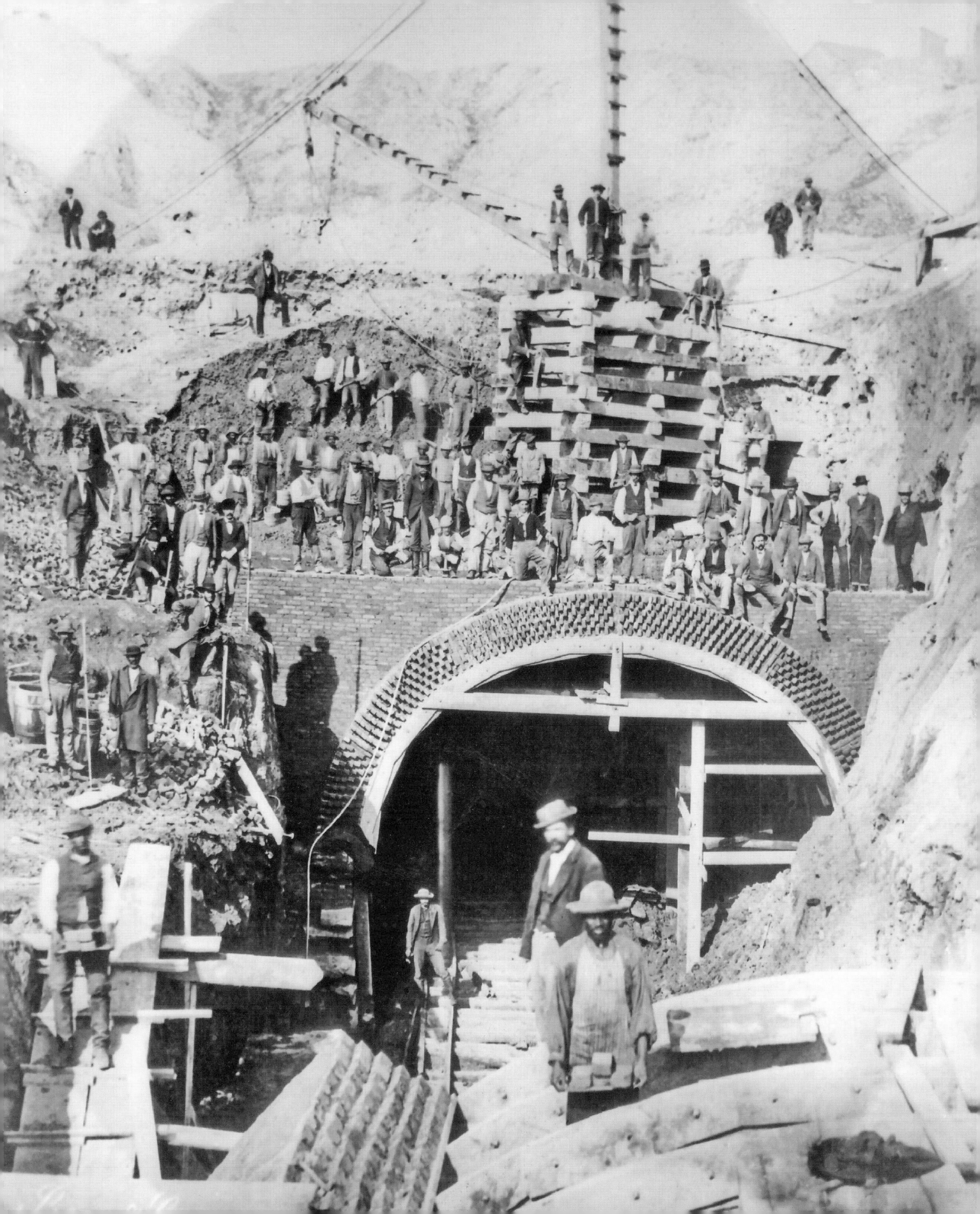

In the final decades of the nineteenth century, modest numbers of black section workers fanned out across the nation from the South. Migration into Kansas and Wyoming has already been noted. When the Illinois Central Railroad faced labor shortages in southern Illinois in the 1880s, it was natural to tap the South because the IC already relied on black track gangs on lines below Memphis. Other Midwestern and northern railroads similarly hired blacks in moderate numbers, not as intentionally perhaps as the IC, but simply to maintain an adequate and mobile labor force. Their section gangs were polyglot crews, with eastern Europeans and Italians predominating. Few blacks helped build the transcontinental lines to the Northwest, however, because of the availability first of Chinese, and later, Japanese, workers, plus others from Eastern Europe. In the Southwest, blacks rarely competed with Mexicans, Native Americans (particularly Pueblos in New Mexico and Navajos in Arizona), and Japanese, who dominated track work by 1900.[40]

By 1910, slightly more than 100,000 black men worked for railroads, double the number of only two decades before. Nearly 85 percent were laborers, most of them on section gangs, with the remainder in shops, roundhouses, freight houses, and passenger stations. And about 85 percent of all black railroaders still worked in the South. World War I changed that. By 1916, with industry booming, foreign immigration nearly halted, and white railroaders taking better-paying factory jobs, railroads in the North and Midwest experienced a critical manpower shortage. Out of necessity, they turned to African Americans and women, particularly for track work.

A flood of black workers onto northern railroads began in the summer of 1916, when several of the largest lines sent agents into the South, offering free transportation to men who would work on their section gangs. The four largest importers of new labor were the four dominant trunk lines of the East. The Erie, Baltimore & Ohio, Pennsylvania, and New York Central railroads brought nearly 40,000 black laborers out of the South in 1916–17, deploying them in boxcar and tent camps scattered along their lines. In the Midwest, the Illinois Central also recruited large numbers.[41] But the railroads almost immediately found these new hires slipping through their fingers. Some migrants accepted free tickets merely to escape the South. Others quickly found non-railroad employers were paying higher wages. Crude housing conditions discouraged others from staying on the job. The turnover was so great that fewer than 2,000 of the Pennsylvania Railroad's 12,000 recruits remained on the payroll after a few months.[42] But despite low retention rates, blacks gained a foothold in northern railroading. Prior to this World War I-era "Great Migration," only about 4,300 blacks labored on northern railroads from Massachusetts to Illinois and Michigan. By 1930, their numbers had increased by more than 300 percent, to 17,500 men. The largest category was MOW laborers.[43]

Many new section workers assimilated themselves into, and contributed to, northern black communities. A remarkable chart compiled by the Pennsylvania Railroad's personnel department in 1924 sheds light on this phenomenon. The Pennsy carried 9,631 blacks on the payroll in 1924, the largest category being 1,796 MOW laborers, including 5 foremen. Only 302 (17 percent) still lived in camp cars or section shanties. The rest dwelt in established black neighborhoods. Their particular housing arrangements were not recorded, but, of the road's entire black workforce, about 20 percent were boarders, 62 percent were renters, and 15 percent were homeowners. And although nearly half of black employees were recent migrants from the South, few were transients, less than 1 in 10 being described as an "unsettled or floating element."[44] So many of those who entered the workforce at the bottom of the pay and prestige scale, as section workers, were putting down roots in local communities. At least up to the Great Depression, even track work offered some opportunity for an improved standard of living and a degree of upward mobility within black America.

Northern section gangs, during and after the Great Migration, continued to differ from those in the South. Very few were all-black. Instead, African Americans typically worked alongside a variety of native and immigrant whites, not infrequently under an Italian or other European-immigrant foreman. Such was the case on the Reading Railroad in New Jersey and Pennsylvania, where blacks made up only a minority of section workers but could be found across the system. In the West, blacks still faced competition from Mexican MOW workers, who were concentrated most heavily in California and Texas, particularly on the Atchison, Topeka & Santa Fe and Chicago, Rock Island & Pacific railways. Mexican section men were imported into other parts of the West by the Great Northern, Northern Pacific, and Denver & Rio Grande Western lines. While more than 17,000 blacks worked on all Louisiana and Texas railroads in the mid-1920s, more than 4,000 Mexicans were employed on the Southern Pacific's lines alone in those states, rendering blacks no longer dominant in section work. Mexicans could be hired for less. Even the Pennsylvania Railroad, whose 10,000-plus route-miles lay east of the Mississippi River, employed 1,200 Mexican track laborers in the mid-1920s and used additional hundreds seasonally. So just as black railroad labor peaked in the 1920s, the seeds of decline were being sown. Although new immigration policies in the later 1920s reduced the number of Mexicans that were admitted legally to the United States by 90 percent, Mexican track workers were now com-petitors to be reckoned with.[45]

The Great Depression of the 1930s hammered railroads and their workers hard. Declining revenues from both freight and passenger trains and increasing competition from trucks and buses meant that personnel costs had to be cut. Although some money-losing branch lines were abandoned, the basic rail network of more than 200,000 miles still needed to be maintained, now with fewer workers who were paid lower wages. Numerous section laborers, of all ethnicities, were laid off. Those who managed to keep their jobs endured pay reductions, seasonal furloughs, and short-term unemployment due to dips in traffic. In 1937, a year before the first federal minimum wage— 25 cents an hour—was established, MOW workers nationwide were averaging only 21.6 cents in hourly pay. The twenty poorest Class 1 railroads, employing nearly three-quarters of the lowest-paid track workers, were all lines that operated exclusively or partially in the South and used mostly African American laborers. When railroads were later forced to pay a New Deal–mandated railroad minimum wage of 40 cents per hour, they turned to mechanization, with the ultimate effect of further reducing the number of track workers. Additional job losses came as 249 short line railroads, primarily in the South, were abandoned between 1921 and 1939.[46] African Americans in the South found one silver lining, however: whites still regarded section work as a black man's occupation, and did not murder them for their jobs, as they did black brakemen and firemen.

Unionization had not helped African American section men. The Brotherhood of Maintenance of Way Employees, established by white workers in the nineteenth century, barred blacks from membership until 1917. Thereafter they could join "allied lodges," but these had no real voice in the union. White men "represented" them at conventions and "negotiated" on their behalf. In the South, many of these "representatives" were the very same white foremen who supervised them. Should black workers challenge the union's sincerity regarding their welfare, or seek to form an independent organization or affiliate with a less racist union, the foreman/union representative could simply fire the dissidents for "insubordination."[47]

The realities of job insecurity can be observed in the career of Allen Brown, who worked in maintenance of way on the Chesapeake & Ohio Railroad for 42 years. After retirement, he felt free to describe the favoritism and nepotism that dampened workers' protests. He started in 1926 at the age of 16 on an extra gang near his birthplace in West Virginia, one of about three dozen black laborers. The only whites were the boss, assistant foreman, timekeeper, and a water boy. Race did not guarantee acceptance by his fellow laborers. One of them warned that if he didn't carry as much weight as the others, "I'm going to throw a rail on you." As Brown put it, "if you didn't work [as hard as the rest], you'd get crippled up." Hard work it was. When asked what type of equipment he used in his career, Brown replied that for most of the time from 1926 to 1968, "there wasn't no equipment—it was manual labor. Pick and a shovel, pick and a shovel, and a [ballast] fork."

New section men often started on extra gangs, because those with seniority claimed the stable jobs, particularly those that were situated close to home. Tie gangs were similar. Brown worked on such a crew for two years after a reduction in force on the C&O's Hinton Division deprived him of a job where he could be home every night. The tie gang worked along the entire 350-mile-long main line from Hinton, West Virginia, to Newport News, Virginia. Brown's work train, including the camp cars in which they lived, left Hinton on Sunday evenings, returning home on Friday after-noon. It was "pretty rough. I was tempted two or three times to quit. My wife begged me to quit . . . But I weathered the storm," finally getting a regular job on a section gang that was responsible for a 28-mile coal branch.

Section men were at the mercy of their white bosses. Brown remembered clearly the days before civil rights protections, when one didn't get a track job by submitting an application to a personnel office but in being chosen by a foreman. "It used to be, a lot of these gangs, . . . like working track, if a foreman didn't like me, if he got mad at his wife or something, and I didn't look to suit him, he could just fire me, on the spot. And he come right along, he'd hire his cousin, or hire his son, hire his daddy, hire anybody . . . I know a lot of gangs, there wasn't nothing but just in-laws." And they had no job security, working only for that day's wages.[48] This was not invariably to the detriment of black workers. On some track gangs, every one was related. Fathers and sons, brothers and cousins, and brothers-in-law worked as teams, knowing one another's strengths and weaknesses from long years' experience.

Race circumscribed the lives of southern black section men. For the most part, they could not aspire to become foremen (section masters); only a very few attained that position, and then usually only temporarily.[49] If their gangs included white laborers, they had to be addressed as "Mister." Some section masters refused to pause the task when men had worked past the point of exhaustion, when if one were driving a mule, it would be prudent to let it rest and catch its wind. Other bosses simply manifested contempt for those under them. Retired track man Frank Carrington still remembered a very hot day when his gang, working with only their muscles, unloaded extremely heavy new ties that were dripping with the chemical preservative creosote and stacked them on a wheeled cart, which they had to push 2 miles up the line. The boss was so unfeeling he sat on the cart, adding to the weight, rather than walk alongside the sweaty, exhausted men. No wonder some contemptuous track-lining calls were sung only when the white foreman was yards away, sighting along the track:

> Boy can't read, boy can't write,
> boy don't know when his track is right.
> Look at the boss, how he stands,
> stands more like a farmer than a boss man.

Abused gandy dancers had few means of protest available. One was the passive-aggressive tactic of aggravating a foreman by "straightening" a rail too far, so that it would have to be pulled back again. This irritation could be amplified by doing it shortly before a train was to pass, forcing the boss to order a man out to flag it down, thus incurring a dispatcher's displeasure for delaying the train.[50]

World War II generated a brief spike in maintenance of way work for blacks, but this merely reinforced the pattern where blacks remained consigned to low-pay, no-promotion job categories. On the Reading Railroad, the only black MOW foremen were in charge of a handful of all-black female crews. The Pennsylvania Railroad again claimed to be the nation's largest employer of African Americans, with more than 16,000 on the payroll in 1942. The biggest group, 38 percent (6,214), was track laborers. The employment of only 29 black section foremen did not signify genuine improvement. And the policy of forming all-black and all-white extra gangs was a step backward. For example, in 1943 the railroad stationed a black gang in camp cars at Carnegie, Pennsylvania, and a white gang in similar accommodations at Dennison, Ohio.[51] The Pennsy's rival, the New York Central, employed 9,282 blacks by the end of that same year. The greatest proportion, 32 percent

(2,913), was in maintenance of way, including 3 foremen and 14 assistant foremen.[52] Progress at the supervisory level on both roads was still at a glacial pace.

Although railroad employment rose to nearly 1.5 million workers in 1945, this was not a hopeful trend. The number of railroad jobs overall declined 17 percent from 1940 to 1960, with the rate of loss for blacks being 20 percent. Track workers and other less skilled laborers experienced the greatest losses. Many had been hired during the war, and, lacking much seniority, couldn't retain their jobs. Overall, the MOW ranks were thinning as railroads moved to further mechanize track laying and maintenance. By the 1960s, some blacks were operating machines and a few were being promoted to section foremen. But penetrating the supervisory ranks was painfully slow, failing to keep pace with the loss of jobs to machines. In a survey of 19 railroads operating in New York and New Jersey in 1957, 1,813 blacks constituted 24 percent of all section laborers, but only 3 percent of foremen.[53]

The enactment of fair employment laws in the 1940s, 1950s, and 1960s (in states outside of the South) began to whittle away at labor union discrimination. The Brotherhood of Maintenance of Way Employees removed its bar to full black participation in 1946. But some railroads remained guilty of blatant racism. In the late 1940s the Massachusetts Fair Employment Practices Commission identified several lines that hired only white track workers.[54] Mechanization brought new obstacles. Not only were fewer workers needed, but blacks were sometimes told, "that ain't no nigger job, that's a whiteman job." Even when civil rights legislation required that they be considered for operating machinery, they might be repeatedly "disqualified" even though they were, in fact, competent. Many a man had to stick it out on the bottom rung. With children and spouses to support, "you couldn't just walk off a job."[55]

Today, construction of new railroad lines is rare. The only significant mileage added in recent decades opened up western coalfields. Maintenance of way tasks are highly mechanized; for example, track is kept in alignment using laser-guided machinery. Lining track by hand, with a gang leaning into heavy steel bars at the urging of a caller, is an archaic art that is preserved only by aging veterans and re-enactors like Virginia's Buckingham Lining Bar Gang. Their performances, featuring lining and spiking as well as the folklore and songs of African American section men, have been enjoyed by crowds at railroad museums and folk-life festivals across the nation. They are the last remnant of the old-time black track workers. Retired C&O laborer Allen Brown remembered "they did every job like they thought the railroad belongs to them. And they didn't want to be criticized about their work. So you didn't do this, you didn't do that. Everybody taken pride in their work . . . Your best track, maintaining them, was did by hand."[56]

The lives of black construction and section men typify the African American railroad experience. They, like most black railroaders, worked in place, enjoying no upward mobility into the more skilled crafts or the supervisory ranks. Their entrenchment at the bottom was enforced at first by their outright exclusion from labor unions and later by their consignment to powerless black union auxiliaries. Railroad work, particularly on section gangs, didn't promise affluence or even, in many cases, job security. But MOW paid more reliably than sharecropping, and that is the key to understanding why, at any given time from 1865 through the 1950s, tens of thousands of blacks laid and lined track. Railroad employment, even at the lowest ranks, was, simply, a step above the worst exploitation suffered by blacks in the post-slavery era.

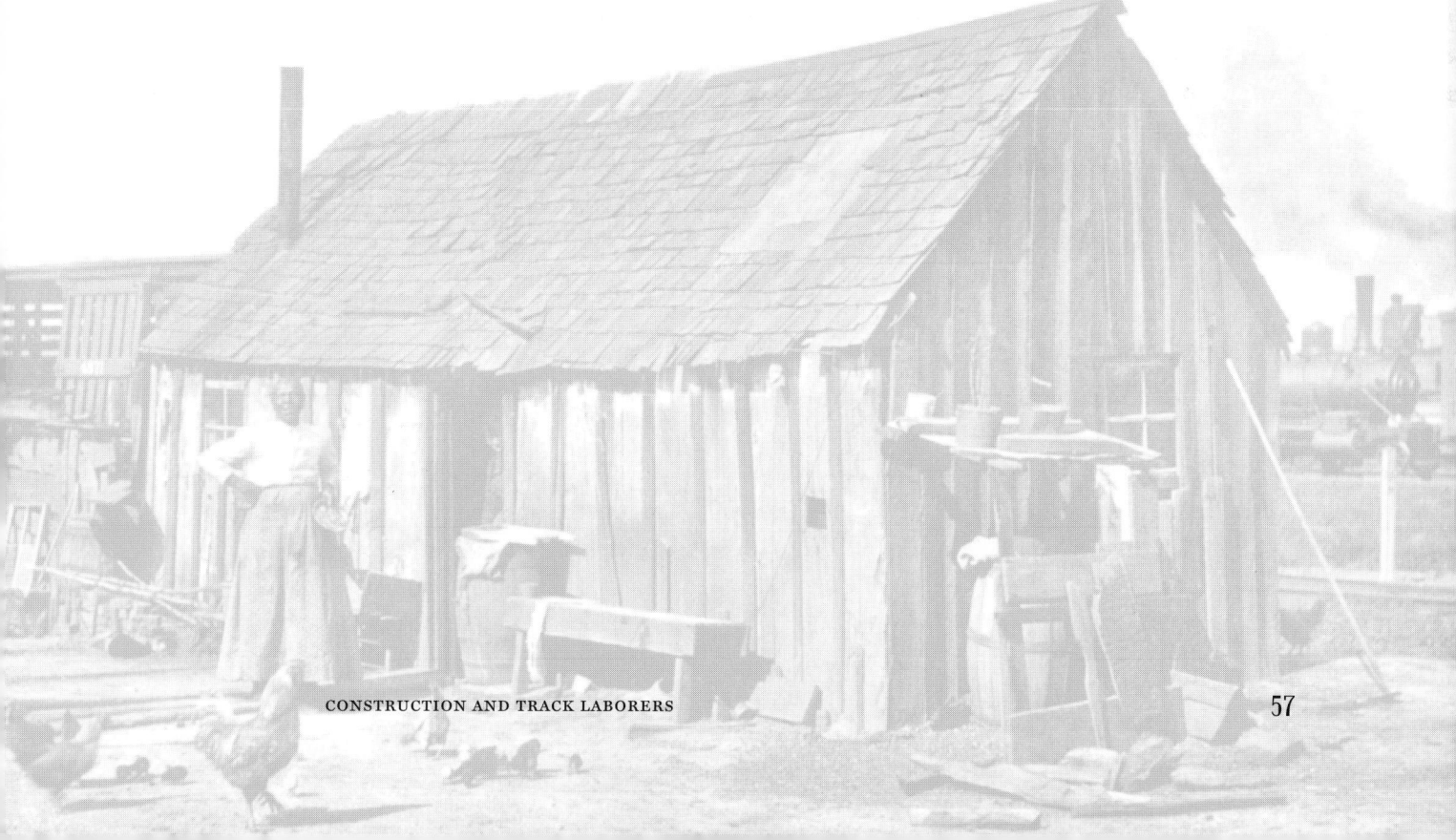

Blacks found railroad employment in the West after the Civil War, although not in large numbers compared to Asian, Mexican, Native American, and white workers. Judging from the streaks on the wall, this Union Pacific Railroad black cook (seated in the doorway) *seems to have had the habit of throwing dishwater or garbage out of the kitchen car's window. What work the gang performed is not clear, but they obviously wanted the camera to record their tonsorial styles, having all doffed their hats. Theodore Kornweibel collection*

(OPPOSITE) *An ornate dining car on the "Pacific Railroad," the popular name for through trains on the Union Pacific and Central Pacific between Omaha and Sacramento, in the 1880s. After the Civil War, dining cars gradually became standard equipment on longer-distance trains. Well-heeled passengers came to expect service by African American waiters and cuisine equal to that found in fine restaurants. Theodore Kornweibel collection*

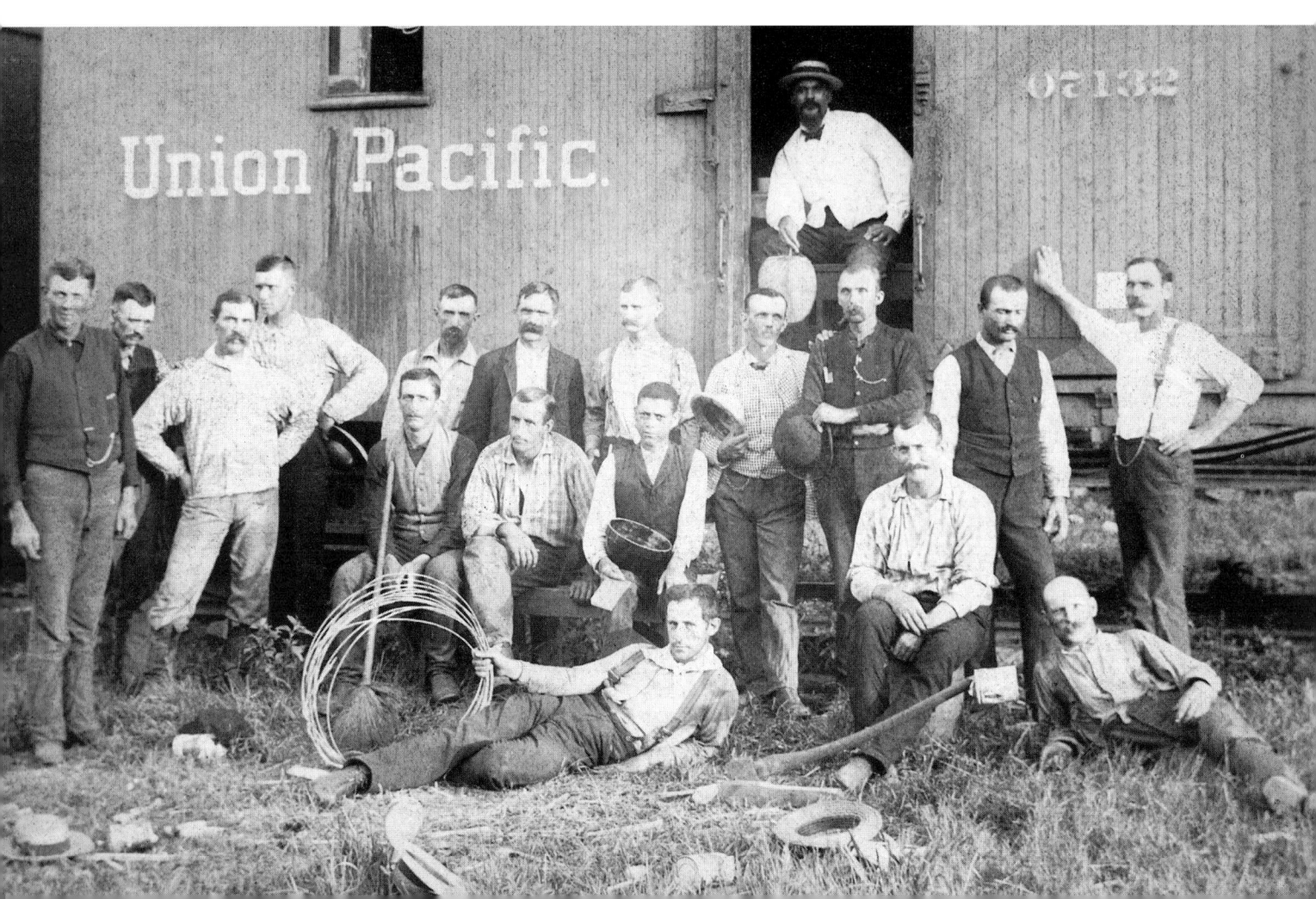

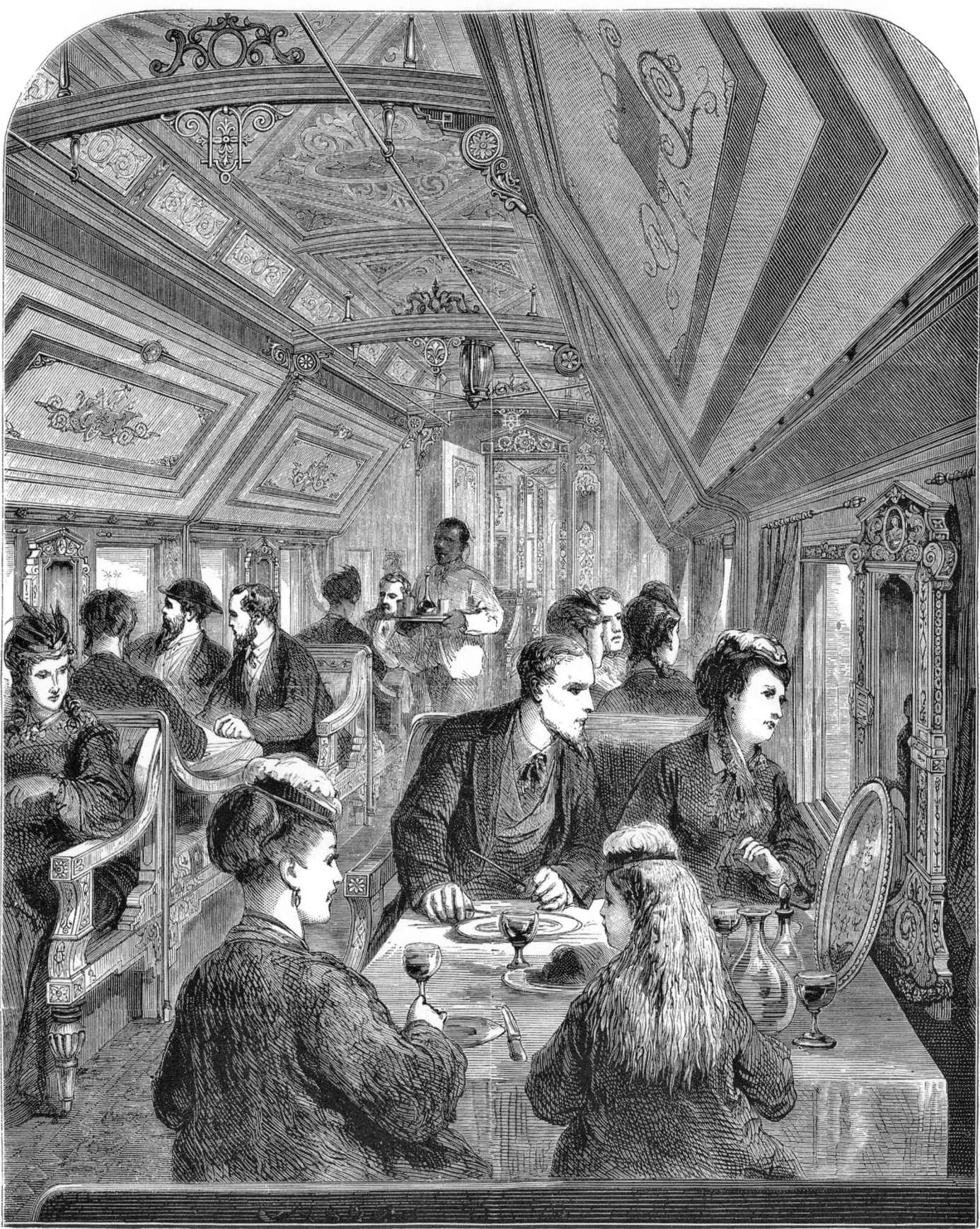

For over a century, racism dictated that blacks live and work on the "wrong side of the tracks." Sometimes the culprits were the railroads themselves, sometimes white railroaders, and sometimes how society at large regarded and stereotyped black railroaders. This 1880s scene illustrates the imprint of railroads on blacks' lives, geographically, environmentally, and socially. *Virginia Historical Society*

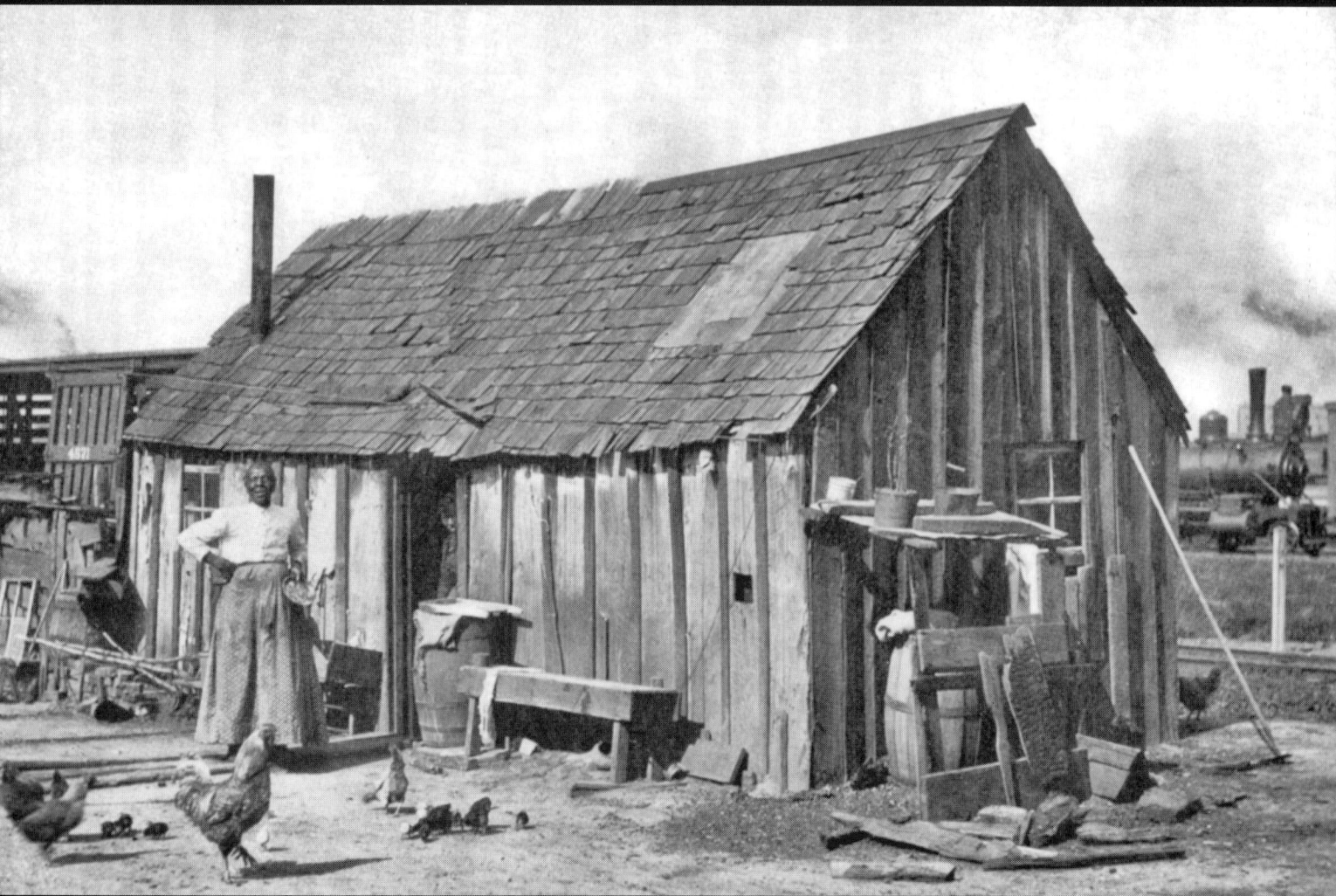

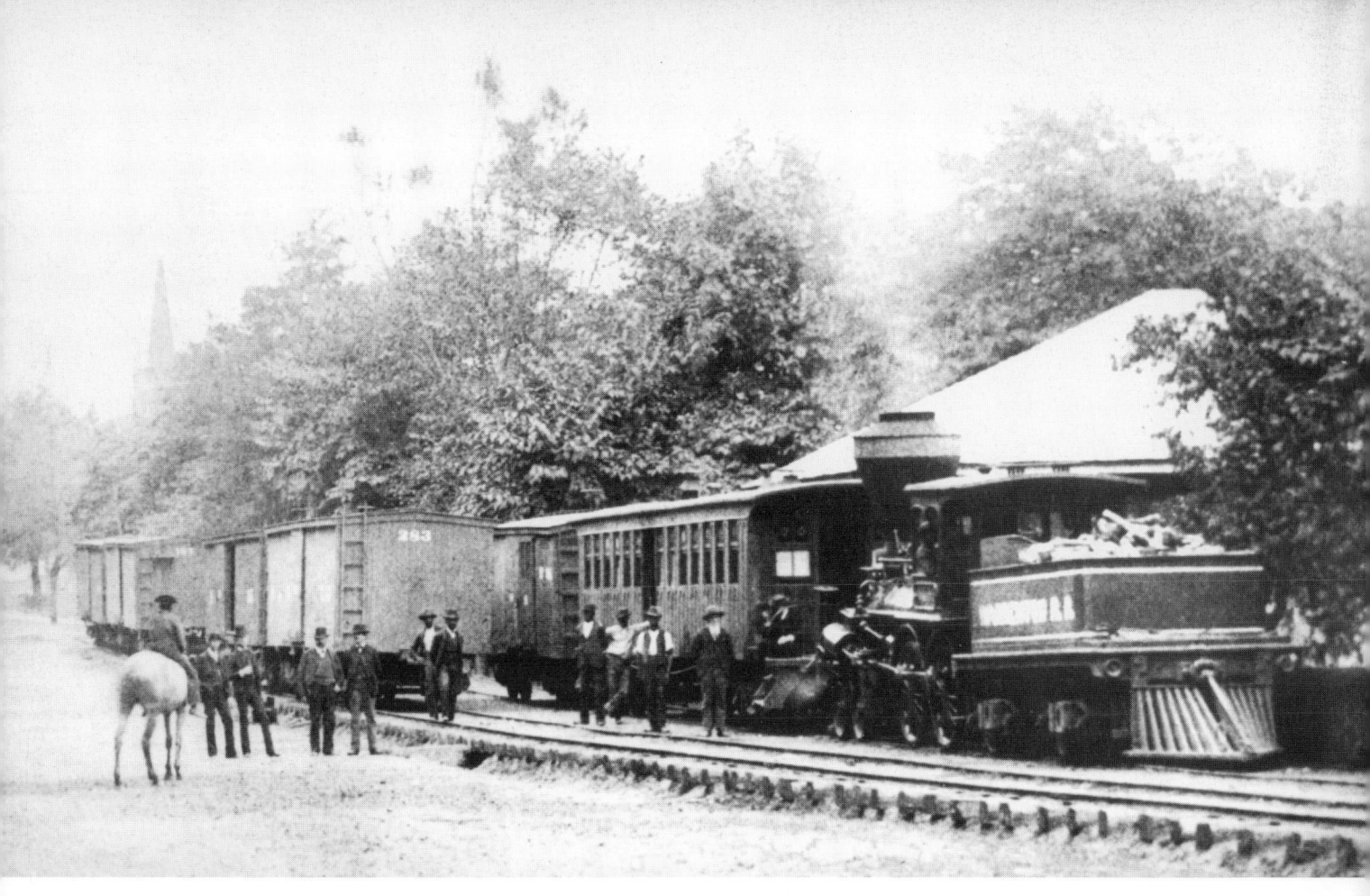

An early Jim Crow car of antebellum vintage, with compartments for the two races separated by a middle baggage section, at Warrenton, North Carolina, in 1888. The Warrenton Railroad ran 3 miles to Warrenton Plains to meet the Raleigh & Gaston Railroad. As the locomotive was not turned at either destination, but merely coupled onto the other end of the train, it has a pilot (cowcatcher) on the tender for running backward. Southern Historical Collection, Wilson Library, The University of North Carolina at Chapel Hill

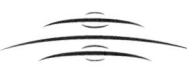

"WITH HIS STRONG ARM AND A SHOVEL"

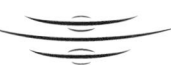

Locomotive Firemen and Engineers

They gave him his orders at Monroe, Virginia,
Saying, "Steve, you're way behind time.
This is not thirty-Eight, but it's Old 97,
You must put her into Spencer on time."

He turned and said to his black greasy fireman,
"Just shovel on a little more coal.
And when we cross that White Oak Mountain,
You can watch Old 97 roll."

Next to the ballad of "Casey Jones," "The Wreck of Old 97" is probably America's best-known train-wreck song, describing what happened to one of the Southern Railway's fast mail trains in 1903. Engineer "Steve" Broady and two firemen died in the cab as the speeding train ran onto a curved trestle posted for 15 miles per hour outside of Danville, Virginia, and plunged into a ravine. Second fireman Robert Dodge, the "black greasy fireman," was an African American. So was Sim Webb, Luther "Casey" Jones's fireman when he crashed the Illinois Central Railroad's *Cannonball Express* into a freight train at Vaughn, Mississippi, in 1900. Neither Webb nor Dodge was an anomaly. For a century, from the beginning of American railroading, many firemen in the South were black, although blacks didn't fire for northern or western railroads. Steam locomotives required a two-man crew: an engineer (sometimes called a driver) and a fireman, to stoke the firebox with fuel so as to raise steam. On particularly fast trains traversing hilly terrain, like Old 97, two firemen worked in tandem.

"The Wreck of Old 97" is scant help in understanding the lives and work and importance of black firemen. "The Ballad of Fireman Dodge," although neither commercially recorded nor in wide oral circulation, fills in key details, despite its racist caricatures:

> His name was Dodge, Robert Dodge,
> And he was black as sin.
> But his heart was full of love and light,
> Not sooty as his skin.
>
> His home was in Catawba—
> A red-bank railroad hovel,
> And he earned his family's living
> With his strong arm and a shovel.
>
> He loved the shanty Gospel sings
> And oft to church did go
> And never did he ever think
> With Steve and Al [first fireman Albion Clapp] he'd blow.
>
> He was just a Colored fireman
> But he reached the gates of Heaven
> When with Broady and with Clapp that day
> He pulled Old Ninety-Seven.[1]

A fireman certainly required a strong arm. Yet what whites disdained as a hovel might reflect the limitations imposed by segregation and racially determined pay rates rather than character or lifestyle. He was more likely to be a church-going, solid-citizen member of his community than a "boomer" section hand or brakeman. But to whites, he was "just a Colored fireman."

The job of fireman was traditionally the stepping-stone to becoming an engineer. Although some white firemen didn't want to become engineers, and others didn't gain the requisite skill or seniority, many did become "hoggers." But not African Americans. For the century and a quarter of American steam-powered railroading, with but rare exceptions, black firemen remained firemen. Upward mobility to engineer was blocked by racial barriers, at first in unorganized opposition, but then systematically by the Brotherhood of Locomotive Engineers (founded 1864), which decreed that only Caucasians could be members. When firemen subsequently unionized (the Brotherhood of Locomotive Firemen and Enginemen was established in 1873), they likewise barred blacks, but were unable to gain a racial monopoly because southern railroads already used firemen of both races and were not about to forfeit the advantage of paying blacks less.

Engineers became American cultural icons: brave engineers; dying engineers; reckless engineers (such as Casey Jones). They achieved heroic or mythic status not only on account of their deeds, but also because they were white men in an age when gender and race determined who was esteemed. Engineers held an elite position in the running trades, exercising personal autonomy, amassing highly admired technical skills, and drawing higher pay, all of which made them, in the eyes of many, a "labor aristocracy."[2] Firemen, on the other hand, labored unheralded on the left side of the locomotive cab, only rarely hinted at in folksong or folklore. In fact, firemen held such mean stature among operating railroaders that only a freight brakeman was of lower status.

Exhausting physical work was the lot of locomotive firemen. For the first half-century of railroading, they literally used their hands to feed split cordwood into fireboxes. When larger boilers consuming hotter-burning coal came into widespread use by the 1880s, firemen often shoveled two tons of "black diamonds" per hour through narrow firebox doors while standing on the swaying, bouncing footplate bridging the locomotive and tender. Louisville & Nashville Railroad fireman William Bestor Steele testified that, on a 412-mile round-trip between Birmingham, Alabama, and Nashville, Tennessee, firing a heavy, fast passenger engine, he would sling 4 to 6 shovels of coal per minute into the firebox, each scoop containing up to 141 pounds of coal. At the end of his 14-hour day, "very weak from perspiration [and] extreme exertion," he would have heaved about 30 tons.[3] Not until the introduction of mechanical stokers on some larger locomotives in the 1910s, which fed coal from the tender to the firebox by means of a mechanical screw, did some firemen's jobs lighten, but many steam engines remained stoker-less "hand bombers." On oil-fired locomotives, firemen operated an atomizer to spray fuel oil onto the fire, much easier work than shoveling coal.

Firemen (as well as engineers) led hard and dangerous lives. Until seniority was accrued, they worked off the "extra board," having no steady, predictable schedule, subject to being called at any time to take a run. And until the federal government limited the number of consecutive hours of service, engine crews were lucky to put in only 6 16-hour days per week. They might be summoned by the callboy to double back with little or no sleep. Enginemen missed family birthdays, holidays, and funerals. Theirs were perilous occupations. Firemen and engineers died in derailments, collisions, and boiler explosions that were caused by bad weather, inadequate maintenance, equipment failure, or human error. Black firemen bore particular disabilities. They would never be promoted to engineer. While white firemen in the South traditionally earned 50 percent of an engineer's pay, black firemen earned 40 percent. They were often expected to "wait on" the engineer. And they might arrive at a distant terminal only to find no accommodations that would accept "colored," leaving them little choice but to sleep on straw in an empty boxcar.[4]

Despite a fireman's lowly status in the railroad pecking order, he shared responsibility with the engineer for the safety of the locomotive and train. He had to watch the track ahead from his side of the locomotive for misaligned switches, rockslides, livestock or vehicles on the track, and red signals. At service or station stops, the fireman polished the locomotive's boiler jacket and joined the engineer in "oiling around"—lubricating the engine's moving parts. "The Wreck of Old 97" had it right: by the end of the run, the fireman *was* likely to be greasy.

Firing a locomotive was an art. So, too, was getting along with engineers, who ranged from paternalistic to tyrannical. The former helped a novice fireman learn the ropes. Railroad historian John H. White, Jr. describes the opposite type: "There were enough mean-spirited engineers to go around. These fellows looked with contempt on their firemen [whether black or white] as inferiors deserving of no kindness or accommodation. Such a driver would not speak to his fireman unless to complain about some deficiency in his performance. He would then work his engine hard to use up steam and thus make the poor lad shovel that much faster."[5]

Great endurance was required in firing a coal-burning locomotive. When a young white man hired on with the Seaboard Air Line Railway in Tampa, Florida, in 1917, he found only four other white firemen; all the rest were black. "Back in them days firing wasn't work, it was just murder … White people wouldn't do those jobs." Neither poor coal nor fatigue was an excuse. "You would do the job and like it, or they would get somebody else. Was up to you how much you could take physically." One had to be able to "stand a lot of punishment."[6] Whites endured such punishment because they were attracted by the romance of railroading, were desperate for a job, or, mostly, because it was the required purgatory on the road to engineer. Blacks endured because it was the highest one could get in the running trades.

African American firemen who held steady jobs with the same railroad were considered middle class by other blacks. Class status within black communities was traditionally measured not by the color of one's collar or the amount of one's wealth, but by the reliability of one's income and the probity of one's lifestyle. Since the labor market prevented access to higher-prestige jobs, a fireman attained status within his community that a white man would not similarly enjoy. Although they were blue-collar workers who came home sweaty and grimy, steadily employed firemen generally enjoyed respect in their communities, in the same measure as whites generally respected engineers. And even though they were among the poorest-paid employees in the railroad industry, their regular paychecks and, by the 1920s, retirement checks put them on a par with black schoolteachers. Charles Hamilton Houston, who fought groundbreaking lawsuits on behalf of firemen, observed that "hour for hour of service the firemen and brakemen make more money than most white collar and professional workers" like teachers. Profiles of firemen in company magazines portrayed them as responsible and dependable family breadwinners, owning cars and homes, paying to educate their children, supporting community institutions, and assuming civic and church responsibilities. Community leadership often required experience in navigating the racial pitfalls of the South, skills that black firemen acquired within the white-dominated, hierarchical world of railroading.[7]

While no record exists of black firemen working on antebellum northern railroads, enslaved firemen were commonplace in the South in the three decades before the Civil War because they were cheaper than whites and could be disciplined more effectively.[8] Some lines relied exclusively on black firemen, others on a multiracial force, while a few employed only white firemen. Slaves (and free blacks) were generally regarded as capable firemen, despite an inauspicious start: the first locomotive boiler explosion took place on the South Carolina Canal and Rail Road Company's engine *Best Friend of Charleston* when the black fireman, annoyed by the hissing of steam from the safety valve and having not been instructed in its purpose, "ventured on the expedient of confining it by pressing the weight of his body on the lever-gage."[9] This fireman, whose name is lost to history, was the first American railroad fatality. The tragic incident reflected only inadequate training, not a race's capabilities. No sustained argument appeared in the South against the use of enslaved firemen. In fact, a few railroad executives, recognizing the savings in using slaves, advocated promoting some to engineers, although this was never done.[10]

Relative labor costs made black firemen attractive to antebellum southern lines. The majority were slaves hired on a yearly basis from individual owners. Even though the railroads bore the expense of food, clothing, shelter, and medical care, hiring slaves was still cheaper than paying a white fireman's wages. A frequent complaint of railroad officials, however, was that once the railroads trained slaves as firemen (or for other skilled positions), their owners withheld them the following year until the railroads paid an increase in the hire. So if railroads had sufficient capital to purchase slaves outright, they did so, confident in recouping their investment in only four or five years.

Nearly 15,000 slaves worked on southern railroads by 1860, hundreds of whom were firemen. A noteworthy example was the North Carolina Railroad, which operated a 223-mile main line. In 1858, it employed 20 white engineers and 30 firemen: 3 whites, 6 free blacks, and 21 slaves. The white firemen were undoubtedly apprenticing for engineer. Several of the black firemen were actually "woodpassers" who worked on larger engines, handing cordwood from the tender to the fireman stationed at the firebox door. They also assisted firemen and black train hands (brakemen) in replenishing the tender at wood yards situated along the line. If locomotives ran out of wood between fuel stops, firemen and woodpassers scavenged for brush or other flammables, or even chopped down trees, alongside the track.[11] On the 206-mile Virginia Central Railroad, three-quarters of the firemen were slaves and freedmen, a practice that continued into the Reconstruction era because experienced, newly freed firemen would work for less than whites.[12] By the Civil War, the 22-mile Richmond & Petersburg Railroad relied exclusively on enslaved and free black firemen, with blacks continuing to monopolize this position after emancipation.[13] On the other hand, the Virginia & Tennessee Railroad used white firemen exclusively up to 1861, but Confederate manpower demands forced it to supplement its force with free black and enslaved firemen by the middle of the war.[14]

Emancipation brought a brief labor crisis as many formerly enslaved workers left jobs or plantations to test their freedom. But whites' irrational fears that freed slaves would not work at all proved to be groundless. The North Carolina Railroad's experience reflected the shifting labor situation. In 1865 and 1866, it employed a dozen free black firemen and roughly half that number of whites. The next year's payroll included only white firemen. But by 1868, 10 freedmen and only 3 whites fired locomotives. Only 1 white was so employed in 1869, alongside 11 blacks. And in 1870 and 1871, all of the road's dozen firemen were black.[15]

While whites continued to work as firemen in the postwar South, firing a locomotive was often considered a "Negro job" because of its extreme physical demands, dirtiness, and the preference of many white engineers for black firemen. Veteran "hoggers" drove their "own" engines, which they embellished with names, pin stripes, deer antlers, or fraternal emblems. And they often shared the cab with the same black fireman for years. Experienced firemen could handle the throttle in an emergency, at a service stop, or if the engineer took a nap. They were sometimes compelled to perform disagreeable maintenance that white firemen were reluctant to do. According to a Florida engineer, "[he] will inspect the under portion of the engine, under the supervision of the engineer, looking for loose nuts, missing cotter keys, collar pins, etc. . . . He will fill the headlight, signal lights, gage light, oil cans and lubricators, and although against the rules on some roads will fill the rod cups." And black firemen were, to varying degrees, the engineers' personal servants, icing their water jugs, shining their shoes, and filling their pipes. In their off hours, some ran personal errands, cut firewood, and mowed the grass at their engineers' homes. Undoubtedly, some firemen found these duties demeaning. But they ensured job security and personal association with a man of stature in the white world who might be one's protector or advocate in dangerous circumstances. Southern whites approved such paternalism because it reinforced the conceit that they really did care for the "better class of Negroes." Finally, white engineers preferred black firemen because they weren't a job threat. They could never compete for the engineer's position. Such preferences, however, did not occur elsewhere. In the early 1900s, only a single African American—in Ohio—is known to have fired a locomotive outside of the South.[16]

From southern railroad managers' perspectives, African Americans were as capable of firing a locomotive as whites, were up to 50 percent cheaper, and were believed to be by nature more compliant. A president (and former slave owner) of the Illinois Central Railroad praised his black firemen and brakemen as "smart active men," "generally amiable, docile, and obedient," and skilled "in learning quickly the duties they are to perform." In firing a locomotive and coupling and uncoupling cars, there was "no better labor among any race in the world."[17] Paying lower wages to black firemen had the additional benefit of depressing the pay of white firemen and retarding their efforts to unionize. So long as railroads could replace them with blacks, white firemen had to accept infe-

Railroads in the African American Experience

rior pay, compared to firemen outside the South, and think long and hard about risking their jobs by striking.

Not surprisingly, southern white firemen resented their black counterparts and insisted that they were intellectually unqualified. In part, this was an effort by whites to transform "dangerous, dirty, and hard" blue-collar work into a more exalted occupation by defining only themselves as competent. But it was equally an attempt to gain a white monopoly. Resorting to the crudest racial stereotypes, white firemen claimed that blacks lacked "moral stamina and mental quickness"; were deficient in ambition, "pride, or fair intelligence"; and were "untrustworthy" and "shiftless."[18]

Throughout the late nineteenth and early twentieth centuries, southern railroads had the upper hand over white firemen. New lines in Texas, Oklahoma, Louisiana, and Arkansas were particularly inclined to seek the cheapest labor. On some railroads' divisions, nearly all firemen were African Americans. Even on older roads east of the Mississippi, the number of black firemen grew to 90 percent on the entire Seaboard Air Line Railway and on certain divisions of the Illinois Central, Louisville & Nashville, and Southern railways. Economics and anti-unionism shaped their employment practices. As one white railroader bitterly complained, "Every time the firemen ask for an increase in wages or for overtime due them, they are told by the superintendent, 'Why I can get a Negro in your place for one dollar, while I am paying you $1.50 per day.'" While wage differentials underscored white supremacy, white railroaders couldn't put additional bread and butter on the table with such spurious advantages.[19]

Because they could not become engineers, black firemen typically stayed at their jobs longer and built up more seniority than white firemen. The Brotherhood of Locomotive Firemen and Enginemen had but two choices. Bring black firemen into the ranks of organized labor and unite to resist the railroads' attempts to depress wages. Or strong-arm the railroads into eliminating blacks from the ranks of firemen. Tragically, they chose the latter path. One white Texas fireman vowed, "we would rather be absolute slaves of capital, than to take the negro into our lodges as a equal and brother." The BLFE's Grand Master was blunt, hoping to see the day "when every locomotive in the country would be fired by a white man." But forsaking labor unity proved costly. The L&N brought in black strikebreakers, awarding them permanent jobs, in breaking a strike of white firemen on the Birmingham Division in 1893.[20]

The most infamous strike against black firemen occurred on the Georgia Railroad in 1909. With black firemen already 42 percent of the force, the railroad began to replace white hostlers (firemen who only moved locomotives around the shops and prepared them for their runs) at the Atlanta Terminal yards, permitting a reduction in wages from $1.75 to $1.25 a day. The white hostlers struck and were joined by white firemen, who for their part were outraged that black firemen had been granted equal seniority rights with the opportunity to replace lower-seniority whites on preferred runs.[21]

The Georgia Railroad's firemen shut down the line for two weeks by inflating this dispute into a "race strike" and inflaming much of the white population. Tracks were blocked. Black firemen

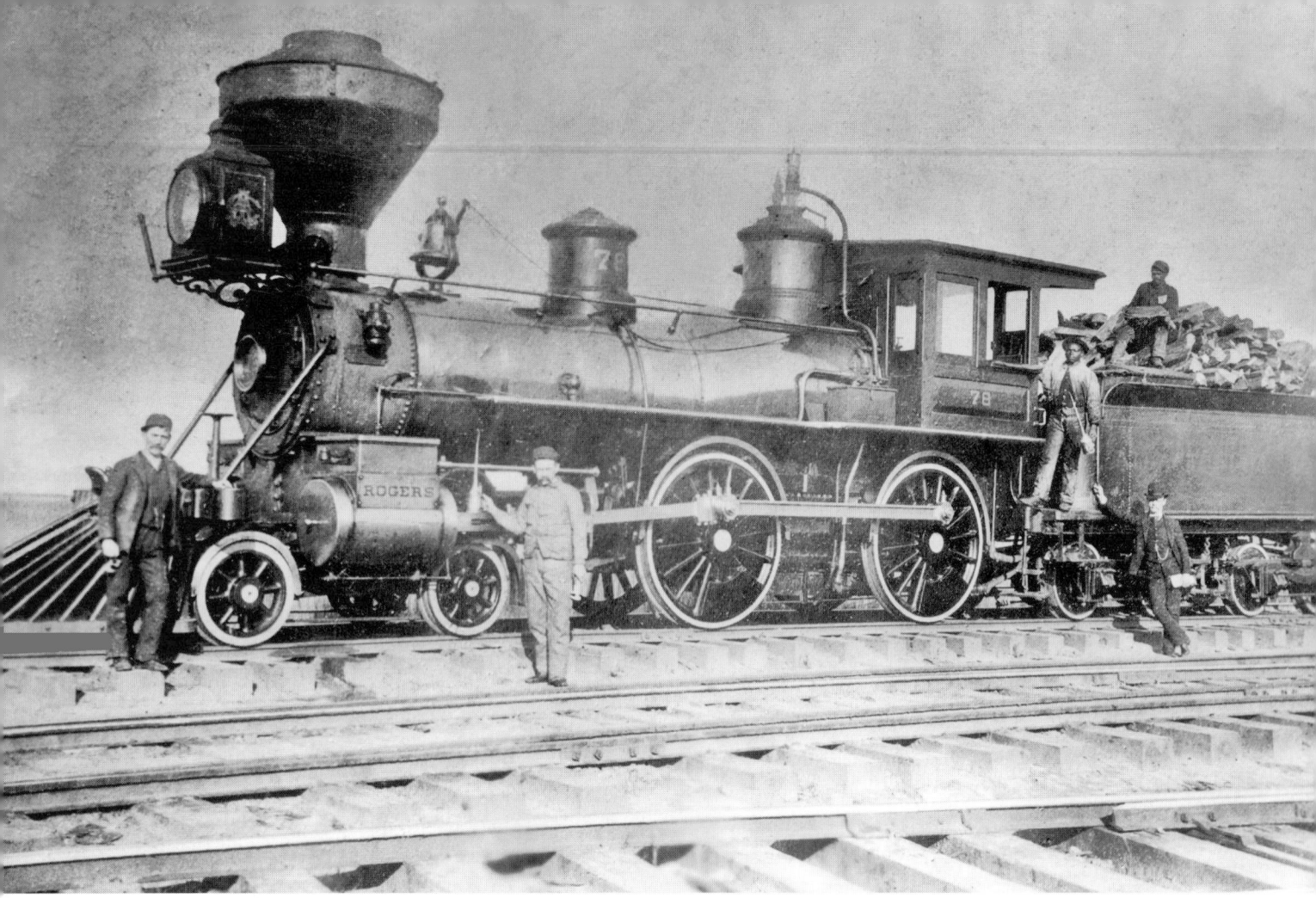

During the antebellum years, fast passenger engines frequently required two men to stoke the firebox, a fireman plus a woodpasser. The practice continued after the Civil War until coal replaced wood as fuel. In this late nineteenth-century scene, an Atlantic Coast Line Railroad fireman stands in the gangway, oil can in hand, ready to perform his customary routine lubrication of the running gear, while the woodpasser has loaded the tender to the maximum and enjoys a moment's respite. E. L. DeGolyer, Jr. Photograph Collection, DeGolyer Library, Southern Methodist University and their white engineers were assaulted. Local and state authorities failed to uphold law and order. Eventually, the white firemen and the railroad, excluding black firemen from the process, agreed to federal mediation. The firemen's union got a number of engineers to testify that black firemen were inefficient, often fell asleep on the job, and were unable to read or understand train orders. (Undoubtedly, some firemen were illiterate.) The railroad responded that blacks had sufficient capabilities for the job and admitted, "if we can get what we want cheap, is it a crime to take it? We give the Negro less because his scale of living is lower. We give the white man more because we do not wish to bring his scale down to the level of a Negro." The arbitration board rejected the charges of black incompetence and supported the railroad's retention of its black firemen and hostlers, but also ordered that black and white firemen be paid equal wages for equal work. The BLFE claimed victory, hoping that equal pay would eliminate the incentive to hire blacks. Such was not the case: the Georgia Railroad and other lines retained their black firemen. Overall, about one-third of all firemen on southern railroads were black in 1910.[22]

Other railroads directly challenged white firemen. Two years after the Georgia strike, the Cincinnati, New Orleans & Texas Pacific Railway (the Queen & Crescent Route) granted its 200 black firemen equal rights with whites, placing everyone on a single seniority list. Then, when the railroad replaced three white firemen holding prized passenger and freight runs with higher-seniority but lower-paid blacks, white firemen and engineers went on strike. Sympathetic whites in Tennessee and Kentucky beat up railroaders of both races who dared to operate their trains. Snipers firing into locomotive cabs murdered 10 black firemen and wounded several others. Finally, a federally mediated agreement between the railroad and the BLFE settled the dispute, but at the expense of the black firemen, who were not included in the negotiations. Their number was capped, their opportunity to hold preferred runs was restricted, and they were prohibited from operating any trains at all north of certain points on the system.[23]

The early twentieth century witnessed the beginnings of a shift in the balance of power between capital, labor, and the state that would ultimately bring permanent gains for many workers during the New Deal. The creation of the Department of Labor during the Wilson administration was indicative of the waning influence of long-powerful business forces and the ascending of the House of Labor. During World War I, white railroad unions, in particular, gained "unprecedented authority" under federal management of the nation's railroads. Yet the end of the Wilson years and the renewal of a conservative Republican agenda again skewed the labor-capital balance toward the latter. In all these momentous shifts, black railroaders were largely disregarded. Even when federal control brought improvements, they were temporary and came at the cost of further embittering white railroaders against them.[24]

Nonetheless, World War I proved to be a watershed for African Americans. A "New Crowd Negro" was born, insistent on full rights.[25] Black railroaders challenged racially based job exclusions, demanding equal pay for equal work. The federal government assumed control of the railroads after the nationwide rail network become chaotic, with traffic growing dramatically, labor in short supply, and serious delays in delivering war materiel to East Coast docks. Blacks appeared to find an ally in the U.S. Railroad Administration. Northern lines recruited tens of thousands of southern blacks for track work. A few got jobs as hostlers, but the BLFE was adamant that the racial-labor status quo be honored: because no blacks had ever worked as firemen in the North, the union argued, they should not now be introduced, despite the need for enginemen.[26]

The USRA assigned a federal manager to each line or group of lines. But it was concerned with assuring a stable labor supply, not revolutionizing race relations in the industry. Nonetheless, in decreeing that all railroaders receive equal pay for equal work, the USRA greatly advanced the position of blacks. General Order 27, issued on June 1, 1918, mandated that "colored men employed as firemen, trainmen, and switchmen shall be paid the same rates as are paid white men in the same capacities." As a result, some of the poorest-paid railroaders saw their wages increase by as much as 43 percent, although the equal pay provision had been pushed by the BLFE to remove the low-wage incentive to hire black firemen. And pay equalization did not represent a commitment on the part of the government, much less the railroads, to scrub the industry's racist practices. Many railroad officials "simply ignored directives from Washington ordering wage increases, overtime pay, or retroactive pay raises. In other cases, they implemented the changes for whites while denying them to blacks, or giving the black workers less." And the USRA capitulated to BLFE demands in decreeing that blacks not be hired as firemen, brakemen, switchmen, or hostlers on northern railroads where they had never before held such jobs. Even though this odious directive was rescinded after protests from civil rights organizations, it was a clear signal that federal authorities, where possible, would heed the wishes of the white unions on matters of race.[27]

A byproduct of wartime nationalization was an upsurge in black unionization. The "Big Four" railroad brotherhoods (the engineers', firemen's, conductors', and trainmen's unions) all restricted membership to whites, although black brakemen and firemen could, in theory, obtain charters as American Federation of Labor affiliates. But such "federal" locals were impotent, having no bargaining power. So out of both pride and necessity, blacks formed independent unions. The most ambitious, the Railway Men's International Benevolent Industrial Association, sought to unite all black railroaders, irrespective of job, into one industrial union, in opposition to the AFL. Other fledgling unions organized along occupational lines. The Colored Trainmen of America represented firemen and brakemen on the Missouri Pacific Railroad's Louisiana and Texas lines and achieved a rare, if modest, victory. The MoPac signed an agreement with its "colored firemen," preserving their runs not only on switch engines and local and through freight trains, but also on its two main Gulf Coast Lines passenger trains, the *Houstonian* and the *Orleanean*. But because other railroads refused to recognize or bargain with black unions, groups like the CTA were almost invariably reduced to appealing for fair play, which white managers might or might not grant. None of these organizations sought to break the white monopoly on engineer and conductor positions but merely to retain firemen and brakemen jobs where blacks already worked. And none tried to use strikes to advance their issues; in fact, the RMIBIA counseled members to remain loyal to their employers during times of industrial conflict. In the end, whatever longevity black unions enjoyed was due more to their fraternal and insurance benefits than to increased numbers of jobs or improved working conditions.[28]

In the South during World War I, animosity toward black firemen continued unabated. General Order 27, which dealt only with wages, nonetheless seemed to whites to place blacks on the same social plane as them, although black firemen asked only for equitable employment, not political rights or "social equality." This hostility erupted in early 1919 into a wildcat strike by white switchmen on the Illinois Central and other railroads in Memphis, Tennessee, who demanded that only Caucasians be employed in yard service. The walkout, essentially a hate strike, was not sanctioned by the switchmen's union and soon ended, but white railroaders, calling themselves "Zulus," began killing black switchmen and brakemen. A young white man confessed to agreeing to kill blacks for $300 per murder. The violence eventually abated, but the unions won a tremendous victory in persuading several southern railroads to hire no more "nonpromotable" firemen, switchmen, or brakemen. In other words, no more blacks would be taken on because they were ineligible for promotion to engineer, yard foreman, or conductor. By 1920, the proportion of firemen in the South who were black had slipped from 33 to 27 percent in a decade.[29] Matters would only get worse.

One reason why southern whites coveted firemen's jobs more, by the World War I era, was because the work was becoming less arduous. In earlier days, all coal-fired engines were handfired. New engines now often had mechanical stokers and devices that protected firemen from the extreme heat of an open firebox door. Runs were shorter, with higher speeds, so that the workday was shorter. Firemen no longer had to climb off their locomotives to open and close switches or wipe (polish) their engines. For all these reasons, a fireman's job was now more desirable.[30]

African American railroaders' brief wartime wage gains further stimulated white railroaders to drive them from their jobs. White firemen flexed their muscles, negotiating new contracts during the 1920s that limited even more the number of black firemen and the districts in which they could operate. The most dramatic erosion occurred on the mighty Southern Railway. Before the war, 80 percent of its Central Division firemen were black. By the end of the 1920s, they constituted only 10 percent. Their numbers on the Seaboard Air Line Railway were halved. Smaller decreases took place on the Illinois Central and Atlantic Coast Line systems. Yet the BLFE was not satisfied. It gained a powerful new weapon in 1926, the Railway Labor Act, which guaranteed workers the right to choose their own representatives, with which employers were required to negotiate. This empowered the BLFE to negotiate new contracts that curtailed yet more the number of black firemen and the districts in which they could operate. By the end of the decade, it had persuaded the St. Louis–San Francisco, the Norfolk & Western, and other lines to fill all job vacancies with whites. On the N&W, this led to the "virtual extinction" of black firemen within 15 years.[31]

Then, when the Great Depression decimated railroad employment even more, some unionized white firemen determined to purge their ranks of black trainmen by tried-and-true southern tactics. Ten men were assassinated and another 11 wounded or fired upon in a reign of terror in Mississippi from 1931 to 1934. White firemen (and indeed, much of the state's white population) found it intolerable that some of them were furloughed while black firemen having decades of seniority continued working. Their first victim, Illinois Central fireman Frank Kincaid, was wounded from ambush in August. Three other trainmen also survived gunshot wounds that summer and fall. Kincaid must have known he was a marked man, but either out of economic necessity or a refusal to be cowed, he returned to work, only to become the first fatality, late one November night in Canton, as he got into the cab on the southbound *Creole.* "Against the lighted window he made a perfect target . . . A shotgun belched a load of buckshot into [his] head and he fell back into the coal tender to die." Was it coincidental that a white substitute fireman was on the spot? Certainly, the IC had no hesitancy in replacing murdered blacks with whites. Three months later, IC brakeman Ed Cole was killed in the Water Valley, Mississippi yards. A month after, in McComb, fireman Turner Sims was shot while in his cab, but survived. Next to die, in March 1932, was Aaron Williams, "the oldest [black] fireman on the Mississippi Division, [who] was exercising his seniority rights to hold his job, despite warnings . . . that to do so meant death. As his locomotive halted in the Vicksburg yards, Williams made a perfect target in the cab window. The shotgun roared and Williams fell dead. A white man, of course, took his place." Two more IC firemen were assassinated in Mississippi and another in Tennessee within the next three weeks. In one case, the fireman saw his attackers approach, appealed for protection from his engineer, but was pushed away and told to run for his life. At year's end, a black brakeman on the Southern was murdered in Georgia. And in Louisiana, Grant Johnson, a longtime fireman on the Yazoo & Mississippi Valley Railroad (an IC subsidiary), was wounded and recovered, only to be killed while coaling his locomotive in the Baton Rouge yards. His father, Frank Johnson, also a fireman, had been killed at the same spot six months earlier.[32]

Terrorism tapered off after Grant Johnson's murder, not because of vigorous efforts to apprehend the culprits—blacks believed the white firemen, railroad police, and local police were in cahoots—but on account of bad publicity and the black railroaders' heroic refusal to abandon their jobs. When arrests were finally made, it became clear that white firemen were either the actual assassins or were behind those who did the shooting. The violence was not random: $100 had been offered for a killing and $25 for a wounding. But Mississippi whites were not inclined to deal harshly with those whose victims were black. Only two whites were convicted, both pleading to assault, not murder, and receiving light sentences. All-white juries acquitted five others. Appeals to the Justice Department were turned aside, even though the assassinations interfered with interstate commerce. Violence was averted on the Gulf, Mobile & Northern, which ran north-south through Mississippi, to the east of the IC, only because company officials promised the unions that, in return for rejecting assassinations, black firemen and brakemen (of which there were many) would soon be eliminated. In the end, all across the South, white privilege trumped black seniority. The Big Four unions had already muscled the railroads into hiring only whites for new jobs. By 1940, 95 percent of locomotive firemen nationwide were white.[33]

New Deal labor legislation further strengthened the hand of white railroaders at the expense of blacks. Amendments to the Railway Labor Act in 1934 required employers to abandon company unionism and bargain with unions. But only one union, whichever was chosen by a majority of workers, would be recognized in a given craft. Thus, the hostile-to-blacks BLFE "represented" black firemen. According to labor historian Eric Arnesen, "representation by the exclusionary white brotherhoods was worse than no representation at all. The white unions legally negotiated contracts and secret agreements that reduced the percentage of blacks in the labor force, excluded them from key job assignments, disregarded their seniority, and ensured that few if any African Americans would be hired in the future." If a black fireman filed a formal labor grievance, which might be against the BLFE itself, he first had to bring it before the very union that had refused him membership and sought his ouster. And if it got to the National Railroad Adjustment Board for consideration, white unionists and railroad officials adjudicated the matter. Often, the black firemen's only recourse was to humbly appeal to railroad managers, stressing their loyalty to the company, renunciation of striking, and willingness to accept low wages. But by the 1930s, railroad executives were increasingly disinclined to play the role of paternalists. "The forces eroding black workers' job security and even access to employment . . . were the white railroad brotherhoods, railroad company managers, and government officials who debated, negotiated, and implemented strategies designed to advance the interests of whites at blacks' expense." By the end of the 1930s, black firemen (and brakemen) were an endangered species. In fact, in Virginia, none at all were left.[34]

World War II brought few gains for black railroaders. Racism remained entrenched in the industry. As railroad business boomed, even acute labor shortages failed to weaken traditional hiring barriers. The Baltimore & Ohio Railroad, among many, desperately needed trainmen but openly admitted that it was "not even considering the hiring of colored men for fireman and brakeman jobs." Employers and unions were equally to blame. When Charles W. Brooks was promoted from laborer to hostler in the New York Central Railroad's Chicago yards, the BLFE demanded his removal, and the company complied.[35]

The Fair Employment Practice Committee, birthed by President Franklin D. Roosevelt's Executive Order 8802, proved to be nearly impotent. Roosevelt was no champion of African American rights. Rather, credit for FEPC goes primarily to A. Philip Randolph, head of the Brotherhood of Sleeping Car Porters union and the preeminent civil rights leader of the day, as well as to numerous militant blacks at the grassroots. Knowing that neither Congress nor FDR would voluntarily institute anti-discriminatory measures, Randolph organized a massive March on Washington in the summer of 1941 to pressure the president into action. Unwilling to risk the possibility of tens of thousands of black demonstrators clogging Washington and conducting civil disobedience, Roosevelt authorized the FEPC with an inadequate budget and staff. Although empowered "to see that war production and war activities are not hindered because of the refusal to utilize fully all available labor," the FEPC was a paper tiger, lacking authority to compel employers to alter discriminatory practices. Obstructed by high-level bureaucrats and opposed by southern congressmen, it was largely ineffective, even after Roosevelt revamped it in mid-1943.[36]

A seemingly invigorated FEPC gave blacks unprecedented opportunities to expose prejudice in the workplace, holding extensive hearings in 1943 on discrimination in the railroad industry, particularly regarding locomotive firemen. Their ranks were being ravaged even more as a result of the infamous 1941 Washington Agreement between the BLFE and 21 southeastern railroads. This cruel bargain defined black firemen as "nonpromotable" and reserved all jobs on new diesel locomotives for "promotables" (whites) only. Even where steam locomotives were still used, on any new runs or runs whose start time or mileage changed, firemen's jobs were to be offered first to "promotables." Hostlers, who serviced steam locomotives and moved them from the roundhouse to the ash pit to the ready track, were similarly to be barred from handling diesels. This was an "occupational death sentence." Numerous black firemen were "almost instantly" demoted or furloughed by what they called the "Hitler Agreement." Seemingly up against Goliath, black trainmen organized a Negro Railway Labor Executive Committee and filed charges with the FEPC. In 4 days of hearings, 50 victims of discrimination—firemen, plus brakemen, switchmen, train porters, dining-car waiters, and car cleaners—testified to the multiple injustices they suffered. No white union officials dared to appear, leaving it to railroad attorneys to lamely defend the industry. The hearings exposed more fully than ever the racism of white railroaders and the willingness of railroad executives to sign discriminatory agreements with them. The FEPC invalidated the Washington Agreement and ordered 7 unions and 20 railroads to end racial preferences for whites and to fairly apply seniority. The railroads rejected the FEPC's findings, while the unions ignored them.[37]

Unable to gain compliance from the railroads or unions, the FEPC referred matters back to the president. Roosevelt directed a new committee to find a solution that would be agreeable to all sides, but blacks were excluded from the negotiations. Then, when the war ended, urgency on the part of the government evaporated. The FEPC's findings were never implemented. A final report in 1946 admitted that its railroad directives "must be counted among the Committee's outstanding failures." Tragically, "black railroaders' demands for justice [were] sacrificed on the altar of industrial peace."[38]

What little southern black firemen were able to salvage in the 1940s came through litigation. Two independent unions, the International Association of Railroad Employees and the Association of Colored Railway Trainmen and Locomotive Firemen, had recruited former Howard University law professor and NAACP special counsel Charles H. Houston, the foremost civil rights lawyer of the day, to their cause in the late 1930s. His first case involved Gulf, Mobile & Northern Railroad fireman Ed Teague, who held decades of seniority. But when a steam locomotive with a mechanical stoker was assigned to his run, a white man with much less seniority displaced him. Teague lost his suit when a court ruled that interpretation of union contracts was not subject to federal jurisdiction.

But the Washington Agreement was a bigger target. To Houston, that infamous bargain "was born in iniquity and conceived in sin."[39]

Seeking a new plaintiff, Houston was blunt: "If you fight, you take a risk. If you stand still, you take a risk. Since your rights are being taken away while you do nothing, you can hardly lose more by fighting than you are losing standing still." His man was William Bestor Steele, a Louisville & Nashville fireman since 1910, son of an L&N fireman, and a militant leader among Birmingham's black railroaders. Steele had been bumped from his prime passenger run by a junior white fireman, then demoted to freight service, and finally relegated to a yard engine.[40] *Steele v. L&N* (1944) sought damages and protection of black firemen's seniority. A state court dismissed the suit, and the Alabama Supreme Court affirmed that decision. By this time Norfolk Southern Railway fireman Tom Tunstall had filed a similar suit, *Tunstall v. BLFE* (1944), after losing his passenger run to a lower-seniority white fireman. Both suits charged that the BLFE, which theoretically represented black firemen, was in fact "persistently hostile" and intent on eliminating them from locomotive cabs. Tunstall, like Steele, failed to prevail in lower courts. Houston, arguing both cases before the U.S. Supreme Court, gained a reversal of their decisions, in effect invalidating the Washington Agreement. In *Steele*, "the single most significant decision it would ever issue on the question of race and railroad labor," the Court ruled that the BLFE, under provisions of the Railway Labor Act, was obligated to accord even nonmember firemen "fair representation" because it was the exclusive bargaining agent for all firemen. Yet the Court did not go so far as to ban the railroad union's racially exclusionary membership criteria. Nor did the federal government rigorously enforce the decision.[41]

Steele and *Tunstall* should have signaled the end of discrimination by the railroads and the BLFE. But the firemen's union, not about to give up, devised a new ploy. It would drop all percentage agreements limiting the number of black firemen and the concept of nonpromotable firemen. Now all firemen would face the same requirements. *All* firemen would be required to test for engineer, and those who failed would be dismissed. Black firemen saw through this "forced promotion" ruse. Many had for years performed their firemen duties satisfactorily or even superlatively, but now faced losing their jobs because they were barely literate. And not all black firemen were interested in being engineers. They knew how violently whites would react to a black man in authority over a white fireman. But they did want access to secure and much less arduous firing jobs on diesel locomotives. Fortunately for their cause, a federal district court, in *Mitchell vs. Gulf, Mobile and Ohio Railroad Company* (1950), ruled that black firemen held valid reasons for rejecting forced promotion. In fact, every black fireman on the GM&O had been furloughed when the road went all-diesel. This ruling finally forced the BLFE to accept blacks' seniority, allowing the dwindling number of old-timers to keep their jobs. The senior fireman on the Central of Georgia Railway had been hired in 1904, and was "not about to be deprived of employment in old age" after giving 46 years of service. But no new black firemen were being hired. With dieselization, the railroads needed fewer firemen, and any unexpected vacancies could be filled from the sizeable pool of furloughed white firemen.[42]

The final hurdle for southern black firemen was forcing the Brotherhood of Locomotive Firemen and Enginemen to admit them into membership. Throughout the 1950s, the Provisional Committee to Organize Colored Locomotive Firemen, led by A. Philip Randolph, argued that a union that was mandated to represent all firemen could not bar certain of them from membership. The legal fight was discouraging. Lower courts held that only Congress, not the judiciary, could require "private associations" like the BLFE to admit blacks. As late as 1959, the Supreme Court refused to reverse lower court decisions upholding the right of the BLFE to deny membership to blacks. And that same year Randolph was again unsuccessful in his perennial effort to persuade the AFL-CIO to threaten the BLFE with expulsion for maintaining its color bar.[43] Not until the Civil Rights Act of 1964 were unions categorically prohibited from discrimination.

The struggles waged by black firemen in the 1940s and 1950s brought mostly Pyrrhic victories. The few remaining men who managed to move into cleaner, quieter, diesel locomotive cabs were nearing retirement age. Ironically, because of their extremely high seniority, they held down some of the choicest runs, like "Coffee" Rivers's job on the Seaboard Air Line Railroad's streamlined passenger train, the *Silver Meteor*, out of Miami. He needed to be as vigilant as before, calling out signals to the engineer and watching for hazards, but he no longer slung coal and now returned home without the grime formerly bestowed by smoke, cinders, coal dust, and grease.[44] A singular exception in the industry was the Florida East Coast Railway which, despite its location, was governed by mostly northern corporate leadership. For decades, every locomotive, diesel and steam, had a black fireman. Since the road's steam engines were oil-fired, they had an easier job than the coal-slingers on other southern lines. The FEC never eliminated its black firemen, a handful of whom were eventually promoted to diesel locomotive engineer. The Louisville & Nashville assigned a modest number of black firemen to road diesel locomotives in the Deep South, while most other southern Class 1 lines, when they allowed blacks on diesels at all, confined them to switch engines in yards.[45]

In the decade and a half following World War II, tens of thousands of steam locomotives went to scrap. Coupled multiple-unit diesel locomotive sets with a single crew powered longer and heavier trains than even those previously pulled by double-headed steam engines with a crew in each cab. Yet despite such technological progress and labor savings, the railroads lost a great deal of passenger traffic to airlines and struggled to compete with interstate truckers for freight. Railroad employment plummeted 32 percent in the 1950s and another 30 percent from 1960 to 1968. The number of firemen nationwide declined from 56,000 in 1950 to 39,000 in 1960, and then to a mere 14,000 in 1970. In 1960, only 7 percent of the South's firemen were black, probably only a couple hundred. By the time civil rights legislation began to take effect in the late 1960s, too many laid-off white firemen existed for the railroads, whether in the South or elsewhere, to consider new hires. Firemen were a dying breed. That position disappeared forever in the 1980s as railroads won the war against "featherbedding," the practice of keeping a fireman in the locomotive cab although universal use of diesel or electric units meant that he (and now occasionally she) had few duties to perform.[46]

New legislation did, however, break the lock on engineer and conductor jobs. Those had been off-limits to African Americans from the dawn of railroading because they were positions of authority and autonomy. The conductor was the actual boss of the train, and the engineer was the boss of the locomotive. Racism, as expressed in both the North and the South, forbade blacks to give direction to or supervise whites. Management and labor were united on this matter. The Norfolk & Western's general counsel freely admitted, "the reason is racial . . . The sentiment of the employees of this company and the public in the territory in which it operates condemns the placement of a Negro in position of command over white men . . . That sentiment controls the management."[47] Both the conductors' and engineers' unions restricted membership to Caucasians. As a result, only a tiny number of blacks worked as engineers for the first century and a half of railroading. In 1883, the *Railroad Gazette* could identify only a single black engineer in the North, operating a switch engine for the New York & New England Railroad.[48] Another late nineteenth-century rarity was David Moore, who ran a switcher in the Grand Rapids, Michigan yards of the Lake Shore & Michigan Southern Railway, but was not allowed to operate road engines out on the mainline.[49] In the twentieth century, occasional southern short lines like South Carolina's Rockton & Rion Railway and the Magnolia State's Mississippi & Alabama Railroad reduced costs by employing non-unionized African American crews, both engineers and firemen. And blacks occasionally ran engines within industrial plants and quarries and on southern logging lines. During World War I, the Scullin Steel Co., which cast locomotive frames at a large complex in St. Louis, replaced striking white engineers, firemen, and switchmen with blacks on its yard and engine crews. This became a permanent practice, at least through World War II. All of them were supervised by a white yardmaster.[50]

The possibility of becoming a Class 1 railroad conductor or engineer was hinted at in Title VII of the 1964 Civil Rights Act, which banned discrimination by employers and labor unions. The act also created the Equal Employment Opportunity Commission, which had authority to investigate complaints and mediate between parties, although no power to enforce its findings or file lawsuits on behalf of those who had suffered discrimination. But "Title VII and the EEOC proved to be slow, imperfect vehicles for challenging past and continuing discriminatory practices, seeking black employment rights, and promoting black employment." Proactive measures were needed. They resulted from President Lyndon Johnson's 1965 Executive Order 11246, which, initially applying only to government contractors, required employers to take "affirmative action" (and document their steps) in hiring and employing minority workers. President Richard Nixon later stressed this didn't require racial quotas, but instead "goals of increasing minority employment."[51]

Three pioneers who managed, against the odds, to obtain engineers' jobs on Class 1 railroads after World War II stand out for their courage and persistence. Astonishingly, James Reed got a fireman's job on the Illinois Central in 1960, upon the recommendation of his great-uncle, an IC brakeman, at a time when almost no new firemen were being hired anywhere in the country. The civil rights movement was just entering the militant sit-in phase, prompting hostile remarks from white co-workers. Reed harbored a secret ambition, to become an engineer, but other black trainmen thought he was crazy and counseled him not to make waves. The 1964 Civil Rights Act, however, compelled the IC to let black firemen seek promotion to engineers. When Reed and fellow fireman Eddie Smith began training, their biggest obstacle was the racism of white engineers, who believed that a black man at the throttle signified a job lost by a white man. The railroad, unenthusiastic about promoting the pair, refused to require white engineers to train them. The only one willing to do so was damned as a "nigger lover" by his peers. Reed and Smith persevered, becoming, in 1967, the IC's first black engineers.[52]

John Wesley Whitaker, a Tuskegee Airman, secured a fireman's position on the Central of Georgia Railway following his discharge. Linking his own progress to civil rights, he helped found a union to fight discrimination on the job. As a result of civil rights legislation, and, of course, his own abilities, Whitaker became the C of G's first black engineer. After the Southern Railway absorbed that road, he achieved another "first," as its pioneer black transportation officer (road foreman of engines).[53] But such breakthroughs opened no floodgates. With traffic and employment generally in decline in the 1980s, railroads were adding few new engineers. As for the North and the West, because blacks didn't even work as firemen earlier in the twentieth century, there was no possibility they would become engineers until the civil rights era.

The Brotherhood of Locomotive Engineers finally admitted its first black member in 1966, but this did not signal an avalanche. The number of engineers nationwide hemorrhaged from a peak of 113,000 in 1920 to a mere 50,000 a half century later. During the huge World War II traffic increase, many young firemen on the Louisville & Nashville were promoted to engineer, only to be bumped back to fireman after the war. Two decades later, in the mid-1960s, when older engineers were offered early retirement, these firemen exercised seniority to finally get their hands back on the throttle, now on diesel locomotives. So anti-discrimination laws were at first of little practical effect, with so many experienced white enginemen in line for whatever jobs opened up. Initially, the door barely cracked open for blacks. Not for another decade, with the retirement of many career white enginemen and increasing freight traffic creating expanding needs for engineers, did broader opportunities occur.

Today black female as well as male engineers are working on the nation's mega-railroads nationwide, earning the same pay and holding the same seniority rights as white men and women. In 2004, on the 351-mile-main-line Florida East Coast Railway, the sole woman engineer was an African American.[54] In the South, retirements of white old-timers, as much as civil rights and affirmative action protections, opened the door. But opportunities came far too late for blacks to establish a tradition as "highball artists." The "brave engineer" of lore was always white. And only in the South did a "black greasy fireman" give his locomotive a full head of steam.

Railroads in the African American Experience

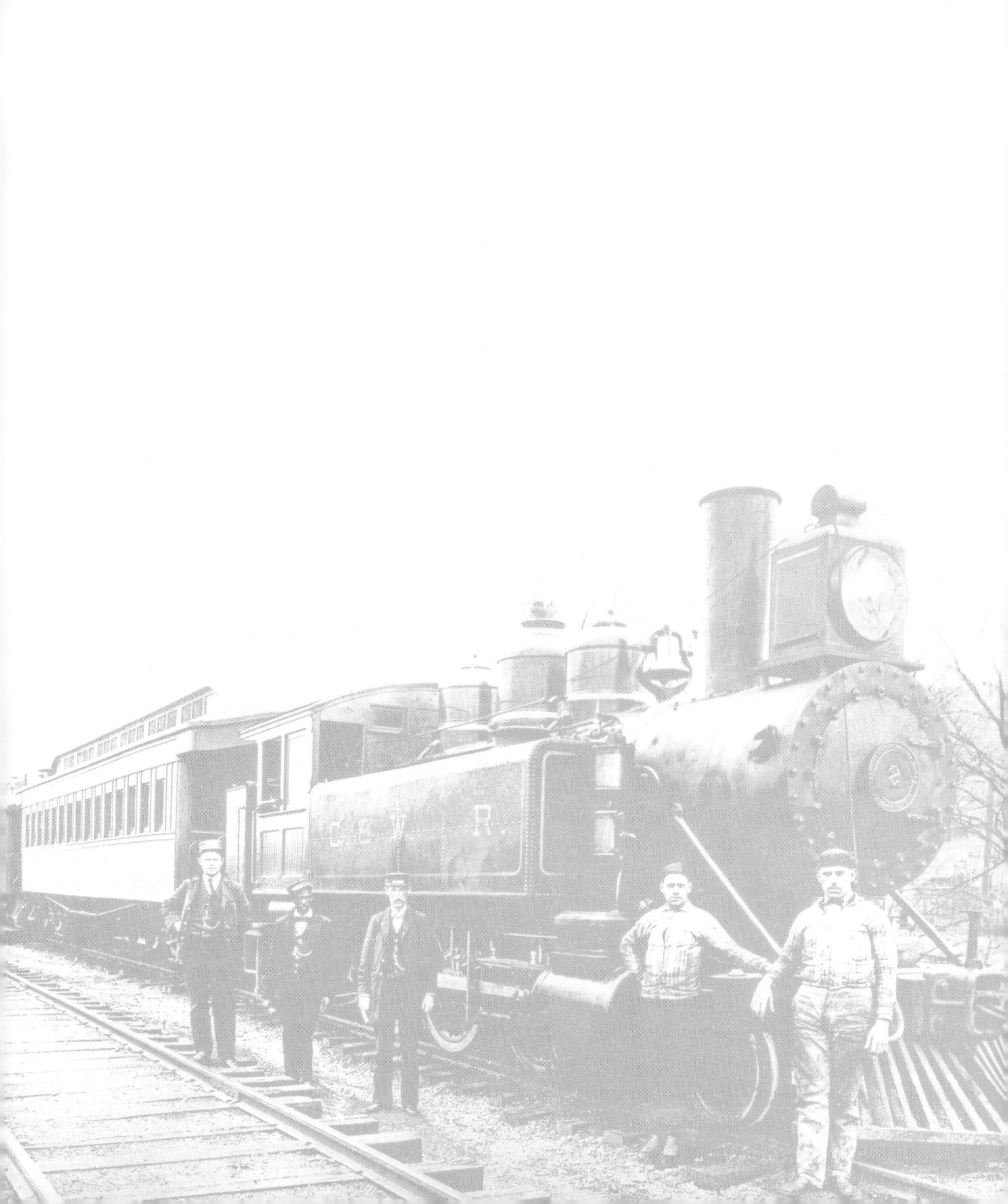

Southern railroad stations made it crystal clear where black people belonged, and where they didn't. At the Littleton, North Carolina depot on the Atlantic Coast Line Railroad, sometime around the turn of the twentieth century, the black station porter stands, broom in hand, below the sign identifying the entrance to the "Waiting Room for Colored People." Courtesy of the North Carolina State Archives

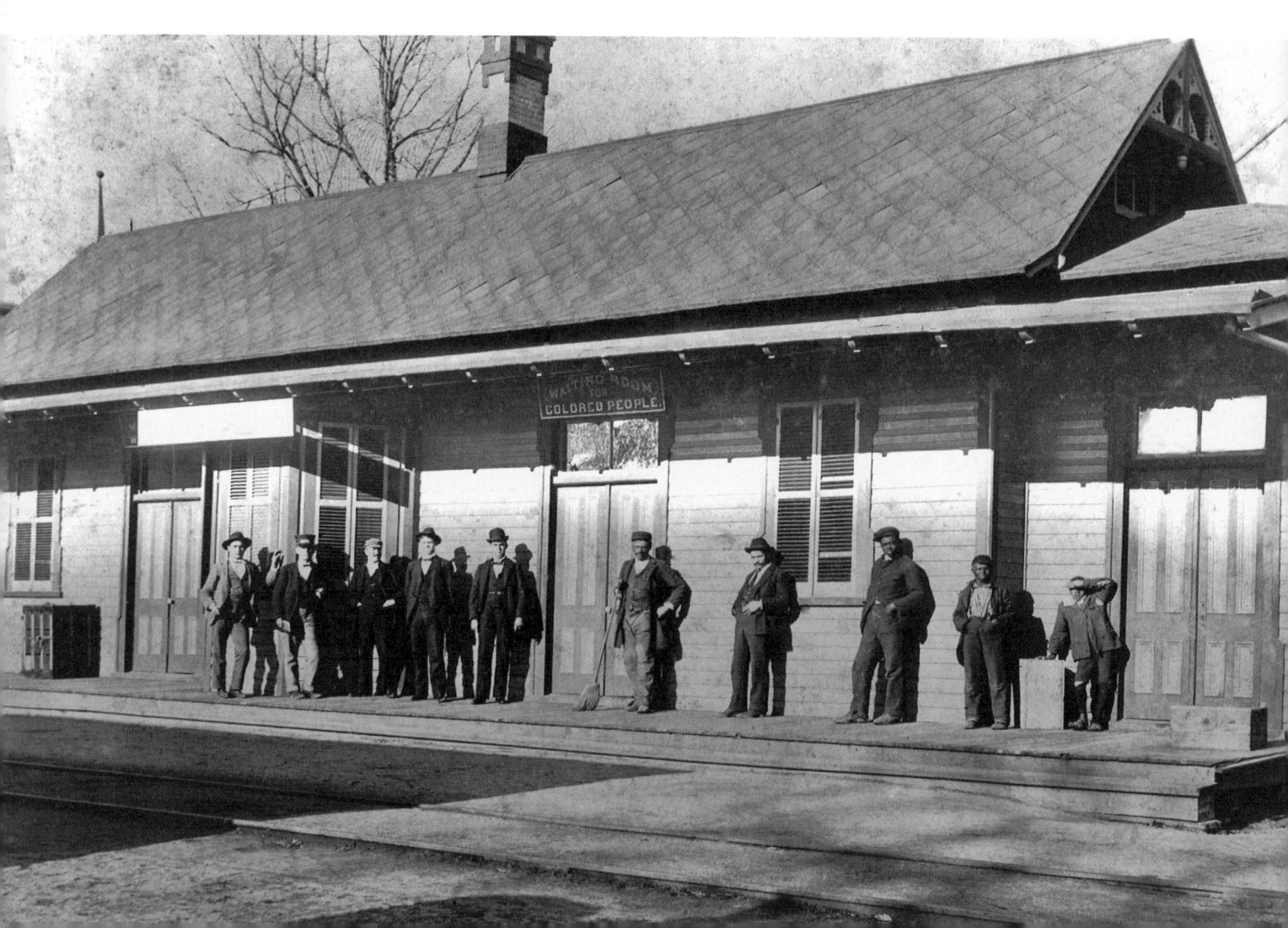

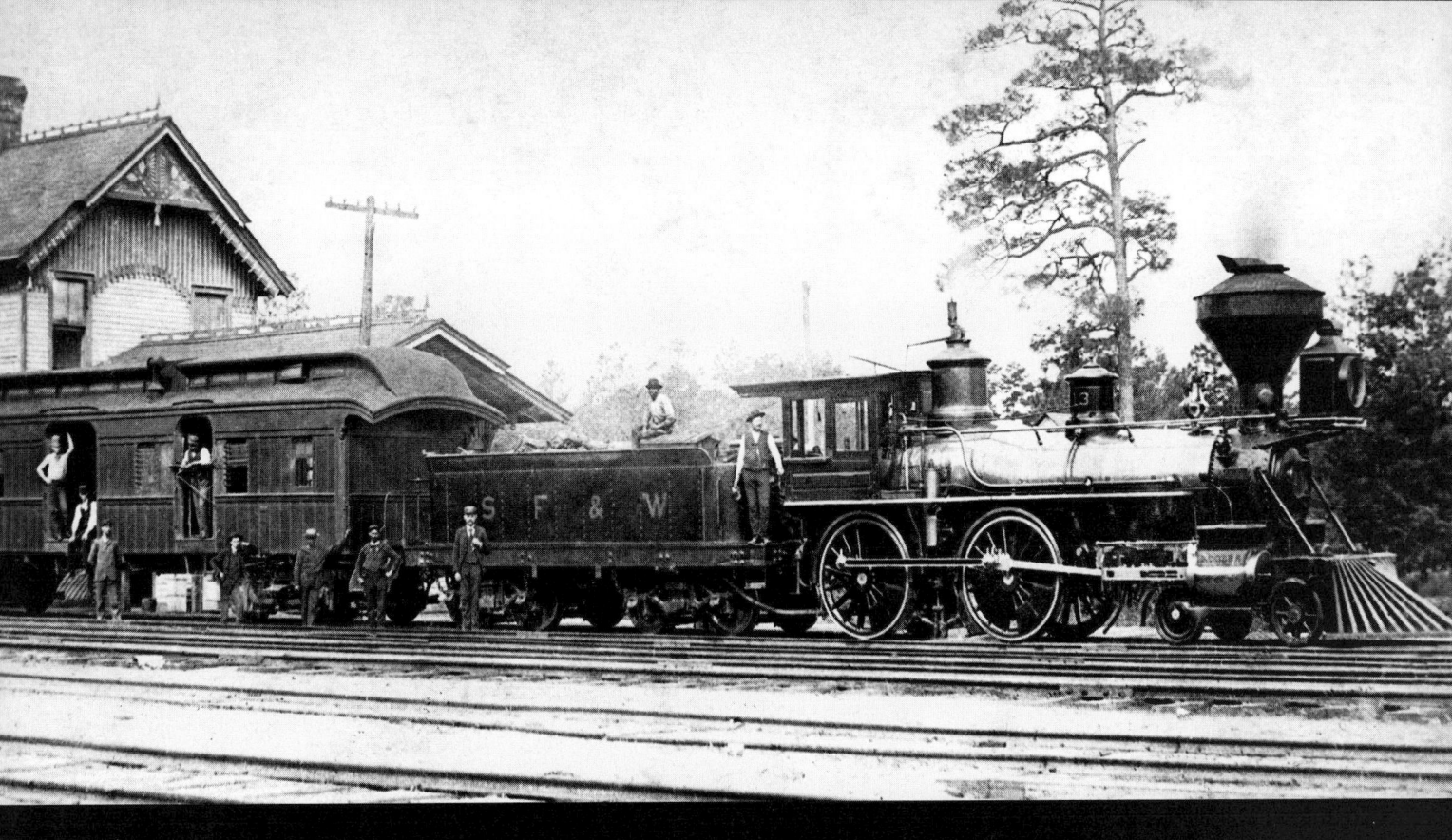

A black Railway Post Office clerk leans on the catcher arm in the open doorway of his car on a Savannah, Florida & Western Railway train at Waycross, Georgia, c. 1893. By that decade clerks of both races staffed thousands of post office cars that were part of passenger train consists. They worked side by side as federal employees in relative harmony until the Woodrow Wilson administration introduced segregation into the federal bureaucracy, poisoning race relations in the Railway Mail Service for many years. Don Hensley collection

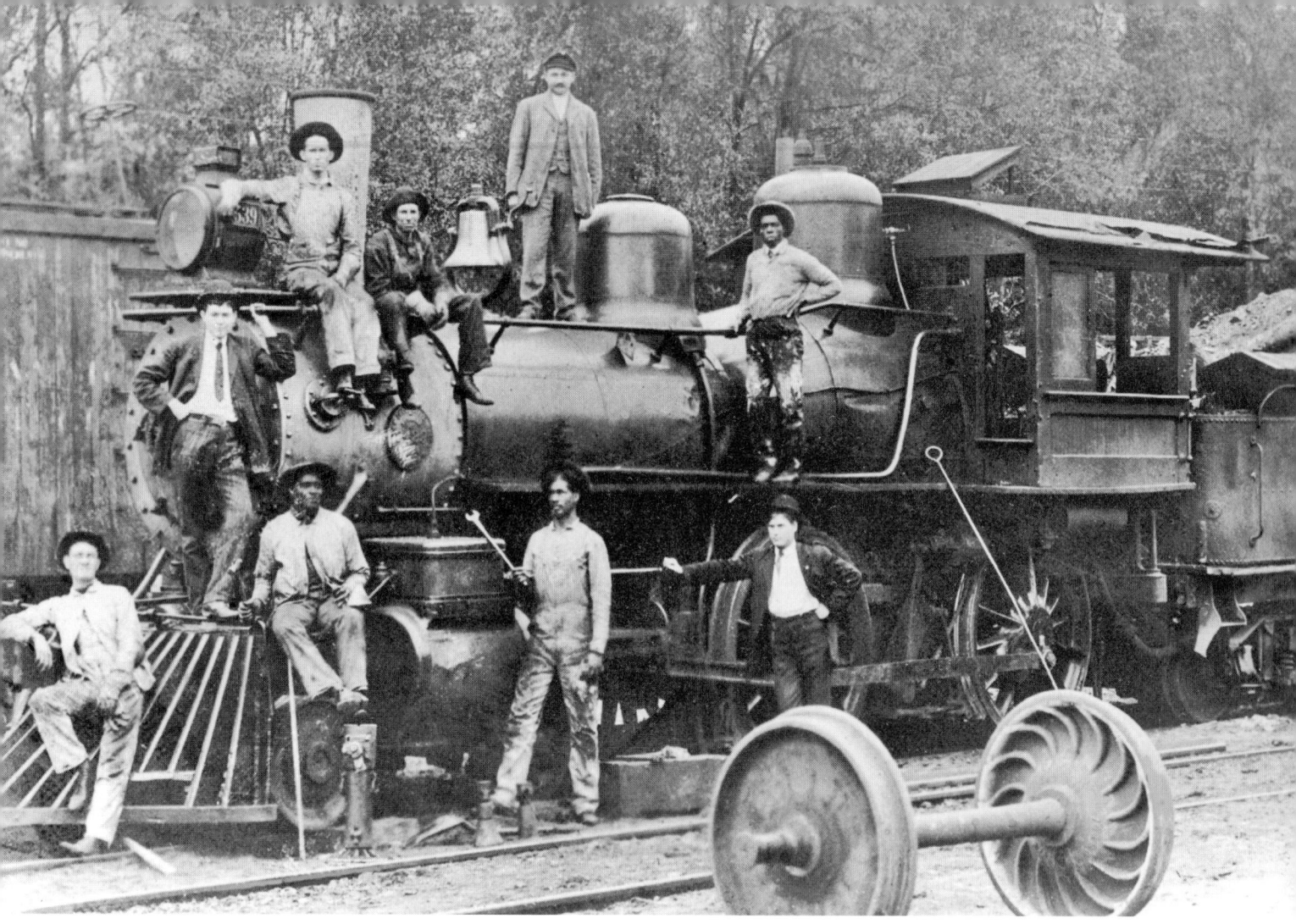

Black helpers and laborers pose with white mechanics on an Atlantic Coast Line Railroad locomotive around the turn of the twentieth century. Southern railroad shops relied heavily on blacks for unskilled and semi-skilled labor, although those who worked for years as laborers— the lowest rank—undoubtedly became quite knowledgeable in their craft. E. L. DeGolyer, Jr. Photograph Collection, DeGolyer Library, Southern Methodist University

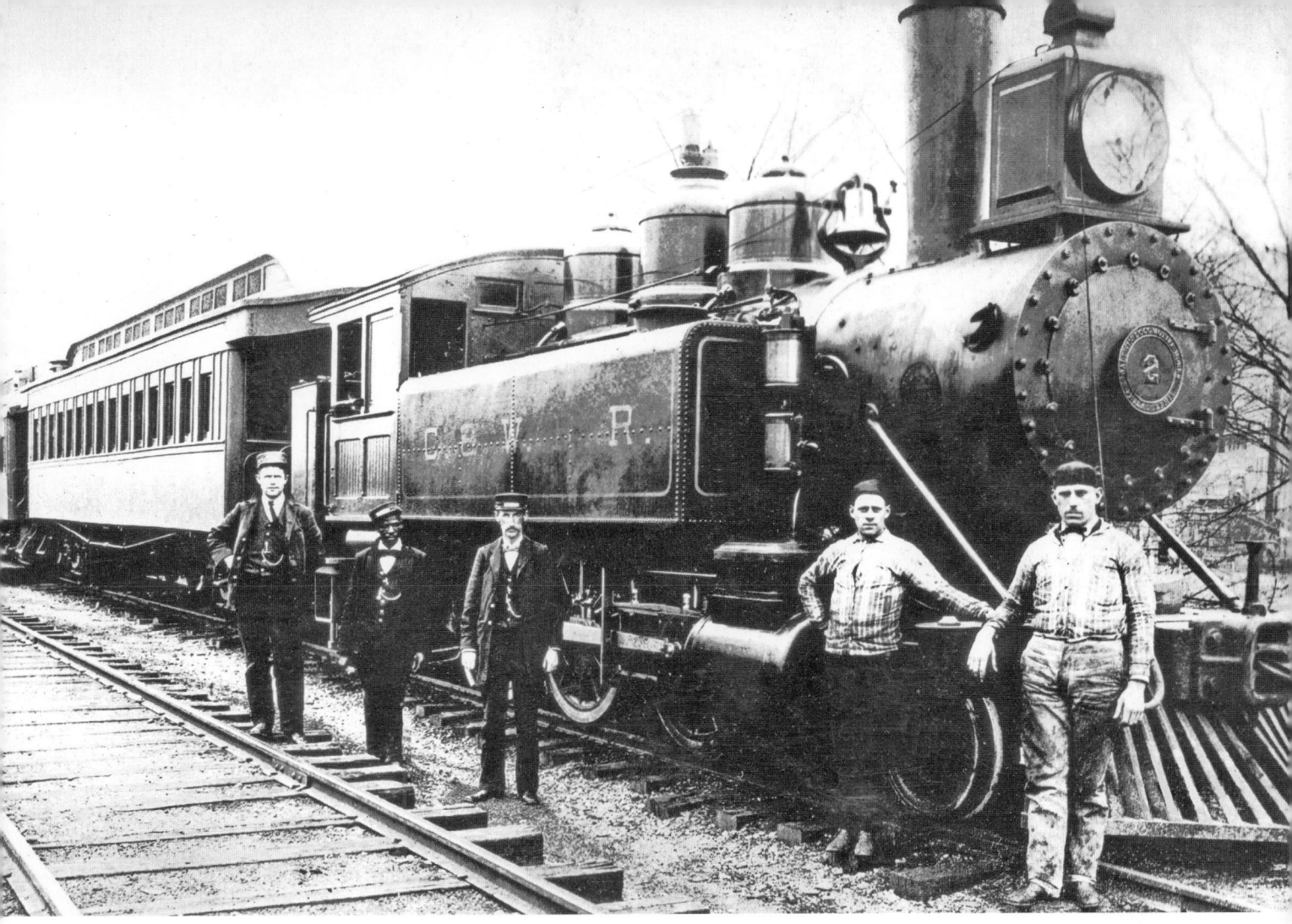

By the late nineteenth century, the public had come to expect train porter service. Even the Cincinnati & Westwood Railroad, a suburban commuter line, employed a nattily uniformed porter, shown standing between a conductor and a brakeman. The C&W ran from the Brighton station of the Cincinnati, Hamilton & Dayton Railroad 5 1/2 miles to Glenmore from 1876 to 1886, and again from 1891 to 1896, when a trolley line won over passenger business. Cincinnati & Westwood Collection, reprinted by permission, Railroad Museum of Pennsylvania

"WARY FEET, AN ALERT MIND, AND CHILLED NERVES"

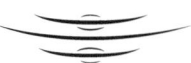

Brakemen and Switchmen

An old folksong, "The True and Trembling Brakeman," recounts, in grim detail, the all-too-common deaths of those who practiced the most dangerous of all railroad occupations:

> See that true and trembling brakeman, as he signals to the cab,
> There is but one thing for him, and the train it is to grab.
>
> See that true and trembling brakeman as the cars go rushing by,
> If he miss that yellow freight car, he is almost sure to die.
>
> See that true and trembling brakeman as he falls beneath that train,
> He had not a moment's warning before he fell beneath that train.
>
> See the car wheels rolling o'er him, o'er his mangled body 'n head,
> See his sister bending o'er him, crying, "Brother, are you dead?"[1]

There was good reason for brakemen to tremble. Many were "fortunate" to have lost only fingers; others limped along for the rest of their lives on one leg. The number who lost their lives falling from the tops of moving freight cars or under a car's wheels while trying to board a moving train, or who were crushed between cars when coupling, shows how cheap was the life of railroaders, particularly in the nineteenth century. It's no wonder that in the South many brakemen were African Americans. As with so much of black railroad history, they began in slavery.

Brakemen (also known as "train hands" and "couplers" on southern railroads) were essential for stopping both freight and passenger trains for the first half-century of American railroading. Automatic air brakes, which allowed an engineer to apply each car's brakes almost instantaneously and simultaneously, were first widely adopted in the 1880s but did not become mandatory in interstate commerce until 1900, as required by the Railroad Safety Appliance Act (1893). Before then, if a train was to be stopped quickly or if its speed was to be controlled safely on a descending grade, each car's brakes had to be manually applied by brakemen upon hearing a "down brakes" whistle signal from the engineer. Before the train could start again, or resume normal speed on level track, the brakes had to be manually released. Passenger train brakemen merely had to step from the open platform of one coach to another to "tie down" the brakes. But freight train brakemen—usually both a head-end and a rear brakeman, or flagman, plus a "swing" man in the middle of a particularly long or heavy train—had to leap across space from the top of one swaying boxcar to another, or climb down from such a car, step over the couplers, and get on a flat or hopper car. While performing such dangerous acrobatics, the brakeman had to keep a grip on his wooden brake "club," which was inserted between the spokes of a brake wheel, giving him leverage to overcome friction in mechanically applying the brakes. If brakes were tightened too much, they would lock up at low speeds, causing wheels to slide along the rail and wear flat spots that would thereafter "walk" (thump, thump, thump) rather than roll smoothly. If brakes weren't tightened sufficiently, the train could not stop soon enough and might run through a switch or into another train.[2]

The Baltimore & Ohio Railroad's 1866 rulebook made a train hand's duties appallingly clear: "The brakeman must understand that his proper position on the train while it is in motion, is on the top of the cars in the center of the train, except if they are empty coal hoppers, when he must place himself on the bumpers [end sills] near the center of the train, so as to be able to use as many brakes as possible in case the engineer or conductor shall call for brakes by the known signal." One could be on top of the cars day or night, in the baking heat of summer, and in rain, sleet, or snow of winter, for 12 to 16 hours of duty.[3] These were certainly valid reasons to tremble.

Equally hazardous was the job of coupling cars. Until automatic knuckle couplers, also mandated by the Railroad Safety Appliance Act, allowed brakemen to join or separate cars while standing safely to the side of a train, they risked their lives every time they had to couple cars with link and pins. The same dangers faced switchmen (also called yard brakemen) who coupled and uncoupled cars in yards and terminals but did not ride trains out on the line. A heavy oval iron link, fastened to each car with a removable iron pin, kept cars together. Nineteenth-century brakeman Harry French recalled the intricacies of link and pin couplings, before they were finally outlawed in 1900:

Railroads in the African American Experience

Perfect coordination of mind and muscle were an absolute necessity. The link was first fastened with a pin in one car. Then a pin was "cocked" at a slight angle in the other car to be coupled. As the two cars came together, the trainman [i.e., brakeman or switchman] guided the link into its slot. The impact of the coupling usually shook down the cocked pin, completing the coupling. If the pin did not shake down, the trainman stepped in between the cars and pounded it down with a spare pin. Oftentimes it was necessary to walk between the two moving cars. Wary feet, an alert mind, and chilled nerve were needed every instant. A man lived only long enough to make one mistake. The uncoupling of the cars was always the most dangerous job. Often it was necessary to uncouple with the cars in motion, especially in making some of the more intricate switching movements. The switchman had the choice of running along between the cars and pulling out the pin at the proper time or of lying on the beam that held the coupling slot . . . If there was any miscue, or if the pin could not be pulled, the trainman stood a fine chance of being thrown under the car.

Even after the introduction of automatic couplers, a switchman or brakeman could slip while trying to climb onto the step of a moving freight car and lose his legs beneath the wheels. Or he could be jarred off the catwalk on top of a car when slack ran in or out and fall to the ground or between cars.[4]

It is part of the perverse genius of capitalism that a dangerous job does not usually warrant a compensating high wage. Among the operating crews, brakemen were paid the least. Even firemen, whose work could be more exhausting, were paid more. An indication of the low status and low pay for brakemen in the antebellum period is that southern railroads hired, where they could, free black brakemen. Slave owners were often reluctant to rent their surplus slaves to railroads if they were to be used in dangerous situations. Free blacks, on the other hand, voluntarily consented to the hazards of such work, and their labor could be obtained for less than the going rate for slave hires. And both slaves and free blacks were cheaper to employ than white brakemen.

Surviving records for antebellum railroads are rarely complete, but it is possible to determine the hiring preferences for a number of larger roads. From 1860 through 1864, the Virginia Central Railroad employed about 33 brakemen per year—seven-eighths of whom were either slaves or free blacks—on its main line from Richmond westward into the foothills of the Blue Ridge Mountains. It hired a handful of white brakemen, likely to train them as conductors, jobs that were reserved for whites.[5] The Virginia & Tennessee Railroad depended almost entirely on black brakemen. In 1856, the year its main stem between Lynchburg, Virginia, and Bristol, Tennessee, was completed, it employed 41 free black and enslaved train hands. In 1862, the road used 14 enslaved and 5 "free colored" passenger train brakemen, as well as 33 enslaved and 1 white freight train brakemen. At the end of September 1864, the road had a total of 47 black brakemen, all slaves.[6] Shorter lines likewise preferred black brakemen. The Richmond, Fredericksburg & Potomac

Railroad used them exclusively throughout the slavery period and up to 1874; thereafter both whites and blacks performed such work.[7]

Although dealing with free workers required some adjustment, southern railroads continued to employ black brakemen after the Civil War. The freedmen, for their part, avidly sought railroad jobs as an alternative to sharecropping. This phenomenon is apparent in the hiring patterns of the North Carolina Railroad. It used the labor of 18 black and 2 white brakemen in 1865, the last year of slavery. In the next 2 years it employed about the same number, but only white men. By 1868 and 1869, however, it was hiring black and white brakemen in nearly equal numbers. In 1870, only one-quarter of the brakemen were white, and by 1871, all 19 brakemen were black.[8]

Thus, by the end of the slavery era, the job of brakeman was often associated with black labor in the South. This pattern would endure for decades to come because the work was dangerous and often unpleasant; blacks could be paid less than whites; and hiring them served the railroads' interest in undermining labor unionization. While it made sense for railroads to continue employing sizeable numbers of black brakemen, it was still necessary to hire white brakemen to guarantee a supply of candidates for conductor. In the South, it was customary for a freight train to have a black head-end brakeman, plus a white conductor and rear brakeman, or flagman, riding the caboose at the end of the train.[9] But because northern and western railroads did not begin with black brakemen—finding sufficient exploitable workers in the ranks of immigrants and poor whites—blacks rarely found such jobs open to them.

Until link and pin couplers were outlawed, brakemen and switchmen were the most frequently injured operating railroaders. A sampling of North Carolina statistics illustrates the point. Each railroad operating in the state was required to file annual reports with the secretary of state, including a 4-page form listing workplace injuries and fatalities. In one period in the 1880s, the 40-mile-long Piedmont Railroad reported 10 injured employees: 5 brakemen, 3 firemen, and 2 section laborers. Four of the brakemen fell from moving cars, and the other was hurt in a coupling incident. On the 223-mile-long North Carolina Railroad, out of 32 accidents, half occurred to brakemen and switchmen. Most of the former either fell off cars—often in icy weather—or their hands and arms were "mashed" in coupling. (Of the other half of accident victims, most were section laborers who were hurt by tools or by ties and rails dropping on their feet.) The Western North Carolina Railroad, which operated 470 miles of track, recorded 120 injuries and 12 fatalities. Nearly half the injuries occurred in coupling and uncoupling cars, or in riding atop cars. Four of the 6 fatalities to operating personnel occurred between cars.[10]

By the turn of the century, North Carolina lines were required to report accidents not only on the road but everywhere else. The Atlantic Coast Line Railroad, whose main line stretched from Richmond, Virginia, to Charleston, South Carolina, reported 437 industrial accidents in the Tar Heel State from January 1899 through October 1901. Forty-two percent of victims were operating personnel; the others were mostly white shop employees and black and white section laborers. Three-quarters of the killed and injured operating employees were blacks, mostly brakemen, cou-

Railroads in the African American Experience

plers, and train hands. So on the ACL, as elsewhere, blacks worked particularly in the most hazardous occupations, and were most frequently endangered while riding on the tops of cars, applying brakes.[11] Similar conditions prevailed farther south. Over a 24-month period early in the twentieth century, the 150-mile-long Mississippi Central Railroad recorded 71 on-the-job injuries and fatalities. Brakemen, switchmen, and flagmen sustained one-third of these casualties, the largest proportion of any labor category.[12]

The proportion of accidents in switching, braking, and flagging declined by World War I because of the universal use of air brakes and automatic couplers and greater emphasis on safety. Railroads formed employee safety committees, held safety rallies, and pushed safety in company magazines, particularly by urging the wearing of goggles and steel-toe shoes. The Illinois Central system reported about 1,500 employee injuries and 8 fatalities in the first 2 months of 1919. Most injuries now resulted from failing to wear goggles; using tools improperly; or handling heavy materials, freight, and baggage. All of the deaths occurred while employees were switching or riding on locomotives and cars, but with brakemen no longer having to remain on car tops to set brakes for their entire runs, and switchmen and brakemen able to couple and uncouple while standing to the side of cars, the risk to life and limb had been permanently reduced.[13]

Despite the hazards, a brakeman's steady pay attracted many blacks in the South. Employee magazines recorded the careers of numerous long-time "faithful" trainmen. Some worked unscathed to retirement, while others sustained repeated injuries. Jim Osborne started as a brakeman in 1897 and five years later became a switchman in the Illinois Central Railroad's Memphis Terminal. Finally retiring after 46 years on the job, he was noted for never having suffered an injury that resulted in lost time. Brakeman James Gardner was not so fortunate. Born shortly after slavery, he entered train service in 1888 but soon left the railroad after losing a finger in a link and pin coupling accident. He returned to the IC in 1903 and worked until retirement in 1926, during which time he was hospitalized after falling from a freight train and also broke an ankle in falling from a locomotive tender. These accidents notwithstanding, Gardner "had the reputation among all the trainmen as being a faithful brakeman, one that could be depended on, and gave no trouble with his superiors." Henry Hansbrough also devoted his entire working life to the railroad. One of 16 children who were born to parents just recently liberated from slavery, he "practically grew up with the Illinois Central," starting as a water boy on a section gang while literally only a boy. In his teen years, he graduated to laborer until, at the age of 18, he was personally selected by a conductor to be his regular brakeman. He never again changed jobs, stepping down after 50 years of continuous service in 1943. The IC became a family tradition: three brothers and two cousins had accumulated more than 100 years of service by the time Hansbrough retired.[14]

Brakemen and switchmen were disciplined for numerous mishaps. Suspensions—for days and even weeks—were meted out for failing to properly line switches or set derails, resulting in cars or locomotives leaving the tracks. And if, while switching, they did not apply brakes hard or soon enough, cars might strike others with such force as to derail or damage them. They were also censured for neglecting to tie down brakes securely to keep cars from rolling away, and for failing to make a solid "joint" of coupling, resulting in a train breaking apart. So not only was the work dangerous, it also carried numerous opportunities for miscues and errors, the blame for which would be laid at the trainmen's feet. It is ironic that they were paid so little for a job that entailed great responsibility for both lives and property.[15]

The numbers of black brakemen and switchmen in the South increased from the Civil War into the early 1900s. On some roads or on some divisions, such as the Missouri Pacific's Gulf Coast Lines, nearly all brakemen were black. Railroads knew that blacks worked without effective union protection, had "no means of resisting any wrong, no matter how grievous," and could be paid considerably less than whites. Despite this, they were good workers. In excluding them from the Brotherhood of Railway Trainmen, white brakemen almost guaranteed that blacks would identify with management more than with their white fellow workers. Again and again, company magazines lauded the brakemen's "loyalty." While this should not automatically be assumed to be devotion to one's employer, or even gratitude, where else did black trainmen have to turn, when faced with the hostility of unionized white trainmen intent on seizing their jobs, than to the goodwill of their employers, gained in exchange for faithful service? In fact, appeals to the "rich white man's sense of justice" appeared to be, at times, their only insurance.[16]

But ominous trends began to emerge in the South in the 1880s. Just as mechanical stokers would eventually make firemen's jobs more attractive to whites, the introduction of automatic couplers and air brakes made braking and coupling more appealing to whites, although the use of air brakes was a double-edged sword. It saved brakemen's lives, but it reduced the need for brakemen, particularly on passenger trains. The result was increased racial competition for a declining number of jobs, with white brakemen beginning organized efforts to oust their black counterparts two decades before white firemen took similar action.[17] In 1884, the Southern Pacific Lines fired almost 300 black brakemen at the insistence of unionized white workers. Similar racial firings occurred on at least five other roads. Seven years later, when the Louisville & Nashville Railroad hired a few black brakemen on a division that had been the exclusive domain of whites, its angry white brakemen shot at the newcomers. White switchmen on the Houston & Texas Central Railroad (an SP subsidiary) demanded the firing of their black counterparts in 1890, hoping that, without lower-paid competition, their wages would rise more quickly. When management refused to budge, the union backed down. The white engineers' union periodical posed the question: "What shall we do with the negro train hands?" It admitted that they were poorly treated, without union representation, forced to accept low pay, and thus lived "more miserably" than their white counterparts. "To demand their dismissal is manifestly unjust," acknowledged the engineers' magazine, but it could not advocate their admission to the white brotherhoods, noting that "the color question, in the Southern States is a mighty hard thing to handle."[18]

The railroads, on the other hand, had no difficulty handling the savings. In mid-1902, 9 white and 22 black switchmen were employed in the New Orleans & North-eastern Railroad's yards in

Meridian, Mississippi, and in the Crescent City. Only 1 white worked more than 20 days in the month; altogether, the 9 averaged only 10 days per month, being paid between $2 and $2.15 per day. Nearly half of the black switchmen worked more than 20 days in the month; altogether, the 22 blacks averaged 18 days, receiving $1.65 to $1.75 in daily wages. In other words, black switchmen were paid about 18 percent less than their white counterparts. If the railroad hired an all-white switching crew, it would have tallied a monthly payroll of $1,040. But by employing mostly blacks, its monthly payroll was $878, shaving 16 percent off its switchmen's expenses.[19]

In the North, so few opportunities for black brakemen existed that they never got a true toehold in the occupation. A few black brakemen and even conductors worked on Ohio railroads up into the 1880s, but with the ascendancy of the Big Four railroad brotherhoods, these positions became defined as "white." The handful of black conductors now found that many white engineers and brakemen were unwilling to work under them. And as these conductors retired, they were not replaced by other men of color. Thereafter, black brakemen were generally hired only in times of sudden labor shortages. During the 1894 Pullman strike, which tied up nearly all Midwestern lines, the Chicago, Rock Island & Pacific Railway was forced, for the first time, to hire black switchmen, but they were not retained once labor peace was restored.[20] Most black brakemen remaining in the North by the turn of the twentieth century were passenger train porter-brakemen. Although they possessed the requisite brakemen's skills, their primary purpose was to assist passengers and keep the cars clean. In fact, true black brakemen in the North and West were so rare after 1900 as to be almost a novelty.[21]

The situation was dramatically different in the South, however. By 1910, southern railroads employed nearly 7,000 black brakemen, switchmen, and flagmen. But despite their presence on every major system, their jobs were in serious jeopardy. Unionized white brakemen, like white firemen, were determined to drive blacks from the craft. At the Brotherhood of Railway Trainmen's 1899 convention, the organization formally called for "clearing our lines of this class of workmen."[22] The Georgia Railroad firemen's strike in 1909 spurred brakemen to likewise try to purge their ranks of black competitors. The following year, the BRT gained agreement from the southern railroads' bargaining body that the percentage of black brakemen would never exceed that of the number employed on January 1, 1910. In addition, no blacks would be henceforth employed as flagmen. Pay differentials were also negotiated. On the Central of Georgia Railway's Thomaston branch, for example, white brakemen would be paid $2.75 per day, while black brakemen would earn only $1.50. But such concessions did not satisfy militant white railroaders. In 1916, trainmen on the Yazoo & Mississippi Valley Railroad tried to terrorize black brakemen out of their jobs. A number were killed, and more wounded, as trains were abruptly stopped at night in remote locations and the brakemen shot while they were inspecting their trains to find why they had halted. No one doubted that white railroaders were behind these acts, but no perpetrator was ever apprehended. One victim was Alex Harris, brakeman on a train between Vicksburg and Hamburg, Mississippi. His widow sued the railroad for $20,000, which offered to settle for $500. Mrs. Harris refused that offer and the case went to trial, but a jury found the railroad not responsible. This verdict strengthened the company's insistence that it was not liable "every time anything happens to an employe on duty."[23]

World War I brought to a head the issue of persecution of black brakemen. U.S. Railroad Administration General Order 27 mandated that black and white trainmen receive equal pay for equal work. Southern white railroaders interpreted this as putting blacks on an equal social plane and they determined to end the nearly 75-year-old practice of employing black switchmen and brakemen. Defying federal authority, white switchmen on the Y&MV and parent Illinois Central in Memphis staged a wildcat strike, demanding that crews switching flat yards, typically consisting of a white foreman, a white switchman, and a black switchman (called a "helper"), now be all white. At the IC's more modern Nonconnah Yard in Memphis, where cars were pushed over a "hump" to roll by gravity down onto designated tracks in the "bowl," a typical shift required 2 foremen, 7 "liners" who threw switches, and 18 black "car riders," who rode each car or cut of cars, slowing them to a stop by applying hand brakes. Here, too, all-white crews were demanded. Soon other switchmen working for the Frisco, Southern, and Union Railway of Memphis walked off their jobs, joining the Memphis hate strike. Switchmen threatened to kill any blacks who showed up for work. This put the Brotherhood of Railway Trainmen in a bind because it had not authorized a strike. Finally, when conductors and firemen refused to walk out and thus paralyze the railroads, the wildcat strike collapsed. This only increased the white trainmen's resolve to achieve a racial monopoly, the BRT now alleging that black brakemen and switchmen were accident-prone, impulsive, unsafe, and "unfitted mentally" for such work.[24]

Predictably, Y&MV and IC trainmen in Mississippi and Tennessee again turned to terror. Supposedly, a price of $300 lay on the head of every black brakeman and switchman. Letters bearing the signature "Zulus," sent through the company mail, threatened death if they did not quit. White thugs stopped trains and beat black brakemen, warning them of worse if they persisted in working. Other men were attacked on their way to work. When the superintendent of the Mississippi Division sought the assistance of civil authorities and put up reward posters all over the railroad, he, too, was threatened. Brakeman Bob Grant was lucky to escape with his life. When his freight train stopped for water after dark in Lambert, Mississippi, he and the white flagman began inspecting the train. Three white men accosted him at gunpoint, but he was spared when one of the kidnappers vouched for him as "a good old Negro." After being threatened if he continued working, he was released, his train having already departed. But luck ran out for other black brakemen. Four of them were murdered by the "Zulus," including Horace Hurd, whose body was shredded by a huge load of buckshot. On his clothing was pinned a note: "Let this be a lesson to all nigger brakemen." Two more were killed in short order. Not surprisingly, many responded to this "carnival of blood" by quitting their jobs, while others requested demotion to train porters, with loss of seniority, rather than risk death.[25]

Railroads in the African American Experience

Two black Norfolk & Western Railway yard switchmen are ready, lanterns in hand, for working at night. The white man holding a lantern is probably a yard conductor, while the man in the suit and derby hat may be the yardmaster. The 0-6-0 locomotive was built for switching, with footboards in front on which a switchman could stand and a "swallow tail" tender to give the engineer better visibility behind him. While switching, the crew might have performed the dangerous maneuver of "poling," moving cars on a parallel track using the pole hanging from the tender. The photograph was taken sometime between 1893, when the engine was built, and 1906, when it was renumbered. Norfolk & Western Historical Photos, Digital Library and Archives, University Libraries, Virginia Polytechnic Institute and State University

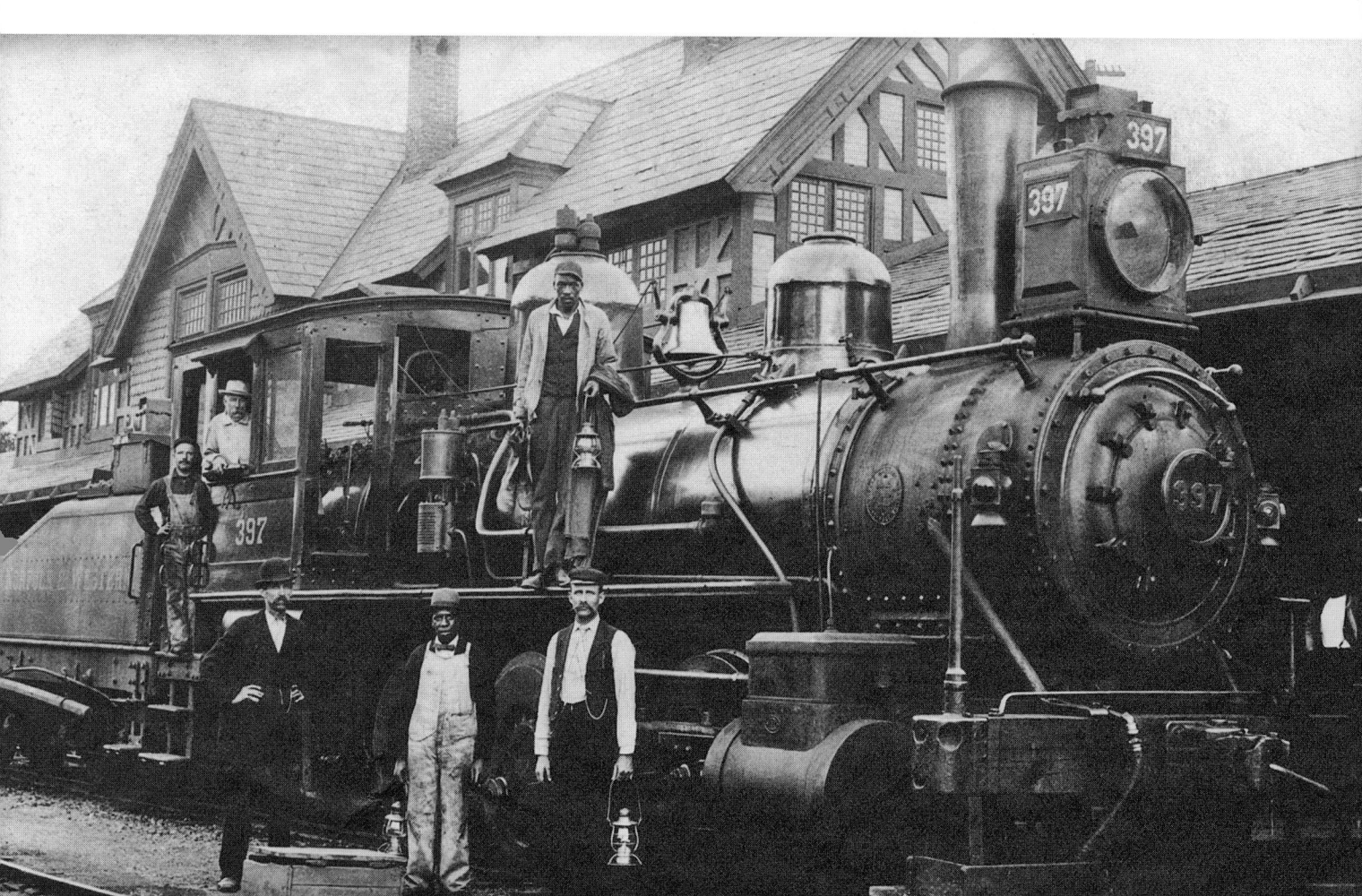

Ultimately more effective than violence was the white trainmen's success in 1919 in negotiating with the USRA new work rules for southern lines. All new brakemen, switchmen, and flagmen would henceforth have to pass a literacy examination. This alone would reduce the proportion of blacks. Furthermore, blacks were now prohibited from working as rear brakemen.[26] Separate racial seniority lists, which had protected the jobs of blacks with many years of service, were abolished, giving senior white flagmen the opportunity to bump experienced black head-end brakemen. Almost immediately, 150 blacks lost their jobs on the Central of Georgia, with similar losses on its affiliates, the Atlanta & West Point Railroad, Western Railway of Alabama, and Georgia Railroad. Black brakemen suffered additional losses on the Georgia Southern & Florida and Atlanta, Birmingham & Atlantic railroads, and even more drastic cuts in 1920 on the Missouri Pacific system. In addition to the IC and its subsidiaries, the Y&MV and Gulf & Ship Island lines, this situation also prevailed on the Southern Railway, Louisville & Nashville, and Nashville, Chattanooga & St. Louis Railway.[27]

Black trainmen could only very cautiously protest, usually beseeching railroad managers to reward their hard work and loyalty by guaranteeing the percentage of jobs that they traditionally had held. But appeals to paternalism, which had at times achieved modest success in the past, were now unavailing. None of the railroads officially recognized the weak independent black unions because they feared only the power of organized white workers. Blacks' interests were disregarded. The Missouri Pacific had long employed all-black freight train crews (with the exception, of course, of conductors and engineers) and black switchmen on its Valley and Louisiana Division, between Alexandria, Louisiana, and Little Rock, Arkansas. Among the brakemen were a number of aging veterans who found it difficult to do their jobs with longer and more frequent trains, the result of swollen wartime traffic. In 1919, their union appealed for lighter duties for these faithful employees, but the company ignored the request. A year later, their union protested the merging of white and black seniority lists, which resulted in whites claiming positions previously held by blacks but which were now attractive because of USRA-mandated wage increases. The MoPac again rebuffed the black brakemen, advising them to file any grievances with the Brotherhood of Railroad Trainmen—which, of course, was actively seeking their jobs.[28]

Black brakemen's jobs continued to erode in the 1920s. Their numbers on the MoPac's Valley and Louisiana Division declined from 250 to 180, while 70 new white brakemen were hired. The cumulative effect nationwide of agreements between railroad managers and the BRT was that, even while overall black railroad employment more than doubled between 1910 and 1924, the proportion of black brakemen declined 5 percent. The Railroad Labor Board continued to permit the BRT to negotiate away black trainmen's rights while ostensibly acting on their behalf.[29]

The plight of black brakemen grew even worse in the 1930s. New Deal labor legislation worked against them. Amendments to the Railway Labor Act in 1934 established that whatever union was selected by the majority of workers in a particular craft was entitled to bargain on behalf of all workers in that occupation. Although this theoretically gave black brakemen the right to vote for union representation, the much greater numbers of white brakemen were represented by the Brotherhood of Railroad Trainmen, whose mission was to eliminate black brakemen. This guaranteed that a small independent union like the Colored Trainmen of America, most of whose members were MoPac brakemen, could never officially represent them unless the railroad voluntarily agreed to recognize it. Otherwise such a union could only appeal to railroad managers to act benevolently on their behalf in a trade-off for lower wages.[30] Such a situation occurred when the coal-hauling Virginian Railway saved 23 percent in labor costs in an agreement with the Association of Colored Railway Trainmen and Locomotive Firemen to pay car riders (switchmen) $6 per day, while neighboring Chesapeake & Ohio and Norfolk & Western railways paid their BRT-member car riders a $7.82 daily wage.[31]

In such a hostile environment, a valiant voice spoke up for black trainmen. Thomas Redd had been a brakeman on the Illinois Central's Louisville District since 1895, and by the 1920s was a persistent pain in the neck to management, regularly complaining about the ill treatment of black railroaders, himself included. A remarkable correspondence reveals his tenacity in seeking personal justice in a case that dragged on for three years. On December 21, 1918, Redd was brakeman on a train between Central City and Louisville, Kentucky, when he was ordered to fire the locomotive at West Point for the remaining 20 miles to the home terminal. The railroad paid him for 100 miles as a brakeman and for 20 miles as a fireman. The standard minimum mileage for firemen, however, was 100 miles, and Redd alleged that, if a new fireman had been called at West Point, that man would have been paid for 100 miles, even though he would only have worked 20 miles. His white engineer agreed with Redd's interpretation, but the company balked at compensating him according to the formula previously agreed upon by management and the BRT. Redd wrote five appeal letters, finally giving up after the railroad's general manager curtly denied his request. While respectful, each letter was forthright, the final one declaring that money was not the main issue; rather, justice was at stake.[32]

Redd also took up the cause of fellow workers, firing off numerous letters on their behalf. In a number of instances, he wrote forcefully for black brakemen who were disadvantaged by a cynical seniority agreement between the southern railroads and the BRT. This rule allowed a white brakeman to exercise his seniority to displace a junior black head end brakeman, but prohibited a black brakeman from bumping a white rear brakeman with lower seniority. The purpose of this was plain: it was "a scheme to eliminate the colored men, from train and yard service on the railroads of the United States." Redd continued with as frank language as a southern black man dared use with whites: "This discrimination against colored men, comes not as a matter of general qualifications, merit and ability to perform the duties prescribed for trainmen or brakemen, but it does come as a matter of race prejudice, which is wrong from start to finish, and it is unjust and unfair in the extreme." Redd futilely challenged the IC to "sign a joint statement of facts, with the colored brakemen of the Kentucky Division to place before the United States Railroad Labor Board, that this question may be adjusted with justice and fair play to all employees, irrespective of race, creed or color."[33]

Brakeman Redd kept up a drumbeat of protests each time a black brakeman was "rolled," writing to everyone up the corporate ladder, including the president. Hoping to lay such matters to rest, vice president-operations A. E. Clift invited Redd to a personal meeting at IC headquarters in Chicago "for the purpose of straightening him out." Clift was obviously peeved that Redd had gone over his head in writing to the railroad's top executive. Redd did not budge, saying that he wanted only "to see that the colored men got their rights."[34]

Illinois Central managers occasionally acknowledged, privately, their racist practices. In a confidential internal communication, the superintendent of the road's Southern Lines wrote that "Thomas Redd is well known to officers on the Kentucky Division as well as to me, as it has been the practice of Redd to write letters to almost every one for quite a long time, and while Redd is a smart negro, many of his communications are ill advised." But the IC official then admitted the real source of the problem: "I wish to be very frank about colored train and engine men matters and say to you that there is discrimination being practiced against this class of employes and the employing officers believe that it is a warranted discrimination for the reason that rules have been promulgated and interpretations placed within the past three or four years that means the gradual elimination of these men from our service." Although Redd was not privy to this confession, he was well aware of the company's resolve. Nonetheless, he persisted in seeking justice for his fellow trainmen. Protesting another case of a black brakeman being rolled by a white trainman with less seniority, he employed a sarcasm rarely uttered by blacks in addressing whites: "I am bring these specific cases to your notice because the unfair provisions of the seniority rule are so very plain that the most indifferent man in the ranks of our officials cannot fail to see the injustice thereof, and as it has always been the policy of this company to treat all of its employes, just, fair and right, irrespective of race, creed or color, hence we can not believe for one moment that you are going to depart from the fair example set by our predecessors in office."[35]

Redd was the grievance chairman of the Louisville local of an independent black brakemen's and firemen's union, but because the IC recognized only the white Brotherhood of Railroad Trainmen, it responded to him merely as an individual. The BRT's grievance chairman claimed that his union was complying with contracts that had been duly negotiated with the railroad, and that Redd was "evidently dumb or, to say the least, very persistent" in asking for the impossible.[36] The black trainmen's complaints covered unfair application of seniority rules, the exclusion of blacks from certain divisions, and the overall erosion of employment. Of the 250 black brakemen and switchmen employed in and around Memphis by the IC and the Y&MV in 1927, fewer than 100 remained by 1933. Furloughed workers lost all seniority after not working off the extra board for six months, while laid-off whites were not similarly penalized. So desperate were the times that Redd even urged the IC to reestablish different pay rates for black and white workers so as to preserve black jobs. But the railroad was deaf to the pleas of blacks. Abandoning appeals to paternalism, Redd in 1934 organized the International Association of Railway Employees to combine the efforts of all existing black railroaders' unions. The IARE tried to persuade federal railroad boards to investigate blacks' complaints, but government officials consistently maintained that the white railroad unions were the only legitimate representatives of brakemen and firemen, irrespective of race. This forced Redd to conclude that the only remaining avenue for redress was the courts. Indeed, litigation would bring significant victories to black railroaders, but not until a decade later. Redd's activism on behalf of brother trainmen in the 1920s and 1930s, while not quixotic, was clearly in vain. Neither railroad officials nor federal bureaucrats would challenge the "right" of white unions to deprive black railroaders of their jobs.[37]

The decline in employment caused by the Great Depression, white railroaders' threats and violence against black workers, and cynical deals between the BRT and southern railroads together shredded the ranks of black brakemen and switchmen. While black firemen were the principal targets of assassination on IC lines in Mississippi in 1931, a brakeman was also murdered and two others were wounded.[38] But more significant were the cumulative effects of the unholy alliance between unions and management dating from early in the century. After the BRT's 1910 agreement with southern lines, some railroads thereafter hired no new black brakemen at all. Thus, on the Norfolk & Western's Radford Division, the dozen remaining "colored road brakemen" in 1937 all had seniority dating from 1891 to 1907. Systemwide, the N&W hired no black road brakemen after 1908.[39]

The Southern Railway achieved similar results by ceasing to hire new black trainmen and isolating those it still employed in fewer and fewer locations. By 1931, only a handful of black yardmen (switchmen) continued working on its Danville and Winston–Salem divisions, all of them having been hired before 1919. No black yardmen at all remained at Lynchburg or Danville, Virginia, or High Point, Durham, or Selma, North Carolina. Elsewhere in the Tar Heel State, the only significant number remained at the Spencer, North Carolina yards. Out of 100 yardmen still working as the Depression worsened, 11 were black. Holding the highest seniority was Jack Pearson, who entered service in 1896. The other 10 blacks also had many years with the company, while most white yardmen hired in the early 1900s had long before been promoted.[40]

The Southern's Asheville Division likewise refused to hire new black trainmen. According to a 1943 seniority list, only 14 of its then 228 currently working flagmen and brakemen—6 percent— were black. Three-quarters of them had hired on before or during World War I. Of the 54 brakemen and flagmen added between 1940 and the end of 1942, only one was black. The yard at Asheville, North Carolina, employed 140 switchmen, with Walter Bruell being the lone black. He held the second highest seniority on the division, having worked continuously since 1906.[41] The triumph of the BRT is revealed in the 1953 Asheville Division seniority list. Flagmen and brakemen numbered 118, only 5 of whom were black, 4 of them hired before 1919. More than 60 men hired between 1941 and 1948 were still in service, not one of whom was black. And all 128 Asheville Yard switchmen were white.[42]

Short-line railroads sometimes followed the example of the big carriers, but others resisted union demands for white monopolies. The 94-mile-long Atlantic & North Carolina Railroad illustrates the former. It employed 14 trainmen in 1939, the oldest in service being a black man whose seniority dated to 1905. The only other African American was hired in 1917, during the World War I traffic increase.[43] But other lines played hardball with the unions in order to keep labor costs low. When the BRT insisted that the 57-mile-long Durham & Southern Railroad employ only brakemen who were eligible for promotion to conductors, it rebuffed that demand. With plenty of North Carolina railroaders furloughed in 1935, the D&S's remaining white trainmen concluded they were lucky to have jobs at all and agreed to work without a union contract and accept the employment of black brakemen at a rate of $4 per day, with white brakemen receiving a $5 daily wage.[44]

The cumulative effects of white unionists' hostility to black trainmen leap out of census figures. In 1920, railroads employed 8,275 black brakemen, yardmen, switchmen, and flagmen, nearly all of them in the South. By 1940, they numbered only 2,739, a two-thirds decline, and attrition continued throughout that decade. Racism even trumped the need to win World War II. The St. Louis–San Francisco Railway experienced an extreme labor shortage in 1944 at a time when, in the sarcasm of famed black attorney Charles H. Houston, "the United States was straining every nerve and sinew against Germany and Japan," but the white unions categorically opposed the hiring of any new black brakemen or firemen, even on the line from Birmingham to Memphis, where blacks had held such positions since the nineteenth century. Evidence that the IC followed a similar practice is found in a 1943 photograph of a class of student switchmen, brakemen, and firemen. Many of them appear to be mere boys. All 32 were white.[45]

The World War II–era Fair Employment Practice Committee offered a glimmer of hope for black trainmen, but in the end its damning findings were simply ignored by both railroads and unions. FEPC hearings revealed systematic discrimination against black switchmen and brakemen by the Brotherhood of Railroad Trainmen and on the Southern Pacific and Missouri Pacific in Texas. Brakemen of both races had long worked on the MoPac's line from Baton Rouge, Louisiana, to Kingsville, Texas. White brakemen had been represented by the BRT for many years, while the blacks, ever since the World War I years, had relied on their own organization, the Colored Trainmen of America. The CTA had negotiated independently with the railroad, appealing to the paternalism of company officials while accepting lower wages than those paid to white brakemen. To these black railroaders, the FEPC appeared to be something of a revival of the U.S. Railroad Administration, which had mandated equal wages for equal work during World War I. The CTA appealed to the FEPC to do what it could to equalize wages. Black brakemen were paid 9 percent less than whites in the same class of service, while black switchmen received 40 percent less. But the FEPC had no authority to order wage adjustments, and, ironically, reminded the CTA that the union had signed binding wage agreements and would have to live with them until they might be renegotiated.[46]

The FEPC found substantial discrimination against black switchmen at the Southern Pacific's Houston Terminal. Early in the Great Depression, the SP reduced the number of black crews while retaining all of its white switchmen. Then, in 1937, the railroad signed an agreement with the BRT to thenceforth hire only whites for yard jobs. And as furloughed switchmen were recalled for work, whites were granted seniority from the date of their original hiring, while blacks' seniority stemmed from the date of their recall. Two furloughed men, however, were not recalled because they exercised leadership among the black switchmen. FEPC attempts to confer with the SP were rebuffed. Meanwhile, the road experienced a severe shortage of switchmen in mid-1944 and placed newspaper advertisements in El Paso, Fort Worth, and Houston reading: "Switchmen, brakemen and firemen urgently needed by Southern Pacific. If inexperienced and you are between the ages of 18 and 44 we will train you." Yet the SP refused to hire experienced and qualified black trainmen. FEPC hearings in the spring of 1945 availed nothing, however; both the SP and the BRT stonewalled the matter.[47]

Northern lines, too, came under FEPC scrutiny. The New York Central Railroad admitted that it had for decades refused to employ blacks as brakemen or trainmen, "regardless of their qualifications or ability," but denied it was on account of race. Rather, the NYC claimed to employ blacks and whites where each could do their best. The railroad had to take into account "the nature of the relationship that will exist among the several men who will work on the job and their contacts with the public." Thus "the present feeling or state of mind of a large majority of the [white] employees of the New York Central and of the public served by its railroads makes it inadvisable to employ Negroes in certain railroad occupations." The Pennsylvania Railroad mounted the same defense, denying "any policy of racial discrimination." Rather, "a railroad cannot take the initiative in introducing practices which it knows will produce an opposite effect on the employes and create not only a serious deterrent to the efficient performance of the service the Company is rendering but make it impossible to perform that service."[48]

It was not until 1953 that the first black was admitted to the Brotherhood of Railroad Trainmen. He was not even a brakeman, and did not work for a southern railroad. N. C. James was already a pioneer, being one of the first black dining-car stewards, running out of New York City on the Pennsylvania Railroad. Another steward who previously sought membership had been rebuffed even though he obtained the assistance of the New York State Commission Against Discrimination. James, however, was admitted to one of the BRT's local New York lodges without the intervention of the commission.[49] Finally, also in 1953, the first black brakeman was hired in the Northeast in modern times, by the Pennsylvania Railroad, although not entirely willingly. It took pressure from the same state commission and black railroaders to crack this barrier. Four years later, the PRR employed nearly 100 black trainmen in New York and New Jersey. But its affiliated Long Island Rail Road only hired its first black passenger brakemen at that time, in 1957. And elsewhere in the Northeast, no blacks yet held brakemen jobs on the New York Central; Baltimore & Ohio; Delaware, Lackawanna & Western; Erie; and New York, New Haven & Hartford. The only other area road to hire them was the Jersey Central Lines.[50]

No black brakemen were hired by southern Class 1 railroads from World War II to the civil rights era. Braking had become a white man's job, period. Only pressure resulting from Title VII of the Civil Rights Act of 1964 began to break the logjam, but by then the number of switchmen and yard brakemen was declining with the construction of automatic hump yards in which cars being classified onto various yard tracks were slowed by mechanical retarders, not car riders. Resistance to change still existed. Eugene S. Johnson had worked for 23 years as a train porter on the Louisville & Nashville until his job disappeared with the reduction in passenger service. Train porters often had experience throwing switches, flagging trains, and directing engine moves, and Johnson was well acquainted with such duties when he applied for openings as flagman or brakeman in 1964. Over the next two years, his application was ignored while several whites—new employees without railroad experience—were hired. Johnson finally found work as a shop laborer, while filing a grievance with the federal Equal Employment Opportunities Commission. Two years later, under pressure, the L&N grudgingly declared him qualified to be a mail handler, bridge tender, laborer, or watchman. Not satisfied, Johnson lodged a more formal complaint with the EEOC, which negotiated a settlement from the L&N. While admitting no violation of civil rights, the railroad agreed to thereafter adhere to the new law's non-discriminatory hiring requirements, abolish segregated workplace facilities, and consider Johnson for the next available openings in all occupations where he met the objective qualifications. In the summer of 1969, the L&N held its first affirmative action training class to qualify 30 former Nashville Union Station mail handlers as switchmen and road brakemen.[51]

Ever since the dawn of railroading, white brakemen were promoted up to the conductor ranks, but brakeman was almost invariably as high as blacks could go. The few black conductors before modern times were anomalies. Those of which there is record worked in the Northeast, where racial attitudes were slightly less rigid. Henry Vanness worked for the New Haven as a branch-line passenger conductor for more than 40 years, retiring before World War I. A unique example was a father and son, Thomas and Charles Morris, who worked themselves, respectively, up to yardmaster (in charge of several switch crews) and yard (freight) conductor at the Boston & Albany Railroad's Hudson, New York facility.[52]

Civil rights legislation finally opened the position of conductor to African Americans. Some railroads responded grudgingly, seemingly intent on making new black conductors fail rather than on helping them succeed. Under legal duress, the Southern Railway suddenly put black recruits in the midst of veteran whites who often resented their new colleagues. James Harrison was rushed through a six-week training course in December 1964, where, he recalled, "the instructors tried to dishearten you rather than inspire you." When he was assigned to Asheville, his fellow workers waited and watched for him to mess up. Confrontations occurred, once with a trainmaster who demanded that he immediately double out after making a trip, without observing the federally required hours of rest. When he cited the law guaranteeing him a rest period, his supervisor wrote him up for having a chip on his shoulder.[53]

Today the ranks of brakemen are fewer than ever, just as railroad employment is at near-record lows, about a quarter million. Cabooses no longer bring up the rear of freight trains. Many trains do no switching and have only a two-man, engineer and conductor, crew. Even local freights that perform switching en route have only a single brakeman. Blacks make up about 12 percent of the railroad workforce, about the same as their proportion of the general population, and they make up nearly the same percentage of railroad "operatives" (engineers, conductors, and brakemen). In 2003, railroads employed 4,912 black male and 264 black female operatives. (The largest category of black railroaders today is craft workers like machinists, mechanics, and electricians.)[54] By contrast, in 1924, railroads employed about 14,000 black switchmen, flagmen, brakemen, and firemen. One thing has remained the same, however: the operating positions are still the most dangerous jobs in railroading. According to the Federal Railroad Administration's yearly compilation of workplace accidents, almost half of railroad employee injuries and fatalities occur in train and engine service. Certainly trainmen jobs are less dangerous today. Brakemen no longer clamber over the tops of moving cars. (For safety reasons, roofwalks on freight cars were banned several decades ago.) Switchmen do not hustle between tracks, and mechanical retarders have replaced car riders in hump yards. But otherwise, the major causes of accidents have changed little over the past century and a half: overexertion, derailments, fingers pinched or crushed while manipulating couplers, injuries caused by slack action, and slipping on irregular surfaces or ballast and in icy or rainy conditions.[55] Blacks are no longer underrepresented in the ranks of brakemen and switchmen, and they have broken into previously off-limits work as conductors. Perhaps most startling of all, they hold positions as officers in the same rail unions that once barred them. But this progress came way late. Today, railroaders make up only a tiny fraction of all black workers.

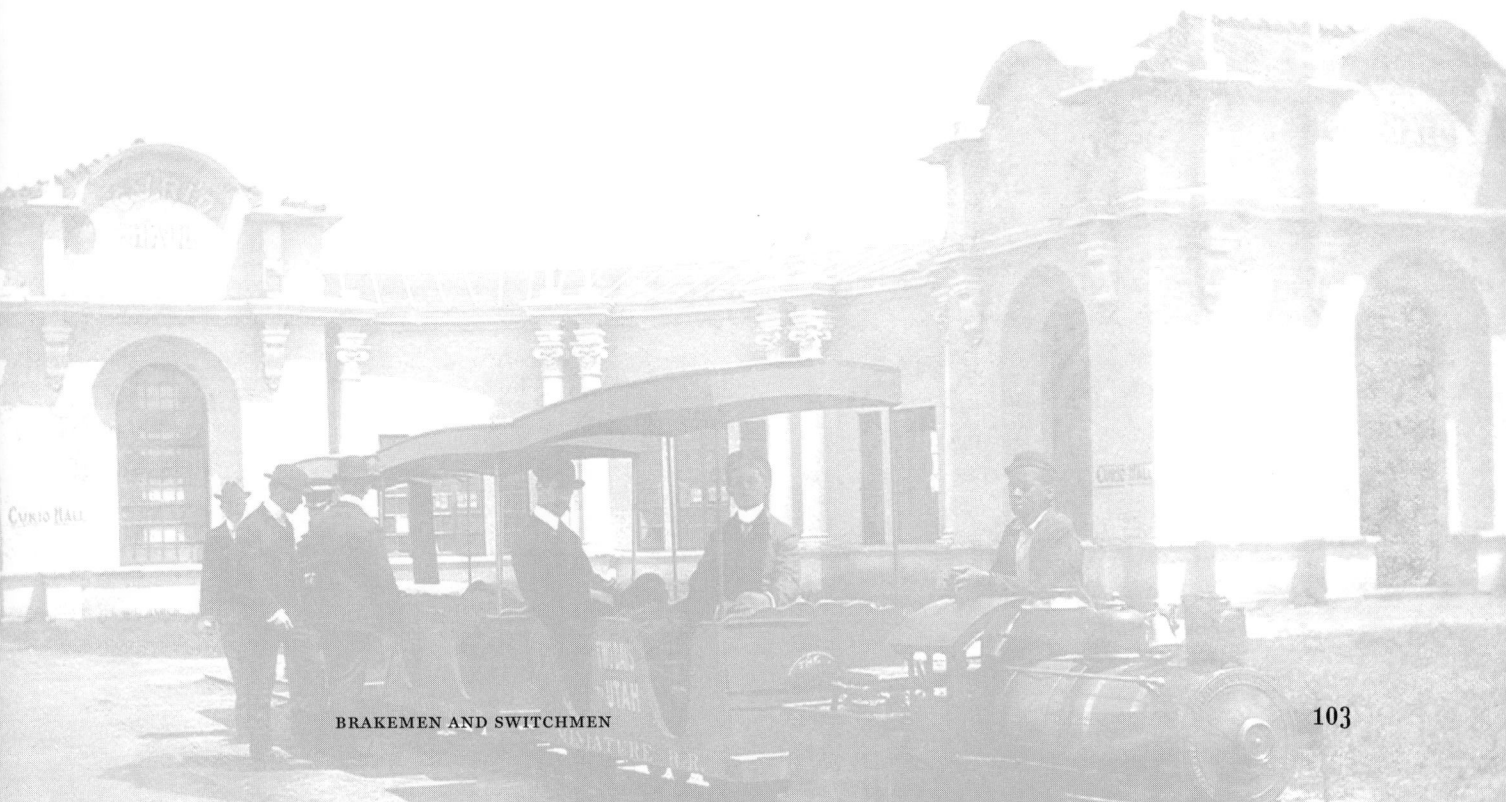

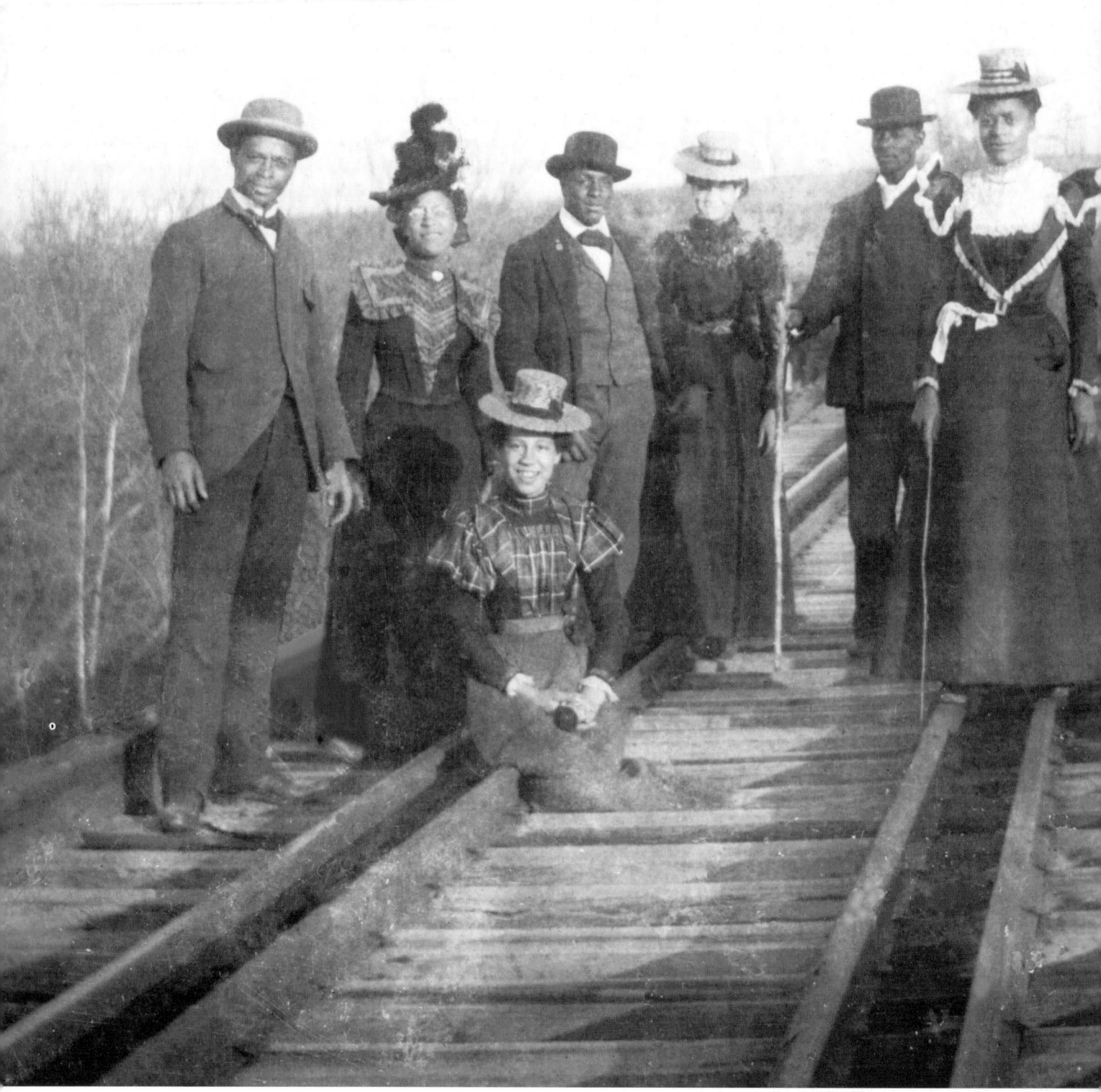

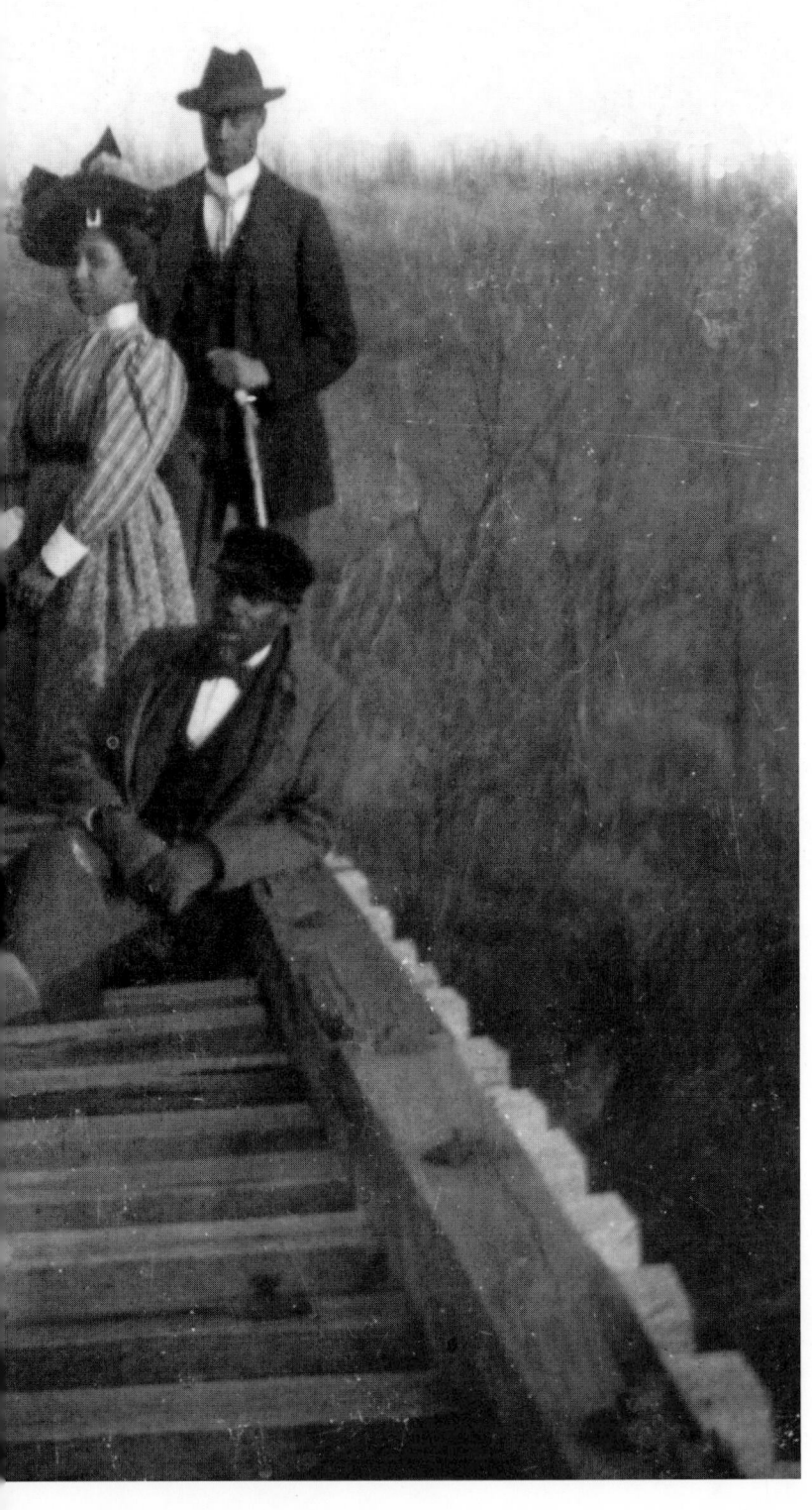

African Americans in the South had few commercial entertainments available to them. Hence picnicking, strolling, and visiting, free of racial indignities and of little or no cost, were popular. Why has this group, probably enjoying a Sunday afternoon after church sometime in the 1890s, gravitated to the railroad tracks? Walking on a trestle was foolhardy, unless one knew train schedules intimately. Perhaps, then, some of the gents are section men, taking pride in their accomplishments. Railroads and railroading exerted a powerful influence on generations of southern blacks, both individually and collectively. Theodore Kornweibel collection

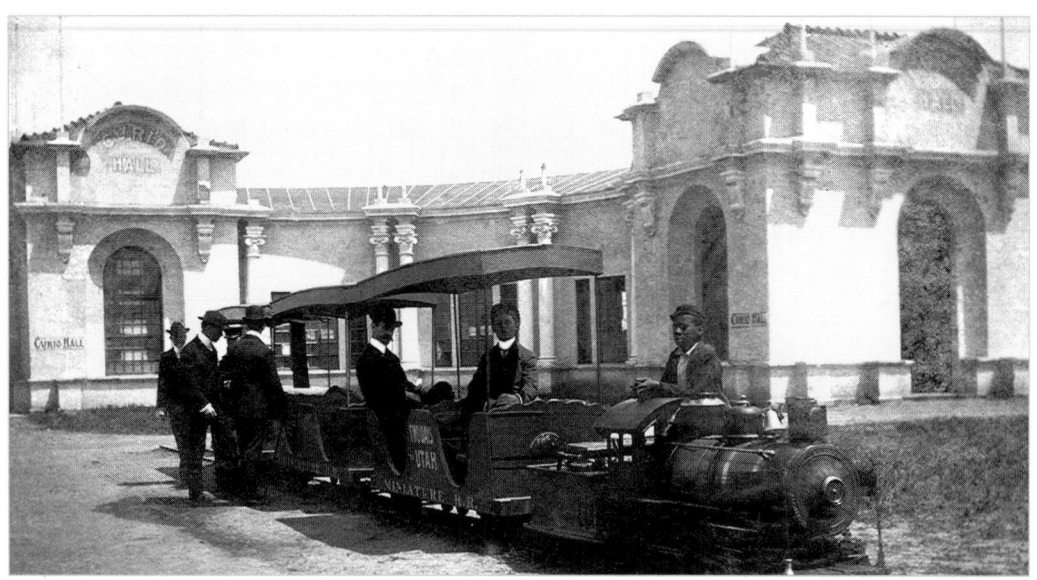

(ABOVE) *For most of its history, the railroad industry barred blacks from the prestige operating positions, engineer and conductor. If the white men in this early twentieth-century postcard photograph came to this amusement ride from any distance, they likely rode a train whose engineer was assuredly white. But it was somehow all right that their toy train engineer was black. Theodore Kornweibel collection*

(BELOW) *A classic photo of a dining-car crew, from an early twentieth-century postcard. The racial hierarchy of dining cars dictated, until the post–World War II era, that only white men be stewards, the "bosses" of the cars. Blacks deeply resented this discrimination. Many waiters were educated men, quite capable of handling a car's receipts, keeping inventory, and supervising the crew. Theodore Kornweibel collection*

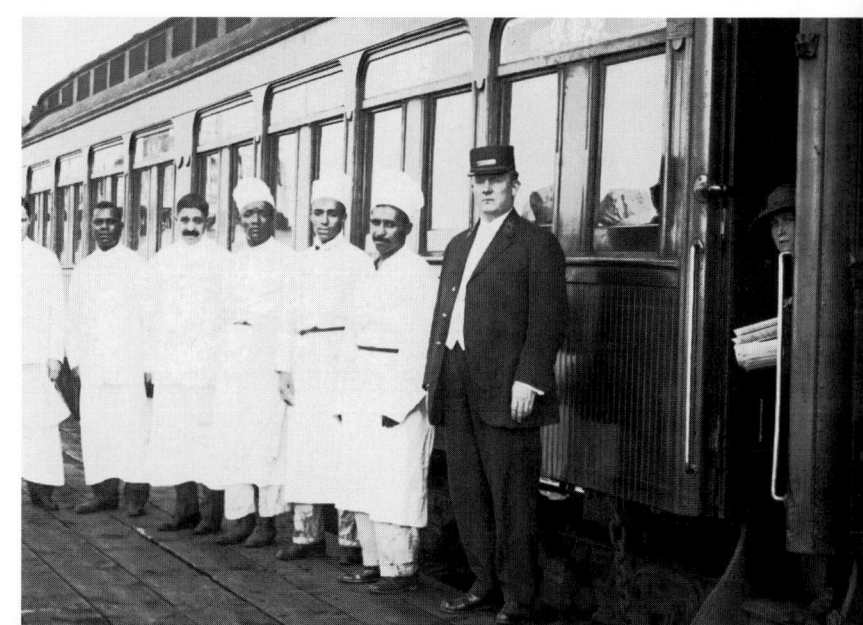

For maintenance purposes, railroads were divided into "sections" of several miles of track, each with a foreman and a labor gang. Numerous sections constituted a division, which was presided over by a roadmaster who periodically surveyed the line to ensure the appropriate standard of workmanship. In the nineteenth century roadmasters were propelled along the line on handcars powered manually by "crank hands" who, in the South, were typically black. In this early twentieth-century photo on an unknown railroad, that hand—now called a driver or chauffer—has a much easier job. Theodore Kornweibel collection

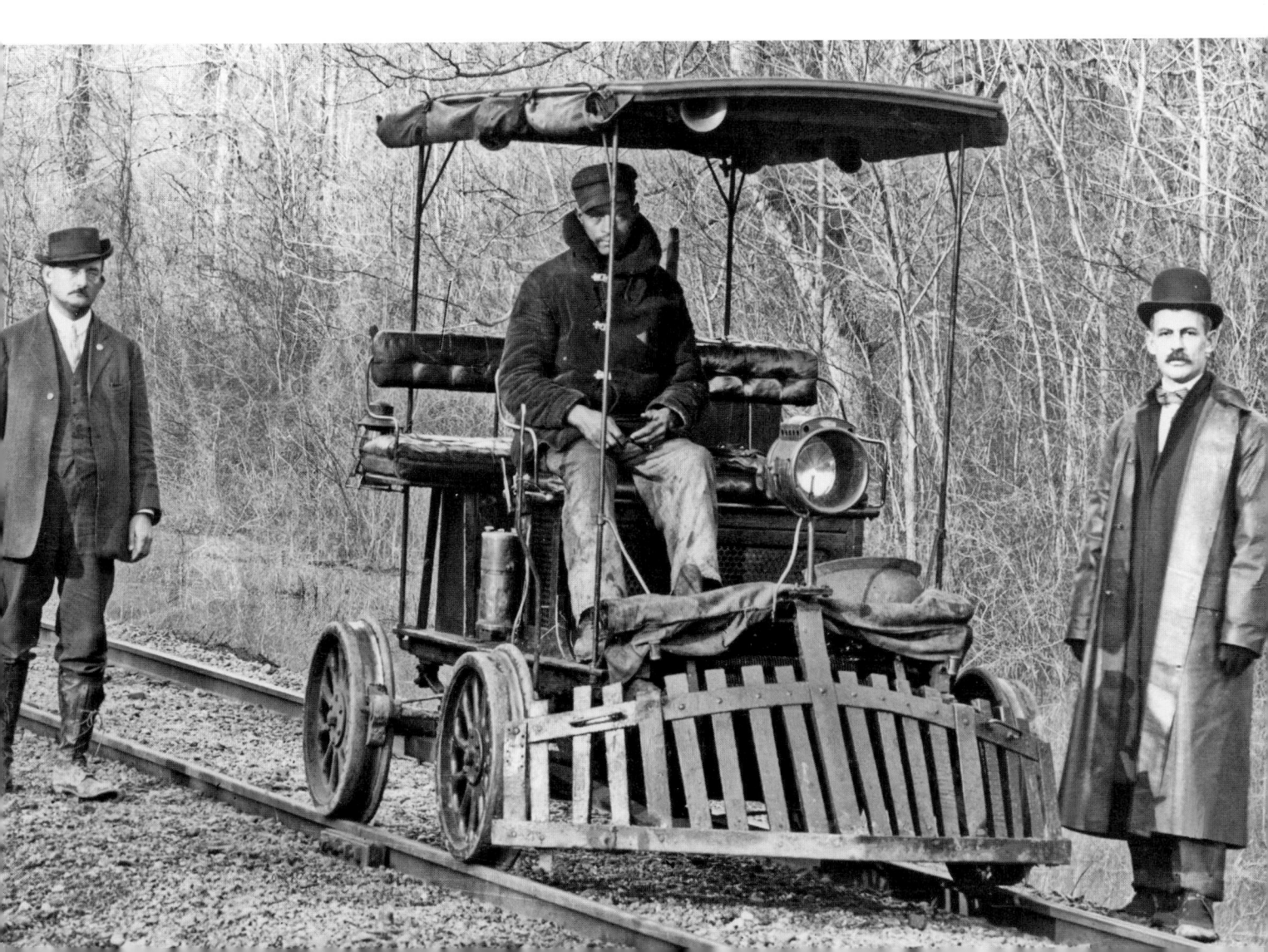

Porters, sometimes doubling as cooks and waiters, staffed railroad executives' business cars. Rubbing shoulders with the railroads' elites, they were men of dignity and discretion. Mitchell Parker stands proudly in front of Mobile, Jackson & Kansas City Railroad private car 100 in the very early 1900s, as that line built north from Mobile toward Hattiesburg, Mississippi. *Gulf, Mobile & Ohio Collection of the John W. Barriger III National Railroad Library, University of Missouri—St. Louis*

(OPPOSITE) Black locomotive firemen were commonplace on southern railroads, while other black firemen, like this one holding his shovel, fed fireboxes on wrecking cranes and steam shovels. Although details of this early twentieth-century mishap are missing, the cause was likely improper lifting, not a derailment, as the road-bed appears intact. Black laborers with their white foreman await a wrecker to right the heavy machine. A similar job performed by blacks was that of stationary fireman, tending boilers in railroad power plants at large shop complexes. On most non-southern lines, this was the only fireman position a black could obtain. Experience and skill gained at such work did not qualify one for advancement to the cab of a locomotive. *Theodore Kornweibel collection*

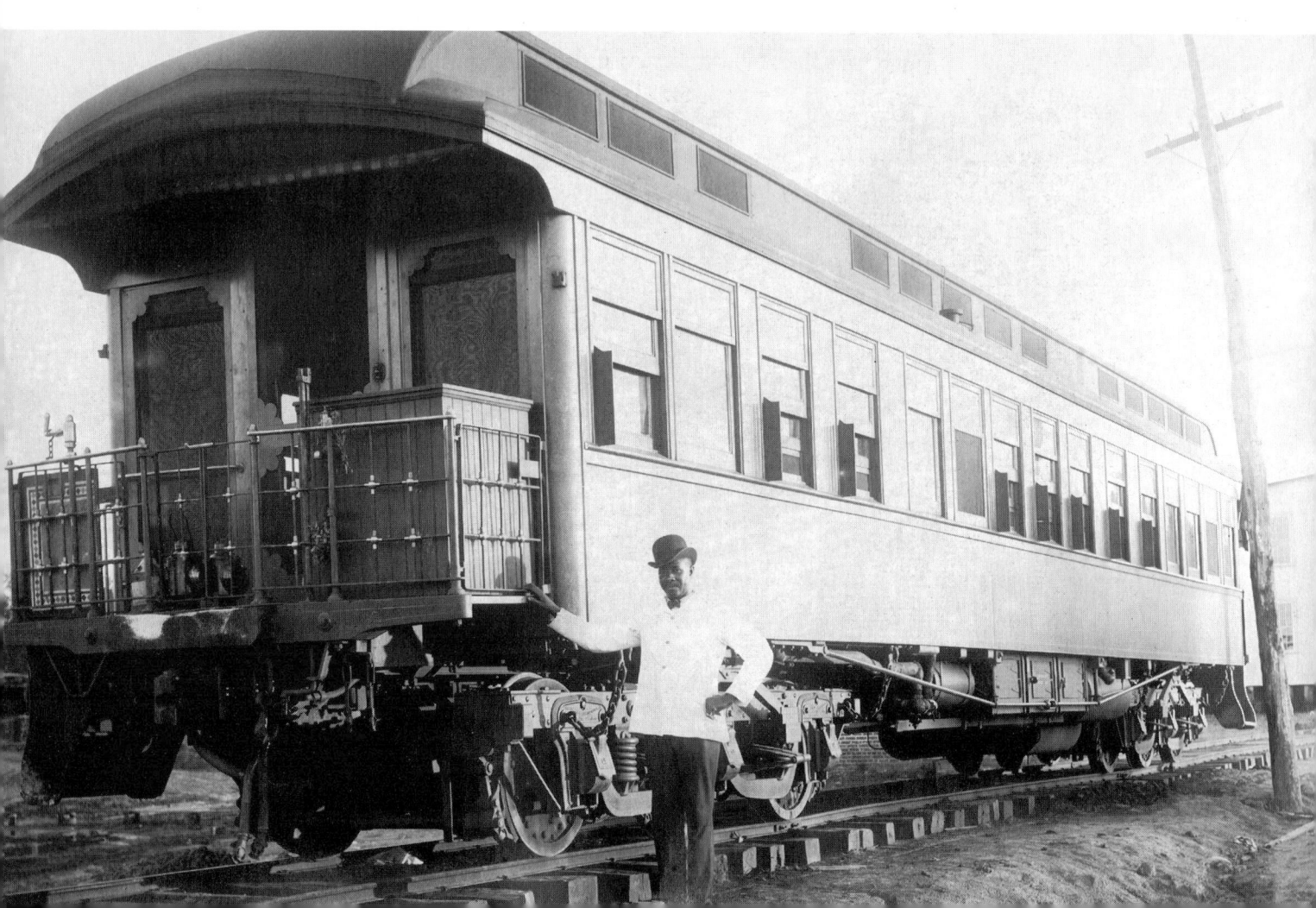

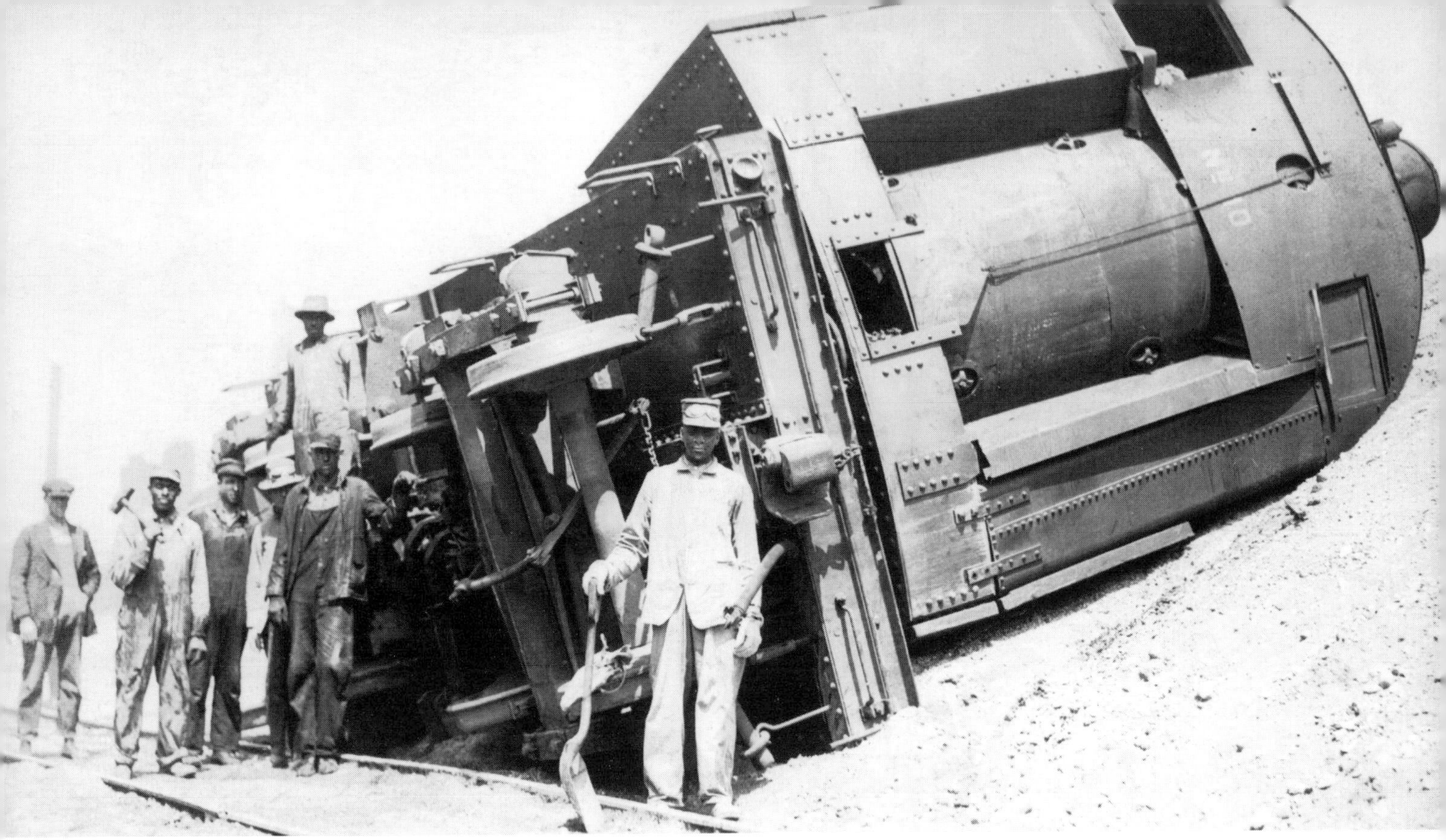

(BELOW) Southern municipal electric streetcar lines, like the steam railroads, relied predominately on black labor for track repairs and maintenance. This crew, employed on the Macon Railway & Light Company, posed with hats off in the early 1900s while the work car's uniformed motorman looks out the cab window. Tools and trim like tie plates can be seen on the car. Courtesy of the Middle Georgia Archives, Washington Memorial Library, Macon, GA

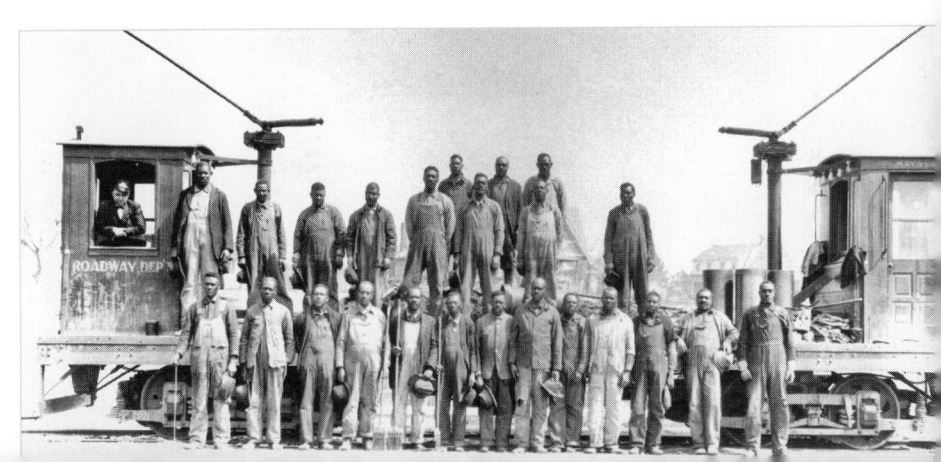

Perhaps the most famous railroad scene, reproduced in numerous books in the 1940s and 1950s, showing the "triple crossing" near the Richmond, Virginia station in 1905, with a Chesapeake & Ohio Railway train on top, its first car a Jim Crow combine; a Seaboard Air Line Railroad passenger train in the middle; and a Southern Railway train on the ground level, with a black fireman standing in the locomotive's gangway. Book captions rarely, if ever, mentioned the African American elements of this or other photographs. E. L. DeGolyer, Jr. Photograph Collection, DeGolyer Library, Southern Methodist University

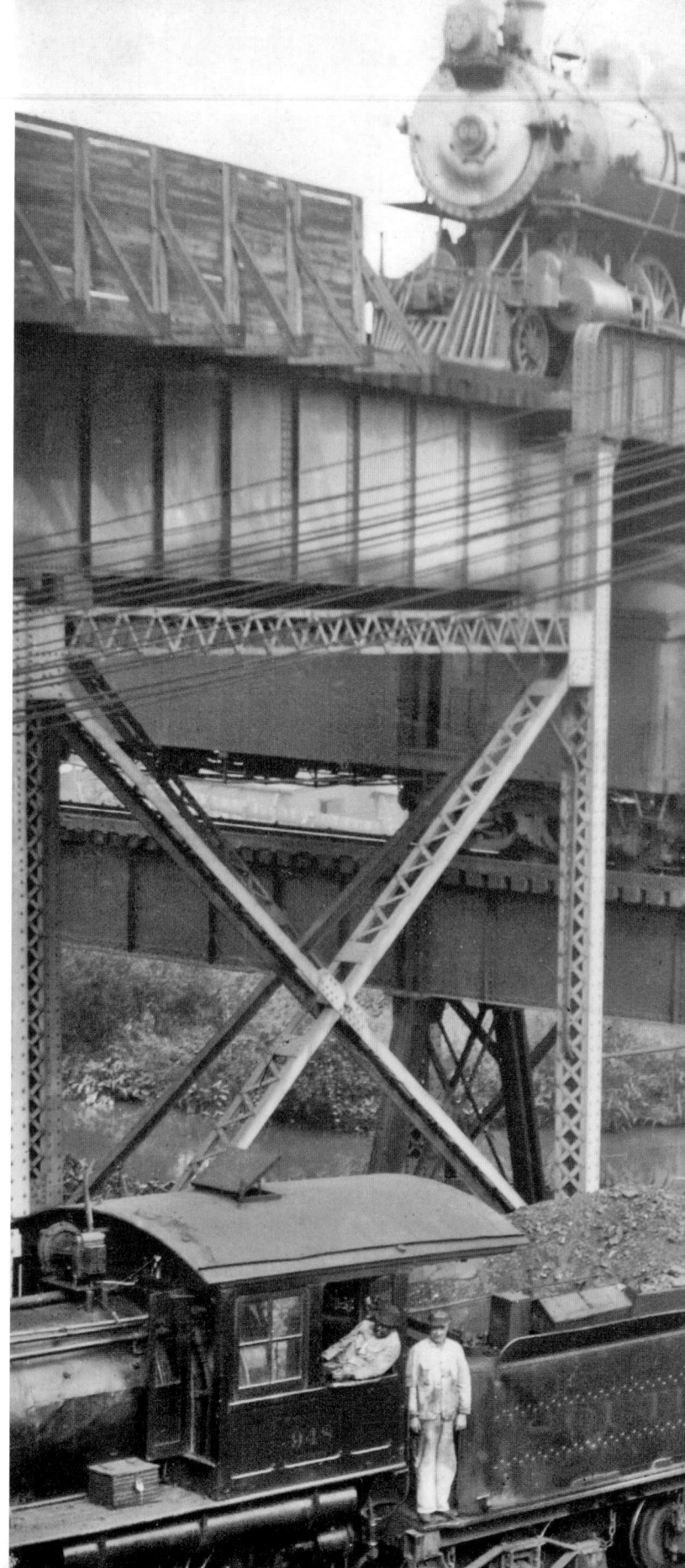

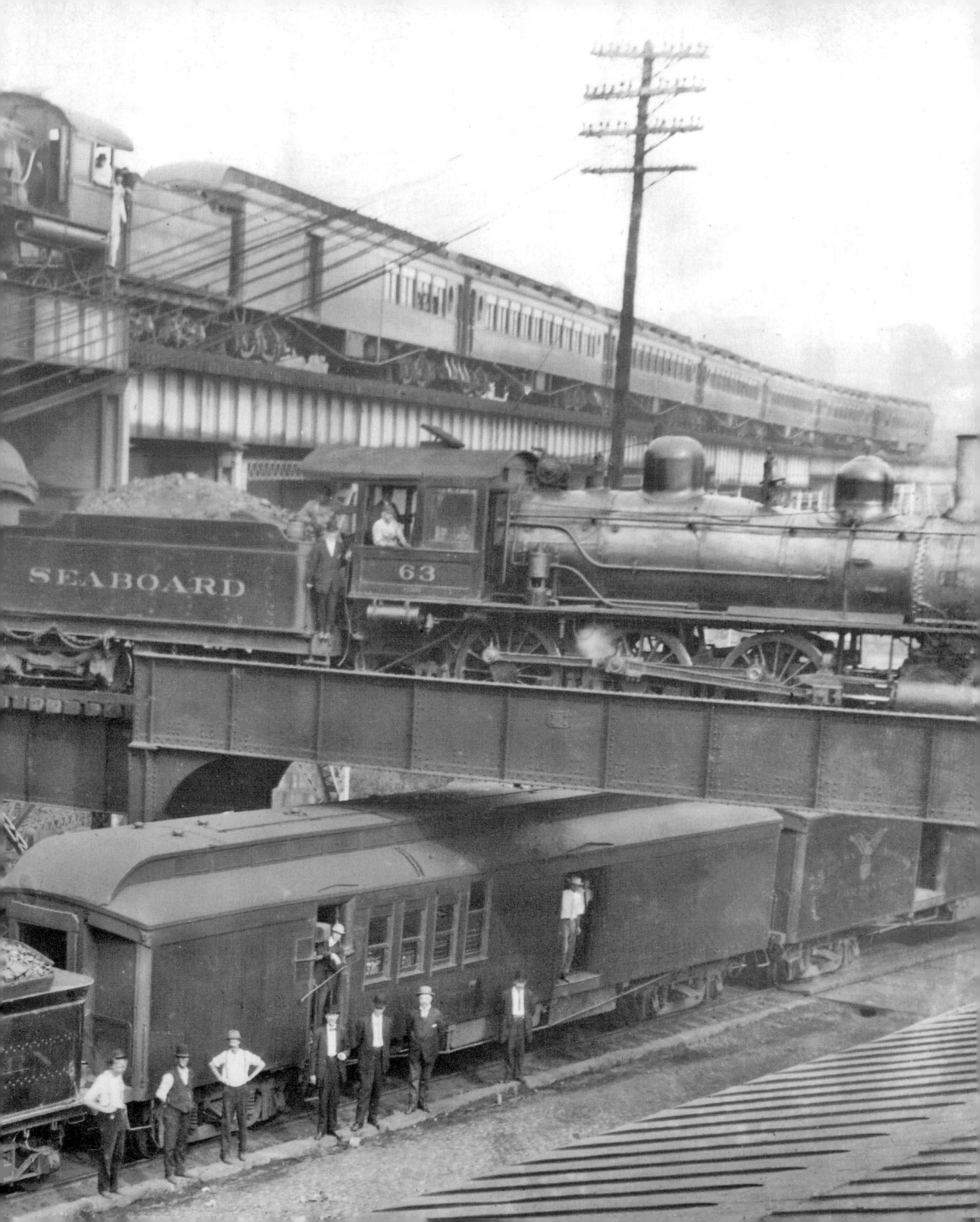

"THE WORLD'S MOST PERFECT SERVANT"

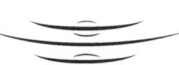

Pullman Porters

The story of Pullman sleeping-car porters is filled with pathos and irony. Although train wrecks hardly made good advertisements, the Pullman Company nonetheless highlighted the selfless heroism of its employees in such disasters. During a heavy summer storm in 1922, a Philadelphia & Reading Railway passenger train speeding toward Atlantic City, New Jersey, hit a switch mistakenly set for a siding, overturning the cars. Porter James Owens was tossed violently in the impact and fell unconscious with a concussion. When he revived, cut and bleeding, he crawled through a window in the darkness to find the conductor. Together, the two of them rescued the passengers. To the Pullman Company, this was expected of its employees, to "show supreme devotion to duty" while disregarding their own safety. One other employee, however, deadheading "summer porter" Theodore M. Seldon, tragically perished in the wreck. His body was so disfigured that it was identified only upon discovery of his Phi Beta Kappa key, earned at Dartmouth College that spring.[1]

From the earliest antebellum decades of railroading, African Americans were assigned servant roles on passenger cars. In the South, enslaved women worked as maids on express trains. Enslaved firemen whose locomotives pulled passenger trains were sometimes also required to handle travelers' baggage. And all passenger trains were staffed by "train hands," usually slaves, who in addition to applying brakes, helped travelers on and off the cars, dispensed water to the thirsty, and kept oil lamps and stoves lit. In the North, free black "water boys" (and sometimes girls) were commonplace on passenger trains before the Civil War. So railroad travelers were accustomed to being waited upon by blacks well before emancipation.[2]

African Americans were cemented into the role of railroad servants soon after the Civil War. As four million slaves entered a tentative freedom, they represented a vast labor pool that, although concentrated in southern agriculture, formed a potential source of workers for new, non-rural occupations. This coincided with the success of George Mortimer Pullman and other pioneers in providing sleeping accommodations for passengers who were now traveling longer distances than before. To what extent Pullman coldly calculated that ex-slaves, under the prod of economic necessity, would willingly become passengers' servants cannot be definitively resolved. Clearly, he believed that blacks were temperamentally suited to serve others. That he was nobly inspired to offer a helping hand to a newly liberated race is doubtful. Having experimented unsuccessfully first with white conductors and women to attend to passengers, Pullman by 1867 was hiring only African Americans.[3] Individual railroads that operated their own sleeping cars, like the Central Pacific's Silver Palace Cars between Sacramento, California, and Ogden, Utah, likewise used black porters.[4] From scattered references, it appears that most, if not all, of the early sleeping car firms, which were later absorbed by Pullman, also adopted the practice.[5] And African Americans worked only as servants (porters, parlor car attendants, maids, valets). The job of Pullman conductor was reserved for white men.

Working the postwar sleeping cars was an arduous task. Not only did porters make up berths, but they also carried pails of drinking water, prepared and sold sandwiches and coffee, and peddled newspapers, magazines, fruit, and candy. As sleeping-car conductors had not yet been introduced, porters also collected tickets and handled the necessary paperwork. Coal-burning stoves located at each end of the cars had to be tended. Candles illuminated the first cars, so the introduction of kerosene lamps was an improvement, but porters had to keep them filled and burning through the night and clean the sooty globes at daybreak. At the end of a run, porters cleaned the cars themselves. While en route, the train might stop with the cry of "wood pile," meaning that everyone— porters, brakemen, engineer, and fireman—helped refill the tender. And when the engineer blew the whistle signal to apply brakes, in the absence of a brakeman, porters ran to the end platforms to manually turn brake wheels.[6]

George Pullman was no philanthropist; in fact, he was a paternalistic autocrat to his employees, white as well as black. The decision to hire only black porters reflected four intertwined business and racial decisions. He recognized that whites would feel that their travel was more luxurious and their status enhanced if black servants waited upon them, especially because most passengers did not have the wealth to keep servants in their homes. The Pullman Company was not just selling transportation. It was, above all, selling service. Second, as sharecropping put legions of blacks into economic bondage in the postwar South, plenty of black men were willing to trade a mule and plow for almost any other employment. Pullman's earliest porters received no wages

Railroads in the African American Experience

at all. Their only income derived from tips and the sale of food and sundries. Third, the racial gulf between the races ensured that blacks could work in intimate proximity to whites without narrowing the caste divide or posing the possibility of later social encounters. And finally, George Pullman believed that blacks were "by nature adapted faithfully to perform their duties under circumstances which necessitate unfailing good nature, solicitude, and faithfulness." So as later generations of porters saw it, the earliest porters continued to be slaves, only now to the Pullman Company, having to act like slaves in order to earn the tips on which they depended.[7]

By the end of the nineteenth century, the number of private sleeping car fleets had been reduced to two: the Pullman Company and its weaker rival, the Wagner Palace Car Company. Wagner could not survive the Pullman juggernaut, and was bought out by the stronger company, ending corporate existence on the last day of 1899. By the early 1920s, at the peak of railroad mileage and passenger travel, more than 9,000 blacks worked as Pullman porters, serving 31 million travelers annually. At the same time, the individual railroads employed another 11,000 men as coach porters (also known as train porters), nearly all of whom were blacks.[8]

The sleeping-car porter's job was "a cross between a concierge, bellhop, valet, housekeeper, mechanic, baby sitter, and security guard . . . prepared at any moment day or night to be a good listener, answer questions, find lost articles, and handle emergencies."[9] The routine was exhausting. He had to report hours before departure to ensure that his car was clean (this was supposed to have been done by Pullman car cleaners) and fully stocked with supplies. When his train pulled into the station to receive its first passengers, he assisted them onto the car and to their seats in an open section (which would be made into upper and lower berths at night) or into their private compartments, at the same time carrying and stowing their luggage. A call bell in each compartment or section summoned him at any time. While en route, he performed numerous errands: dispatching letters or telegrams; setting up tables for card playing, meals, or office work; fetching a drink; warming an infant's bottle; pressing suits and dresses; brushing passengers' hats and clothing; making down beds and stowing them away the following morning; and in general, anticipating passengers' needs and desires. Magazine advertisements encouraged parents to leave older children in the porter's care while they enjoyed a nightcap in the lounge car. In addition, porters were responsible for their car's cleanliness during the journey: sweeping carpets and mopping floors; cleaning toilets and wash basins; replenishing towels and soap; washing out cuspidors; and quickly removing trash. Passengers had to be warned of the approach of their destinations, where the porter assisted them off the train and handled their baggage. If someone detrained at night, the bed might have to be quickly made up anew for the next passenger. Nighttime duties included shining passengers' shoes. The company did not *require* them to do this; they simply encouraged it and expected that passengers would pay for the service. This explains the fact that a porter had to buy his own shoe polish. When the last passenger had detrained at the end of the run, the porter scouted his car for lost belongings, restocked all supplies, and ensured that all beds were properly stowed. In short, "Pullman Porters know that passengers want to be treated as individuals and receive careful attention to their particular needs and requirements . . . Courtesy, kindness, willingness to serve, and careful attention to detail . . . That is the formula that has made the Pullman Porter a symbol of outstanding service and gracious hospitality known throughout the land."[10]

Pullman porters' smiling faces in posed photographs hid the ugly realities of their work. Although white travelers assumed that they were well paid and well treated, in fact they were among the most exploited black workers outside of agriculture and domestic service. When porters launched a new unionization effort in the mid-1920s, their grievances were legion, even considering the wage gains granted by the U.S. Railroad Administration during World War I. The Pullman Company expected them to work nearly 400 hours a month, about double that of industrial workers. Many additional unpaid hours were spent making up their trains before departure, and preparing them for storage or the next run after the last passengers were gone. As historian William H. Harris notes, this represented "millions of dollars that porters donated to the company annually." While an urban family needed a yearly income of $2,088 to live adequately in 1926, the porters' base pay was only $810, and they averaged $600 annually in tips, for a combined average income of only $1,410. Yet even that figure was not net income: until they had put in 10 years of service, porters had to buy their own uniforms. If no Pullman Home was available, they had to pay their own expenses while laying over until their return trip. These expenses consumed about $33 of their base $67.50 monthly wage.[11]

Low pay for long hours wasn't the porters' only grievance. They were not guaranteed sleep during their runs (although Pullman conductors were granted six hours of rest).[12] Day or night, at every stop where a passenger would entrain or detrain, the porter had to be on duty to assist those getting off and escort each new passenger to his or her compartment or berth. Even after an exhausting five-day transcontinental run, porters could be "doubled back" on the next train, without a rest period. Then there was psychological abuse. Malicious whites sometimes required porters to perform demeaning or "comical" acts. Porters were often called "George," probably a shortened version of "George Pullman's boy," rather than their real names. And they were under the stress of being fired or suspended for a legion of infractions, such as being disheveled or upon passenger complaints that they were not properly courteous or obsequious.

Efforts by Pullman porters to organize in the early 1900s all fizzled.[13] The company, reflecting George Pullman's notions of industrial paternalism, insisted that it benevolently considered the porters' interests and knew best what they needed. This translated into adamant opposition to independent unions. Suspected union activity was grounds for firing. Unionization efforts were further hampered by a lack of solidarity within the porters' ranks. Some credited the Pullman Company with keeping "milk on the tables of thousands of black families" and chided those who urged improvements. Some porters so identified with the company that they became stool pigeons, reporting those who were involved in organizing efforts. And the Pullman Company sponsored a company union—the Employee Representation Plan—that provided just enough welfare and benefits to convince many porters, and many pro-business blacks, that the nation's largest private employer of African Americans was in fact doing right for the race.[14] The porters were caught in a dilemma: most of them recognized that they were exploited, and that family life suffered from the demands placed upon them by the company, but where else could educated black men find steady employment and even $1,400 in annual earnings at a "clean," non-manual labor job?[15]

The story of the Pullman porters' 12-year struggle to unionize and extract decent pay and working conditions from the Pullman Company has often been told. The most prominent figure in the Brotherhood of Sleeping Car Porters union was its charismatic leader, A. Philip Randolph. Previously an opponent of American involvement in World War I and a socialist radical dubbed "the most dangerous Negro in America" by the (federal) Bureau of Investigation, he was chosen to lead the new union in part because, not being a porter, he could not as easily be intimidated or bought off.[16]

Yet when Randolph helped found the BSCP in 1925, failure was probable. Much of the black press and business leadership was in the Pullman Company's pocket and attacked the BSCP as well as Randolph. Porters who joined the new union, if detected, were fired. To intimidate all porters, the company began hiring Filipino lounge-car attendants in 1925. This was particularly threatening, as "almost every porter aspired to [an attendant job] because it paid better money, . . . the work was easier," and the tips were better.[17] And Pullman refused to negotiate with the upstart BSCP. When these tactics failed to make the membership buckle, it sent Randolph a blank check, but he wouldn't be bought off. The low point came in 1928, when Randolph gambled that the threat of a strike would alarm the traveling public and the president and bring federal intervention. But the Pullman Company and a federal mediation board called his bluff. The strike had to be called off, and many porters abandoned the crippled union.[18] The BSCP limped on, supported and encouraged by a strong Ladies Auxiliary that included porters' wives and sisters as well as Pullman maids. Not until pro-labor New Deal legislation forced corporations to negotiate with unions chosen by their workers did the BSCP revive. (Ironically, these were the very laws that crippled the black firemen's and brakemen's independent unionization efforts.) Yet even when forced to meet with the BSCP, Pullman announced "we ain't recognizing no union."[19] Two long years later, on the 12th anniversary of the founding of the BSCP, the Pullman Company finally agreed to a contract that would improve wages and working conditions. While most porters supported the BSCP, a minority distrusted Randolph and continued to support the old company union.[20] Nonetheless, the BSCP's achievement was not just a labor settlement; it was also a civil rights victory. Ironically, though, the ranks of Pullman porters would never again equal the number employed in the 1920s. Automobiles, buses, and airplanes were already ending the dominance of rail travel.[21]

To the Pullman Company, whether they worked in the United States or Canada,[22] the ideal porters were definitely not union men. Rather, loyalty to and identification with the company were most highly prized. The pages of the *Pullman News* often drew upon racist stereotypes in identifying the porters' exemplary traits. Its first issue described blacks as "a singing race" whose music "adds to their cheerfulness and contentment." Seeking to capitalize on this, the company hired a black bandleader to organize porters' choruses, orchestras, and bands across the country.[23]

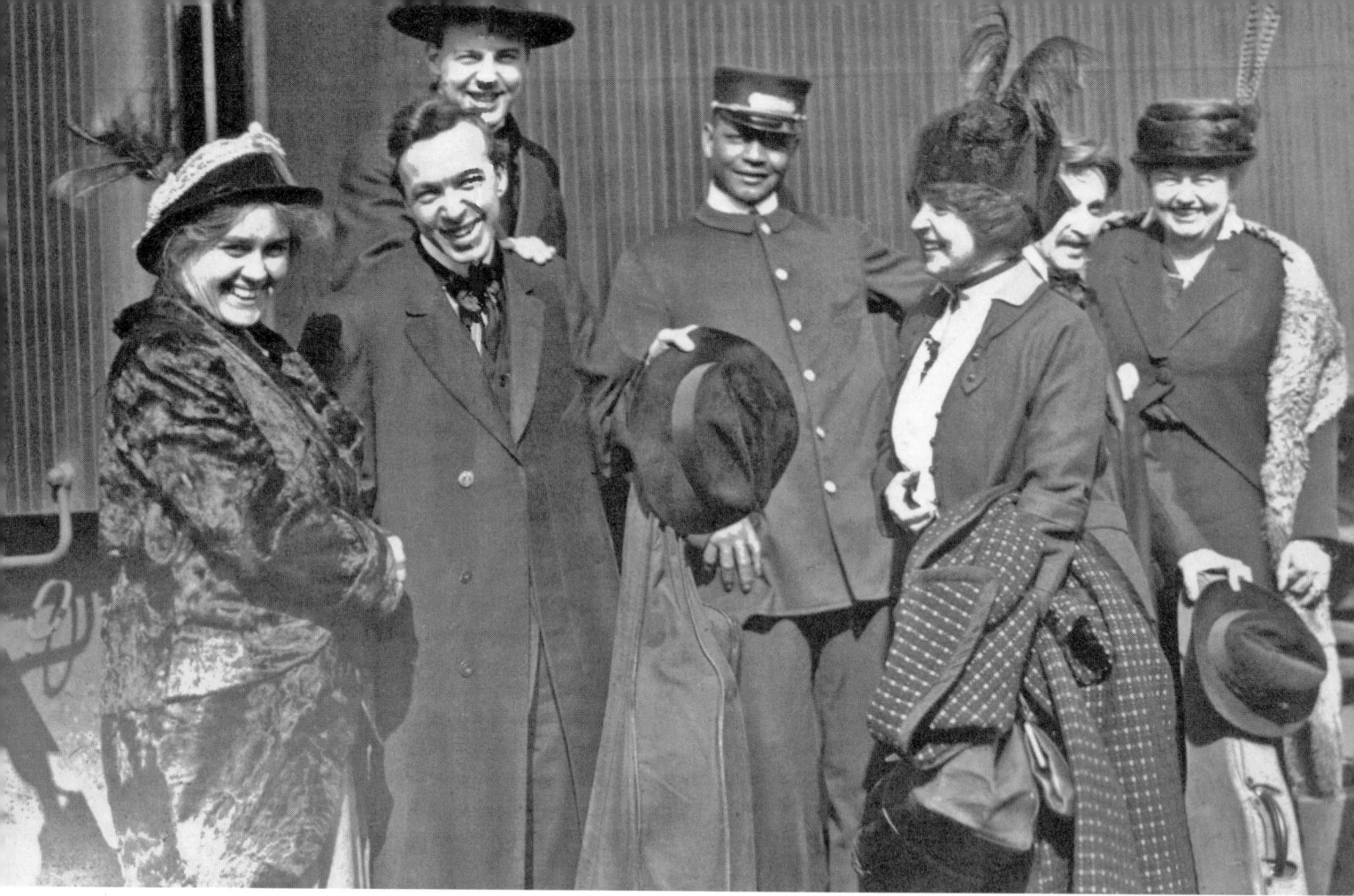

White travelers frequently photographed the porters who waited upon them, often including them in group pictures. "Our favorite porter" genre photos reinforced whites' sense of social preeminence and their belief that blacks found gratification in serving them. This photo dates from about 1900. Theodore Kornweibel collection

Forty-five-year veteran David G. Scott, noted for his "faithful service" and for keeping his cars "spotless," was hailed as the "World's Most Perfect Servant."[24] Others were praised for integrity—exemplified by turning in lost pocketbooks, wads of cash, jewelry, and even a $120,000 ring.[25] Senior porters who served presidents, millionaires, and generals were noted for their discretion. Heroic porters who risked (and sometimes sacrificed) their own lives to save others also found prominence in the *Pullman News*.[26] And a company spokesman added another ideal trait: "To all the millions who annually ride Pullmans the porter is regarded as a dependable and indispensable friend. He often is guide and counselor to the perplexed or the ill; his instinctive fondness for children relieves harassed mothers; hundreds of letters testify to his care of invalids and the suddenly stricken."[27]

Passengers' expectations, too, helped define the ideal Pullman employee. Cincinnati Division porter John R. Lucas served a party of teachers and students on a four-week round-trip to California who composed a song extolling the virtues of a perfect servant:

> John was our porter, and he was good and true,
> Faithful, untiring in all he had to do,
> It was "John, bring a pillow,"
> Or "John, please black my shoes,"
> Or, "John, please put my window down,"
> "Now do, do, do."
>
> Chorus:
> John did it, John did it,
> And no complaint made he;
> John made the finest porter
> That could ever be.[28]

To many whites, porters should be "natural" servants, a quality that, they believed, only blacks truly possessed. When Pullman began hiring Filipino attendants for buffet and lounge cars (which also had bedrooms), passengers on the Pennsylvania Railroad's premier *Broadway Limited* complained that they were not as attentive, were less likely to anticipate a traveler's needs, and were less outgoing than "happy-go-lucky" blacks. Some passengers went so far as to demand accommodations only in cars on which blacks served. The Pennsy worried about the impact of Filipino attendants because the rival New York Central Railroad used blacks exclusively on its competing *Twentieth Century Limited*. Pennsy management ultimately concluded that a Filipino made a competent lounge-car waiter, but "he is lacking in the attributes of a servitor; he seldom smiles, and while attentive to duty, appears mechanical." On the other hand, "the Negro is a natural servitor . . . Affability is a racial trait . . . The proper type of Negro, rather than the Filipino, . . . make[s] a patron feel that he is an honored guest and that his renewed patronage is fully appreciated." Thus, stereotypes of blacks as "natural" servants ensured their predominance not only in Pullman's employ, but also as lounge attendants on cars owned by the individual railroads. The Atlantic Coast Line Railroad was an exception. It found Filipinos "far superior" to blacks as lounge-car attendants.[29]

The Pullman Company blithely displayed cruel stereotypes in early issues of the *Pullman News*. A slave-born porter was described as having been, as a child, a "Virginy pickaninny." Dialect stories, meant to be humorous, were also included. One, about a "darky preacher," elucidated his theory of the operation of the universe: "De earf, breddern, revolves on its axles, and it takes a right sma't ob grease to keep it lubricated. So de good Lord put petroleum inside de earf to keep de axles greased."[30] Another early issue featured a cartoon about mixing up pairs of shoes that lampooned the porters' language and suggested their stupidity.[31] And a porter who went to the aid of a dying passenger, staying up with him and buying medicine with his own money at a station stop, was described as "a Samaritan With a 'Pure White Soul.'"[32]

In fact, the Pullman Company was convinced that it did right by its black employees through corporate welfare, setting up a Pullman Porters Benefit Association that granted sick pay of $10 a week and equally modest death benefits to employees who had paid into the program. It also trumpeted its generosity in providing 118,741 free uniforms over a 34-year period.[33] The company encouraged a variety of porters' social organizations and sponsored field days in which hundreds of porters and their families participated in parades, musical competitions, and athletic events. Most significant, however, was the company union, which "granted" wage hikes to try to forestall independent unionism. The *Pullman News* underscored all these efforts, giving liberal press to porters' activities and a positive spin on the company union, like the article headlined "Million Dollars Wage Increase for Porters and Maids." In fact, this "raise" amounted to little more than $100 per year.[34]

Becoming a Pullman porter was no simple matter. The quickest route was through relatives who already worked for the company. It was an advantage to have a father, brother, or uncle who had proven to be a reliable employee. Virgil Smock's grandfather, father, and older brother were porters, and so a good family reputation opened the door to employment.[35] But in most instances, prospective porters (and maids) were subject to perhaps the most rigorous scrutiny of any black job seekers. Pullman investigators individually contacted references to determine the applicant's character, personal habits (like alcohol use), and past job performance. Once he passed this hurdle, a 14-day course in the fundamentals of Pullman service gave the new man the basics, which he put to use on student trips under the supervision of experienced porters. Recruits were on probation for the first six months; only after compiling a satisfactory record was one fully hired.[36] Lacking seniority, the new man often did not draw a regular run. Instead, he might work only an irregular schedule, with unpredictable gaps between runs, like trainmen on the extra board. Or the opposite could occur: he might be required to double out on a new run as soon as he returned from a trip, without opportunity to bathe or rest. It took years of seniority for porters to obtain the best runs on premier all-Pullman trains catering to the rich and famous. John H. Tibbs, who began portering in

1928, remembered his arduous first year: "Extra men were likely to go to Florida one day, and when they came back they might go to Montreal, St. Louis, Chicago, or anyplace where a car was going. It was real tough to plan anything when you were working like that."[37]

Sleep deprivation was a given. For decades, porters were on call 24 hours a day. If a porter fell asleep on duty, he might be disciplined by one of Pullman's undercover "spotters," some of whom took malicious delight in surprising an exhausted, cat-napping employee. When off duty, porters were expected to find rest in the men's smoking room. If passengers occupied that room late in the night, the Pullman conductor could permit the porter to rest in an upper berth at the end of his car, but only if no lady passenger occupied the lower berth beneath him. After they unionized in the 1930s, the Pullman Company agreed to allow porters four *unpaid* hours of sleep per night, while the man in the next car covered his car as well. An upper berth was reserved for their use, but requiring them to use special blue-colored blankets reinforced their social inferiority. The traditional brown-colored Pullman blankets were reserved exclusively for passengers. If he was found by an inspector with a brown blanket, a porter would likely be suspended for several days.[38]

Pullman spotters didn't simply look for rules violations; they also used entrapment. Some tested porters' honesty by planting "lost" jewelry or pocketbooks to see if they would turn them in. And white female spotters attempted to lure porters into compromising situations. Inspectors lurked nearby, eager to catch the culprit. Pullman had strict rules regarding leaving the door to a compartment ajar when serving a female passenger traveling alone, and most porters complied, both out of personal integrity and for fear of losing one's job. Some, however, could not resist temptation. "One guy, this lady had left her curtains open where he could see her, and he'd come right in and peek. Then she would ring the bell like she wanted something, see. And he'd go there, you know, and she'd just show him everything. He'd get ready to crawl in there, then the inspector is over here . . . We got ya! You get *fired!!*"[39] Other instances weren't set-ups. More than one white woman used the anonymity of the train and proximity to a black male to satisfy a sexual fantasy. James Steele recalled the situation where a woman ordered a scotch and soda delivered to her compartment. When he started to enter, he discovered she had no clothes on. Steele retreated, but she kept ringing her bell, so he summoned the conductor to go with him. When the conductor knocked, she said to come in, and he entered first. "She grabs her robe and puts it on right quick. "'Oh, I'm sorry' . . . The conductor tells her, 'Look, I don't want this happening no more, or we'll put you off the train.'" A female passenger might feign pity for the porter who had no place to sleep and offer him the unoccupied upper berth in her room. As Steele remembered, "You got to have damn good willpower not to get yourself messed up."[40]

At times porters were "invisible men" to female passengers. Because they were servants, neither social nor racial peers, women sometimes ignored propriety and modesty around them. On one occasion, a group of wealthy college girls chartered a car on which Garrard Smock, Jr. served. "They'd run through that car with no clothes on and everything else. 'Will you all get dressed.' 'Shut up!' All college students. I don't think they's more than 21, 22 years old." Other incidents were just plain embarrassing. "Lots of times the bell would ring, I'd knock on the door, they said, 'Who is it?' I said, 'This is Garrard, the porter. You rang for me?' 'Yes, come in here. Would you get my bag from underneath the bed?' And she's sittin' on the damn toilet."[41]

Whether they wanted it or not, porters were drawn into the intimate details of white travelers' lives. It was not uncommon for passengers, including women, to become inebriated in the lounge car, which sometime necessitated the porter leading them back to their rooms, undressing them, and putting them to bed. So frequently did women experiencing menstrual discomfort seek help from porters that some of them carried appropriate medications in their grips. Tending to sick passengers was commonplace. Garrard Smock's oldest brother, George, recalled one sufferer who asked, "'Porter, could you help me? I don't have a medication, and my hemorrhoids are down' . . . 'Well, let me go back [to the dining car] and get you some bacon grease, and I'm sure that will take care of it, until you get to a doctor.' The next morning he gave me a $50 tip!"[42]

The Pullman Company was justifiably proud of porters who were at times nurse, doctor, or midwife, and included numerous testimonials from grateful passengers in the *Pullman News*. One such individual, stricken with appendicitis on a train from upstate New York, wrote that "Your porter Hilary G. Jones, nursed me all the way into Chicago with a tenderness almost equal to a trained nurse." I. H. Hill similarly went beyond the call of duty when an elderly woman boarded his car in Spokane, Washington, and soon took sick. As described by another passenger, "the old porter cared for her as tenderly as if she was a baby." A few porters even *delivered* babies although railroads tried to deny tickets to women who were that far advanced in pregnancy. Garrard Smock, Jr. recalled, "I had them die on me. I had them born on me. I'd run to tell the Pullman conductor, 'Hey, we have a new passenger about to come aboard.'"[43]

Race influenced all Pullman employment. Pullman conductors were always white. Neither education, aptitude, nor experience qualified African Americans for that position. Many conductors regarded porters as inferiors and also as potential competitors, so dealing with them could be dicey. A train with several sleepers had both a Pullman conductor, who collected and sold tickets for the sleeping accommodations, and a train conductor employed by the railroad who handled tickets for transportation from all passengers and who was boss of the entire train. To one black newspaper, the Pullman conductor was useless. "The money paid those *ornaments*, the sleeping car conductors, ought to be paid the hard-worked porters, and their offices abolished . . . The porter can, and in many cases does, perform his own and also the conductor's duties." Many blacks would have agreed that if Pullman got rid of the conductors, it could pay its porters a living wage and relieve the traveling public from having to tip them.[44]

Pullman conductors often resented porters who were "running-in-charge." Such porters performed the basic conductor's duties of taking tickets, selling tickets to those who had not pre-purchased, assigning spaces, and filling out car diagrams showing occupancy of each berth or room. They received the same type of training and followed the identical Book of Instruction as issued to conductors.[45] Porters ran in-charge when no Pullman conductor was available for a particular train, or for a segment of a long-distance route, or on shorter daylight runs. On the Santa Fe's Chicago–Los Angeles trains, cars destined for Phoenix were cut off at Ash Fork, Arizona, and a porter would run in-charge on this seven-hour leg of the journey. New York Central trains from Buffalo to New York often had a porter-in-charge as far as Syracuse, where a white conductor boarded and took over. In 1931, to cut costs during the Depression, the Pennsylvania Railroad substituted porters-in-charge on its parlor car lines between Washington and New York.[46] Porters also ran in-charge when there were only one or two sleeping cars on a train. Naturally, Pullman conductors, realizing that porters-in-charge did the same job for a fraction of what they were paid, felt threatened. In 1920, conductors worked less than half the hours of porters, but were paid $120 per month, double the porters' wages. Porters-in-charge earned a mere $12 per month extra.[47]

Pullman conductors held power over the porters, and could use it to their advantage. Leon Long remembered, "most of [our] run-ins were with conductors. You know how some people want to push you around and put hardships on you and have you to do part of their work and all like that. Instead of them doing their own work, they'd push the work onto the porter." If a porter objected, "if you said any smart words or anything like that, well, they'd have you up on the carpet and lay you off for a trip or two. You couldn't stand up to them." William Harrington's memory was even more vivid: "The conductors was some of the worst sons of bitches there ever was . . . We had some of the nastiest people in the world out there. And me especially, because they didn't want to see me run in charge, take those tickets." Porter Ernest Ford's assessment was blunt: "The conductor was like a gestapo over the porter. The Pullman conductor was *worse* than the gestapo."[48]

The conductor-porter relationship replicated that of plantation overseers and slaves. The white man was in charge and held sole authority. Some conductors actually referred to the porters as their "boys."[49] As James Steele remembered it: "You had to swallow so much. The conductors are right, you're always wrong." But there were limits to what porters would take from Pullman's white employees. One inspector habitually bragged that he was an ex-cop and "had kicked a million niggers' ass." But "he said that to the wrong porter one time, and this porter laid him out. And they squashed it. Nothin' was said about it." Steele had his own run-in following an incident in which a passenger tried to hit him with a whiskey bottle and then lodged complaints against him with the Pullman conductor. He believed the passenger's fabrications without asking Steele for his side of the story, and suspended Steele from duty on the spot. The train conductor vehemently objected, however, and told Steele to resume his duties, saying, "If this son of a bitch [the Pullman conductor] tries to hurt you, you kill him." Later, when he gave Steele a dirty look, the emboldened porter replied: "Look, man, you heard what the [train] conductor told you, didn't you? Don't you mess with me, 'cause I'm gonna tear you in two." Several women passengers who witnessed this confrontation wrote letters in Steele's defense, and the superintendent at his home terminal exonerated him.[50]

Not every African American had a strong enough constitution to stomach either the Pullman conductor's authority or passengers' abuse. While his grandfather, father, and two brothers made careers of Pullman service, George Smock lasted only four years, being fired and rehired twice before finally quitting for good. One firing occurred after he slugged a passenger who insisted on calling him "Gawge," even after being corrected.[51] Porters generally believed that low-class whites were more likely to be offensive. Virgil Smock, George's brother, stated that "I could tell you when a passenger comes down the platform at night or in the daytime, the way they approached you, that he was either gonna have hell with him or he's gonna be a gentleman clerk of the county."[52] Fortunately, the Smock brothers worked on California trains. Many porters dreaded the behavior of passengers on New York-to-Florida runs. Once the train crossed the Potomac River into Virginia, some passengers no longer addressed them as "porter," but "nigger."[53]

Passenger abuse took many forms—verbal, psychological, and physical. A snappy verbal riposte was often the only defense. On occasion, they would call for the porter or lounge car attendant by whistling, as one would call a dog. In response, one attendant would look under tables and chairs. When somebody would invariably ask if he had lost something, he'd reply, "No, this man [the whistler] be calling for a dog." When a group of businessmen asked where they could get some black girls to show them a good time, a Pullman attendant replied, "Well, I tell you, I just can't put my finger on it. You see, my wife is white, and all my friends are white."[54]

On occasion, a porter stepped out of his customary role in dealing with obnoxious passengers. Homer Glenn became entangled in unwanted conversation with an inebriated Texan who claimed to love blacks, but damned black men for raping white women and asked Glenn what he thought should be done to such brutes. Glenn asked whether he should respond as a servant, or as a man. When the drunk gave permission to answer as a man, Glenn replied that black women came in all shades of color, "as black as a shoe" to "as white as a white woman." "But in the white race, I never see a black white woman. Now ask yourself the question. Who is the rapist?"[55]

In most instances, however, porters and attendants had to ignore provocation. James B. Newsome, who was one of George Pullman's first black employees, working from 1870 to his death at age 76 in 1925, adopted his own "Golden Rule of Service": "My mother taught me never to quarrel with a fool."[56] Years later, another porter remarked, "You are supposed to take everything the passenger puts on you—you're supposed to take it. I swallowed a lot of times to keep from losing my job, cause I had Sears to pay . . . So I'd walk away. A lot of times, because you don't say anything, that doesn't mean you're a coward, if a man is cursing you . . . Oh, I've been cursed out a lot. I just look at you and laugh."[57]

Being called "George" was particularly galling to porters. Not until the 1930s did the company issue them nametags. Eventually, cards were posted reading, "This car is being served by porter ____." But even this didn't stop the use of "George." Some porters simply ignored passengers who addressed them that way. But Hunter Johnson was unwilling to allow that insult to pass. After a female passenger boarded at Columbia, South Carolina, she called out, "Hey George, will you get me a Coca-Cola, please?" Johnson got the card with his name on it, waved it in front of her face, and said, "You can call me porter, or you can call me Johnson, but *George* is not on the train today."

Needless to say, she didn't get her Coke. Other passengers tried addressing them as "boy." Virgil Smock had a standard response: "Boy's not on this trip. He stayed at home."[58]

Porters sometimes suffered psychological abuse. One recalled doing many extra chores for the Duke of Windsor, who tipped him a measly 10 cents each time. By the end of the run, all the now-resentful porter had to show for performing extraordinary service was a few dimes. Then the Duke asked for his money back! The porter complied—all 80 cents—at which the Duke "rewarded" him with a $50 tip. But, years later, it was being humiliated and reminded of his inferior status, not the size of the tip, which stuck in the porter's memory. Such mind games were not uncommon. Porter Glenn Green described a "classification of tippers that were known throughout the Pullman Company . . . They were this class that would get on the train, take a five- or ten-dollar bill, tear it in half, give you one half, and he keeps the other. That was to ensure that you give him good service. You're going to give him all the service you can to get that other half."[59]

Another form of abuse was being falsely charged with theft. Although dishonest porters undoubtedly existed, the vast majority were upright, either out of personal moral convictions or the need to keep the job to support one's family. Sometimes an allegation was a scam. Hunter Johnson was accused of stealing two rings from a woman who claimed that she had left them on the bed while she went to the washroom. Fortunately, the conductor had confidence in Johnson and wired ahead for police, who boarded at the next station and found the rings in her purse. In another instance, a passenger claimed that Johnson had stolen a pack of cigarettes. In this case he defended himself: "Mister, the Pullman Company don't have no rogues out here. We weren't hired as rogues, we were hired to *protect* your stuff." Other passengers tempted porters, leaving money where they could easily find it. The wise porter immediately returned the bills to their owner.[60]

As historian Jack Santino notes, porters "could resist bribes and temptations; drunks they could finesse." But how should one respond to actual physical threats? Sometimes a porter chose not to react, as when Ernest Ford was "booted" by a cruel passenger who was showing off to friends how one treated a "nigger" in the South. That the abuser's companions felt guilty about his conduct, and gave Ford a generous tip, made up for the attack, in Ford's mind. At other times, however, porters would not remain passive. L. C. Richie worked a troop sleeper leaving Arkansas when a number of soldiers—"these boys were just rednecks, crackers"—repeatedly called him "nigger." Then, when his back was turned, one of them aimed an apple at his head. Richie grabbed the window jack, a heavy implement resembling an axe handle, shouting, "Goddamn you, every son of a bitch in here." After walking down the aisle, brandishing his weapon, "nobody on my car after that used the word nigger . . . And when we got to Atlantic City, every one of those sons o' bitches wouldn't open their mouth. Just as quiet as they can be." Some porters responded to threats with counter threats: Hunter Johnson carried an ice pick, for its customary use, but was ready to employ it to defend himself. Others carried knives, one porter retaliating for being slapped by slashing a passenger with his blade.[61]

A porter's decision on how to respond to cruelty was influenced by the prospect of earning or losing tips. The Pullman Company paid such low wages that one couldn't possibly make a decent living without them. For many years, tips were money free and clear. But when a porter published an article in the *Saturday Evening Post*, telling how he put his children through college on his tips, the Internal Revenue Service took notice. Thereafter, it required porters to declare tips as income. Pullman rationalized its low-wage exploitation by insisting that it was doing blacks a favor simply by employing them. In fact, the custom of tipping gave whites the opportunity to abuse porters, because if they didn't have to depend on tips, they would not have put up with maltreatment.[62]

Some passengers had never ridden on a sleeping car before, and didn't know how much to tip. Even regular travelers could be uncertain. Fortunately, some passengers were wealthy or generous, customarily giving liberal or even extravagant tips. But others were stingy and offered only a few small coins, or nothing at all, even though Emily Post could have been consulted for guidance. In the 1920s, she advised at least 50 cents per person per overnight, more if the porter shined one's shoes, drew a bath, served food or drink, delivered a telegram, or mailed a letter.[63] Given the unpredictability of tips, porters couldn't afford to leave things to chance. They became actors. At least in theory, the better the performance, the better the tip. As Happy Davis remembered, "You had to con a lot of them, get inside them and make them feel like they were the boss . . . When a passenger entered my car, I had him. I had ways. I was way *ahead* of them." Flattery was one method. On one occasion, Mrs. Will Rogers was on Davis's car, so ill that she traveled with a nurse. Davis had to physically lift her into her bed. She asked him, "Porter, how much do you think I weigh?" Although she had wasted away to almost nothing, Davis answered, "You weigh 135 pounds." At the end of her journey, she gave him a $135 tip. According to Davis, it was all about making passengers feel good.[64]

The amount earned from tips varied with the type of passengers. Those who rode trains the most—businessmen and salesmen—were dependable if not extravagant tippers. Some of the best tips came from newlyweds, when a groom tried to impress his bride with his unselfishness. Reputedly, drunks were the best tippers, but keeping them happy was no easy task. Mobsters and hookers were likewise generous. Some celebrities were good to the porters, while others—particularly baseball players—were miserly tippers. Solitary female travelers were said to be not only hard to please, but also cheapskates. Since those who rode tourist sleepers were less affluent, they were more likely to tip sparingly. For that reason, the base pay for porters on such cars was slightly higher. Some wealthy travelers were cheap, while others, like Mrs. H. J. Heinz, the catsup heiress, were lavish. After Garrard Smock, Jr. cared for her on a trip from Chicago to Phoenix, she sent a truckload of Heinz groceries worth $10,000—every variety, from beans to pickles—to his home.[65]

African Americans have long employed "trickster" strategies—exemplified in black folklore by the Brer Rabbit character, who uses his wits to outsmart bigger or more powerful animals—to combat racism or just get by. The necessity for tips fostered trickster behaviors among porters. Ernest Ford learned a bit of French when running to Montreal, so that he could pass himself off to

Canadian travelers as a French-speaking Louisiana Creole and build a foundation for large tips.[66] Tom Standard, who began his Pullman service in 1886 on the Mexican Central Railway's trains from El Paso to Mexico City, learned to speak Spanish and play the guitar. This paid off handsomely on one memorable trip. On discovering his musical talent, 16 female passengers requested that they be awakened with a *fandango*, lulled to sleep with the *cachucha*, and serenaded hourly in between. Each woman rewarded him with a $2 bill, a munificent tip for that era.[67]

Porters referred to trickster strategies as "hustling" and perfected their art in serving the Hollywood crowd, some of whom were among the very best tippers. The glitterati favored all-sleeping car luxury trains like the *Broadway Limited* and *Twentieth Century Limited* from New York to Chicago, the *Super Chief* from Chicago to Los Angeles, and the *Lark* overnight between Los Angeles and San Francisco. Many celebrities were generous, although Jack Benny was a cheapskate in life as in character. Bing Crosby was "one of the best passengers a man ever wanted to have," who frequently bestowed a $20 tip every time he ordered a cocktail or sandwich. Naturally, porters and attendants were eager to please, refining their hustle to an art. Crosby often wanted to enjoy the privacy of his drawing room, bringing a bottle of whiskey nestled in his golf bag. James Steele knew his wants, and would bring him glasses and ice as soon as he boarded, continuing the personal attention until Crosby went to bed. In the morning, Steele awakened him with a glass of freshly squeezed orange juice and two pots of fresh coffee.[68] Virgil Smock polished his hustle by learning the names of businessmen who regularly commuted between their offices on the *Lark*. "We knew those fellas, you know . . . We had all kinda ways to hustle. You could be standin' receivin' [passengers] and I ask, 'How you doin', Mr. Dave? Oh, hi gentlemen.' They used to go by, give me five dollars! They weren't even in your car!"[69]

While white passengers perceived Pullman porters as servants, they were regarded highly within their own communities. A steady income was not easily achieved by educated black males— among the few alternatives were teaching, working for the post office, and the ministry. Porters often earned more than schoolteachers.[70] The fact that it was a low income, measured in compensation per hour worked, did not diminish the job's status. Being a Pullman porter placed one securely in the black middle class, which valued respectability as well as income. The uniform identified one as a professional. Their earnings paid not only for homes and a modest "good life" but also for higher education for many of their children. To numerous women, a porter husband was a good catch, even given his frequent absences. In African Canadian communities in Montreal and Toronto, they "were the most eligible bachelors and parents often encouraged their daughters to marry" them.[71] Porters were also more urbane and sophisticated than many other blacks, esteemed for the breadth of their experiences, including rubbing shoulders with the high and mighty. They provided other blacks with a window into the wider world, entertaining families and friends with tales of faraway places and famous people. Yet they paid heavy costs: accepting a servant role and the abuse that came with it; sacrificing family life to long runs and doubling out and 400-hour work months; enduring abysmal working conditions and the tyranny of superiors. And it was ultimately "a blind-alley job. You went there as a porter and you left there as a porter. There was no advancement."[72]

Many porters devoted the best part of their lives to the Pullman Company. Their longevity is explained primarily by economic factors. By the 1920s, all Pullman employees could retire on pension after 20 years. Many worked far longer. In a 1923 list of the 50 porters with the most service, 3 had worked more than 50 years, 5 more than 45 years, 18 more than 40 years, and 24 more than 37 1/2 years.[73] Death benefits were paid to dependants of any employee who had paid into the plan, even if he worked only for one year. But economics aside, there was, for some, the satisfaction of serving (and sometimes getting to know) the rich and famous. Numerous porters featured in the *Pullman News* proudly related their acquaintance with presidents and senators; tycoons like J. Pierpont Morgan, Cornelius Vanderbilt, and John D. Rockefeller; and celebrities like Wild Bill Hickok, Buffalo Bill Cody, and, in later days, Hollywood notables.

Not a few men, of course, could stand being a porter only for a few months. The job put too much stress on family life. It paid too little for too many hours. For those lacking seniority, working the extra board was too irregular or exhausting. Some simply lacked the temperament to be "George" to white passengers. Many undoubtedly identified with poet Langston Hughes's fictional porter who wearily complained, "All my days / Climbing up a great big mountain / of yes, sirs!"[74] Others wanted only part-time work. Until the Great Depression shrank train travel, as many as 4,000 men were "summer porters" who worked during school vacations to finance their collegiate educations. In the mid-1920s, one porter claimed, "thirty percent of colored doctors are ex-porters." Many lawyers and teachers had done the same.[75]

How hard did the porters work? The labor they performed was so physically exhausting that Pullman recruiters were skeptical that small men could handle the job. Some career porters racked up astounding statistics. Fields Johnson toiled for 49 years, retiring at the age of 70. He estimated that, working 300 days per year, he assisted 576,000 passengers while himself traveling more than 3 million miles. Another porter, Golden William Smith, accumulated even greater mileage, logging more than 3 million miles in just 17 years on the premier *City of Los Angeles* to Chicago. This worked out to 50 60-hour weeks per year. Smith worked other trains for 24 years before that, almost certainly compiling at least 2 million more miles. Probably the record was the 5.8 million miles traveled by James B. Newsome, the 52-year "Grand Dad of all porters." And Joseph "Little Joe" Tompkins estimated that in his nearly half-century of work, he shined more than a half million shoes.[76] Fortunately, working conditions for all porters and maids improved significantly after 1937, when the Pullman Company finally signed its first contract with the BSCP, reducing the monthly workload from 400 to 240 hours as well as improving wages.[77]

Porters labored extra long and hard during World War II, when every seat was sold and the call buzzer rang incessantly. Passengers still asked them to run errands, like getting off at a stop to run into the station to purchase magazines or bringing them a meal from the diner. Cars were dirtier, ice water and paper cups ran out, yet, as the travel editor for the *New York Sun* wrote, "through this disorder and man-made confusion the Pullman porter moves with majestic aplomb, doing his job not only well but better than anyone has a right to expect. When we get around to war monuments something should be done about the Pullman porter." Others drew assignments on troop trains. They had to be philosophical to keep up the wartime pace. According to M. Kincade, "You just gotta haul folks as they come, some's good, some's bad, some's nice and some's crabby." But the war took its toll. "I like folks and I liked my job, but I feel a little tired, so now the war is over I'm quitting."[78] As for the suggested monument, the porters' wartime heroics went unrecognized.

Career porters constructed a group identity that they maintained into retirement and even after the demise of Pullman service. Although they worked more or less alone, each man in his own car, they regarded themselves as a fraternity, living communally while on layovers away from home. If their runs ended at one of 35 (in 1922) major terminals, they received free lodging in Pullman Homes, YMCAs, hotel rooms, or old sleeping cars furnished by the Pullman Company. Some of these "accommodations," however, were unpleasant and to be avoided if possible. Not a few porters paid for their own lodging so as to find cleaner and quieter surroundings. Porters and Pullman dining-car crews did not always get along—waiters and cooks tended to feel superior—so it was not uncommon for the two groups to be housed on different floors to avoid arguments and fights.[79]

Dozens of porters might be laying over at any time in a city like New York. They came from many different districts, but the layovers threw them together and created bonds of brotherhood. While some men went off in search of drink or women, many stayed in the quarters, playing marathon games of checkers and cards. Bid whist was their favorite, in teams of two, with a crowd of spectators invariably commenting on the play. According to William Harrington, "Very seldom anybody'd gamble. But that bid whist, checkers, everybody's raising hell playing cards." Other group activities included baseball and harmony singing: a vocal group of any number was called a quartet, and might imitate the style of the Ink Spots or Mills Brothers. Then there was "conversational storytelling . . . [with] its own unarticulated rules in which men took turns contributing their own narratives." Former porters remember with fondness how they "played" during their layovers. They also "played" on "deadhead" moves, returning in an empty car or train after a special one-way trip, like a troop movement from one coast to another. Such a ride might produce a four-day marathon game of bid whist.[80]

Working out of the same region also fostered brotherhood. One of the largest concentrations was in New York, where, even after the Great Depression had depleted their ranks, over 2,000 porters were based in the Penn Terminal, New York, and Grand Central districts. Porters wrote weekly columns in the *New York Age* for several years, reporting weddings, deaths, news of "old timers," and who got plum private car assignments; listing the sick and chastising those who neglected to visit their ill brothers; promoting fund-raising balls, benevolence funds, and the porters' baseball team; and urging attendance at safety programs.[81] Retirement did not end their camaraderie. Many porters continued to meet to keep up ties, share reminiscences, and play cards. Wives were not present during such get-togethers.

One matter not fondly remembered was the Pullman Company's exploiting them as porters-in-charge while refusing to promote them to the rank of conductor. Even as the racial climate began to change in the civil rights era, the railroad industry did not readily embrace change. But Pullman porter Earl Love had had enough. He first got the Colorado Civil Rights Commission to rule in his favor, in 1965, but the price of victory was too high. The Pullman Company offered to promote him to conductor, but he would have to forfeit his decades of seniority. The railroads were shedding passenger trains right and left. Numerous Pullman conductors, all of whom had seniority over Love, were out of work. There was simply no chance he would ever get to work as a conductor if he accepted the offer. Love appealed to the federal Equal Employment Opportunity Commission, but the Pullman Company was intransigent that he waive his seniority. So in 1968, Love and other porters-in-charge filed a class-action lawsuit. Another seven years elapsed before a U.S. district court ruled that they had suffered discrimination because "Pullman maintained racially segregated job classifications and that promotions of qualified [black] employees were foreclosed on racial grounds." By this time, however, the Pullman Company had been out of the sleeping car business for six years, so there were no conductor jobs for the plaintiffs. Nevertheless, 1,293 men who had worked as porters-in-charge following passage of the 1964 Civil Rights Act shared a $5.5 million settlement.[82]

In the 1950s and 1960s, even as they slashed the number of passenger trains, individual railroads took over from Pullman the operation of sleeping and lounge cars. In most cases, they continued to be staffed by the same men, just no longer Pullman employees. Amtrak assumed most of what remained of intercity passenger service on May 1, 1971, and with this step, the role and identity of Pullman porter began to disappear. Amtrak's sleeping-car personnel were called "attendants," and while many initially were former Pullman men finishing their working careers, new hires were of all ethnicities and included women.[83] Traditional duties like shoe shining disappeared. With relatively decent pay, the necessity to hustle for tips declined. The surviving ex-porters were often tired, not just physically, but tired of being servants. Sons no longer followed fathers into their work. Railroad passenger service was too closely identified with servile roles to be attractive to many black men who grew up in the civil rights years. Thus the type and level of service performed by Pullman porters for a century faded into history. Some travelers lamented this loss, while others, sensitive to the civil rights revolution, recognized that requiring African Americans to humble themselves to Caucasians, offering "miles of smiles" in hopes of cadging a good tip, was an affront to their dignity.

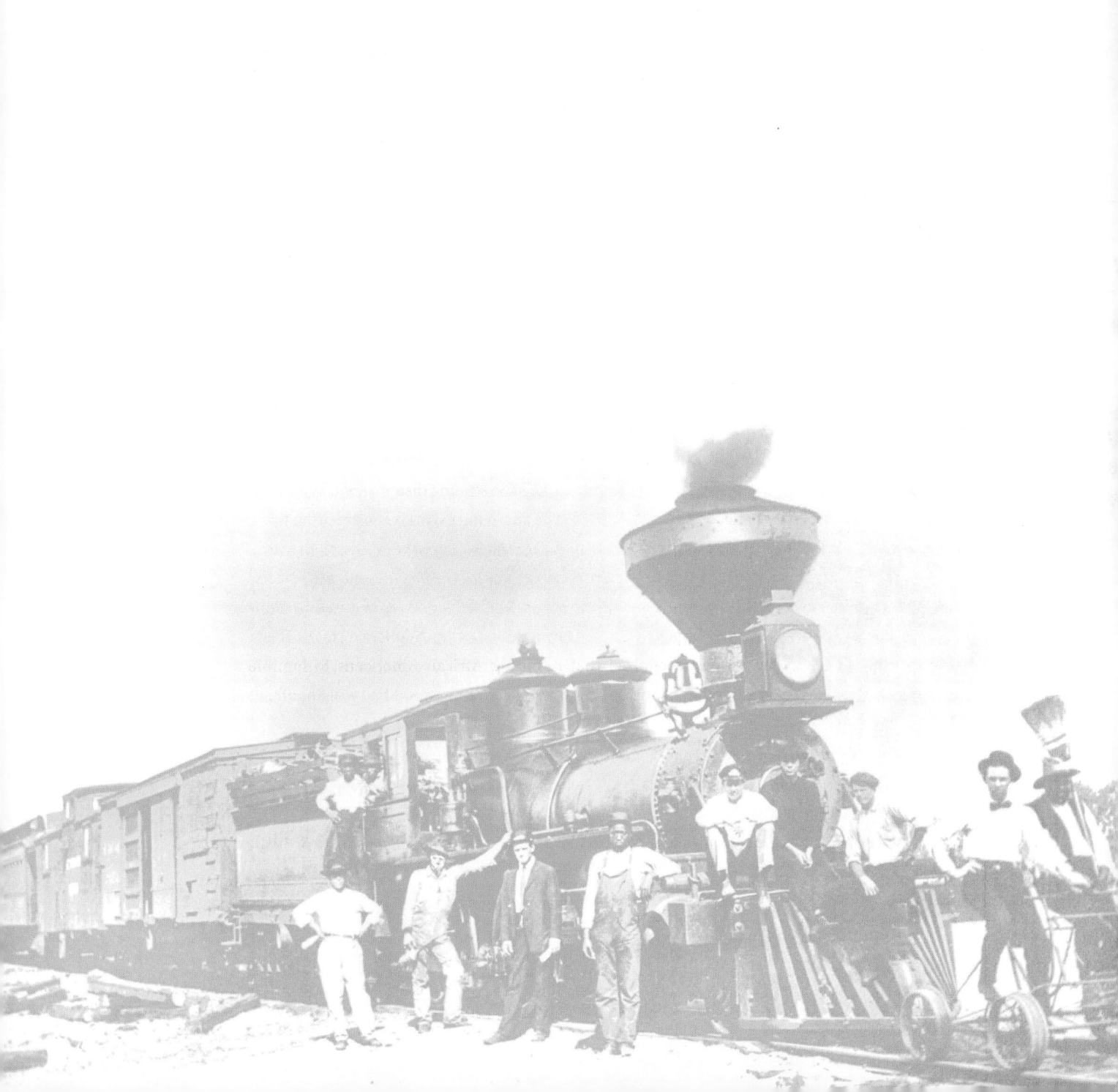

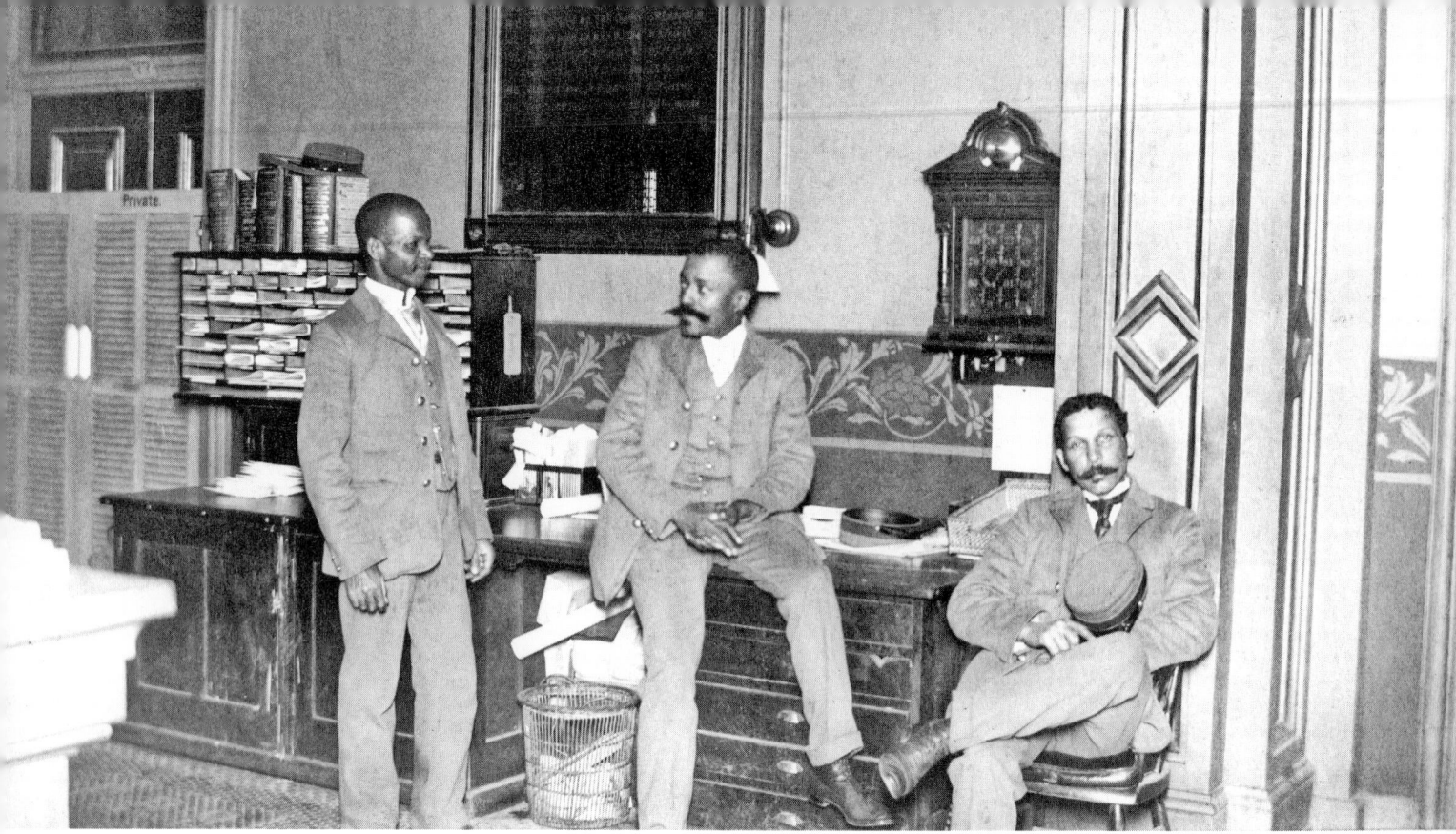

Early twentieth-century Pennsylvania Railroad office porters or messengers, whose duties ranged from filing documents to carrying paperwork between offices to custodial tasks, pause between assignments. Their uniforms identified them as functionaries and menials, distinct from white-collar employees. Longtime porters were often praised for their discretion and "faithfulness." Penn Central Railroad Collection, courtesy of Pennsylvania Historical and Museum Commission, Pennsylvania State Archives

(OPPOSITE) Perhaps the single greatest American railroad construction project was tunneling under the Hudson River to allow the Pennsylvania Railroad's passenger trains direct access from New Jersey to New York City at Pennsylvania Station. Before this link, all passengers from the west (railroad south) had to cross the Hudson on ferries. Construction on two parallel bores began in 1902 and was completed in 1910. Workers tunneled through sand, mud, and rock, linking successive 23-foot diameter tubes while compressed air kept out water seeping from the riverbed above. Pennsylvania Railroad Collection, courtesy of Hagley Museum and Library

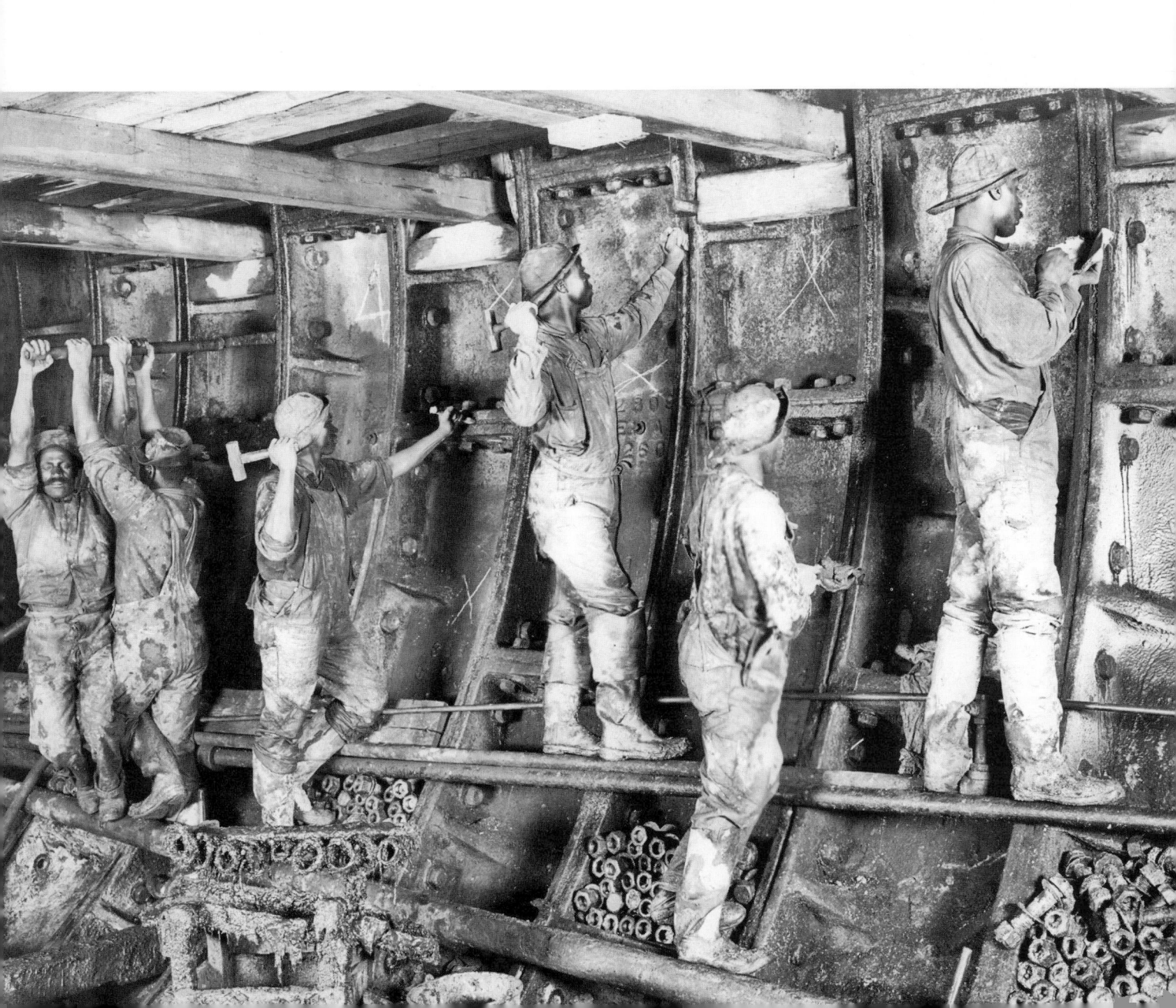

Construction workers led less settled lives than most other railroaders, usually absent from their families. These men, relaxing after work building the Tallulah Falls Railway south from Franklin, North Carolina, into Georgia around 1904, have the benefits of spouses and, possibly, better-prepared food. North Carolina Collection, University of North Carolina Library at Chapel Hill

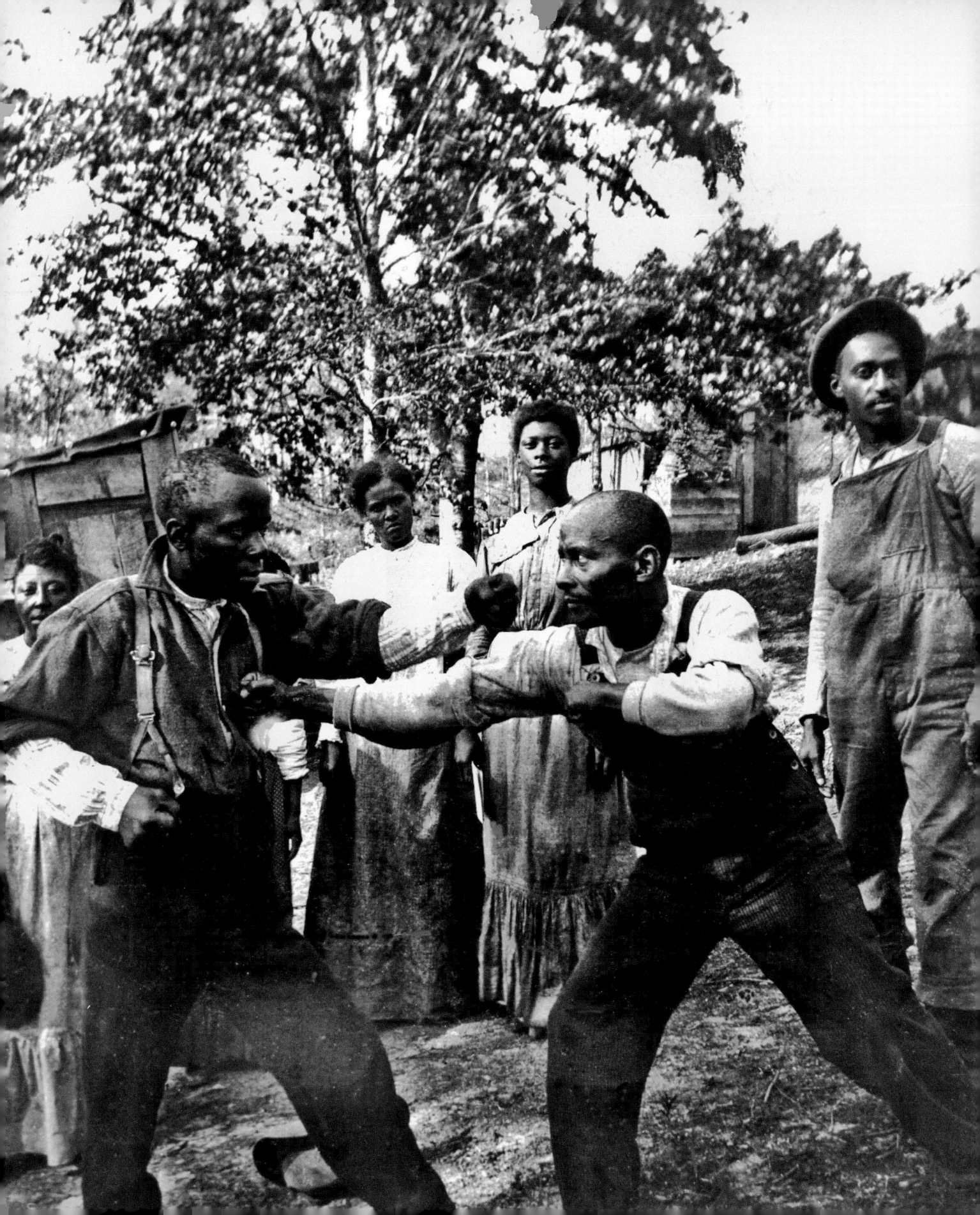

A black labor gang, with white overseer, building the Tallulah Falls Railway from Franklin, North Carolina, to Cornelia, Georgia, c. 1904. Railroad construction in the South, where labor was cheaper, remained largely manual work throughout the nineteenth century. It was not unusual to employ youths as water boys or mule drivers, their sharecropper families grateful for even a tiny cash income and one less mouth to feed. This lad had probably learned to handle mules while plowing on the family's tenant farm. North Carolina Collection, University of North Carolina Library at Chapel Hill

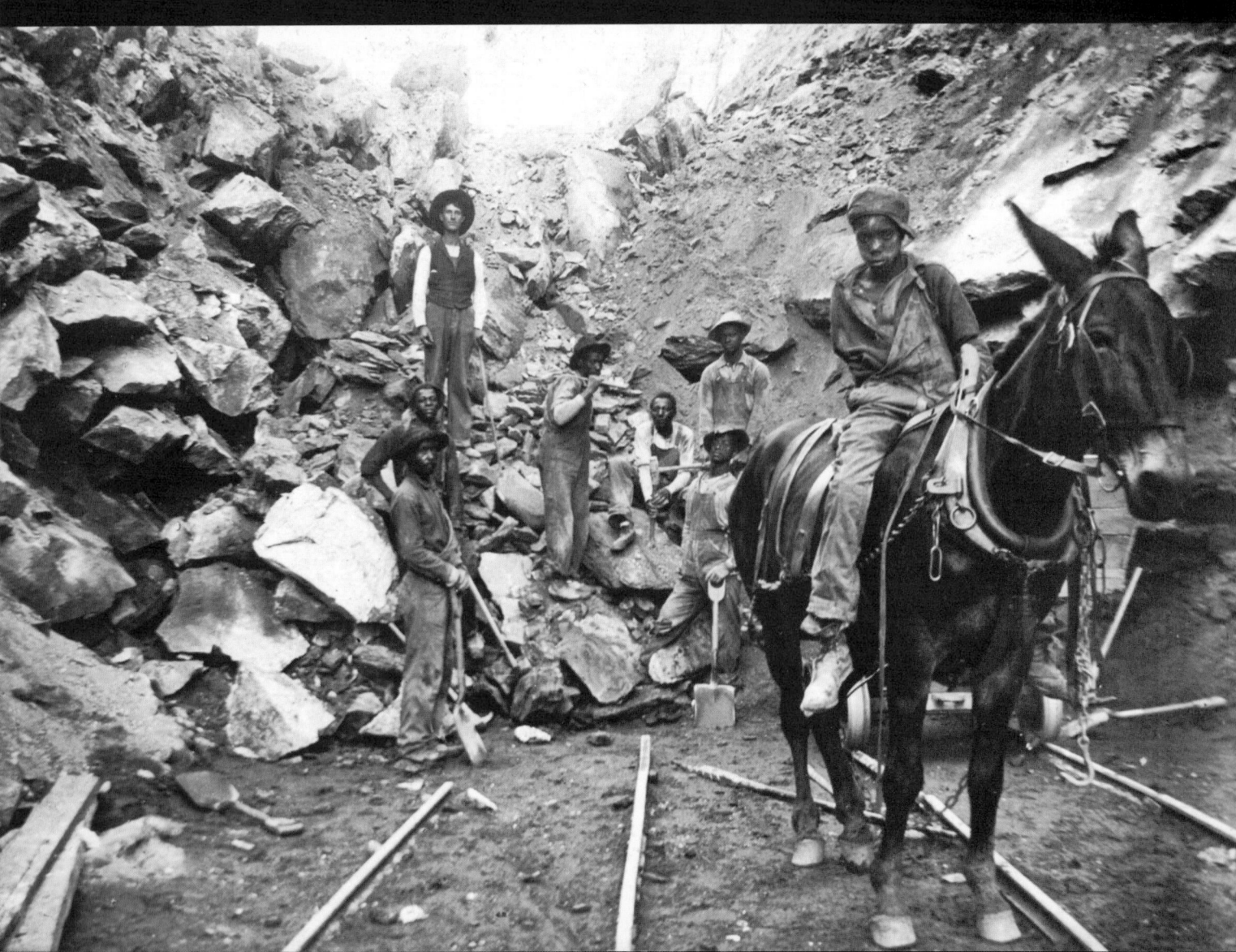

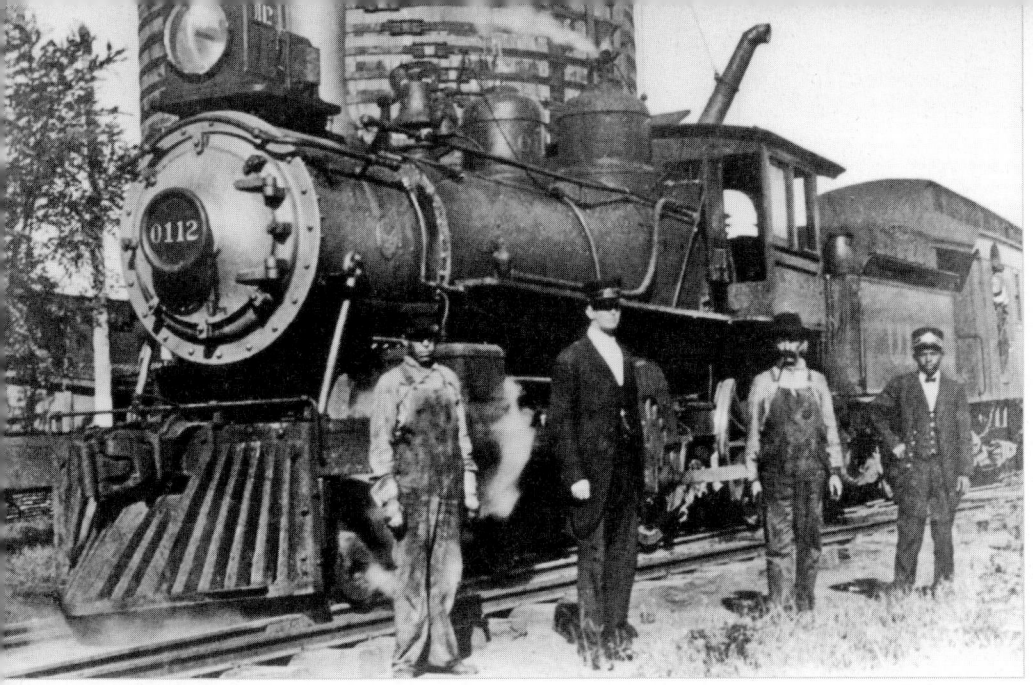

(ABOVE) *Black firemen were found almost exclusively on southern railroads. The most common exceptions were on western roads that also had lines in Texas, Oklahoma, or Louisiana. Here is an Atchison, Topeka & Santa Fe Railway fireman (far left) as well as a black train porter or porter-brakeman (far right) at Crescent, Oklahoma, in 1904. The firemen would have been barred by union contract from running north of Oklahoma. Santa Fe Railroad Collection, Special Collections and Archives, Cline Library, Northern Arizona University*

(BELOW) *Trackwalkers were maintenance of way employees tasked with inspecting several miles of roadbed daily and making needed light repairs. Although some literally walked their sections of track, this Florida West Shore Railway employee has a rail bicycle for propulsion. Among the train crew looking on in this 1908 view are a black fireman and brakeman. Don Hensley collection.*

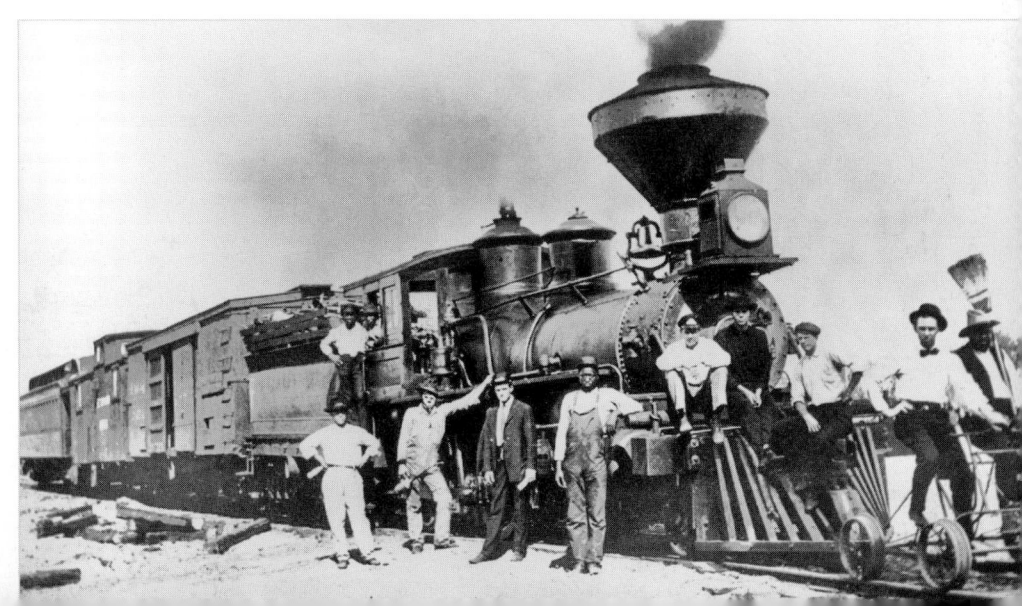

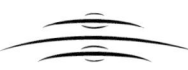

"CAPABLE OF WORKING IN ANY FINE RESTAURANT"

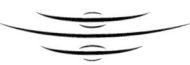

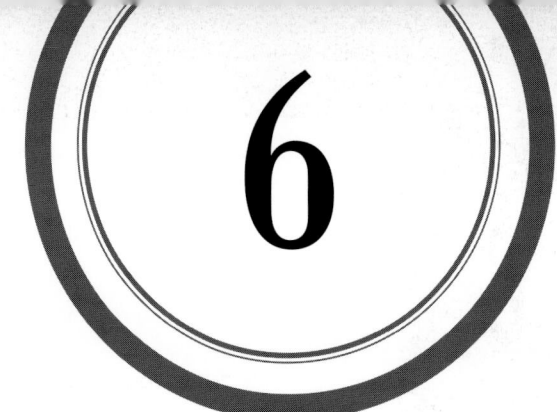

6

Dining-Car Cooks and Waiters

For the first three decades of railroad travel, passengers got off trains to eat at meal stops, with food ranging from abysmal fare served at crude frontier depots to hotel-quality cuisine at substantial station restaurants. After several experiments with serving meals on board trains, the first regular dining cars were introduced on the Philadelphia, Wilmington & Baltimore Railroad during the Civil War, although food was prepared at terminals and kept warm in steam boxes. The first waiters were black men, wearing white jackets. Thus was established a pattern that lasted to the end of railroad-operated dining-car service. Dining cars themselves underwent a number of evolutions. In 1867, George Pullman, who was successfully launching a sleeping-car fleet, introduced "hotel cars," which combined dining facilities and a kitchen with a lounge section and sleeping compartments. Waiters doubled as porters. But such cars were not the best way to feed travelers. Food odors lingered in the compartments, making some passengers travel sick. The dining room and kitchen were too small to feed everyone who might wish to have a meal. Above all, expansion of train routes made it more efficient to separate sleeping and dining functions, so that sleeping cars could be uncoupled from one train and added to another, allowing passengers departing from one terminal eventually to reach many different destinations without having to change cars. It made no sense for each sleeper to provide meals. A separate dining car could feed passengers on an entire train.[1]

George Pullman introduced the first true dining car, the *Delmonico*, in 1868, but such service was rarely profitable and the Pullman Company exited the dining-car business in the early 1900s, although it continued to operate parlor, buffet, and lounge cars offering beverages and a limited menu, staffed with Pullman waiters and cooks. The individual railroads gradually picked up the dining-car concept and accepted revenue losses as the cost of doing business: first-class passengers expected superior service, including a dining experience comparable to that found in a fine hotel. At the peak of passenger travel, the number of meals served was prodigious. Even during the Great Depression, dining cars served 25 million meals yearly, passengers consuming 15 million pounds of meat, 24 million eggs, more than a million loaves of bread, 9 million pounds of potatoes, a million pounds of coffee, and nearly half a million quarts of ice cream. Each railroad sought to create its own unique dining identity, vying with one another to hire famous chefs, devise gourmet meals served on custom-designed china, and offer opulent accommodations and amenities. Blacks gained a near-monopoly as waiters. Kitchen crews were not so uniform. On some railroads, the entire staff was black; on others, the chef (head cook) was a white man, with the cooks being African Americans. The entire operation was presided over by a white steward. Until very late, racism barred blacks from managing dining cars.[2]

Railroading was one of the few steady nonagricultural jobs open to southern black men after slavery,[3] so it is not surprising that many of them made careers as cooks and waiters. Northern blacks, too, gravitated to such work, particularly before industrial work opened up during World War I. In Buffalo, New York, home to a dozen long-distance railroads, one of every 12 adult black males in 1905 was a dining-car waiter or cook.[4] Like the Pullman porters, dining-car workers often encouraged family members to follow in their footsteps. Railroad recruiters enlisted others. Such was the case in 1920 of 19-year-old George McLain, who encountered a Southern Pacific Lines waiter in San Antonio, Texas, recruiting blacks for car cleaning and dining-car jobs. An immediate opening existed: that day's westbound *Sunset Limited* was short a cook. Asked if he had ever worked in a kitchen, McLain replied that he had learned "a whole lot about cookin'" from his mother. So he hopped on board, "and that's all I ever did in my life." When the *Sunset* reached El Paso, Texas, the diner was cut off for its return on a later eastbound train. The rest of the crew headed for Mexico in search of "Spanish girls." Heeding his mother's warning about avoiding bad places and associates, McLain remained behind and was approached by an official looking for a cook for the next westbound to Los Angeles, who promised him a pass back to El Paso. At the Los Angeles commissary to collect his pass, he learned that a cook was needed on the *West Coast* up to Portland, Oregon. Upon returning, he prepared to go home when he was offered a trip on the *Golden State Limited* to Chicago. "By the time I made that trip and come back, I had a couple checks, and I wasn't thinkin' about goin' back to Texas." McLain wasn't an exceptional case: In his estimation, "a third of the people that immigrated out here in California, the railroad immigrated 'em."[5]

Starting out young in a dining-car kitchen was not unusual. Sam Turner secured employment on the Atchison, Topeka & Santa Fe Railway on his 18th birthday in 1946 and worked until the end of its passenger service in 1971. Jimmy Clark was only 17 when he was hired in the fall of 1917, and Thomas Fleming was 19 in 1927. Both had careers on the Southern Pacific. Sometimes it merely took hanging around the commissary for a few days before a cook failed to show up and the first person available would be hired on the spot. Practically everyone started as fourth cook (primarily a dishwasher). Jimmy Clark recalled his rude awakening: "There was a whole lot of dishes on a dining car, more than what Mama had at home in her kitchen. Oh, man!!" About 1,000 dishes had to be washed each meal period, in a sink measuring less than 2 feet square.[6] The "forty" (fourth cook) also cleaned vegetables and peeled potatoes. Thomas Fleming had to shell a 50-pound sack of peas on his first trip. Not surprisingly, some men soon quit. Third cooks sometimes prepared vegetables and washed pots and pans too, but they were mostly fry cooks on the range. The second cook worked the range at breakfast, preparing omelets, ham and eggs, hotcakes, and the railroad specialty, French toast. For other meals, second cooks made soups and roasts. On the New York Central Railroad, because for many years the chefs were white, the second cook was the broiler man. On the Santa Fe's *California Limited* during the peak summer tourist season and at Christmas, two second cooks were required. The chef was boss and manager of the crew, and was stationed near the pantry where meals were passed to the waiters, making certain that the food looked as good as it tasted. Southern Pacific chefs also manned the charcoal broiler, cooking fish, chicken, and steaks. It required leadership as well as culinary skill to graduate to chef. In extraordinary cases, men became chefs in only a few years, but, for most, it took decades. Even after attaining that rank, one might have to work the extra board for years before gaining enough seniority to land a desirable permanent run. Third cook Joe Turner, who was also a prizefighter, made an extraordinary leap in rank on the SP. On one occasion, the commissary superintendent attended a fight and got so enthused that he shouted, "Knock the bum out and I'll make you a chef tomorrow." Turner did just that, and the next day he was indeed promoted over the second cook.[7]

Although railroads employed traveling chef instructors, the kitchen staff mainly learned from one another. Jimmy Clark remembered "the training of those good men, those wonderful men that I'd worked with, took me by the hand and trained me just like a father would in the home." When he finally became a chef, he did the same: "I'd take the dishwasher, put him in the third cook's place. Third cook, I'd put him in the second cook's place. The second cook, I'd put him in my place." Years later, many cooks still called him "Daddy" out of respect for his mentoring. Railroads with large dining-car fleets established formal cooking schools, the New York Central's at first in an old coach in the Mott Haven yard, outside Manhattan, and later in Grand Central Terminal.[8]

Most cooks, of course, never became chefs. Only a limited number of such jobs existed on a given railroad, and seniority ruled. So did racism. For many years, Santa Fe chefs were German or French immigrants, because Fred Harvey, who made the railroad's meal service famous both on its dining cars and in his Harvey House station restaurants, didn't believe that blacks could cook well enough to be leaders. It wasn't until such foreign chefs began to retire or leave for less arduous and better-paying hotel jobs during World War II that African Americans became Santa Fe chefs.

The Southern Pacific also employed white chefs, many of whom worked for decades and had the seniority to claim the best runs. For years most black SP chefs were on the extra board, available to be called whenever the need arose but having no regular run. New York Central chefs, too, were for many years white and, according to future chef James Heyliger, sometimes mean to the black cooks. "Then the company started getting good recommendations on the colored cooks, and let us be promoted to chef. In some places they'd say the passengers would rather have a colored crew on there instead of a white one." The Union Pacific Railroad discriminated among cooks, maintaining separate lists of "A" (white) and "B" (black) cooks, assigning preferred runs to the former.[9]

The more glamorous the train, the greater the culinary opportunities. Some chefs, kitchen artists whose recipes became legendary, would not work on a train where their creativity was stifled by plebeian ridership and pedestrian cuisine. It took a number of years for chefs, cooks, and waiters alike to gain seniority on trains like the Santa Fe's new streamlined all-Pullman *Super Chief*, introduced in 1937, which traveled from Los Angeles to Chicago in the unprecedented time of 39 1/2 hours. By the time they gained such positions, they were highly trained. "We were capable of working in any fine restaurant," remembered Thomas Fleming, although "most fine restaurants didn't hire black chefs." Workhorse trains, on the other hand, like the Santa Fe's *Scout*, which carried only tourist sleepers and coaches and had a lower fare, featured a basic bill of fare. Eggs were always scrambled—one couldn't get them cooked any other way—and the entire meal—eggs, meat, toast—came on one plate. Cooks and waiters referred to the *Scout*'s diner as the "greasy spoon."[10]

Until only a few years before Amtrak, dining-car crews prepared nearly every dish from scratch. The home terminal commissary stocked all needed supplies. In the 1920s, the SP commissary "had everything the public would get in a luxury hotel—lamb chops, pork chops, filet mignon, Chateaubriand, fresh green vegetables, milk in 10-gallon cans, cases of eggs, fresh fish, shrimp, oysters, and lobsters . . . The commissary bakery made pound cakes and raisin bread, and it packaged special flour mixes for biscuits, shortcake, muffins, and hot cakes—all you had to do was add milk and stir. They even gave us dough for pies." Aside from the flour mixes, crews had few shortcuts. The third cook had to French-cut the string beans; the second cook had to filet the trout. Soups were made from scratch in big stockpots. Hamburger was freshly ground on the train. Applesauce was likewise train-made.[11]

A hallmark of Southern Pacific dining cars was fresh Parker House rolls. Either the chef or second cook set a sponge (dough) in the evening, and, after it had risen, punched it down before closing up the kitchen at night. He got up at 3:00 a.m. to punch the dough down again, knead it, roll it out, cut out, and fold the dough into shape, and have the rolls baked by 6:30 a.m. Most desserts were made fresh on board, including bread, raisin, and rice puddings; cakes; and at least two kinds of fruit pies. Jimmy Clark recalled that "the only time we'd get any assistance in cooking from the [SP] commissary would be when we'd stock up in the afternoon when we reported, say, for three o'clock, and we gonna be leaving about five-thirty or six o'clock, and we're serving dinner leaving town—the commissary would give us a supply of pies." The same practice prevailed on the New York Central's luxury *Twentieth Century Limited*, leaving New York and Chicago in the late afternoon. Some passengers didn't even go into their sleepers, but instead went directly to the dining car.[12]

Working a dining car required considerable physical stamina. Like Pullman porters, cooks and chefs reported for duty several hours before departure. The chef, as kitchen manager, conferred with the steward and the commissary regarding the necessary supplies, which were hauled to the cars in two-wheeled carts pulled by a cook and a waiter. Meanwhile, other commissary employees (often blacks) loaded ice, coal, and charcoal. Before the introduction of propane-fueled stoves, one of the cooks started a fire in the range, which burned hard coal, and another in the broiler using charcoal. Jimmy Clark sometimes worked the SP's *Daylight*, which ran every morning between Los Angeles and San Francisco. If he was doubling back the next day, he laid fires at the conclusion of the run so that they would be ready to light early the next morning. This required Clark to arrive at 5:00 a.m. for an 8:00 a.m. departure. Propane gas ranges were introduced in the early 1940s and before long, no cooks wanted to work on the older diners with coal ranges.[13]

One innovation particularly disliked by kitchen crews was double-unit dining cars, first introduced by the Union Pacific and Pennsylvania railroads. They consisted of one car with nothing but tables, seating 68 rather than the customary 42 patrons, coupled to a car with an extra-large kitchen and a dormitory with bunk beds for the crew. Waiters who served the last tables, farthest from the pantry, worked particularly hard. Even worse were the Southern Pacific's triple-unit diners on the popular *Daylights*. A single kitchen car was bracketed by a 68-seat dining car on one end and a full coffee-shop car at the other. The addition of more cooks and waiters did not appease the crew. George McLain was blunt: even with eight cooks, "they were hell."[14]

Although sleeping-car porters also got little sleep, no passenger train crew members worked more physically exhausting jobs than cooks and chefs. On a lengthy train during busy tourist or holiday seasons, they might work 18- to 20-hour days, all on their feet. If the diner was to open at 6:30 a.m., the cooks had to get up at 5:00. With luck, breakfast would be finished by 9:30 or 10:00, but if someone came in later wanting breakfast, she or he would be served. So sometimes breakfast merged with lunch, without a break. By the time lunch was finished in mid-afternoon, preparations were well under way for dinner, and it might be 10:00 p.m. before the last patron had finished, and midnight before the last pots and pans were scrubbed, the kitchen cleaned, and preparations made for the morning. On the *Twentieth Century*, some passengers stayed up most of the night. According to James Heyliger, "If they wanted to eat until two o'clock in the morning, you fed them. They'd have parties in the dining car . . . As long as they wanted to party, we stayed . . . They'd tell the waiter, 'Ask chef if he can make us a cake,'" which Heyliger would do, from scratch.[15]

Cleaning the kitchen was a laborious task. Thomas Fleming described the procedure on SP diners: "The kitchen floor had a sheet of copper bolted in place, fitted with wooden slats that covered every square inch. I had to wash and scrub the slats until they were almost white, then stand them on their sides while we mopped the copper flooring. We oiled the stove on top, cleaned the range and charcoal grills, polished the coffee urn, and cleaned and put away the crocks on the steam table, so everything was shining bright." The *Century*'s crew arrived for duty five hours before departure, because the cooks had to get down on hands and knees and scrub the copper floor with Bon Ami until it shone. This was necessary because the door to the kitchen, along the hallway that passengers used to get into the dining room, was kept open on account of the heat in the kitchen. People would look into the kitchen, so it was important for everything to be extra clean and polished, and the cooks smiling.[16]

This grueling regimen exacted both a physical and a psychological toll. Kitchen temperatures reached way over 100 degrees in summer with meat roasting, bread and pies baking, and steaks and chops grilling. Until after World War II, many dining cars were not yet air-conditioned. And in even the most modern cars, the air conditioning only efficiently cooled the dining room. Many cooks got swollen legs. Sweat ran down into their shoes. Some fainted from the heat and were dragged to the vestibule to get fresh air and have wet towels placed on their heads. Even after reviving, they were often too weak to work the rest of the day. Drinking lots of ice water only made matters worse. Instead, they made their own version of Gatorade by placing raw oatmeal in a jar filled with water that was kept cool, but not cold. Others coped by imbibing other beverages. Santa Fe cook Sam Turner saw it all: "A lot of cooks drank—drank a whole lot." Problem drinkers were sooner or later found out and made to attend Alcoholics Anonymous classes. But the Santa Fe, at least, was forgiving: "If you did anything wrong, they'd put you on the ground [suspension] for a few days, but they'd always let ya come back. They would always give you another chance."[17]

Many cooks, like porters and waiters, sacrificed family life for the opportunity to make a decent living. Some repeatedly doubled out. Others, however, managed to ensure regular family time by concentrating their schedules. Leland "Sugar" Cain worked on the Chicago & North Western Railway's *400s*, from Chicago to Green Bay, Wisconsin, and return, for half a month straight, racking up the maximum-allowed 180 hours. During this time, his family saw little of him, but he had the other half of the month completely off. Cain's father often worked for two different railroads in the same year, on an eastern line like the New York Central until traffic slowed with the approach of winter, then on to a southern road like the Atlantic Coast Line for the Florida season. Other chefs worked for many days away from home because railroading was in their blood. Such extended absences, including at Christmas and other holidays, were a major reason for failed marriages.[18]

Like other black railroaders, the cooks' accommodations while laying over away from home were limited. The SP's *San Joaquin* out of Oakland, California, arrived shortly before midnight in Los Angeles. Thomas Fleming, along with other cooks and waiters, stayed at a black-owned "fleabag hotel" across from the station. Pool sharks infested the downstairs "recreation room," while prostitutes plied their trade on the floor above. The railroad paid for these accommodations—two men per room—and at least the sheets were clean. But sleep was all too short, with the crew caller knocking on doors at 6:00 a.m., for an eight o'clock departure. Dining car stewards, of course, stayed at a white hotel.[19]

While some cooks and chefs merely put in time or cut corners whenever possible, others, like 32-year SP veteran Jimmy Clark, took genuine pride in their work. As a chef, he ran a tight but fair ship. It was not uncommon for an order to get mixed up, provoking an argument between a cook and a waiter. His authority was clear: "I'll come down and straighten it out. You keep on cookin'." Clark knew that his job depended upon satisfying the traveling public: "Put your best into it because these people that's riding these trains and eating in the dining car, they're the ones who are supplying our jobs . . . [If] we please those passengers, they gonna recommend Southern Pacific." Clark's pride in his work was related to his assessment of his employer. "The Southern Pacific was like a father—just like a wonderful home and all the employees that I worked with and worked under, coming up from dishwasher to chef." Unlike some others, he didn't feel that race limited his opportunities: "I didn't know anything about discrimination, although there was discrimination. But for some reason or another, I didn't even think about it." Clark's claim to have avoided prejudice can perhaps best be understood in light of how he assessed his life's progress overall: dining-car work was "the greatest experience I could've ever had coming up from the bottom like I did."[20]

Dining-car kitchen crews seldom encountered passengers, so they didn't customarily earn tips. But a special train could be different. Fraternal organizations or wealthy individuals might charter a train for a few days, or even take several weeks to travel around the country. Jimmy Clark drew a special for Hollywood film stars Douglas Fairbanks and Mary Pickford and a dozen of their friends, just from Los Angeles to San Luis Obispo, then on to publisher William Randolph Hearst's *La Questa Encantada* (Hearst Castle) by car. In such private circumstances, celebrities let down their hair because they would never encounter the cooks, waiters, and porters—their social inferiors—in any other situation. Fairbanks donned a waiter's jacket and walked into the kitchen, shouting out orders and pretending to wait on his guests. Each of the kitchen crew got a $25 tip each way for a half-day's run.[21] Some gratuities were not monetary. Sam Turner remembered a group of Elks who "had all the whisky in the world you wanted on there, all that good food. They give you a lot of stuff. Those groups would be so good, a lot of times they didn't care about no color or nothin' 'cause they be drinkin', having a good time."[22]

Chefs and cooks were also largely spared the kind of personal racism from passengers that waiters and porters had to endure. But the kitchen was not an impregnable sanctuary. Pullman lounge-car attendant George Smock witnessed an explosive incident involving his cook, 200-pound Harold Carr. The lounge was full of Hollywood actors and executives, including C. A. Brown, vice president of Universal Studios. He ordered wheat toast, but received white toast by mistake. Calling the cook into the midst of the crowd, he shouted, "Goddamn, you dumb sonofabitch, I told you I wanted wheat toast." Suddenly "everything got quiet as hell," as Carr went up to him. "Mr. Brown, can you bake a cake?" "No, I can't bake a cake." To which Carr replied, "You dumb sonofabitch," and turned on his heels. Everyone started laughing, including Brown, adding, "Come here, Carr. Thank you very much," and handed him a $40 tip.[23]

In fact, discrimination defined and circumscribed cooks' and chefs' jobs, as it did for all black railroaders. On one occasion, George McLain questioned the economy of supplying whole roasted turkeys from the commissary kitchen for the *Morning Daylight*, since that train served only turkey sandwiches at lunch, the legs being discarded, to which one of the white commissary employees retorted, "Hey, you think that nigger know what he's talkin' about?" McLain's response was the black railroader's classic posture: "I ignored it . . . All through life you have to ignore an ignorant person." McLain wasn't an Uncle Tom. On the contrary. "You know the setup. You see, the average Negro that's got any kind of education or anything like that, he know from whence he come, and he know where he's tryin' to go, and so he's got to use the best psychology to get there . . . That's the way I got advanced on the dining car, by studyin' and figurin' out people."[24]

McLain advanced all the way to traveling inspector, a key position in ensuring the safe handling of food and the prevention of disease. "I rode one train to the other train. I got on, and I inspect the meat, the food, watch 'em serve some dishes, and rode to the next station, got off, and caught another train" to observe a different crew. "Very seldom I'd grab one crew [again] 'lessen I found something bad on there, then I'd double back and catch 'em, see if they correct it, tell 'em 'bout it—and they liked me for that, because I didn't have 'em all the way on the carpet [reported to the superintendent] . . . I don't always start writin' 'em up, but I tell 'em what I want, and they'd do it." But even with authority to instruct anyone, white or black, regarding compliance with standards, McLain encountered senseless hatred. One steward on the *Lark* told him, "Ain't no nigger come tell me how to run my diner." McLain exercised grace by not reporting the steward to the superintendent: "If I'd been the person to get upset, I could have dealt him a whole lotta misery. But I said to myself, 'Those people [the dining car crew] need help' [in raising their standards]. And so the next time I saw him, why, he apologized." In the years before the civil rights era, particularly in the South, one had to be an adept "psychologist" and exercise self-control. When McLain was sent to Houston in 1950 to show crews how to operate the state-of-the-art diner on the streamlined *Sunset Limited*, a superintendent retorted, "You tell me, with this brand-new train, they send a nigger down here to tell us how to run it?" McLain remembered that "I just ignored him like I didn't see him . . . You got to know how to handle those people."[25]

Cooks and chefs also faced prejudice from the railroads, which proved as willing as the Pullman Company to exploit them. Thomas Fleming believed that the SP deliberately recruited blacks from the South because it could get away with paying them less. Wages *were* low: a fourth cook starting out on the New York Central in 1921 worked 240 hours a month at 50 cents per hour, earning $120 a month (about $1,415 in 2009 inflation-adjusted dollars), minus charges for broken or lost dishes. (By comparison, passenger train "colored brakemen" on the Missouri Pacific's DeQuincy Division earned about the same monthly pay in 1929, but for an 8-hour day/206-hour month). For decades the railroads actually charged cooks and waiters "room and board" for sleeping and eating on the train while en route.[26] Their accommodations were miserable. For many years they slept in the dining car on bedrolls and wood frames that were stowed in the "possum belly," a cavity beneath the floor, or simply on chairs lined up together with a folded blanket for a mattress. Only relatively late were dormitory cars introduced, often an old open-section tourist sleeper, placed at the front end of the train.[27]

Despite occasional friction, waiters and cooks looked after one another. Any food consumed by the crew was supposed to be paid for, at one-third or one-half the menu price. Sympathetic cooks sometimes fed the waiters without cost, though. Steaks were precut in the commissary, and were quite thick, to appease the appetites of male passengers. But if a lady ordered a steak dinner, the cook might slice the steak in half, and save the other for the crew. By the end of the night, there might be enough steaks for four or five men. And before steaks were cooked, the ends could be cut off, thrown in a pot, and made into Mulligan stew (which was not on the menu).[28]

Although less often than Pullman porters, cooks and chefs were occasionally drawn into the intimate details of passengers' lives. SP chef George McLain recalled that the "biggest experience" in his railroad career was not cooking for a president, but delivering a baby. When a woman on the *Imperial* went into labor, news of the emergency reached the diner. McLain's mother had been a midwife, so he knew a bit about the procedure. Getting his butcher knife, "I went up there [to the Pullman car], pump that woman's stomach, and tied that cord and cut it . . . So I delivered that baby. And years after that baby was growed up, his mother would write. She never got through thanking me for it. But they had no business lettin' her on the train."[29]

Other interactions with whites involved business of a different sort. During Prohibition, some dining-car workers supplemented their earnings by selling bootleg liquor, which was readily obtained in Chicago's South Side, the black ghetto. McLain discovered that servicemen were eager for hooch. "I made some good money during that Prohibition time . . . You get a [gallon] jug for about two or three dollars and put it in some half-pint or pint bottles. Then every time you had a trainload of soldiers, you could sell it to 'em . . . I sell those pints for a dollar, half a pint for 50 cents . . . You couldn't carry too much, 'cause you wouldn't want the commissary man see you packin' a whole lotta stuff down there [onto the train]. But what's in your grip you could take." A $5 net profit from a $3 investment was a good income in light of one's $30 monthly base pay.[30]

A dining-car kitchen, prior to the Amtrak era, was exclusively a man's world, except during World War II. The military draft, busy defense industries, and dramatically increased passenger travel created labor shortages that could ultimately only be filled by women. The Southern Pacific opened an employment office in Watts, Los Angeles's black community, seeking male help, but few applied. To employ women, however, meant observing California labor laws limiting the number of consecutive hours they could work. The solution was to split their shifts, with guaranteed rest periods in between. Black women were hired as dishwashers (fourth cooks) and third cooks (only two females became second cooks on the SP). They got along better with the men than with one another. "All those guys tryin' to make love to those women and help them and wash dishes for 'em. You put a guy on there, and he's second cook . . . the woman's up on the range cookin', and he's down there washin' dishes." Despite the addition of women during the war, labor was still short. By 1944, the SP was limiting dining-car service to breakfast (until noon) and dinner (after 4:00 p.m.), with box lunches available in between. It claimed to "serve more meals to men of the armed forces than any other two railroads combined." But when millions of servicemen returned to civilian life after the war, female dining-car employees were unceremoniously discharged.[31]

Despite encounters with prejudice, not a few cooks and chefs looked back on their careers with satisfaction. Some, like Sam Turner, were particularly proud of working on crack trains like the *Super Chief*. Others were selected, on account of their culinary skills and personal probity, to prepare meals for presidents and other dignitaries. Franklin Roosevelt long used a B&O chef when he traveled by train, on whatever railroad. When FDR returned from the Yalta Conference in early 1945 via San Diego, the Southern Pacific took charge of his transportation eastward toward Warm Springs, Georgia, where he died soon thereafter. The president's menu included abalone, but the B&O man wasn't familiar with that West Coast seafood. Hearing this, SP's president informed a Roosevelt aide that "I've got a man that'll cook anything that'll swim, crawl, or fly" and summoned George McLain to prepare what turned out to be the president's last meal in California. Roosevelt gave him an autographed $50 bill for a tip. McLain was also chef on Harry Truman's 1948 campaign special from Seattle to Douglas, Arizona. And nearly 12 years later McLain cooked for Nikita Khrushchev on a trip from Los Angeles to San Francisco. Although a Russian menu was also offered, the Soviet premier ate McLain's American food and shook his hand in appreciation.[32]

Top chefs also served on railroad executives' private cars, attaining such positions not by kowtowing but by working with dignity, diligence, and discretion. According to George McLain, "when you are associating with professional people, you have to be professional yourself." Of course, they also wanted chefs noted for their culinary art. Tom DeMerritt, "dean" of office car chefs, cooked for five presidents on the Central of Georgia Railway. Over the span of nearly half a century, business-car chef James H. "Jim" Jones prepared food for four Louisville & Nashville Railroad presidents. Chesapeake & Ohio Railway chef James H. "Jim" Peters staffed Office Car 6, used by a long succession of MOW superintendents and chief paymasters. He also cooked for board chairman Collis P. Huntington. And John Sanders likewise cooked for a variety of officials for over three decades on the Santa Fe.[33]

The ranks of dining-car cooks and chefs thinned dramatically in the 1960s as the railroads dropped more and more passenger trains in a futile effort to staunch the flow of red ink. On some trains, diners were replaced by café (lunch counter) cars, which required only a single cook and one or two waiters. In a further erosion in service, a number of railroads offered only "automat" cars with vending machines. (The SP's once splendid but now woebegone *Coast Daylight* in 1968 featured such a car, offering pathetic "meal and beverage service" on the author's honeymoon trip from San Francisco to Los Angeles.) Elsewhere, "food service" meant packaged sandwiches sold from carts pushed down the aisles by a lone attendant. And on other lines, all food service was discontinued. The number of dining cars in operation in 1970 was half that of 1960.[34]

The takeover of passenger routes by Amtrak thinned still more the cooks' ranks. A few senior men hung on as private-car chefs for railroads that retained a small passenger car fleet for business purposes. But this rarely meant steady employment. After a stint on the Chicago & North Western's office cars in the early 1980s, longtime chef "Sugar" Cain abandoned food preparation for manning club and bar cars on Chicago-area Regional Transit Authority commuter trains, a job that at least allowed him to return home nightly.[35] Today's long-distance Amtrak runs do not require old-school on-board cooks or chefs. Most dining-car entrees are pre-plated and reheated just before serving. The proud legion of African American railroad cooks and chefs is no more. *Sic transit gloria mundi.*

From the beginning of railroading, dining-car waiters were black. It was the railroads' insistence that food service was a black man's job that established his predominance. They sought to hire "men with black skins and white habits" who would cheerfully work extremely long hours under circumstances—swaying cars, cramped spaces, rushed time, hard-to-please patrons—which were far more difficult than those posed by restaurant work. Railroad officials, echoing the Pullman Company's assumptions, believed that blacks were a race that was naturally suited to providing personal service. Besides, even immigrant whites would shun such work because one was not just a waiter, but also a bus boy, silver-polisher, car cleaner, and more.[36]

The railroads' racism is clear in policies that regarded waiters as objects. Some lines deliberately assembled crews of like-skin coloration. According to a New York Central steward, "they try to put the same kinds of niggers in a squad. Medium mulattoes go in one car, tall blacks in another. It sort of helps dress the car in a uniform fashion."[37] In other words, waiters were part of the decor. Furthermore, the roles of blacks and whites had always to be distinct. Even though they wore white jackets identifying them as servants, Seaboard Air Line Railway waiters were to stand stiffly at attention at station stops, if they were not actually serving food, so that no one outside the train might mistake them for passengers and accuse the railroad of "mixing the races."[38] And, until late in the dining-car era, blacks were barred from the position of steward, the actual boss of the car and supervisor of both waiters and cooks.

Dining-car waiters worked slightly fewer hours than kitchen crews, who had to be on duty earlier in the morning to fire up ovens and begin baking. On the other hand, lounge-car waiters worked until the cut-off of legal liquor sales—midnight or 1:00 or 2:00 a.m., depending on the state—and sometimes beyond. Waiters earned more than cooks because they received tips, although they had to pay for any dishes, silverware, or napkins that were stolen as "souvenirs" by passengers. And their direct interaction with whites made them vulnerable to rude or racist behavior. Many a waiter had to hold his temper and wait until he was back in the pantry to curse out an abusive guest.[39]

A typical 42- or 48-seat dining car had 6 waiters. Most travelers didn't realize that a hierarchy prevailed among them. On the Illinois Central Railroad, for example, the highest position was first (or chief) waiter, who on other lines was known as the pantry man. He managed the pantry where side dishes were kept, salads were made, and entrees were passed from the kitchen to be "dressed" so as to make a pleasing presentation. The first waiter also served patrons at the two tables closest to the pantry. The others likewise had their assigned tables and extra tasks. An IC second waiter was responsible for polishing the silver serving pieces, keeping the buffet clean, and mopping the passageway alongside the kitchen. The third waiter was in charge of replacing tablecloths and napkins before new guests were seated and inventorying the soiled linens before they were sent to the laundry. The fourth waiter had the large responsibility of polishing all the silverware—more than 1,000 pieces on some diners. He also attended to the general cleanliness of the dining area, dusting everything and sweeping the carpet. Cleaning, polishing, and filling all condiment containers—salt, pepper, cream, sugar, vinegar and oil—was the task of the fifth waiter. And an IC sixth waiter, in addition to serving the tables that lay most distant from the pantry (and thus walking more steps each day), kept all serving trays, china serving pieces, and glassware spotless, while also ensuring the cleanliness of the refrigerated lockers at the far end of the dining room. In peak seasons, some long-distance trains with many Pullmans had a seventh man, called the "upstairs waiter," who served sleeping-car passengers who did not wish to eat in the diner.[40]

Waiters worked extremely hard. On longer runs, especially from the Midwest to the West Coast, they served three meals (with two or more sittings for lunch and dinner) for three straight days. At the end of each 16- to 18-hour work day, they and the equally weary cooks retrieved their bedding from the possum belly, mounted drapes to provide a modicum of privacy, and caught a few hours of sleep. One of the waiters became the steward's personal servant, making up his cot at the end of the car. Waiters on day trains likewise labored without respite. The SP's *Shasta Daylight* left Oakland shortly after 8:00 a.m. in the early 1950s with as many as 500 passengers. Alex Ashley recalled his exhausting 18-hour day: "We started seating [before the train actually departed]—train loaded—and you know, I didn't sit down till I got to Portland. That's facts. *Didn't sit down!* . . . You get into Portland around eleven o'clock at night. You get over to the hotel around twelve o'clock. You get to bed—look like before you get to sleep good, they're waking you up five o'clock in the morning to get back on this train, see. No, you could never get a good full night's sleep."[41] On one Baltimore & Ohio Railroad special, taking conventioneers from Jersey City to Louisville, waiters got no sleep at all. No sooner were dinner guests finished than card players wanted sandwiches. Then night owls wanted coffee and more sandwiches. By the time they went to bed, the first breakfast eaters arrived. And the final breakfast guests vacated their seats just in time for the first lunch patrons.[42]

In the South, state segregation laws had to be observed. Waiters and stewards followed rulebook instructions on "Serving Meals to Colored Persons."[43] They were either to be excluded entirely, served only after all whites had finished eating, or seated behind portieres (curtains) at the last two tables at the end of the car. In these ways, whites maintained their color line that denied blacks the dubious privilege of "social equality" with them. So a 42- or 48-seat diner contained, at most, 8 seats for African Americans. But even these were not guaranteed. The steward was at liberty to keep the curtain back and allow whites to occupy the last tables. On the Louisville & Nashville, an occasional "good" steward would allow the curtain to be moved forward to accommodate a larger number of

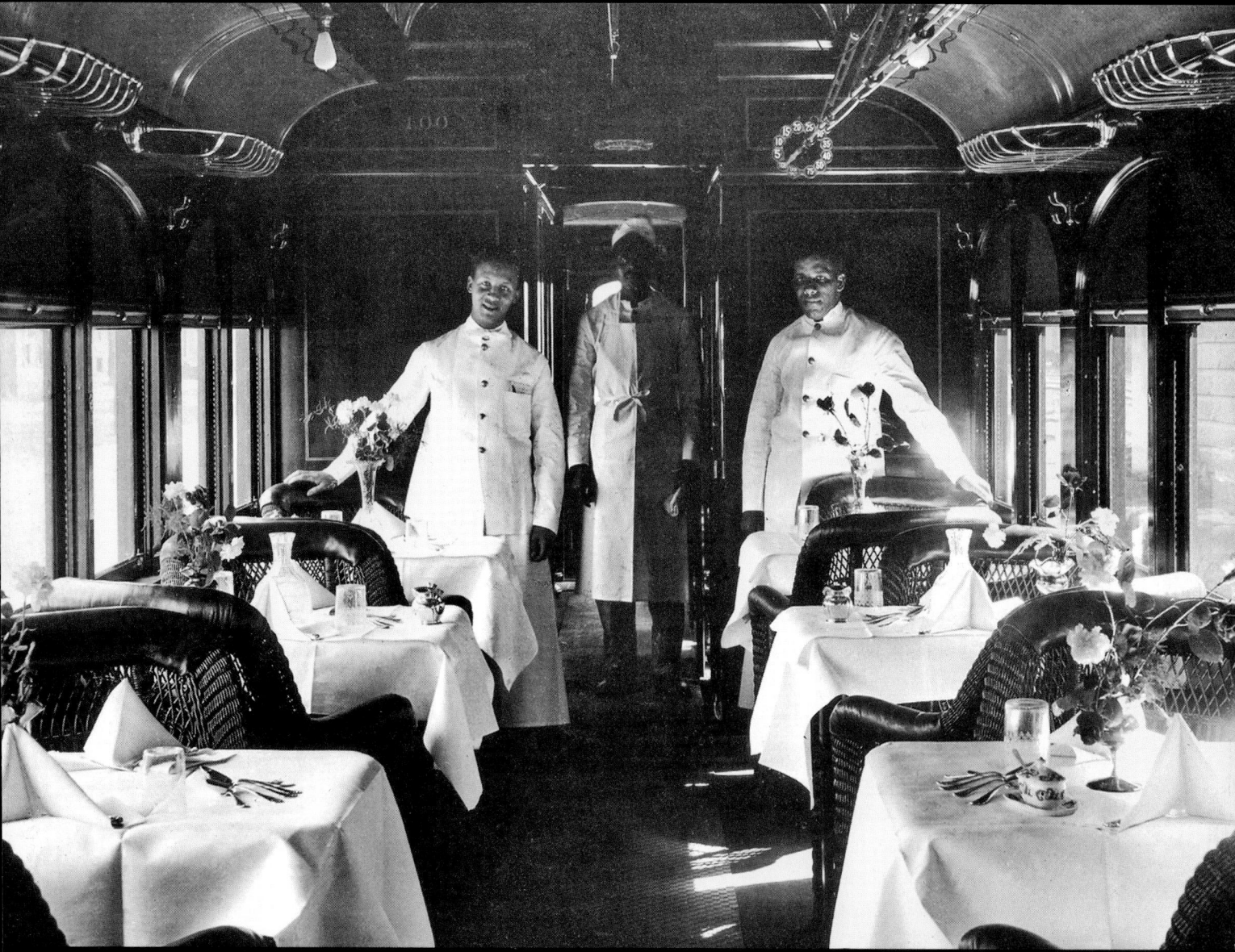

A few electric interurban lines offered luxurious dining amenities. The Chicago & Milwaukee Electric Railway took as much pride in its dining services as many steam railroads. Two black waiters and a cook pose inside parlor-buffet car 100 in 1909. They had to work efficiently, as a trip between the two cities took little more than two hours. *Arthur D. Dubin Collection, Special Collections, Donnelley and Lee Library, Lake Forest College*

blacks who wanted to eat, but it was more common for blacks to have to wait for one of the eight seats while numerous tables in the rest of the car were completely vacant. Some railroads tried to discourage blacks from using the dining car at all by offering tray meals at their coach seats. The illogic of dining-car segregation is revealed in the Seaboard Air Line's special instructions: "Colored nurses accompanying white families may be seated in the dining car at the table with such white families for the purpose of taking care of children, such nurses to be allowed to have their own meals at the same time." Even after dining car segregation was outlawed, some southern railroads still ordered stewards to avoid seating whites and blacks at the same tables.[44]

Like other railroaders, dining-car waiters built up seniority, gaining regular runs on the more prestigious (and lucrative) trains. Generally speaking, better tips came from all-Pullman and "limited" trains whose passengers tended to be more affluent. Secondary trains with a mixture of coaches and sleepers, or only coaches, carried passengers of more modest means, some of whom had rarely, if ever, eaten in restaurants and needed to be coached in which utensils to use, or even how to order. Such patrons also might not be familiar with tipping.

When waiters secured a good run, they often became well known to business travelers who might call them by their first names. And if a waiter could greet a patron personally, "Good Evening, Mr. So and So," and know what that person liked to eat, a good tip was much more likely. Very few Americans had personal servants, so the experience of being offered a classy meal by a properly liveried servant was delicious in more than one sense, and in many cases elicited the appropriate noblesse oblige: a generous gratuity. Businessmen, politicians, and celebrities who regularly traveled the same route sometimes specifically booked a train and car on which a familiar waiter or porter worked.[45] Not all passengers were easy to please, however, even on luxury trains. Some were extremely particular concerning the number of minutes their eggs should be cooked, or the cut and doneness of their steak. Nothing less than perfection pleased them, and a mistake or miscue by either cook or waiter could result in one being verbally abused or "stiffed."

Tips made the difference between poverty and a living wage because the railroads expected travelers to make up for the miserly sums they paid their waiters. Pennsylvania Railroad waiter James Corbett worked the *Congressional Limited*, which catered to businessmen and politicians traveling between New York and Washington. He sometimes made $100 in tips in a single day from well-heeled passengers. Corbett also served actors, musicians, and baseball players, but celebrity did not always equate with generosity. The worst tipper in his book was actor Mickey Rooney: "He was one of those guys that was the life of the party except when it ended." Like the Pullman porters, waiters sometimes gained an intimate view of passengers' lives, including a tempestuous moment in Elizabeth Taylor's marriage to Richard Burton. As they lingered in the diner, Corbett recalled, "she was talking loud and making a fuss and he kept telling her to quiet down. Finally he smacked her. [He] kept reading the newspaper the whole time."[46]

Waiters with seniority and reputations for discretion and rectitude, like certain chefs, were tapped for charters and presidential specials. James Corbett proudly served every president from

Harry S. Truman to Ronald Reagan. The former was his favorite: "He was the best person ever. He would come back and sit with the crew . . . He could curse and swear with the best." Richard Nixon was the opposite: "Nothing was ever good enough for him." But whether for president or plebeian, waiting tables was often challenging to one's dignity and pride: "As a black man, you had to take a lot . . . You smiled even if you wanted to cut somebody's throat." L&N waiters had a saying: "When you go to work then leave your feelings at home."[47]

Before waiters obtained regular runs, they often spent years on the extra board. Because they worked only when a shortage or absence of more senior crew members occurred, their incomes and time spent with families were much less predictable. In order to make a decent living, some "extra men" had to keep doubling out. If they were married, they sacrificed home life. And as passenger service (and consequently the number of dining cars) began to decline in the 1950s, even some with considerable seniority found themselves lucky to be working from the extra board and not laid off.[48]

The humblest "waiters" on passenger trains were the food vendors who plied the aisles of coaches. They were the descendants of the news butches (or butchers) who sold candy, snacks, newspapers, and cheap paperback books to coach passengers. By World War II, a "sandwich man" could be found on many a short-distance train. During the war, 16-year-old Malcolm Little, years before he became Malcolm X, lied about his age and got a job on the New York, New Haven & Hartford Railroad's *Yankee Clipper* between Boston and New York, walking up and down the rocking aisles carrying a shoulder-strap sandwich box and 5-gallon aluminum coffee pot, calling out, "Get'cha gooood haaaaaam an'cheeeeeese . . . sandwiches! Coffee! Candy! Cake! Ice Cream!" So successful was the red-haired Malcolm that the waiters and cooks dubbed him "Sandwich Red." But he was also wild, too wild, and eventually lost his job for mouthing off too many times to passengers.[49]

Although the Pullman Company got out of the dining-car business at the turn of the twentieth century, it continued to operate lounge cars that offered a limited menu and beverages (often a full bar). This fleet peaked at nearly 1,200 in 1930, including parlor, buffet, and club cars. Some of them also included sleeping compartments with porter service. Lounge cars were places for first-class passengers to socialize, shielded from their social inferiors in the coaches. Naturally, food and drink were essential to this experience.[50] One to three employees staffed lounge cars, depending on how many people could be accommodated and the extent of the menu. Waiters were trained in basic food handling, so they could pinch-hit in the kitchen if necessary. A single cook, sometimes called an attendant, worked the kitchen. If the car included rooms, the third person was a porter. Pullman lounge-car workers' instruction manuals were extremely detailed, even down to the precise way to pour a bottle of beer or mix a Tom Collins. From the beginning, those who staffed lounge cars were black, but in an effort to intimidate them in the 1920s and 1930s, when porters and attendants were trying to unionize, the Pullman Company began to hire Filipino attendants. In a further experiment in dividing workers, Pullman brought in a handful of Chinese attendants at higher wages than were paid either blacks or Filipinos, for observation lounge-car service on the Union Pacific's *Spokane-Portland Limited* in 1930. Its strategy backfired when passengers complained of inferior service.[51]

Pullman lounge-car employees who were fortunate enough to hold jobs on luxury trains earned good tips. Such was the experience of the remarkable Smock family. At one time father Garrard Smock, Sr. and three sons all worked the rear buffet cars on the Southern Pacific's *Lark*. Sometimes all three brothers pulled the same run.[52] One was the porter, because in addition to the lounge, a car also had a drawing room and five bedrooms. He also worked "upstairs," taking food and drinks to passengers in sleepers who did not wish to mingle in the buffet car. Another brother was a combination cook and bartender, while the third was the waiter. They generally earned more in tips than from their salaries. Business executives who commuted between San Francisco and Los Angeles, before air travel was common, found overnight trains to be the most efficient and generally restful way to maximize their time. Traveling on expense accounts, they tended to be generous tippers, especially when train personnel remembered their names.[53]

Tips varied (although the Smock brothers pooled them and split the total evenly). "It was nothing for a person to get off and give you a dime, and it was nothing for a person to get off and give you twenty, thirty, or fifty dollars even." On plebeian trains, like the SP's all-coach *Coaster* between Los Angeles and San Francisco, lounge-car waiters' tips for a round trip in the 1930s might not even total $3. Out of necessity, they adopted strategies to stretch their earnings. George Henry Smock remembers smuggling a dozen oranges on board. It took two oranges to make a 14-ounce glass of fresh juice, which sold for $1. The first six juice orders of the day came from his own supply, netting him $6 less the cost of the oranges. He also might sneak a pound of bacon and some tomatoes on board and pocket the proceeds from BLT sandwiches made from them (less the cost of the orders for "toast"). Although he later admitted, "it's another form of stealing," he justified it as being necessary to pay his layover expenses.[54]

Luxury trains, like the Union Pacific's *City of Los Angeles*, routinely carried celebrities up through the 1940s. Some of them were stingy, but others were munificent tippers. When Bob Hope rode the *City* to Chicago and back with a group of University of Southern California alumni to attend the USC–Notre Dame football game, he occupied a suite in the lounge car and ran a tab the entire trip. Upon returning to Los Angeles, he tipped the crew the same sum as his tab, about $1,000. Good tips also derived from exercising discretion and overlooking the rules. On the overnight *Lark*, the lounge-car waiter and porter derived a good income from the activities of a beautiful woman in a black dress who would flirt with a passenger, encourage him to tip generously, and then accompany him to his bedroom for the night. She traveled back and forth, never buying a ticket, with the Pullman conductor pocketing an especially "fat tip."[55]

A genuine familiarity sometimes developed between lounge-car crew members and passengers. A business executive who commuted between offices on the *Lark*, learning that the lounge-car waiter or attendant would double back the following evening, might say, "Well, it looks like it's gonna be a good day in San Francisco. Would you keep my coat for me tonight?" The Pullman

Company's reputation for honest employees assured passengers that they could leave most of their belongings on the train. Some passengers even had waiters' home telephone numbers so they could call to determine who was going out on what train. If they weren't going to be served by their favorites, some passengers postponed their trips.[56]

The lounge car was the train's bar, and more than once, bartenders (cooks) and waiters ignored state liquor laws in order to win large tips. G. W. "Babe" Smock, youngest of the three brothers, quickly learned the ropes on the *Lark:* "There was a two o'clock law as far as sellin' whiskey is concerned, but as long as the train is runnin' and the train conductor is on your side, you don't have to worry about nothin'. You can just buy whiskey all night long." One night, when James Steele worked the SP's *West Coast*, crooner Bing Crosby got on at Bakersfield at 2:00 a.m. with a reservation for the lounge-car bedroom. Crosby, who knew Steele by name, asked him to fix a highball. Steele reminded him that it was past the liquor cut-off, "but you know I'll bring it to you." Crosby did not disregard Steele's risk, giving him a $25 tip.[57]

Pullman lounge-car waiters and cooks had an advantage not enjoyed by their sleeping-car brethren: sometimes they worked together to "hustle" their passengers in order to get large tips. A well-lubricated poker game, with lots of money on the table, was such an opportunity. "So they'd be drinking a while, and maybe you'd take a box of Black & White [whiskey] or whatever they're drinkin'—ten [miniature bottles] in a box—set it on the table and say, 'Now, you fellas have been real nice to us. We wanna buy this round.'" If the gambit worked as planned, one of the men would reply, "Oh, hell no," and laid down a $20 bill, twice the cost of the beverages, and a clean $10 tip.[58] Malcolm Little (Malcolm X) observed about this strategy, "We were in that world of Negroes who are both servants and psychologists, aware that white people are so obsessed with their own importance that they will pay liberally, even dearly, for the impression of being catered to and entertained."[59]

Lounge-car employees had no intention of giving away food or drink, because they, like the dining car personnel, had to meticulously account for all supplies. At one time, the Pullman Company valued a lemon at 30 cents, and prescribed that a glass of lemonade required the juice from only half a lemon. But if the lemon wasn't juicy enough, and it took the entire lemon for the beverage, the waiter owed the company 15 cents. A lemon slice for tea was supposed to be one-eighth of the lemon, but if a waiter's meal checks only showed seven orders and the remaining slice was not to be found, his pay was docked. Lounge cars served breakfasts and lunches, and a loaf of Pullman bread was supposed to yield so many slices. If the number of sandwiches or pieces of toast showing on meal checks did not equal the amount of bread used—perhaps the toast got burned—the cook had to pay. As "Babe" Smock recalled, "They were so stinkin' tight that they could tell me that, 'G.W., you're using an excessive amount of sugar this time.'"[60] The Pullman Company was more than simply "tight." It treated its black employees as if they were delinquent children, not to be trusted.

Passenger theft, even of a single spoon or napkin, was another problem, not of their own making, for which lounge-car personnel and dining-car waiters were made to pay. Sugar bowls and silverware were commonly appropriated as "souvenirs." Confronting a passenger was a no-no, however. Virgil Smock described the attendants' helplessness. "Why I've known people to take a sugar bowl at night, and I'd tell the conductor, 'When [the porter is] puttin' away the bed, I wanna go back and take it.' He said, 'No, you can't do that, Smock.' 'But, oh, yes sir, that's the man that took it.' But you're afraid to approach the passenger. If you [the passenger] say you don't have it, the Pullman Company's in jeopardy of a suit." So the black employee had to pay for the missing item.[61] It would have been just as "logical" for the white dining car steward to be responsible—after all, he was the boss of the dining car—but only the black employees were liable for such losses.

Lounge-car staff had to deal with more passenger abuse than any other crew members, because their car was the train's bar. Liquored-up passengers had to be handled with care. James Steele recalled that, "in them days, if the white man could kick your butt, he did. But if you showed him that you'll kick his butt back, he wouldn't bother you." Waiters always announced the cut-off of liquor sales at least 10 minutes ahead of time. Once, during World War II, an already-inebriated military officer, who had been boasting of killing Japanese with his bare hands, ordered drinks after closing. When Steele refused, the officer followed him back to the kitchen, making threats. "So I reached and got the steel that I sharpened knives [with]. And I got a French bread knife, and I hit it four or five times [to sharpen it]. I told his wife, 'If you don't want his guts emptied on this floor, you better come and get him,'" which she did. Fortunately, the conductor wired ahead to the next station, where MPs hustled the officer off the train. On another occasion, a passenger approached Steele, saying "Hey, nigger, give me a scotch and soda." He replied: "My name is on the door out there: 'Steele,' see? And I don't appreciate you callin' me that. And if you don't want to get knocked on your you-know-what, don't call me that again." Whereupon the passenger apologized and gave him a $10 tip. In relating such incidents, Steele admitted that "I swallowed a lot of times to keep from losing my job, 'cause I had Sears to pay."[62]

One battle a lounge-car crew couldn't win concerned the Pullman Company's wage rip-off. They weren't paid for the hours between the end of liquor sales and the car's reopening in the morning. This was supposed to be their rest period. When the *Lark* left San Francisco at 9 in the evening, the waiters and cook had already been on duty for a couple of hours. The car could stay busy right up to the end of liquor service at 2:00 a.m. But that didn't necessarily mean that passengers left the car. "We say, 'we have to close up at two o'clock. We can give you three or four boxes of [miniature bottles of] scotch or bourbon or whatever you're drinkin', and you can keep on partyin', and then we can open 'em for you.' We'd be busy cleaning up and feedin' 'em, or they'd leave at four-thirty or five o'clock. Then it's time to start breakfast, so you didn't go to bed. But the company wouldn't pay you for that though, see, 'cause you're supposed to close down. But if the tips were good, oh, say your guys had an eight-dollar check. He'd give ya three dollars." By the time the train arrived in Los Angeles at 9 in the morning, and the crew had closed and cleaned their car, they had been on their feet for 15 or more hours, although they would not be paid for 4 of them.[63]

The Pullman Company used World War II as an opportunity to further squeeze work from its employees. Citing the manpower shortage, it reduced lounge-car staff to two, leaving only a cook and one waiter, with no additional pay but record numbers of passengers. The waiter now had to serve as porter to the room passengers as well as wait on tables, while the cook not only worked the kitchen, but also went out front to serve food. Once the war was over, the union requested the return of the third man, but the company replied, "Well, you worked it for four years without him, why should we put him back?"[64] Even worse was how the New Haven Railroad capitalized upon the successful use of women waitresses on its grill cars during World War II. In 1949, the road cut costs by replacing 10 diners with grill cars, laying off 79 veteran black waiters (one-third of the force), and hiring white waitresses off the street.[65]

Dining- and lounge-car cooks and waiters, in common with other black railroaders, had to battle for almost every improvement in pay and working conditions, not to mention promotion beyond the race ceiling. Apart from USRA pay increases during World War I, nothing came without struggle. But dining-car employees were more successful than nearly all other black railroaders in unionizing and achieving gains through collective action. A number of independent unions and associations formed during the World War I years, with several merging in 1920. By 1926, the Brotherhood of Dining Car Cooks and Waiters represented 3,000 workers on 7 lines, including the nation's 2 largest, the New York Central and Pennsylvania Railroad, plus 2 of the 3 major southeastern carriers, the Southern Railway and Atlantic Coast Line. Other small independent unions spoke for waiters and cooks on roads west of Chicago. Although neither powerful nor national in scope, these organizations nonetheless negotiated modest improvements in grievance procedures, benefits, and pay for their members, concrete progress that no other black railroad unions could yet claim. Their successes rested on the fact that each railroad individually negotiated with its own employees. The cooks and waiters did not confront a giant corporation, like the Pullman Company. And in some cases, individual railroads were not resistant to small unions that did not make threatening demands and accepted nominal improvements.[66]

Not all waiters and cooks were satisfied with the BDCCW, however, and began to establish locals affiliated with the American Federation of Labor's Hotel and Restaurant Employees International Alliance. SP employees in Los Angeles and Oakland, deeply angry over being forced to work an extra 45 unpaid hours a month, organized HRE locals and won a fair contract with a 5.5 percent pay increase. As other HRE locals sprang up across the country in the 1930s, they used the amended Railway Labor Act to win representation elections and supplant the BDCCW and other independent unions as the cooks' and waiters' representatives. Then, in order to achieve greater power within the HRE, which represented mostly white, mostly non-railroad service workers, and to gain a uniform, nationwide wage covering all lines, black activists established a Joint Council within the HRE that succeeded, by the mid-1940s, in "dramatically transforming labor-management relations." With 15 locals representing 9,000 members working on 47 railroads, many cooks and waiters for the first time had guaranteed grievance procedures, secure seniority rights, reduced weekly hours, paid vacations, and incremental wage increases. Not all HRE locals satisfied their members, however, and in the late 1940s an independent Dining Car and Railroad Food Workers Union took over representation of nearly 3,000 Pennsylvania Railroad employees, plus others on the Milwaukee Road.[67] Considering both the HRE and DCRFW, only the sleeping-car porters gained as much from collective action as did the waiters and cooks. Only where blacks controlled their own unions (or in the case of the HRE, their own locals) and monopolized jobs, could they hope to win meaningful, lasting concessions from corporate or labor giants. The persistent opposition of white unions and railroads to promoting black waiters to dining-car stewards, even though many had good educations (some were college graduates) and ample experience, proves this point.

The position of steward evolved in the late nineteenth century as dining-car operations increased, menus became more complex, passengers demanded higher levels of service, and the railroads sought to minimize expenses by careful allocation of food and meticulous record keeping. Judging from the number of anticipated passengers, stewards requisitioned the appropriate supplies from the commissary. During dining hours they seated guests, saw that they were properly served, accepted payment, and made change. Throughout the journey they supervised both cooks and waiters. At the conclusion of the run, stewards filled out forms to account for all supplies consumed and remaining.[68] Numerous waiters could have capably exercised these responsibilities.

The railroads had long followed the penny-pinching practice of making black "waiters-in-charge" responsible for some dining cars.[69] They were expected to carry out the steward's tasks while also waiting on tables. Despite the added responsibility, they were paid only a pittance more than other waiters. And being "in charge" was an occupational dead-end because stewards were by definition white. The Brotherhood of Railway Trainmen represented stewards and sought the enactment of state laws requiring stewards in charge of all cars—dining, lounge, club—where food or drinks were served. Although unsuccessful, they persisted in maintaining that stewards must be white, and to this the railroads agreed. Waiters-in-charge sought to improve their position in the 1930s by joining the HRE, which fought for a steward's pay. Events came to a head during World War II. The FEPC ordered a number of roads to promote waiters-in-charge to steward. Only the Chicago and North Western acted more or less willingly, upgrading five waiters-in-charge and adding them to the stewards' seniority roster in 1944. It was the first line to hire black stewards. The Pennsylvania Railroad was already facing an adverse ruling from the Railway Adjustment Board, but was prepared initially only to grant steward's pay to waiters-in-charge, but not promote them. Seeing the FEPC handwriting on the wall in 1944, however, it advanced several experienced waiters-in-charge to steward. But the New York Central didn't budge under FEPC censure. Its subsidiary, the Boston & Albany Railroad, hired new white stewards lacking railroad experience while ignoring the applications of seasoned black waiters-in-charge. In fact, the NYC didn't appoint any black stewards until after the war, and then only men of light complexion. They weren't allowed to work on prestige trains like the *Twentieth Century Limited* until years later. The Delaware, Lackawanna & Western, Louisville & Nashville, and Missouri–Kansas–Texas railroads likewise refused to promote waiters-in-charge during the war. The Erie Railroad was particularly stubborn, stonewalling into the mid-1950s. When veteran workers Benjamin A. Thompson and Edward Williams filed a complaint and the New Jersey civil rights commission ordered the Erie to "cease and desist from discriminating in employment and upgrading of employees," the unrepentant road simply abolished the position of steward.[70]

Following the World War II spurt in train travel, the number of passengers declined and then plummeted in the 1960s. By then, the railroads had tried numerous expedients to cut costs. One was to prepare simpler food, requiring fewer cooks, served in more spartan settings than in traditional dining cars. Not only trains geared to the common folk, now even first-class trains had a café car, staffed by one cook, a waiter-in-charge, and a second waiter. Diners ate at a lunch counter, sitting on stools. Menu selections and prices were more in tune with coach passengers' pocketbooks. The cook and waiters shared dishwashing duties.[71]

The civil rights revolution of the 1950s and 1960s eroded longstanding racial barriers, but it was too late for most train-service employees. Railroads slashed passenger trains and dining cars. Some, like the Southern Pacific, deliberately made travel unpleasant or inconvenient so as to drive away riders and justify ending service. As the era of white tablecloths and gleaming silverware faded, so, too, did waiters' jobs. Only a few blacks finally entered the ranks of steward. For some, such an opportunity was hollow. Louie Stewart refused the Louisville & Nashville's offer to become its first black steward because he would lose his waiter's seniority and regular employment to become an "extra" steward, working only when a white steward was sick or took a day off.[72]

Today's Amtrak waiters and stewards are female as well as male and from all ethnic backgrounds. The reasons why generations of African Americans became dining- and lounge-car waiters—particularly, the paucity of good-paying jobs for educated black men—thankfully no longer exist. And understandably, many blacks today shun jobs that carry an historic servant connotation. To most black dining-car employees now, it's not a heritage, it's just a job.

Although most southern broad- and narrow-gauge railroads were standard-gauged in 1886, the 74-mile Gainesville Midland Railway, in northeast Georgia, did not do so until 1908 and 1913. Here a section crew has just laid heavier standard-gauge rails outside the 3-foot narrow-gauge tracks, which will soon be taken up. Some lines simply moved one rail to change the gauge, but the GM opted to upgrade the rail weight to accommodate heavier locomotives and cars. Short-line railroads occasionally elevated blacks to responsible positions, and it appears that the crew boss is the black man in the middle back, with the watch chain hanging from his bib overalls. The white man was an acquaintance of the photographer, not a railroad employee. Cicero C. Simmons photograph, Theodore Kornweibel collection

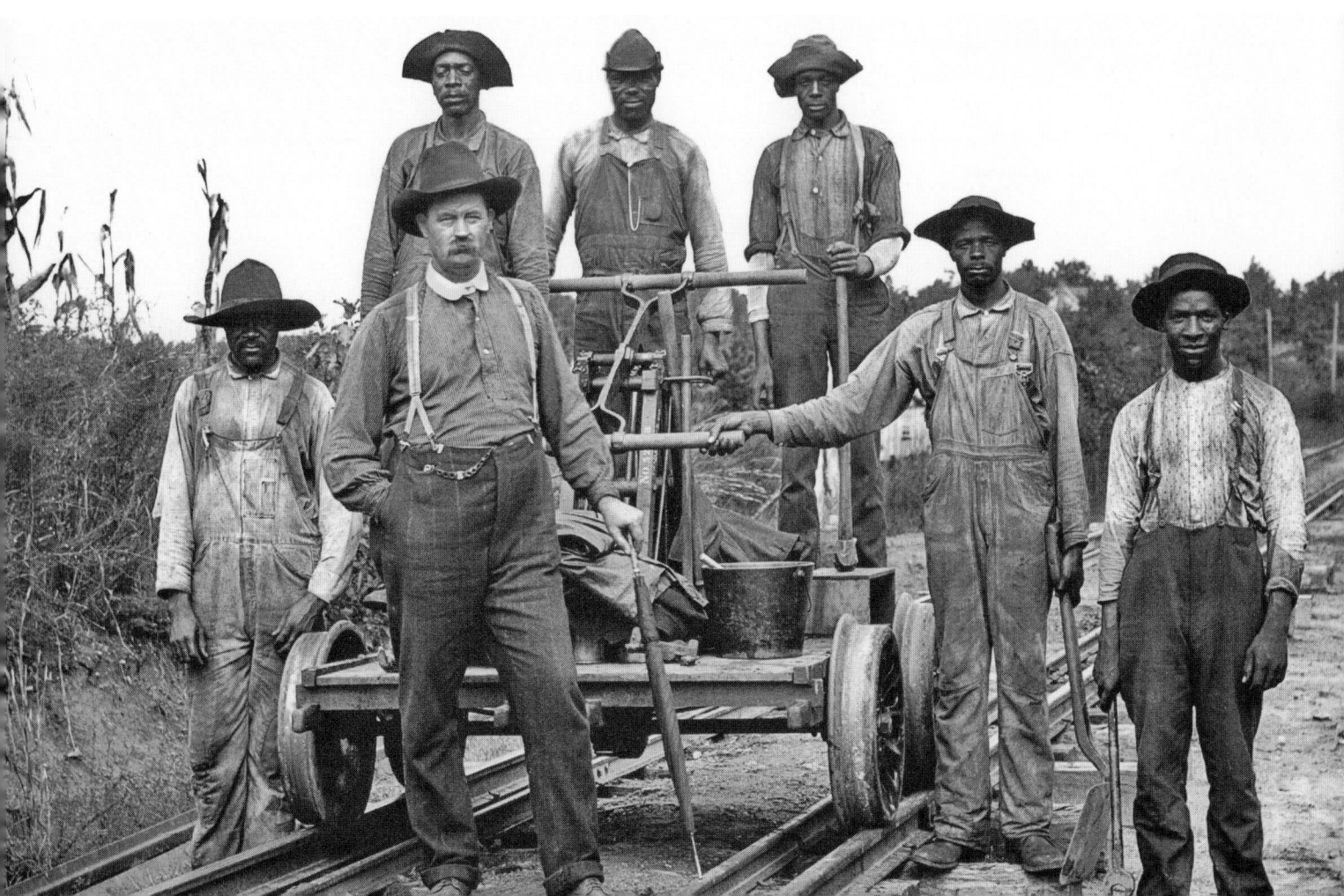

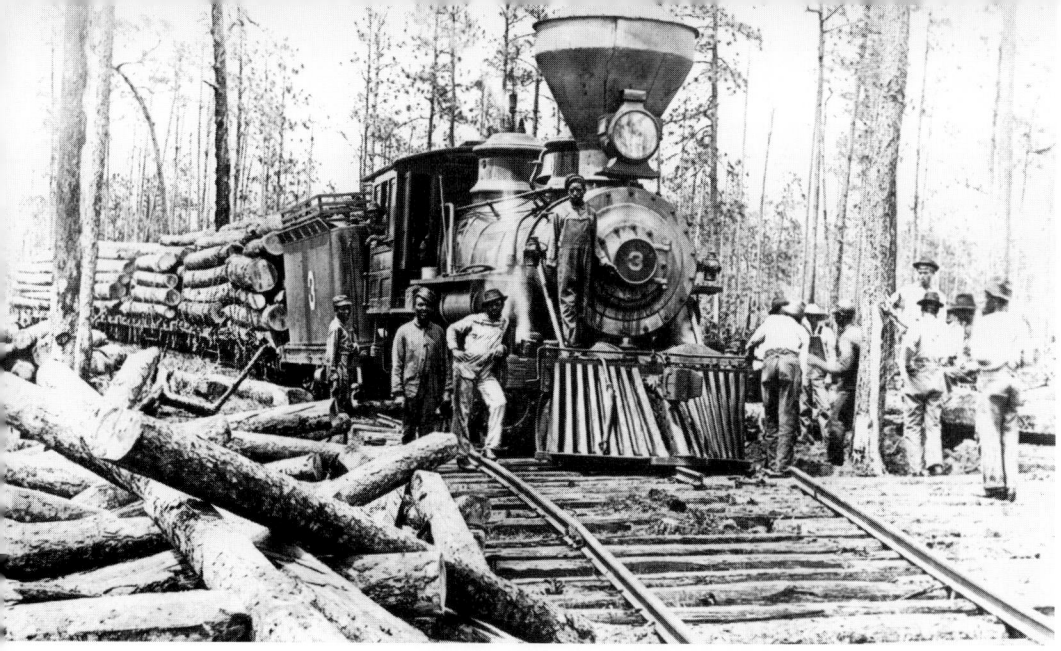

(ABOVE) *Black engineers and firemen could be found on southern logging railroads, which were not common carriers and not unionized by the white railroad brotherhoods. Here, c. 1910, the Bagdad Land & Lumber Co.'s all-black train crew, plus several loggers, ponder how to re-rail their locomotive, a second-hand 2-8-0 unsuited for running on the rickety trackage in the woods near Svea, Florida. State Library and Archives of Florida*

(BELOW) *Where large track maintenance jobs required many more laborers than a regularly assigned section gang, an "extra gang" was called in. This Norfolk & Western Railway extra force was laying steel on the Columbus line near Lucasville, Ohio, in 1910. Nearly 175 men were on the job, about 60 of which appear in this picture. Most of them were black, including the cooks standing in the doorways of the second and third outfit cars. The foremen were white. Norfolk & Western Collection, Digital Library and Archives, University Libraries, Virginia Polytechnic Institute and State University*

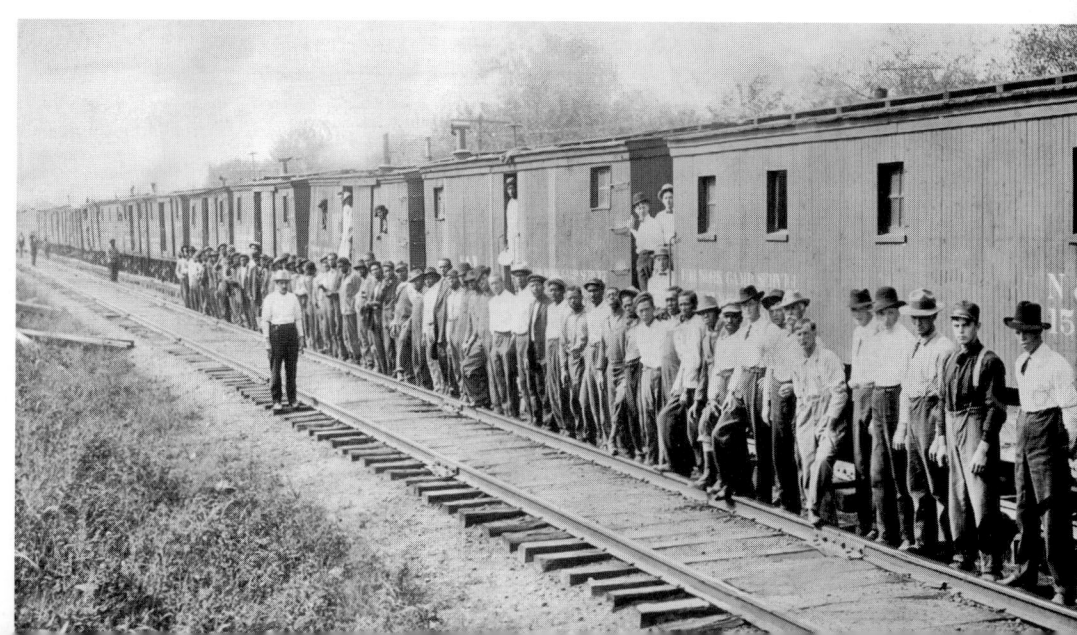

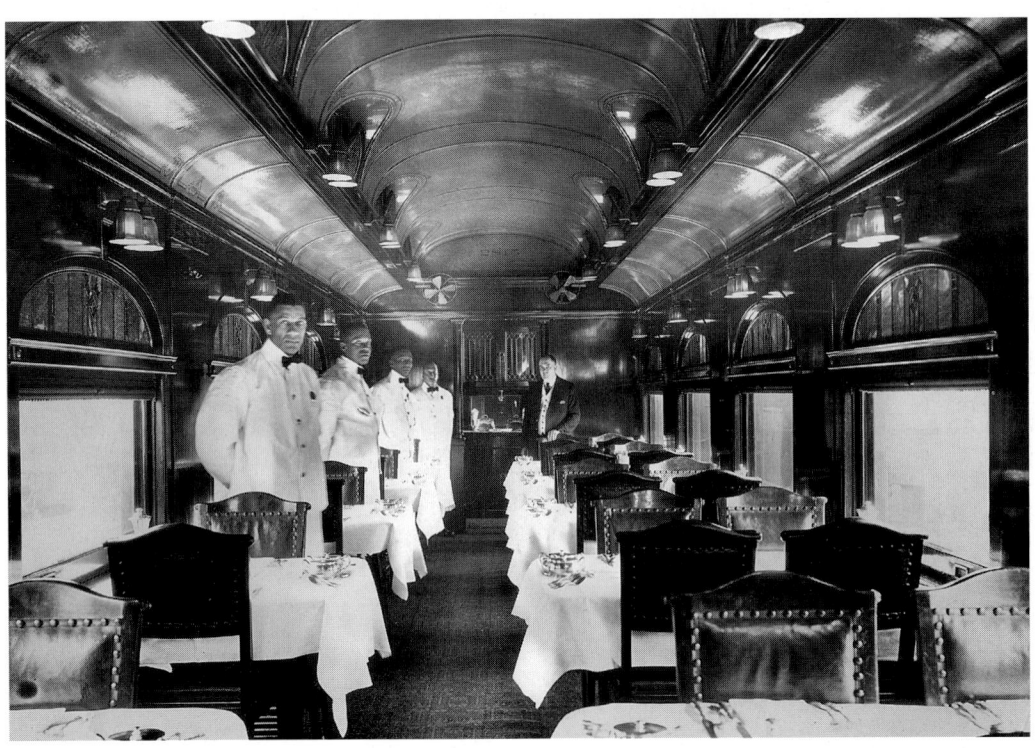

Blacks found work as dining car waiters on the Canadian Northern Railway, seen here c. 1916, and other lines north of the border, although they did not come close to achieving a racial monopoly as they did in the United States. Arthur D. Dubin Collection, Special Collections, Donnelley and Lee Library, Lake Forest College

(OPPOSITE) *Pullman porters worked in Canada as well as the United States, including runs on the Temiskaming & Northern Ontario Railway, whose train 47, traveling up from North Bay to Englehart, wrecked on March 9, 1914, near the town of Cobalt. All but this last car overturned. The "Cobalt Special," as it was known locally, carried through Pullman sleeping cars from Toronto, which reached North Bay on the Grand Trunk Railway. Theodore Kornweibel collection*

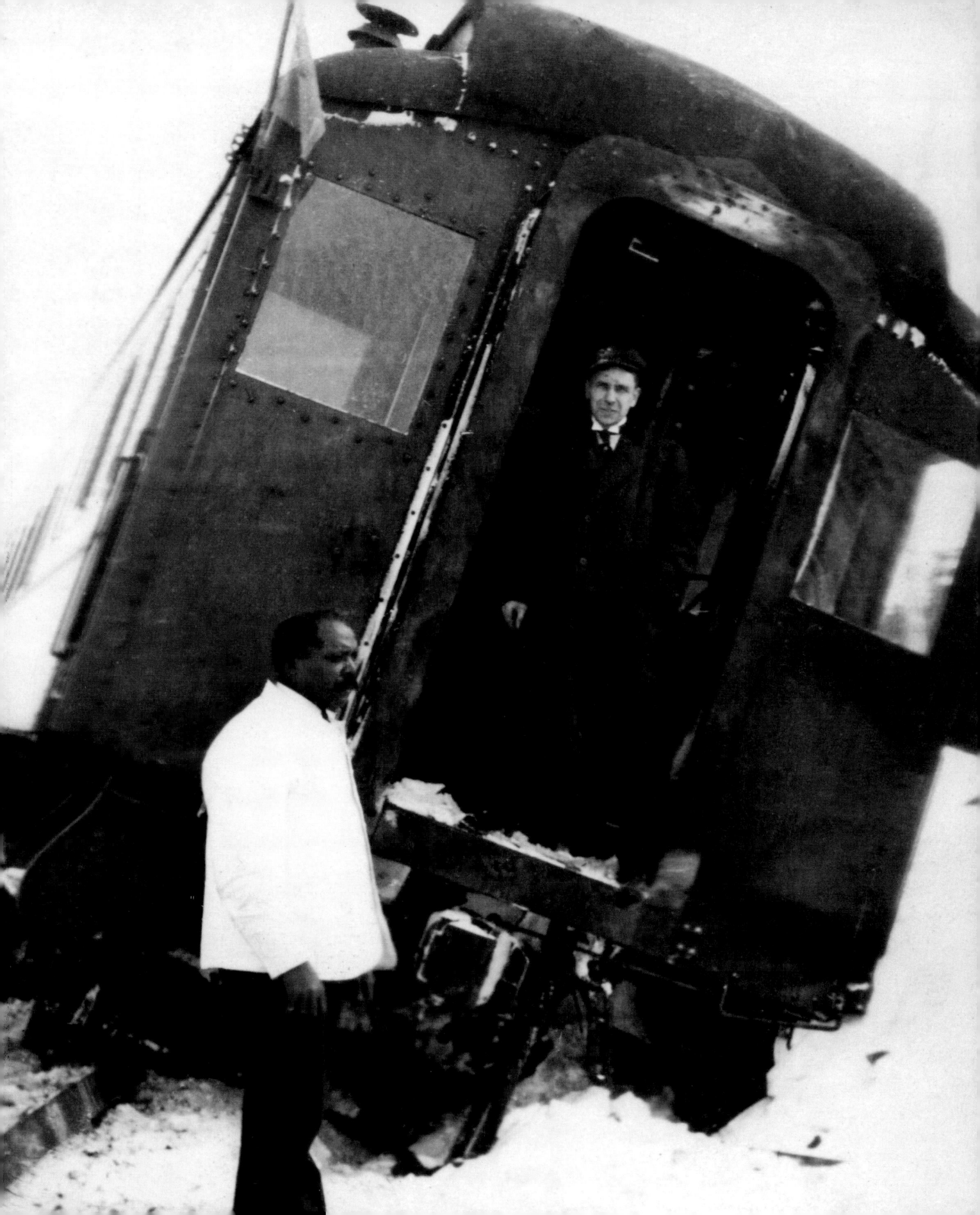

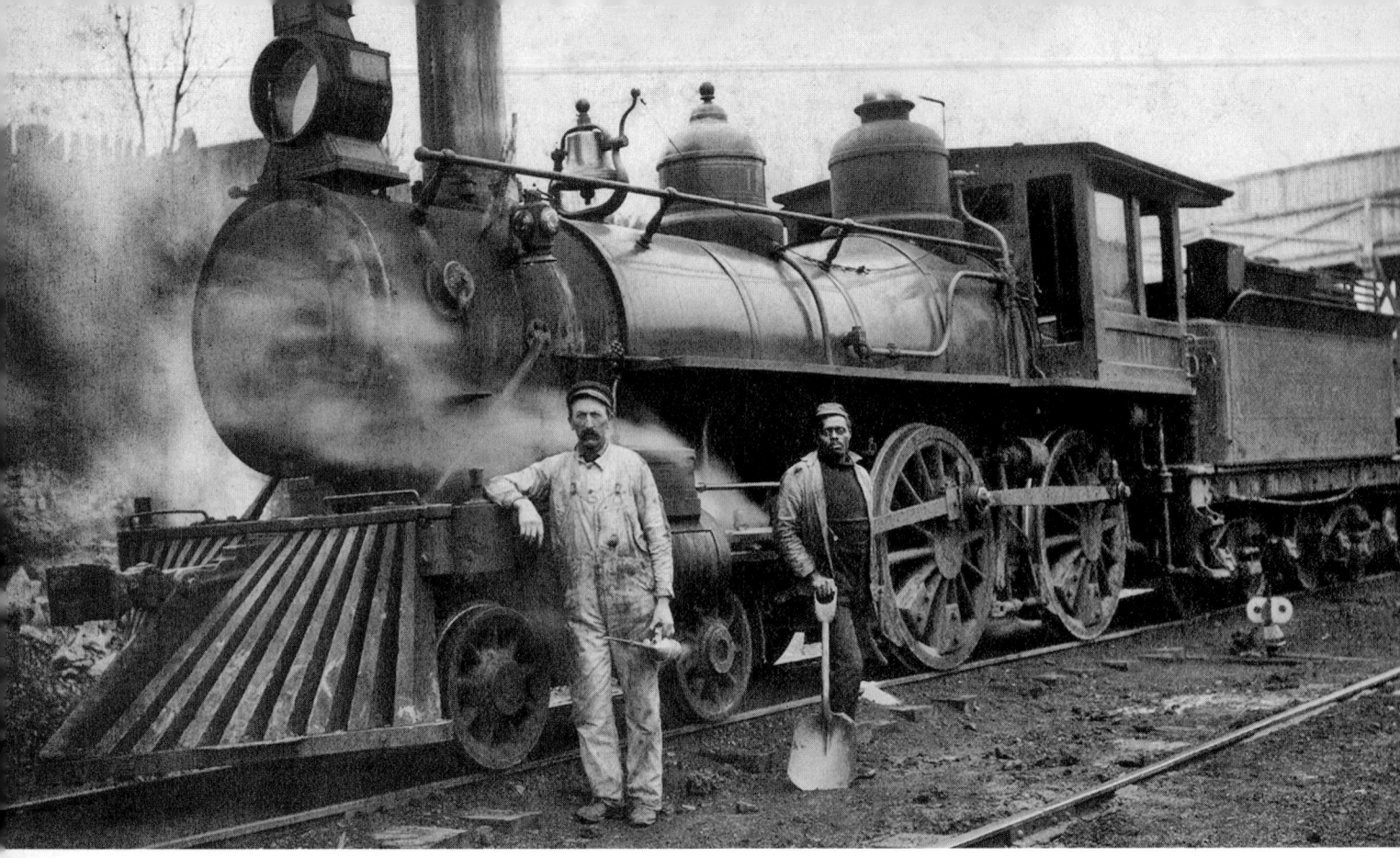

Southern railroads' black firemen frequently worked for years on the same locomotive and with the same engineer, developing a close, if socially unequal, relationship. Mobile & Ohio Railroad fireman Will Terrill and engineer William F. McKnight display the classic tools of their trades, coal scoop and oil can, at Meridian, Mississippi, in 1911. Their elderly locomotive, leaking steam, needs to go to the shop for repairs. Gulf, Mobile & Ohio Collection of the John W. Barriger III National Railroad Library, University of Missouri—St. Louis

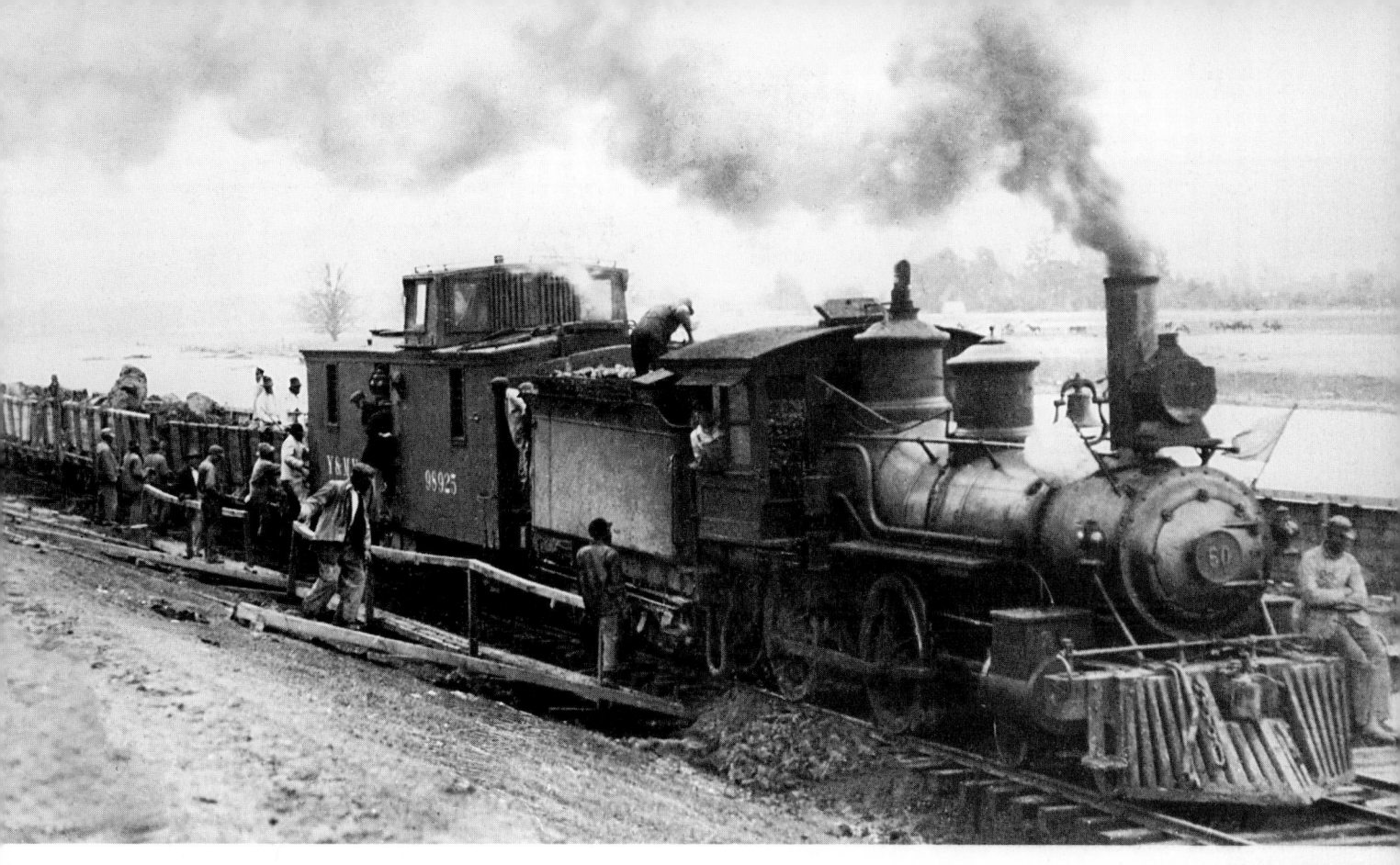

If a single photograph could typify the African American railroad heritage, it might be this of a Yazoo & Mississippi Valley Railroad work train near Greenville, Mississippi, in 1912. Aside from the engineer leaning out of the locomotive cab, every other individual is black, from the brakeman on the pilot to the fireman on the tender and the numerous section men preparing to strengthen a levee with the boulders in the gondola cars. The Y&MV could not have existed without black muscle-power. W. A. Lucas Collection, reprinted by permission, Railroad Museum of Pennsylvania

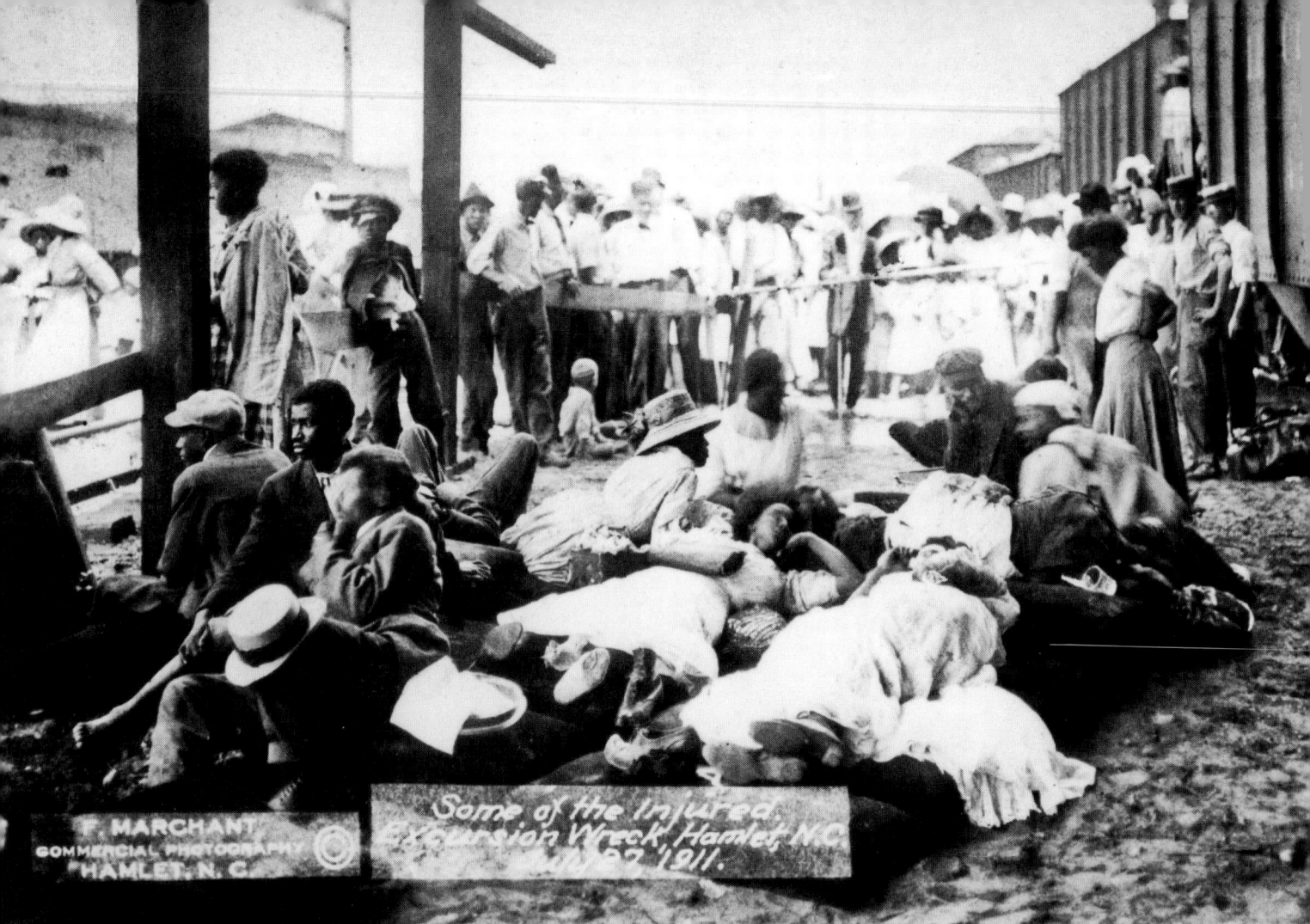

Some of the Injured.
Excursion Wreck Hamlet, N.C.
June 27 1911.

F. MARCHANT
COMMERCIAL PHOTOGRAPHY
HAMLET, N.C.

A crowded excursion train on the Seaboard Air Line Railway crashed head-on into a freight train at the town of Hamlet, North Carolina, in 1911, killing nearly a dozen and injuring many more. As was often the case, the railroad assigned old wooden coaches for use by black excursionists. Such cars crushed horribly in such an impact, resulting in many more casualties than if more modern steel cars had been used. Courtesy of Durham Historic Photographic Archives, North Carolina Collection, Durham County Library

Segregated station facilities in the South were more likely to be equal for both races at small depots where accommodations were basic. The 435-mile (main line) Virginian Railway, hauling coal out of West Virginia to Hampton Roads, near Norfolk, built rural depots from a standard plan in which the waiting rooms were the same in size and amenities. Such stations were scattered all along the line, which was completed in 1909. Flush toilets were not provided for either race, although there would have been separate outhouses. Theodore Kornweibel collection

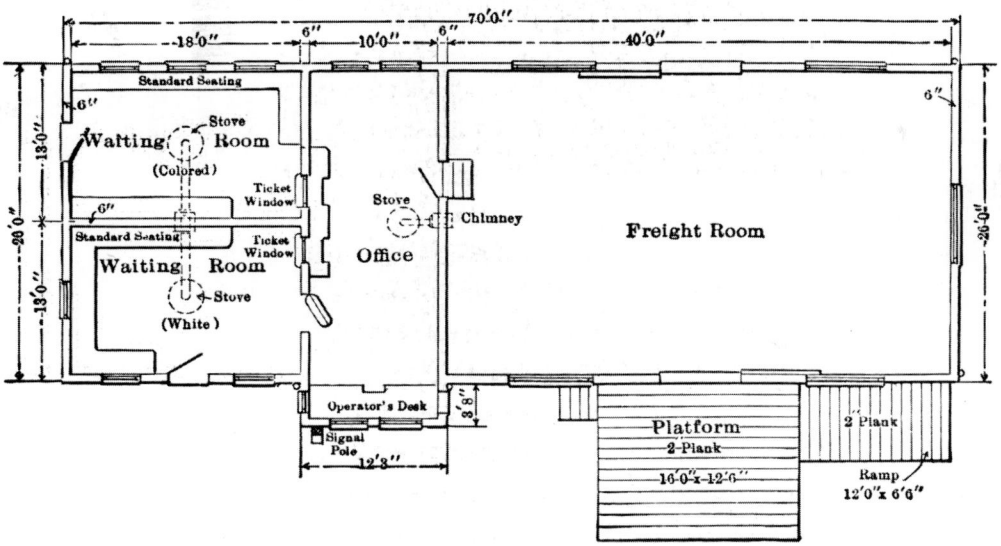

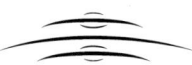

"FAREWELL— WE'RE GOOD AND GONE"

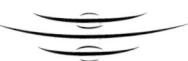

7

Railroads and Black Migration

R obert Horton's barbershop in Hattiesburg, Mississippi, like such establishments all over black America, was a neighborhood center where community issues could be safely discussed away from the ears of whites. Throughout the fall of 1916, particularly on Saturdays when the latest copy of the *Chicago Defender* arrived, the pros and cons of migration were increasingly debated. When Horton decided to move to Chicago he had little difficulty persuading nearly 40 others to join him in a "migration club." Taking advantage of the Illinois Central Railroad's discounted group fares, they transplanted themselves the following January to the Windy City, where Horton opened the Hattiesburg Barber Shop, which became a gathering place for former Mississippians.[1]

Horton was a participant in the Great Migration, the most important African American phenomenon in the first half of the twentieth century. A hundred years ago, 90 percent of blacks lived in the South, overwhelmingly in rural areas. Today, only half the black population is southern, and the vast majority of all blacks dwell in cities. Credit the railroads with making these momentous shifts possible. Railroads offered new jobs to tens of thousands of blacks while simultaneously providing more than a million with a cheap and efficient means by which to liberate themselves from southern racism and poverty. But this was not the first notable black migration, nor the first in which railroads played a role.

The geographical center of slavery in the Revolutionary era was Virginia; by the Civil War, three decades into the railroad era, it was in Georgia. Most of this transplantation took place after 1815 as rich new agricultural lands in the Deep South beckoned settlers, many of them slaveholders. This demographic shift was also stimulated by the interstate slave trade. Earlier slave traders had to march their human wares overland, taking weeks and months to reach new markets. By the 1840s, they could transport their captives by rail in a matter of days. Sometimes riding in coaches, sometimes simply in boxcars, ultimately hundreds of thousands of slaves left declining agricultural economies in the upper South to take up involuntary residence in the Cotton Belt and beyond. So in the three decades before the Civil War the economic viability of slavery was in good measure dependent upon railroads, not just to move agricultural products toward distant markets, but also to funnel fresh workers into newly opened regions.

The South's railroads also figured in slaves' resistance. For a fortunate few, it was their path to freedom. Runaways either concealed themselves on trains or rode openly in coaches, having disguised themselves or carrying false identity papers. The most famous flight was that of William and Ellen Craft, who traveled from Georgia to Boston in 1848 on a succession of trains and steamboats. She was light-skinned enough to disguise herself as an invalided white gentleman who was accompanied by "his" faithful manservant.[2] One of the most-traveled escape routes was between Maryland and Pennsylvania. Dressed as a sailor, Frederick Douglass boarded a train in Baltimore carrying forged seaman's papers, but no free papers. When the conductor asked to see proof he was a free man, he replied, "No sir; I never carry my free papers to sea with me," while handing him the sailor's document. Fortunately, the conductor did not examine it painstakingly.[3] The Philadelphia, Wilmington & Baltimore Railroad eventually required that blacks departing from Baltimore appear at the ticket office by 8:00 a.m. to allow sufficient time to check the authenticity of their free papers, without which they would not be permitted to board.[4] Despite such precautions, runaways continued to use this line, then to be taken in hand by well-organized abolitionists in Philadelphia. This group also received fugitives traveling on the Philadelphia & Reading Railroad's cars between Harrisburg, Reading, and Philadelphia. Other abolitionists helped slaves flee westward on the Baltimore & Ohio Railroad to Pittsburgh and on to Erie, Pennsylvania, or Cleveland and, if necessary, Canada.[5]

On at least one occasion, an entire group of fugitives took a train for the last part of their flight. The general superintendent of the Michigan Central Railroad was an abolition sympathizer and friend of detective and abolitionist Alan Pinkerton. When 11 escapees reached Chicago, Pinkerton arranged with that railroad official for a passenger car, stocked with food and water, to carry them on the final leg of their journey to Detroit and then across the border to safety in Canada.[6] Other systematic Underground Railroad efforts utilized the Illinois Central. Near Tamaroa, in southern Illinois, an abolitionist had a siding installed on his property, concealing fugitives in empty boxcars that were then picked up by northbound trains. Several IC employees in Centralia, including a freight conductor, likewise hid runaways in boxcars, supplying them with food to last them until they got to Chicago.[7] During the Civil War, many more slaves were able to take advantage of unsettled conditions and use trains to make good their escape, especially from Missouri and Maryland.[8]

The burden of denying passage to runaways was usually on the railroad, although it was often very difficult for conductors or ticket sellers to determine the status of a passenger. Georgia law stipulated slaves could travel only with an owner, employer, overseer, or a written permit from such persons. If a runaway escaped successfully, the railroad was to reimburse the owner for the market value of the slave.[9] Missouri law permitted masters to sue a railroad for twice the slave's value if the slave was carried without the owner's permission.[10] Understandably, the North Carolina Railroad's regulations stated that conductors "shall not allow any servant to pass on the Cars without a written pass, unless in company with the owner; and the pass shall be returned to the Ticket Agent" at the slave's destination.[11]

Southern courts disagreed, however, on the culpability of the railroads for successful escapes. The South Carolina Supreme Court ruled that the South Carolina Railroad was not liable for the flight of two brothers because railroad employees could not be expected to detect that someone passing for white was actually black. The Georgia Supreme Court, in 1861, ruled similarly that requiring conductors to question "every white passenger having a dark complexion, and refusing . . . conveyance unless he could prove his descent from Caucasian parents" unduly burdened a railroad. But six years later the Georgia court took the opposite position, ruling, "however white in color, as it seems she [the runaway] was (though she had negro blood in her veins), we have no power to regard that fact as excusatory or altering the right of the owner to recovery of damages." The Tennessee Supreme Court ruled that a railroad was required to ascertain if one presenting a written pass was in fact the slave so named in the pass.[12]

As involuntary servitude ended, many former slaves did not feel truly free until they tried out their liberties. Train travel became an important expression of one's new status. All over the South, freed people congregated at stations. Some were actual travelers. Others lacked the financial means but fantasized of departing or nursed dreams of better opportunities elsewhere. During slavery, blacks had begun to associate the awesome power of steam engines with freedom and escape. No less now, they excited the imaginations of young and old, representing longings, hopes, and new beginnings. "As the train passes, the negroes gather in groups to gaze at it, until it disappears in the distance." At a small town in Virginia, "the negroes . . . swarm day and night like bees about the trains." Where once the Underground Railroad inspired dreams of escape, now the actual railroads did the same, for far greater numbers.[13]

No sooner had the war ended than the availability of railroad jobs began to influence black demographics. War-ravaged southern lines had to be rebuilt. At the same time, northern investment capital stimulated new southern railroad construction. Many ex-slaves who knew nothing but farm labor eagerly exchanged hoes, plows, and the scant earnings of sharecropping for railroad picks, shovels, and cash wages. Tens of thousands left the Deep South for railroad work west of the Mississippi. Railroads also facilitated the redistribution of labor into newly opened agricultural regions. The Vicksburg & Meridian Railroad, for example, transported thousands fleeing crop failures in Alabama to rich new farms in the Mississippi Delta. Railroaders themselves were sometimes the pioneer members of new black communities. The first black settlers in Fort Lauderdale, arriving in 1895–96, were laborers for the Florida East Coast Railway. Railroads also facilitated micromigrations, where blacks took flight following a spate of racial violence. In early 1890 *Frank Leslie's Illustrated Newspaper* reported on a "Negro Exodus" from the Carolinas as a result of "recent murderous outrages perpetrated upon negroes by brutal whites." Large crowds were congregating at many railroad stations, and thousands of blacks had already left the state.[14]

Another type of railroad-propelled migrant was the hobo.[15] African Americans testing their new freedom, as well as itinerant railroad and sawmill workers, may have been the first black hoboes. Traveling from job to job, they snatched rides in "side-door Pullmans" (boxcars). Others were escaping the exploitation of sharecropping or the brutality of chain gangs. Some were musicians who would do much to spread the blues. Whenever the economy plunged into depression the number of hoboes swelled. Black and white hoboes generally got along well, even in the segregated South, "'cause everybody was poor," although altercations took place like the one that led to tragic accusations against the Scottsboro boys in 1931 in Alabama.[16] The races generally ate, drank, and slept together in hobo "jungles" (encampments), sharing not only grub, cigarettes, and bottles, but also a hardship-strewn life, time spent in jail, an inability to "fit in" with conventional society, and a preference for living "on the road." According to one authority, "the hobo jungle was seemingly one of the most racially integrated institutions in America," but another scholar believes that, at least in the Midwest, black hoboes were more likely to be singled out for mistreatment. On Harry Haywood's first hoboing venture, railroad police evicted him and a dozen whites from a train in LaCrosse, Wisconsin. While the others were let go, the locomotive's fireman told the officers to "let me have that young colored boy there to slide down coal for me into Minneapolis." Overall, proportionally fewer blacks than whites were hobos because railroad "bulls" and local police were more harsh toward the former, especially in the South, where white hobos caught by local authorities might spend a night in jail, but blacks could end up on the chain gang.[17]

From 1915 to 1930, one and a half million blacks streamed out of the South to escape discrimination and find better economic opportunities in the North and Midwest. This massive interregional Great Migration would not have been possible without railroads. For most, the only efficient means of long-distance travel was by train. And the first good industrial jobs for blacks outside of the South were on the railroads.

Most migrants traveled up the Mississippi Valley to the Midwest on the Illinois Central, Mobile & Ohio, Southern, and Louisville & Nashville lines, or up the eastern seaboard to the Northeast on the Atlantic Coast Line, Seaboard Air Line, and Southern railways. Those who didn't live near such trunk lines took trains to railroad hubs like New Orleans, Birmingham, Jacksonville, Savannah, and Memphis, and thence traveled northward. Migrants headed particularly for industrial cities like

Chicago, Cleveland, Detroit, Akron, Ohio, and Gary, Indiana. Commercial centers like New York and Philadelphia also experienced tremendous black population growth.[18]

The Great Migration was set in motion by the onset of World War I in Europe. Emigration to the United States dried up as men were conscripted into their national armies. Soon, America began to produce munitions for the western Allies, and eventually for its own rearmament. This surge in industrial and transportation activity required many new laborers. And when America entered the war in early 1917, legions of factory and railroad workers volunteered or were drafted. Northern industries and railroads, for the first time, had to consider employing blacks and women. In short, new job opportunities as well as greater social freedoms provided the necessary "pull" to start a large-scale migration, while longstanding southern "push" factors—lynching, segregation, peonage, disfranchisement, poor schools—supplied additional motivation.

Three stimuli were particularly important in energizing the migration: the railroads; the mail; and an extraordinary black newspaper. The vast majority of migrants rode trains, with the remainder traveling by steamship up the Atlantic seaboard. Although they typically journeyed in groups of two or three, larger aggregations were also common because 10 or more traveling together could purchase group tickets. They usually paid for their own transportation, although in 1916 and 1917 labor agents offered "free" tickets to men (and a few women who disguised themselves as males) who agreed to have their fare deducted on their first payday. Most people left home only after careful deliberation, but a few acted on the spur of the moment, like Clem Woods, lounging at a Mississippi station one night as a northbound train pulled in. When a migrant called out, "Good-bye, bo, I'm bound for the promised land," Woods jumped on board.[19]

The U.S. mail was also a significant stimulus to migration. Northern transplants wrote back home and encouraged others to join them. Letters frequently contained money for train fare or prepaid tickets. Correspondents promised to find jobs and lodging for those who would join them. The arrival of a letter with a northern postmark was a matter of intense community interest. Advances in literacy in the half century since slavery made possible this greater use of the mail. Literacy also promoted the greater influence of black publications.

The *Chicago Defender* played a singular role in promoting the Great Migration. Publisher Robert Abbott made his flamboyant weekly newspaper a voice for all black Americans. Its national edition was widely distributed throughout the South by local agents and dining- and sleeping-car crew members who delivered bundles of the paper to small towns. The fact that the *Defender* had more than 200,000 paid subscribers—far more than any other black publication—does not fully indicate its influence. Each week, thousands of copies were read aloud or passed from hand to hand in southern barbershops, crossroads stores, churches, and fraternal lodges. The *Defender*'s furious rhetoric condemned every instance of southern racial barbarity. It also carried enticing advertisements for northern jobs. When white southerners became aware of the paper's influence in promoting migration, they sought to bar its circulation and, in some instances, forced it underground.[20]

The *Defender* promoted a "Great Northern Drive" to take place on May 15, 1917, exhorting people to board trains on that date. An observer in Savannah wrote three months before the appointed day that "the word has been passed along from father to son, from mother to daughter, brother to brother and sister to sister, prepare for the day is coming." Many did not wait. A Birmingham correspondent reported a month later that "the Great Northern Drive . . . is taking place long before the time set by the paper. They are leaving here by the thousands." Numerous individuals wrote directly to the *Defender*: "There is a great many of us that wants to come and the depot agent never gives us any satisfaction when we ask for they don't want us to leave. Please put in your paper Saturday, just what time the train will be here, and the fare so we can be there on time." In fact, northern train stations received many more arrivals from the South than usual in the days following May 15. In the words of one woman from New Orleans, "Nearly the whole of the South is ready for the drive . . . We are sick to get out of the South."[21]

Northern industries worked directly with the railroads to import new laborers. In 1917, Pittsburgh steel mills used an employment agency in Richmond to arrange transportation on the Baltimore & Ohio and Pennsylvania railroads for an average 150 black workers weekly.[22] But in addition to the many corporations looking for new sources of unskilled hands, northern railroads were also desperate for labor. Because defense industries offered better-paying jobs, northern railroads found themselves chronically short of white workers on their maintenance of way, roundhouse, shop, yard, and freight-house gangs. Of necessity, not benevolence or enlightenment, they turned to the southern black labor pool, recruiting first in Florida and southeastern Georgia, then from North Carolina and Virginia. Soon the Mississippi Valley was tapped for its human resources. The railroads' advantage was their ability to bring in new workers from distant locations at little cost, but, ironically, they were unable to keep most of their new workforce. Because they paid lower wages than other industries and because track gangs often lived in rude bunkhouses made from old box cars, isolated from black communities, the majority of migrants summoned north by the railroads did not long stay in their employ. In mid-1917, while northern railroads paid 19 cents an hour for common labor, construction jobs offered up to 30 cents. The Pennsy was able to retain only 15 percent of the thousands of blacks it had imported in the previous 12 months.[23]

Although the first recruitment of southern blacks began nearly six months before the world war broke out in Europe, when the PRR addressed an immediate labor shortage by bringing five trainloads of laborers up from Savannah in early 1914, a large-scale exodus didn't start until the summer of 1916, when the Erie and the Pennsylvania railroads "promiscuously picked up trainloads of Negroes" from St. Augustine, Pensacola, and Jacksonville, Florida. Future NAACP leader James Weldon Johnson was witness to "the sending North from a Southern city in one day a crowd estimated at twenty-five hundred. They were shipped on a train run in three sections, packed in day coaches, with all their baggage and other impediments."[24]

Why were so many willing to travel so far from home? Georgia farm hands got less than a dollar a day, and even those with industrial jobs earned only about $1.25. Day laborers in Alabama

Railroads in the African American Experience

Black Belt counties averaged no more than 60 cents a day. In contrast, northern unskilled industrial laborers earned as much as $3 daily. Pay on a northern railroad section gang was sometimes four times as much as a southern farm worker's wage.[25] Some white southerners leaned toward more conspiratorial explanations, alleging that blacks were being imported into politically "doubtful" northern states to be ushered to the polls to vote Republican. Attorney General Thomas Gregory, a Texas Democrat, instructed U.S. attorneys in the South to collect the names, hometowns, and destinations of blacks found to be traveling in "suspicious numbers." The Labor Department, however, recognizing the operation of supply and demand, advised southerners that they could slow the exodus by raising wages.[26]

The Pennsylvania Railroad was the largest recruiter of black southerners for railroad work in the North. From July 1, 1916, through July 31, 1917, alone, it provided transportation vouchers for 13,223 blacks. In a 2-week period in mid-August, the Seaboard Air Line hauled 5,000 new Pennsy workers out of Florida and 3,000 from Georgia. Eleven hundred black men, accompanied by more than twice that number of relatives and friends, assembled at Savannah's Union Station at five o'clock one morning to board two special trains destined for maintenance of way camps near Philadelphia. According to a "race" newspaper, "There was nothing of the sorrow of parting in the crowd, everybody who left being in an excursion mood, and those who stayed behind being sure that they would be well taken care of by the wages sent home." The PRR used its white employees, including railroad policemen, as recruiters, sometimes with black intermediaries, although the railroad claimed it didn't pay them directly. While attempts were made to select men between the ages of 21 and 45 who were free from venereal diseases, on some occasions the railroad simply resorted to "backing a train into a southern city and filling it as quickly as possible." Before long, opposition arose from southern political and business interests, including large employers alarmed at the exodus of workers and upward pressure on wages. Recruiters were harassed while the railroad was sued for violating local anti-enticement laws. As a result, the Pennsy claimed to have halted recruiting at the end of July 1917, although in the following two months, carloads of workers were dispatched from Texas.[27]

The Pennsy invested more substantially in black workers' housing than other northeastern lines. By mid-1917, it had erected 35 camps (a few of them housing white workers) in its 5 divisions east of Pittsburgh, each housing from several dozen to several hundred laborers in tarpaper-covered wooden sheds that had steam heat. Similar huts had showers, washrooms, and flush toilets. Workers ate commissary-prepared food in other sheds, paying $4 to $7 per week for meals and only $1 to $2 monthly for the use of a bunk bed. (Less fortunate workers were housed in converted boxcars parked on sidings.) To keep them happy, the company furnished postcards, musical instruments, and phonographs, and later offered to bring their wives up to them. A Department of Labor investigation found these camps to be mostly clean and sanitary. The Pennsy also spent more than other railroads on workers' health, providing at least minimal medical services in all camps. Yet no matter which railroad, or whether workers lived in boxcars, tents, or more permanent

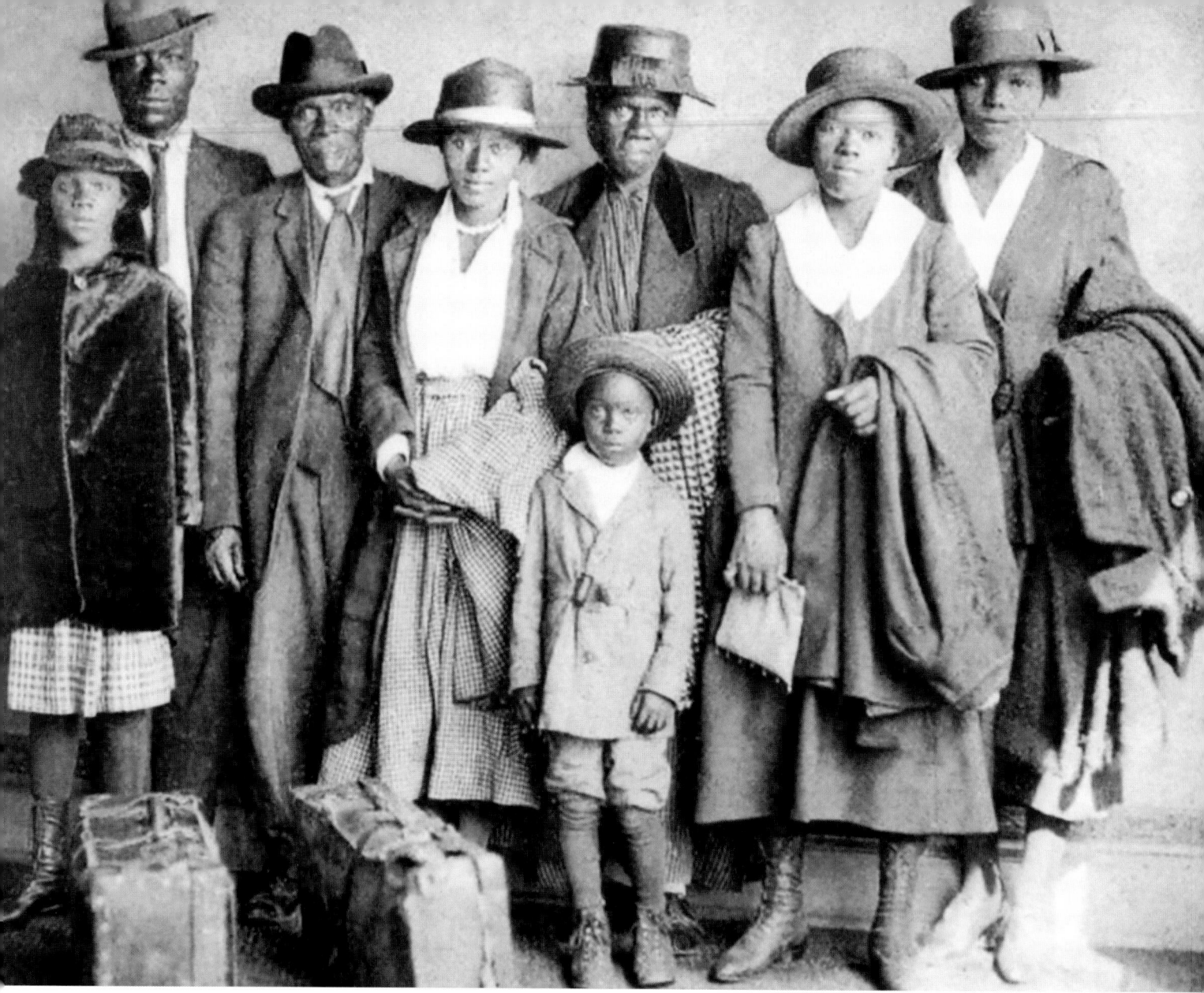

Although initially single men pioneered north-ward black population movements, the Great Migration during and after World War I eventually transplanted entire families, as this three-generational group that has just arrived at a train station in Chicago from the rural South. Theodore Kornweibel collection

housing, health conditions were often poor because migrants brought diseases with them and lived in crowded environments. One railroad's physicians examined 800 workers at a large camp, discovering 70 percent of them to be infected with tuberculosis, syphilis, and especially gonorrhea.[28]

Rarely were the Pennsy's camps full, however, because of the continuous high turnover. In extreme cases, within 10 days of arrival, half of a new batch had already disappeared; more usually, half remained after 2 months. According to a federal investigator, "most of the new Negroes, with the exception of favored cooks and janitors, remained in the camps only long enough to draw a first pay, or until they learned of the opportunity for high wages in the steel and construction fields." Nonetheless, by mid-1917, the PRR employed 4,800 black laborers from Pittsburgh eastward, including some black women track and roundhouse workers doing somewhat lighter tasks than the men.[29]

Another significant importer of southern black laborers was the Erie Railroad, which disputed the Pennsy's claim to having initiated direct recruiting in the South. In the summer of 1916 the Erie brought 9,000 workers up from Florida and Georgia on Clyde Line steamers to New York and from Kentucky to the road's terminus in Cincinnati on special trains, from which they were assigned to track gangs and shops across the system. After investing considerable effort in selecting suitable workers and giving them adequate supervision, only 2,000 stayed long enough to work off the full cost of their transportation. One reason may have been their housing, old wooden coaches converted into sleeping and commissary cars. And when new recruits brought to Hornell, New York, protested the 17 1/2 cent hourly wages for a 10-hour day (expecting the 34 cent wage for skilled shop labor) they were shipped off to isolated section camps to lessen the likelihood of their absconding. So severe was the continual disappearance of new laborers that by mid-1917 the Erie hired 600 black women for work on tracks and in yards.[30]

A third major importer of labor directly from the South was the Baltimore & Ohio, transporting 10,000 blacks on steamers to Baltimore and then to MOW camps across the system. The B&O also paid lower wages than many industries and was able to retain only one-tenth of its recruits. Track workers' housing was sometimes as primitive as that on the Erie. The camp at Hazelwood, near Pittsburgh, consisted of 10 converted boxcars plus "seven old two-story houses." In mid-1917 the B&O was "futilely seeking to fill the depleted ranks of the laborers by new importations from the South," including black women for roundhouse and track labor.[31]

The New York Central was another large railroad offering blacks "free" transportation from the South, importing nearly 10,000 but retaining fewer than 1,000 of them. It established particularly large MOW camps in Cleveland, New York City, and Weehawken, New Jersey, housing workers in converted boxcars that rarely reached 60 percent of capacity because the crude dwellings discouraged workers from staying long. In the constant search for replacements, like other roads, the NYC also hired black women for unskilled labor.[32]

Eastern roads that imported smaller numbers of black workers from the South included the Wabash, Delaware & Hudson, Lackawanna, and Lehigh Valley. In Philadelphia, the Reading

Company employed 1,000 black workers in 1923, one-tenth of its workforce in that city, 20 percent of whom held skilled and semi-skilled jobs. The New York, New Haven & Hartford Railroad, like other New England lines, had long relied on European immigrants for common labor, but when the war dried up that source it tentatively imported 100 blacks from Norfolk, Virginia. When they proved to be satisfactory, the New Haven brought up another 1,400 from that state and nearly 800 from North Carolina.[33]

Midwestern lines that penetrated the South extensively recruited blacks from the Mississippi Valley, with the Illinois Central importing hundreds at a time on "free" transportation. Twice a month in late 1916 and early 1917, the Mobile & Ohio Railroad brought about 15 new employees up to East St. Louis, Illinois, on "gang passes." The Louisville & Nashville also fed new workers into East St. Louis, from which they were dispatched in groups of 50 to work as roundhouse laborers and section hands. Blacks were concentrated in particular locations, not spread equally across entire systems, because northern and Midwestern railroads insisted on segregating their housing and shop washrooms.[34]

Black labor also migrated to railroad jobs in the West. A contractor widening a tunnel for double tracking on the Union Pacific Railroad's main line between Cheyenne and Laramie, Wyoming, imported 3,000 men in 1917 from Georgia and Alabama. When the project was done, some of them remained in the region and helped found black communities in railroad towns across the southern part of the state. By 1930, more Wyoming black men were railroad laborers than any other occupation. Blacks also migrated in significant numbers to Council Bluffs, Iowa, and Omaha, Nebraska, where the UP was a major employer. Davenport and Des Moines, Iowa, on the Chicago, Rock Island & Pacific Railroad's main east-west stem also drew many migrants. And in the Midwest and Northwest, the Great Northern Railway, no longer able to tap traditional sources of immigrant labor, resorted to hiring blacks to fill labor gaps, keeping them in segregated crews, living in separate boarding camps. Some of them eventually settled in Spokane, Washington, helping to establish a community there.[35]

New railroad employees during the Great Migration encountered a nearly impermeable job ceiling. Most lines used black workers almost exclusively as section hands, unskilled roundhouse and shop laborers, freight-house truckers, and waiters, cooks, and coach porters in passenger train service. An exception was the Pennsy shops in Erie, which employed 400 blacks in April 1919, half of whom were skilled. No wonder, then, that turnover was constant, even with much higher wages than in the South. Ironically, the railroads' recruitment efforts supplied labor primarily to other industries, leaving themselves chronically short of workers.[36]

It was common for railroads to deduct the cost of transportation from new workers' first wages. In accepting a "free" ticket, migrants signed agreements like the following:

It is hereby understood that I am to work for the above-named company as _____,
the rate of pay to be _____. The _____ Railroad agrees to furnish transportation and food to destination. I agree to work on any part of the _____ Railroad
where I may be assigned. I further agree to reimburse the _____ Railroad
for the cost of my railroad transportation, in addition to which I agree to pay _____
to cover the cost of meals and other expenses incidental to my employment. I autho-
rize the company to deduct from my wages money to pay for the above expenses. In
consideration of the _____ Railroad paying my car fare, board, and other expenses,
I agree to remain in the service of the aforesaid company until such time as I reimburse them
for the expenses of my transportation, food, etc.

As an incentive, contracts often stipulated that, after a year's satisfactory employment, the cost of
the ticket would be returned to the employee. For a while the Erie Railroad was more generous,
requiring only 60 days' work.[37]

Not surprisingly, blacks' desire to escape from the South made them vulnerable to bogus white
labor agents who sold "registration" cards that supposedly entitled one to train fare and a job. In
one instance in late 1916, 37 blacks purchased such cards and assembled at Douglas, Georgia, where
their "agent" told them he had their tickets to Pittsburgh in hand. They boarded the Jim Crow car,
believing that he was on a "white" coach. But when the conductor came to collect the migrants' tickets, the "agent" was nowhere to be found and the disappointed party was put off at the next station.
In another case, 1,800 Louisiana blacks who were promised jobs in Chicago paid a crooked "agent"
$2 each.[38]

African American migration, when railroads were the primary means of transportation,
involved more than moving one's residence or seeking a better job. It was fundamentally about
raising one's expectations, anticipating more out of life, achieving an improved status in society.
Migration profoundly influenced the psychology of black Americans. And this was often mediated
through their spiritual experiences. The Great Migration took on a distinctive religious tone. Blacks
called it an Exodus, God's appointed time to leave bondage in Egypt (the South), cross the Jordan
River (the Ohio), and reach the Promised Land (the North). Migrants left en masse, as though they
were fleeing a curse. Some chalked slogans reading "Bound for the Land of Hope" and "Bound for
the Promised Land" on the sides of coaches carrying them north. An observer noted the biblical
context of this mass migration: "There are also Negroes of all classes who profoundly believe that
God has opened the way for them out of the restrictions and oppressions that beset them on every
hand in the South; moving out is an expression of their faith." Entering the North took on spiritual significance for many migrants. As a party of 147 from Hattiesburg crossed the Ohio River on
an Illinois Central train, they "knelt down and prayed; the men stopped their watches [signifying
an end to their old life in bondage] and, amid tears of joy, sang the familiar songs of deliverance,

'I done come out of the Land of Egypt with the good news,' . . . 'Beulah Land' and 'Dwelling in Beulah Land.'"[39]

The Great Migration was a folk migration. As southern blacks understood that God had finally appointed the time for their escape, they responded in communal fashion. Although early departures were mostly single men, as it gained momentum entire social entities left together for a common destination. Compared to European immigrants, a greater proportion of blacks journeyed as families. Church congregations, Masonic lodges, and social clubs sometimes emigrated en masse, taking advantage of group rates to charter their own railroad cars. An influential woman in a community often led such efforts. "Neighbor was soliciting neighbor and friend persuading friend" as a group psychology propelled them forward. Many were like the woman from a small town in Mississippi who feared she had missed the Exodus: "If I stay here any longer, I'll go wild. Every time I go home I have to pass house after house of all my friends who are in the North and prospering . . . There ain't enough people here I now know to give me a decent burial."[40]

The railroads of the South made this folk migration possible not merely by running trains, but in pricing tickets so that even the poor, with sufficient planning, could afford transportation. In 1918 it cost $22.50 to ride from New Orleans to Chicago on a standard ticket (the equivalent of about $315 today). Some migrants bought tickets using savings, while others sold household possessions to raise cash. But railroads offered excursion rates during the slack summer months, plus group rates for large parties. Friends and neighbors formed migration clubs in order to get reduced fares, particularly on the IC, which probably carried more migrants than any other railroad. Around the time of the Great Northern Drive in May 1917, group rates from New Orleans to Chicago were as low as $6.[41]

Railroads profoundly influenced the demographics of black America, making possible the great rural-to-urban and South-to-North (including the Midwest and West) transformations of the twentieth century. But the migration also had a deep effect on the South. Numerous black belt communities were emptied of from one-quarter to one-third of their male working-age populations. The Alabama experience is illustrative. From Eufaula, Sunday trains on the Central of Georgia in September 1916 were packed with blacks from the surrounding countryside who took advantage of labor agents' free passes. Between August 1916 and June 1917, Selma's depot agents sold 81 tickets to Detroit; 31 to Pittsburgh; 51 to Akron; 51 to Cleveland; and 47 to Chicago; plus 159 to Memphis, from which many migrants entrained for Midwest cities. In October 1916, the first large-scale migration from Mobile occurred when the L&N transported two trainloads of blacks to work on section gangs and in yards at points farther north on that line. Birmingham was a particularly important staging point for northward migration. Many rural Alabamians first bought tickets to that city, from which they had the choice of riding the IC, SRR, St. Louis–San Francisco, and L&N to the Midwest, or the SRR and SAL to the Northeast.[42]

The exodus directly affected southern railroads, which soon experienced their own labor shortages. In Georgia, shop foremen and section bosses on the Central of Georgia, Georgia Southern &

Florida, Atlanta, Birmingham & Atlantic, and Atlantic Coast Line found it difficult to keep laborers for any length of time. From March through May 1917, when labor agents for northern railroads and industries were recruiting nearby, the C of G's Macon shops lost on average one-third of their 600 black laborers monthly, twice the normal turnover rate. To halt this attrition, railroads had to raise daily wages from $0.75 to $0.80 in 1916 to $1.25 to $2.00 a year later, although even this didn't guarantee sufficient workers. Roundhouses and freight houses all over Mississippi experienced similar shortfalls. In Brookhaven, every man on an IC section gang dropped his tools and hopped a train for the North without even waiting to collect his pay.[43]

Once it became apparent that the labor exodus was no short-lived phenomenon, southerners did all in their power to prevent blacks from departing. In August 1916, when 500 or more blacks gathered at the station in Tampa, Florida, believing they could get free passes, the police—instigated by large employers—attacked the crowd, clubbing many before arresting them. They were released the following day, the migration having been only temporarily blunted. No whites were more determined to halt the exodus than those in Mississippi. Landowners persuaded sheriffs to yank their sharecroppers off trains. Towns hastily passed laws to restrict blacks' freedom of movement. In Hattiesburg, when police barred them from the ticket office and arrested those who boarded Gulf & Ship Island Railroad trains without tickets (i.e., intending to purchase them from the conductor), determined migrants climbed aboard moving trains as they left town. When passengers were dragged off northbound Yazoo & Mississippi Valley Railroad trains arriving in Greenville, local blacks hiked 12 miles up the line to Leland to board for Memphis. Blacks in Jackson had to do likewise. Other migrants stole away under cover of darkness. Brutal treatment of would-be migrants by Greenwood police at the Y&MV depot only prompted more to escape. At Meridian, the chief of police held up a Mobile & Ohio train until a federal marshal arrested him for delaying it. When Brookhaven whites learned that a labor agent had lured blacks away from local lumber mills, police arrested the agent and forced IC trainmen to switch out 2 coaches carrying 125 migrants, leaving them stranded on a siding. This action resulted in another 100 blacks congregating at the depot, hoping to go north. Police used considerable brutality in driving them away. Finally, after three days, the cars with their passengers were allowed to depart for the North.[44] Such efforts were ultimately counterproductive. As one Greenville resident declared, "Our pepel are tole that they can not get anything to do up there and they are being snatched off the trains . . . but in spite of all this, they are leaving every day and every night."[45]

Georgians were also harsh in attempting to halt the migration. Police blocked migrants' departures at dozens of stations. A state law enacted in 1917 required labor recruiters to be licensed, cough up a $1,000 bond, and pay local fees which, in Macon, meant a $25,000 permit. In case that wasn't enough, labor agents operating in Macon also had to gain the endorsement of 25 local businessmen, 10 clergymen, and 10 manufacturers. While these obstacles deterred recruiters, they did not stop the migration. In one instance, Macon police used force to drive several hundred blacks trying to leave for Chicago away from the station. Then the city purchased 40 repeating rifles to control future crowds. Undeterred, other blacks walked 7 miles to a station up the line where they succeeded in boarding. In Americus, police boarded trains and removed large numbers of blacks, crowding them in jail on trumped-up misdemeanors until their train had left, although those accused of being leaders suffered additional police mistreatment. Albany police simply tore up blacks' tickets. Harassment was recurrent in Savannah. In one incident, police blocked the entrance to the "colored" waiting room and arrested more than 100 migrants for loitering, even though they held tickets. And two blacks were sentenced to a month at the county prison farm for publicly reading a "subversive" poem titled "Bound for the Promised Land."[46]

Railroad officials in the South were ambivalent about the Great Migration. While it was in their interest to sell tickets, it was not in their interest to deplete their own labor supply or, in general, their region's pool of low-wage workers. After the initial large-scale movement of migrants on special trains arranged by the Erie and Pennsylvania railroads, the Southern Railway refused to furnish special trains or to accept prepayment from northern railroads so that labor recruiters could simply hand out tickets to migrants. And the SRR eventually refused to sell discounted group-rate tickets to recruiters although it still sold blocks of straight-fare tickets, as many as 200 at a time. The ACL and SAL did not adopt such policies.[47]

The Great Migration permanently changed the demographics of black railroading. African Americans established a secure foothold on northern and Midwestern railroads. The return of soldiers and a brief postwar depression temporarily reduced their ranks, but as the economy improved in 1922 and new federal legislation curtailed Eastern European immigration, a scarcity of unskilled workers forced railroads to continue importing blacks from the South. Black railroad employment nationwide reached its all-time peak in 1924, with over 136,000 workers. While southern states continued to employ the most—Georgia leading the way with more than 10,000—Illinois, Ohio, and Pennsylvania each counted several thousand.[48]

New black railroaders helped build and strengthen communities all over the nation. The majority of blacks who fled the South for railroad jobs never returned, instead establishing residences and contributing to their new communities (although many eventually found employment in other industries). No clearer example is the influence of Pullman porters and dining-car waiters and cooks. Cities that were crew bases, like Oakland and Los Angeles, California, received strength from the incomes and civic participation of such passenger service men. When the Pennsy imported thousands of MOW laborers in 1916, they not only greatly increased the population of South Philadelphia, but also laid the foundation for new colonies along the main line to Pittsburgh. Union Pacific contract construction laborers helped plant black communities at several places along its main line in Wyoming.[49]

The Great Migration slowed to a trickle with the onset of the Great Depression, but migration began to pick up again in the mid-1930s as desperation drove rural black southerners to cities, not only in the Northeast and Midwest, but the South as well. The World War II defense boom then ignited a second Great Migration, transplanting another million blacks. For the first time, large numbers of southerners trekked to the West Coast, there to build large communities in Seattle, Portland, Richmond–Oakland–San Francisco, Los Angeles–Long Beach, and San Diego. All of these cities had rapidly expanding defense industries. California drew more migrants than any other western state, most of whom came from Louisiana, Texas, Oklahoma, and Arkansas. More of them traveled on the Southern Pacific than on any other line.

In marked contrast to the World War I period, southern whites did not crudely attempt to block the outmigration of blacks during this second railroad-facilitated exodus. The South's economy was changing. New Deal price-support policies had reduced cotton acreage, which made share-croppers less necessary. Mechanization of southern agriculture further decreased the need for cheap farm labor. So white southerners who a generation before would have attempted to prevent large numbers of blacks from leaving now registered no alarm.

As in the previous war, railroads desperately sought new labor during World War II. The draft and better-paying defense-plant jobs again depleted the existing workforce. Some railroads again stimulated migration by recruiting blacks. The SP imported about 3,000 men from the South for track labor, carrying them to California on its own trains. Neither the railroad nor some of the prospective workers were averse to exploiting the other. The SP broke its commitment not to hire minors, failed to ensure that workers were medically fit, defaulted on agreements to return minors and "physically defective" recruits to their homes, and had not planned housing or efficient trans-portation to work sites for hundreds of arrivals. The problems would have been even more acute had not one-eighth of the recruits deserted before getting to Los Angeles. An equal proportion was unwilling, on arrival, to go to work. Others lasted only a few days, particularly those repairing tracks in the blazing Arizona and California deserts. More remunerative defense jobs lured others. In the end, scarcely half of the migrants remained SP employees for any length of time.[50]

The Pennsy, viewing the SP's troubles, decided against systematically recruiting black labor in the South. It was already struggling to keep northern blacks in its employ. Superior defense-plant wages caused significant attrition in the ranks of African American section men. The PRR claimed that many of them "quit without giving any reason," but living in converted boxcars far from female companionship, when a man could get a better-paying factory job close to home, was undoubt-edly sufficient reason for taking one's leave.[51] Although many new World War II railroaders were blacks, including significantly more women than during the previous war, by far the largest number of new workers was the 100,000 Mexicans imported to work for more than 30 lines in the railroad bracero program.[52]

The opportunity for blacks to move long distances during the World War II era still rested largely on train travel, although bus lines had grown significantly during the 1930s, seizing the chance to serve small towns more cheaply than railroads. Some blacks began "riding the dog" (Greyhound bus) because it was generally less expensive, but railroads had long before captured their imaginations and they never forsook trains. A black travel writer observed in 1950 that rail-roads still kept black patronage not because of speed but on account of dependability and comfort.

An elderly lady said, "I ain't in no big hurry to git there, but I needs plenty of room so I can stretch my feet. Ain't no *room* on them buses." The writer went on to state that "the Negro is just naturally railroad-minded."[53] While much less so today, trains still carry numerous blacks to and from southern homes and roots.

The migration story is incomplete without exploring the cultural significance of African American train travel. Some of the most meaningful social occasions were enacted at southern stations as families separated and reunited. Migration was a communal phenomenon, even if only one person was leaving, because the hopes and dreams of entire communities rode on the success of individuals in newer, freer locales. Bidding farewell was an experience that was rich in meaning for all concerned. Greeting visitors from the North was likewise a social ritual in which hopes for a better life might be validated.

Clifton Taulbert, who grew up in tiny Glen Allan, in the Mississippi Delta, recalled his youthful impressions of train stations and travelers in the late 1940s. One passenger train a day ran from Vicksburg to Memphis on the Yazoo & Mississippi Valley line, a subsidiary of the IC, the closest station to Glen Allan being Greenville. The grandly named *Delta Express* was in reality an all-stops, coach-only train that took 4 1/2 hours to meander 150 miles. Visitors from the North—few who came back, stayed—made an indelible impression on Taulbert. "Everyone getting off the train seemed to have found the dream. Colored men in striped suits and beaver hats carried matched luggage beside beautiful colored ladies with amber rouged faces and red lips. The ladies' hair was pressed to their heads and clusters curled at the back or side. They wore brightly colored dresses and carried coats with bits of fur. They said, 'Pardon me' as they whisked by with their train cases in their hands. They quickly walked to the colored side of the station, but with the air of 'I am only doing this to keep these red-necks happy. Why, in Chicago, there's no such thing as separate.'" Just the sight of such travelers kept alive the dream of a freer life beyond Mississippi.[54]

Other social rituals attended travel from Glen Allan to visit friends or family in the North. When entire families would go to Greenville to see someone off at the station, excitement reigned. Northbound travelers, too, wore their best clothes, although not such finery as was displayed by those coming back from the North. Women were as carefully coiffed, if not as stylishly. The facts that their luggage was held together with belts or neckties and that they carried fried chicken and slices of cake in brown paper bags made them no less respectable than more nattily dressed visitors from the North. They endured Jim Crow only for the present, lining up at the "colored" ticket window and boarding the Jim Crow coach, because once their northbound connecting train crossed the Ohio River, they could choose seats anywhere they wished. Emotions swelled, Taulbert recalled, as train time approached: "Relatives would be crying as if the train were taking the loved ones to those eternal green pastures. Some who were departing would cry too. I don't know if the tears were for joy, because now they had a chance to go north and be somebody, or for fear that once they boarded the old Illinois Central, they might never return again." As his family drove slowly back to Glen

Allan, young Cliff would fall asleep, "dreaming that maybe some day I'd be boarding that same train heading north."[55]

Another observer caught similar rituals still being enacted in the late 1960s at Kingstree, South Carolina, on the Seaboard Coast Line Railroad. The northbound all-coach *Gulf Coast Special* (cheaper than the railroad's reserved-seat streamliners) stopped at Kingstree at 2:15 in the afternoon and arrived in New York at 7:00 a.m. the next morning. As it approached the station, a reporter noted, the waiting crowd's mood shifted.

> The youngsters who have been noisy suddenly become quiet, and old people who have been quiet suddenly feel the need to talk. Portable radios are clicked off. Bags are lifted. Hands are held and shaken. Cheeks and lips are kissed and clung to. Eyes mist. Faces smile. People say good-by, take care and write me or call me; be a good boy, be a good girl, stay out of trouble . . . Along Main Street, people stand under awnings and look at the train and, in their mind, beyond it—to where it is going and where it has come from . . . For a few moments . . . this unthinking machine stops the life of the town, pulls dreams and curses out of the people, moves on to the next town. And when it is gone, with its noise and its nuisance and its passengers looking out the windows, the town seems strangely quiet for a little while.

What would become of migrants going to Baltimore, Philadelphia, Newark, or the Big Apple? Would they ever return?[56]

Migrants did return to southern homes for visits, reunions, and funerals. Their narratives emphasized the wonders and successes of the North, not their hardships and how the "Promised Land" was agonizingly elusive. These "tales of glory" shaped the hopes of those remaining behind, who realized that their dreams were not likely to come true in the old home place. As a teenager in the early 1960s, Clifton Taulbert found his imagination spinning scenes of good jobs and exciting cities. "I could hardly wait to go North, and I knew it would be the train, the 'high class' mode of transportation, that would make it all reality . . . I spent my days mentally alone, riding the train. That train seemed to me like a grand uncle with a huge cigar, coming to take me North." In fact, "my lifetime ambition had been to view the world from the windows of a train." When that day finally came, in 1963, sadness and apprehension and excitement were inextricably mixed as he boarded a coach for St. Louis, leaving behind kin, friends, and the community that had nurtured him.[57]

For many African Americans, even though railroads shed passenger services as fast as they could in the 1960s, trains remained the preferable mode of transportation into the Amtrak era. Poor folk might take buses. But as one of Clifton Taulbert's relatives stressed, "the bus stops for everybody whether they can breathe or not. A better class of people rides the train." Parents were more comfortable entrusting their youngsters traveling alone to a train's coach porter, avoiding the risk of a child being left behind when everyone piled off the bus for a meal stop. On many northbound journeys, one could board a train in the rural South and arrive at New York or Chicago or Detroit without even having to change cars.[58]

Although the volume of migration out of the South declined after 1950, railroads continued to be the pipeline funneling the young to hoped-for better lives. Black high school graduates in declining rural-economy towns like Kingstree found few decent jobs awaiting them. In the weeks following graduations, the SCL's *Gulf Coast Special* from Jacksonville to New York began with six or eight coaches, rather than the usual two or three, and often added up to six more at Florence, South Carolina. As many as 300 passengers, nearly all blacks and many teenagers, would jam the cars at Kingstree, some having to stand in the baggage car, clutching tickets for northern cities where relatives or friends were already planted.[59]

What roles did railroads play in the momentous twentieth-century rural-to-urban, South-to-North transformation of black America? Nearly everyone bought a one-way ticket, literally or figuratively. Many would return, briefly, for weddings, or a family crisis, or even to help with the harvest. But most who settled in a northern or Midwestern or western city stayed there, although not a few *did* come home again, in a pine box, because "home" was always "down South," even though one may have lived "up South" for decades. For some, their last wish was to be buried "back home." Williamsburg County, South Carolina, of which Kingstree was the seat of government, had only 40,000 residents in the late 1960s, but the SCL delivered 300 caskets a year from New York, Newark, Philadelphia, or anywhere else blacks had transplanted themselves.[60]

The migrants' experiences were often bittersweet. Some called the train they rode the "Chickenbone Special" because travelers were so poor they carried their own food. Jazz trumpeter Louis Armstrong remembered that "colored persons going North crammed their baskets full of everything but the kitchen stove." Even if they could have afforded a meal in the diner, segregation usually prevented their being served. Many times, they rode in inferior or decrepit Jim Crow coaches. And because the fares were cheaper, they often took slower, non-streamlined, secondary trains. But the hardships of their journey did not overshadow the significance of their self-liberation. Waves of migrants, numbering in the millions, streamed out of the South from the 1910s to the 1950s. Most never found the "Promised Land" in the North. But at least they had escaped the "land of bondage." They found "a bit of equality north of the Mason-Dixon Line. So rigid were the rules of their former segregated South that they cherished the light of integration coming from the slightly-ajar northern door."[61] Railroads kept that door ajar.

Railroads in the African American Experience

Railroads continued to use construction contractors into the twentieth century to build new lines or upgrade existing ones. Such companies, like the firm of Yale & Reagan, brought in their own equipment, often obsolete steam locomotives purchased from the railroads, as well as their own employees. Here a crew works on the Illinois Central Railroad in the World War I era. Theodore Kornweibel collection

(OPPOSITE) *Seaboard Air Line Railway wreck clean-up crew, with cook, 1919. Wilmington–Charlotte passenger train no. 63, pulled by 4-6-0 engine no. 613, derailed near Lilesville, North Carolina, on May 2. The "colored fireman" lived only long enough to tell rescuers that the engine had run over something before plunging down an embankment. Investigation revealed sabotage: someone had clamped a coupler knuckle over the rail. It sometimes took several days to clean up a big derailment, necessitating a cook and outfit cars to feed and house the wreck crew. The photograph also starkly illustrates the dangers faced by firemen and engineers. Courtesy of the North Carolina State Archives*

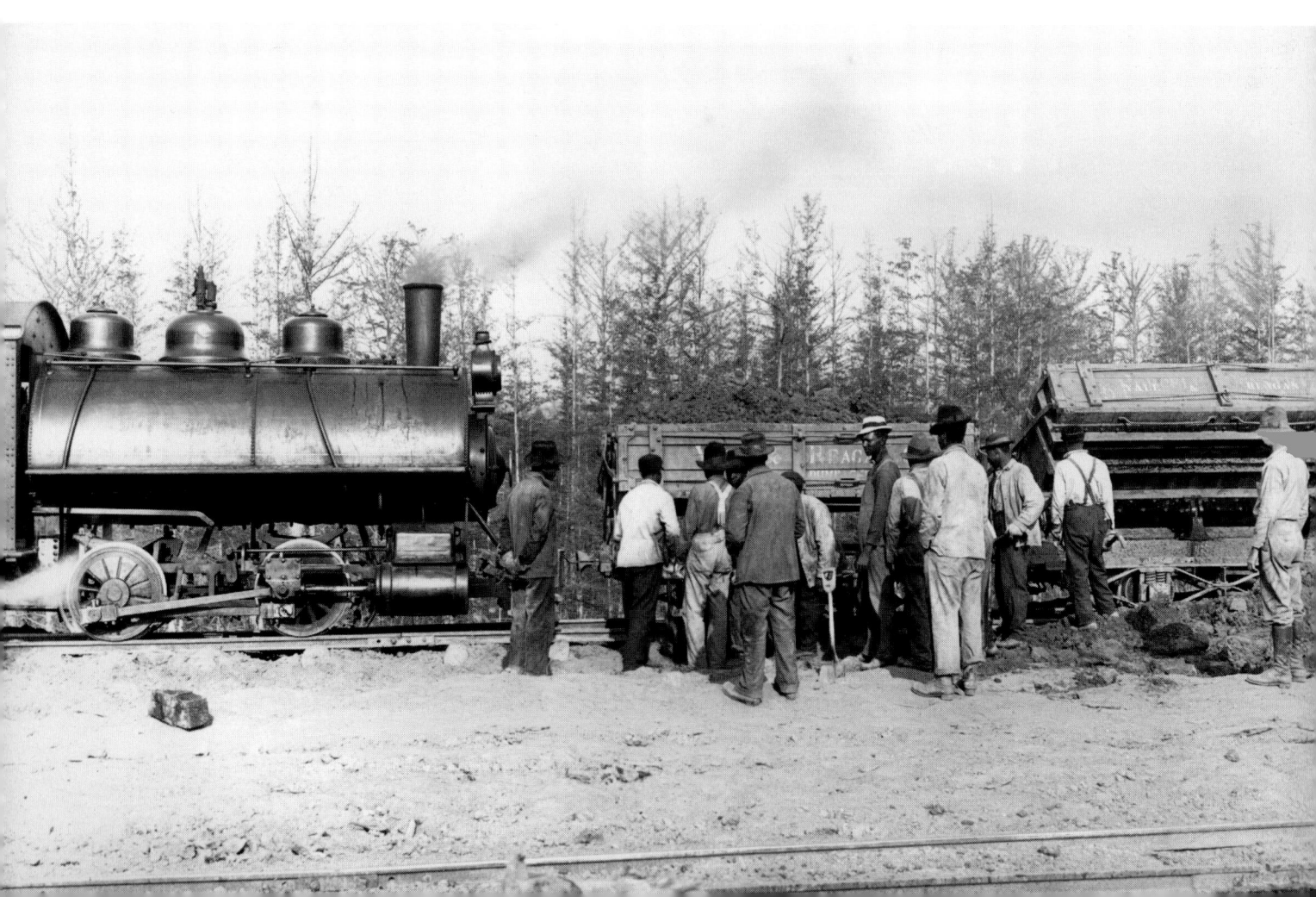

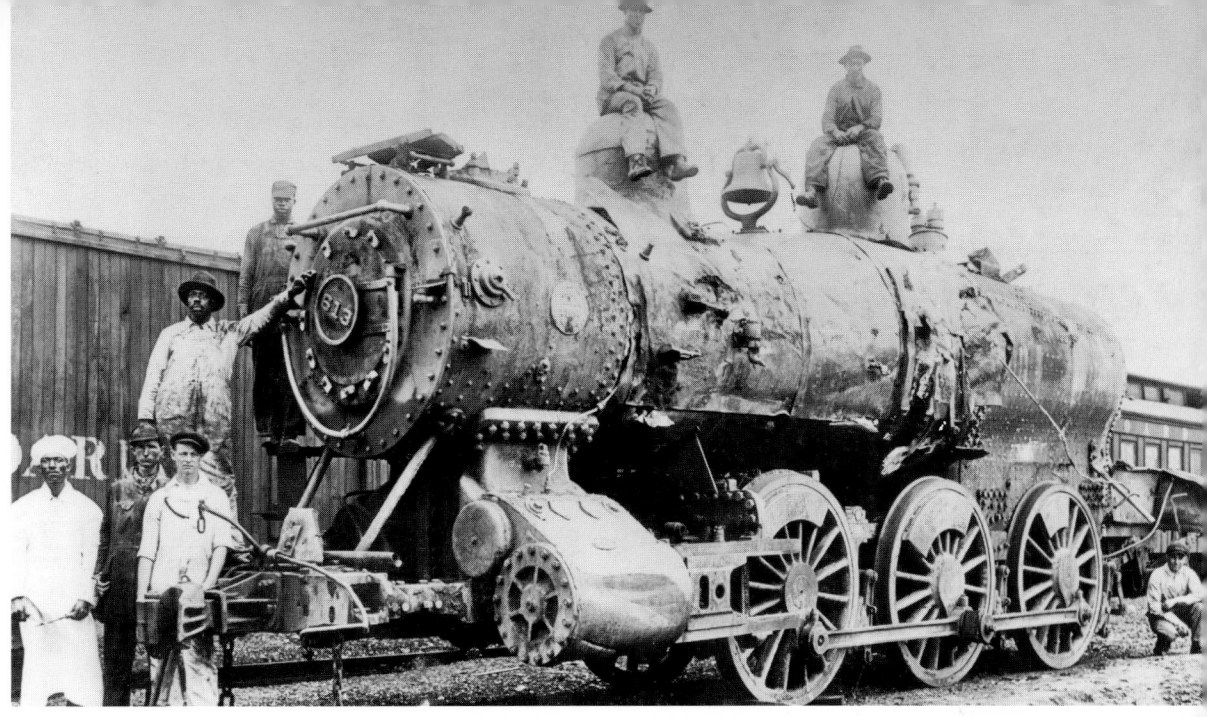

(BELOW) *Railroad work was a source of pride for many African Americans. Sons frequently followed fathers' footsteps. This proud engineer working for the Louisiana Sand & Gravel Company in the early twentieth century may already be utilizing his older son—oil can in hand—as fireman, while a younger child is learning to ring the bell. Theodore Kornweibel collection*

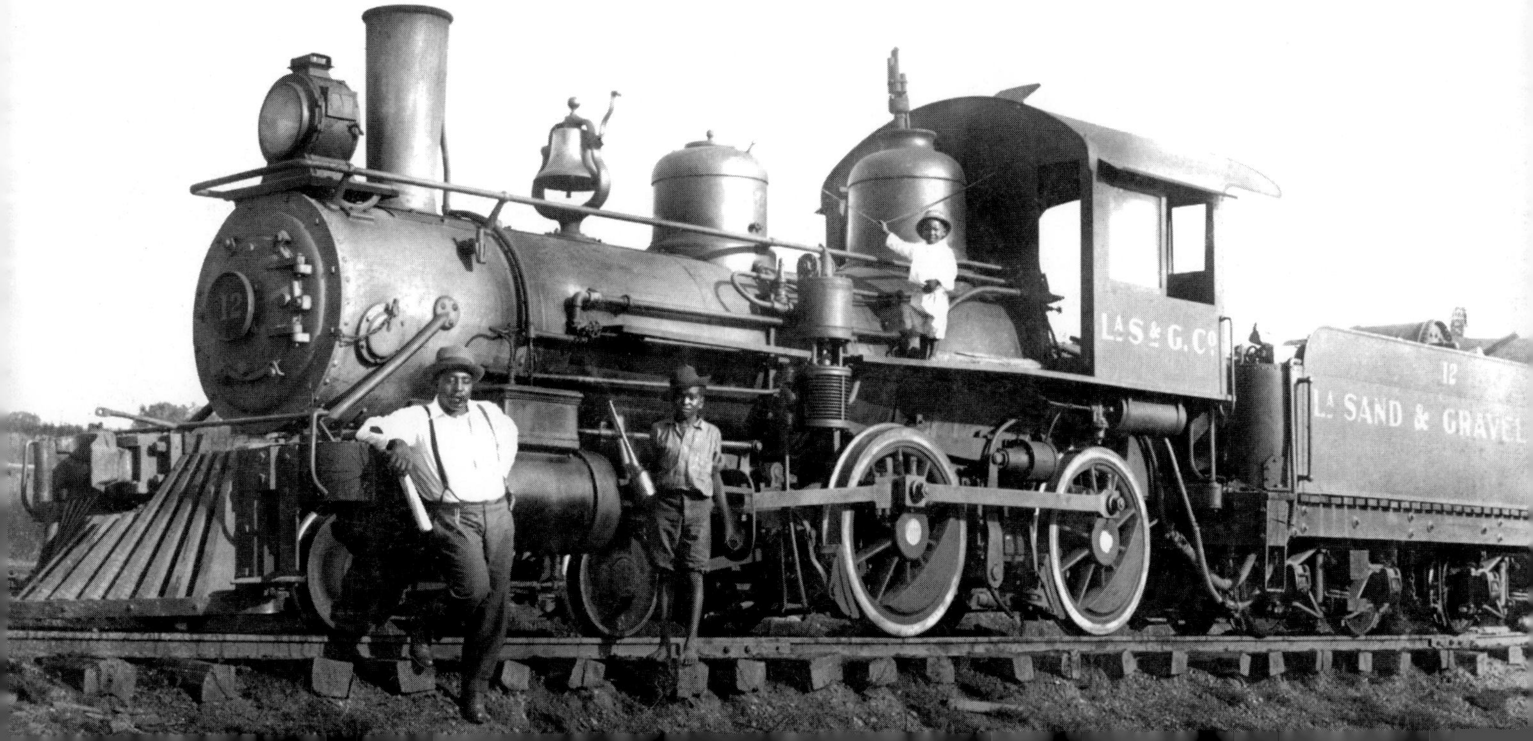

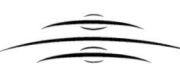

"REPRESENT THE BEST IN COLORED"

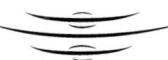

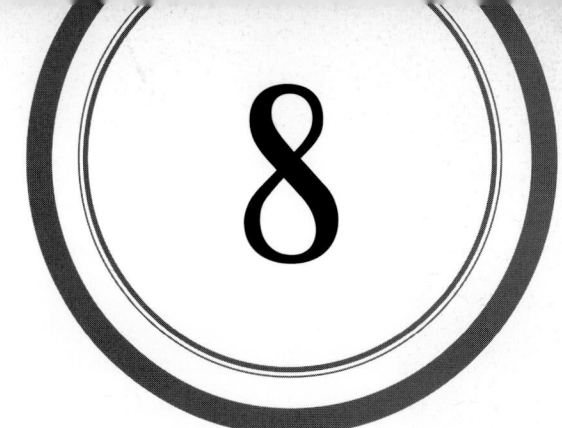

Train Porters, Porter-Brakemen, Railroad Ferry and Steamship Porters, and RPO Clerks

As prominently as the Pullman porters figure in railroad history and photography, train travelers who either could not afford sleeping accommodations or who took short trips in coaches were more familiar with another category of service personnel: train porters, also known as coach porters. By the mid-1920s, at the peak of passenger travel, they totaled about 11,000, or 2,000 more than the number of Pullman porters.[1] Blacks did not have a monopoly on train porter jobs, but they predominated because the position had servant connotations.

Each railroad owned its own coaches, whereas the majority of sleeping cars were owned and operated by the Pullman Company. So train porters, unlike Pullman porters, were employed by the railroads themselves. While Pullman porters cared for passengers in a single car, coach porters were responsible for several cars, because the level of service was much less. Coaches were used on a great variety of trains. Local trains used coaches exclusively. Even faster, limited-stop and express trains traveling relatively short distances—between Los Angeles and San Diego, or New York and Boston—usually carried no sleepers. The same was true for many medium-distance trains that traveled during the daytime, as between Minneapolis and Chicago, or between St. Louis and Detroit. And beginning in the late 1930s, in order to compete with airlines, some railroads offered all-coach, reclining-seat, long-distance trains like the Baltimore & Ohio Railroad's *Columbian* between Chicago and Washington, the Atchison, Topeka & Santa Fe Railway's *El Capitan* between

Los Angeles and Chicago, and the Texas and Pacific Railway's *Louisiana Daylight* between El Paso and New Orleans. Train porters served passengers on all of these types of trains except locals that stopped at every town and village along the route. And many rural short lines, if they accommodated passengers at all, operated only mixed trains, with a single passenger car coupled to the end of a freight train that switched cars at industries along the route. The only assistance to passengers on locals and mixed trains came from the conductor or brakeman/flagman.

The train porter evolved from the antebellum train hand and water boy. The former was basically a brakeman in the era before automatic air brakes, but he also helped passengers on and off the cars and kept the lamps lit and the stove burning. Black train hands were common in the antebellum South although whites also held such jobs. No record exists of black train hands working in the North at this time. Black water boys could be found in both regions before the Civil War, assuaging the thirst of passengers and sometimes selling sundries. Some trains still featured water boys in the late nineteenth century. Future Pullman porter Fred D. Wright remembered his start in passenger service: "I came to New York from Chester County, Pa., in 1892, when I was 12 years old. Went to see Mr. C. P. Clark, then president of the New Haven Railroad, and asked him for a job. He hired me as a water boy. You see, at that time the day coaches were not supplied with coolers or tanks, and passengers slaked their thirsts, when the water boy appeared with a large can and tumblers. I got the water from a hogs-head in the baggage car." If he was lucky, passengers tipped him a few pennies.[2]

After the Civil War, as rail journeys lengthened and sleeping-car accommodations were added, even coach passengers began to expect more comfort, cleanliness, and service. Conductors were preoccupied with tickets, paperwork, and giving permission to depart each station. Brakemen might logically have offered passenger services, especially after air brakes lessened their duties, but they were not hired because they were personable. One peeved traveler in the 1880s described a passenger brakeman who was both lazy and seemingly deliberately inconsiderate of passengers.[3] So in addressing the need for better service, the railroads created a new job category and sought new personnel.

The introduction of train porters followed the use of sleeping-car porters. Water boys became obsolete by the end of the century when new coaches were equipped with cold-water dispensers. But cars still got dirty, even dirtier as trains now crossed half a continent. Train porters were first employed on the Pennsylvania Railroad when it introduced through coach service from New York to Chicago and St. Louis. They eliminated the necessity for car cleaners to be brought on board at intermediate stops. Not only were train porters expected to keep their cars swept, cuspidors emptied, and the bathrooms clean and supplied with soap and towels, but they also were to assist passengers getting on and off the train, carry and stow their baggage when they could not do it themselves, and offer them pillows. Unlike Pullman porters, who discreetly notified individual passengers when their station stop was near, coach porters made general announcements in their cars. One Southern Railway porter was noted for the poetic license of his announcements:

Salisbury, Salisbury. The next station stop will be Salisbury.

Change trains here for Raspberry, Blueberry, Elderberry, Huckleberry;

Come back next week, and we may go to Strawberry.

But the next stop now is Salisbury.[4]

The train porter position became identified with African Americans because whites were loath to accept jobs that combined janitor and servant roles. Although some porters were indeed white, coach travelers came to anticipate being attended by an African American. Most whites, particularly those residing outside of the South, had never been waited upon by blacks. (Although black hotel waiters were common, most dining room patrons were commercial travelers or the affluent.) Many whites' first experience with black servitors was on a railroad coach. By the early twentieth century, it seemed entirely natural, to both the railroads and the white traveling public, that both train porters and their Pullman counterparts be black servants.

The fact that train porters had become regular fixtures in passenger travel is evident in their being as properly attired as white crew members or Pullman porters. The Chesapeake & Ohio Railway's 1889 uniform specifications required a single-breasted summer coat, double-breasted winter coat, vest, and cap identical to that worn by conductors except for silver, rather than gold, braid.[5] Pay varied from railroad to railroad, even within the same region. In 1894, the Norfolk & Western Railway paid train porters $30 to $40 per month, the Southern Railway $30 to $35, but the Richmond & Danville Railroad only $20 to $30.[6] Differences in pay often reflected whether or not porters had the "pillow privilege," the right to revenue from rental of railroad-supplied pillows. Porters on the Pennsylvania Railroad made $57.70 per month in 1910, without that concession, while those on the Chicago Great Western, Illinois Central, and Chicago & Eastern Illinois railroads made no more than $45 monthly, but also enjoyed pillow revenue.[7]

World War I brought significant, although temporary, improvements to the wages and working conditions of train porters. The U.S. Railroad Administration doubled their pay, but the increases— from $50 to $55 to $120 per month—prompted southern whites to redefine the train porter position as a "white" job.[8] It was less physically demanding and less dangerous than a freight brakeman's work, and now, with relatively decent pay, it seemed no longer too menial or servile for whites to perform, under certain conditions. What happened on the Central of Georgia Railway illustrates the intricacies and illogic of railroad racism in the South.

White trainmen on the C of G began to bump less senior black train porters, and African American travelers immediately suffered a reduction in service. While black train porters had gladly served members of both races, the new white porters were disinclined to assist black passengers getting on and off a train, even if they were female or elderly. In fact, some of the new porters were downright rude to blacks. The road's federal manager ordered white trainmen to curb offensive behavior, but it was one thing to tell southern white men to treat blacks as courteously as one would whites, and another matter for them to change lifelong habits. The greatest resistance came to offering black women the same respect one gave to white women. Most white train porters simply would not take a black woman's arm to help her on and off the cars, nor handle her packages or baggage. Not every one behaved in such prejudiced fashion: porter L. F. Glenn asserted that he "cheerfully assisted" black passengers in all ways to which they were accustomed. Such examples, however, were rare, as Georgia blacks testified. In desperation, they petitioned the USRA to require railroads to provide, at the least, a porter for each race. Such an added expense, however, the railroad was loath to bear.[9]

Following the war and the end of federal control, railroads everywhere began to slash the federally mandated wages. Nor surprisingly, whites on the Central of Georgia now abandoned the ranks of train porters, thus defining the position once again as a black job. But the situation did not return to the status quo ante. Black train porters reappeared in the 1920s, but on fewer trains than before. On other runs, only white conductors or flagmen remained to assist passengers, and they typically ignored blacks' needs altogether. African Americans pleaded in vain for restoration of black train porter service. But the Model T was eroding short-distance rail travel. Local trains operated at a loss. Only on more heavily traveled runs could the C of G now justify train porters. The Great Depression made matters worse. More porters were furloughed with the result that, on many C of G trains, no one was willing to assist black passengers. They continued to plead with railroad management to require white trainmen to offer them courtesies, but their protests availed nothing.[10]

Ironically, as railroads further cut back on train porter services in the 1930s, some misguided officials were urging blacks to think of such careers. As the need for farm labor declined with the introduction of New Deal crop reduction programs, many young men of both races found in the Civilian Conservation Corps a lifeline providing food, shelter, medical care, and vocational training. But whereas white enrollees could hope to capitalize on the clerical, technical, construction, and trade skills they acquired in segregated CCC camps, blacks faced exclusion from all but service occupations. Addressing this reality, the educational advisor of an Arkansas "Negro" CCC camp prepared a curriculum for instruction in portering.[11] But as railroads struggled to emerge from the Depression, increasing payrolls for money-losing passenger service was not in the cards.

Train porter service was just one of the factors making passenger operation so costly. The public had become accustomed, by the early twentieth century, to a high level of on-board amenities from a multitude of personnel. Counting a chef, cooks, a steward, waiters, and train porters, plus a Pullman conductor and porters and attendants (and sometimes a Pullman maid and valet), a long-distance train could have close to 20 service crew members. In addition, a train carried the railroad's conductor, head-end brakeman, and rear brakeman/flagman. Such high labor costs could not forever be sustained. Although passenger counts soared far beyond Depression-era levels during World War II, personnel costs were closely watched. Pullman porters worked harder than ever before. So did train porters. On the Gulf, Mobile & Ohio Railroad, per a 1942 agreement between the railroad and a small independent black union, only two train porters served the many coach passengers on its streamliners from St. Louis, the *Rebel* to New Orleans, and the *Gulf Coast Rebel* to

Mobile, Alabama. They worked 56-hour weeks at 50 cents per hour ($6.48 in 2009 if adjusted for inflation) before overtime kicked in, and had to pay out of pocket for their uniforms.[12] Obviously, the amount of tips determined whether or not they earned a living wage.

Passenger numbers after 1945 never again equaled the wartime level. Travelers increasingly turned to their automobiles and then to airplanes, despite the railroads' efforts to lure them with cleaner diesel-powered trains, streamlined equipment, and, at least on the Baltimore & Ohio, a 10-day training school to make coach porters more courteous and efficient. By the late 1940s the Brotherhood of Sleeping Car Porters represented train porters on many lines, and negotiated decent wage and hour packages for them.[13] But in the 1950s, in efforts to stanch the flow of red ink, railroads discontinued numerous trains and on the remaining runs, cut costs where they could, including reducing the number of coach porters. Even crack streamliners, like the Chesapeake & Ohio's *George Washington* from Cincinnati to the nation's capital, curtailed service, sometimes running eight coaches with as few as two porters. This meant overworked porters and less than the personal service to which even coach passengers on premier trains were accustomed. The Atlantic Coast Line Railroad cut costs by replacing train porters with lower-paid car attendants.[14] A dwindling number of train porters nationwide continued working down to the end of passenger service by the individual railroads in 1971. With Amtrak's assumption of most of the remaining passenger runs, the traditional name disappeared, and members of all races and ethnic groups, plus women, now worked as "coach attendants."

Another category of train porters had expanded duties. These men were variously called "porter-brakemen," "flagmen porters," or "colored trainmen." In addition to helping passengers, keeping coaches clean, and calling out station names, they worked as brakemen, throwing switches, coupling and uncoupling cars and steam and brake hoses, and relaying signals to the engineer. In fact, they were more brakemen than porters, yet the railroads paid them far less than white brakemen.[15] They worked from the front end of passenger trains; the position of rear passenger brakemen always remained a white monopoly because, when a train backed up, this person gave orders to the engineer, which would have been impermissible for a black man to do. Although relatively few in numbers, porter-brakemen were intensely disliked by white brakemen who, for decades, variously tried to bar them from such dual roles, sought to abolish the job itself, and agitated to guarantee that passenger trains carried only white brakemen. The white brakemen's weapons were their union, the Brotherhood of Railroad Trainmen (which restricted membership to Caucasians), and, by the 1930s, the National Railroad Adjustment Board. Although smaller railroads that were not unionized continued to employ black porter-brakemen because they would accept lower pay rates and perform two jobs, the BRT was largely successful in persuading the major railroads not to hire them and in some cases getting them to fire those who were already in their employ. One of its early struggles was against the Gulf, Colorado & Santa Fe Railway (the Atchison, Topeka & Santa Fe's Texas lines) in the late 1890s. With automatic couplers and air brakes now standard on passenger cars, the road figured to cut costs by replacing both white brakemen with black porter-brakemen, paying them $45 a month compared to the white brakemen's $50 wage. The outraged BRT protested and persuaded the GC&SF to staff passenger trains with a white brakeman and a black porter-brakeman, the same formula that the Santa Fe had recently adopted on its lines in Oklahoma and southern Kansas. Even so, more than 100 white brakemen lost their jobs on the GC&SF.[16] To the BRT, the handwriting was on the wall. Black porter-brakemen were clearly the enemy.

A decades-long struggle between the BRT and the Pennsylvania Railroad on its lines west of Pittsburgh shows how black porter-brakemen were caught between forces far more powerful than they. Despite generally acceding to the union's demands, the Pennsy reserved the right to employ porter-brakemen, getting them to perform two jobs for half the wage paid to a single white brakeman. To counter this, unionized white railroaders persuaded seven eastern and Midwestern state legislatures to pass "full-crew" laws, ostensibly to promote greater safety, which required passenger trains having at least five cars to be staffed with a conductor and two true brakemen. Porter-brakemen recognized the scarcely hidden agenda of such legislation—to ensure that all brakemen were white—and tried to fight their enactment. But they could not match the white railroaders' political muscle.[17]

Indiana and Ohio were full-crew states where the BRT fought the Pennsy over the issue of "colored trainmen." Initially, the railroad complied with the full crew laws and replaced its relatively few porter-brakemen with white brakemen. But the PRR's legal department subsequently concluded that lower-paid porter-brakemen, if they were instructed and assigned as brakemen, could be employed to comply with the full-crew laws. Hence white brakemen were replaced by "colored trainmen" on a number of runs. They were paid a porter's wages—only about half the white brakeman's pay—yet they performed all the duties of a head-end brakeman. The white brakemen counterattacked by insisting that the "colored trainmen" be paid the same as them, since their duties were nearly the same, they were almost identically uniformed, they had to carry and synchronize railroad-approved watches, and they had to pass the same rules examination. The railroad naturally rejected this proposition because of the additional cost, and even increased the number of "colored trainmen." But the white brakemen did not give up, eventually forcing the railroad to retreat. The PRR, beginning in 1911 on its subsidiary Pittsburgh, Cincinnati, Chicago & St. Louis Railway (the "Panhandle" road), agreed to replace most "colored trainmen" with white brakemen, while the few remaining ones (only on long-distance trains with lots of coaches and thus in need of porters' janitorial services) would be paid the same as white brakemen but not be granted seniority. The BRT was transparent about its intentions: it had, according to PRR officials, "no interest whatever in the colored 'trainmen' personally but . . . to have these colored 'trainmen' paid brakemen's rates and then secure their positions through the exercise of seniority rights."[18]

In the meantime, several Pennsy coach porters who had performed brakemen's duties for a number of years without being classified as "colored trainmen" sued to collect the difference between the two rates of pay. Although some of them won judgments in 1917, the railroad appealed.

The cases dragged on until 1924, when appellate courts dismissed the suits and ordered the porters to pay the railroad's legal costs. There is no record that it managed to collect, but this was a bitter defeat for the porters, who were really pawns in a high-stakes game between the unionized brakemen and their employer.[19]

The BRT was never interested in a compromise over the "colored trainmen" issue: it wanted every brakeman to be white. Thus, it maintained pressure on the Pennsylvania and other railroads. White brakemen's dissatisfaction increased during World War I when the USRA decreed that if train porters performed *any* brakemen's duties, they must be paid a brakeman's wage. Nonetheless, white brakemen saw a ray of hope. If this actually took place, white men could then bid on the porter-brakemen jobs, exercise their seniority, and displace the blacks. BRT locals filed grievances to this effect, but they were not upheld. The PRR, for its part, continued to insist that it shouldn't have to pay blacks the standard brakeman's wage by claiming an absurd technicality: the "colored trainmen" didn't perform brakemen duties at the direction of the company, but only at the command of individual conductors! Meanwhile, many black railroaders—not just porter-brakemen— were emboldened by the USRA to seek pay equality with whites.[20]

After the war, the BRT continued its campaign to eliminate the Pennsy's "colored trainmen," while the company continued to resist, even asserting that blacks were often superior railroaders, performing equally capably both the brakemen's and porters' duties. To their credit, a number of company officials admitted that, should the blacks ever be displaced, fairness required that jobs with equivalent pay be found for them elsewhere on the system. The situation changed in mid-1921, however, when Indiana's full-crew law was repealed. "Colored trainmen" were immediately demoted back to porters and prohibited from performing any brakemen's duties, their pay dropping from $130 to $95 a month. They protested that this was far too little to support families, plus pay layover expenses. Someone in the company must have had a conscience, because in early 1922, the PRR increased their monthly salary back to $120. Ohio remained a full-crew state, however, so "colored trainmen" continued to be paid as brakemen, prompting the BRT to renew its campaign in that state. Elsewhere, unionized white brakemen were more successful. During and after the war, a number of other railroads tried the Pennsy approach and replaced white head-end passenger brakemen with porter-brakemen. But the BRT and its ally, the equally lily-white Order of Railway Conductors, persuaded the U.S. Railroad Labor Board to order that white brakemen be restored to their previous positions.[21]

In the South, up to World War I, white unionists were unsuccessful in getting full-crew laws passed. Thus, southern railroads more fully exploited black porter-brakemen (and angered white brakemen) through race-based pay differentials. During the war, however, the USRA's equal-pay-for-equal-work order inspired black railroaders to seek parity. Six Southern Pacific porter-brakemen, operating on Texas and Louisiana lines, complained to the USRA that while they performed the same work as white brakemen, plus handled baggage, mail, and express shipments, they still got only $71.50 per month, compared to the $115 earned by white brakemen. On the Southern

Railway's Memphis Division, a porter-brakeman even had to "climb up on the tender of greasy engines with his nice uniform on, and pull the [water] tank spout down and take the water for the fireman."[22] Unfortunately, USRA General Order No. 27 backfired for blacks in the South. On the Missouri Pacific Railway, for example, they had enjoyed a racial monopoly since the 1880s on the Valley and Louisiana Division, where all firemen, brakemen, flagmen, switchmen, engine foremen, and porter-brakemen were African Americans. Now, with equal pay for equal work, whites suddenly found trainmen jobs desirable. Despite the porter-brakemen record of loyalty to the company—that is, not striking—the MoPac negotiated a new contract with the BRT in 1920 that consolidated the two races' seniority lists, resulting in senior white brakemen bumping blacks from their long-held porter-brakemen positions, while blacks were not commensurately allowed to bid on flagmen and brakemen jobs that were historically reserved for whites. The same thing happened on the Illinois Central and its subsidiary the Yazoo & Mississippi Valley Railroad.[23]

Pay differentials and racial job categories reappeared in the South after the end of the USRA. On the Missouri Pacific's Gulf Coast Lines, pay was cut, resulting once again in blacks monopolizing porter-brakemen jobs, with seniority limited to one district or division, thus restricting lateral mobility. On the St. Louis–San Francisco Railway (the Frisco), porter-brakemen's wages were slashed to those of train porters.[24] White railroaders continued to blame black railroaders for the generally lower southern wages compared to the rest of the nation. But rather than addressing this problem by admitting blacks into the House of Labor, they blocked blacks' entrance into their unions. The Great Depression's shrinkage of railroad jobs brought even more bitterness and, finally, an "all-out assault" against black porter-brakemen by white unionists.[25]

The Brotherhood of Railroad Trainmen had battled the Santa Fe since 1899, when it replaced some white brakemen with black porter-brakemen. The two groups' wages were equalized during World War I and remained so afterward, although they were carried on separate seniority lists. Several times in the 1920s the brakemen tried to appropriate the blacks' jobs, but because they would not perform porters' duties, the Santa Fe refused to use them in such positions. The BRT eventually agreed to accept an arbitration board's decision that its members had no right to claim the blacks' jobs. Nonetheless, the BRT again took the offensive against the Santa Fe in 1939,

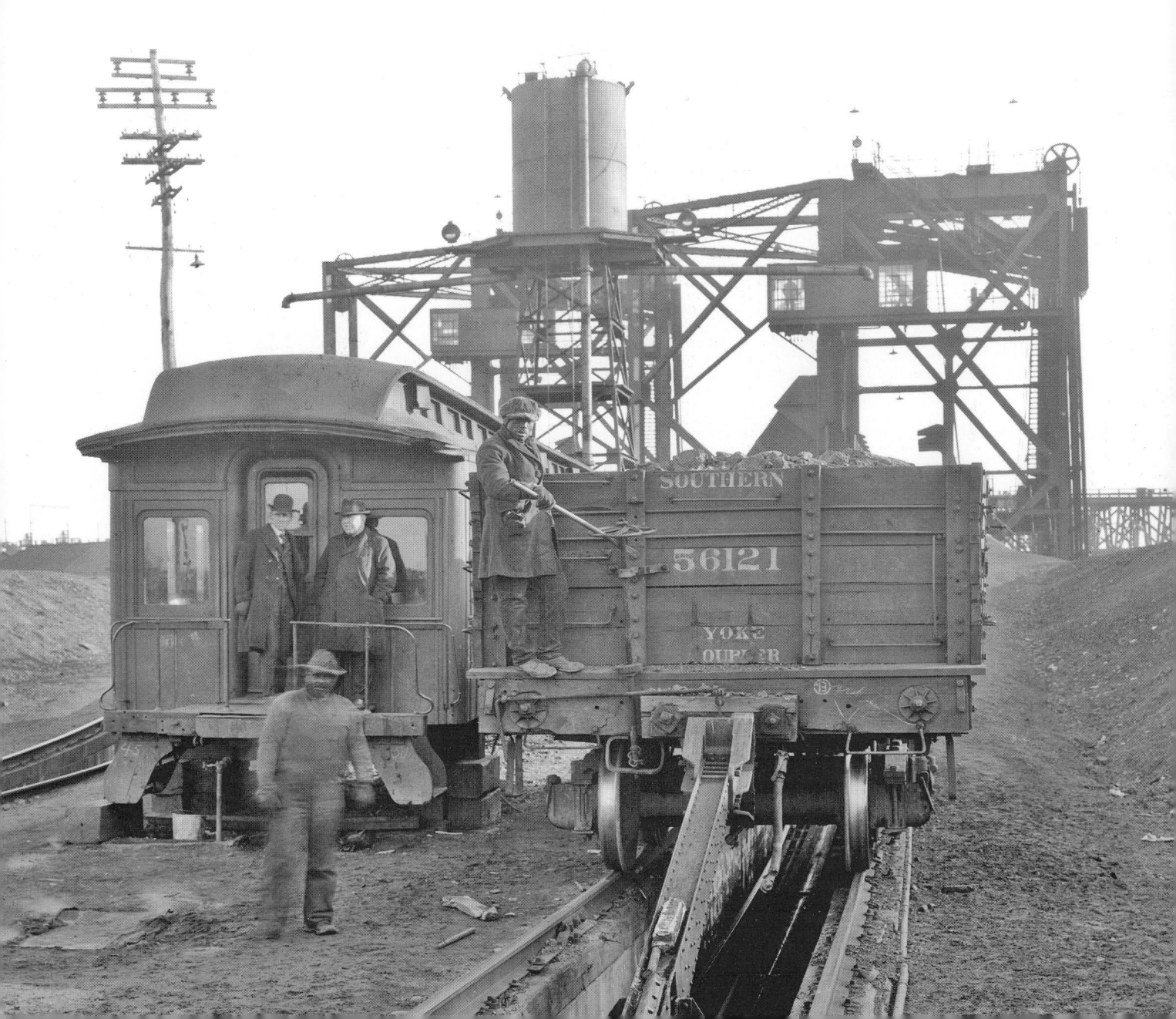

charging that the jobs held by black porter-brakemen belonged, by union contract, to whites. The National Railroad Adjustment Board, "made up of five representatives of Negro-excluding brotherhoods, a 'neutral' referee, and five railroad representatives," sided with the union, ordering the Santa Fe to end 43 years of practice and fire its black porter-brakemen, handing their jobs over to white brakemen. Labor economist Herbert Northrup, observing this dumfounding decision unfold, wrote that the Board "declares that [white] brakemen *own* certain jobs. Negroes, who do the same work, and in addition, perform other duties, are *porter-brakemen,* not brakemen. Consequently, they have no *right* to perform brakemen's work, and the management has no *right* to hire them to perform brakemen's work." The Santa Fe appealed the ruling, and the black trainmen prepared to go to court.[26]

Next to face the union's "threats and intimidation" was the Missouri–Kansas–Texas Railroad (the Katy), which had employed black porter-brakemen for more than 60 years, and the Frisco, which counted 111 porter-brakemen on its payroll. Some of the Katy railroaders had over 40 years' seniority. When both railroads bowed to the BRT's demands, the porter-brakemen, now affiliated with A. Philip Randolph's Brotherhood of Sleeping Car Porters, saw their only recourse in the federal courts. Injunctions and appeals consumed several years. Not until 1950 were the Santa Fe and Katy porter-brakemen's jobs secure. Other events were more dramatic. Former NAACP Legal Defense Fund attorney Charles H. Houston declared that "Hell has broken loose on the Frisco" when it buckled under a BRT strike, firing a number of porter-brakemen and demoting others to train porters. A federal appeals court recognized this act for what it was, the BRT's "predatory seizure" of another distinctly different railroad craft. The Supreme Court agreed, Justice Hugo Black writing in *Brotherhood of Railroad Trainmen, et al. v. Simon L. Howard, Sr., St. Louis–San Francisco Railway Company* (1951) that the BRT was after the blacks' jobs simply "because they are not white." While the porter-brakemen's jobs were saved, the *Howard* case was a lone victory: the Supreme Court did not for many years hear another railway labor discrimination case. And the steep declines in the number of passenger trains in the 1950s meant that porter-brakemen were working on borrowed time.[27] Those who managed to retain their jobs sometimes found themselves working even harder. On the Richmond, Fredericksburg & Potomac Railroad, their responsibilities were further enlarged by the addition of flagmen's duties, "protecting" trains that made unscheduled stops by walking a half-mile down the track to warn approaching trains and prevent collisions.[28]

The 1964 Civil Rights Act came too late to help many porter-brakemen. Their ranks had already been dramatically reduced by the decline in rail travel and resultant "train-offs." But it was not entirely too late to obtain justice for past wrongs. Such was the crusade of Joe Vernon Sears, who had been employed since the age of 22 on the Santa Fe as a porter-brakeman. Several times he applied for a trainman job, but was told, "you can't become a brakeman until your skin changes color." Sears's job was saved by the *Howard* decision, but as the Santa Fe's passenger service dwindled—only six long-distance trains survived to Amtrak—even porter-brakemen like Sears, with three decades of seniority, were bumped back to chair-car attendant, the Santa Fe's term for train porter. Inspired by the civil rights struggle in the South and the 1965 Watts riot, however, Sears applied for a brakeman job, only now to be turned down because he was "too old." Unwilling to accept defeat, he filed complaints against the BRT and his employer, first with his state's civil rights commission and then with the EEOC. The latter found that his Title VII rights had been violated. Thus emboldened, Sears and 72 other porter-brakemen filed a class-action suit against the union and the railroad. A federal court ruled in their favor, but appeals consumed several more years. Finally, in 1984, at the age of 71 (9 years after his retirement), Sears and his fellow plaintiffs were paid damages by the Santa Fe and the union, averaging $85,000 per man. A parallel case filed by Santa Fe chair-car attendants took even longer. Not until 1993, 22 years after the Santa Fe ceased passenger service, did 120 former attendants and the survivors of an additional 80 men win similar damages.[29]

Although to whites, black train porters and porter-brakemen were simply anonymous members of a passenger train's staff, to African American travelers they were often much more. The railroads were owned by whites and run by whites, and the issues of whether or not black passengers rode in comfort or discomfort, could obtain food or receive personal assistance often depended upon the presence of a black porter. Families at times had to send their children to distant places unaccompanied by adults, and it was to the care of train porters that young travelers were entrusted. Sometimes a child would be taken to one point, the porter then seeing that the youngster was put in the hands of a porter on a connecting train. To black southerners, in particular, "the colored porter was just as important to the colored traveler as the conductor was to the train." For years, Clifton Taulbert's aunt Ma Ponk had ridden the Illinois Central's inaccurately named *Delta Express* (it took 4 1/2 hours to run 150 miles, stopping at every whistle stop and hamlet) from Greenville, Mississippi, to Memphis. She knew the train porters, and they knew her. When she went to the station to see her sibling off, Taulbert recalled, "Ma Ponk introduced the porter to her sister and made him swear that after the whites had been served, he'd slip her some hot coffee and get her a pillow without charging. Of course he said yes. How could he, our conductor, say no with so great a cloud of witnesses?"[30]

Black train porters, like the Pullman porters, were frequently respected members of their communities. Theirs were good jobs, considering the limited opportunities for non-manual work, even though they were paid half or less the wages of a white passenger brakeman. "When I grew up," remembered Taulbert, "I thought, I might want to be a porter. The porter seemed to represent the best in colored. His shoes were highly polished, and his white shirt, stiffer than a board, stood out elegantly against his black suit furnished by the railroad. We called him Mister as he looked at his gold watch and assured us (our private conductor, you might say) the train would be leaving on time."[31] Like his Pullman counterpart, he might be a church deacon, a Masonic lodge officer, and a home and automobile owner. In addition, he was a window onto the wider world, having been to Chicago or Harlem, where black and white sat next to one another on the streetcars. He read the

Chicago Defender or *Pittsburgh Courier* and could interpret the news of the day. On top of all this, he was a good marital catch: "When you marry, marry a railroad man."[32]

African American porters were not confined to passenger train service. Others worked on vessels operated by the railroads. Railroad passenger ferries plied the waters of Boston, Philadelphia, Baltimore, Norfolk, and the San Francisco Bay. Canadian railroad ferries linked the Maritime Provinces in the east and ran from Vancouver to Vancouver Island in the west. But the greatest number of railroad-operated passenger ferries was in the New York City region, where all of the major railroads maintained marine departments on the Hudson River. Passenger trains from Washington and Philadelphia could reach Manhattan's Pennsylvania Station through the "tubes" under the river. But for decades, legions of commuters from New Jersey into the Big Apple took ferries from railroad terminals in Jersey City, Hoboken, and Weehawken. The Delaware, Lackawanna & Western, Erie, Pennsylvania, New York Central, and Central of New Jersey railroads all ran passenger ferries (as well as fleets of car floats and tugboats for transporting freight cars) that plied the Hudson. Other ferries, operated by the Long Island Rail Road, ran from Long Island City to lower Manhattan. And Baltimore & Ohio ferries plied routes from Staten Island to Manhattan as well as from South Amboy, New Jersey. Ferries employed porters, many of whom were African Americans or black immigrants from the Caribbean, although they had no racial monopoly.

Some ferry porters, like their counterparts on trains, were uniformed with easily recognizable coats and caps. Others, however, dressed like deck hands in work clothes. Whatever their attire, porters' duties were largely custodial: sweeping, cleaning restrooms, and the never-ending task of washing windows. Peak rush hours on Erie passenger ferries were 7:30–9:10 a.m. and 4:50–5:55 p.m. on weekdays, so it was not uncommon for porters to work 11- to 12-hour shifts. Since the number of midday passengers was much fewer, some of the railroads' boats tied up for two or more hours, with their crews being unpaid for the idle time. This was called a split watch. As a result of a grievance filed by Erie porter Ulysses Shell with the National Railway Labor Relations Board, split watches were abolished on the New York waterways, with the additional requirement that employees be paid time and a half after working eight hours.[33]

The Reading and Central of New Jersey railroads' fleets also employed black porters. The former operated passenger ferries across the Delaware River between Philadelphia and Camden, New Jersey, while the CNJ spanned the Hudson in the New York region. The two lines were under joint operations for a number of years and thus shared the company magazine. It occasionally printed photos of Reading porters at work, including a weary Tom Dickens holding his broom, and porter-window-washers Edward Drummond and Holbert Fister, the latter wielding a long-handled squeegee. Two photos of CNJ ferry *Westfield* porter Walter Williams show the seasonal differences in attire. During the summer, he was neatly uniformed with cap, white shirt, and necktie affixed with a clasp to prevent its blowing in the wind. In winter, in addition to the clothing just described, he was handsomely dressed in a double-breasted dark coat festooned with brass buttons plus shiny brass CNJ logos on each lapel. Porters performing custodial duties also worked in the ferry terminals. Another CNJ photo shows terminal porters Edward Scott and Walter Ray alongside similarly uniformed doorman William Marshall.[34]

Blacks performed other jobs in the operation of the railroad ferry fleets. While ferries burned oil for propulsion in the West, eastern vessels consumed coal. At least as late as the 1920s, fuel was hauled to the Reading's ferries in horse-drawn coal carts, as seen in photos of coalers Isaac Durrett and Oscar Knight. Durrett's four-legged steed was "Tom," described as "a faithful Reading worker for sixteen years." Other goods were brought on board by supplymen such as James Anderson, who pulled high-wheeled carts.[35] Few blacks were able to find jobs beyond laborer and porter, but at least two worked as CNJ bridgemen on the Hudson River, lowering gates on the slips when a ferry was about to depart and raising them upon a vessel's arrival. The photo of Henry Sneid and a white co-worker show both in caps, white shirts, ties, and slickers. Bridgeman Leslie Surgeon, who worked on the New York side of the Hudson, is shown in full winter garb, wearing a mid-thigh-length double-breasted coat, gloves, and a watch and chain. The latter was required because ferries ran on as precise schedules as did the trains.[36]

Many ferries offered lunch counters that provided quick meal service. Because railroads traditionally employed black cooks, waiters, and dishwashers, it is not surprising to find African Americans doing the same in their maritime divisions. One of the quickest food services was on the electric interurban Sacramento Northern Railway, whose railroad car ferry crossed Suisun Bay on its route between Oakland and Sacramento, California. An entire passenger train, broken into three-car segments, was loaded onto the ferry *Ramon*, which had tracks on its deck. A lunch counter, staffed by a black kitchen crew (two waiters and a cook), provided food for passengers, as well as for the captain and four deck hands. Thomas Fleming, soon to be a Southern Pacific dining-car waiter, got his first taste of railroad employment on the *Ramon*. Waiting for trains to arrive was boring. Living conditions were primitive: the three blacks lived in a "one room hut on stilts over the water" lacking indoor plumbing. The shack was infested with marsh mice that had to be shaken out of one's bed before retiring. And the pay and tips were meager.[37] To what extent blacks were employed as cooks and waiters on other railroad ferries cannot be determined, but because nearly all passenger ferries provided some manner of food service, it is likely that they were common fixtures to morning commuters fortifying themselves with coffee and a pastry in New York, Philadelphia, and elsewhere.

In the South, blacks found wider employment in railroad marine operations. The Chesapeake & Ohio operated both passenger ferry and car float service across Hampton Roads, Virginia. The *Virginia*, known to locals as the "Smokey Joe," employed black cooks and waiters as well as deck hands as it carried passengers between the railroad's terminals in Norfolk and Newport News. The C&O also owned the tugs *Alice* and *Louise*, with black firemen tending their boilers and line tenders (deck hands) to secure freight-car-laden car floats (barges with tracks) to be hauled across the channel.[38]

From the post–Civil War years into the early twentieth century, numerous steamship lines were owned or controlled by railroads. Some of the most important fleets sailed across Long Island Sound between New York and New England cities; along the southern Atlantic Coast, linking ports like Savannah, Charleston, Norfolk, and Baltimore; along the Gulf Coast and across to Cuba; and threading through and across the Great Lakes. Passenger steamers on overnight voyages offered staterooms to first-class passengers, who expected the same level of attention they would receive on a Pullman sleeping car. Such service was provided by messmen and messboys, the maritime equivalent of railroad waiters and porters, who were frequently black. The Anchor Line, a Pennsylvania Railroad subsidiary, sailed the palatial *Octorara*, *Tionesta*, and *Juniata* in the early 1900s on a Buffalo, New York-to-Duluth, Minnesota route. A huge dining room offered formally attired passengers a menu with fish, fowl, meats, other entrees and an impressive dessert selection of pies, cakes, and puddings, all served by white-jacketed African American waiters. For an additional 25 cents, messboys would take meals to one's stateroom.[39]

The lengthiest southern railroad maritime routes were operated by the Ocean Steamship Company of Savannah, also known as the Savannah Line, a subsidiary of the Central of Georgia Railway. It survived longer than other railroad ocean-going fleets because the railroad itself operated only within the state boundary and was thus exempted from the 1915 Panama Canal Act's requirement that interstate railroads divest themselves of passenger ships. The Savannah Line plied only two routes, four-day (three-night) nonstop voyages between Savannah, Georgia, and New York, and five-day (four-night) nonstop sailings between Savannah and Boston. While taking longer than rail travel between these points, the line promoted luxury. Its advertising extolled its "elegant saloons, finished in highly polished hardwoods. Commodious and well-ventilated staterooms, lighted by electricity. Table d' hote, including delicacies of the northern and southern markets." Plus, fares were one-quarter to one-third less than first-class rail tickets.[40] By the mid-1920s, it operated a fleet of eight modern passenger vessels named for southern metropolises, one of which, the *City of Rome*, carried only first-class passengers. They, of course, expected first-class service, which was provided by black chefs, cooks, messmen, and messboys. The line attained a remarkable seven-decade longevity, from its acquisition by the C of G in 1872 to cessation of operations during World War II. Contributing to its demise was the requisitioning of vessels for troop transportation and the sinking of the *City of Atlanta* by a German submarine off the coast of North Carolina on January 19, 1942. Only 3 of the 45-member crew survived. Both black cooks and all four black messmen and messboys perished.[41]

For more than a century, first-class rail travel and at least some steamship sailings included service by African Americans. Passengers paying premium fares enjoyed the ministrations of Pullman sleeping-car porters, lounge-car attendants, and steamship messboys. It seemed only natural for railroad and shipping managers to employ blacks in these capacities. After all, African Americans were viewed as a servant class. Black train travelers rarely went by Pullman, finding it difficult—and often impossible—to secure sleeping-car reservations. And for most blacks, first-class accommodations were prohibitively expensive. As a result, few of them enjoyed Pullman service provided by members of their own race. But millions of blacks traveled by coach, and, at least in the South, if they received any assistance from railroad personnel, it was from a black train porter. Short ferry crossings did not involve personal service, although porters, often black, were essential to maintaining cleanliness.

Many passenger trains carried other black railroaders who were rarely, if ever, seen by travelers. African American railway postal clerks were not, strictly speaking, railroad employees, but they were part of the black railroader fraternity. As employees of the Railway Mail Service, they were federal government workers, sorting and distributing mail on board especially designed Railway Post Office cars that were operated at the head end of passenger trains or assembled with similar cars into fast mail trains that carried no passengers. By the 1890s, 3,000 RPO cars traversed the nation, staffed by more than 6,000 clerks. With the implementation of the federal civil service system, many blacks were appointed as clerks, although the proportion of employees of each race is not captured in surviving postal personnel records. At the RMS's peak in the late 1920s, 18,000 clerks worked on 10,000 mail cars. Significant numbers of African Americans worked in the South. In 1915, 60 black RPCs ran out of St. Louis and an equal number out of New Orleans. Atlanta was home base to 90 more. Their monthly salaries averaged about $120, compared to the base salary of $27.50 for Pullman porters.[42]

Among all postal workers, railway postal clerks were considered the elite, but theirs was an exacting job. They earned premium pay, but only after passing periodic examinations testing distribution knowledge for as many as 10,000 post offices. Until passage of the Steel Car Act in 1911, their wooden cars were death traps in collisions and derailments. Clerks worked on their feet in swaying cars for as many as 16 hours at a time. A recent retrospective asserts that whites and blacks worked together in a "relatively integrated" environment, even on RPO runs in the South, yet evidence suggests that jealousy and even attacks tainted their relationships. In the first half of 1912, at least three black clerks were assaulted in Mississippi, while two years later, in Virginia and North Carolina, white clerks finagled assignments so that they got all the day runs, leaving the less desirable night runs to the black clerks. Reflecting such hostilities, the largest labor organization, the Railway Mail Association, added a "Caucasian clause" to its constitution and excluded blacks. This prompted black clerks to form their own brotherhood, the National Alliance of Postal Employees.[43]

Conditions worsened for black RPCs with the election of Woodrow Wilson in 1912. This first Democratic administration in decades ushered in segregation and white preferences throughout the federal bureaucracy. New Postmaster General Albert S. Burleson, a Texan, ordered that black RPCs be permitted to continue working only where their presence "would not be objectionable." Although existing jobs were generally protected by civil service procedures, new regulations, intended to subvert the merit system, required job applicants to submit photographs. Fighting to keep employment opportunities open for other blacks, the NAPE contested the photo requirement for years, finally gaining its abolition in 1940.[44]

White RPCs drew the color line against their black brethren in a number of ways. The Railway Mail Association was a fraternal and insurance organization and functioned much as a union even though postal employees were prohibited from unionizing until 1970. Nonetheless, like most railroad unions, the RMA excluded blacks because admitting them would grant them "social equality," which was unthinkable to most Caucasians.[45] White postal clerks also sought to establish an on-the-job racial hierarchy. The RMA repeatedly opposed the appointment of blacks as clerks-in-charge because they would exercise authority over white clerks. A typical protest complained that "this does not create harmonious relations between clerks and clerks-in-charge . . . We believe that no colored clerk-in-charge can supervise the work of clerks of Caucasian birth to best advantage." On the Norfolk & Raleigh RPO in 1913, after white clerks complained about a black clerk-in-charge, he was demoted and a white subordinate, who had a lower examination score, was elevated to his position. During World War II, veteran black clerks on the Longview & San Antonio RPO documented how the Railway Mail Service repeatedly passed them over and promoted whites with shorter periods of service to clerk-in-charge.[46]

Despite racial hostility from white clerks and the Post Office Department, black RPCs clung to their jobs. Mail by rail declined dramatically in the 1950s and 1960s, however, with the last RPO route ending in 1977. Promotions, particularly to office administrative positions, were rare for black clerks. Postal historian Frank R. Scheer notes that "it must have been ironic to work shoulder-to-shoulder with whites in the confines of an RPO car, yet deadhead to and from home in a segregated car in the South, or stay in a separate hotel and eat in a different beanery" when laying over.[47] The working experiences of black RPCs were in this respect little different from those of dining-car waiters, brakemen, and train porters. They had steady work, received what was, by black community standards, good pay, and were members of the black middle class. And they were more fortunate than other black railroaders in one key respect: although they also endured the hostility of organized white workers, they were federal civil servants. Even though the photograph requirement limited the availability of new employment for 25 years, those who managed to get RPO jobs worked in an at least theoretically merit-based system. A few blacks were advanced to clerk-in-charge decades before blacks gained supervisory or leadership positions like foremen or conductors on the railroads. Many others, whose lives depended upon the railroads, were less fortunate.

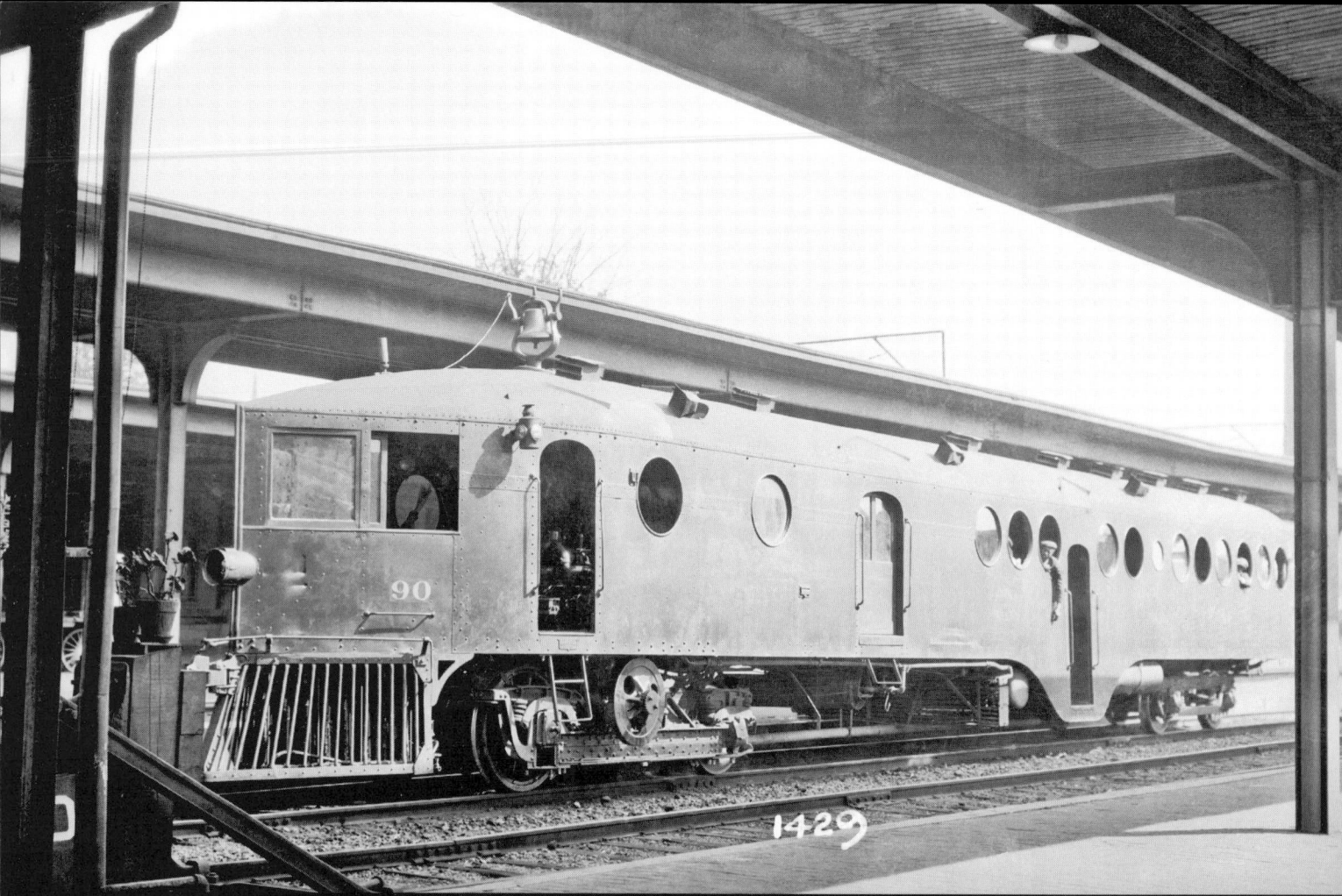

The Norfolk Southern Railroad's McKeen gasoline-engine motor car no. 90 has a black passenger leaning out of the forward, Jim Crow section. Other southern motor cars had both a middle entrance, for blacks, and a rear entrance, for whites. Such vehicles operated mostly on branch lines or on shorter railroads. This photograph was taken sometime after the 1909 delivery of the car and its conversion, in 1923, into an electric trolley car. Norfolk Southern Railway Collection, reprinted by permission, Railroad Museum of Pennsylvania

A black porter-brakeman, in vest and jacket, holding on to the locomotive handrail on the 20-mile Greene County Railroad in Georgia, c. 1920. African American porter-brakemen were common in the late nineteenth century, but unionized white railroaders drove them nearly to extinction on Class 1 lines in the first half of the twentieth century. They were more apt to retain employment on short lines such as this. All the equipment, including the Jim Crow car, is ancient and second-hand.
Don Hensley collection

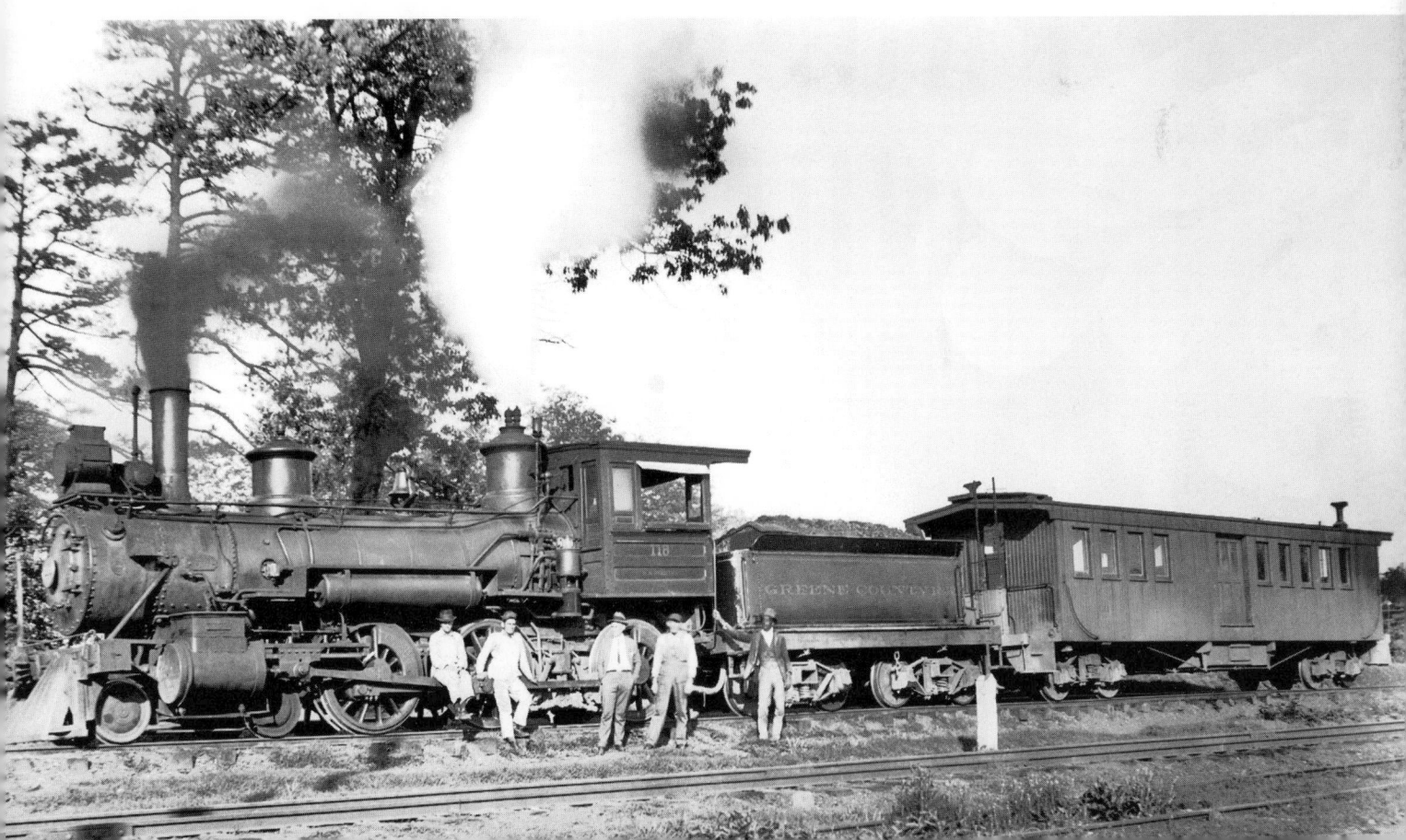

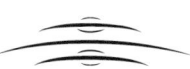

"NOT AT ALL PROPER FOR WOMEN"

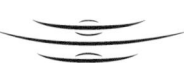

9

Female Railroaders

African American women railroaders? Women railroaders, period? Hasn't railroading always been a man's job, given its heavy outdoor labor and dangerous working conditions? Even railroad historians would be hard-pressed to identify many female railroaders beyond telegraphers, station agents, switch-tower operators, and the Harvey Girls. Some might recall the white "hostesses" (aka "stewardess-nurses") who graced some of the luxury trains from the 1930s to the 1960s. Others might know the story of 15-year-old Kate Shelley who, in 1881, braved a violent storm to flag down a passenger train shortly before it would have plunged into the Des Moines River after a bridge gave way. Only women's studies scholars and a few labor historians are likely to know much about the thousands of women who briefly filled men's shoes during World Wars I and II. But if you really want to stump the experts, ask about African American woman railroaders.

Women's entrance into railroading is usually dated to 1855, when three white females were employed as charwomen and another as a "restaurant keeper" at the Baltimore & Ohio Railroad's stations in Baltimore.[1] But female slaves began railroad work two decades earlier. Because slaves supplied most of the physical labor for building the antebellum South's railways, and because enslaved women were assumed to be capable of as much plantation labor as men, it isn't surprising to find them occasionally working alongside males on railroad construction crews. Others cooked for such crews and for section gangs. Some were owned outright by the railroads, while others were hired from owners who had a surplus of laborers. The most unfortunate enslaved female railroad builders were convicts. No white women, not even the despised Irish, were considered to be suitable for such dangerous and exhausting work. As historian Deborah Gray White observes, "black women did not experience sexism the same way white women did. Owing to their color white men saw black women differently and exploited them differently." Black women, including railroad workers, "were unprotected by men or by law, and they had their womanhood totally denied."[2]

The numbers of female slaves involved in antebellum railroading were not large, but their treatment and the tasks they performed established several patterns that persisted after slavery. The most odious was the inclusion of female prisoners in convict leasing to railroad construction contractors, which expanded all across the South after the Civil War. Other antebellum precedents led to decent, if narrow, opportunities. A few railroads employed enslaved women as matrons (janitresses) to keep stations clean and to assist in handling baggage. Not only did free black women continue this work in the South after slavery ended, but the idea spread to other parts of the country. At least two antebellum lines, the Richmond & Danville and the Philadelphia, Wilmington & Baltimore railroads, assigned maids to passenger trains, specifically slaves to staff the ladies' cars on the former line, and probably free black women to work on sleeping cars for the latter.[3] This practice disappeared after the end of slavery, but was revived shortly after 1900, when the Pullman Company began to employ ladies' maids on long-distance luxury trains.

One final antebellum custom that continued after the end of slavery was the sale of food to travelers at station stops by slaves and free blacks. Dining cars were practically unknown before the Civil War and station restaurants were infrequent. This gave female entrepreneurs the opportunity to sell pastries, meat, bread, and fruit, displayed on trays, through open coach windows. Such commerce persisted after emancipation because dining cars were still in their infancy and southern black women were eager to earn cash incomes without subjecting themselves to the exploitation of domestic service. Station vendors eventually disappeared when dining cars became commonplace and the fare at station restaurants improved. Although they were excluded from work on dining cars, black women eventually found occasional employment as waitresses, bus girls, and dishwashers at depot eateries.[4]

Some southern station matrons and waitresses held their jobs for years, as did Laura Rutland, janitress at the Southern Railway's Memphis station. She began in 1880, quit work for a while, but resumed the position and was still there 36 years later, in 1916, when she was awarded a 25-year service medal. Identical medals were also presented to Sarah Walker, who worked 34 years in the same capacity at the Danville, Virginia depot, and to matron Maggie Lattimore, who for 30 years cared for passengers and premises at the village of Coster, Tennessee. What such women earned was a pittance—a black waitress at the North Carolina Railroad's depot restaurant in Durham and a dishwasher at the Richmond, Fredericksburg & Potomac Railroad's Milford Hotel earned a mere $5 per month in the 1880s.[5] But steady work for cash wages in the post-Reconstruction South beyond domestic service and laundering was not easily found. Then, as travel became more refined and cars more commodious, black women began to secure employment as coach cleaners in southern cities where passenger cars were serviced. Before long, the Pullman Company was relying almost entirely on black women to clean the interiors of its growing fleet of sleeping and dining cars at its southern car yards.[6]

Perhaps the most barbaric aspect of southern convict leasing during and after Reconstruction was compelling black female prisoners—many of them teenagers—to live and labor alongside males. Women, nearly all black, made up 7 percent of the southern prison population in the late nineteenth century. In some instances, they were chained to men and slept in the same bunks. If male convicts were treated brutally by their keepers, and sometimes each other, how much more vicious must life have been for women facing equally punishing labor, savage correction, and the near certainty of rape.[7]

Examples of the tragic fates of African American female convicts can be found in almost every state in the South. Georgia's published statistics are graphic. From 1880 through 1882, of 1,243 convicts trapped in the state prison system, 112 were white men, 1 was a white woman, 30 other women were black, and the remaining 1,100 men were also African American, ages 12 to 78. The state furnished 211 of these unfortunates, without charge, to grade and construct more than 80 miles of the Marietta & North Georgia Railroad. Nine of that number were black women. Nora Daniel, age 20, arrived in 1881 to begin serving a 10-year sentence for simple larceny. The capriciousness of sentencing is seen in the fact that Lula Jones, age 14, received a 4-year term for the identical offense. Ada Maddox, 15, was serving 5 years for robbery, although Emma Williams, the same age, had drawn a 3-year sentence for burglary, while 22-year-old Martha Shallmon was serving an identical sentence for stabbing. Elizabeth Givins, Rose Henderson, and Mary Wood were serving life terms for murder.[8] Official prison reports are silent on the treatment of individual prisoners, but it is hard not to conclude that these women had no protection from assaults.

Outside of the South, African American women were absent from railroading in the late nineteenth and early twentieth centuries with the exception of a small number of car cleaners, crossing guards and station cleaners, and the earliest Pullman maids. Then, World War I opened railroad employment to women, nationwide, as never before. While many white females found office work, black women were stereotyped as being capable of only manual labor.[9] Despite this barrier, railroading offered numerous black women their first industrial jobs, plus, for some, an opportunity to escape the South.

The war in Europe, months before Americans were drawn into the conflict, exerted a dramatic influence on the American economy and on the lives of women. With customary sources of new unskilled workers all but vanished, industry turned to its largest untapped labor pools, women and blacks. Because of federal control of the railroads, black females found some of their best new opportunities in that industry, earning more than double the pay for unskilled laborers in other sectors of the economy and benefiting from U.S. Railroad Administration–mandated eight-hour work-

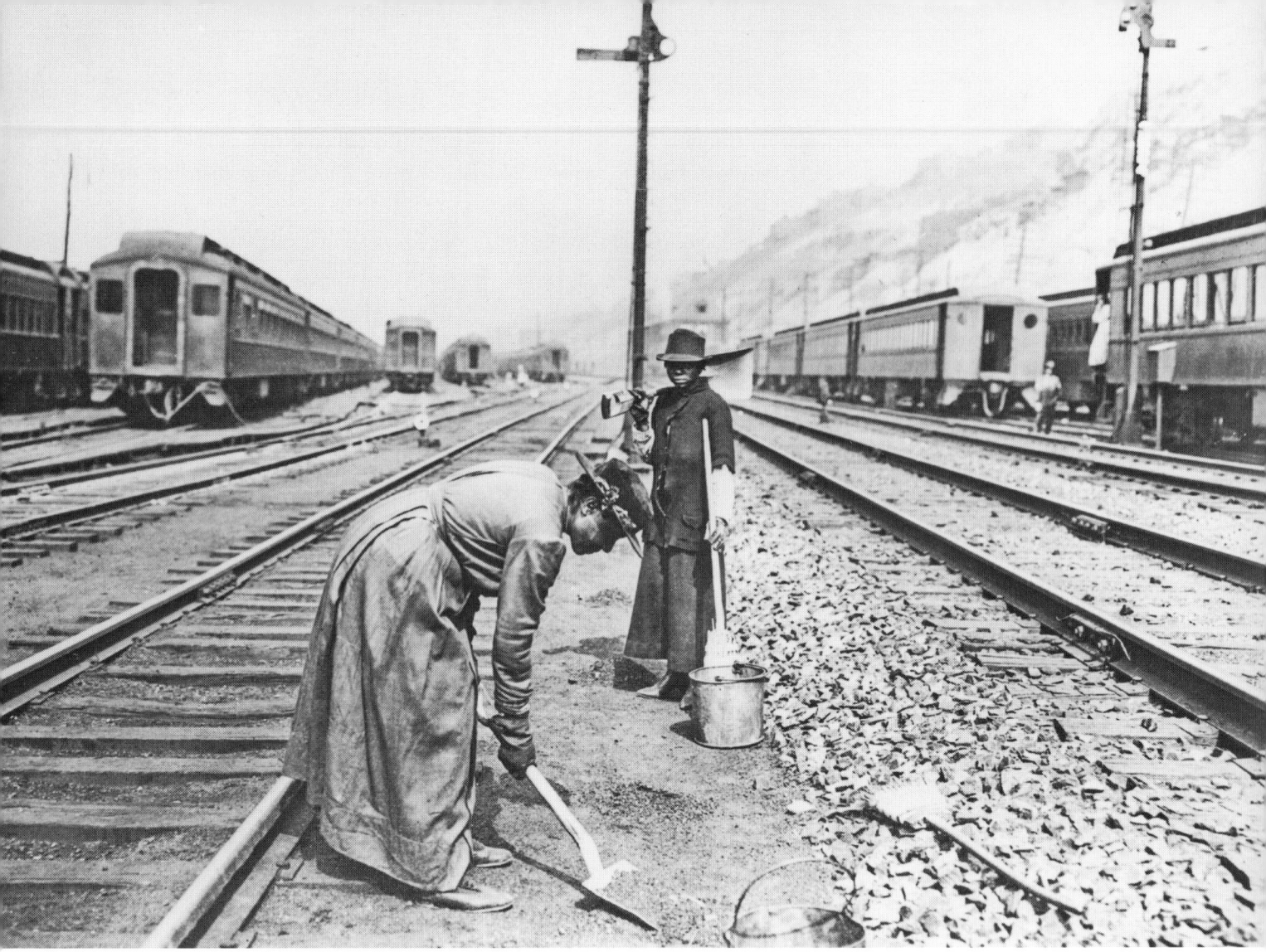

*Members of a black female Pennsylvania
Railroad "floating" gang in 1917, during World
War I, dressing the right of way on the Pittsburgh
Division, between that city and Altoona. This
was reputedly the first all-female section gang on
any railroad. The U.S. Railroad Administration
eventually barred women from heavy work,
including maintenance of way. Reprinted by
permission, Railroad Museum of Pennsylvania*

days and a standard of equal pay for equal work. The USRA's Women's Service Section investigated hiring practices and working conditions and in cases helped ensure the payment of fair wages, but the middle-class reformers who staffed it also ended up reducing black women's opportunities by defining a number of manual labor jobs, like maintenance of way and freight trucking, as being too physically demanding for them.[10]

When northern railroads experienced acute labor shortages in 1916, they initially recruited only black men. Then, as the migration widened to include whole families, black women began to find railroad jobs. The door was hardly opened wide, however. Even as female railroad employment more than tripled, eventually topping 100,000 in October 1918, white women got the vast majority of the jobs, and they monopolized white-collar work. Newly hired black females were destined for manual labor, with which they were already familiar, having worked in domestic service, laundries, restaurants, and hotels, as well as agriculture. In fact, many came right from the farm, their industrial work clothes being the same dresses, aprons, and bandanna head coverings they had traditionally worn. Others switched to bloomers and "womanalls."[11]

Although a tiny number of black women worked in train operations as switchmen and flagmen, most were restricted to tasks in shops and roundhouses or along the right of way. More than 150 were employed on the Pennsylvania Railroad's Baltimore division, clearing tracks of trash, cleaning passenger cars, guarding crossings, and doing unskilled shop labor. Other new Pennsy employees replaced male baggage handlers at a suburban Philadelphia station. Several railroads reported "very satisfactory" black female engine wipers and roundhouse laborers who washed locomotives, cleaned headlights and marker lights, and painted smoke-boxes. Others shoveled out ash pits where steam locomotives dropped their fires. In the shops, black women were restricted to sweeping and other custodial tasks, while white women performed skilled and semi-skilled labor. Freight houses in the North and the South utilized considerable numbers of black women. Nearly two dozen worked for the Atchison, Topeka & Santa Fe Railway in Kansas City, Missouri, as truckers under the supervision of a black male foreman. The Wabash Railway found several dozen suitable black female replacements for male truckers, including 25 working in Chicago who earned $3.09 for a 9½-hour day, decent wages for black women in the Windy City. But when the Missouri Pacific Railroad hired 25 female truckers in Little Rock, Arkansas, their black male co-workers objected because abusive white foremen supervised the women.[12] No matter who was the boss, this was hard physical labor; on some railroads, male truckers were expected to move more than a ton of boxed freight per hour.

Although women, white as well as black, worked on tracks during World War I, they were rarely true section laborers. Reportedly, black women did genuine maintenance of way in the Illinois Central Railroad's East St. Louis yards. And slavery-era definitions of black women's physical endurance resurfaced in 1918, when the Central of Georgia Railway hired a number of them to, the company implied, collect scrap metal along the right of way. Once on the job, the women found themselves carrying 150-pound crossties. Apparently they had sufficient physical strength, because on the basis of this one-day experiment officials assembled an entire black female section gang with a white male foreman. Before noon of the second day, however, the women quit, fearing that if they were expected to work this hard in the yards close to home, they would have to toil even harder when they were dispatched to a remote section of the line.[13]

The USRA eventually forbade the use of female section laborers and freight truckers, regardless of race, ruling: "This class of work is not at all proper for women and that in view of the [increased] wages now paid for such work, it should be possible to secure men." Even those female track workers who merely dressed ballast, picked up scrap and rubbish along the right-of-way, and kept switches free of ice during winter eventually lost their jobs. Some discharged track workers and freight truckers strongly protested the ruling, but to no avail. Following the edict, on one railroad alone, more than four hundred truckers and track laborers were reassigned or found themselves unemployed.[14] At least some male workers must have applauded such restrictions. In a number of yards and freight houses, women were paid one-third less than men.[15]

The number of black female car cleaners increased dramatically during World War I, not only because of labor shortages, but also because the railroads perceived black women as being particularly fit for the task, such work being similar to domestic service. Their ranks eventually numbered in the thousands. Many worked in the Pullman Company's yards, cleaning sleeping and parlor cars, while others worked for railroads that operated their own fleets of coaches and diners. Black women labored alongside black men and whites of both sexes, many of whom were immigrants. Men generally washed the exteriors, while a mixed force of women and men performed the more meticulous inside tasks: sweeping up trash and litter; mopping floors; disinfecting spittoons; cleaning hoppers (toilets); brushing seats; washing windows; dusting woodwork; cleaning carpets by hand, on one's knees; and polishing metal surfaces. Women were generally paid less than men, and racial differentials were common in the South. Where there were acute labor shortages, black women were sometimes hired as outside cleaners. The Pullman Company paid them more than inside cleaners, but still less than male outside cleaners.[16]

Car cleaning was hard and sometimes nasty work with long shifts and, until late in the war, very low pay. On numerous railroads, northern as well as southern, employees worked 10 hours per day (including a 1-hour meal break), 6 or 7 days a week. Seventy-hour work weeks were common. The USRA eventually shortened the work week to 5 or 6 days, and reduced some shifts to 8 hours. More significant were its pay increases. Before these improvements, the Southern Railway paid black female inside cleaners at its Charlotte and Greensboro, North Carolina, coach yards only 6 cents an hour for 6-day, 10- to 11-hour shifts. (Black males earned 11 cents per hour.) The women's $3.50 weekly wage was no better than the earnings of a domestic servant, who at least could expect the added "payment" of the "service pan" (leftovers). If female car cleaners agreed to work every day of the week, they were awarded a 10-cent-per-day bonus. Wartime labor shortages forced railroads to raise women's and men's hourly wages to 11 and 13 cents, respectively, in early 1918, but USRA-mandated increases really made a difference. By July 1918, women were earning 28 cents an hour, and men 2 cents more. And by early 1920, car cleaners' wages peaked at 45 cents for men and women alike. Once the railroads were free of federal control, however, wages for both sexes dropped by 40 to 50 percent.[17]

Black women car cleaners often experienced racial prejudice on the job. In Council Bluffs, Iowa, a spiteful white forewoman on the Union Pacific Railroad replaced an all-black gang with whites. Not only was segregation of black and white workers the norm in the South, even in most northern coach yards black women had to use separate toilets and locker rooms, which were often inferior to those reserved for whites. Some yards had no women's washrooms, forcing them to use toilets in the cars that they were cleaning, or walk long distances to a station restroom. On the Long Island Rail Road, black women were not allowed to clean dining cars, only coaches. The use of white supervisors in the South was based on racist notions that blacks could not effectively lead other blacks and that whites best knew how to "handle" them. In fact, where black car cleaners (male as well as female) were supervised by members of their own race, they performed satisfactorily and sometimes superlatively. Such black forewomen or foremen were, however, rare. One such supervisor was Katey Hogan, employed at the New York Central's Cleveland yards, who directed several pairs of women inside cleaners, each of which completed 30 to 40 coaches per shift. Her teams were known for the excellence of their work, due undoubtedly to the fact that their supervisor understood their traditional work habits and knew how to motivate them. And Hogan stood up for her workers. Rather than require them to use the cold, unsanitary outhouses designated for them, she allowed them to take advantage of toilets much closer, even though this was against company regulations.[18]

Black women station matrons had become more common by the World War I era. They had done such work in the South as far back as during slavery, and by the early twentieth century, northern blacks also began to take such jobs, sometimes working alongside white women. A matron's primary duty was to keep the station spotless: sweeping, dusting, mopping, polishing brass, and cleaning restrooms. She might also be recruited to handle luggage in the absence of a Red Cap. Although the railroads depicted matrons as friendly helpers to female travelers, they were essentially janitresses, their low wages reflecting that fact. Before federally mandated wage increases, black matrons working at the Delaware, Lackawanna & Western Railroad's stations in New Jersey earned only $32 per month. By mid-1919, they were earning $70 and working fewer hours. Whether in the North or the South, such women were expected to be "courteous, old fashioned Negroes," humble and obsequious.[19]

The largest concentration of black women railroaders during World War I was in the nation's capital, where the Washington Terminal Company operated Union Station and performed switching duties for the five railroads whose passenger trains departed from and arrived there. It employed more than 50 black women common laborers in the roundhouse, many as engine wipers (one of the dirtiest jobs in railroading). Another 55 kept the station clean, and about 30 more worked as waitresses, bus girls, and kitchen cleaners in the station restaurant. By the end of the war, after the USRA raised wages nearly 70 percent, these women were much better able to support their families.[20]

Cleveland typified the range of occupations open to black women during the war. The Baltimore & Ohio, Pennsylvania, and New York Central began adding them to freight dock, coach yard, round-house, and scrap yard forces when men left for higher-paying factory jobs. Despite the fact that they had to brave cold winds whipping off Lake Erie in winter, they felt their wages were worth the hard-ship. Married women in particular appreciated going to work before dawn, allowing them to return home to care for children and their households in the afternoon. Until the USRA banned them from such work, freight truckers sometimes struggled with crates beyond the weight limit allowed by state law for women in factories, but managed to handle them by working in teams. Railroad offi-cials stereotyped black women as stronger than white women, or having already suffered gyneco-logical injuries and thus not in danger of further damaging themselves with overly strenuous labor. In short, whites who hired black women tended to believe that, as historian Kimberley Phillips notes, "black women could work more like men because their lives differed inherently from those of white women."[21]

What drew African American women to railroading during World War I? Although some may have sought employment out of patriotic zeal, as did many women during World War II, in general blacks were lukewarm about the war.[22] For most, the primary motive was pay. The highest wages available to black women during World War I—as much as $15 to $20 weekly—were earned in government munitions factories, in the garment industry, and on railroads.[23] Those working at the Santa Fe's Corwith yards in Chicago reported: "This is the best pay they can get anywhere." As Pearl Jones, a 21-year-old Santa Fe freight trucker in Kansas City, Missouri, put it, "All the colored women like this work and want to keep it. We are making more money at this than any work we can get, and we do not have to work as hard as at housework [domestic service] . . . Eight dollars [a week] is considered good at housework. Nine dollars is good in a laundry and that is the hardest work a woman can do . . . With three dollars a day, we can buy [Liberty] bonds . . . , we can dress decently, and not be tempted to find our living on the streets."[24]

Real upward mobility, or even longevity, was illusory. A few Missouri Pacific car cleaners who had worked since before the war moved up to better-paying, heavy-labor work in trucking oil bar-rels and 250-pound couplers and storing bulky castings and forgings. Others graduated to freight trucking jobs. Black women accepted such hard work because they aspired to a better life for their families. A scrap dock laborer in the New York Central Railroad's Cleveland shops added her pay to that of her husband, who worked as a roundhouse ash pit man, so that she could clothe her children well and live respectably.[25] Female employment was essential for family survival in urban economies where the cost of living far exceeded that of the rural South. But postwar demobiliza-tion proved disastrous for black women railroaders. Although car cleaners, station matrons and restaurant help, and office janitresses generally retained their jobs, Pearl Jones and other truck-ers and laborers were soon "last hired, first fired." Even though the USRA recognized the right of female workers to accrue seniority, many lines ignored it and dismissed them to make room for male employees. The Pennsylvania Railroad violated women's seniority rights more than any other line, discharging many for "inefficiency." Women railroaders generally accepted the legitimacy of allowing demobilized veterans to reclaim their old jobs but they deeply resented being fired so that men with no prior experience could be hired in their places.[26] The railroads did not contemplate more than a handful of black women in their permanent workforce, and at times displayed little regard for their welfare. When the New York Central built a new freight office building in Cleveland in 1919, it provided modern restrooms for white women clerks, but only a dank windowless basement facility for the black cleaning women. Of the Pennsylvania Railroad's 9,479 black employees as of January 1924, only 152 (1.6 percent) were women. Despite exceptions like the four black women telegraphers on the New York Central in the mid-1920s, female railroaders remained overwhelmingly white.[27]

As most black women were losing their wartime jobs, the era of the Pullman maid was about to reach its peak. Maids were first hired to work on luxury trains in the early 1900s. The heyday of their service was the 1920s, when, the *Pullman News* reported, they served "on all the celebrated limited trains that run between New York and Chicago, to the Florida East Coast, from Chicago to the South and to the Pacific Coast and the Northwest."[28] They were a hand-picked lot, subjected to rigorous scrutiny. Company investigators checked every reference in person. Particular stock was put into whether the applicant's home was neat, clean, respectable, and located in a decent neighborhood. Her personal character was probed to ensure that a prospective maid was morally upright and not likely to fraternize with either passengers or crew members. Obviously, prostitution or promiscuity on its cars would shatter the Pullman Company's carefully cultivated image of safe, respectable, family-friendly travel. Once hired, the maids' performance was continually reviewed to ensure their moral probity and servant demeanor along with the satisfactory performance of their assigned tasks.

Pullman maids were, overall, an educated, poised, and mature lot. What attracted them to a job requiring long hours and days away from home? Simply put, even urbanized African American women had few good employment prospects. Men reclaimed most industrial jobs after the Armistice, thereafter limiting them again to commercial laundries or domestic service. Well-educated black women were unlikely to get clerical or sales jobs that now were being filled, increasingly, by white women. Most maids had attended high school and some had college experience. In physical features, they were generally matronly rather than the thin, bust-less "flappers" of the era. Most were in their late 20s or early 30s when they were hired, had been born in the South, and had previously worked as hotel and domestic maids or as manicurists and hairdressers. Some were trained nurses. Single women predominated, but Pullman did not discriminate against those who were married. The fact that more maids were single reflects the hardships of maintaining family life while being "on the road." Newly hired maids might be required to "double out" or even "triple out" without even the opportunity to return home to see one's family or change clothes. Frances Albrier, a single mother whose two young children stayed with a neighbor, recalled "running wild" for a year before she was able to bid on a regular run. Another reason why more maids were single was the unpredictable nature of their jobs. Trains were added and dropped from the railroads' schedules due to growing or declining traffic. And some luxury trains were seasonal, so maids could expect periodic furloughs.[29]

The Great Depression hit Pullman maids particularly hard. About 300 were employed in 1929, but their numbers dropped below 200 by mid-1931 and were down to about 100 a year later. With business and leisure travel eroded, Pullman figured manicures weren't essential and porters could assist women with children. The passenger boom of the World War II era brought a modest revival in employment, but the service ended in 1948, at which time only 16 maids remained on the payroll. A few railroads continued, on their own, to staff luxury trains with maids. The Atlantic Coast Line Railroad had offered female passengers "southern hospitality" since 1939, but canceled the service in 1951, laying off its last 17 maids.[30]

Despite service interruptions, some Pullman maids enjoyed lengthy careers. Etta Banks began working in 1909 at the age of 31 and remained on the payroll until retiring in 1943. Because of her seniority she was one of the few maids who was immune to furloughs. And her seniority guaranteed a job on one of America's most famous trains, the Pennsylvania Railroad's all-Pullman *Broadway Limited*. The Pullman Company logged all complaints and commendations, and Banks was periodically cited for providing "indifferent service," reading a magazine while on duty, and failing to be as "conspicuous" and "useful" as she should. But she also received "credit letters," and upon her retirement the company lauded her "fine service record." Mabel Taylor worked for many years on the *Broadway Limited*'s rival, the New York Central's equally luxurious all-sleeping-car *Twentieth Century Limited*. She had already been a chambermaid and manicurist prior to joining the Pullman Company in 1906 at the age of 21 and she worked for 36 years until retiring in 1942, when wartime traffic demands brought the suspension of many luxury services on trains.[31]

While Taylor's and Banks' overnight trains took only 20 hours to get from New York to Chicago, other maids' runs lasted up to three days on Midwest-to-Pacific Coast luxury trains like the *Golden State Limited* to Los Angeles and the *Oriental Limited* from Chicago to Seattle. The shortest run with Pullman maid service was the Southern Pacific's overnight all-sleeper *Lark* between San Francisco and Los Angeles, featuring, for a time, Chinese "winsome maidens" with new "American names" like Virginia, Barbara, and Dorothy. They were hired primarily in 1928 and 1929, when the Brotherhood of Sleeping Car Porters was threatening to strike, in an attempt to intimidate those maids who had joined the union or were sympathetic to it. The Chinese maids were considerably younger women, and most of them worked less than two years.[32]

Like Pullman porters, maids were expected to be servants. The company's "Instructions for Maids" specified that "the most important requisite of our service to be observed without exception is to please and satisfy passengers." Their uniform reinforced their role: a one-piece black dress embellished with white cuffs and collar, over which was worn a bibbed apron. So that there be no

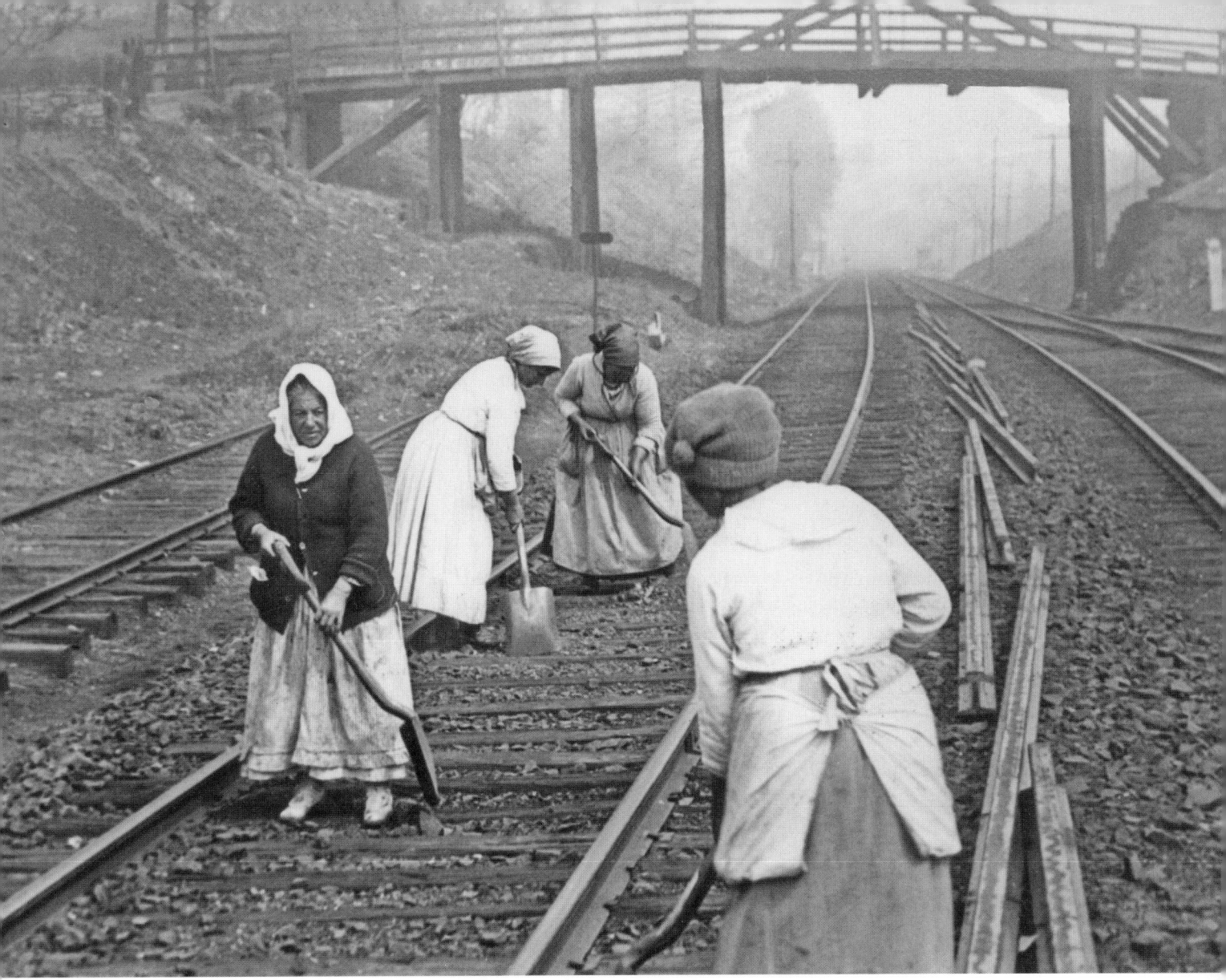

An Erie Railroad female gang dresses the right of way somewhere in New York in March 1919, during the World War I male labor shortage. Wearing traditional rural clothing, they appear to be recent migrants from the South. They will not work long: troops are already being demobilized, and men will quickly reclaim such railroad jobs. Women's Bureau Records, National Archives

hint of sexuality, they were forbidden to use powder, rouge, or any other cosmetics. Their main responsibilities were to attend to the "wants and comfort of women and children," beginning with assisting them in boarding and, when necessary, offering first aid. If more urgent duties did not interfere, they were to give free manicures and hair-dos (the equivalent of the porters' "free" shoe shines). Some trains had baths for women, which the maids were to keep "scrupulously clean." They were also required to keep passengers' rooms tidy, collect trash, remake beds, repair garments, and perform any other personal service. Like the porters, maids had little time for rest; if they slept at all, it was on a couch in the ladies' lounge. Pullman's expectations were clear: "Maids should thoroughly understand that the reputation of the service depends upon their efficiency; consequently, in their contact with passengers [they] should be obliging, courteous and alert to anticipate their wants." For all this, the Pullman Company paid them less than $80 per month in the 1920s, justifying this exploitative wage with the belief that well-served passengers would be generous tippers. But a maid only attended to travelers when they requested her assistance, and generally only women, the elderly, and the infirm, so she earned less in tips than did a porter.[33]

The Pullman maids' struggle for decent pay and working conditions required them to confront not only the anti-union Pullman Company, but also the sexism of porters. Although their union was initially named the Brotherhood of Sleeping Car Porters and Maids, the "and Maids" was dropped in 1929. Despite the fact a number of maids supported the union—and a few were fired for union activism—they were expected to join one of the Ladies' Auxiliaries, which also included porters' wives and other female relatives. The Auxiliaries' purposes were to help build the union and bolster the morale of porters. Bolstering the morale of maids was not on their agenda. Maids did not attain BSCP leadership. BSCP leaders tended to downplay maids' issues, while Auxiliary leaders often disregarded them. Basically, the BSCP and even many Auxiliary members did not see women as a fundamental and permanent part of the labor force. If black male workers achieved a decent wage, they could fully support their families and women could leave the world of work. So the BSCP was not a strong advocate for Pullman maids as working women, even though it did bargain on their behalf and win improvements in wages and working conditions.[34]

Passengers encountered Pullman maids and porters, but they never saw those who labored behind the scenes to make their travels pleasant, like Pullman's car cleaners and laundry workers. At first, commercial laundries cleaned Pullman linens and uniforms, but in 1923, the company began to establish its own plants all around the country, as well as in Mexico and Canada. Men did the hardest work, transporting sacks of soiled linens from passenger yards, loading them into huge washing machines, and then putting them into extractors that spun out most of the moisture. Women then took over, shaking out the damp linens and feeding them into ironers. Damaged items were sent to seamstresses for repair or conversion into other articles (a torn tablecloth could be made into napkins, for example). Then, either men or women folded and packed the clean linens into bags, ready to be returned to stockrooms near the yards. At the peak of passenger travel, nearly 10 million pieces of linen were required to supply the company's 8,600 cars. A million pieces of soiled linen were washed daily. The Pullman Company proudly called itself "the world's greatest housekeeper." Even in 1931, when the Great Depression had greatly eroded passenger traffic, about 60,000 travelers slept in Pullman sleepers each night, or the equivalent of one-fifth of the country's population in the space of a year.[35]

Pullman's laundries placed African Americans in the hottest, heaviest, and least-skilled jobs, although the racial mix varied from laundry to laundry. In the South, blacks held practically all nonsupervisory jobs. In northern and Midwestern cities black women and men predominated in sorting, washing, ironing, and folding, but mostly white women, many of immigrant background, worked in the sewing rooms. In western cities white women were as likely to shake, iron, fold, bundle, and tie linens as were blacks, while whites monopolized the seamstress positions.[36]

African American women continued to work in station restaurants throughout the first half of the twentieth century. Some railroads did not add dining cars until the 1920s, in which case passengers still ate at meal stops. The most famous restaurants were the 74 Harvey Houses, located along the Santa Fe's lines. These eateries were known for their consistently good food and proper waitresses, the single, white "Harvey Girls." But in El Paso, Texas, at least during World War II, black women worked as waitresses although they may not have borne the title "Harvey Girl." It is possible that at the other 14 Harvey restaurants in Texas, black women were similarly employed. More widely, Harvey Houses used black women as pantry girls and dishwashers while black men worked as bus boys and dishwashers.[37] And the Fred Harvey lunchroom at Chicago Union Station employed a nearly all-black staff of female waitresses and male bus boys during World War II. Black women served food to passengers at station stops in many other places. In World War II, they staffed mobile trackside canteens at Illinois Central stations in Jackson, Mississippi; Fulton, Kentucky; and Champaign, Illinois, selling coffee and sandwiches while trains paused for engine servicing. This food service was necessary because dining cars could not accommodate all passengers. Some of the servers manned platform carts as others carried baskets and sold throughout the coaches. While black women performed these tasks, white women supervised them.[38]

The modest number of black women who performed railroad work between the wars had one thing in common with all other railroaders: the Great Depression wiped out many of their jobs. By mid-1933, total railroad employment was down 44 percent, and those remaining on the payrolls were earning 20 percent less than in the 1920s. Pullman maids won wage increases after the porters unionized, but fewer of them were left to enjoy this victory. And Pullman's car cleaners who were lucky enough to have retained their jobs were still earning less in 1938 than in April 1929, before the stock market crash.[39]

World War II once again opened nontraditional doors to black women as industrial expansion and the military draft drained manpower from railroads that were already straining under tremendous increases in freight and passenger traffic. The numbers of women railroaders and the variety of jobs they performed were much greater than in the previous war. Almost any Class 1 line could illustrate the labor crisis in the months after Pearl Harbor. In less than a year, the Southern

Pacific lost 7,200 male employees to military service, necessitating that "Women Take Over Tough Jobs to Relieve [the] Manpower Shortage." They were "a new source of emergency power . . . WOMANPOWER."[40] By September 1942, 40,000 women nationwide were employed by railroads. That number jumped to more than 100,000—7.5 percent of all railroad employees—by the end of 1943. About two-thirds of them were white women clerks and secretaries. A small number of white women also joined the ranks of operating employees as brakemen and assistant passenger conductors (i.e., ticket takers). Black women were concentrated in five areas. They remained a large proportion of the more than 5,000 female car cleaners employed by the individual railroads, facing a seemingly endless number of "muddy and litter-strewn coaches." At least as many others cleaned the interiors of Pullman cars. Black women, particularly in the South, constituted a considerable portion of the 5,000 female unskilled shop laborers. They were also among the growing numbers of female section gang laborers. And they were part of the "armies of charwomen, black, brown and white, who descend on . . . terminals by night."[41]

One of the largest wartime railroad employers was the Pennsylvania Railroad that in mid-1943 had 17,951 African Americans, nearly 11 percent of its workforce. One in 4 black workers was a woman. The largest group was 1,008 coach cleaners, followed by 990 shop and roundhouse laborers, and 828 "section & extra gang men." Another 415 toiled as freight-house truckers and loaders, and more than 100 had broken the male monopoly on dining cars, working as waitresses and cooks. But not a single black woman on the Pennsy held a clerical job; their only presence in offices was as messengers, elevator operators, and janitresses. And although it was the nation's busiest railroad, operating thousands of steam locomotives requiring frequent servicing and a fleet of tens of thousands of freight and passenger cars needing periodic maintenance, no black women were either journeymen or apprentice mechanics and only 81 became boilermaker, machinist, car repair, and pipefitter helpers. By comparison, hundreds of white women were entering the helper ranks. By May 1944, the number of PRR black female employees had grown another 25 percent, to 5,484, but they made no significant breakthroughs into mechanical occupations although hundreds of black men were being hired or promoted to helpers. The limit of black women's opportunities had peaked. By June 1945 their jobs were in free-fall, having slipped 28 percent (to 3,954) in 13 months. And by January 1946 their ranks were down to 2,741.[42] Similar patterns occurred on smaller lines. The Reading Railroad employed black women only as section hands, engine and car cleaners, lamp cleaners, and unskilled roundhouse laborers and scrap sorters, and only so long as the war lasted.[43]

The Pennsy did not regard all women employees the same. Some jobs like track repairs, believed to be inappropriate for white women because they required "brute strength," were nonetheless allowed for black women.[44] Other tasks were demasculinized so that white women could perform them, but such considerations were not deemed necessary for black women, supervisors generally being of the opinion that they alone, of all women, were capable of heavy labor. The PRR segregated female employees' bathroom facilities, at times simply failing to see black women as women. When women were introduced at Cincinnati's Fifty-ninth Street engine house, new restrooms were built for white women but none at all provided for black women. And Pennsy managers tolerated abysmal conditions in the Chicago coach yards where 261 car cleaners (90 percent of whom were black) had to use a small, foul toilet facility infested with bedbugs and cockroaches. Officials in Detroit had to be repeatedly prodded before they ordered windows in the black women's bathroom and changing area to be covered so that men could not peek in. This tendency to ignore issues of modesty applied only to black women.[45]

"Firsts" were ballyhooed when women entered previously male bastions. Baltimore & Ohio porterette Maggie Hudson was "the first girl to crash the ranks of train porters." (In fact, she was the third porterette hired.) She held down runs between Washington and Cumberland, Maryland. Porterettes earned the same pay as porters, shared the same seniority list with them, and became permanent employees, some continuing on the payroll into the 1960s. They could not work in Ohio after the war, however, because a labor law prohibited women from lifting more than 25 pounds and porterettes, like porters, assisted passengers in stowing luggage that at times exceeded that weight. Union Pacific porterettes lasted only for the duration of the war, however, and those on the Seaboard Air Line Railway were likewise considered wartime replacements and discharged once the conflict was over.[46]

Dining cars suffered labor depletion at the same time as they were deluged by record numbers of patrons. The result was a modest number of black women in kitchens, mostly as fourth cooks (dishwashers) and as waitresses. The Pennsy introduced them on short runs, like the Philadelphia–New York turn, where they would not have to lay over away from home. Nearly 200 were employed by November 1943, constituting 9 percent of the railroad's 2,181 dining-car servers. Apparently, public reaction was positive and the women were gratified to earn good pay and tips.[47]

Scattered across the country were veteran black car cleaners like Rosetta Jones, employed at the Southern Pacific's Houston coach yard since World War I. But as World War II travel soared in 1942, many new black women were added to cleaning crews nationwide. Cars were packed to the gills, leaving them dirtier. And with a shortage of cars, they had to be prepared for new runs more quickly than before. At the SP's Mission Coach Yards in Los Angeles, an all-black 50-woman crew led by "foreman" Katherine Mayo cleaned the coaches of seven regularly scheduled trains plus three military extras every four-to-midnight shift. The Chicago & North Western Railway's California Avenue coach yard, in the Windy City, employed 218 car cleaners in mid-1943. Half of those hired since Pearl Harbor were black women.[48]

The need to stir the patriotism of all Americans led government and railroad photographers to document women's labor more thoroughly than ever before. A favorite subject was female engine wipers. Not to be outdone by Rosie the Riveter, Rosetta the Railroader posed patriotically in front of or atop gleaming engines, wearing men's overalls with her too-long cuffs rolled up and cap or scarf protecting her "do." Photographs showing women polishing headlights and boiler jackets do not reveal the grease and grime that adorned them by the end of their shifts, nor the heat endured in working on a steaming locomotive. Some wipers worked in integrated gangs, but it was common, not just in the South, for women to work in all-black gangs, as did Rosetta Nash, Erma Lee Walker, Grace McNeal, Jennie Ford, Glozell George, and Mittie Mae, holding the tools of their trade for the camera at the SP's West Oakland, California roundhouse.[49]

Women frequently replaced men as roundhouse and shop laborers, although sometimes this meant opportunities only for whites. The Pennsylvania Railroad, experiencing an acute labor shortage in Pittsburgh in 1942, hired numerous white women shop workers but refused to add blacks because "they had no rest rooms for colored women."[50] The Pennsy reversed course in its East Baltimore, Maryland shops, employing more than 50 black women, including a number of fire and water watchers who kept locomotives steaming while the engines awaited their next assignments. At the Kingsville, Texas shops of the Missouri Pacific Lines, black women similarly kept up locomotive fires. Sizeable numbers of black women were concentrated in some areas; by the spring of 1944, 100 were at work in the SP's Galveston, Texas shops. Some female laborers ventured into new territory, although once again muscle was emphasized. Black women operated grease guns to lubricate the moving parts of locomotives' running gear. Others manhandled bulky hoses to clean engines, using chemicals mixed with steam. Some simply did general "housekeeping" chores in dirty roundhouses. Only a few penetrated the skilled trades as helpers, like the New York Central passenger-car generator mechanic in Detroit.[51]

As one employee magazine admitted, "it took World War II to breach the traditionally masculine strongholds" of shops and roundhouses. But while both white and black women made these gains in the North, only black women performed truly heavy physical work in the South. The Louisville & Nashville Railroad's story is illustrative. When a severe labor shortfall developed in mid-1943, more than 200 black women began work at its South Louisville, Kentucky roundhouse and shops where the only previous female employees had been white stenographers and clerks. Called "L&N WACS" by the shopmen, they were largely consigned to stereotypical roles deemed appropriate for black women: engine cleaners, tender washers, and boiler jacket wipers in the roundhouse; and tool cleaners, scrap sorters, sweepers, and material handlers in the shops. A few performed a less arduous task, operating the roundhouse turntable. The L&N, as did other railroads, patronized its new employees, noting that "the women have adapted themselves to the orderly hurly-burly of shop life in a surprisingly short time." And it credited their supervisors with "true psychological insight" in assigning them "to jobs at which the female of the species is traditionally adept, such as cleaning, straightening, sweeping, etc." The closest any came to a skilled trade was rivet catching in the car repair shop. Rebecca Smith recalled that this required both dexterity and guts. "You had to catch those [red hot] rivets in a cup . . . your nerves had to be awful good . . . You had to keep your collar fasten[ed] up, sometimes they would go down in your shirt pocket, sometimes they would go down your gloves, and it would be so high up there [on scaffolding], a lot of women couldn't climb because if they looked down they would get dizzy."[52]

Who were these 200 black L&N railroaders? Ranging in age from 18 to 40, about half were married. Most previously worked as laundresses, dishwashers, and maids, rather than as field hands or factory workers. They were a hardy and, at times, a rowdy bunch. Rebecca Smith remembered being afraid of some of her co-workers. "Some of them came from the South . . . they would fight, they carry knives, and the bosses didn't fool with them too much, some of those women had those big old bras, straw hat on, chew tobacco, dip of snuff, maybe cigarette in their mouth, load them wheelbarrows down so heavy, whew, ain't no way [I could have done that]." Black male employees could be as chauvinistic as whites, saying ,"Yawl ain't got no business out here[,] said we ain't no women working down there."[53]

Just as in the earlier war, black women again found work as freight truckers. It was not easy, however, for some railroads to break with masculine traditions. The Southern Railway's Spencer, North Carolina freight transfer sheds resorted to "womanpower" after most of its black male truckers were drafted. By the middle of the war, 42 women, mostly blacks, had replaced men. They had to be literate and, because the work was so strenuous, in good health and weigh at least 130 pounds. Background checks ensured that only "good citizens" were employed. Most of them appeared to be happy to make a personal contribution to the war effort while earning good wages. Unlike most wartime female railroaders, many of them kept their jobs after the war.[54]

African American women also found employment on section crews during World War II, filling in for the depleted male workforce. The degree to which they actually performed the heaviest tasks, like replacing ties, spiking rails, and lining track, is hard to determine. Publicity photographs commonly depicted them holding shovels and ballast forks. But some did truly rugged work. Mozel Boyd, Annie Ullis, and Mary Ellen Jackson were credited with keeping 139 switches free of ice and snow in the Baltimore & Ohio's Toledo, Ohio yards. Black women utilized time-honored methods to endure exhausting, monotonous labor. A number of them toiled alongside kinswomen, mothers and daughters or sisters together on the same crew. Singing together also helped make the hours pass more quickly. Other women displayed patterns that originated in slavery and sharecropping, like refusing to work up to one's physical limits to avoid exhaustion. A PRR official complained that, after standing aside for passing trains, a female MOW gang did not resume working within seconds of the track being clear. He ordered that "any women who are not producing must be told either to work or quit." Given a better alternative, many probably would have quit. Resistance took other paths as well. Women at the Pennsy's Spruce Street engine house in Columbus, Ohio, all asked for Sundays off, a communal and family day that they were loath to sacrifice for their employer. When, as was frequently the case, their requests were denied, they simply absented themselves without permission.[55]

Black female railroaders benefited little from either unionization or the FEPC during World War II. White railroad unions were adamant that women, of either race, be hired only at low-skilled positions and be regarded as temporary workers whose seniority, if granted at all, would disappear when the war ended.[56] The women best positioned to organize were Pullman car cleaners and laundry workers, because the Pullman porters and maids were already unionized and their BSCP could, in theory, take interest in unionizing them. But when laundry workers, aggrieved over long shifts and abusive "southern bosses," asked the BSCP to organize them, union president A. Philip Randolph rejected the overture and suggested they affiliate with an AFL laundry workers' union that had no competency or prior interest in railroad workers. Black women who worked in Pullman car yards had multiple grievances. "Southern bosses" violated seniority in giving preferential promotions to white men and penalized assertive women. Pay rates varied arbitrarily, from city to city. In the South, whites earned more for performing the same job. As the war came to an end, white men summarily replaced black women employed as electricians' and machinists' helpers. The BSCP proved helpless to remedy these situations.[57]

Black women Pullman employees tried to use the FEPC to break the lock on jobs reserved for white women, like upholster apprentice-helpers in the yards, and clerical jobs in offices and commissaries. But Pullman opposed any new positions for blacks, particularly clerical jobs that would survive postwar demobilization. When two women were refused work as commissary checkers in 1943 and filed an FEPC race discrimination complaint, top Pullman officials knew the applicants were qualified. Vice President Champ Carry, at least, had "no great feeling" against hiring them, although he feared opening the floodgates. But, in the assessment of historian Melinda Chateauvert, "the President's Committee on Fair Employment Practice was not interested in discrimination against African American women in the railroad industry . . . Pullman's foot-dragging illustrates that employers could undermine the Executive Orders through simple procrastination and when that failed, through due process delays." In the end, no black women obtained Pullman clerical jobs during World War II. Six years after the war ended, all Pullman's black female employees still worked at low-level jobs in its yards and laundries.[58]

Rosetta the Railroader and her sisters pitched in to do their part during World War II, but most of them were discarded afterward. Few remained in roundhouses and shops and they all but disappeared from section work.[59] Many males objected to working alongside women once the wartime necessity for their presence had passed. Most women who were not abruptly laid off were demoted. Rebecca Smith hired on as a helper in the L&N's South Louisville Shop 14, the freight-car repair department, but when the war ended, she was downgraded to laborer, where she remained, never to be promoted, for 33 years. That she and a few others managed to hold on to their jobs was due, ironically, to union membership. In an unusual move, the local shop chairman of the Firemen and Oilers Union insisted that newly hired women be added to the seniority roster. The union certainly wasn't color- or gender blind—it negotiated higher wages for males than for females doing the same jobs—but to Smith, the union was "the only thing that kept us there." The L&N was hardly benevolent. Black women were simply cheaper labor. And seniority still ruled. Of the more than 200 women employed at South Louisville during the war, only about 50 remained after massive layoffs in 1949. Before long Smith was the only black woman in Shop 14 and remained so up to her retirement in 1977.[60]

As black women lost maintenance of way and shop jobs after World War II, railroad work regressed to predictably stereotypical patterns. By 1953, of 12,622 African Americans on the Pennsylvania Railroad payroll, only 620 (5 percent) were females. Sixty-six percent of them were coach cleaners and 18 percent were janitors. Only 2 women were helpers in the skilled trades.[61] Matters for black women railroaders went from bad to worse in the 1950s and 1960s. Large metropolitan stations continued to employ a few matrons, but at smaller stations nonessential employees were cut as the public increasingly abandoned rail travel. Black females still performed janitorial services in railroad office buildings, but operators disappeared with the advent of automatic elevators. The Pullman Company employed a dwindling number of black women car cleaners until it got out of the sleeping-car business in 1969, by which date only 2 of its laundries remained in operation. Railroads abandoned money-losing trains as quickly as the Interstate Commerce Commission granted approval, further reducing the need for car cleaners. While 20,000 passenger trains plied the rails daily in 1929, only 500 were left in the fall of 1970. As for true office work, black female secretaries, even in the North, were still rare before the 1970s.[62]

The struggle to obtain more meaningful railroad employment—especially in white-collar jobs and the operating crafts (engineers, conductors, brakemen)—began with the Civil Rights Act of 1964, which prohibited job discrimination on the basis of race. Even after that date, it was still a hard fight, particularly in the South, as Joyce Howze found out. In 1970 she applied for jobs as a clerk-typist and stenographer in the Gulf, Mobile & Ohio Railroad's accounting department, only to become yet another victim of the company's systematic denial of white-collar employment to blacks. Howze had completed more than three years of secretarial college, had been employed as a secretary for nearly four years, and had passed company typing, shorthand, spelling, math, and business English tests—but was rejected upon failing a "mental alertness" test. The accounting department employed 270 whites and only 2 blacks, both in the lowest category, office assistants. At least one recently hired white employee had also failed the mental alertness test, while more than half of the white clerical force had not been required to take it at all. An Equal Employment Opportunity Commission hearing officer found that, in a 1-year period, the GM&O hired 182 clerical and office personnel, only 5 of whom were black. Racial barriers still blocked equal access to white-collar jobs.[63]

Black women have obtained good railroad jobs since 1970, although overall railroad employment has declined. Today they hold 13 percent of office and sales jobs, the same as blacks' percentage of the national population. Progress has also been achieved at higher levels: 20 percent of all female railroad officials and managers are African American, although women represent only 11 percent of all workers in these positions. Among craft workers and skilled operatives, 20 percent of all female employees are African American. One-third of all female laborers are black, but their overall numbers are very small as few women of any race or ethnicity seek arduous outdoor manual labor. A telling statistic, however, reveals that black females hold 54 percent of all railroad service jobs performed by women, like janitresses and waitresses.[64]

Black women have struggled successfully to break out of traditionally stereotyped jobs in the railroad industry. It is no longer startling to see a black female engineer at the throttle of a freight engine or an Amtrak passenger locomotive. Female brakemen, switchmen, and conductors of color are no longer novelties, though they still are not commonplace. They didn't get there by luck or government fiat: they had to overcome harassment and prejudice at nearly every turn. Railroad operating departments have seemingly forever been bastions of masculinity. Only the strongest women have retained jobs and gained promotions.[65] But black women are still over-represented, as they have been since women entered railroading, in the least skilled, least remunerative, and least prestigious positions. Black women railroaders have had to battle exploitation, persevere against odds, and fight for their dignity. May those today remember this legacy as they pursue railroading in the twenty-first century.

Railroads in the African American Experience

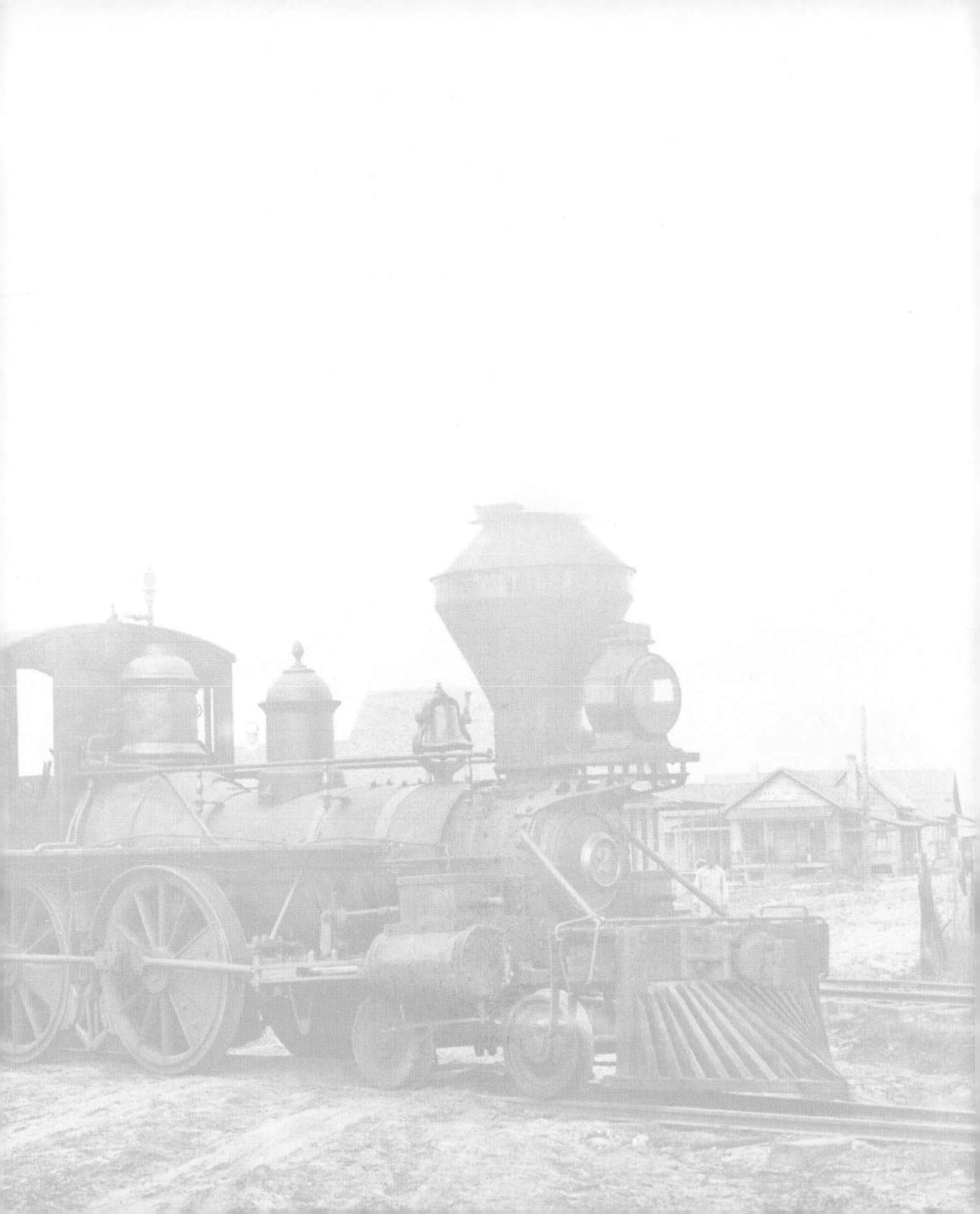

Even small railroads, like the 168-mile Tonopah & Tidewater, imbibed the racism of the era. To publicize the 1907 opening of its line from a connection with the Atchison, Topeka & Santa Fe at Ludlow northward to Death Valley and mining towns in Nevada, a souvenir pamphlet featured a cruel caricature of a Red Cap. Douglas Wornom collection

TONOPAH & TIDEWATER RAILROAD COMPANY

1907 CIRCULAR No. 45

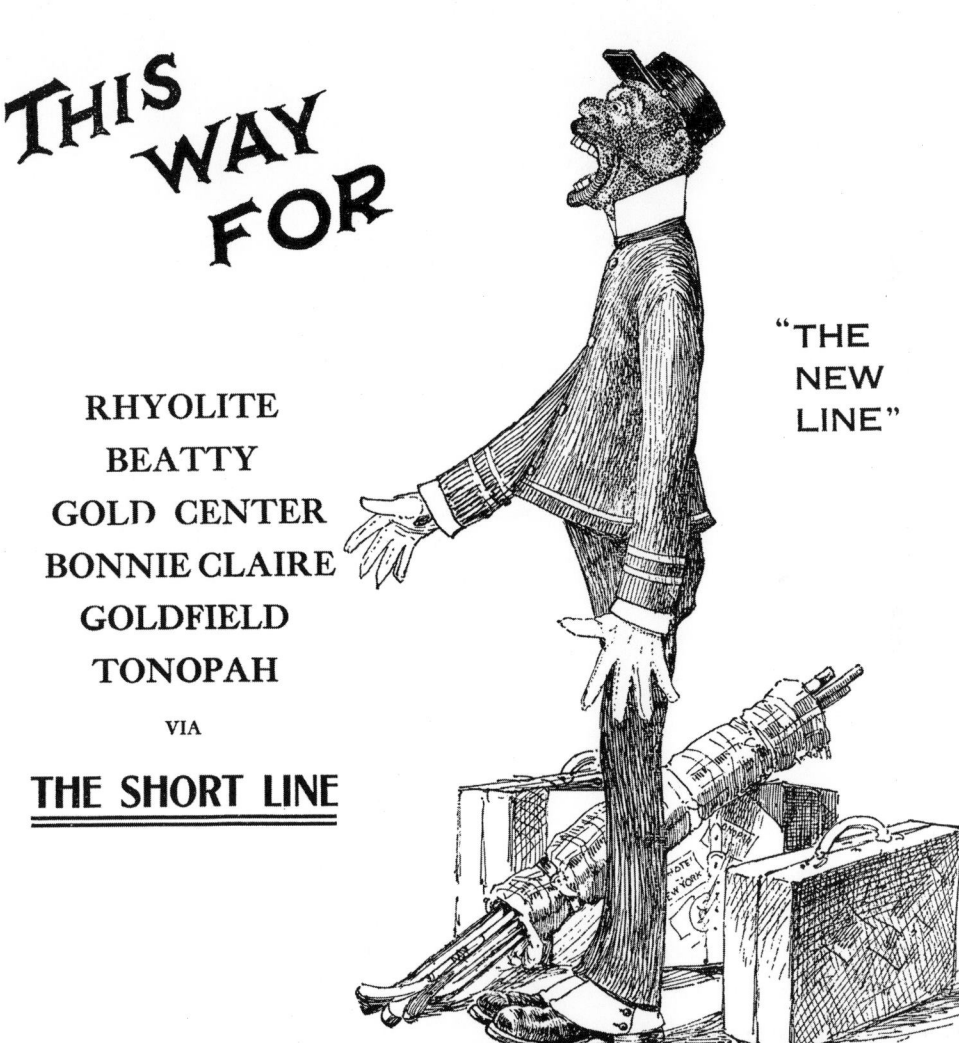

THIS WAY FOR

"THE NEW LINE"

RHYOLITE
BEATTY
GOLD CENTER
BONNIE CLAIRE
GOLDFIELD
TONOPAH

VIA

THE SHORT LINE

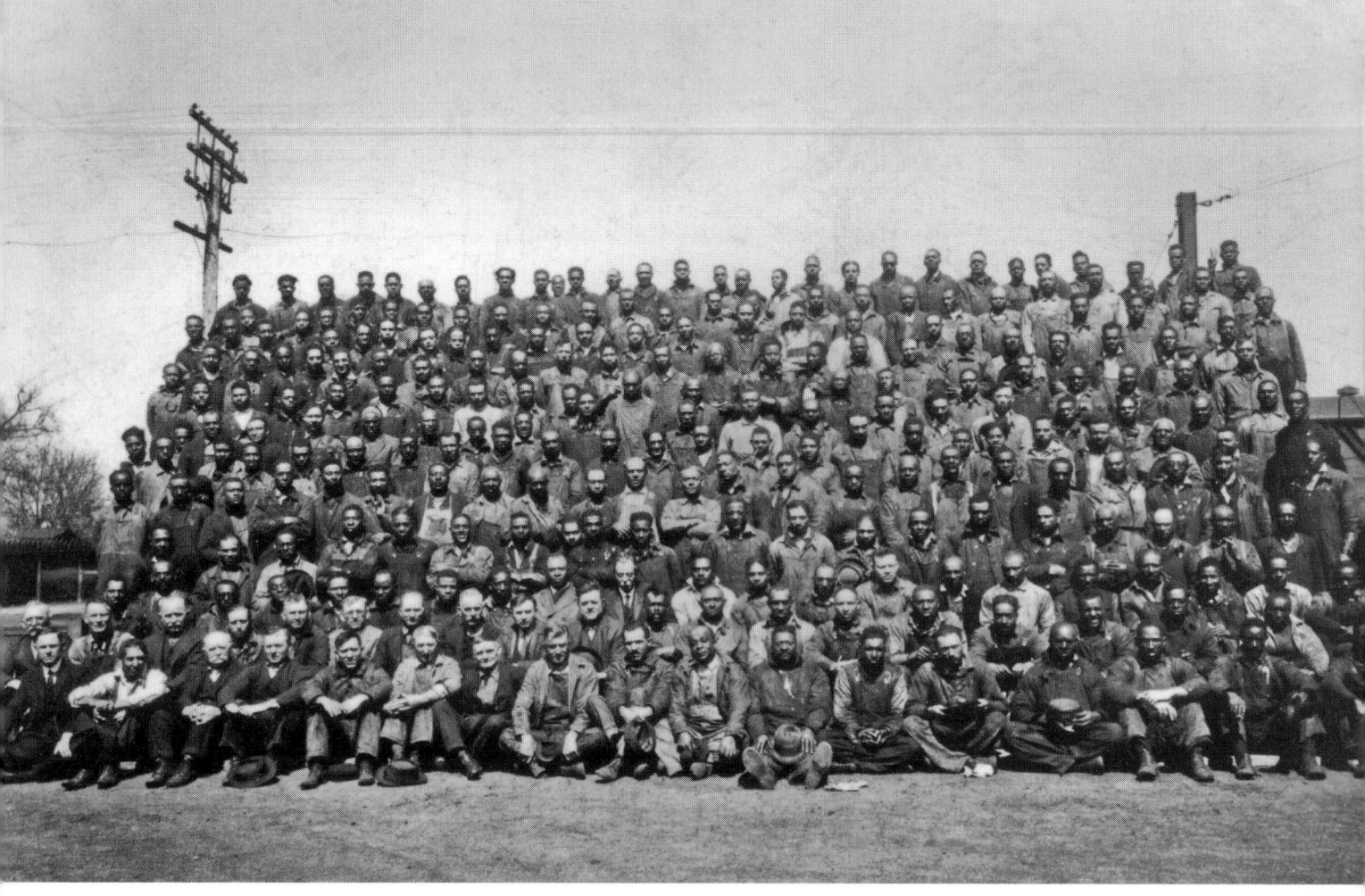

The 1922 nationwide shop workers strike opened up skilled jobs for blacks, including this group of over 200 Atchison, Topeka & Santa Fe Railway workers recruited for the Topeka, Kansas shops. Unfortunately, few blacks, on any railroad, were able to retain their newly won skilled positions after the strike was settled. *Atchison, Topeka & Santa Fe Collection, Kansas State Historical Society*

234

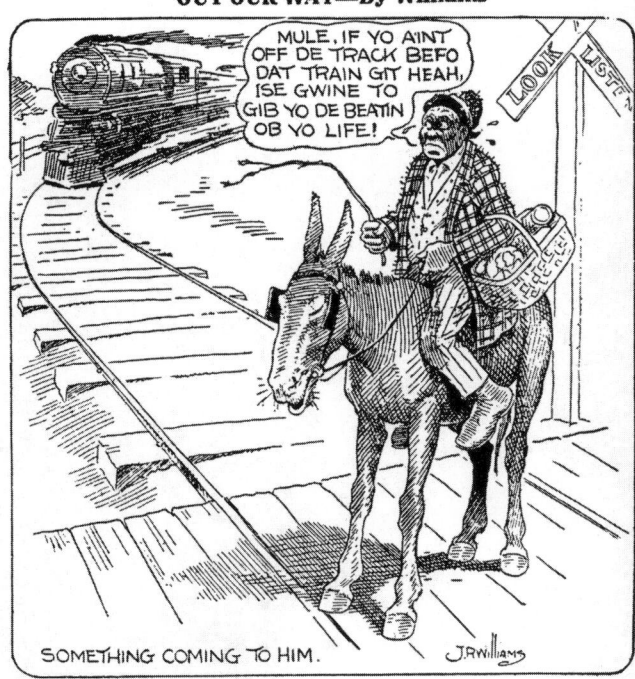

OUT OUR WAY—By Williams

MULE, IF YO AINT OFF DE TRACK BEFO DAT TRAIN GIT HEAH, ISE GWINE TO GIB YO DE BEATIN OB YO LIFE!

LOOK LISTEN

SOMETHING COMING TO HIM.

J.R.Williams

The Chesapeake & Ohio Railway's company magazine, like many others, featured racist jokes and cartoons like this one dating from 1923. Was the editor oblivious to the feelings of the road's black workers, or simply unfeeling in portraying blacks as stupid? Theodore Kornweibel collection

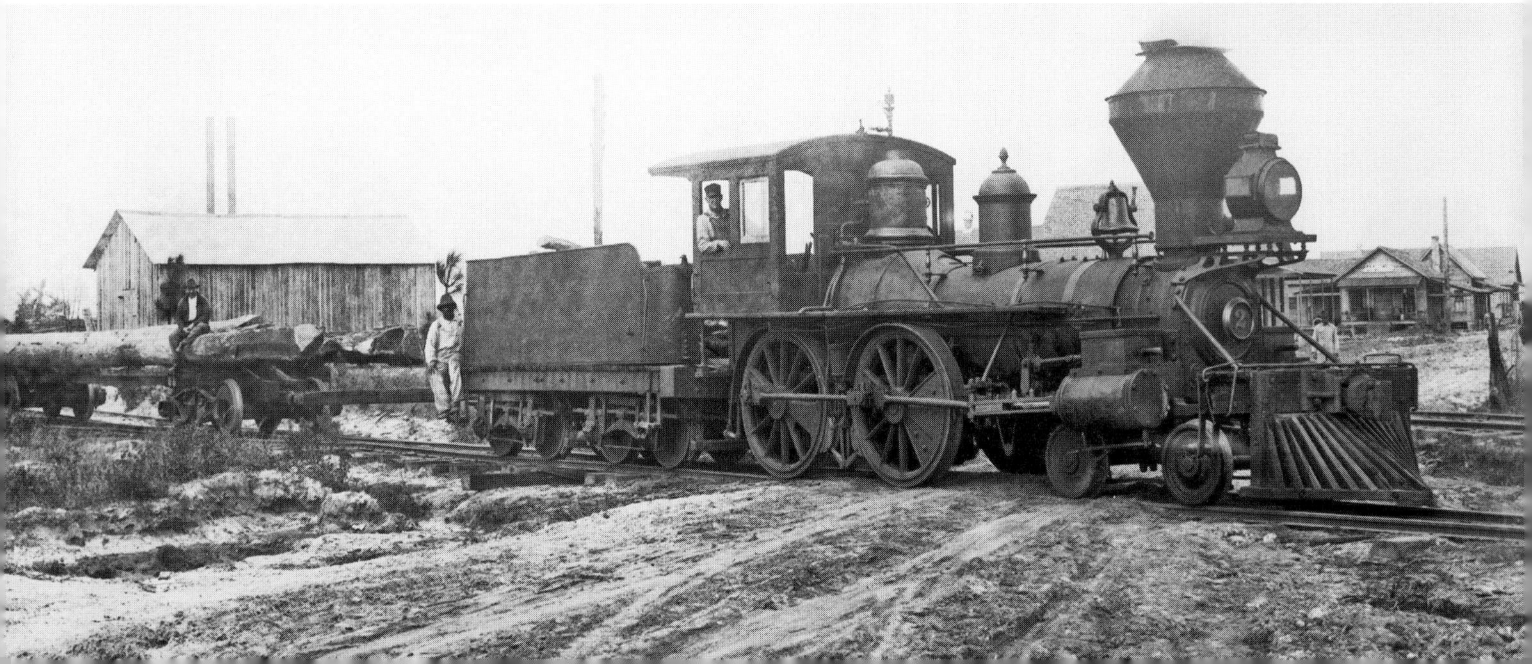

Whites did not generally threaten black brakemen's jobs on logging and industrial railroads because no line had a significant number of operating employees and such roads were not unionized so the pay was lower. The J. N. Bray Lumber Company's brakeman, photographed at Valdosta, Georgia, in 1923, is riding behind a real relic, a 4-4-0 locomotive built by Matthias W. Baldwin in 1856. It was definitely not designed for hauling logs out of the woods. Don Hensley collection

"NOBODY RIDE BUT DE CHOCOLATE TO DE BONE"

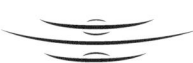

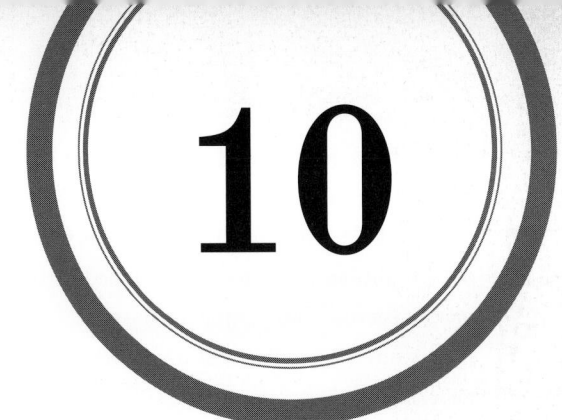

Jim Crow Segregation

Jim Crow. The humiliations of segregation went hand in hand with the development of American railroads. The term itself derived from a white minstrel actor's racist caricature of blacks. How it came to be attached to segregation remains a mystery. But there is no mystery in the quick development of separate—and inferior—accommodations for black passengers, in the North as well as the South, well before the Civil War. When Austrian civil engineer F. A. Ritter Von Gerstner traveled throughout the United States in 1838–40, at the end of the first decade of American railroading, he observed that in the South, some free black passengers paid half fare and rode in a baggage car equipped only with plain wooden benches, while others paid full fare and sat in coaches along with whites. While journeying through the North, however, he found separate cars to be the rule.[1]

Black travelers frequently rode in "second-class" cars, paying lower fares for more rude accommodations. But poorer whites did likewise. Second-class cars were not Jim Crow cars; rather, they segregated by class, not by race. Truly segregated cars arose from the desire to separate the races without having to dedicate an entire car for blacks when it was likely that relatively few of them would ride. The solution was the combination car, or "combine" (COM-bine), which had two or three sections, one or two for passengers and the other for baggage and sometimes mail. Occupants of an antebellum combine generally sat on benches along each wall.[2] When a railroad had no combine, blacks (and white smokers, drinkers, and gamblers) simply stood or sat on crates or trunks in a baggage car. Should there be an extraordinarily large number of black passengers—perhaps a slave trader transporting his wares—an entire coach might be designated as a "negro car" or "servants car."[3] A custom developed early of placing baggage cars right behind the locomotive, in part to serve as buffers for the passenger cars should a collision or boiler explosion occur. A parallel custom thus evolved, in which Jim Crow cars were coupled closest to the locomotive, therefore exposing their occupants to greater danger and more smoke and cinders.

What was it like for free blacks to travel on southern railroads in the three decades before the Civil War? Although in some instances they sat in the same first-class coach with whites, refusing demands to move to another car was risky. The issue, for whites, was ensuring social distance. Proximity to one's own servants did not imply social equality, but it did among strangers, as New Orleans free blacks learned when they attempted to use a Pontchartrain Railroad streetcar that was reserved for whites. A ruckus ensued, during which they shot at those who sought their removal, but the "trespassers" were outnumbered and the ringleader was pummeled and hauled off to jail. In response, the railroad added segregated cars.[4]

Slave passengers were regarded differently. If they accompanied masters or mistresses as personal attendants, they rode along with them. If not, they rode in whatever Jim Crow accommodation was provided. According to the South Carolina Railroad's "Regulations for Passenger Carriage," "Servants not admitted [to coaches], unless having the care of Children, without the consent of all the Passengers."[5]

Black passengers in the antebellum North frequently encountered discrimination when they traveled by train. Although slavery was abolished above the Mason-Dixon Line by the early nineteenth century, prejudice was not eradicated. Before the coming of railroads, blacks were often forced to sit on top of stagecoaches, not in the enclosed carriage, and were segregated on steamboats. The first railroads in Massachusetts appeared by 1835, and segregation quickly followed, with the vehicle for blacks being known commonly as the "dirt car." By 1841 it was being called a "Jim Crow car," the first usage of that minstrel-show term to refer to a railroad car.[6]

In that year, the issue of segregation burst into the public arena in Massachusetts when, in separate incidents, black abolitionists David Ruggles and Frederick Douglass refused to move to Jim Crow cars and were forcibly ejected. In yet another fracas, when Douglass and a white abolitionist sat together and Douglass refused to leave, the conductor rounded up "eight or ten toughs" to "snake out the d——d nigger." The pair was dragged headfirst out of the car and thrown to the ground. Then black abolitionist Mary Newhall Green, traveling with her husband and baby, was unceremoniously removed from the "white" car with the infant in her arms. For trying to protect his family, Mr. Green suffered a beating, and the baby was injured in the melee.

These well-publicized incidents helped galvanize public opinion against railroad segregation in Massachusetts. That state was a hotbed of abolitionism and during 1842, mass protest meetings, sympathetic letters and editorials in newspapers, and calls to boycott the railroads generated pressure for legislative relief. One of the most persuasive arguments was the irony that visiting southern slaveholders were allowed to bring their servants into the very same coaches from which free blacks were ejected. Numerous petitions reached lawmakers. Although a bill outlawing railroad segregation was twice defeated, the tide of public opinion persuaded the railroads, in 1843, to end segregation.[7]

That was not the final chapter of railroad segregation in Massachusetts, however. At least one line reverted to old practices. The popular train from Boston to New York in 1847 carried three coaches and a Jim Crow car, all of them crowded. But apparently, this was the last gasp of the practice, Frederick Douglass informing fellow abolitionists in 1849 that "not a single railroad can be found in any part of Massachusetts, where a colored man is treated and esteemed in any other light than that of a man and a traveler."[8]

The rest of the North (and far West) was not so progressive. Even the City of Brotherly Love held no affection for interracial mingling in the mid-1850s, as was depicted in a contemporary engraving entitled "Negro expulsion from Railway Car, Philadelphia." An occasional protest brought a measure of justice, as in the case of a man who was ejected from a passenger car and forced to ride in a freight car. When the conductor demanded the standard fare, the indignant traveler replied, "You count me as freight, and I'll pay you as freight; weigh me, and I'll pay by the pound." The conductor acquiesced to the logic of his argument. But victories were few. As horse-drawn street railways were introduced in a number of northern and southern cities, blacks sometimes found themselves banned outright or forced to stand on the end platforms, exposed to the elements.[9] Not until after the Civil War did segregation on northern and western railroads and streetcars end, due in part to a change in sentiment generated by the war and the destruction of slavery, and to the courageous protests of African Americans themselves.

With emancipation, antebellum half fares disappeared, but payment of a full fare for a seat in a southern segregated car was galling. Objections were unavailing: "You're free, ain't you? Good as white folks, ain't you! Then pay the same fare, and keep your mouth shut."[10] Not surprisingly, blacks began to challenge segregation. For a season, Jim Crow was pushed back, although victories were not easily won. The first obstacles were "Black Codes" enacted by unrepentant white southerners to resurrect slavery in all but name. Several states mandated segregation of first-class cars. Even where no laws were passed, whites pressured railroad companies to separate passengers by race and some carriers complied with such demands. But blacks fought back, utilizing the federal courts, the backing of Union army commanders, and their own militant actions. The most notable successes occurred in Louisville, Charleston, and New Orleans where they boarded streetcars, blocked tracks, and filed federal lawsuits. Turmoil brought results, and Jim Crow was for a season abolished.[11]

The freedmen attacked railroad segregation as they participated in state constitutional conventions and the new legislatures that were established during Radical Reconstruction. A majority of the states enacted laws barring discrimination in all forms of public transportation. Blacks also won lawsuits against individual railroads. And persistent black political pressure finally brought enactment of the Civil Rights Act of 1875 that guaranteed "full and equal enjoyment of the accommodations" of all modes of transportation "on land and water." These gains were unevenly obeyed and enforced, however. In several states, blacks could ride in first-class cars alongside whites into the 1880s. But elsewhere railroads ignored civil rights laws when state officials were loath to vigorously pursue cases against them. In general, blacks encountered segregation more in the Deep South although even there it was not total. While excluded from first-class cars in Texas and Mississippi, no segregation existed in second-class cars and the railroads in those states did not yet operate separate Jim Crow coaches.[12] While southern railroad officials were white men who believed in the appropriateness of segregation, as businessmen they disliked the practice because it would impose an economic burden, requiring extra cars, hence longer and heavier trains, necessitating larger locomotives and more fuel.

By 1877, whites had regained political control of every southern state, bringing Reconstruction to an end. Even so, patterns of train travel did not immediately change. Segregation continued where it was already established. Yet in the upper South, blacks who could afford the fare generally rode in first-class coaches alongside whites. And protests still occasionally brought reversals of segregation. Opposition from New Orleans blacks forced one railroad to quickly abandon separate waiting rooms in 1882. Elsewhere, blacks organized boycotts. But the most militant actions were lawsuits filed by bold black travelers, including a number of women. "The railroads of the 1880s were contested terrain."[13]

Ida B. Wells was a 21-year-old schoolteacher who boarded a train from Memphis to Woodstock, Tennessee, in 1884, taking a seat in the ladies' coach. A conductor ordered her into the smoking car, occupied by white men and blacks of both sexes, but she refused. When the conductor tried to eject her, she sunk her teeth into the back of his hand. With two other white men, he dragged her out, to the applause of the white "ladies and gentlemen" in the car. Filing suit against the Chesapeake, Ohio & Southwestern Railroad, she was awarded damages of $500. But the state supreme court reversed the verdict, concluding that since she was traveling only 11 miles, she would not have been denied comfortable seating by riding in the smoker. Believing that she was simply trying to harass the railroad, the court ordered her to pay its legal costs.[14] Why did Miss Wells object to being moved? First-class and ladies' cars were smoke- and tobacco-free. Second-class cars reflected the uncouthness of ordinary men of both races. Spit and tobacco juice covered the floor, despoiled the seats, and even decorated the ceilings. The air was rank with cigar smoke and vulgarities. One white traveler pronounced such cars "absolutely uninhabitable."[15]

Another brave soul was 16-year-old Mary Church, the daughter of a well-known Memphis businessman. With a first-class ticket in hand, she boarded a train, only to be directed into the Jim Crow car and told, "this is first class enough for you." She tried to leave the train, but was blocked by the conductor, who demanded to know what she was doing. "I am getting off here to wire my father that you are forcing me to ride all night in a Jim Crow car. He will sue the railroad for compelling his daughter who has a first class ticket to ride in a second class car." In fact, her father, Robert R.

Church, Sr., was well connected politically and her threat had the desired effect. The plucky Miss Church took a seat in the first-class car.[16]

A few blacks even succeeded in recovering damages. A Galveston, Texas resident, Thomas W. Cain, was on his way home in a Pullman sleeping car from St. Louis in 1893 when an International & Great Northern Railroad conductor informed him that a new Texas law prohibited his presence in the same car with whites. Cain accepted a $2 cash refund and moved to the "colored" coach, but then sued the railroad and the sleeping-car operator. A Galveston court found in his favor, ruling that the Pullman Company's acceptance of payment of a first-class fare obligated it contractually to provide first-class accommodations. The Texas Court of Civil Appeals upheld the $100 damages awarded to Cain, instructing railroads to either allow blacks to occupy the same cars with whites or provide separate sleepers. No railroad, of course, could do the latter. Thus, trains entering Texas from western and Midwestern cities retained non-segregated sleeping cars for the duration of the Jim Crow era.[17] Blacks also challenged exclusion from dining cars. Rev. Henry T. Johnson, editor of the African Methodist Episcopal Church's denominational magazine, won damages of $500 from the Pullman Company, which operated the Seaboard Air Line Railway's diners, after being refused breakfast service while traveling north from Richmond in 1902.[18]

Isolated legal victories could not, however, halt the steamroller of segregation. Jim Crow spread all across the South at the turn of the twentieth century. Railroads disliked the economically burdensome practice but powerful political forces prevailed. Southern whites were particularly apprehensive that railroad coaches were amorphous public spaces, not easily conformable to white supremacist patterns. What was the nature of race relations in second-class cars that indiscriminately mixed the races and sexes? According to one newspaper, "a man that would be horrified at the idea of his wife or daughter seated by the side of a burley negro in the parlor of a hotel or at a restaurant cannot see her occupying a crowded seat in a car next to a negro without the same feeling of disgust." Alabama legislators disingenuously called their new segregation law "An act to promote the comfort of passengers on Railroad Trains." To many whites, segregation was necessary for the protection of white female virtue. "In the late nineteenth century, sexual relations did not have to end in intercourse or even physical contact to be considered intimate and dangerous to a woman's reputation and self-respect."[19]

Segregation also increased in response to southern whites' perception of a new and dangerous generation of African Americans. Older "respectable" blacks allegedly knew their assigned racial roles and places and would not think of transgressing the South's long-established folkways. But many whites recognized a new generation of blacks, either born during the last years of slavery or after emancipation, who had not been socialized by that institution into obsequious and fatalistic responses to white power. "Educated and assertive blacks, especially those of the younger generation, chafed at every restriction against them and looked for opportunities to exercise their legal rights to attack the very assumptions and presumptions of segregation." A Georgia black newspaper urged readers to call the bluff of white trainmen who tried to force passengers to move into Jim

Crow cars. So many whites were not content with only partial segregation. More uniform policies and laws were needed.[20]

The path to South-wide railroad segregation was short. Although federal courts ruled in the mid-1880s that those who paid first-class fares had to be granted first-class accommodations, they also approved separate accommodations so long as they were equal. The recently established Interstate Commerce Commission likewise stressed a standard of "equality of accommodations." In an unequivocal 1907 order, it ruled that "carriers may not discriminate between white and colored passengers paying the same fare in the accommodations which they furnish to each other," yet "segregation of white and colored passengers on interstate journeys is a reasonable regulation of interstate traffic."[21] In reality, the ICC and the courts "simultaneously stressed equality and sanctioned segregation, giving with one hand and taking away with the other." Nine states had already passed segregation laws between 1887 and 1891, despite opposition from the railroads that alone would bear the added costs. But no definitive ruling on the legality of segregation yet existed. Louisiana blacks forced the issue with a test case involving Homer Adolph Plessy, who boarded an East Louisiana Railroad train, sat in the white car, and defied the conductor's order to leave. He was duly arrested for violating Louisiana's railroad segregation statute. In its fateful *Plessy v. Ferguson* decision (1896), the Supreme Court rejected Plessy's contentions that segregation violated the due process and equal protection clauses of the Fourteenth Amendment. Whether blacks could ride in the same railroad car as whites was merely a "social privilege," not a legal right. The Supreme Court had spoken, and those southern states that had not yet enacted segregation laws lost little time in doing so. And not just railroad cars were henceforth to be strictly segregated; so were station facilities.[22]

By the turn of the twentieth century, segregation had fastened its grip on practically every arena in the South where the races might come into public contact. Enforcement was capricious, but that very uncertainty led blacks to increasingly conservative behavior because while some breaches might be overlooked, other challenges to the racial status quo were met with violence. In 1900, Representative George H. White of North Carolina, the last black member of Congress until 1928, boarded the white compartment of the partitioned Jim Crow car on an Atlantic & North Carolina Railroad train. When ordered by the conductor to repair to his proper compartment, he refused, whereupon "six or eight white men gathered around and told the conductor not to say another word, that they would take pleasure in throwing the scamp off the train." White quickly moved as directed.[23] Militant protests in the South would no longer be tolerated. When Virginia's Jim Crow law took effect in 1900, a newspaper observed that no organized protest had surfaced because "even if the Supreme Court should decide that the law was unconstitutional, it would in reality avail the negro race but little. They know that force has practically disfranchised the negro in certain of the Southern States . . . and they realize that the temper of the Virginians is such that having once obtained these [segregated] cars they will maintain them."[24]

New Orleans's Union Station, built in 1908,
reveals, like many larger stations in the South,
the lie in the "separate but equal" segregation
formula. While whites had separate men's and
women's waiting rooms, all blacks had to share
a common space. And the restaurant was for
the enjoyment of whites only. Theodore
Kornweibel collection

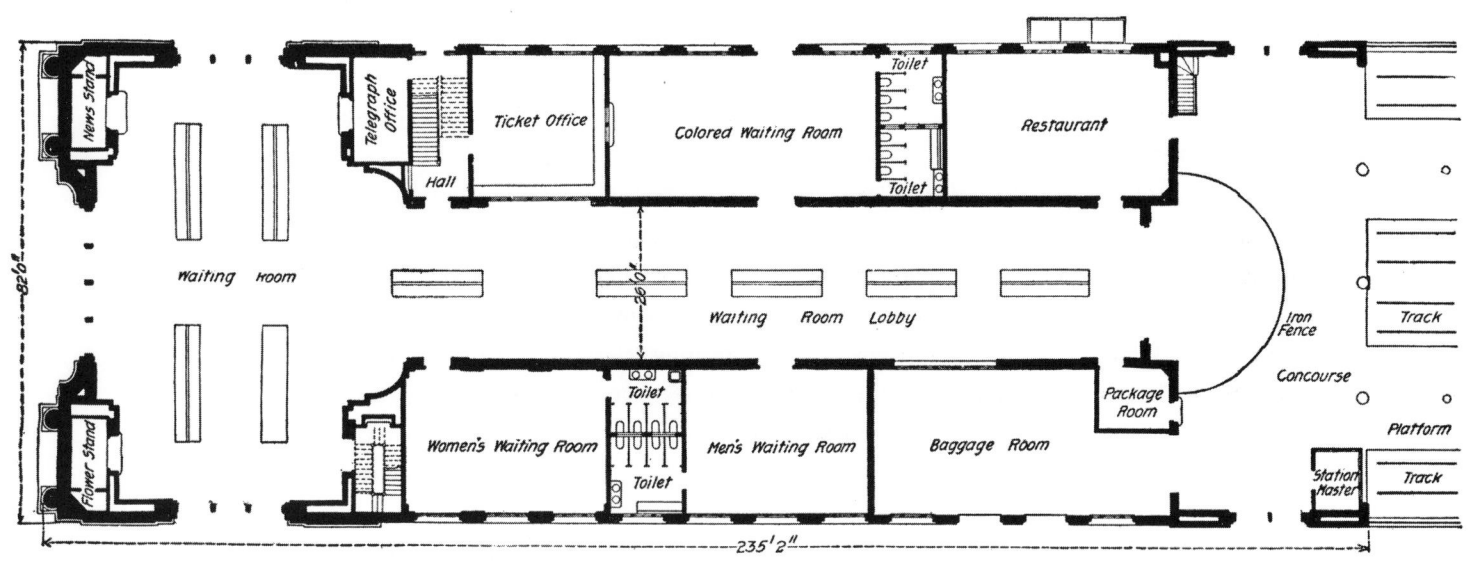

Complaining directly to the offending railroad rarely brought improvement, so blacks often petitioned state regulatory agencies. Occasionally, they found sympathetic ears. In 1906, the Texas Railroad Commission reprimanded the Atchison, Topeka & Santa Fe Railway for maintaining unequal accommodations: "The idea of compelling people to ride 218 miles in a car without water cooler or water closet [toilet] for the benefit of passengers, who are not permitted to enter other cars, is a violation of the purpose and intent of the laws of this state . . . It would not be tolerated for a moment in a car devoted to white passengers and under the laws of this state there can be no difference made as to the necessary comforts on account of race or color."[25] This was a rare victory for equal treatment. But it did not disturb the principle of segregation.

The files of the North Carolina Railroad Commission, which became the Corporation Commission, reveal the range of indignities that blacks faced and the unlikelihood that state regulators would insist that any "separate but equal" principle be scrupulously observed. Railroad officials routinely permitted conditions for blacks that they would never have allowed for whites. This was particularly grievous for the more well-off members of the race who wanted the same class-differentiated accommodations enjoyed by whites. If certain whites could insulate themselves in higher-fare cars from the unwashed masses who smoked, drank, and gambled, then why shouldn't respectable blacks have the same amenities to shield wives and daughters from coarser members of their own race? Disregard for their dignity rankled these blacks almost as much as segregation itself.

A persistent critic of North Carolina's railroads was J. W. Jones, a medical doctor in Winston-Salem, who found much lacking in the Southern Railway's practices. Writing to the Corporation Commission, beginning in 1906, he noted that the local train to Charlotte carried "only one car for Col. People & our ladies have to ride with all classes & conditions of Col. Passengers regardless of the fair they pay. We don't want to ride with white people but want equal accommodations for our ladies just what the law allow us & nothing more." On a recent journey, although they had purchased first-class tickets, his family was "crowded in a dirty little car with the drunkards & whiskey drinkers subject to insults smoke & everything." The Commission referred the matter back to the railroad, which delayed three months before changing one train's consist to two partitioned cars, one of them first-class, with separate sections for blacks and whites.[26]

But the Southern Railway did not commit to a policy of equal accommodations. Two years later, Dr. Jones again complained to the Corporation Commission, this time concerning the Greensboro–North Wilkesboro local that had "only one little dirty compartment for Negro passengers in that all classes & conditions of us must ride." Blacks were willing to pay for "a first class car where our best people can ride free from drunkards & smokers." Prodded by the Commission, the Southern added an additional coach.[27] But this was no promise of a new policy, as evidenced by another complaint from Jones about the Charlotte train, which once again had only a "little dirty [partitioned] car," one half for blacks, smokers and non-smokers alike, the other half an additional smoker for whites. Railroad officials explained that blacks could light up in the "white" (smoking) half of the partitioned car. Obviously they didn't feel comfortable doing so. The Commission nonetheless found these accommodations to satisfy the requirements of the law.[28]

Two years later, Dr. Jones complained once more about the same train. Blacks still had only one-half of a partitioned car where smokers and drinkers mingled with more abstemious folk, while whites had one and a half cars. On a recent journey, Jones was one of 36 blacks who were crowded into the compartment having only 28 seats. He was plainly fed up with state officials. "Now, the law says that there must be separate and equal accommodation for the races on all trains. This is your law, made by your legislature and is on your statue books . . . We pay the same as white people and are crowded together like cattle in a box car. This we cannot stand and if something is not done, we will have to go to the courts for a remedy." Of course, courts all over the South winked at the unjust application of separate but equal, so this was a hollow threat. Once more, the Commission failed to order the Southern to make permanent changes. A National Association for the Advancement of Colored People investigation a few years later concluded that the Southern, compared to the Atlantic Coast Line and Seaboard Air Line, had the vilest Jim Crow practices of the major roads running south of Washington.[29]

The inequality of segregation at times imperiled blacks' lives. Not only was it customary to assign older, more decrepit, and less comfortable cars for use by blacks, but in the early 1900s, as railroads replaced many wooden passenger cars with new steel cars (or added steel underframes to wooden cars), travel in unmodified wooden cars became all the more dangerous. When collisions occurred, steel cars telescoped through wooden cars, killing many passengers in the latter, while, relatively speaking, sparing those in the heavier, sturdier cars. A petition was sent to the North Carolina Corporation Commission in 1914 regarding these perils, asking that passenger trains be made up entirely of either steel cars or wooden ones.

This appeal was prompted by an incident on October 10, 1914, when some of those who signed the petition were aboard a Southern Railway train from Raleigh to Greensboro when a wreck was narrowly averted. Many black casualties would have occurred because the wooden coach in which they were riding was trailed by a string of steel cars. "We do complain that we are not only assigned the most dangerous portion of the train [directly behind the locomotive and head-end cars], but we are forced to ride in the weakest coaches that make up the train. Because of this, some of us have lost friends and kinsmen in wrecks, while the other passengers in the same train, but in stronger coaches, were not damaged enough to need hospital attention. For this reason, your petitioners beg to assure you that the law guaranteeing to us equal accommodations in travel is not being observed." The SAL was praised for not mixing wood and steel cars, but the Commission was urged to require the ACL and Southern to follow the same practice. Both railroads skirted the issue. The ACL pontificated that it was "an established policy of this Company to treat its colored patrons with equity and fairness." The SRR responded similarly: "We appreciate the patronage of the colored race as passengers and certainly want to give fair and proper consideration to their comfort and best interests."[30] But racism meant that blacks' "best interests" were subordinate: their safety was of less importance than the comfort and security of whites in modern steel cars.[31]

Blacks also frequently complained to North Carolina officials about inadequate depot facilities. Early in 1895, petitioners detailed the abysmal conditions at Raleigh Union Station, jointly operated by the Seaboard Air Line and the Southern. The "colored waiting room" was ill-lit and -ventilated, with seating for only a dozen persons in back-to-back rows of six seats. One bank of seats directly faced the toilets. When the toilet doors were opened, "the urinals and stools in said closets are plainly exposed to all persons in the room . . . [and] in warm weather the odor of the closets enters the waiting room." This was a particular affront to the sensibilities of refined black women holding first-class tickets who were denied sanctuary in the "ladies waiting room," which was reserved for white women.[32]

The Southern freely admitted that facilities were inferior, but excused the lack of equal amenities by citing the "considerable trouble and expense" of arranging "double accommodations." It offered, if the SAL agreed, to make "any reasonable and proper" changes that the Corporation Commission ordered. But no compromise could be reached because blacks insisted on the same gender-separated waiting rooms that whites enjoyed. In 1898, commissioners approved the railroads' plans for rearranging waiting rooms without requiring separate facilities for black women and men. A final protest was unavailing. The offensive toilets remained for a decade until a further station remodeling.[33] Clearly, railroads were not committed to providing equal station facilities. The comfort of blacks never weighed as heavily as the needs of whites. When pressed by state regulators, railroad officials would promise improvements that in some instances were forthcoming, and in others, not.

African Americans weren't the only ones to complain to state officials. Whites objected to having to "suffer" being mixed with blacks when railroads did not offer separate waiting rooms. Remodeling such country depots was an unwanted expense, and the railroads sometimes argued that there was no justification where there was no regular black patronage. But the Commission usually demanded expanded station facilities and the railroads mostly complied, although some stalled, like the 95-mile Atlantic & North Carolina Railroad, which repeatedly ignored complaints from whites in Newport, a town of only a few hundred inhabitants. Larger railroads also had to furnish segregated waiting rooms at tiny whistle stops. Over the space of 13 years, the Commission dictated new or remodeled depots in 34 towns, with the ACL, SAL, SRR, Norfolk & Western, and Norfolk & Southern roads all complying. Separate waiting rooms sometimes came at a cost to whites, as (white) "ladies waiting rooms" were often the only space that could be converted to use by blacks.[34]

Rarely were segregated station facilities equal. The grand Southern Railway station built in 1908 in Salisbury, North Carolina, and now preserved as an historic landmark, is an example of the fiction of separate but equal. A brass railing divided the large general waiting room into "white" and "colored" sides, the former being twice the size of the latter. One ticket office served both races, with multiple ticket windows for whites but only one for blacks. White women had their "*ladies* parlor" (with an attached spacious three-toilet bathroom) where they could nurse children or simply relax in seclusion. White men had their own "smoking room," with an equal-sized bathroom. The station also offered a separate waiting room for "colored *women*," the same size as the one for whites, but with a smaller two-toilet bathroom. The bathroom for black men was similarly small and accessible only by leaving the station proper and using an exterior door. Eating facilities for whites included a large dining room plus a lunchroom with an elegant L-shaped counter. An order window in the lunchroom wall opened onto the "colored" side of the general waiting room, but no tables or counters allowed blacks to sit down for meals. About the only thing "equal" in this station was its modernity. This general pattern was repeated many times over, such as at the new union station built in 1919 in Richmond. Whites enjoyed a spacious waiting room and rest rooms, separate smoking and retiring rooms for men and women, and a full dining room plus lunchroom. Blacks had only one small waiting room, fewer toilets, and a tiny dining room and lunchroom with a pantry but no kitchen.[35]

Ironically, truly equal separate accommodations were most likely to be found in small country depots. Typical was a combination freight and passenger station on the Mississippi Central Railroad at Sandersville. The smaller end of the rectangular structure was for passengers, with the agent's office in the middle, and a freight room occupying the remaining two-thirds of the structure. The passenger area was divided exactly down the middle by a wall, with each waiting room having its own door to the platform outside. Each also had its own identically sized ticket window. The two waiting rooms and the agent's office all had fireplaces, sharing a common chimney. Neither race had an inside toilet; outhouses (not on the blueprint) must have sufficed. Railroads used standard depot plans, and similar layouts were to be found on the Missouri–Kansas–Texas Railway's combination stations all over Oklahoma and Texas, the Virginian Railway's combination freight and passenger depots in West Virginia and Virginia, as well as the Mobile & Ohio Railroad's tiny 15-by-30-foot non-agency (unstaffed) depots in Mississippi.[36]

Railroads could not ignore state segregation laws, no matter the economic burdens they imposed. But in border state Maryland, partly because white public opinion was not so militant on the question, they managed to minimize the costs of compliance by distinguishing between interstate and local travelers. Maryland's Jim Crow law went into effect in mid-1904, having a potentially serious impact on the Baltimore & Ohio, Western Maryland, and Pennsylvania railroads that operated both long-distance trains across and local trains within the state. The B&O began to install partitions in "old smoking coaches" for local trains, one end for black passengers, with smoking prohibited, the other for white smokers. The other two roads made similar arrangements for locals, while all three classified trains originating outside of Maryland (including in Washington, D.C.) or traveling beyond the state as "through express trains" and thus exempt from the Jim Crow requirements. As a Frederick newspaper admitted, "according to the construction of the law by officials of

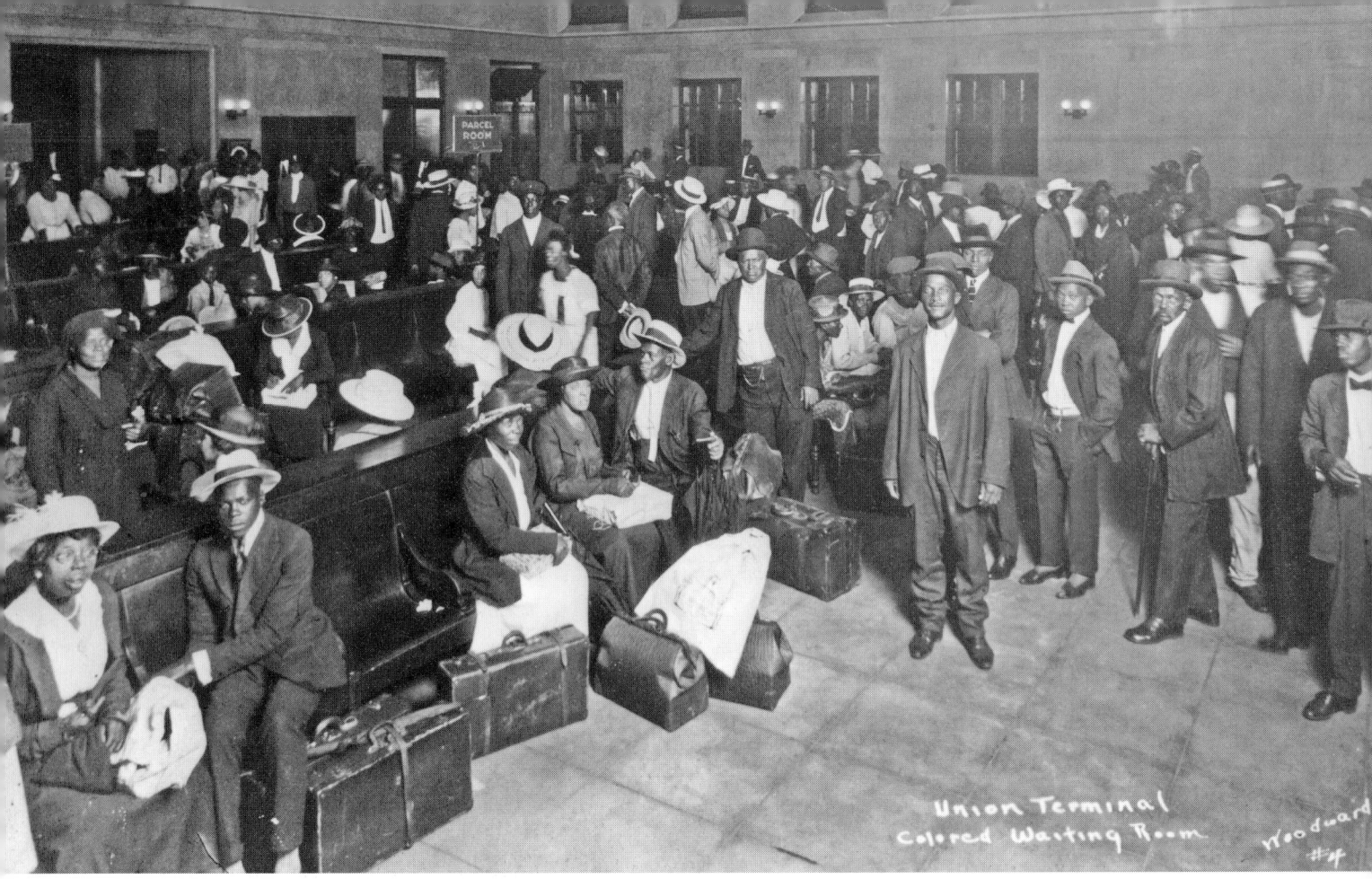

The union terminal at Jacksonville, Florida, photographed in 1921, served all five passenger railroads. It had segregated waiting rooms that opened onto a broad concourse with newsstand and shops, which in turn led to the tracks where travelers boarded trains. Note how people dressed up to travel in those days. Many of them may be heading north, swept up in the Great Migration. Woodward Photo, State Library and Archives of Florida

[the] railroads, colored passengers can enjoy the same privileges as heretofore on through express trains and trains doing an interstate business."[37]

Blacks lost no time in challenging Maryland's new law. The first to do so was, surprisingly, a woman from Pittsburgh, Pennsylvania, visiting relatives near Frederick. She and her husband boarded a B&O local at Ijamsville to travel the dozen miles to Mt. Airy, taking seats in one of the white coaches. When the conductor ordered them into another car, the wife took offense. According to the local newspaper, "when the conductor attempted to use force, she hit him in the face with her fist, and then drawing a hatpin from her hat, attempted to stick him with it." The entire family was put off at the next stop. When brought to trial, the woman claimed that since there were no Jim Crow cars in Pennsylvania she was unaware of such a requirement in Maryland. The judge imposed a light fine, on account of the fact that her husband would have to bear the cost of her indiscretion. Clearly the B&O did not relish enforcing the new state law, as the same newspaper soon reported, for public information, that conductors had been instructed to allow black passengers traveling from Philadelphia or Washington into Maryland to take seats in white coaches if they objected to sitting in the Jim Crow car.[38]

The Pennsylvania Railroad similarly faced an unwanted Jim Crow situation when Virginia's Jim Crow law went into effect in 1900. It controlled the Cumberland Valley Railroad from Harrisburg, Pennsylvania, to Winchester, Virginia, which passed through Maryland and West Virginia before its last 7 miles in the Old Dominion. Clearly black passengers would not assent to being segregated where no state law required it, and the railroad did not want to be burdened with extra equipment. So its shops constructed two "light partitions made of wood and covered with cloth," one to be kept in Winchester, the other in Martinsburg, West Virginia. As soon as the northbound train crossed into West Virginia, the partition was removed and stowed in the baggage car, then dropped off in Martinsburg. Partitions on southbound trains were loaded on at Martinsburg, but not actually installed until the last stop in West Virginia. The CV's crew undoubtedly disliked having to mount and dismount the partition and move passengers back and forth between cars.[39] These awkward maneuvers lasted until the end of passenger service south of Hagerstown, Maryland, in the late 1940s. Railroad segregation was rare, but not untried, in the North. In 1913, the Central Railroad of New Jersey inexplicably started separating black and white patrons in the lunchroom at its Jersey City station. Within weeks, after many African Americans had shifted patronage to the Pennsylvania Railroad, a committee of 100 local blacks persuaded railroad officials to abandon the odious practice.[40]

By the dawn of the twentieth century, blacks recognized that possession of a Pullman ticket was no guarantee that they could enjoy such accommodations. When whites objected to the presence of blacks in their midst, they often had to give up their first-class seats and repair to a Jim Crow coach. The NAACP documented a number of cases in which violence accompanied such action. In one, the supreme chancellor of the Colored Knights of Pythias purchased a seat in a Pullman open section for a day trip from New Orleans to Jacksonville, Florida. When white passengers complained, the conductor "advised" him to go to the Jim Crow car. For his return trip, he purchased space in a drawing room so that he could remain unseen by other passengers. But a white crewmember took offense and wired the news to stations ahead. Sensing danger, the passenger took refuge in the Jim Crow car but was seized by a mob in the town of Milton, Florida. Counting himself lucky to be jailed and not strung up, he paid a $25 fine the following day and boarded the next train, careful to occupy the segregated car. In another case, during World War I, a Texas constable summoned by the conductor of the Missouri Pacific's *Sunshine Special* ejected a black army officer from a Pullman at gunpoint.[41]

Jim Crow was more than segregated cars and stations. It was also the humiliating and infuriating experience of being treated as an inferior. At times, railroads were the unwilling participants in segregation,[42] but in other instances, they actively took it upon themselves to uphold what whites regarded as their "sacred" way of life, the system of white supremacy. This can be seen in microcosm in the files of the Central of Georgia Railway. By the early twentieth century, blacks no longer hoped for an end to segregation but they pleaded frequently for the implementation of "equal" in the separate but equal formula. The C of G, which stonewalled desegregation to the very end, was the only railroad to actually promote segregation in its timetables.

A drumbeat of black discontent can be traced in the Central of Georgia's executive correspondence file. In a 1912 letter composed carefully so as to avoid the racial offense of being "uppity," the Rev. H. J. Peeples wrote to president C. H. Markham, "I have notice the inadequate accommodation to colored peoples." Specifically, while a step stool was placed on the ground for passengers getting on the white coaches, none was furnished for blacks entering their segregated car. "Our women have to climb up in your trains the best they can . . . They have to raise their dresses to reach the top step [which] is disgraceful for ladies." A second grievance was the absence of separate toilets for the two sexes in partitioned cars. It was undignified for both men and women to have to share the same toilet. (Southern whites were routinely oblivious to such sensibilities. Many places had only three public toilets, for "white women," "white men," and "colored.") And a single restroom was inadequate. Peebles confessed that "just a few days ago I like to have disgrace myself . . . I went to the toilet [for] the third time [while] the lady was still in there." His plea to use the toilet in the smoker was, not surprisingly, denied by the white conductor.[43]

Rev. Peebles's complaints were forwarded to the general passenger agent, but went unheeded. "As we cannot give this man assurance of equipping the coaches in accordance with his suggestions, it would be better not to make him any reply. If reply be made, he may use it to our disadvantage" in a lawsuit, since other Georgia railroads did provide toilets for both sexes in partitioned cars. Regarding the stools, known as step boxes, the train porter placed such stools on the ground at each stop. But many C of G trains had only a single train porter, whose priority was to serve white passengers by placing the step box for their use. [44]

Protesting to the Central of Georgia was futile. All across the South, the number of complaints about the unfairness of segregation declined in the early 1900s, not because conditions improved but because such indignities became so firmly entrenched. But government control of the railroads during World War I generated hopes that federal managers would be more receptive to pleas for fairness, if couched in the need for patriotic unity. Such expectations, however, would be bitterly disappointed.

The C of G's "Negro Complaints" file reveals that the U.S. Railroad Administration was more attentive to white sensibilities than to blacks' grievances. The USRA received numerous letters from southern blacks, some complaining about Jim Crow cars, but a "large majority" concerning discourteous treatment by white trainmen. Director General William Gibbs McAdoo declared that "the Negro should be treated with courtesy and consideration." But this was fatally compromised by the fact that numerous USRA bureaucrats were "Southern men" who did not believe white railroaders should be "taken to task for alleged discourtesies to a Negro." To his credit, McAdoo believed in "the necessity of improving the conditions under which Negroes travel," but USRA actuary Theodore H. Price admitted that disciplining individual trainmen "would probably generate ill feeling rather than remove it."[45] The C of G's federal manager saw no solution acceptable to the dominant race: "I don't see how we can mend this matter by issuing instructions to our white employes. A white man feels his superiority and will not tolerate any talk about equality." So why were blacks often treated discourteously? "I think it is true that the station and train employes are somewhat impatient with the negroes, but this is not due to the difference in race or color but to the difference in mental status. The stupidity of many of the negroes is exasperating."[46]

Increased discourtesy to black travelers was an indirect consequence of changes instituted by the USRA. Having imposed higher wages and abolished racial pay differentials, the position of train porter, formerly a monopoly for African Americans in the South, was now attractive to whites. This was a phenomenon that blacks knew all too well. Whatever occupations whites chose not to fill were defined as "Negro jobs." If such work became desirable on account of higher pay, they became "white jobs." A train porter's duties included helping female and elderly passengers on and off the train, which meant holding their arms, when necessary. But rarely were southern white men willing to give personal assistance to a black person. Naturally, blacks expected the same cheerful service from white porters as they had gotten from black porters. So when white porters did not offer personal service, blacks urged that trains carry porters to serve each race separately.[47]

Other complaints also became more common during the war. Many trains were crowded[48] and blacks felt that not enough coaches were assigned for their use, forcing many to stand for hours in the aisles. The absence of separate black smoking compartments forced tobacco users onto the cars' exposed open end platforms, yet white men felt free to come into the segregated cars to drink, smoke, and behave offensively in the presence of black women. If the cars for whites were crowded, conductors and news butchers appropriated seats in the blacks' cars for their "offices." Each porter had only one step box, so when the sole porter was a white man, only white passengers were able to board or alight from trains with ease. And the Central of Georgia had not added additional toilets to partitioned cars, so black women and men still shared the same facilities.[49] Summing up the humiliations of Jim Crow, Benjamin J. Davis, editor of the *Atlanta Independent*, wrote McAdoo that "railroad travel for colored citizens is a nuisance, disgrace and rises but little above barbarism."[50]

Federal manager W. A. Winburn was at least willing to resolve the toilet issue, recommending that a second lavatory be added to all 58 coaches used by black passengers, at a cost of only $120 per car. But the line's general manager vetoed this solution. Meanwhile, the railroad attempted to evade the problem of step boxes by eliminating their use entirely, but the state Railroad Commission voided this plan. Fundamentally, the C of G refused to take discriminatory treatment seriously. The USRA went no further than ordering it to ensure "sufficient accommodations," cleanliness in coaches and station facilities, and the separation of smokers and non-smokers. In response, the general passenger agent claimed that the railroad complied with all these requirements, including adding more toilets to partitioned coaches when they were shopped for major maintenance.[51]

In the fall of 1919, however, the railroad was forced to respond anew to "numerous complaints" that white trainmen were not "assisting colored women and children on and off of trains." In fact, they were often downright rude, treating blacks in an "abrupt manner."[52] The USRA demanded immediate improvements, while C of G general manager H. D. Pollard reaffirmed that trainmen knew full well what their duties were and no excuses were acceptable. Knowing one's duties was one thing; discarding delusions of racial superiority was another matter. Trainmen were now placing step boxes for blacks but were still unwilling to "assist the negro women by the arm in getting on and off or help them with their packages and bundles as probably was the practice with the negro porters."[53] This was precisely the problem. Blacks demanded that they be treated with the same dignity as any other passengers.

The C of G's federal manager reported what he deemed to be progress in the fall of 1919, noting that white trainmen were "expected to perform the same duties as have heretofore been performed by the colored trainmen" so that now "there should exist no just cause for complaint." A division superintendent added: "I am frequently on the road riding our passenger trains, and my personal observation is that every white train porter on this division is handling the colored patrons of our company in exactly the same manner that the colored train porters did."[54] What he didn't state was that when railroad bosses rode trains, their employees tended to follow the rules more scrupulously than when they were left unmonitored.

The short period of federal supervision did not, unfortunately, alter southern folkways. What did change was that white train porters were now a permanent fixture on the Central of Georgia, although black porters were still employed as well. Complaints regarding white trainmen continued in the 1920s. A black insurance agent and frequent traveler between Savannah and Macon wrote to president L. A. Downs condemning the refusal of white trainmen to fulfill the road's advertising promise of "Courtesy and Service." In one incident, a flagman gave "utmost attention" to "a number of rank foreigners" while refusing to help black women with children and baggage. Like other complainants, he could recommend only one solution: the employment of black porters on all trains. In a letter published in Savannah's black newspaper, Downs promised an investigation, but at a meeting with "representative colored men" the Savannah Division's superintendent agreed to look into allegations of discourtesy only if blacks supplied exact dates, train numbers, places, and times of the incidents. As the black delegation bitterly noted, it was now up to blacks "to remedy existing unsatisfactory conditions."[55] In fact, discourteous treatment continued through the decade.[56]

Other complaints against the Central of Georgia in the 1920s concerned the difficulties encountered in obtaining sleeping-car accommodations. Travelers bought train tickets and sleeping-car reservations at the same time, most often from station ticket agents. The majority of beds were upper and lower berths that offered privacy behind curtains but not in separate compartments. During the daytime, berths were stowed away and passengers sat near one another in "open sections." Many whites felt squeamish about blacks sharing such intimate social space, even though the porter who served them was also an African American. Black travelers, particularly in the South, had no guarantee that they could purchase such accommodations. Ticket clerks might erroneously inform them that all spaces were already booked. Sometimes one had to have a person light enough to pass for white or someone "important" actually purchase the ticket. When blacks could not be denied reservations they were put in a private compartment at the end of the sleeping car even though they had paid for a less expensive berth. This resulted in a rare paradox by which they got more of a bargain than whites because of racism. But should no compartments be available, even those holding berth reservations were often forced to ride in a segregated coach.[57]

Complaints typically came from black professionals whose business required overnight travel. Federal agricultural extension agent T. M. Campbell wrote to C of G president Downs in 1925, suggesting that relations between the races had become sufficiently harmonious that "a plan whereby accredited colored passengers may secure sleeping accommodations" could be implemented. Downs did not buy the race relations improvement argument, however, and nixed the proposal.[58] Two years later, the head of one of Atlanta's black Masonic lodges wrote to protest the Central of Georgia's unwillingness to sell sleeping-car space to its members. Grand Master H. R. Butler added his personal experience: "For thirty years I have been traveling to and from Savannah, and if my trip was at night I have had to sit up all night, with money in my pocket to pay for sleeping accommodations." New president J. J. Pelley responded by claiming that the C of G "is doing the best it can for you, and is doing as well by you as any other railway operating within the State of Georgia."[59] In fact, it would be another two decades before it became easier for blacks in the South to obtain sleeping-car accommodations.

Grievances identical to those in Georgia could have been found in any of the southern states. The governor of North Carolina, acting on a resolution of the General Assembly, appointed a Commission on Negro Legislation to examine, among several issues, the transportation laws. It identified five prominent issues. Blacks were still frequently riding in wooden cars coupled between steel cars. Even on through trains, the accommodation for blacks was often only one-half of a partitioned car with a single toilet, which provided neither adequate seating nor amenities. Jim Crow cars were typically dirty. Where railroads operated restaurants at station stops, there was usually no provision for blacks to obtain food, even for take-out. Finally, "decent, respectable colored passengers" could only rarely obtain Pullman accommodations. The Commission held hearings in early 1921, with the railroads denying the first and fourth charges, dismissing the seriousness of the second and third issues, and refusing comment on the last. No significant change came from its efforts.[60]

Whether or not a railroad offered courteous service to blacks depended upon a variety of factors, not the least being orders from the top. On a short line like the 168-mile Columbus & Greenville Railway, which spanned northern Mississippi, most white employees had probably met president A. T. Stovall, who appears to have been a classic southern racial paternalist. When a complaint about discourteous treatment by passenger train flagmen reached him, he reminded the road's superintendent that black passengers were entitled to "good and courteous service . . . It is a mighty no-account white man that is discourteous, disrespectful, or unkind to a negro. I would not willingly permit any negro to be more courteous or kind to me than I am to him, and neither can our employes afford to ever do it."[61] On a road with relatively few employees, and a president personally involved in its operation, his instructions could not easily be ignored.

The Great Depression made it even more certain that traveling conditions in the South would not change. When in 1930 the Atlanta branch of the National Urban League sent a list of grievances concerning trains with no porters or with only white porters, Central of Georgia president A. E. Clift's response was pointed. With passenger traffic declining steadily, the road couldn't afford to hire additional employees. But Clift made no apologies. On the contrary: the railroad employed a large black workforce, paying them, he claimed, good wages and generous benefits. "There is no corporation in the country that is a better friend of the negro or accords him better treatment than the Central of Georgia Railway Company." The unspoken message was clear: don't push your grievances, lest you jeopardize the employment of hundreds of blacks. A petition from black Atlantans four months later received an almost identical response: nearly 40 percent of the C of G's workers were black. "It is my conviction, therefore, that the Central of Georgia deals fairly with the negro."[62]

Discrimination was living on borrowed time, however. The tide began to turn at the end of the Great Depression, beginning with the case of Congressman Arthur Mitchell, a Democrat representing Chicago's black South Side. He settled into an immaculate, air-conditioned Pullman one night in 1937 on the Illinois Central's *Louisiane* southbound from Chicago on his way to Hot Springs, Arkansas. The next morning in Memphis, Mitchell's sleeper was switched to the Chicago, Rock Island & Pacific Railway's *Hot Springs Limited*. As soon as it crossed the Mississippi River, a conductor ordered him into a Jim Crow coach, citing Arkansas's segregation law. Mitchell protested that he had paid a first-class fare, adding that he was a U.S. congressman. The conductor retorted, Mitchell recalled, that "it didn't make a damn bit of difference who I was, that as long as I was a nigger I couldn't ride in that car." Knowing that blacks were lynched in Arkansas for being "troublemakers," Mitchell retreated to the Jim Crow coach. It was old, had no air conditioning, and reeked of smoke. The ancient toilet didn't flush, and the car lacked a washbasin, soap, or towels.[63] Mitchell brought suit against the Rock Island. Eventually the case wound its way to the Supreme Court, which ruled unanimously, in *Mitchell v. United States* (1941), that blacks possessing first-class tickets must be accorded first-class accommodations, no matter the number of black passengers. The right to equal accommodations belonged to each individual African American. As the court framed the issue, it was "not a question of segregation but one of equality of treatment."[64]

The next legal victory was *Morgan v. Virginia* (1946), in which the Supreme Court ruled that segregating interstate passengers—those crossing state lines—was an "undue burden on interstate commerce." Irene Morgan had boarded a Greyhound bus in Virginia in 1944, destined for Baltimore, and not only refused to give up her seat for a white person, but kicked the sheriff's deputy who tried to evict her "in a very bad place" and continued fighting him as he dragged her off the bus. The court's decision applied to any mode of transportation. Two pioneer civil rights groups, the Congress of Racial Equality and Fellowship of Reconciliation, undertook a "Journey of Reconciliation" in 1947 to test compliance with the court's decision. Most of these first "freedom rides" were on buses, but four involved interracial teams riding Louisville & Nashville, Norfolk & Western, and Southern Railway trains in the upper South. Although conductors expressed disapproval of whites and blacks sitting together, sometimes threatening arrest, they did not follow through. Greater defiance of the court's decision, including arrests, was encountered on the buses. The riders did not go beyond Tennessee and North Carolina; resistance undoubtedly would have been greater farther south.[65]

Legal progress was significant, but incremental and painfully slow in actual implementation. The next triumph was *Henderson v. United States* (1950), wherein the court ruled that segregation in dining cars violated the Interstate Commerce Act. But if blacks thought that decision would end such discrimination once and for all, they were quickly disabused of their optimism. Plaintiff Elmer Henderson had sued the Southern Railway, and less than a year after his legal victory he learned that the Southern was back to its old tricks. Curtains had been removed but stewards had been issued new instructions to circumvent the court's edict: "When entering [the dining car] singly, women will be seated with women, men with men, young people with young people, elderly persons with elderly persons, white persons with white persons, Negroes with Negroes . . . white passengers should be seated from the buffet or kitchen end of the dining car and Negroes from the opposite end (from the ends toward the middle)."[66] In short, resistance on the part of railroads operating in the Deep South continued to remain stiff. In the border states and the Southwest, however, railroads found less public support for segregation. Eager to relieve crewmembers of distasteful enforcement responsibilities, some lines now disregarded state regulations and allowed dining-car segregation to lapse.[67]

Examination of racial customs and the observance of segregation in Texas illustrates how the South was not monolithic. While the legislature passed a number of Jim Crow laws at the turn of the twentieth century, authorities were not always zealous in their enforcement, nor were a number of railroads operating in the state that were more "western" or "Midwestern" than southern, with corporate headquarters in San Francisco or Chicago. For example, the Fort Worth & Denver City Railway (Chicago, Burlington & Quincy), Rock Island, and Panhandle & Santa Fe (AT&SF) did not segregate their station waiting rooms in Amarillo. West Texas and Panhandle whites were not entirely persuaded that segregation laws were necessary. By the 1940s, Texans generally were more inclined to accept legal decisions like *Mitchell* and *Henderson* than whites farther south. As for the state Railroad Commission, its "resolve to enforce the state's Jim Crow laws completely collapsed" before the end of the decade, prompted by the unwillingness of railroads entering the state from the Midwest, particularly the Missouri–Kansas–Texas (the Katy), Missouri Pacific, and Santa Fe, to uphold segregation. Dining-car protocols were often ignored, and coach partitions were either nonexistent, were lacking doors, or did not extend all the way to the ceiling. Following the *Morgan* decision, the Katy outright refused to attempt to separate travelers. Other lines followed suit. And shortly after *Henderson* the Rock Island ended all segregation. Although Jim Crow retained its grip on railroads in more traditionally "southern" East Texas, it was on life support. The railroads didn't want it, and the Railroad Commission had no stomach for effective enforcement.[68]

The World War II era brought new pressures on segregation. Well-reported incidents fanned the flames of protest, like the case of black soldiers in Mississippi who were forced to eat in the kitchen of a railroad depot restaurant while German POWs with their guards enjoyed their meal in the dining room.[69] No wonder, then, that the Pennsylvania Railroad was roundly condemned by black organizations in mid-1944 for cooperating with southern railroads in segregating black passengers. The PRR handled all of the ACL, SRR, and SAL trains originating in New York, hauling them as far as Washington, D.C., with Pennsy locomotives and crews. Its ticket agents assigned black passengers only to the first (Jim Crow) coach, which typically had a three-faced sign on the wall, one face reading "white," another "colored," and the third being blank. The blank face was displayed until the train left Washington and entered Virginia, when it was turned to the "colored" side. If all space in this car, which became the Jim Crow coach once it entered Virginia, was booked, passengers were informed there were no seats available beyond Washington. If knowledgeable passengers insisted, however, on obtaining seats in the reserved seat coaches (for whites) for a southern destination, they were to be ticketed only as far as Washington and told that they must apply there for tickets beyond that point.[70]

Despite protests, the PRR didn't end this practice until four years after the war when, under "vigorous" pressure from the New York State Commission Against Discrimination and the New York City Mayor's Committee on Unity, it agreed to reserve coach seats on through trains from New York to the South "for all passengers, negro and white alike, in any part of the train," although it could not guarantee they would be politely treated south of Washington by other railroads' crews.[71] In fact, the PRR and its southern-railroad partners worked out a cynical deal, each continuing to respect the other's policies after 1949. The first coach on southbound reserved-seat trains was deliberately kept vacant until Washington, with black passengers boarding between New York and Baltimore seated randomly in other coaches. But at Washington and subsequent southern stops, all blacks entraining would have to occupy the first coach that had become the Jim Crow car. Such trains were thus simultaneously integrated and segregated. On northbound trips originating in the South, all black passengers sat in the first (Jim Crow) car until Washington. In order to avoid any further "social equality," the Southern Railway's deluxe all-coach *Southerner*, from New York to New Orleans, had two club cars, one right behind the first coach, the other at the end of the train. Blacks were encouraged to patronize the former and discouraged from entering the latter, with the opposite suggestions made to whites. This arrangement was a guaranteed money loser. A train with only six passenger cars could at best hope to meet the expenses of one club car, not two.[72]

Black passengers elsewhere traveling from the North into the South likewise found railroads attempting to segregate them from the beginning. The Illinois Central operated a number of trains from Chicago to Birmingham and New Orleans that ran first down through Illinois, entering the South (into Kentucky) after crossing the Ohio River at Cairo, Illinois. A black woman purchased a coach ticket in mid-1950 in Chicago and was handed a card assigning her to the Jim Crow car. Upon boarding, she found it already filled to capacity. Although there were numerous empty seats in other coaches she was barred from them and compelled to stand in the segregated car for much of her trip. Summoned before the Illinois Commerce Commission, the railroad confirmed the facts but claimed that the seat assignment was not compulsory. But officials acknowledged a racial motive: seats were segregated to "follow the desires of [white] passengers as expressed to the Illinois Central." The commission didn't buy the railroad's justifications, pointing out that car assignments could only be construed as compulsory, as there was nothing written on the cards indicating they could be disregarded, and ordered the IC to cease subjecting blacks "to prejudice and disadvantage and discrimination with respect to service because of their race and color." Unfortunately, this order could only be enforced in the state of Illinois.[73]

The Southern Pacific Lines likewise segregated black passengers on trains traveling to and from the South. In May 1954, two women boarded the railroad's premier westbound *Sunset Limited* in Phoenix, which had originated in New Orleans and had long since left segregated territory. Nonetheless, they were assigned to the Jim Crow car. Its toilet facilities and other amenities were inferior to those in the coaches occupied by whites elsewhere in the train. They brought suit against the SP, joining four other women who had previously charged it with violating their California civil rights by requiring them to ride in the *Sunset*'s Jim Crow car all the way from California to New Orleans, even though segregation was not enforceable until the train reached El Paso, Texas.[74]

A major study of railroad segregation in the early 1950s revealed what blacks knew all too well, that Jim Crow train travel was still usually unequal and was often enforced with indignity, capriciousness, and even brutality. (A black newspaper had recently called the Illinois Central's crewmembers "the toughest and most discourteous in American railroading.")[75] The best that could be hoped for was a reserved seat on a new stainless-steel streamliner where at least the segregated car's amenities—air conditioning, reclining seats, adjustable leg rests, lounge type of restrooms— were equal to those in the cars for whites, because all the cars were part of a matching trainset.

But many such deluxe trains required an extra fare. Furthermore, with all seats reserved, once the Jim Crow car was sold out (typically only 7 percent of the total number of seats), no more black passengers could ride. So blacks more often rode secondary trains with a mix of modern and older equipment, the cars they occupied often lacking reclining seats, florescent lights that could be dimmed at night, and spacious restrooms. Open windows might provide the only "air conditioning." And the placement of such cars at the head end meant that blacks were still more endangered, as in the head-on collision of the Southern's *Crescent* and *Southerner* at Woodstock, Alabama, during the Thanksgiving holidays in 1951. Of the 17 fatalities, 15 were black passengers, all in the latter train's Jim Crow combine.[76]

Another form of discrimination experienced by black passengers was the absence of through coach services. Many long-distance trains carried cars that would be switched out at intermediate points and re-coupled to other trains, allowing travelers to reach alternate destinations without having to change cars. For example, in 1950 the L&N's northbound *Georgian* ran from Atlanta to Chicago, but at Evansville, Indiana, the train was split with some coaches and sleepers going to St. Louis. The lone Jim Crow coach remained with the Chicago-bound train, however, so blacks going to St. Louis had to detrain in Evansville, carrying their baggage, and then board a new car. Although this maneuver only took a few minutes, it occurred at three o'clock in the morning. Meanwhile, white coach passengers slept undisturbed while their car was switched to the *Georgian's* St. Louis section.[77]

The implementation of segregation in the early 1950s still took place within the same "hierarchical authority system" that had long demeaned African American passengers. "Not infrequently, the manner of ticket sellers, conductors and passenger agents is derogative of the Negro passenger, reducing him to the status of one whose presence is merely tolerated on the train through the generosity of the powers that be." Ticket agents at southern terminals usually waited on all white patrons first, and even when finished with them, sometimes ignored blacks so that they missed their trains and had to take a later departure. Although certainly not all such employees were mean-spirited, many blacks encountered such hostility. Inquiries regarding train times too frequently brought responses like, "I don't answer nigger's fool questions." Southern ticket agents also often refused to give blacks timetables that were free for the asking to whites.[78]

Once on board a train in the South, the relationship between black passengers and white conductors and brakemen could easily escalate into conflict, particularly when blacks were required to relocate to the Jim Crow car upon crossing the Mason-Dixon Line. While some white trainmen tried to alleviate overcrowding in the segregated cars, others were abusive. According to state laws, conductors were invested with police power to enforce segregation. In addition, they could summon local police at station stops to back them up. One did not have to search long in the black press in the late 1940s and early 1950s for examples of black passengers who were beaten or killed by small-town policemen commandeered by conductors. As the author of the study of railroad segregation observed, "the Negro passenger is charged not merely with failing to obey the orders of the train conductor but with the more serious offense of breaking the law. He is now a criminal . . . the most dangerous of criminals—he has dared to challenge the word and authority of a white man; he has broken the racial code and defame[d] the sacred idol of 'white supremacy.'"[79]

The 1950s were times of trial for both African Americans and the railroads of the South. A new generation of blacks was insistent on full civil rights, and the Supreme Court and Interstate Commerce Commission were increasingly on their side. Would the railroads change? The larger ones were under the jurisdiction of the ICC. All were also beholden to state regulatory bodies and vulnerable to segregationist public opinion and political pressures. Could they sidestep federal court edicts? Within a month of the *Henderson* decision, the Central of Georgia's general counsel had devised a duplicitous strategy. It operated, in concert with other railroads, a number of long-distance Florida-bound trains originating in the Midwest and crossing many state lines. Such trains were subject to ICC jurisdiction. But its own two streamliners, the *Nancy Hanks II* and *Man O' War*, ran only within Georgia and thus were beyond the sweep of the ICC and the recent court decisions. Both trains featured a black maid and porter. Black passengers wishing to eat were served at two tables in the "colored" car, with their orders brought to them by the maid from the whites-only grill-lounge car. However, these trains carried some interstate black passengers. Refusing to serve them in the grill-lounge car would violate the Interstate Commerce Act. But the general counsel nonetheless advocated violating ICC rules: "We run a risk only in the case of interstate negro passengers, and only then in the few cases in which they might be unable to find a seat at the tables set up in the negro car or may prefer to challenge us by going into the lounge car and demanding service. I think we can take that much risk. Proof of damages would be difficult." This was curious legal advice in light of his quote from the *Henderson* decision: "The right to be free from unreasonable discriminations belongs, under Section 3 (1) [of the Interstate Commerce Act], to each particular person. Where a dining car is available to passengers holding tickets entitling them to use it, *each such passenger is equally entitled to use its facilities*."[80] Yet the C of G defiantly intended to maintain segregation on intrastate trains, publishing the notice "Seats for white passengers reserved" in its public timetables.

Following the *Henderson* decision, blacks stepped up their attacks on segregation, seeking to make the separate but equal policy too costly for railroads to maintain. The C of G was already losing money on passenger service, yet in efforts to stave off integration, it invested precious capital into transforming old heavyweight coaches into partitioned cars with two sets of toilets in each end.[81] Financial logic should have dictated jettisoning Jim Crow. But the C of G held on as Atlanta's NAACP chapter and individual complainants battered away at the stubborn railroad.

The C of G's liability was its inability to always provide the same type of equipment to each race. Invariably, rolling stock shortages or spikes in ridership meant that antiquated equipment was pressed into service and assigned for black passengers, while modern "deluxe accommodations," whenever possible were reserved for whites. Older baggage-coach combines typically lacked air conditioning and often the seats did not recline, a major point of discomfort for overnight travelers. In response to an NAACP complaint of "inferior accommodations," the railroad promised only that *some* of the older, "less attractive" cars would be modernized.[82] Such assurances did not pacify southern blacks in the early 1950s, whose appetite for a total end to inequality had been whetted by recent Supreme Court victories.

The Central of Georgia's most persistent critic in the 1950s was Edward McGlockton, who directed most of his protests to J. Monroe Johnson, an elderly South Carolina Democrat who served on the Interstate Commerce Commission. McGlockton's point of view was consistent, from his first letter to that agency in January 1951: "Most of the southern railroads are guilty of cheating colored passengers when it comes to giving them the service that they advertise in time tables." On four consecutive trips, the Jim Crow car on the *Nancy Hanks II*, between Atlanta and Savannah, had too few seats for the number of black passengers, forcing McGlockton and many others to stand for much of the trip. And on five other occasions, local trains between those points featured deluxe coaches for whites while blacks had to ride in older cars, sometimes without air conditioning. The ICC sent McGlockton's letter to the railroad, which responded that it was impossible, during the Christmas rush, to know ahead of time how large the crowds might be, although it did add a second coach for blacks to its locals. In fact the company simply did not have sufficient deluxe cars for all of its trains.[83]

The ICC commissioner overseeing this dispute was not optimistic, writing to McGlockton, "I find it is difficult indeed to compose these differences," and suggesting that McGlockton meet with railroad officials and try to compromise. In the end, the ICC admitted that since C of G trains ran only within the state, it had no jurisdiction. In fact, no agreement was possible if the road insisted on maintaining segregation. And it was not about to make concessions to McGlockton or the NAACP, which it regarded as troublemakers who were trying to "make capital" from the "rare occasions" when unanticipated numbers of blacks rode trains.[84] In fact, the railroad took specific steps to gauge the number of white passengers beforehand but was disinterested in learning how many blacks might ride. In advertising reserved seats for whites on the *Nancy Hanks II* and *Man O'War*, the C of G could anticipate demand and add cars if reservations soared. It meant nothing to inconvenience blacks, while concrete measures were taken to ensure that whites always had sufficient deluxe seats.

Did the Central of Georgia still have a legal leg to stand on? The Supreme Court had not overturned *Plessy v. Ferguson*, but it had strengthened ICC regulations. The railroad was refurbishing older cars with air conditioning and toilets for both sexes, but not reclining seats. Was it in compliance with Section 3 (1) of the Interstate Commerce Act, prohibiting carriers from subjecting passengers to an "undue or unreasonable prejudice or disadvantage"? The general counsel, in a new opinion in mid-1951, pinpointed the C of G's continued liability: "What I am concerned about is the fact that it is unquestionably our deliberate policy, uniformly followed, to supply the deluxe cars to white passengers where we do not have enough deluxe cars to go around, and never to supply them to colored passengers." This, then, was a (confidential) admission that racist criteria were used in assigning cars. Whites' comfort always took priority; blacks received less consideration simply because of their race. The general counsel acknowledged that the C of G could resolve any legal liability simply by alternating "the assignment of our deluxe cars between colored and white passengers." But such a solution was unacceptable to white supremacists. "As a practical matter, we could not do this in this part of the country." Let an aggrieved black passenger sue. "We could much better afford to pay what a [southern white] jury would give him than go to the expense of equipping ourselves completely with deluxe cars, particularly in the face of our waning passenger revenue."[85]

The Central of Georgia's defense became untenable a year and a half later following the Supreme Court's refusal, in November 1952, to review *Chance v. Lambeth*. This circuit court decision reaffirmed that the commerce clause prohibited segregating or otherwise discriminating against interstate passengers. Only the segregation of intrastate passengers might still be legal. The railroad again turned to its general counsel for advice. In fact, he admitted, segregation had already crumbled. On trains from the Midwest carrying passengers to Florida, "we do not disturb a negro who comes into Georgia holding an interstate ticket, though he may be in a car which is supposed to be set aside for white passengers, and I assume that if he buys a ticket in Georgia and is headed for Florida, we would not insist, over his protest, on his going into a car set aside for negroes." But the general counsel urged taking a stand to preserve the sacred white privilege of traveling exclusively among one's own kind: "Though there are certainly some interstate passengers on both the *Nancy Hanks II* and the *Man O' War*, the bulk of the tickets must be intrastate and, since we give the races equal accommodations on both of those trains except in the dining cars, the chances of a claim or suit are rather remote unless one is filed to test the question. I do not think the provable damages would be great simply because a negro is required to sit in a negro coach between Savannah and Atlanta." In other words, the counsel advised risking considerable legal costs, and the possibility of damages, simply to preserve on two trains a practice that was unenforceable on its other (interstate) streamliners.[86]

With the C of G determined to preserve its antediluvian custom, the passenger traffic department quickly issued "Instructions regarding passenger train accommodations for different races" on November 20, 1952. They began with an acknowledgment: "The segregation of interstate passengers according to races has been held unlawful by the Supreme Court." But there were still ways to wiggle around it. Interstate sleeping-car passengers could not be denied seat or berth tickets, but the longstanding custom of putting blacks in more expensive compartments, where they could not be seen by white passengers, was to be followed unless the individual objected, in which case she or he would have to be given a seat or berth. If that were the case, white and black passengers should not be assigned to the same open section (i.e., where they would sit opposite one another and sleep in a berth one above the other). If intrastate passengers requested drawing rooms, bedrooms, or roomettes, they were to be sold such tickets. Should they seek berths or seats in the less expensive open sections, they were instead to be placed in compartments, but charged the lower fare. If no compartment was available, they should be refused a Pullman seat under authority of Georgia's segregation law.[87]

Dining-car seating was to be similarly finessed. Blacks were to eat at the last two tables, behind curtains. If no blacks were being served, and whites occupied all other tables and more whites waited to eat, the curtain was to be pushed back and the two tables occupied by whites. Then, should blacks come to eat, they would be refused and offered tray meals at their seats. Enjoyment of the grill-lounge and club observation cars on the *Man O' War* and *Nancy Hanks II* remained off-limits to blacks holding intrastate tickets. Those possessing interstate tickets could not be banned outright, but "tact and diplomacy should be used in an effort to persuade them not to [frequent those areas]." If blacks holding interstate tickets *demanded* to sit in coaches occupied by whites, they could not be refused although employees should again employ "tact and diplomacy" to get them to change their minds. Blacks entering Georgia on other railroads' integrated cars that were added to the C of G's trains "should not be disturbed." Finally, "interstate colored coach passengers should not be denied same accommodations occupied by white passengers when their demands are such as would create a disturbance when an effort is made to persuade them not to do so."[88]

The tenacity of those who were trying to plug the leaks in their sinking ship is remarkable. Exactly how whites would be tactful and diplomatic in enforcing segregation is unclear. To expect blacks to acquiesce and forsake their manhood and dignity was naïve. Not surprisingly, E. C. McGlockton kept up his drumbeat of complaints to the ICC. On a Christmas Eve 1952 journey on the *Nancy Hanks II*, blacks were crammed "like sardines" into an inferior coach, with others having to stand in the baggage car and in the vestibules. Whites were not similarly crowded nor standing in their deluxe car. And it had been impossible for blacks to get meals delivered from the grill-lounge car.[89]

At times, racists were downright nasty, and McGlockton was not one to let offensive behavior go unprotested. His new complaint went to Harlem's congressman Adam Clayton Powell, Jr., whose willingness to challenge whites was legendary among blacks. McGlockton described a journey in the combination car on the *Nancy Hanks II* in which the white baggageman sat down at the pair of seats with the table where blacks ate meals delivered from the grill. He "put his feet on the table and sat there all the way to Griffin, about 30 miles, smoking and whenever he wanted to spit, he would lean over by the window and spit on the floor. I called this to the attention of the porter and maid and told the maid to cancel my dinner order because I could not eat on the table where the Baggage man had his feet. The maid removed the sugar bowl, salt and pepper shakers from the table, but the Baggage man kept his feet on the table until we reached Griffin." This was no isolated incident. Two months later, McGlockton rode the same train and again lost his appetite when the baggageman repeated the disgusting performance. McGlockton finally summoned the conductor, who merely "talked to him [the baggageman]."[90] This second complaint was lodged with the ICC, which demanded an explanation. C of G president B. J. Tarbutton minimized the baggageman's behavior, although an investigation acknowledged that "there may be some justification" for the complaint that train crew members occupied seats needed by black passengers, while concluding that the baggageman's "actions while occupying this seat were probably not as bad as pictured by McGlockton." No regret was ever expressed. Southern folkways prohibited white apologies to blacks. The only tangible result was new instructions to train crews to stay out of the Jim Crow cars entirely "except in the discharge of their duties."[91]

By this time events were moving rapidly on the national legal front. In late 1953, while Supreme Court justices were deliberating the *Brown* school desegregation case, the NAACP petitioned the ICC to ban all Jim Crow railroad travel and terminal facilities. Twelve southern railroads were named as culprits, but not the Central of Georgia because it was an intrastate carrier. The ICC heard testimony on the NAACP's petition two months after the *Brown* decision was announced. Its attorneys naturally used that ruling to argue that all segregation was illegal. The NAACP's case was bolstered when the Justice Department filed a brief arguing that segregated interstate transportation violated the Interstate Commerce Act. The ICC issued its finding in November 1955, ruling that all segregation of interstate transit, trains and buses, on the vehicles themselves and in station facilities, was illegal: "The disadvantage to a traveler who is assigned accommodations or facilities so designated as to imply his inherent inferiority solely because of race must be regarded under present conditions as unreasonable." Black passengers were "entitled to be free of annoyances, some petty and some substantial, which almost inevitably accompany segregation." While McGlockton's encounters with hostile baggagemen involved intrastate trains and were thus not affected by the ICC's order, its points, and those stressed in *Brown*, would make it increasingly untenable to burden African Americans with the insults and humiliations of enforced segregation.[92]

Four Deep South states reacted swiftly to the ICC ruling, insisting that their segregation laws be fully obeyed, in effect urging defiance of the federal government. Georgia and two other states now required, where before it had been simply customary, that intrastate passengers be segregated in terminals. The dilemma for segregationists, however, was how to retain segregation of intrastate travelers while accepting that interstate passengers could no longer be Jim Crowed. The larger railroads, all of which crossed state boundaries, now placed on trainmen the responsibility of distinguishing between interstate and intrastate travelers and not disturbing the former if they sat in "white" cars. But the Central of Georgia, because it served proportionally more intrastate passengers, ordered its employees to continue to segregate all blacks, using "persuasion" with interstate travelers. Segregated transportation remained alive, and mostly well, in the Deep South in 1955.[93]

Nearly the last nails in Jim Crow transit's coffin were driven home as a result of the Montgomery, Alabama bus boycott. A federal circuit court ruled in mid-1956, in *Browder v. Gayle*, that segregated *intrastate* transport was unconstitutional. The decision was stayed pending Supreme Court review. In December, that body unanimously affirmed the lower tribunal's judgment. This was the effective end to the *Plessy* principle, separate but equal, which had Jim Crowed blacks for more than half a century. Most southern railroads had already ceased segregating interstate passengers and *Browder*, plus the economic drain of operating extra cars, brought an end to most remaining Jim

Crow practices. The railroads did not, however, publicize such decisions so as not to antagonize southern white travelers and not to embolden blacks to demand "social equality." White demagogues continued to thunder against "amalgamation" and claim that Jim Crow laws remained in force. The Justice Department organized an unpublicized conference between ICC commissioners and the major railroad and bus trade associations, the attorney general making clear that all Jim Crow transportation laws were illegal. When the Association of American Railroads communicated this to its constituents, their economic self- interests overrode whatever racial sentiments lingered and total on-board desegregation was agreed to in early 1957. Most southern lines ordered employees to cease segregating passengers, although some trainmen, acting on their own, still tried to enforce it. But the railroads did not abandon segregated station facilities. And the stubborn Central of Georgia continued to try to keep intrastate passengers separate on its trains.[94]

Eighteen railroads[95] operating in the South, bowing to local political pressures, still retained Jim Crow station signs in 1961. In a number of Mississippi towns such signs carried the message "By Police Order." Pressure from the Justice Department was required to get the recalcitrant railroads to allow free access to waiting rooms, ticket windows, toilets, and restaurants. Behind-the-scenes negotiations in mid-1961 with the Illinois Central, Louisville & Nashville, and Southern Railway resulted in those lines promising to end separate facilities. Armed with this apparent victory, the Justice Department threatened the other railroads with legal action if they failed to follow suit. Eager to be rid of the expense of maintaining dual facilities, they quickly agreed. Even so, at the end of the year, segregation still persisted where local authorities insisted that it be maintained, despite another ICC order banning all enforced separation of the races in train and bus stations. Employees continued a "cold war" against black patrons at several L&N depots in Alabama and Mississippi. During the 1961-62 civil rights campaign in Albany, Georgia, an interracial group of demonstrators was arrested for trespassing when it conducted a "sit-in" in the white waiting room of the depot shared by the ACL and the C of G. The latter continued to defy the ICC into 1963. Not until the Justice Department began preparing a lawsuit did it finally abandon all remaining segregation.[96]

Why the Central of Georgia, whose advertising slogan was "The Right Way," so stubbornly clung to the wrong way when the rest of the white South acquiesced to desegregation, is not directly revealed in company files. Georgia did not accept civil rights progress easily. Being essentially a one-state railroad, the C of G could not counterbalance Georgia's reactionary politics with less rigid views from other states, assuming it would have wanted to do so. Implicit statewide political support and grassroots approval emboldened the C of G to maintain segregation into the mid-1960s. The coffin into which the corpse of discrimination had been laid required repeated federal hammering to nail the lid shut. Jim Crow also died a lingering death in Virginia. The 1966 edition of the State Corporation Commission's compendium of statutes and regulations still included all the now unenforceable Jim Crow laws in a booklet whose cover instructed: "TO BE POSTED AND KEPT POSTED CONSPICUOUSLY IN EVERY PASSENGER AND FREIGHT DEPOT."[97]

Railroads inspired segregation, from beginning to the end. Train travel allowed more extensive mingling of the races in public space than ever before. Segregation was a crude attempt to regulate class and racial distinctions. Despite the court's assertion in *Plessy*, it could never be benign, because it was grounded in dehumanizing African Americans. And segregation was, at times, absurdly illogical. Virginia's Jim Crow law was so rigid that a white policeman escorting a black prisoner was prohibited by the train's conductor from riding together with him. At an opportune moment, the prisoner leapt from the car window and escaped. On a number of occasions black passengers with very light complexions were ordered to ride in cars occupied by whites.[98] Native Americans and persons from India were mistaken for being African Americans and forced to ride in Jim Crow cars. And Homer Plessy was seven-eighths white, one-eighth black in racial ancestry. Logic could conclude that he was white, but segregation was never grounded in logic.

Blacks were not the only ones to be intentionally segregated on passenger trains. Across the West, whites made scattered efforts to keep Hispanics and Native Americans separate from them. On the Denver & Rio Grande Western Railroad's famed narrow-gauge line between Durango and Alamosa, Colorado, the *San Juan* permitted nonwhites to ride in only the first passenger car, absolutely not in the tail-end parlor-observation car.[99] But such segregation was neither systematic nor backed by state legislation. Jim Crow's target was African Americans. They hated it. The depth of their bitterness is revealed in an ancient folk blues:

Well, I'm goin' to buy me a little railroad of my own,
Ain't goin' to let nobody ride but de chocolate to de bone.[100]

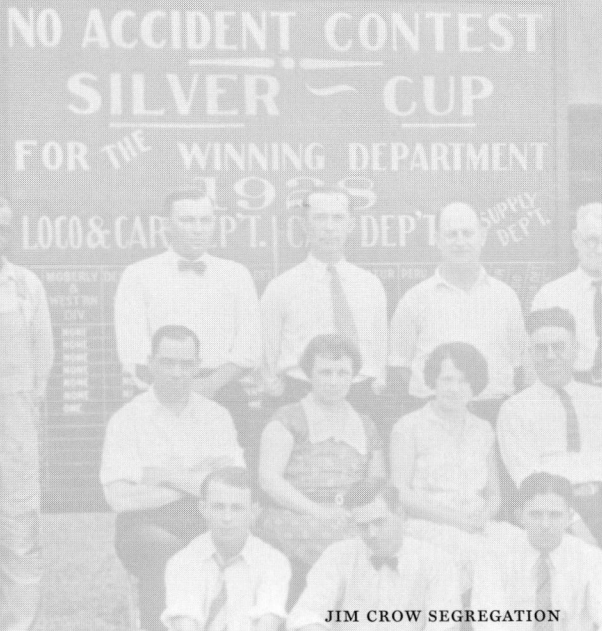

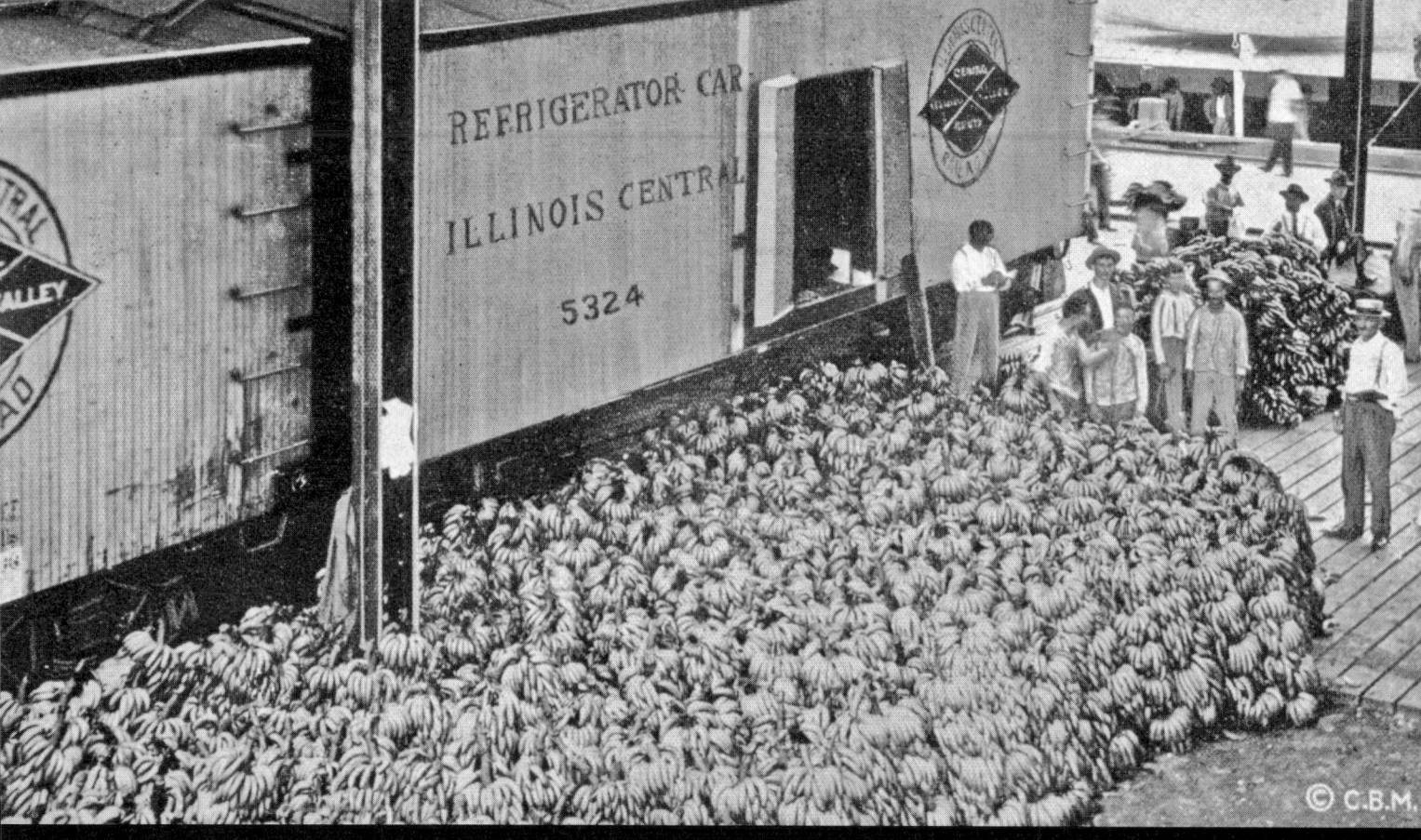

© C.B.M.

Illinois Central Railroad laborers transfer bananas directly from ships to refrigerator cars at New Orleans docks. This postcard, mailed in 1928, touts New Orleans as receiving more banana shipments from Central America than any other port. These IC employees were among the poorest paid Gulf Coast dockworkers.
Theodore Kornweibel collection

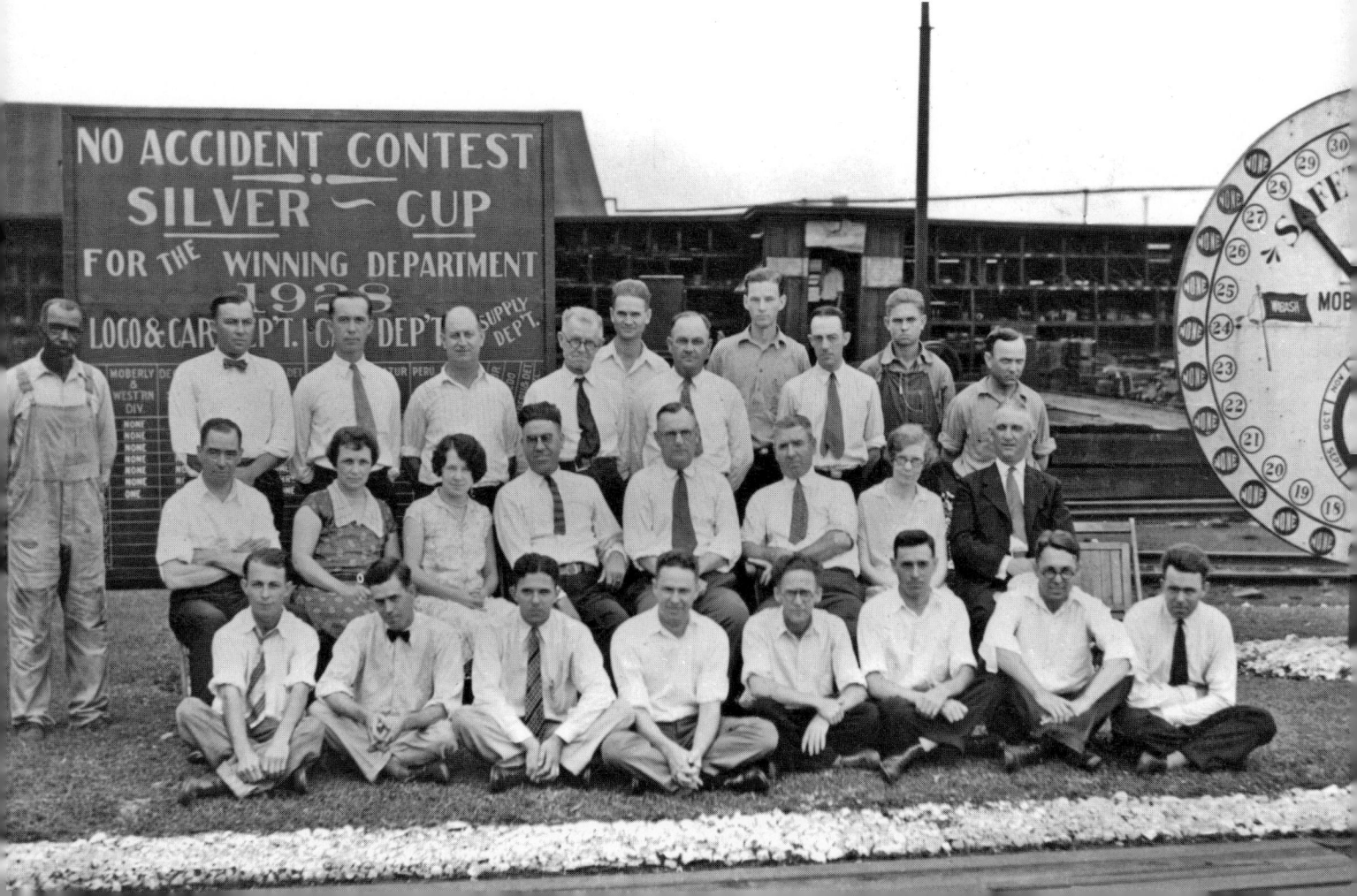

Until the civil rights revolution, the only job open for blacks in most railroad offices was that of janitor. The back of this 1928 Wabash Railway locomotive and car department photograph lists everyone's name, but only janitor Silas Barton's occupation. The physical distance between Barton and the white employees reflects the racial and social gulf prevailing in the railroad workplace. Theodore Kornweibel collection

NO ACCIDENT CONTEST
SILVER CUP
FOR THE WINNING DEPARTMENT
1928
LOCO & CAR DEP'T. | C DEP'T. | SUPPLY DEP'T.

Blacks were fascinated with trains no less than any others, girls as well as boys. Whether climbing on freight cars, like this young woman in a 1930s snapshot, or congregating at stations to watch trains come and go, or lying awake at night listening to locomotive whistles and dreaming of faraway places, railroads symbolized excitement, hope, and greater opportunities for generations of African Americans. Theodore Kornweibel collection

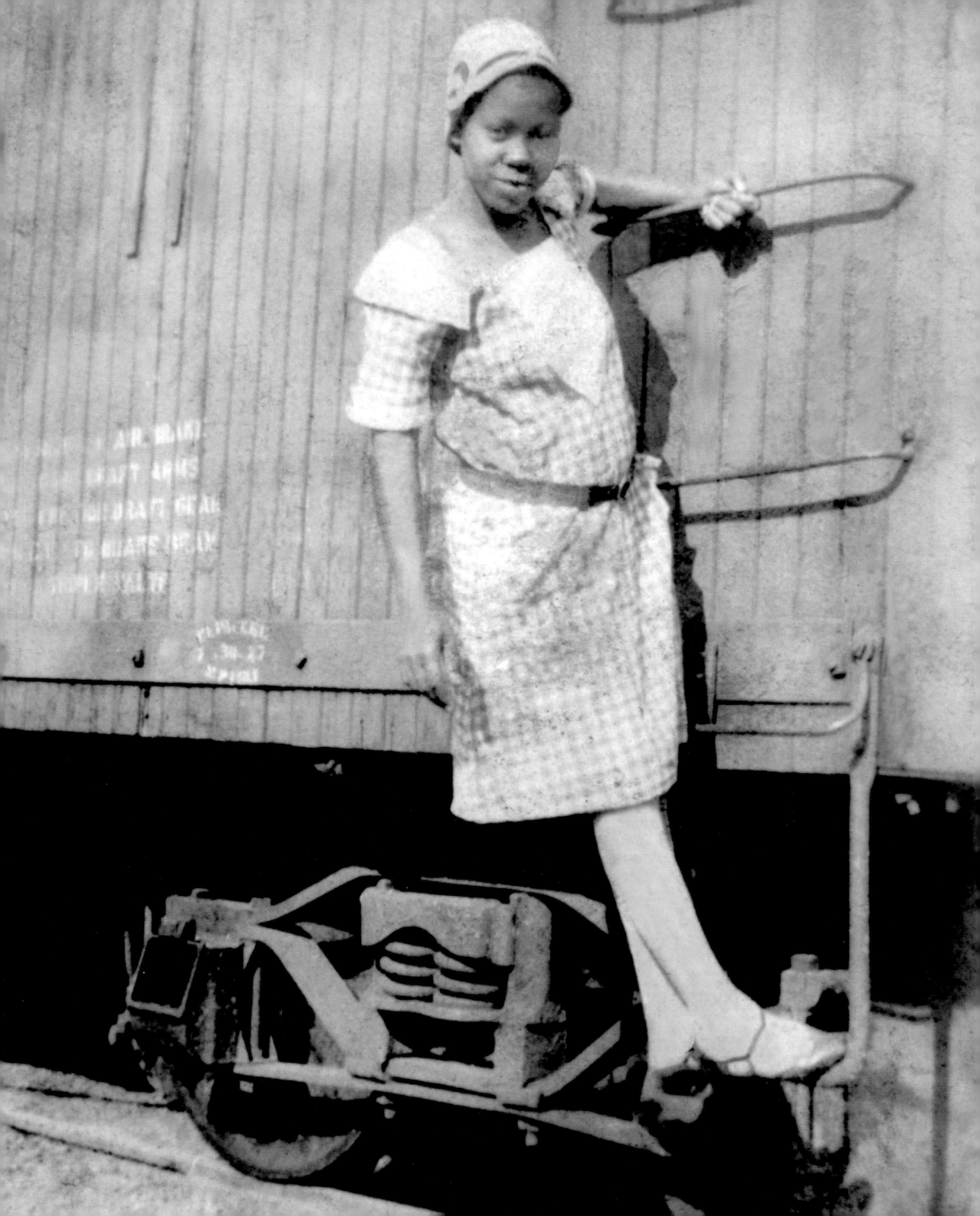

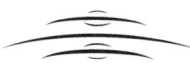

"LITTLE BLACK TRAIN A-COMIN'"

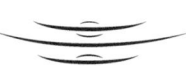

Railroad Imagery in African American Music

No other part of the Industrial Revolution infused African American culture more than railroads. And no other people's culture incorporated industrial imagery as much as African Americans' embrace of trains. Trains symbolized escape, freedom, hope, loneliness, the tension between traditional and modern life, severed relationships, and wanderlust. Railroads generated new forms of culture, like track-lining and train-calling chants, while reshaping others, including work and protest songs and the blues. And although railroads first penetrated the music of rural folk, they went on to influence urban music, including the city blues, big band swing, jazz, even rock 'n' roll.

Why did railroads capture the imagination of African Americans? As was the case for all Americans, the first railroads represented unprecedented (and sometimes frightening) speed. Among enslaved blacks in the South, another meaning quickly emerged. A railroad might lead one to freedom. In many southern newspapers' runaway notices, owners surmised that their slaves had absconded on a train. Many, of course, lived distant from any railroad line and had no firsthand knowledge of this new mode of transportation. But urban slaves, and those living in rural areas through which new lines were laid, soon began to assimilate trains into their thought.

The earliest explicit incorporation of this new technology into the black consciousness was the concept of the "underground railroad." Whether this idea originated with blacks or whites cannot be proven, although it was the latter who first formalized it in print. Appropriate lingo was adopted: fugitives' guides were called "conductors," while those who hid them and arranged for further safe destinations were "stationmasters."

Train imagery quickly entered the spirituals, sometimes by simple substitution. In the familiar "Low [Swing] Down the Chariot and Let me Ride," the mode of celestial transportation is updated:

> Train comin', let me ride
> Oh, low down the chariot and let me ride.[1]

Railroads now symbolized one's life journey. Those who got right with God earned a one-way ticket to heaven. "The Gospel Train" is an invitational spiritual, urging sinners to prepare for the coming judgment before it is too late:

> The gospel train is coming,
> I hear it just at hand;
> I hear the car wheels moving,
> And rumbling thro' the land.
>
> Chorus:
> Get on board, children (x3)
> For there's room for many a more.[2]

Numerous spirituals bear the motif of the trials and tribulations of life being an extended train journey that ends, for the faithful, on a specific route to a heavenly destination. These include "Git on de Evening Train," "If I have My Tickit Lawd," "Oh, Be Ready When the Train Comes In," "How Long de Train Been Gone," and "I'm Going Home on the Morning Train."[3] In "The Train is A-Coming," those who are righteous don't travel alone: "King Jesus is conductor."[4] But if one train led to heaven, another went straight to perdition. According to "Little Black Train," one had best be prepared:

> Oh, the little black train is a-comin',
> I know it's goin' to slack;
> You can tell it by its rumblin',
> It's all draped in black.
>
> Chorus:
> There's a little black train a-comin',
> Get all your business right;

> There's a little black train a-comin',
> And it may be here tonight.[5]

Twentieth-century versions of "Little Black Train" were unambiguous: it picked up unrepentant sinners and took them directly to the "judgment bar." Death would appear unannounced, so one should prepare accordingly. In "Dat Same Train":

> Dat same train goin' t' be back tomorrow, dat same train (x 2)
> Dat same train took away ma mother [father, sister]
> Dat same train goin' t' be back tomorrow
> Dat 'er same train.
> Oh, get yo' ticket ready fer
> Dat same train, etc.[6]

Among the slaves, it was customary to sing admonitory songs to the dying. "Oh, Run, Mary, Run" warns against delaying readiness for departing this life:

> Oh, run, Mary, run,
> The Gospel train is leaving.
> Oh, run, Mary, run,
> I want to get to heaven to-day.[7]

"Goin' Home" depicts a train bringing an end to earthly burdens:

> When the doctor give me out,
> I'm goin' home on the morning train.
>
> When you see me enter my grave,
> I'm goin' home on the mornin' train.[8]

After slavery ended, train-theme spirituals, both traditional and newly composed, continued to speak to blacks' spiritual confidence and their longing for escape, now not from formal slavery but from the burdens of segregation and discrimination. The song that maintained greatest popularity was "The Gospel Train is Coming," sometimes also called "Get On Board." It was a favorite in the repertory of the Fisk Jubilee Singers, the black college choir that, beginning in the 1870s, was first to take the spirituals to white audiences. One stanza of "Gospel Train" took on added meaning in the segregation era, making clear that the heaven-bound train had no Jim Crow car:

The fare is cheap and all can go,
The rich and poor are there,
No second-class on board the train,
No difference in the fare.[9]

For several generations following the end of slavery, African Americans continued the spiritual tradition in their churches, keeping railroad imagery alive. "Git Yo' Ticket" instructed worshipers to be prepared (saved) now, because it would be too late to pay one's fare (accept Christ as one's Savior) when death appeared:

Train's a-comin'
Oh! When, when, when,
Oh! When?

Judgmunt's comin'
Oh! When, when, when,
Oh!, when?[10]

Another slavery-era survivor, "If I Have Mah Tickit Lawd," depicts the struggles of living a Christian life, and wrestling with doubts about whether one is truly saved:

It keeps me always in a move an' strain,
Tryin' to be ready for the Gospel train.
Ever now an' then, either day or night,
I examine my ticket to see if I'm right.
If the Son grant my ticket, the Holy Ghost sign,
Then there is no way to be left behind.[11]

And a twentieth-century Sanctified (Pentecostal) song, "Oh, Be Ready When the Train Comes In," repeated the admonition to get one's life in order:

No harlot nor idolater, neither loafer,
Will be counted in on this holy train;
No pipe-smoker, neither joker are permitted
On this great clean train.[12]

"The Gospel Train" title remained popular throughout the twentieth century. The Reverend Edward W. Clayborn, known as "The Guitar Evangelist," recorded it in 1926 for the "race records" market. His version was more invitational, pleading with sinners to make the decision to follow Christ and be ready for Judgment Day. Each verse ends with the penitent's response:

> Gospel train is comin', don't you want to go?
> Yes, I want to go.
>
> Do you want to know who's the engineer, don't you want to go?
> Yes, I want to go.
>
> Jesus is the engineer, don't you want to go?
> Yes, I want to go.[13]

Jesus or the Lord as engineer was a familiar theme in other songs about the coming judgment, like "He's Comin' This Away."

"This Train," also known as "This Train is Bound For Glory," was recorded four times by vocal groups in the 1920s and early 1930s. Based on an older spiritual, it identified who would and would not be aboard that celestial train:

> This train don't carry no gamblers, this train (x2)
> This train don't carry no gamblers, hobo liars, midnight ramblers,
> This train, my Lord, this train.[14]

When blues man Big Bill Broonzy recorded "This Train" some years later, he included additional verses stressing that God brooked no racism:

> This train don't fit no transportation on this train (x2)
> This train, don't fit no transportation,
> No Jim Crow and no discrimination,
> This train is bound for glory, this train.[15]

Black sacred music continued to use train imagery well past the first third of the twentieth century. During the 1920s, when phonographs first became common in black households, some of the most popular race records were sung sermons with congregational accompaniment, like the Reverend A. W. Nix's "Black Diamond Express to Hell" (1927). It reversed the usual symbolism and made the speeding train a metaphor for ungodly living which, once begun, could not be stopped. "Sin, the Engineer, [is] holding the throttle wide open. Pleasure is the Headlight, and the Devil is the Conductor. You can feel the roaring of the Express and the moanin' of the Drunkards, Liars, Gamblers and other folks who have got aboard. They are hell-bound and they don't want to go.

The train makes eleven stops but nobody can get off."[16] The Reverend J. M. Gates's sermon, "Death's Black Train is Coming," recorded in 1926, stressed the immediacy of changing one's behavior and making a decision to follow Christ:

> There's some men and some women,
> They care nothing for the gospel light,
> Now the bell ring, and the whistle blow,
> Oh the little black train in sight.[17]

Railroad imagery in black sacred music receded in the 1930s as gospel music overtook the spirituals in popularity, although numerous gospel artists and ensembles still included railroad-theme songs in their repertoires. But train motifs remained widespread in secular music, both in the blues and in a much earlier genre, the African American work song. Work songs are vocal music used to give rhythm to physical toil, thereby making the labor easier on one's body and lending encouragement and generating class consciousness through an often satirical commentary on life or one's current situation.[18]

It is impossible to precisely identify the earliest black music reflecting railroad employment, but it must have evolved from slave work songs or field hollers. Agricultural slaves used communal singing to give pace to their labor and to make the long hours go more quickly, so when such slaves were put to railroad construction and track maintenance they undoubtedly continued that practice, particularly when gangs used chants to coordinate each individual's labor in moving heavy rails and ties or tamping ballast. Similarly, slaves in the fields communicated with one another through calls, or "hollers," individual cries to express one's mood or simply to identify oneself. Later nineteenth-century railroad workers and convicts likewise created their own distinctive hollers. And just as agricultural slaves sometimes celebrated their heroes in song, so too did enslaved and later wage-earning black railroaders.

One of the earliest descriptions of black railroaders' songs comes from Frederick Law Olmsted, a northern traveler who observed a group of enslaved train hands singing in unison as they loaded a freight train in South Carolina in 1853: "I could hear one urging the rest to come to work again, and soon he stepped towards the cotton bales, saying, 'Come, bredern, come; let's go at it; come now, [singing] eoho! roll away! Eeoho-eeoho-weeioho-i'—and the rest taking it up as before. In a few moments they all had their shoulders to a bale of cotton and were rolling it up the embankment."[19]

Railroad work songs, according to a pioneering folklorist, required a singing leader who "must have the feel of the work that is being done, an understanding of the men with whom he is working, and the capacity to evoke both music and motor response . . . Although the prime objective of the gang song is not entertainment, it nevertheless must be more than melody, words, and timing; the song that captures the imagination of the workers, that engages them, will get the work done by keeping the men in a working spirit." Song leaders were improvisers, refashioning familiar verses or themes into songs for a particular context while eliciting positive responses from the other workers. The ultimate object is "to convert song into movement and force through proper timing." As an Alabama track worker put it, "singing just naturally makes the work go easier."[20]

Track lining—straightening rails that had been kinked out of alignment by the pounding passage of many trains—required the labor of "gandy dancers" (section men) working as a team. They wedged 5-foot-long steel lining bars, weighing more than 20 pounds, under the rail to be moved, shoving against the foot of the rail in unison until it had been properly aligned. The foreman, or "captain" (who until recent years was usually white), sighted along the rail from several yards distant to spot the kink in the track. The black caller was the one actually prescribing the work. His lyrics often combined rhythm with a sardonic view of the job and the white boss:

> Oh, the Captain can't read, the Captain can't write,
> Captain can't tell you when the track's lined right.
> Mobile, Alabama [the men in unison pull on their bars to move the rail]
> Mobile, Alabama [move rail farther][21]

The number of lining chants was constantly expanding as each caller put his own stamp on familiar texts or composed new ones. Some were ribald, some were religious, some were humorous, and some were complaints. In fact, some of the clearest protests against exploitative working conditions are revealed in the work chants. At times, experienced section men were required to train a white man, without any experience, so he could become their foreman: "Look at the boss, how he stands, stands more like a farmer than a boss man." Pennsylvania Railroad trackman Johnnie Horne sang: "Swing and chain, don't get lost; we don't need no section boss." Section foremen could be heartily disliked: "He boss Southern, L and N, don't know nothing but kill good men." Some section bosses were, in fact, cruel men. Many thought nothing of calling their laborers "niggers." A retired worker recalled with disgust one boss who treated his men worse than work animals. "Now we had a foreman, he's gone, Mr. Smith, he work you 'till you fall out [faint]. He wouldn't do like you drive your mule, be hauling, and see your mule give out of wind, and in my time you let him catch his wind. Now we had fellas like that, who wouldn't give you no slack."[22]

Track work was exhausting, and lining chants commented on the rigor of the job:

> All I hate about linin' track,
> This old bar's 'bout to break my back.[23]

Callers had to have a large repertory, given the long day's work. Some interspersed blues lyrics: "I got the St. Louis Blues, (Ha), I'm just as blue as I can be, (Ha)," while others borrowed from the spirituals: "If I could I surely would, stand on the rock where Moses stood."[24] A good caller also had verses commenting on tensions between the sexes:

> Me and my wife had a falling out;
> Now stop, lemme tell you what the trouble 'bout.
> She jumped at me, I give her load;
> She want me to work on the Southern rail road.[25]

Some callers boasted of exploiting women:

> Ain't no need me workin' so hard,
> When I got a gal in the white folks' yard;
> Boy, I'm livin'; boy, I'm livin'.[26]

Verses on sexual themes were popular, at least among those gandy dancers who were not religious: "Whoa, Susie, Susie don't you know; I can make your belly grow." Other chants revealed the long careers of veteran trackmen: "I been out East, been way out West, believe I like Alabama the best." And many lining chants were simply nonsense verses that rhymed amusingly: "Ten thousand biscuits in my hand, sop my way to the Promised Land."[27]

Track lining chants remained within the world of working railroaders, in part because many of them could quickly turn scatological. Track gangs sometimes "cleaned up" their chants when working within earshot of black residences. Although folklorists made numerous field recordings, only one commercial recording of a lining chant was made, by a Tennessee Coal & Iron Railroad section crew:

> Jack the rabbit, jack the bear, can't you line 'em, just a hair,
> Can't you line 'em, for the captain, can't you line 'em, for the straw [boss]
> Can't you line 'em for the [track] walker, can't you line 'em, for the boss.
> Can't you line 'em, just a little bit, can't you line 'em, to the other side.[28]

The flip side of the record is a song that could have been sung to accompany driving spikes or moving rail in unison. It reveals how workers were exploited by withholding their pay to cover debts for room and board. Like previous examples, the text pushes the limits in criticizing the white boss:

> Oh, captain told the poor boy, "Ain't gonna pay you off," (x3)
> But its payday, captain, and you won't pay off.
>
> I'm gonna make this payday, I'm gonna tip on down the line, (x3)
> If you want me, captain, you got to come and find.[29]

Hammer songs were used to pace the work of driving spikes or drilling holes for blasting tunnels. For the former, songs helped them lift and strike their spike mauls, and even to breathe, in unison. Bosses instructed them not to draw back to hit a spike, but instead to "make a wheel out of that maul," swinging it in a continuous circular motion.[30] A tunnel-boring hammer man sang to rhythm as he swung his sledgehammer, the song informing the "shaker," his partner holding the drill, when the hammer would fall:

> If I had 'bout [grunt] forty five dollars [grunt]
> All in gold, yes [grunt], all in gold [grunt]
> I'd be rich as [grunt] old man Carter [grunt]
> Wealth untold, yes [grunt] wealth untold. [grunt][31]

Closely related is the occupational song in which the singer describes his labor or the nature of the job. Many depict hardships: dangerous work; little pay; living far from home; being cheated out of one's earnings; even death from exhaustion or overwork. While some may have originated as hammer songs, they have come down to the present in ballad and blues forms. While some blacks may have taken pride in the stereotype that they had greater strength and endurance than whites, "Spike Driver Blues" and other songs with the hammer motif take heed of John Henry's self-destruction and draw the line at working beyond one's limit:

> Take this hammer and carry it to my captain,
> Tell him I'm gone, just tell him I'm gone, I'm sure is gone.
>
> This is the hammer that killed John Henry,
> But it won't kill me, but it won't kill me, ain't gon' kill me.[32]

The John Henry narrative ballad and folktale is an amalgam of motifs: pride in the physical strength of black men and women; the struggle of manual laborers against the encroachment of machines; the hazards of railroad work; and the fatalistic view that blacks are doomed from birth to labor under exploitative conditions. John Henry was more than legendary; he was an actual Virginia convict excavating a tunnel on the Chesapeake & Ohio Railroad.[33] Although the earliest published and recorded versions of "John Henry" were written and performed by whites, the ballad was already part of black folklore. The common elements of the song include a premonition, when just a baby, that he would die "with a hammer in his hand"; preparation for the contest against the mechanical steam drill; the contest itself, in which John Henry and his shaker drill more holes, or deeper holes, than the steam drill; John Henry's death and burial; and his woman, who, in some versions, takes up John Henry's hammer to "drive steel like a man."[34]

Of the numerous renderings of "John Henry," these verses sung by prisoners at the Ohio State Penitentiary (others have been omitted) capture the essential elements:

When John Henry was a little boy,
Sitting upon his father's knee,
His father said, "Look here, my boy,
You must be a steel driving man like me,
You must be a steel driving man like me."

The steam drill started at half past six,
John Henry started the same time.
John Henry stuck bottom at half past eight,
And the steam drill didn't bottom till nine,
Oh, the steam drill didn't bottom till nine.

John Henry said to his captain,
"A man, he ain't nothing but a man,
Before I'd let that steam drill beat me down,
Oh, I'd die with the hammer in my hand,
I'd die with the hammer in my hand."

John Henry had a little woman,
And the dress she wore was red,
She went down the railroad track and never came back,
Said she was going where John Henry fell dead,
Said she was going where John Henry fell dead.[35]

Another genre of black folk music is the "bad man" ballad. Just as a number of white folk songs celebrate train robbers and other desperadoes, so, too, could blacks identify with one of their own who defied authority. But the circumstances were different. White antiheroes, like Jesse James, were romanticized by working-class folk for challenging the norms of respectable society. African American bad man ballads, on the other hand, emerged from the experiences of oppressed people seeking heroes who were not intimidated by anyone, whether an abusive boss, racist cop, or cheating spouse. Examples include the liberated Frankie of "Frankie and Johnny," whose man was "doing her wrong"; Duncan, a black bartender who gunned down a policeman in "Brady, Brady, Why Didn't You Run"; and Railroad Bill. According to the most common account, propagated by whites, Railroad Bill (Morris Slater) was a freight train robber in the 1890s who shot and killed two pursuing white lawmen before being gunned down by a white constable and shopkeeper. But

Railroads in the African American Experience

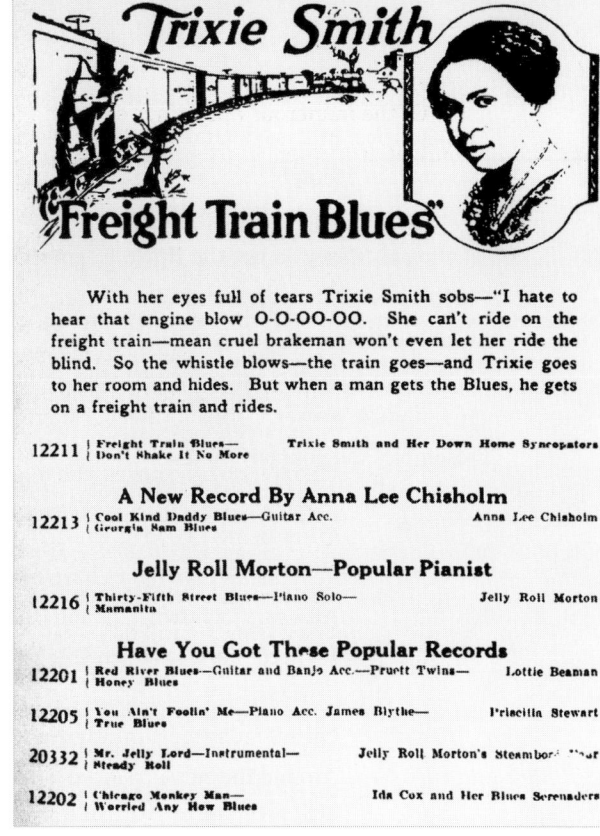

blacks along the Louisville & Nashville Railroad in Alabama regarded him as a wish-fulfillment folk hero who was invincible to ordinary bullets and able to transform himself into animals to elude capture while delivering stolen food to poor blacks. To other African Americans, Railroad Bill was a martyr, an innocent turpentine worker falsely accused of robbing trains, necessitating his taking up guns in self-defense against white pursuers.[36]

> Railroad Bill's a mighty mean man,
> Shot the midnight lantern, out the brakeman's hand,
> Gonna ride old Railroad Bill.
>
> Buy me a pistol just as long as my arm,
> Kill everybody ever done me harm,
> Gonna ride old Railroad Bill.[37]

Perhaps the best-known American ballad is "Casey Jones." Although associated more with white folksingers, the original text was composed by Wallace "Wash" Saunders, a black engine-wiper in the Illinois Central Railroad's Canton, Mississippi roundhouse who had ample opportunity to learn of Casey's fatal run when he tried to make up time, speeding the *Cannonball* southward from Memphis to Canton on April 30, 1900. Saunders never profited from his text, which was appropriated and altered by white vaudevillians T. Lawrence Seibert and Eddie Newton, who launched "Casey Jones, the Brave Engineer" into the national music treasury. In fact, Jones was more reckless than brave, being known as a "fast roller" who habitually ignored speed limits to make up a schedule.

Wash Saunders's original text was never written down. But years later, an aged black Canton roundhouse worker, Cornelius Steen, claimed to remember Saunders's lyrics. Steen's version closely resembles the popularized text:

> Casey being a good engineer,
> Told his fireman not to have no fear;
> All I wan's a little water and coal,
> I'll peep out the cab, and see the drivers roll.
>
> On a Sunday mornin' it begin to rain,
> Around the curve he spied a passenger train;
> Told his fireman he's better jump,
> Cause there's two locomotives that are bound to bump.[38]

Why did a black folk bard celebrate a foolhardy white engineer? There was, by the turn of the twentieth century, a well-established tradition of train-wreck ballads and broadsides in which tragic deaths were sometimes due to unforeseen natural forces, but otherwise to the daring of engineers whose recklessness was apotheosized into heroism. Railroad travel was dangerous, even after the introduction of air brakes, and perhaps Americans wished to believe that the wrecks and deaths that occurred with such regularity were due to the hand of God, not the actions of rash men.

"Casey Jones" entered popular culture via vaudeville and sheet music. It also became a source for other songs, including "J. C. Holmes Blues," a ballad recorded by the greatest female blues singer, Bessie Smith, in 1925. Here the wreck is ignored; instead the engineer and a female passenger represent sexual energy. "J. C. Holmes Blues" is both a parody of the earlier text and a double entendre song of the type that became popular in commercial recorded blues.

> In the second cabin sat Miss Alice Fry,
> Going to ride with Mister J. C. or die;
> "I ain't good looking and I don't dress fine,
> But I'm a ramblin' woman with a ramblin' mind."[39]

The authentic blues did not emerge, like the example just cited, from Tin Pan Alley, but from life experience. For hundreds of thousands of black workers, railroads meant backbreaking toil or smiling for the white man in hopes for a tip. To millions of black travelers, railroads represented both the humiliation of segregation and escape from discrimination. It's no wonder, then, that railroads inhabit the blues, a genre reflecting the hopes and disappointments, lives and loves, of generations of southern-rooted African Americans.

How soon railroad images surfaced cannot be determined because the blues—descended from field hollers, work songs, and prisoners' laments—were sung long before they were recorded. W. C. Handy's "Yellow Dog Blues" is often credited as being the first railroad blues. Handy made no claim to originality, acknowledging that in 1903 he encountered an itinerant musician fretting his guitar with a knife and singing "the weirdest music I had ever heard," which was, in fact, a blues progression. He sang about "goin' where the Southern cross' the Dog," referring to Moorhead, Mississippi, where the Yazoo Delta Railroad crossed a branch of the Southern Railway. The Yazoo Delta was known locally as the "Yellow Dog." Handy published his arrangement as "The Yellow Dog Rag" in 1914, and recorded a blues version with his Memphis Blues Band a few years later, and it also became popular through Bessie Smith's 1925 recording.[40]

With the broad marketing of commercial recordings in the 1920s, including race records targeting black consumers, railroad blues quickly became popular. One source lists more than 400 railroad-themed blues recordings from 1923 to the present. Over 60 blues (e.g., "B & O Blues," "Mean Old Frisco Blues") name an actual railroad in their title. The first recorded railroad blues did not feature rural guitar-picking blues men, but female blues belters backed by small jazz combos. They sang what are variously known as the classic, urban, or vaudeville blues, songs that were for the most part penned by professional songwriters, thus not necessarily reflecting the singers' personal life experiences. These songs often depicted trains as causing family separations or hastening the breakup of a love relationship. More often than not, during the Great Migration, it was the woman who was left behind. Bessie Smith's "Chicago Bound Blues" spoke for many women who found themselves alone when their men hopped a train headed north:

> Lord, mean old fireman, cruel old engineer;
> You took my man, and left his mama standing here.[41]

Women did not always passively accept abandonment. Sippie Wallace's "Mail Train Blues" declared that "I'm gonna ride on the mail train, until I run my man down."[42]

Even when love didn't fail, the North might disappoint. Employment was erratic, life was hard, and people longed for their southern roots and families. Bessie Smith's "Dixie Flyer Blues," referring to a luxury Chicago–Miami train on which the only blacks were cooks, waiters, and Pullman maid and porters, reflects such disillusionment with one's new home:

Dixie Flyer come on and let your drivers roll;
Wouldn't stay up North to please nobody's doggone soul.[43]

Trixie Smith expressed a similar homesickness in "Railroad Blues":

I've got the railroad blues, I wanna see my hometown;
And if the Seaboard don't wreck, I'm Alabama bound.[44]

At least a dozen blues carried the name of famous passenger trains. Three women recorded differing versions of the "Panama Limited Blues," named for the Illinois Central's New Orleans-to-Chicago express that carried only Pullmans and would rarely, if ever, have hauled black passengers:

I've got the choo-choo blues, had 'em all night and day,
Cause the *Panama Limited* took my sweet man away.[45]

Memphis Minnie (Lizzie Douglas) expressed similar sentiments in "Chickasaw Train Blues," named for another IC train:

I'm gon' tell everybody, what that *Chickasaw* has done for me;
She done stole my man away, and blow that doggone smoke on me.
She's a low down dirty dog.[46]

Although more often the female blues singers blamed men (if not the railroad itself) for sabotaging relationships, sometimes women took the initiative and refused to be victimized. In "Leavin' Gal Blues," Bertha Henderson declared her personal independence:

Get my ticket at the junction and flag the 'fore-day train;
I'm goin' to leave this country before I go insane.[47]

But it was more difficult for women to leave home alone because family responsibilities held them back, they lacked cash for a fare, and it was harder for them to hop a train without paying.[48] Clara Smith depicted this plight in "Freight Train Blues":

When a woman gets the blues she goes to her room and hides;
When a man gets the blues he catches a freight train and rides.[49]

Martha Copeland, on the other hand, offered a proposal in "Mr. Brakeman, Let Me Ride Your Train":

Railroads in the African American Experience

> Mr. Brakeman, let me ride your train,
> Pay you, when I get back home again;
> I'll get by the station guard, standing at the gate,
> If you let me ride the rods on that southern freight.[50]

Most female blues singers probably didn't live the lives they portrayed in song. One who did, however, was Bessie Tucker, the "Queen of the Texas Moaners." She sang of bumming freight train rides on the Missouri–Kansas–Texas, Texas Midland, Fort Worth & Denver, and the Atchison, Topeka & Santa Fe roads while working as a prostitute and singing for change on the streets and in juke joints. "The Dummy" narrates an altercation with a railroad "bull" on a boxcar:

> Now, when I got on the Dummy, didn't have no fare;
> The police asked me what I was doin' on there.
>
> Well he caught me by the hand, he led me to the door;
> He hit me 'cross the head with a two-by-four.[51]

Memphis Minnie recorded "In My Girlish Days," recounting how as a teenager she rode freight trains:

> I flagged a train, didn't have a dime,
> Trying to run away from that home of mine.
> I didn't know no better, Oh boys,
> In my girlish days.[52]

Railroad blues depicting black railroaders are few. One fragment reflects the fact that black men with steady jobs and weekly cash wages made desirable mates:

> When you marry, marry a railroad man;
> Every day Sunday, dollar in your hand.[53]

Clara Smith valued both the wages and the strength of her "Steel Drivin' Man":

> Ain't nobody that lives in 'Bam,
> Who can make a hammer ring, like my man Sam.
> Steel drivin' Sam, steel drivin' man of mine;
> He works on the railroad, making them white folks' dime.[54]

But Lucille Bogan's "Payroll Blues" admits to a more opportunistic appreciation of railroaders:

> Mens out on the Southern, they make dollars by the stack,
> An' I have money in my stocking when that payroll train gets back.[55]

Some men saw less than loving motives in such women, according to Walter "Buddy Boy" Hawkins's "Working on the Railroad":

> My black woman, she needs the money, that's why I work so hard (x2)
> And if I don't keep on a' rollin', she'll have another black man in my yard.
>
> When your black woman says, "Bring it home, partner," railroad is all you know,
> When a woman says, "Bring it home, Buddy Boy," railroad is all you know,
> Just get out on your hot track and work your hands till they (sore).[56]

Although black women were the first to widely record railroad blues, by the late 1920s black blues men were finding a commercial audience. While women often sang compositions by Tin Pan Alley songwriters, the men sang their own or traditional rural folk blues with only their guitars and "harps" (harmonicas) as accompaniment. But the genre did not remain static. Some male blues recordings soon became more polished and danceable, compared to the rough-hewn country blues.[57] Even though the Great Depression caused record sales to plummet, that decade was the golden age of railroad blues written and performed by male artists.

Broken relationships predominated in male railroad blues lyrics, just as they did in the women's songs. Dozens of blues describe a man at the station, watching his woman depart. Charlie McCoy's "That Lonesome Train Took My Baby Away" reveals his helplessness:

> Mister depot agent, close your depot down,
> The woman I'm lovin', she's fixin' to blow this town.[58]

In "Big Four Blues" (the Big Four was the Cleveland, Cincinnati, Chicago & St. Louis Railway), Leroy Carr and Scrapper Blackwell spell out the heartache of being abandoned:

> Now I can hear the whistle blowin', but I cannot see no train,
> And it's deep down in my heart, baby, there lies an achin' pain.[59]

Elmore James showed similar emotion in "Sunnyland," about a Frisco Railway train running from Birmingham to Memphis:

Well I feel bad this morning, feel just like I want to cry;
Well my baby rode that *Sunnyland* this mornin', she didn't even once say goodbye.[60]

And sometimes the woman left because she had to shake her own blues, as Robert Wilkins admitted in "Long Train Coming":

She walked down the yard, caught the longest train she seen;
Said she'd ride and ride "till the blues wear offa me."[61]

While many blues depict men as impotent to prevent their women from leaving, relatively few sing of following to bring one's baby back. Charlie Patton's "Pea Vine Special" (local blacks' colloquial name for a Yazoo & Mississippi Valley train) excused himself from trying because, "I ain't got no money, boys, I can't ride the train."[62] And few took responsibility for the turn of events. One who did was Tampa Red (Hudson Whittaker) who admitted in the "Seminole Blues" (named for an IC train) that:

She gimme her love, even let me draw her pay,
She was a real good woman, but unkindness drove her 'way.[63]

Another rare confession appears in Howlin' Wolf's "Who's Been Talkin'." Realizing that his companion has already bought her ticket, he can do no more than lament, "I'm the causin' of it all."[64] Walter Davis's "M & O [Mobile & Ohio] Blues No. 3," on the other hand, shifts blame for his own (likely bullying) actions onto the woman in explaining *his* departure:

My baby got unruly and she called the chief of police,
My baby got unruly, called the police up to my door,
I believe to my soul, gonna have to ride that M & O.[65]

A much more prominent motif in the male blues (also echoed in the female blues) is blaming the railroad or its personnel, not the singer, for the loss of one's lover. Arthur "Big Boy" Crudup disliked two railroads:

Well that mean old Frisco, and that low down Santa Fe,
Well it carried my baby away, and it's blown right back on me.[66]

The "mean old Santa Fe" was also blamed in Lightnin' Hopkins' "Santa Fe Blues," and for the same reason.[67] In a similar vein, Noah Lewis's "Ticket Agent Blues" pleaded with a depot employee to prevent his woman from leaving town, while Ed Bell's "Mean Conductor Blues" castigated not only that official, but the engineer as well. Numerous other songs, like Simmie Dooley's "Every Day in the Week Blues," blame the engine crew:

> Slow down, mean old fireman, cruel engineer,
> Took my good girl and left me standing here.[68]

And a train's whistle simply mocked the man as his woman left on the "mean" railroad or train. Sunnyland Slim had the "Illinois Central Blues" because

> I want to tell you people, what that Illinois Central will do;
> It'll steal your woman, and blow back after you.[69]

The last car on every train, whether a passenger car or a freight train's caboose, carried lanterns called marker lamps with colored lenses to protect the rear of the train like an automobile's tail lights. Many blues used those lamps and colors to portray sadness at losing one's woman. Blind Lemon Jefferson's "Dry Southern Blues" states that

> One train's at the depot with the red and blue lights behind;
> Well, the blue light's the blues, the red light's the worried mind.[70]

Black Ivory King (David Alexander), in "The Flying Crow" (referring to a Kansas City Southern Railway train) identified multiple sources of heartache:

> Yes she's gone, she's gone, with a red and green light behind;
> Well now the red means trouble, and the green means a ramblin' mind.[71]

Another common railroad blues theme sung by men describes them leaving on a train while blaming a woman for poisoning the relationship. Legendary Mississippi blues man Robert Johnson, claiming that his lover "treats me so unkind," made plans to "catch the first mail train I see" although his song's title, "Rambling on My Mind," perhaps reveals his true motivation.[72] "Little" Walter Jacobs was similarly frustrated when he announced his departure in "Up the Line":

> I'm cuttin' out, baby, girl I'm goin' back up the line.
> If I stay another day, you're goin' to drive me out of my mind.[73]

Infidelity was a common problem, as revealed in Big Bill Broonzy's "Southbound Train":

You made me love you, now your man done come;
Now you leave me here worryin' baby, and I'm just the lonely one.

No wonder, then, that he was "standin' at a station, I'm waitin' for a train."[74] But how badly did the men want their women back? Broonzy's "Southern Blues" indicates that at least some did:

I'm goin' to Moorhead, get me a job on the Southern line;
So I can make some money just to send for that brown of mine.[75]

But others had no desire to reconcile, for reasons explained in Blind Willie McTell's "B & O Blues #2":

Now she wants to come back, and I can't use that child no more;
'Cause I got another hot mama, and she lives in Baltimore.[76]

Clearly, some men were ramblers, incapable of sustaining long-term relationships. The hobo blues, like Son Bonds's "Old Bachelor Blues," reflect their lives and perspectives out on the rails and in the hobo "jungles":

I'm a broken-hearted bachelor, travelin' through this wide world all alone;
It's the railroad for my pillow, this jungle is my happy home.[77]

Nehemiah Curtis "Skip" James's "Cherry Ball Blues" (a "cherry ball" is a woman who gives good sex) describes a traveling man who wants life on his own terms:

I'll catch the Southern if you take the Santa Fe;
I'm gonna ride and ramble, tell cherry to come back to me.[78]

John Lee Hooker's "Hobo Blues" expresses little regret concerning the rambling life, stating, "I took a freight train to be my friend,"[79] and Tampa Red had a similarly carefree attitude in "Western Bound Blues": "What's the use of walkin', for when there's a freight train goin' your way."[80] Others who hit the rails, however, were victims of their own bad judgment or addictions. David Alexander admits, in "Standing By a Lamp Post," that "I'm leavin' here tonight if I have to ride the blinds" because he gambled away the rent money.[81]

Many men hopped trains simply because they couldn't afford a ticket. In "Cool Drink of Water Blues," Tommy "Snake" Johnson testifies that:

From the earliest railroad era, trains were linked to sacred images in black music. In the 1920s, when millions of "race records" were sold to African Americans who were avidly purchasing phonographs, some of the most popular recordings were sung sermons, including those depicting the road to hell as a fast express train with plenty of heedless passengers. Theodore Kornweibel collection

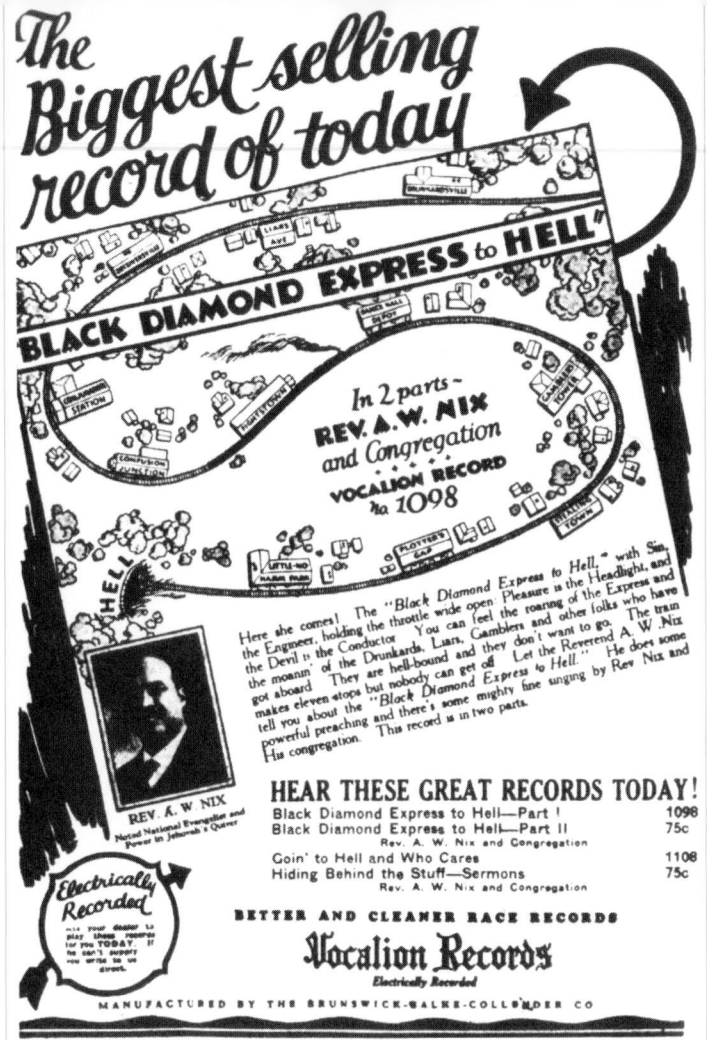

Lord, I asked the conductor, "Could I ride these blinds?"
(Want to know, can a broke man ride the blinds)
"Son, buy your ticket, buy your ticket, 'cause this train ain't none of mine."[82]

In "The Gone Dead Train," King Solomon Hill asks the engineer, "can I ride your train?" to which he replies, "Look here, you oughta know this train ain't mine, and you're asking me in vain."[83] But the hoboes' real adversaries were the railroad "bulls." The two sides engaged in battles of wits and, often, clubs and fists, as was attested in Sleepy John Estes's "Special Agent (Railroad Police Blues)":

Now, them special agents up the country, they sure is hard on a man;
Now, they will put him off when he hungry and won't even let him ride no train.

Particularly cruel police would wait to throw hoboes off until the trains were far from a town.[84]

The Great Depression added new misery for millions of African Americans and increased the number of hobo-migrants. Charley Patton's "'34 Blues" mentions down-osn-their-luck "women and children flaggin' freight trains for rides."[85] Like many others, "Monkey Joe" Coleman, in "New York Central," hoped that riding the rods would improve his prospects:

> They tell me that the New York Central train runs faster than any Greyhound
> bus can run;
> I'm gonna ride it this mornin', just to leave this bad luck town.[86]

Discussion of railroad imagery in the blues would not be complete without its use as sexual double entendre. Numerous early blues women sang delightfully risqué lyrics. Ida Cox's "How Long, Daddy, How Long" declares, "It takes a good engine to pull a fast mail train."[87] Male blues men often compared their prowess and physical attributes to the powerful parts of a steam locomotive. Blind Willie McTell lamented in "Broke Down Engine" that he "ain't got no drivin' wheel" and that he felt "like a broke down engine, ain't got no whistle or bell."[88] Modern-day blues man B. B. King employs the same metaphor in "Driving Wheel": "Yes, I'll give her everything she needs, 'cause I'm her driving wheel."[89] There is no subtlety at all, however, in an extraordinarily lewd song by contemporary rap group 2 Live Crew that uses "Amtrak" and doing "the train" as euphemisms for group anal sex.[90] Numerous blues artists, in contrast, demonstrate that symbolic, rather than graphic, language stirs the imagination and heightens a listener's enjoyment.

No African American singer captured the poignancy of trains better than Leadbelly (Huddie Ledbetter). A lifelong musician who spent years in prison for committing violent crimes, he once obtained a pardon by singing for a governor. One of his most famous songs, "Midnight Special," refers to the Southern Pacific's westbound *Sunset Mail,* which ran past the Texas state prison farm at Sugar Land, west of Houston, around the middle of the night. Convicts believed that if the locomotive's headlight beam shone into their cells, they would soon be freed:

> Let that Midnight Special, shine its light on me;
> Let that Midnight Special, shine its ever-lovin' light on me.[91]

In a less-well-known but more conventional blues, Leadbelly expresses the classic theme of railroads both forming and severing human relationships. "Shorty George" was the name given to trains that took blacks to prison and also brought their loved ones to visit. "Shorty George 2" probably reflects Leadbelly's own emotions at the end of an all-too-brief jailhouse rendezvous:

> Well-a, Shorty George, he ain't no friend of mine;
> He's taken all the women and left the men behind.[92]

Leadbelly popularized "The Rock Island Line," which he learned from Arkansas convicts while accompanying folk song collector John A. Lomax. The Chicago, Rock Island & Pacific Railway had extensive trackage in the state, and it was natural for inmates to fantasize about using that road to escape or to depart for elsewhere upon their release:

> Oh, the Rock Island line, mighty good road,
> Oh, the Rock Island line, road to ride.[93]

As train *imagery* spread through the lyrics of the folk ballads, blues, work songs, spirituals, and sung sermons, the *sounds* of railroads likewise penetrated black music and eventually all of American popular music. Black musicians used their instruments to make train sounds—locomotive onomatopoeia—at least as early as the 1870s. W. C. Handy recalled minstrel musicians, including his father, imitate both the rhythms and sounds of trains on fiddles and harmonicas.[94] Back-up musicians in the blues recordings of Bessie, Mamie, and Clara Smith mimicked the sounds of locomotive whistles and bells, the rhythmic acceleration of trains, and the clickity-clack of wheels on jointed rails. The first country blues men to record in the 1920s also demonstrated numerous ways by which to replicate train sounds on their guitars, fiddles, and harmonicas. A particularly fine example is Mississippi John Hurt's "Talkin' Casey," a "talking blues" version of the Casey Jones story. Throughout, Hurt maintains a rolling clickity-clack rhythm on the bass strings while employing his signature slide guitar technique on the higher-pitched strings to imitate the "voices" of Mrs. Jones and Casey's children, the sound of the bell and whistle, and the wheels of his locomotive "jumping" over the rail joints.

The first black star of the Grand Ole Opry in the 1930s, and one of the first stars, period, on that live radio program, was the "harmonica wizard," DeFord Bailey. He received numerous requests for his signature pieces: "Pan-American" and "Dixie Flyer Blues" (named for premier L&N trains). As a child, he waited for the *Dixie Flyer* to pass each morning, learning to imitate its sounds on his harmonica. He could duplicate the sounds of trains crossing trestles, going through tunnels, or disappearing into the distance. People swore that Bailey's renditions were real train sounds.[95]

During the "swing era" of the 1920s and 1930s, both white and black "big bands" embraced locomotive onomatopoeia. Drummers employed a basic pattern called "the train," which "stylized the rhythm of a steam locomotive pulling out of the station, first accelerating and then rolling down the tracks." This became the bands' "basic dance pulse." Following Count Basie's popularization of train sounds, no big band could expect to be popular without "the train" in the percussion and a locomotive-whistle "'wah . . *WAH* . . . wah . . . *WAH*' call-and-response between brass and reeds," particularly in the use of mutes and plungers in trumpets and trombones. Every successful band had to have a signature song with a lengthy locomotive introduction like the Duke Ellington Orchestra's "Take the 'A' Train."[96] Much of American popular music was now driven by a railroad beat.

Train motifs were perpetuated in rhythm and blues, and from there into rock 'n' roll. The most popular black artist in the 1940s was "jump band" leader Louis Jordan, who had numerous hits not only in the segregated rhythm and blues market, but also in the predominately white pop music world as well. "Choo Choo Ch'Boogie" (1946) was his biggest chart-topper. Thematically, it begins with a sharp-edge blues sensibility, with the narrator arriving by train in a new town, needing work. He peruses the want-ads, "but the only job that's open needs a man with a knack / So put it right back in the rack, Jack." Apparently not too disappointed, he decides to "take me right back to the track, Jack" and live a life of ease, employed or not:

> Gonna settle down by the railroad track,
> Live the life of Riley in the beat down shack.
> When I hear a whistle I can peep thru the crack,
> Watch the train rollin' when it's ballin' the jack.
> Love to hear the rhythm of the clickety clack.[97]

The biggest train song hit in the 1950s, and perhaps for the entire second half of the twentieth century, was the instrumental "Night Train," first recorded by Jimmy Forrest in 1952, when it reached the top of the R&B charts. [98] Forrest "borrowed" it from the last part of Duke Ellington's "Happy Go Lucky Local" but added his own honking tenor sax imitating the sound of a diesel locomotive's horn, which was becoming the most common locomotive sound as railroads rushed to retire their steam locomotives. Since then, "Night Train" has become a jazz standard and was recorded by other artists numerous times in the 1950s and 1960s.

The railroad blues were rooted most deeply in rural southern blacks' experiences. But even though they had passed the peak of their popularity by 1950, and a Greyhound bus was usually cheaper than a train, blues men continued to explore train themes. One of the most remarkable recordings of the decade was Jesse Fuller's loosely autobiographical "Leavin' Memphis, Frisco Bound." Fuller describes his hobo life, including the claim that, although he usually rode freight trains for free, he occasionally "paid" for a ride in the cab of a locomotive by shoveling coal for a tired fireman. Fuller traveled with a guitar on his back, and the song tells of a confrontation with a St. Louis–San Francisco Railway (the Frisco) brakeman: "Oh, hobo, you can't ride this train. If you ride this train, you got to pick that guitar and sing." To which Fuller replied, "I'll pick this guitar for you, but I'm San Francisco bound."[99]

The most important blues man in the 1950s was Muddy Waters, the "King of the Chicago Blues," 14 of whose singles rose into the R&B charts' top 10 in that decade. "All Aboard" recaptured the main themes of earlier male railroad blues: although the "Mean ole Frisco, take my baby 'way," the narrator was clueless as to why she had "left me for another man." Helpless and self-pitying, he could only cry as her train departed. Waters's vocals were backed by twin harmonicas, wailing like a two-chime steam whistle, while drums supplied the clickity-clack of wheels rolling over rail joints.[100]

Even though railroads cut passenger trains drastically in the 1960s, and many more blacks could go from big cities to rural homesteads by automobile on the new interstate highway network, train themes and sounds continued to inhabit the blues and jazz, maintained a toehold in gospel, and even appeared occasionally in rock 'n' roll. Perhaps the best-known example of the latter is blues harmonica player Little Junior Parker's "Mystery Train," co-written with white soon-to-be rock 'n' roll midwife Sam Phillips. Elvis Presley covered the song two years later in 1955, earning far more from it than Parker would ever see:

> Train I ride, sixteen coaches long;
> Well that long black train, got my baby and gone.[101]

Since then, "Mystery Train" has been recorded by several other black blues men and covered by a number of white artists and bands.

At least two early black rock 'n' roll stars tapped into the black railroad heritage. According to "Little Richard" Penniman, the sounds of Central of Georgia Railway steam locomotives climbing Vineville Hill out of Macon inspired the beat of his early hits like "Good Golly Miss Molly" and "Long Tall Sally."[102] In 1955, Muddy Waters persuaded unknown Chuck Berry to sign with Chess Records, one of the foremost blues labels. That year, in addition to his first rock 'n' roll hit, "Maybellene" Berry also recorded a classic sung-sermon for the black market, "Down Bound Train," which depicts a drunkard who dreams he is riding a "down bound train" on which "the devil himself was the engineer."[103] Five years later, still with Chess, the flip side of Berry's R&R hit "Too Pooped To Pop" was another black-audience song, "Let It Rock," describing a section crew at work, unaware that a speeding train is bearing down on it with disastrous consequences.[104]

Blues artists, however, were most responsible for keeping trains in the black musical lexicon in the second half of the twentieth century. A number of men like Muddy Waters, who cut their first records before or soon after World War II, maintained decades-long careers and kept railroad blues in their repertories. And younger black musicians today are ensuring these blues' longevity. A unique conjunction of past and present is a new train blues sung by Alberta Hunter, who sang jazz and blues from the 1920s until retiring in the early 1950s. She made a comeback in the 1980s and recorded "Amtrak Blues," a classic "I don't know what to do about that dirty lowdown man, but I love him still" composition:

> He's ornery, he's trifling, he's just the type of man who don't care,
> He'd pawn the Holy Bible, just to get his Amtrak railroad fare.[105]

Railroad imagery found its way into pop music in the second half of the twentieth century with *Soul Train*, the longest-running black-oriented TV dance show, first aired in 1970, and two mega-hit songs. Inspired by the 1963 civil rights March on Washington, The Impressions recorded "People Get Ready" the following year. Member Curtis Mayfield wrote the song :

> People get ready, there's a train a-comin'
> You don't need no baggage, just get on board.
> All you need is faith to hear the diesels hummin'
> Don't need no ticket, you just thank the Lord.

The song expressed hopefulness. The word "people" was all-inclusive. Despite the still-unfinished agenda of the civil rights movement, blacks would indeed get their due rights. Whites, too, found an opportunity for redemption, if they would leave their "baggage" (racism) behind.[106] The second big hit, Gladys Knight and the Pips's "Midnight Train to Georgia," reflected a darker reality, the shattered dreams of northern ghetto dwellers in the years after the 1965 Watts riot. "L.A. proved too much for the man," so he "pawned all his hopes" and bought a one-way ticket to home. Georgia represented roots, the wellspring of the African American experience. The train represented hope, though: "Said he's goin' back to find the simpler place and time."[107]

Train songs also remained in the repertoires of gospel singers throughout the twentieth century. One of the most popular groups in mid-century was the Golden Gate Quartet. Getting a huge break—national exposure in the famed 1938 "Spirituals to Swing" concert at Carnegie Hall—they soon were broadcasting a weekly radio show drawing millions of listeners seeking spiritual inspiration. One of their most-requested numbers was "Golden Gate Gospel Train," in which the vocalists imitated nearly all of the train sounds.[108] "Gospel Train," "Little Black Train," and "This Train" are the railroad spirituals that have been most recorded in recent decades. Black college concert choirs particularly continue to perform them.

Will railroad metaphors and imagery persist in twenty-first century African American music? Certainly, so long as there is interest in preserving the black cultural heritage, particularly the spirituals, work songs, and blues. "Gospel Train" and "John Henry" will not be forgotten. But because railroads have receded from most Americans' consciousness with the shrinkage of passenger train travel, there will never again be an identification of one's life hopes and trials with arriving and departing trains. But trains captured blacks' imaginations more than 150 years ago, and it is unlikely that this collective cultural memory will ever be eradicated.

Trixie Smith

Southern railroads' timetables, like this Central of Georgia Railway example from the 1920s, referred to Jim Crow cars as "partition" coaches. Three separate railroads handled the Dixie Express *before the C of G picked it up in Atlanta. Black passengers leaving from Chicago could have sat among whites in a "straight coach" if they asserted themselves, but as soon as the train crossed the Ohio River into Kentucky after leaving Evansville, Indiana, they would have to ride in a segregated car. Theodore Kornweibel collection*

(OPPOSITE) *In a time-honored tradition, Pullman porter A. A. Hoggard shines a passenger's shoes while sitting, late at night, on the couch in the men's restroom. The scene dates from the 1920s. Although not required by the Pullman Company, passengers expected porters to shine shoes, and it was an important addition to their incomes. Arthur D. Dubin Collection, Special Collections, Donnelley and Lee Library, Lake Forest College*

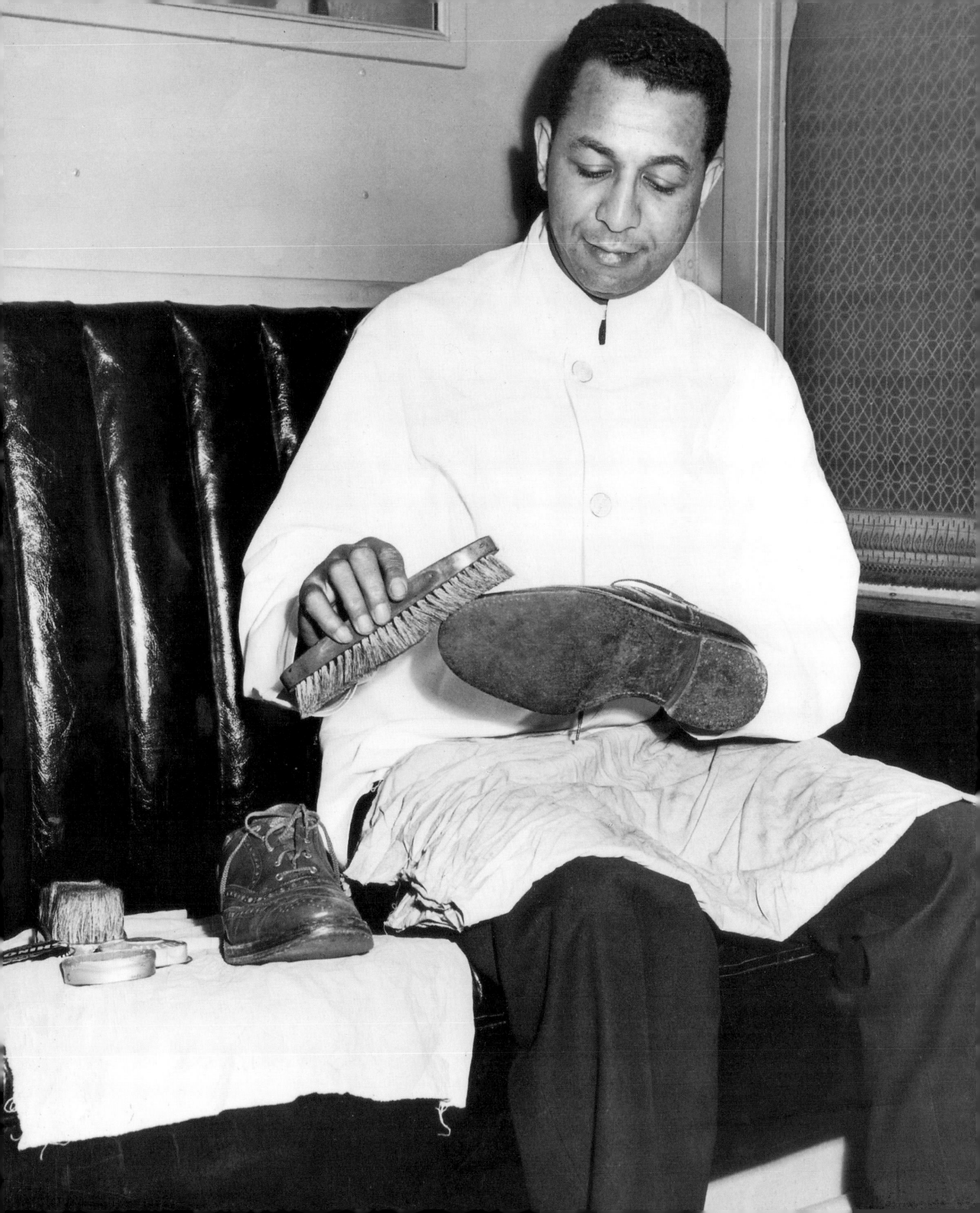

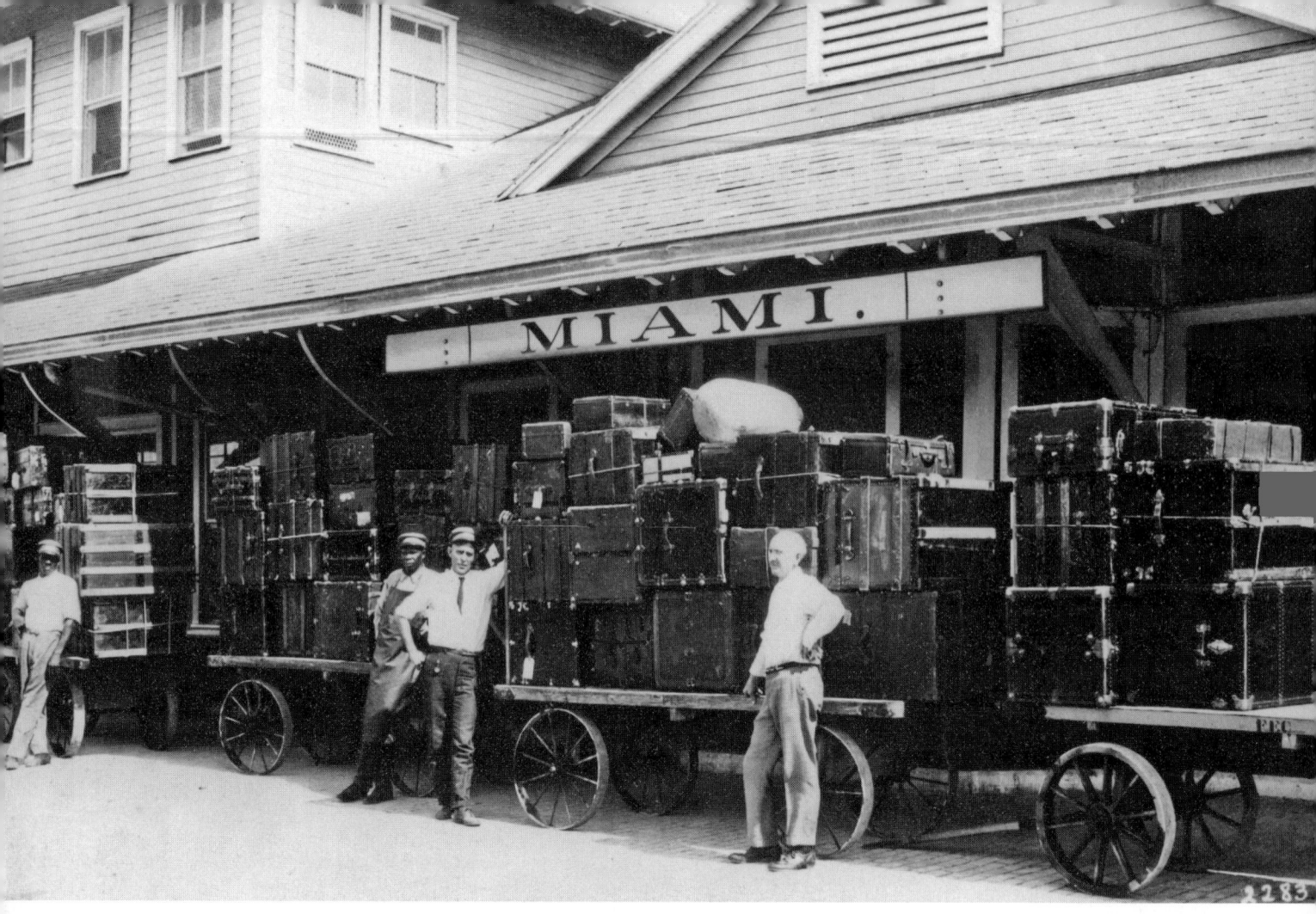

On November 1, 1921, as snow flurries
approached the Northeast, winter vacationers
were already flocking to Miami. These baggage
handlers will be tired when their work is done.
When the well-heeled went to Florida for the season, they didn't just bring suitcases, but trunks
and footlockers as well. *Florida Photographic
Collection, State Library and Archives of Florida*

Segregation put black travelers' lives in greater danger because the Jim Crow car was always the passenger car closest to the engine, and often an ancient wood vehicle. The interior of this St. Louis–San Francisco Railway car reveals where 12 blacks were scalded to death with steam escaping from the locomotive when a passenger train derailed at Henryetta, Oklahoma, in 1929. Hardin Studio photograph, Western History Collections, University of Oklahoma Libraries

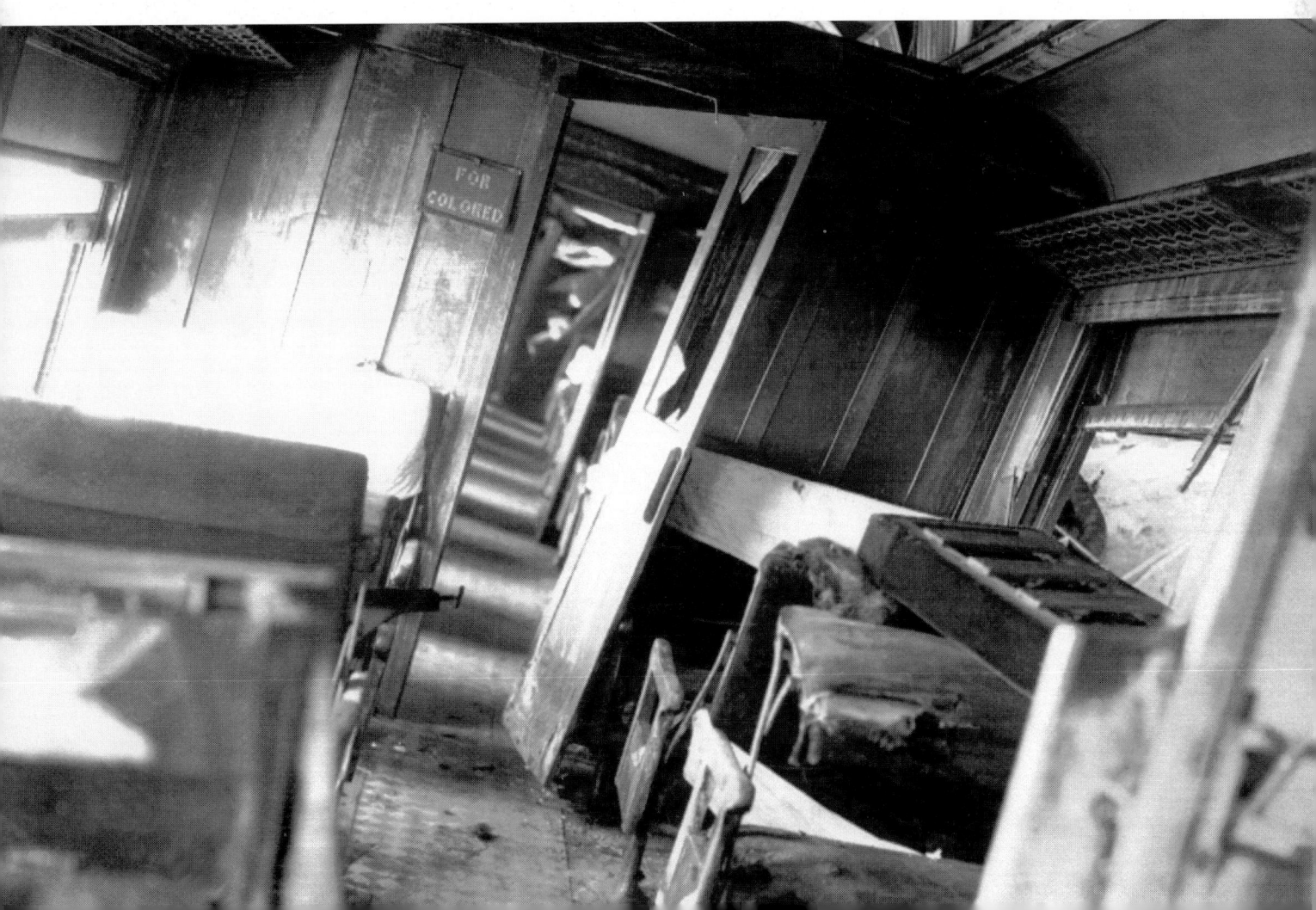

A Pullman maid entertaining or babysitting
children. On her sleeve is embroidered Oriental
Limited, *the name of the Great Northern*
Railway's premier train, shortly before it
was renamed the Empire Builder *in 1929.*
The Pullman Company emphasized that
maids and porters were there to enhance the
comfort and pleasure of passengers, including
watching children while parents enjoyed the
train's famous afternoon tea in the observation-
lounge car. Great Northern Railway Records,
Minnesota Historical Society

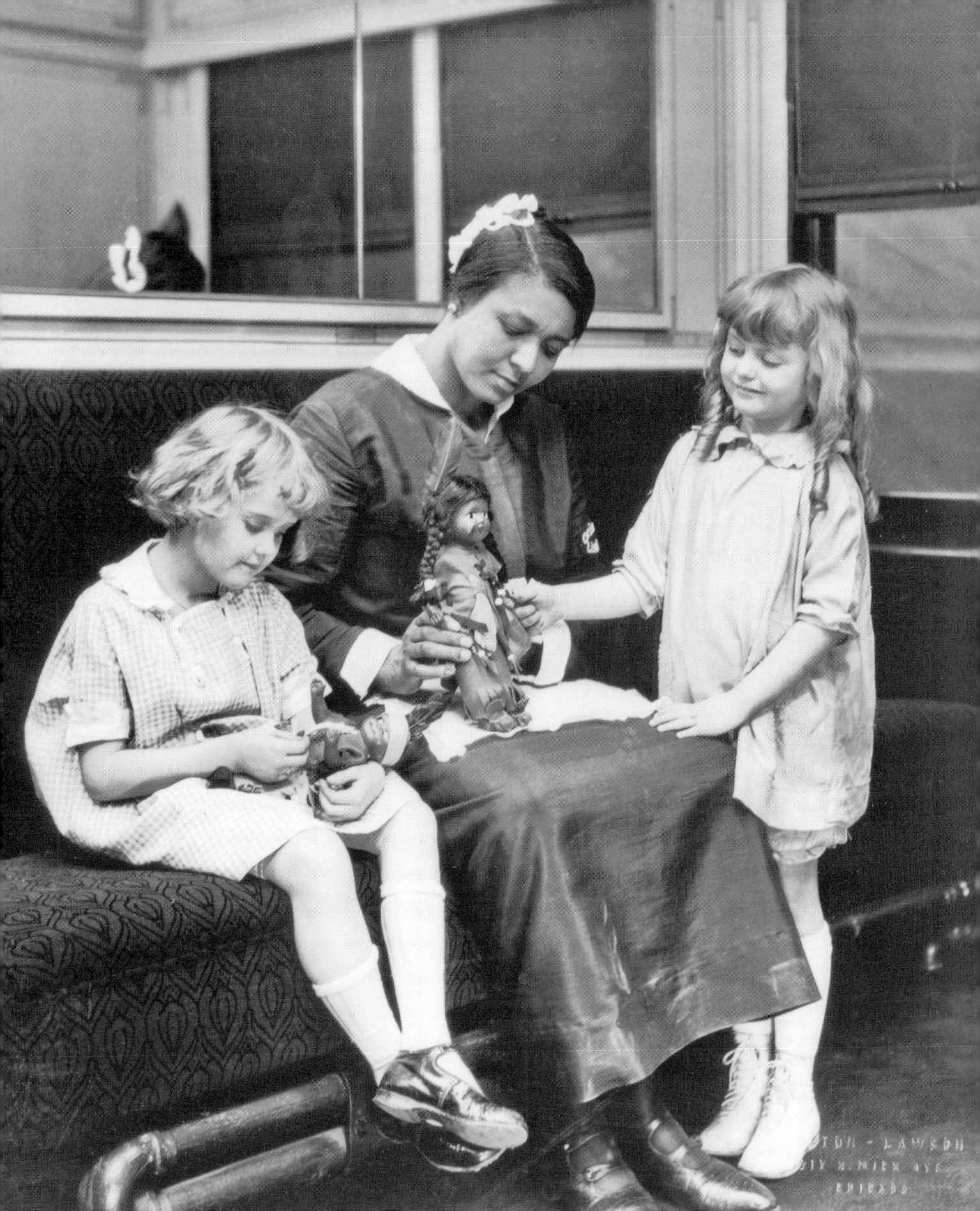

"TOO D--- MUCH FOR A NEGRO TO HAVE"

In the Shops, Freight Houses, and Offices

For its first 110 years, from 1830 into the 1940s, the railroad industry was highly labor-intensive. So long as steam locomotives ruled the rails, servicing and maintaining them required many more workers than the number subsequently needed for diesel locomotives. Most track maintenance was performed by hand, in a ratio of nearly one laborer per mile of main line track. Switching took place in flat yards, where car riders manually applying brakes brought each freight car or cut of cars to a halt. Up to the 1960s, the railroads operated large fleets of passenger cars, employing many workers to maintain, clean, and staff them. And until the advent of containerization and the transport of highway trailers on flat cars, much freight was loaded and unloaded by large numbers of truckers at freight stations across the land.

During the antebellum era, enslaved African American railroaders, including skilled craftsmen like blacksmiths, worked in southern railroad shops. After slavery ended, blacks were more and more concentrated at the bottom rungs of the occupational ladder, losing skilled shop positions to white workers who, as they unionized, drew rigid color lines. Ultimately seven unions gained jurisdiction over shop workers—the Machinists; Sheet Metal Workers; Electrical Workers; Boilermakers; Blacksmiths; Carmen; and the Firemen and Oilers—with only the last (which organized shop and powerhouse workers) admitting blacks to full membership before the 1940s. All the unions reserved apprenticeships and upward mobility into journeyman skills and status for Caucasians. So across the country, blacks were relegated, with few exceptions, to the semi-skilled and unskilled categories in these seven shop fields. The 1930 census counted nearly 100,000 unskilled and semi-skilled laborers out of a total of about 165,000 black railroaders. Seventy-three percent of these laborers worked in the South, forming the backbone of railroad manual labor in that region. The rest were scattered unevenly over the rest of the country with a few lines, like the Pennsylvania Railroad, employing many more than some, and others hiring only very few. Of the 100,000, about 16,000 were shop workers. And of that number, only slightly more than 1,000 were skilled: 600 machinists, 180 blacksmiths, 231 boilermakers, and 62 electricians.[1]

Major railroad shops were huge enterprises, employing hundreds of workers. In the 1920s, principal shops on the Southern Railway in Alabama and North Carolina each had 1,600 employees, while large Illinois Central Railroad shops in Mississippi, Kentucky, and Illinois all employed 1,000 or more.[2] The Louisville & Nashville Railroad's South Louisville complex covered 50 acres, and included a mammoth erecting shop plus pattern, blacksmith, tender, coach, and freight car shops, as well as a foundry, power plant, and scrap yard. Other large facilities found in shop complexes were RIP (repair in place) tracks and car, air brake, machine, and boiler shops. Many other workers labored in roundhouses and at coal chutes, fuel docks, and related engine facilities where locomotives received light repairs and were cleaned, serviced, and readied for their next assignments. Although blacks and whites worked together, they used segregated toilets and washrooms.[3] One excuse given by some railroads outside the South for hiring few or no black shop workers was the supposed necessity for providing such separate facilities. The Minneapolis & St. Louis Railway employed only 4 black laborers at its largest facility in the former city, the 18-stall Cedar Lake roundhouse and shop, but deemed it necessary, as late as 1945, to have them wash up and change in a separate locker room even though they relieved themselves in the same toilet used by white employees.[4]

Railroad shops concentrated on major repairs and sometimes constructed new engines and cars. Locomotive servicing and routine maintenance, including light repairs, took place in roundhouses. Work went on around the clock, on three "tricks" (shifts). In mid-1945, the L&N's Radnor, Tennessee roundhouse employed almost 500 workers to service its division's 140 locomotives, plus hundreds more that passed through but were assigned to other divisions. In one month alone, 1,971 locomotives were serviced and sent back on their way. The Radnor force included skilled craftsmen, particularly machinists and boilermakers, plus their apprentices and helpers. Only a tiny number of blacks managed to become machinists. Both blacks and whites worked as roundhouse helpers, but only the latter could expect upward mobility. And a contingent of laborers was required for the heaviest manual labor. In the South, they were mostly black. How well everyone worked together depended upon several variables, particularly whether blacks had gained higher positions as strikebreakers and whether whites coveted blacks' jobs during periods of unemployment or economic depression. A history of the Southern Railway's Spencer, North Carolina shops asserts, "race relations on the shop floor were usually cordial." Age may blur unpleasant memories, but one white shopman professed to believe that "we got along fine because it was hard work and each man was supposed to do his job," while a black retiree remembered that journeymen stood up for "their" helpers in tense racial situations.[5]

The greatest numbers of African American roundhouse and shop employees were semi-skilled helpers. Somewhat smaller numbers were organized in unskilled labor gangs (sometimes called "bull gangs"). Not all departments were equally receptive to blacks. In the South, blacks were most numerous in the blacksmith forces because, of all the shop crafts, this was the dirtiest and hottest. At Corbin, Kentucky, the L&N's black shopmen were concentrated in the foundry, which was dangerous as well as hot. It was common to place black helpers in hazardous work, like on spring gangs, which required working underneath locomotives with the risk of falling objects. At the opposite end of the occupational spectrum, boilermakers tended to be averse to black helpers because journeymen and helpers worked closely next to one another inside a cramped firebox, and whites stereotyped blacks as less clean and attentive to personal hygiene. As for laborers, blacks were more numerous than whites in southern shops and roundhouses because such work involved much heavy lifting, loading, and unloading of parts and materials.[6]

How blacks regarded their limited occupational options is revealed in the language of L&N "burn-up track" laborers at Albany, Alabama. Their job was to scrap worn-out, wrecked, or obsolete cars and locomotives using sledge hammers and cutting torches. They called this assignment "the penitentiary." Every laborer started there before, he hoped, transferring to one of the shops. If a laborer failed to perform adequately in a new assignment, he was sent back down. This was dirty work, performed outdoors. Blacks were over-represented: nearly all of the 50-member force at the South Louisville shops in mid-1948 were black.[7]

White shop workers used their unions to disadvantage black co-workers. When blacks were allowed to join at all, they were relegated to segregated, subordinate locals controlled by the parent body. Black locals could not negotiate with the railroads, but were instead "represented" by the white local general chairmen. This guaranteed that, in each craft, white workers effectively blocked African Americans' advancement. At times, shop unions even fought against the principle of seniority, usually dear to their hearts, when blacks claimed that privilege. In one such case, 64 white machinists' helpers on the Nashville, Chattanooga & St. Louis Railroad tried to engineer the layoffs of 20 senior black helpers when the railroad reduced forces following the World War I Armistice. Fortunately, the U.S. Railroad Administration ruled that the blacks' seniority should be honored.[8]

The craft unions also determined what specific tasks laborers and helpers could and could not perform. All were precisely defined in agreements negotiated with the railroads. On the Chicago & Alton Railroad, machinist helpers were allowed to operate drill presses, bolt threaders, and other machines, but only for uncomplicated procedures. When locomotives came in for repairs, they assisted in dismantling, oiling and lubricating them during reassembly, and performing very heavy tasks like installing the drawbars that linked a locomotive with its tender. Boilermaker helpers could operate metal shears, but only to cut bar stock or scrap. Otherwise, they performed heavy and dirty

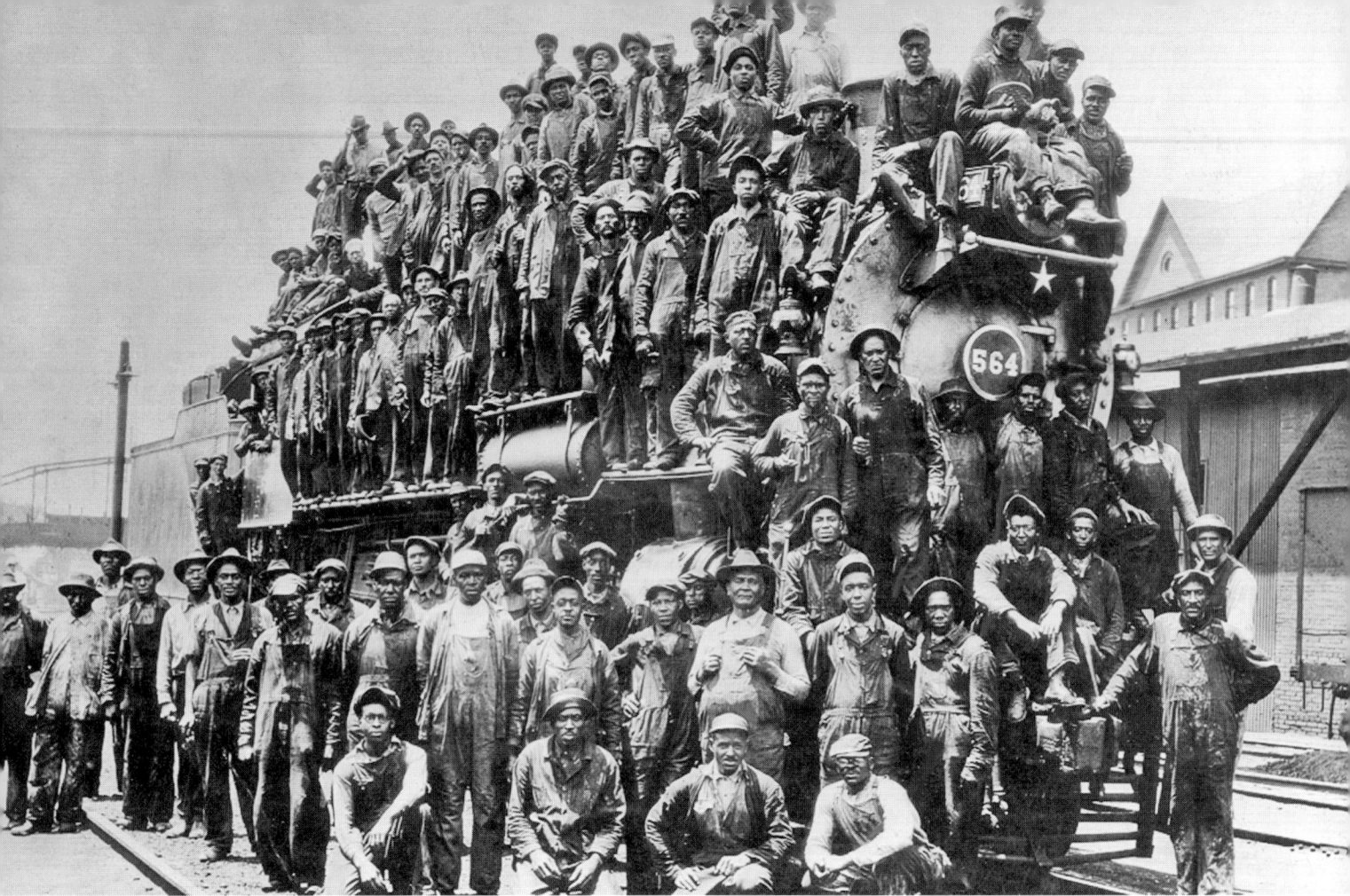

*Over 100 black employees of the Norfolk &
Western Railway's Bluefield, West Virginia
shops, along with a white foreman, gather for a
group photo in June 1929. The railroad was
Bluefield's largest employer and the black community's economic foundation. Their shared
workplace also helped strengthen social bonds
within that community. Norfolk & Western
Historical Photos, Digital Library and Archives,
University Libraries, Virginia Polytechnic
Institute and University*

jobs like removing firebox grates and washing out boilers. Blacksmith helpers could operate steam hammers, drill presses, bolt cutters, punches, and shears (only for scrap and bar stock), but much of their work was unskilled, like straightening bent bolts and rods on anvils (but not by heating), and lighting furnaces and building fires. In short, work rules explicitly prohibited helpers from acquiring advanced skills. Yet in doing their jobs for decades, black helpers learned a great deal about their particular craft. Black labor historian William H. Harris recalled the ironies of a helper's work for the Atlanta, Birmingham & Coast Railroad in Fitzgerald, Georgia: "My father, who knew as much about fixing locomotives as anyone in town, always remained a machinist's helper while younger whites, who learned their work from him, became machinists."[9]

The opportunity for a few blacks to become skilled boilermakers, blacksmiths, and machinists came largely during strikes by white shopmen. In 1911, they walked off their jobs on the entire Illinois Central system when it wouldn't recognize their unions. The railroad refused to negotiate and brought in strikebreakers, mostly blacks. Under the tutelage of white foremen and instructors, many were taught specialized skills, some becoming machinists. After nearly four years, the shopmen called off the strike, having suffered an "unmitigated disaster." Of those blacks recruited during the strike, many were still employed 30 years later.[10]

A much broader opportunity to enter the skilled ranks occurred during the nationwide shopmen's strike in 1922. While many black helpers and laborers walked out with the 400,000 striking shopmen, others, like a large number of L&N black shop employees in Birmingham and Mobile, Alabama, remained on the job. Throughout the South, where skilled workers walked out, some veteran helpers were promoted to mechanic. One stated later that "the Negroes made the company [Southern Railway] able to win the strike because those [whites] that were transferred in from other cities knew very little about this class of work and the Negro helpers had to do most of the work." Other blacks attained skilled positions during the strike in the Cleveland shops of the New York Central and Erie railroads, and the Erie's facilities in Buffalo, New York. But not all those who were promoted kept their positions. Black helpers who were advanced to boilermakers on the IC were gradually demoted in the years following.[11]

Only in the Pullman Company's shops did the 1922 strike permanently transform labor. Its workers had unionized during World War I, and they went out on strike in 1922 along with the railroad shopmen. Pullman turned to its pool of hundreds of former "summer porters," offering them shop jobs and seeking their assistance in recruiting others. The response was dramatic: thousands sought work and were hired as fast as they could be processed, even at a meager 47 cents per hour (only $5.91 in 2009 dollars). These strikebreakers proved to be good learners and good workers. Many remained in the Pullman Company's employ after the strike ended, when the helper's wage was raised 5 cents. It now became company policy to hire and promote blacks from laborer to helper to helper-apprentice to mechanic. By 1930, 60 percent of the shop workers were black, to be found in almost every skilled craft, although all supervisors remained white. This policy was not grounded in benevolence, but in the fact that they were unorganized, the company threatening to replace them with white workers if they unionized.[12]

The Pullman example notwithstanding, few blacks were employed as skilled craftsmen in the railroad industry. It was at the bottom that most blacks began working for a railroad, and at or close to the bottom where they remained. Upward mobility was never easy. Ralph Clements started as a laborer on the L&N, gained promotion to helper, and finally became a freight car repairer through "diligent application to duty,"[13] but most other blacks couldn't advance to the journeymen ranks. At the Norfolk & Western Railway's Bluefield, West Virginia shops, they worked as laborers and helpers in the air brake, blacksmith, boiler, and machine shops. But neither on the N&W nor on any other southern line has evidence been found that blacks worked in the erecting shops where new locomotives were constructed. It appears that they were restricted to repair functions. The same general pattern also existed on railroads outside the South, although, with the exception of the Pennsylvania Railroad, the number of black employees was considerably fewer. On both the Reading and Central of New Jersey lines, a few blacks worked as shop laborers and helpers, but achieved no higher-skilled positions.

Although some blacks worked in partnership with a particular white journeyman for many years, a railroad shop job was no guarantee of steady employment. William Williams, a blacksmith helper at the L&N's Mobile, Alabama shops, spent more than two decades alongside the same journeyman. But anyone could be furloughed or demoted as a result of declining business, personal deficiencies, or the whim of a superior. During his 45-year career in the N&W's Roanoke, Virginia shops, Lee Windsor worked his way up from laborer to helper, in which position he worked for 30 years, only to be demoted back to laborer and later again promoted to helper. Other blacks held a variety of jobs. In his 43 years with the L&N, John Davis, of Flomaton, Alabama, worked successively as an engine coaler, station porter, car oiler, and finally extra (i.e., substitute) coaler and shop laborer. Given the often erratic nature of low-level railroad jobs, it is no surprise that numerous black shop workers toiled into their 70s, and a few beyond that, even after the establishment of a national railroad retirement plan in the 1920s. Laborer Ed Williams did not retire from the L&N shops until 1926, when he reached 85, and 9 years later, Frank Johnson finally ceased work at the age of 80.[14]

On railroads that spanned more than one region, like the Illinois Central, Louisville & Nashville, Chesapeake & Ohio, and Norfolk & Western, black shop employment was not uniform across the system but was more concentrated in their southerly facilities. The IC employed thousands of men from Nebraska to Illinois to Louisiana and Alabama. The company magazine published a number of panoramic photographs of massed shop workers in 1939 and 1940, with as many as 300 assembled for a group portrait. Out of about 175 mechanical department workers in Waterloo, Iowa, only half a dozen were black. Chicago's Burnside Shop employed about a dozen blacks out of roughly 300 total workers. Elsewhere in Illinois, Centralia's car department had about 240 workers, only 3 of whom appear to be black, and the mechanical department in Champaign included 5 blacks out of 55 total workers. But many more blacks found work in the South. Of Jackson, Tennessee shop-men, 72 were white and 35 were black. At the Asylum Shops in Jackson, Mississippi, the mechanical department force included 18 blacks and 44 whites. Vicksburg, Mississippi shop workers totaled about 50 blacks and 80 whites. In McComb, Mississippi, hiring practices apparently barred blacks entirely from the 135-man car department, but included about 30 out of 110 workers in the locomotive department. The degree to which the IC restricted blacks to unskilled and semi-skilled jobs is revealed in a survey of 3 major facilities in 1934. A massive Illinois shop employed 1,150 workers, including 115 blacks (all but 4 of whom were laborers and helpers); a large Kentucky shop had 1,000 employees, including 81 blacks (4 or 5 of whom were craftsmen); and at another large shop, in Mississippi, of 1,000 employees, 180 were blacks, all laborers and helpers.[15]

The Norfolk & Western similarly concentrated blacks in the ranks of the unskilled and semi-skilled. Even during the worst of the Depression, from 1931 through 1934, the Bluefield shops kept food on the table for about 150 black workers and their families. One-third of them were classified as laborers. Another one-third were helpers, with the largest number being machinist and "over-hauler" (car repairmen) helpers. The remainder held a variety of unskilled positions that on other lines would have been defined as laborer, including 19 journal box packers and oilers. The only skilled craftsmen were two boilermakers, and the only supervisor was a labor foreman, reflecting the same job ceiling that existed elsewhere.[16]

In addition to shops, southern railroads' roundhouses and yards utilized large numbers of unskilled and semi-skilled black workers. Once engines were brought by hostlers (sometimes blacks) from the passenger station or freight yard to the roundhouse, they received the attention of several types of laborers, many of whom were black. A "fire knocker" killed the fire, shook out "clinkers," and cleaned the ash pans of as many as a dozen still-hot locomotives on his trick. The cinder pit man shoveled the contents of the ash pits into his wheelbarrow for disposal elsewhere. Locomotive washers used a pressurized spray to clean grease and dirt from the engines' running gear, sometimes themselves being doused as the scalding, chemical-laden water ricocheted back onto them. Parts and tools needed for repairs were brought from tool cribs and storerooms by stores truckers using hand dollies. Other laborers removed heavy parts and muscled new ones into position for reassembly. While skilled craftsmen and their helpers performed repairs, engine wipers removed grime and then polished the upper parts of locomotives. More laborers greased their moving parts. Locomotives received a washout by boiler washers every 30 days, to remove sludge and scale that had built up from impurities in the water. Once servicing or minor repairs was complete, firebuilders returned locomotives to steam, while fire watchmen responsible for a number of engines kept them steaming sufficiently so that full boiler pressure could be raised in a short time to ensure prompt departures. When engines were ready to leave the roundhouse, or needed turning, hostlers ran them onto turntables and then to the water plug and coal hoist or oil dock for refueling, while still other laborers ensured that all needed supplies were onboard.

Some of the most numerous black laborers at southern railroad yards and roundhouses were box and cellar packers. Journal boxes, which housed the bearings on which wheel axles rode, depended upon lubrication to prevent excessive friction and the resulting "hot boxes" (journal box fires). Every car and locomotive had to be frequently inspected to ensure that journal boxes were filled with oil. Walking down a long line of cars, lifting each journal box cover while toting an oil can, was hard work that had to be performed in all kinds of weather. Steam locomotives' driving wheels did not have conveniently accessible outside bearings, and thus the work of cellar packers was even more difficult. For many decades, they had to crawl under locomotives to reach their oil cellars, until the invention of reservoirs and nozzles that could reach into the running gear. Whether at a roundhouse or in the yards, packers were defined as unskilled, hence the concentration of blacks in these jobs on southern lines.[17]

Railroad complexes frequently relied on their own coal-burning power plants to generate electricity. And shops often had their own furnaces. Both needed to be stoked, and for many decades, this was a job for hand labor. Not surprisingly, blacks found employment as stationary firemen, performing the same task as steam locomotive firemen, without, however, facing the hostility of unionized white firemen who never defined this as a "white" job. Roundhouses and shops also required the movement and replenishment of materials and parts. The N&W's Roanoke shops employed a dozen black truck drivers, although they actually drove small motorized tractors. The IC called such men chauffeurs. Both stationary firemen and truck drivers were considered to be unskilled workers.

Although some tasks were less strenuous, or less dirty, or less hazardous, the jobs available to blacks in southern roundhouses and shops required, as whites saw it, brawn, not brains. Job ceilings were almost impenetrable. The appropriately named Wash Cox retired from the Illinois Central after 28 years, managing only to rise to engine cleaner foreman.[18] His counterpart on the Central of Georgia Railway was George Curtis, chief engine washer on the Macon Division, responsible for keeping locomotives assigned to the railroad's flagship train, the *Flamingo*, gleaming and spotless.[19] Perhaps slave-born William Calloway, more than 70 years old in 1924, was lucky to be working at all as a one-armed engine cleaner on the N&W, having lost his limb in a link-and-pin coupling accident three decades earlier.[20] Lewis Baptist, whose favorite literature was the Bible, began railroading as a slave water boy on the Richmond & Danville Railroad, graduating to fireman as a freedman. The R&D was absorbed into the Southern Railway system and by the 1890s Baptist left engine service to work in the roundhouse. When he died in 1928, presumed to be more than 80 years old, he was lead engine cleaner.[21] Old-timers in the shops and roundhouses who continued working past 70 often had comparatively less strenuous jobs as engine watchmen (called steam keepers on the L&N), turntable operators, and stationary firemen.

Northern railroads employed few blacks in shops and roundhouses in the nineteenth century, relying on foreign-born workers to fill entry-level jobs. Such employment didn't open up for blacks until the Great Migration of the World War I era. Even then the range of occupations was more limited than on southern lines. The New York Central was not averse to poaching from southern lines, recruiting Illinois Central laborers like Louisville fireknocker John Malone to perform the same job in Cleveland. Malone secured work for his son as a mechanic's helper, greasing locomotives. The Pennsylvania Railroad appears to have been more willing than other northern roads to advance blacks to skilled shop positions. Its Erie, Pennsylvania, shops employed 400 blacks in April 1919, half of whom were skilled workers. The Erie Railroad imported blacks for unskilled labor in its shops in Youngstown, Ohio, and Hornell, New York, housing them in hotels run by the railroad and feeding them in mess halls. But many such workers did not remain long. Northern railroad pay was often lower than in other industries and turnover was high. A Fort Wayne, Indiana newspaper regularly reported in 1917 that "colored" laborers had quit the Pennsy's machine, boiler, and erecting shops for other employment, sometimes after only one day on the job.[22] Pay wasn't the only reason. Over 30 workers at the Baltimore & Ohio Railroad's East Side Shops in Philadelphia signed a petition protesting segregated drinking fountains, warning that this example of "German propaganda" was bad for morale and could weaken the war effort.[23]

To what degree World War I opened up new shop and roundhouse jobs west of the Mississippi River is difficult to determine. The Atchison, Topeka & Santa Fe Railway had long tapped Kansas' sizeable African American population for such laborers, although there is no obvious explanation why some shop towns employed no or very few blacks while others seemed to welcome them. Over 60 blacks worked in the stores department in Topeka in 1916. These men were probably permanent residents. Elsewhere, railroads imported new workers without intending that they would remain. When the Union Pacific Railroad brought black roundhouse laborers to Sharon Springs, Kansas, it housed them in an old passenger car. But by 1923 they had found housing in town and become residents, so the car was moved elsewhere for occupancy by a section crew.[24]

The Pennsylvania Railroad was not only the largest single railroad employer in the nation in the 1920s, having a daily average of 218,626 workers in 1924, it claimed to be the largest railroad employer of blacks, carrying 9,631 African Americans (including 152 women) on its payroll in January of that year. The proportion of blacks in various job categories was typical of railroads outside the South. Nineteen percent (1,830 total) worked in the shops, 9 out of 10 being helpers or laborers. Less than 1 percent held skilled positions, a mere 74 black craftsmen, principally boilermakers, carmen, machinists, and equipment mechanics. The PRR's occupational ceiling was as rigid as on any southern railroad, although blacks were not the only ones against whom discrimination was practiced; Italians and Eastern Europeans were also excluded from apprenticeship programs. Opportunities for shop jobs were not uniform across the system, however. Thirty percent of black helpers and laborers in the maintenance of equipment department worked in the Southwestern Region—southern Illinois, Indiana, and Ohio, plus St. Louis and Louisville—although that area accounted for only 13 percent of total black employment on the system. Thus, in areas closer to the South, the PRR reflected the shop employment practices of its neighbor railroads like the IC and L&N.[25]

The employment of black roundhouse workers was likewise not consistent outside of the South. Again, the clearest picture emerges from Pennsy statistics. About 20 percent of its nearly 10,000 black workers in the mid-1920s worked in roundhouses. The greatest numbers, in descending order, were laborers (one-third of the total), locomotive preparers, helpers, engine cleaners, ash pit men, boiler washers, and hostlers. The Pennsy employed only 100 hostlers, far less than 1 per roundhouse across the system.[26] Overall, its roundhouse hiring policies were more racially restrictive than on southern lines. Elsewhere, blacks tended to be either very few in number and scattered, or concentrated in jobs that whites did not want, such as the Santa Fe's large force of boiler washers in Chicago and tie creosoting plant employees in Sommerville, Texas.[27] Just as in the South, white unionists' determination to monopolize apprenticeship programs and eventual promotion to journeymen, in concert with the racial stereotypes held by railroad managers, conspired to severely limit blacks' opportunities.

Black shop and roundhouse employment peaked in the 1920s, due to the opening of jobs on northern railroads and some occupational mobility as a result of the 1922 strike. The proportion of blacks holding unskilled positions (laborers) declined between 1910 and 1930, from 83 to 57 percent. At the latter date, 30 percent of black shopmen were semi-skilled, and 12 percent held skilled positions. Yet the vast majority of shop workers nationwide—93 percent—remained white. Pay remained a sore matter. Aside from the brief period of federal control during World War I when racial pay differentials were abolished, black shop laborers and helpers earned among the lowest railroad wages. In the South they also had to endure discriminatory pay rates. A southern helper described for USRA head William Gibbs McAdoo the attitude of the white boilermaker under whom he worked: it was "a hard matter to get along with the man I am helping . . . He says that 45 cents per hour is entirely too d--- much for a negro to have."[28]

The number of black roundhouse and shop workers tumbled from the 16,000 recorded in the 1930 census in the decade that followed. The Great Depression brought major cuts in railroad employment across the board, but shops were particularly hard hit because, in addition to layoffs due to declines in business and fewer trains running, repairs not deemed absolutely essential were postponed to further trim costs. Staff reductions were often not handled fairly. Collusion between management and white workers was common, resulting in proportionally more layoffs of blacks. At times they were told their jobs were abolished, but soon thereafter the jobs were reconstituted and whites hired. Seniority was sometimes ignored in layoffs. In the admission of a white union organizer, active in the IC shops, "the white man's having work is more precious than for the Negro."[29]

A second factor eroding employment in the 1930s was technological change. The introduction of labor-saving machines meant not only fewer manual labor jobs, but also a distinct preference for white men to operate them. At a large IC shop in Mississippi, small electric cranes mounted on trucks displaced 20-man lifting gangs. Mechanization of engine cleaning likewise reduced the number of unskilled blacks. Outsourcing of manufacturing of replacement parts to non-railroad suppliers diminished employment of craftsmen (particularly blacksmiths) and their helpers. When

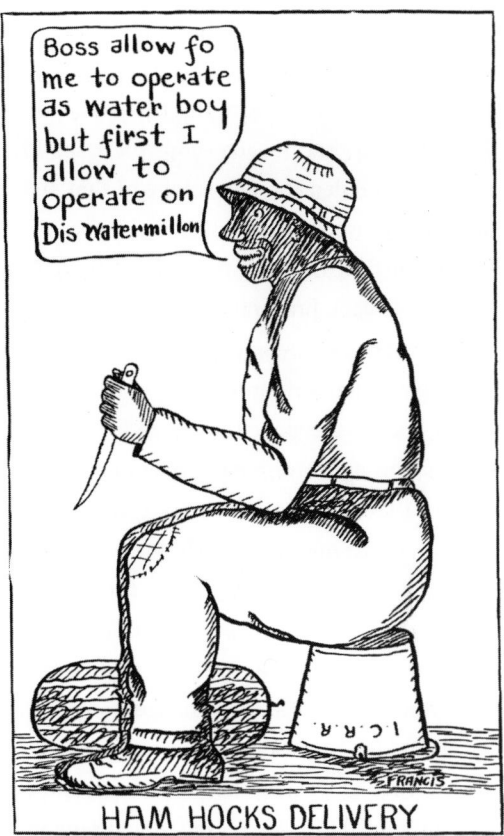

For the first half of the twentieth century, railroads irrespective of region thought nothing of demeaning their black workers by including racist cartoons and jokes in employee periodicals. For a number of years the Illinois Central Magazine ran cartoons drawn by one of its white employees featuring the buffooneries of a black worker named "Ham Hock." This one dates from 1926. Theodore Kornweibel collection

expensive new machines appeared, "the established southern rule [was] that the white man gets work of that nature."[30] In short, whether due to the impersonal economic forces of the Depression itself, the actions of managers and unionists to give preferences to whites, the continued exclusion of blacks from apprenticeships and promotion opportunities, or the reduction in manual labor due to technological progress, shop and roundhouse work became increasingly scarce for blacks. And as diesel locomotives drove steam engines to scrap after World War II, hosts of engine servicemen were rendered obsolete. The new internal combustion engines required new men with new training, once more beyond the reach of most blacks.

World War II renewed the possibility of federal intervention in railroading, but the Fair Employment Practice Committee proved to be no USRA. The FEPC lacked authority to compel recalcitrant lines or unions to give a square deal to black shopmen or to other railroaders. The Pennsylvania Railroad employed over 5,000 blacks in roundhouses and shops (out of a total 17,200-black workforce), but only 2 percent were skilled, with another 12 percent helpers. When admonished by the toothless FEPC to do better, the Pennsy took out newspaper ads claiming that no discrimination existed while also stating the "necessity" for "selecting employes who must work with others effectively." In other words, if white blacksmiths decided they could not work well with African American blacksmiths, there was nothing the railroad could do about it. Furthermore, the PRR claimed that in each shop where the FEPC alleged discrimination, the percentage of black workers exceeded the percentage of that state's black population. How, then, could the railroad justly be accused of discrimination?[31]

While the FEPC's attention to southern lines was mainly concentrated on their imminent elimination of black brakemen and firemen, its investigation of six northern and western railroads, including the Pennsy, underscored discrimination in shop and roundhouse work. The Union Pacific was a particularly interesting case. In Cheyenne, Wyoming, following the 1922 shopmen's strike, it had opened the skilled trades to Mexicans, Mexican Americans, blacks, Japanese, Italians, and Greeks, through vocational classes and promotions. All went well until AFL unions organized the shop in 1934 and began to exclude minorities from apprenticeships and promotions, even to helpers jobs, in the machinist, boilermaker, sheet metal, carmen, blacksmith, and electrician trades. At the conclusion of testimony before the FEPC, UP officials admitted "the existence of conditions not recognizable within the employment policy of the Union Pacific Railroad" and two days later hired a Mexican as boilermaker and upgraded three Mexicans as helpers.[32] There is no evidence, one way or another, whether serious changes took place systemwide.

FEPC investigation of the Chesapeake & Ohio Railway's employment policies at Huntington, West Virginia, revealed that blacks were not advanced to machinist helpers. In response, the company upgraded Charles Wilson to that rank in May 1943, but after three days he was demoted back to laborer at the insistence of the machinists' union. Higher management eventually restored his new position, but no other black was promoted to helper. The machinist helpers' seniority roster included no blacks hired since 1927. A FEPC order to take ameliorative steps was ignored.[33] The Baltimore & Ohio Chicago Terminal Railroad was similarly found at fault for colluding with the carmen's union in refusing to allow black car cleaners to apply for positions as carmen helpers. The B&OCT excused itself as merely following custom, while the union simply ignored the FEPC.[34]

The New York Central was second only to the Pennsy as a source of railroad jobs for blacks during World War II. But as FEPC investigators learned, at two of its largest facilities—Mott Haven Yards in New York and Sixty-Third Street Yards in Chicago—it had long refused to hire or upgrade existing black employees to helpers in the machinists, boilermakers, and carmen trades or as hostlers and hostlers' helpers. The railroad admitted that "a custom has grown up, through no fault of the company, to refuse Negroes such positions in disregard to their qualifications and ability, but the New York Central denies such custom has become an established procedure." All but one of the unions simply refused to respond to the FEPC's charges. The FEPC sought, where possible, voluntary compliance, to gain friendly settlements, and in December 1943 the NYC proposed cleaning up discriminatory practices "in its own way." The following February it reported that one out of four

Railroads in the African American Experience

new shop hires were black, some of whom were semi-skilled and skilled workers.[35] Whether progress continued once the FEPC spotlight moved elsewhere is unknown.

Only the Chicago & North Western Railway proved truly cooperative, although, given the recalcitrance of so many railroads, the FEPC was satisfied with very modest gains. Its chief complaint was that C&NW car cleaners were not allowed promotion to carmen helper jobs. After some defensiveness and blaming black workers for not pressing their applications vigorously, C&NW officials began to promote a few men into the helper ranks, allowing them to carry their seniority with them. Putting the most positive spin on this development, the FEPC declared its efforts to upgrade blacks to mechanic helper jobs on the C&NW "satisfactorily adjusted."[36] On the whole, the FEPC was impotent. The railroad labor unions ignored its directives as did nearly all the railroads.[37] World War II did not bring as much improvement for black railroaders as World War I, primarily because the federal government did not reestablish the U.S. Railroad Administration. The racially structured employment status quo remained fundamentally undisturbed.

In addition to roundhouses and shops, all major railroads maintained coach yards where passenger cars were cleaned and serviced. (The Pullman Company likewise operated yards where its sleeping and lounge cars were given attention.) Familiar racial employment patterns prevailed. Whites performed mechanical repairs, but cleaning was another matter. In the South, most car cleaners were African Americans. Elsewhere, whites predominated, many being recent immigrants who, along with blacks, encountered narrow employment options and were thus compelled to accept low-paying manual labor. Women were primarily inside cleaners, while men were more likely to handle pressure hoses and long-handled squeegees to wash car exteriors. For both black men and black women, car-cleaning was a dead-end job.

Crossing watchmen—sometimes called crossing guards—were a common sight in urban areas in the late nineteenth and the first half of the twentieth centuries. Today, all significant railroad-street crossings are protected by flashing lights and, often, crossing gates as well. But for many decades, most crossings had only a "crossbuck" (X-shaped) warning sign. Urban crossings required a watchman who blew a whistle and blocked traffic with a round "Stop" sign mounted either on a short handle, like an oversize ping-pong paddle, or on a staff. Manually operated gates protected particularly busy crossings. Blacks and whites, women as well as men, guarded crossings. Their hours on duty varied according to the schedule of trains passing that point. Some guards occupied their time between trains by tending a flower garden to beautify the adjacent railroad property, and by talking with small boys who were fascinated with trains.

Since the work was not physically arduous, crossing guards were often elderly but still in need of income in their declining years. "Uncle Charlie" Evans was a fixture on the IC in Memphis in the early 1930s. He didn't know how old he was, but the gray-haired man had started working for the railroad decades before as a boy of 16 on a section gang. Now in his twilight years, he was on the extra board substituting for crossing watchmen who were sick or wanted a day off. Another aged guard was slave-born Dandridge Stevens, who began working for the C&O in 1871 as a 14-year-old yard brakeman and died 56 years later, working as a crossing watchman in Richmond, Virginia.[38]

Amputee watchmen were also a common sight. John Black was a Santa Fe freight house trucker at Atchison, Kansas, when he lost his arm in 1874. Upon recovering, he flagged a downtown crossing for 50 years. IC brakeman Robert Cavitt had lost a leg while coupling air hoses. His responsibility was the busy crossing on Baltimore Street in Jackson, Mississippi. The company magazine commended "Flagman Cavitt's exceptional success in winning the friendship of those who habitually use his crossing, both white and colored." Richard Cade was a 27-year-old brakeman when he lost his left leg in an accident. Upon recovering, he was assigned to guard an IC crossing in Memphis, where he worked for 37 years until retiring in 1947.[39]

Crossing watchmen (and women) were especially necessary in northern cities with street congestion and extensive commuter operations. The Reading and Central of New Jersey operated numerous suburban lines radiating from Philadelphia and Jersey City, New Jersey, with many crossings needing protection. Both railroads employed black as well as white flagmen who halted traffic with hand-held signs and gatemen who manually lowered and raised crossing gates with a hand crank. In the mid-1920s, the Pennsylvania Railroad included among its African American employees 144 male and 41 female crossing guards, nearly all of whom worked on its busy Maryland and New Jersey routes.[40]

Railroads operated a number of downtown facilities besides passenger stations where blacks were variously employed. A major center-city hub, until the era of freeways and containerized cargo, was the freight station or freight house. Small-town freight houses were usually attached to or close by the depot and did not employ a legion of workers. Not so the large 'round-the-clock freight "platforms" that employed dozens of men on each trick to handle "less than carload lot" (LCL) freight, individual crates and barrels sent from a number of different shippers to a variety of customers. At the turn of the twentieth century, the IC's Paducah, Kentucky freight house loaded and unloaded 35 to 40 boxcars a day with a force of 43 truckers wielding hand trucks that themselves weighed 150 pounds. Accidents were common, particularly fingers and feet being mashed by falling or dropped objects.

Freight houses in the South depended heavily on African American muscle; elsewhere, the labor force was more varied. In southern freight operations, a white receiving clerk checked in outbound shipments. Thereafter, the freight was mostly in black hands. Break-out men unloaded it from the delivery vehicle, placed it onto a cart, and trundled it into the building. With the introduction of motorized tractors, tractor operators pulled carts around the facility. Callers (also known as tallymen or pickers) directed truckers to move each individual shipment into its correct boxcar. Stowers (packers) then arranged heavier boxes and crates on the car floor and lighter ones on top, bracing items so they could not shift in transit. Upon arrival at a destination, the operation was reversed. Truckers moved cargo from one car to another elsewhere on the freight platform, or into the freight house for pickup by local customers. At the largest freight operations, an army of black workers performed these tasks, 175 of them in the L&N's Nashville Union Station freight terminal in 1949.[41]

As in the rest of the railroad world, blacks found themselves relegated to the lowest-status, poorest-paid, and heaviest freight house jobs. The freight agent stood atop the occupational hierarchy, followed by his assistant and various accountants, rate and bill clerks, and cashiers, all of whom were white. By the time equal opportunity legislation was enacted in the 1960s, freight house shipments had all but disappeared as trucking and package delivery companies captured the business of LCL shipments. What remained for the railroads was bulk cargo not requiring trans-loading. Traditionally, the only freight-house "office" job open to blacks was janitor or porter. Blacks didn't wear white shirts, ties, or eye shades. Overalls and gloves were their uniform. Colonel Blanks, who started working at the age of 17 and put in more than 50 years at the IC's Paducah freight house, remained a trucker his entire career. Ben Dalton and Coley Thornton worked until the ages of 75 and 74, respectively, as L&N truckers in East St. Louis. But the record for longevity may belong to Hugh Merritt, who did not retire as an IC freight handler in Paducah until the age of 86.[42]

Blacks also found employment in freight houses outside of the South, both on multi-regional railroads like the IC and L&N, and on strictly northern lines like the Reading and Pennsylvania. The Reading's employee magazine included photographs of black truckers, freight handlers, cartmen, electric truck operators, platform men, and janitors. Nowhere outside of the South did blacks predominate on freight platforms, although the Pennsy employed 891 black truckers plus 60 stowers and tallymen in 1924. They did not work equally all over the system; 4 out of 5 truckers worked in Philadelphia, New York, or Norfolk. Fully 40 percent of all Pennsy truckers—358—labored at the huge Philadelphia Terminal.[43]

African American freight truckers were largely unsuccessful in employing labor unions on their behalf. They remained unorganized until World War I, when the Brotherhood of Railway Clerks, which restricted membership to Caucasians and had no sincere regard for their welfare, nonetheless claimed jurisdiction over them. Truckers were enrolled in "federal" locals that were impotent to control their own affairs, pursue grievances, or influence the course of the BRC. These locals had all but disappeared by 1930 because the clerks took no interest in them or in removing their whites-only policy. In the mid-1930s, however, the BRC reversed course and again organized federal locals and began to negotiate on behalf of truckers, actually winning some improvements in wages and working conditions. But the truckers were not satisfied with being "represented" by a union in which they were denied full membership and participation. Consequently in 1941 they organized an independent National Council of Freight Handlers, Express and Station Employees, only to have the National Mediation Board refuse to recognize it as their legitimate bargaining unit and reiterate that the BRC was their only authorized representative. This spelled the doom of the NCFHESE. By 1943 the BRC had won more wage and working conditions gains for the nation's 20,000 freight truckers, but constituting less than 10 percent of the membership and placed in Jim Crow auxiliaries, black truckers had no real voice in the national body.[44]

The BRC, in concert with the railroads, also blocked promotions to higher job categories. During World War II, FEPC investigations revealed such collusion between the union and the New York Central. Experienced black truckers applied for talleymen jobs, which were awarded instead to white truckers with less seniority. These were defined as entry-level clerical positions even though the work was performed on the freight platform. The BRC and the railroad united to bar blacks because talleymen accrued clerical seniority, which might eventually lead to an office job. It was unthinkable that blacks would work in railroad offices, other than as janitors or messengers. A similar situation existed at freight houses on various railroads in Kansas City, Kansas. On the Union Pacific, 20-year veteran black truckers applied in vain for jobs as freight callers and stowmen while new white employees were hired off the street. In both the UP and NYC cases the railroads fell back on the excuse that it had never been the "custom" to promote blacks to higher-level positions. Pleas for a fair shake, in the interests of national defense, were unavailing.[45] After the war, the BRC continued to oppose the interests of its black members. In 1954, it colluded with the Texas and New Orleans Railroad (Southern Pacific Lines) when the jobs of 45 black freight house workers in Houston were supposedly abolished. In fact, most of the positions were immediately refilled by whites. The Supreme Court ruled that the BRC failed to afford the black workers the "fair representation" to which they were entitled from their bargaining agent.[46]

Thousands of railroad dock workers, whose tasks were similar to that of freight truckers but more arduous because they toiled outdoors, labored at southern seaports. Ever since railroads began to funnel agricultural goods and forest products from the interior to seaports in the antebellum period, small armies of blacks toiled on southern wharves, loading and unloading ships. Not all docks were owned by railroads, so only those under railroad control are discussed here. Such dock hands were railroad employees and thus at a disadvantage in attempting to use strikes, since the railroads employed hundreds of other outdoor manual laborers—section hands—who could be quickly imported to take the place of those who walked off the job in a labor dispute. And if these numbers did not suffice, the railroads had the ability to quickly transport strikebreakers to the docks.

Nowhere was the railroads' advantage more powerfully felt than in Savannah, in the late nineteenth century, where the Central of Georgia carried over a million bales of cotton from the hinterland to the wharves of its subsidiary, the Ocean Steamship Company. The C of G's hands who unloaded the cars and loaded the ships were underpaid, not guaranteed a full day's work, and sometimes required to work overtime without overtime pay. Seeing no alternative but collective action, the workers organized a union in 1891 and called a strike. When scabs were brought into the city, the organized dockers persuaded them over to their side. With unloaded cars clogging the port, the C of G reluctantly agreed to raise wages, although to only half the union's demand, and it refused to sign a union contract guaranteeing the increase. When the union rejected this "compromise," the railroad brought in more than 1,000 new strikebreakers, isolating them from the strikers, and ship loading resumed. Now fearing permanent loss of their jobs, the strikers returned to work, the C of G gloating over its victory.[47]

Black dock workers in other southern ports also confronted powerful railroad employers. Some New Orleans docks were owned by ship lines, while others were owned by "economically powerful, resourceful, and determined railroad companies" like the Southern Pacific, Texas & Pacific, and Illinois Central. They were able to keep wages much lower than on the steamship companies' wharves, impose more harsh working conditions, and break strikes, thus keeping their workers in a worse economic position than any other waterfront workers other than Mississippi River roustabouts. When workers struck, the railroads secured the docks with armed guards and proceeded to bring in trainloads of scabs. Longshoremen on the steamship docks in the mid-1880s earned 40 cents an hour for a 10-hour day, while their counterparts on the Southern Pacific docks earned only 25 cents per hour with no guarantee of a full day's work. A similar situation occurred in Galveston, Texas, although some railroads had all-white dock worker crews, others all-black. Black railroad dock workers in Mobile, Alabama, were the worst paid of any on the Gulf Coast.[48]

When African American women and men managed to find employment in railroad offices, it was in menial, blue-collar positions. Secretarial and clerical jobs remained beyond reach until the end of the 1960s. Thus, blacks worked only as "office boys" and messengers (porters), janitors, matrons or maids, and elevator operators. For some, such work was compensation for an on-the-job injury. James Henry Griffin was a brakeman on the Norfolk & Western when he lost his right arm in an accident. He became a highly valued messenger in the Norfolk Terminal office, undoubtedly grateful, especially in the depths of the Great Depression, to have a railroad job at all. Noted the company magazine: "For years Jim has been charged with the duty of seeing that the coal report leaves the coal office at Lambert Point coal piers for the telegraph office at Norfolk promptly at 6:00 a.m., each day, for transmission by wire to [company headquarters in] Roanoke . . . He permits nothing to interfere with getting the report to Norfolk on time." In one instance, "a deep snow had fallen during the night and that, together with a gale, had put street cars, buses and even automobiles out of commission. Jim came through with the coal report, walking the entire five miles regardless of the weather." Yet after 50 years, such diligence had earned him no promotion; he remained a messenger.[49]

African American office messengers and porters received frequent mention in company magazines, undoubtedly because editors knew them better than those in other work categories and because they interacted on a daily basis with the higher echelons, from company presidents on down. Some were genuinely revered, but not, unfortunately, for their intelligence. Instead they were remembered for "faithfulness" and "humbleness," character traits that one was wise to cultivate if occupational longevity was a goal.

Porters' and messengers' duties varied widely. Some were assigned to particular offices or officials, others to an entire building. All performed multiple tasks. Some were part-time mail clerks. Others marked and bound office files and records. Messages and documents were hand-carried from one office to another. Some also ran elevators. A number were competent chefs, and when their bosses went out on the road in a business car, they accompanied them to prepare meals. At least one knew shorthand and took dictation. But many office porters were also janitors or custodians. A 1941 photo spread on the L&N's general office building in Louisville showed office porter Les Samuels stocking the men's restroom, an unnamed porter bringing food to employees who didn't want to leave the building for lunch, and night porter John Harris hauling mops for distribution to custodians.[50] Jacob Thompson's B&O obituary shows the range of his duties and what whites valued in the "little, gray-haired porter who, with his long-handled broom and a large bag, went from vault to vault (restrooms) throughout the building. Here he swept the floors and gathered into his bag the waste-paper from the boxes and baskets. Again he would be found in the cellar of the building, where the many precious files and important documents are kept, tidying up the storage vaults, gathering up scattered waste-paper, picking up bits of twine, and always busy. Sometimes he was a bit slow; sometimes he would grumble a bit when some person had carelessly left open a package of files for him to tie up, or if his load was unusually large, but for all that, he never shirked his job or left work undone."[51] The line between porter and janitor was often blurred.

Family life sometimes had to yield to one's employer. The B&O employee magazine was unabashed in admitting that Central Office Building porter Joseph Jenkins worked from 1914 to 1923 "every single day, including Sundays, except for his vacation days."[52] Aaron Govan, a porter in the L&N superintendent's office in Montgomery, Alabama, had to retire after 47 years of "faithful service" because of a nervous breakdown caused at least in part by the fact that "I hadn't had a vacation but once in the past five years, due to the fact that my duties were of such nature as to cause inconvenience by my getting off, hence I did not ask it."[53]

Railroad officials seemingly had no qualms about exploiting black office porters, defining their long hours as exemplary loyalty. The adjective used over and over to describe these long-serving men was "faithful." Many were also described as a friend. The B&O's James A. Turner was "our faithful porter and friend" whose "courtesy to all, his faithfulness to duty and willingness to oblige, have made him many friends" at the office.[54] Tom McDonald, who worked in the L&N's law department in Montgomery, was a "winner of friends." and "an old and esteemed member of the colored race." Many a visitor to the office where he worked "had their hearts warmed by sunshine from this natural diplomat, and loyal, faithful railroad employe."[55] Yet his obvious capabilities never qualified him for greater responsibilities and higher positions; after all, he was only a "member of the colored race."

Railroads outside the South also employed African American office menials, although since northern whites did not see themselves as racial paternalists, they did not describe such black workers as loyal and faithful servants. In the mid-1920s, the Pennsylvania Railroad's black employees included 87 office messengers, 29 elevator operators, and 144 office porters. No other non-southern line employed as many blacks in its offices.[56] Black janitors were, of course, commonplace all over the country and across the industrial spectrum, where they often worked into old age. Those who were profiled in railroad company magazines tended to be the favorites of whites, having demonstrated such appealing (and non-threatening) traits as loyalty, faithfulness, humility, and cheerfulness. A poetic paean to Johnnie Benn, a Reading Railroad janitor, illustrates these themes, along with a strong dose of racial stereotyping:

> When Johnnie washes windows
> With his bucket, soap and mop,
> He makes them shine like crystal
> From the bottom to the top;
> And when Johnnie's at the washing,
> Plying hard his soap and mop,
> Johnnie whistles and he whistles,
> And his whistle just won't stop.
>
> When Johnnie goes about his work
> Among the rest of us,
> However mean the job may be,
> You never hear him cuss;
> You never see him rant and rave
> Or fume like some of us;
> Johnnie whistles and he whistles,
> That's his only kind of fuss.
>
> When Johnnie in his even way
> Lives till he's ninety-seven,
> He'll waste no time in rolling bones
> For "seven, come eleven!"
> He will work and smile through all the years,
> Right up to ninety-seven;
> Then he'll whistle and he'll whistle
> Till he's plumb inside of Heaven.[57]

African American women found office employment options to be even more limited than did men. Although white women made great inroads in clerical work in the first half of the twentieth century—most railroad clerks and secretaries were male in the nineteenth century—black women were refused such employment, in the North as well as in the South, because it would have placed them in the same social sphere with white women. Centuries-old stereotypes of black women as unclean and promiscuous served to bar them from "social equality" although not, illogically, from cleaning areas where whites performed intimate functions. Black female cleaners were common in southern railroad offices. Those who served for many years and played the expected subordinate racial roles might be "honored" like Hattie Moore, janitress at the Central of Georgia's freight traffic office in Savannah, as "a faithful and efficient employe, always cheerful and eager to give good service." Older women were often called "Aunt," following a venerable white southern paternalist custom. Whether she appreciated that appellation is unknown, but "Aunt" Nettie Ross undoubtedly worked hard, keeping the C of G's Macon shops' washroom clean. Few laborers got dirtier than those working in roundhouses and shops and on steam locomotives. "No one appreciates her faithful and efficient service more than the engineer, whose first thought upon concluding a long journey is the water, soap and towel to be found in the wash room."[58]

Black female employees' families often paid a price. When Mollie Stewart was widowed and left to support four young children, she obtained a cleaning job at the Pennsylvania Railroad station in Baltimore. "She cooked and sewed at home, and after a day's work mothering her children, she went at night to work with the Railroad people." Soon she was mothering them, too. "For 39 years Mrs. Stewart 'kept house' in the station, tidying up and polishing, sometimes bringing the telephone girls coffee, often being called on for advice or sympathy by people who saw her courage, and remaining unfailingly cheerful." Certainly she was an example of fortitude: she managed to pay for her home and put two daughters through college.[59] That she was a confidante to the young white female employees is proof that the role of "Mammy" persisted long after slavery ended, but these women would not have dreamed of inviting her into their homes for a social visit. Women like Mollie Stewart had to depend on their peers for emotional support. Thus black women cleaners and elevator operators at the Pennsy's 30th Street and Suburban stations in Philadelphia established a Friendly Protective League for fellowship among themselves and to support various charities.[60]

African American women held no monopoly on office cleaning jobs. In the North, immigrant women took such work as a steppingstone to something higher. In the South, poverty blurred racial distinctions in employment. Even before the Great Depression, the L&N's proximity to Appalachia ensured a supply of impoverished white women who were willing to do what elsewhere in the South was considered blacks' work. At Louisville's massive General Office Building, the custodial force in 1928 consisted of about 40 white women.[61]

It would take a civil rights revolution to propel black women from blue-collar to at least pink-collar office jobs. As late as the mid-1950s, doors were still closed to clerical work. Val Davis was the Chicago & North Western depot and division office janitress at Huron, South Dakota, in 1954, even though she had some college credits, was a licensed cosmetologist, and had taught U.S. history for the United Service Organizations in Germany. Like southern railroads' magazines, the *North Western Newsliner* lauded her "genial disposition, cheery whistle, and infectious laugh" while claiming that she was "proudest of all" to be a C&NW employee.[62] She would certainly have been even prouder to be a rate clerk or telegrapher or station agent.

Today's railroads employ only a small fraction of the labor force utilized in the first half of the twentieth century. Maintaining steam locomotives and passenger-car fleets was highly labor-intensive. Today's diesel locomotives can idle for days without needing human attention. While there are many fewer jobs, unions and railroad managers can no longer bar blacks from apprenticeships and upward mobility in the skilled trades. Containerization and package delivery and trucking companies, however, doomed freight houses and their legion of laborers, and roundhouses are largely relics of the past. If modern diesel engines are turned at all, it is usually on a "wye" track. Locomotive maintenance is centralized in a few major shop facilities rather than at division points every 100 miles or so. Corporate mergers, downsizing, and the advent of computers have drastically cut the number of offices and the size of staffs. At the same time, black railroaders today can find opportunities in the clerical, managerial, and executive ranks of which their ancestors dared not dream. Although blacks are still over-represented in railroad service occupations, they no longer have to perform a humble, faithful, and cheerful racial dance.

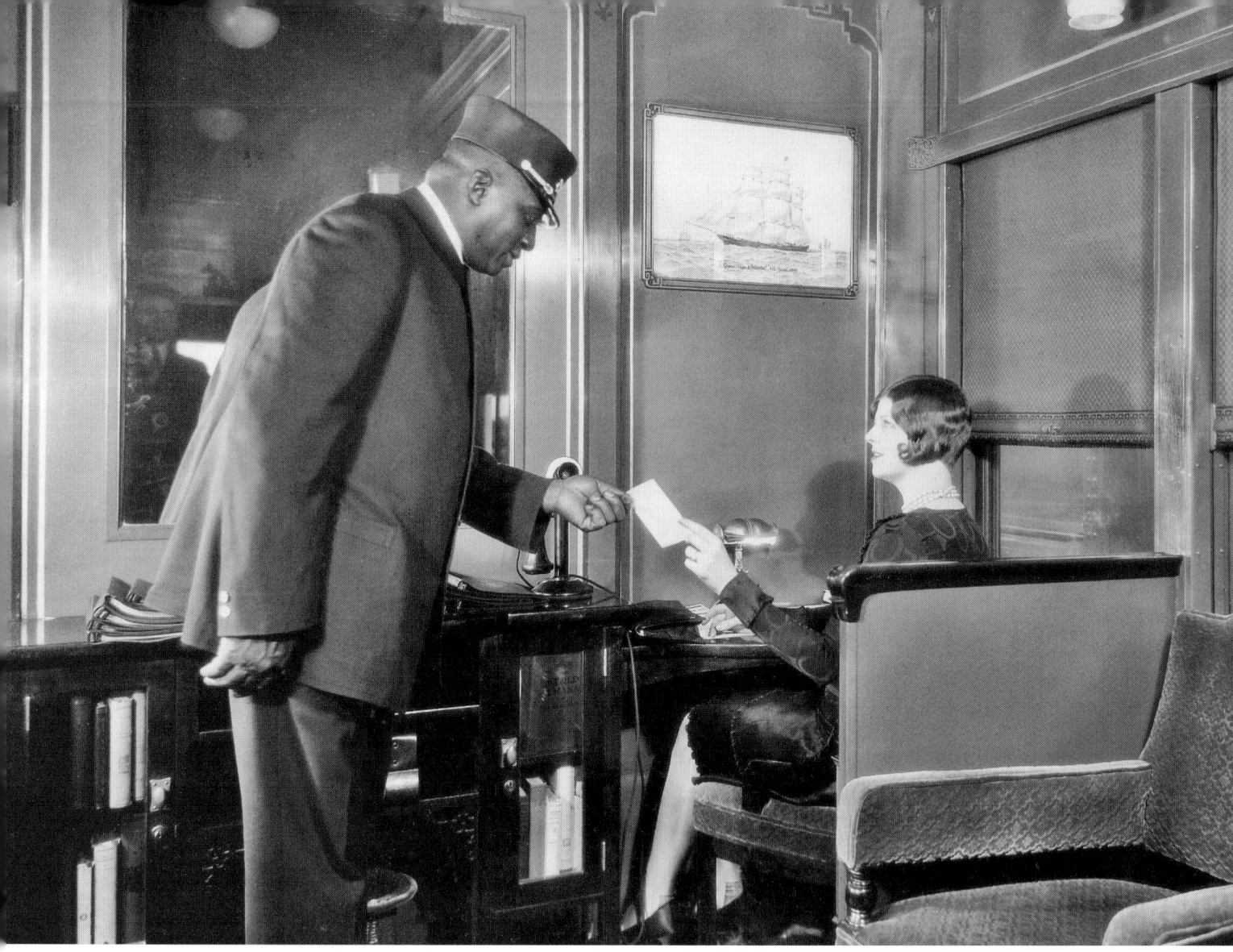

*Pullman porters and attendants working in
lounge cars had multiple duties. This porter
on the observation car of the Great Northern
Railway's* Oriental Limited *in 1929 will drop off
the lady's telegram at the next station stop for
transmission by telegraph. Arthur D. Dubin
Collection, Special Collections, Donnelley and Lee
Library, Lake Forest College*

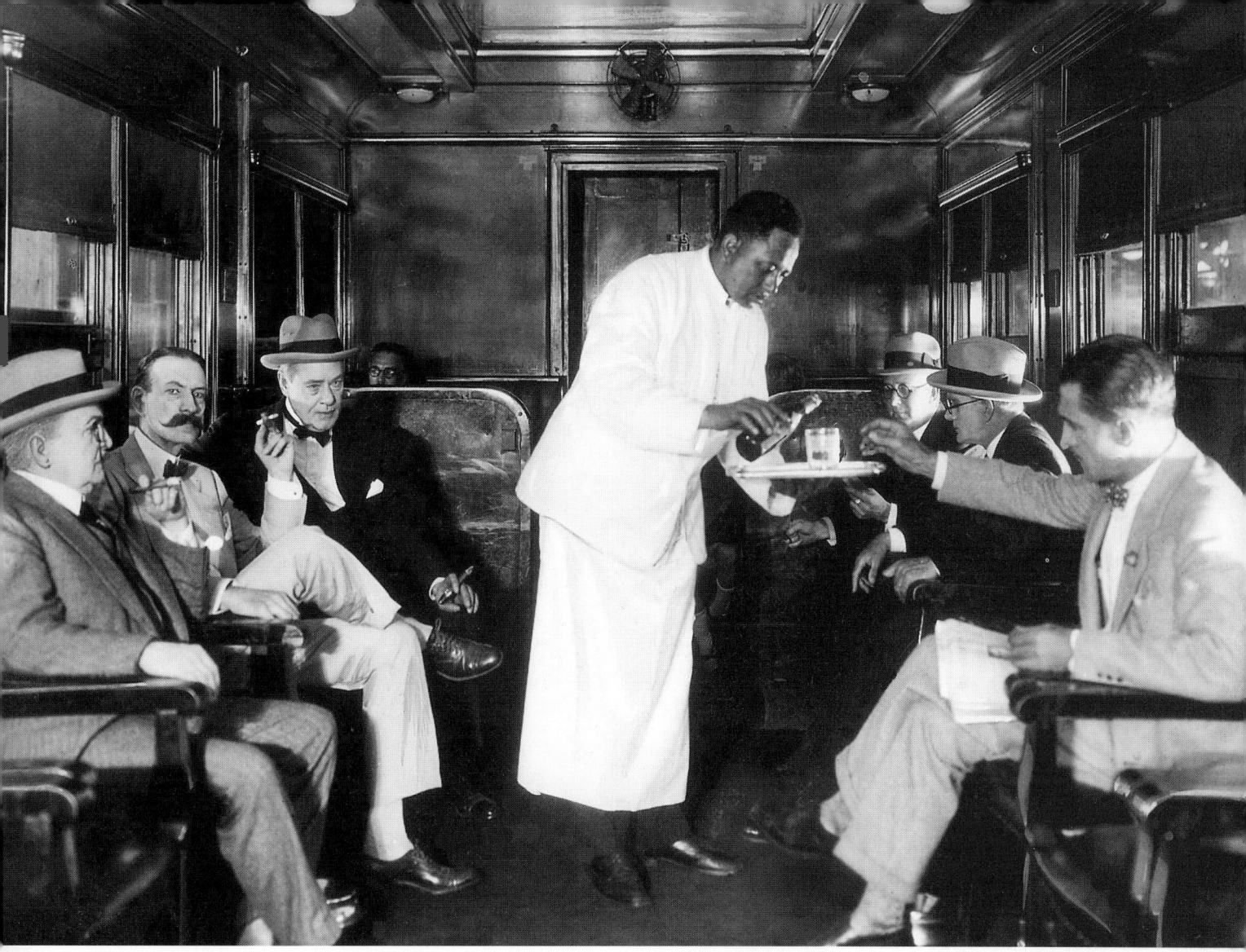

Some waiters worked in lounge or club cars instead of dining cars, offering beverages and food from an abbreviated menu. This waiter on the New York Central Railroad's famed Twentieth Century Limited *is serving "near beer" (or ginger ale) during the prohibition era. The only liquor sales permitted on NYC lines were on its Michigan Central route across Ontario, Canada. Arthur D. Dubin Collection, Special Collections, Donnelley and Lee Library, Lake Forest College*

For the greater part of the Pullman era, most sleeping-car passengers rode in "open sections," which were cheaper than compartments, drawing rooms, or bedrooms. During the day they sat in common, but at nightfall the Pullman porter pulled down upper berths, converted seats into lower berths, separated sets of berths with wooden dividers, and hung curtains for privacy. This porter is hanging curtains on the Great Northern Railway's premier Empire Builder *from St. Paul to Seattle in 1929 or later. Great Northern Railway Records, Minnesota Historical Society*

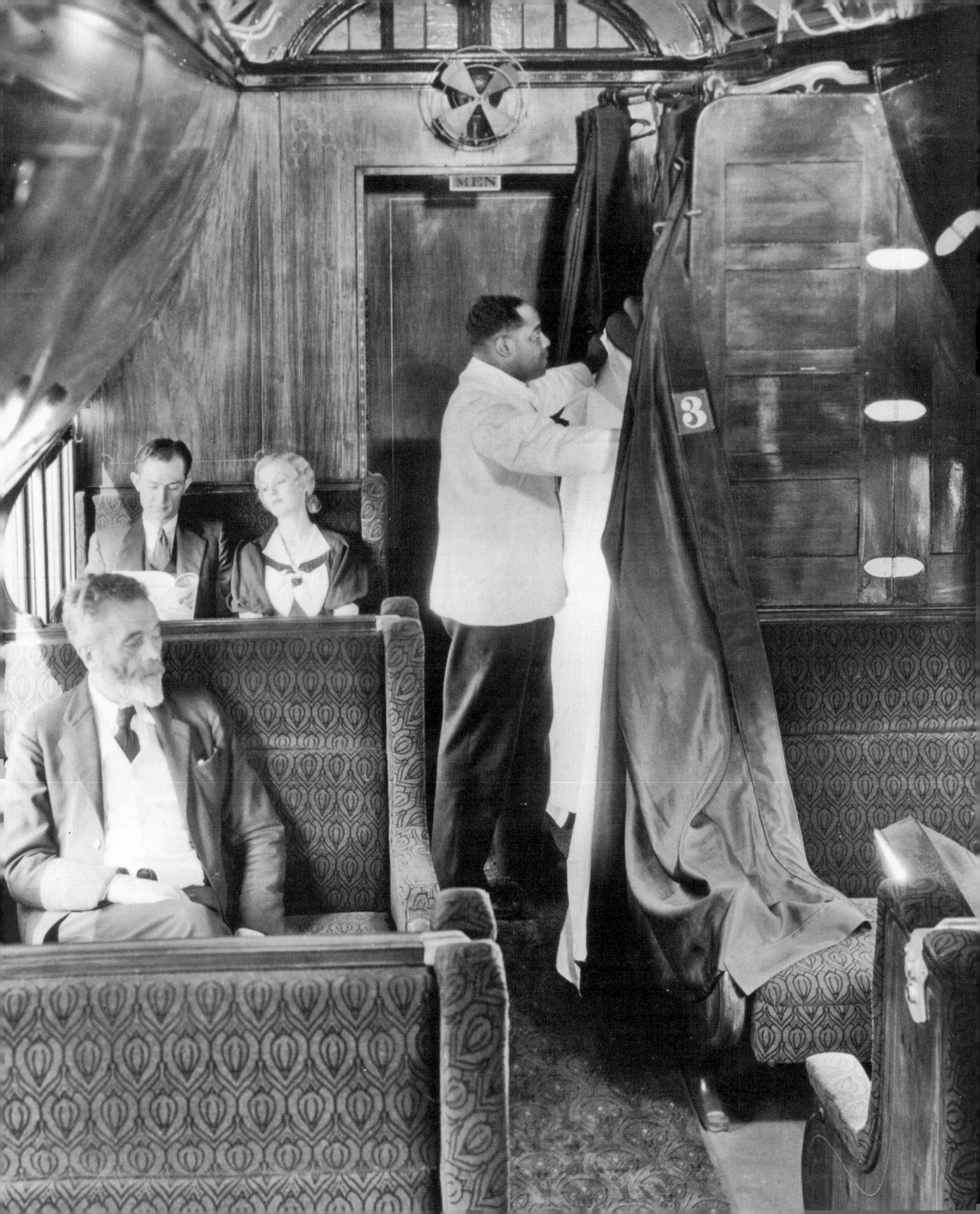

Blacks rarely predominated on section gangs outside of the South. Multiracial gangs were common, however, particularly on roads that could recruit laborers directly from the South. This Illinois Central Railroad MOW crew north of Du Quoin, Illinois, in August 1929, is putting in heavier rail, as evidenced by the tie plates on the motor-car trailer. Theodore Kornweibel collection

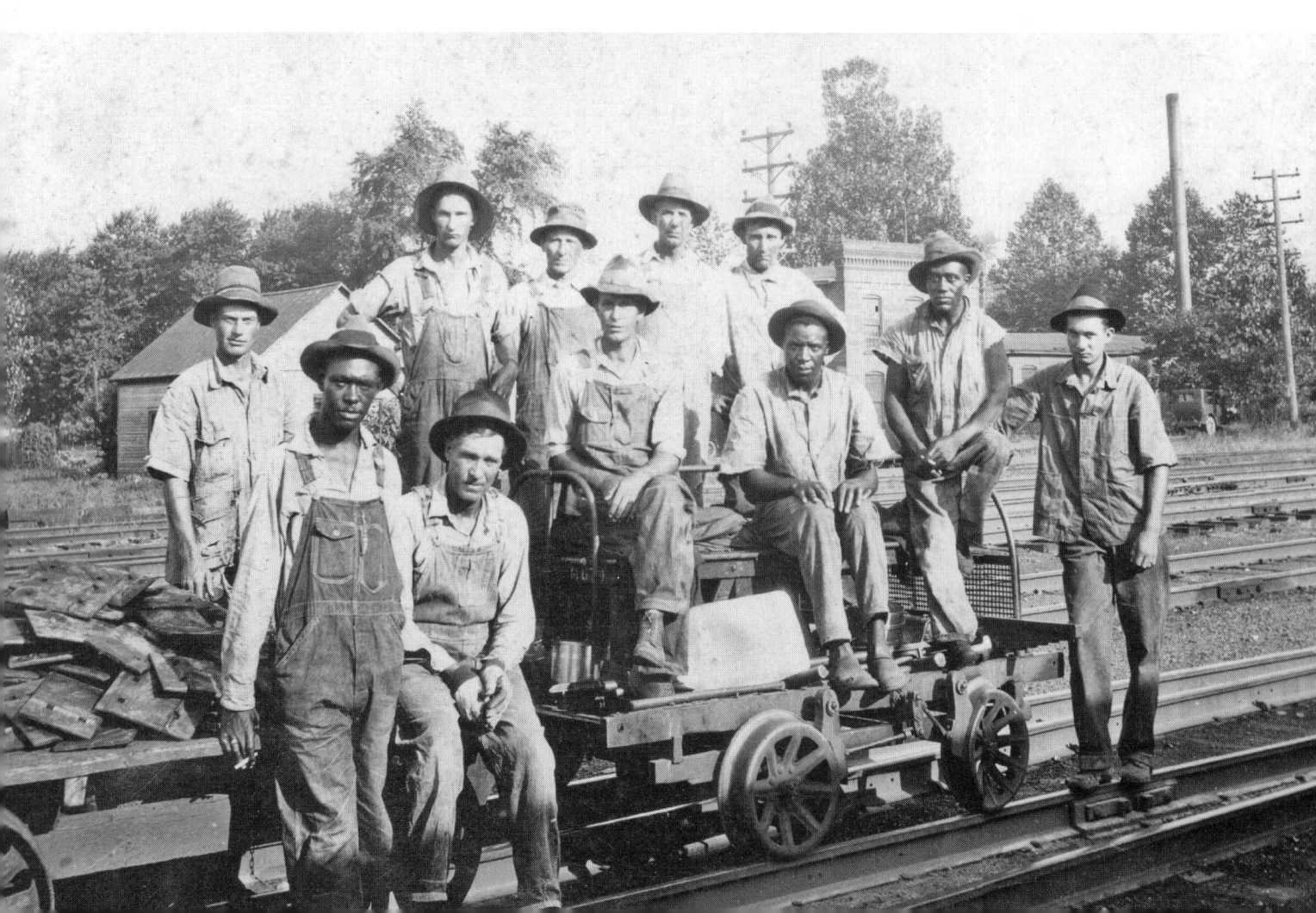

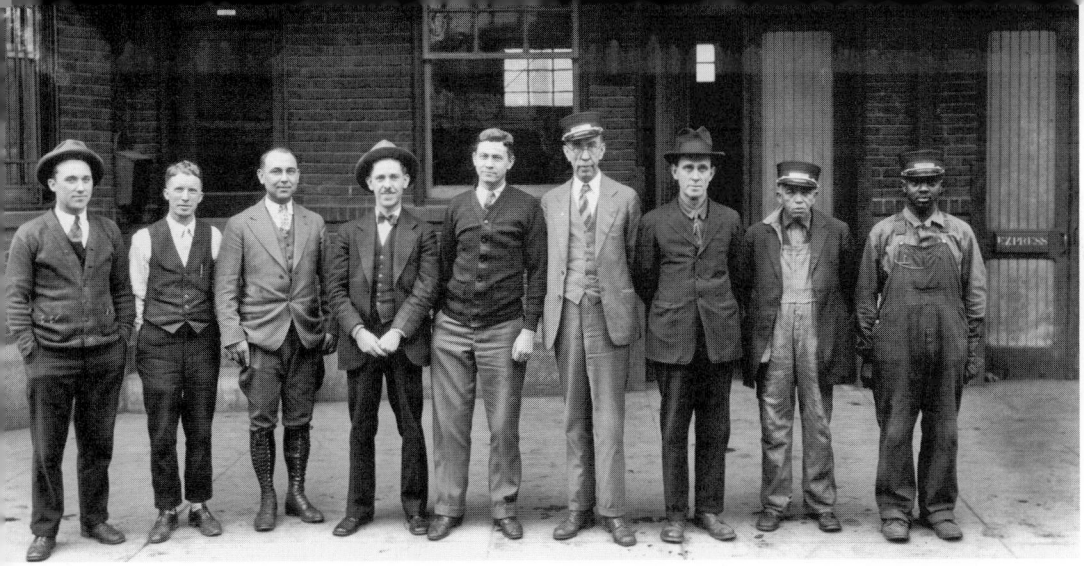

(ABOVE) *During the steam era, even many rural localities had a sizeable "station force," like this group of Norfolk & Western Railway employees in the 1930s at North Fork, West Virginia, a tiny spot on the Virginia–Ohio main line. The white men included the stationmaster, passenger and freight agents, and telegrapher. The two blacks performed multiple tasks as station porters, janitors, and handymen. Norfolk & Western Historical Photos, Digital Library and Archives, University Libraries, Virginia Polytechnic Institute and State University*

(BELOW) *The Pullman staff of the* Liberty Limited, *the Pennsylvania Railroad's premier Washington–Chicago train, photographed sometime after Pullman started hiring Filipino lounge-car attendants in the 1920s in an attempt to threaten porters who were trying to unionize. The crew consists of porters Bruno Watson, R. Smith, H. Jones, C. Harris, and W. Lindsay; attendants A. Domingo and F. de Guzman; and Pullman conductor P. A. Steele. Arthur D. Dubin Collection, Special Collections, Donnelley and Lee Library, Lake Forest College*

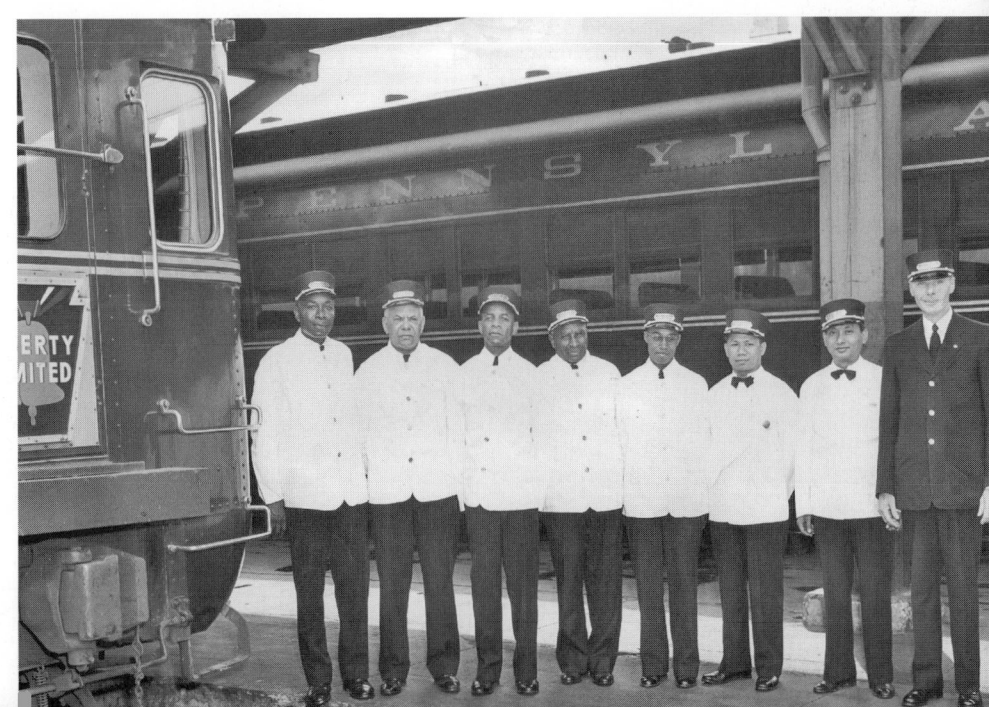

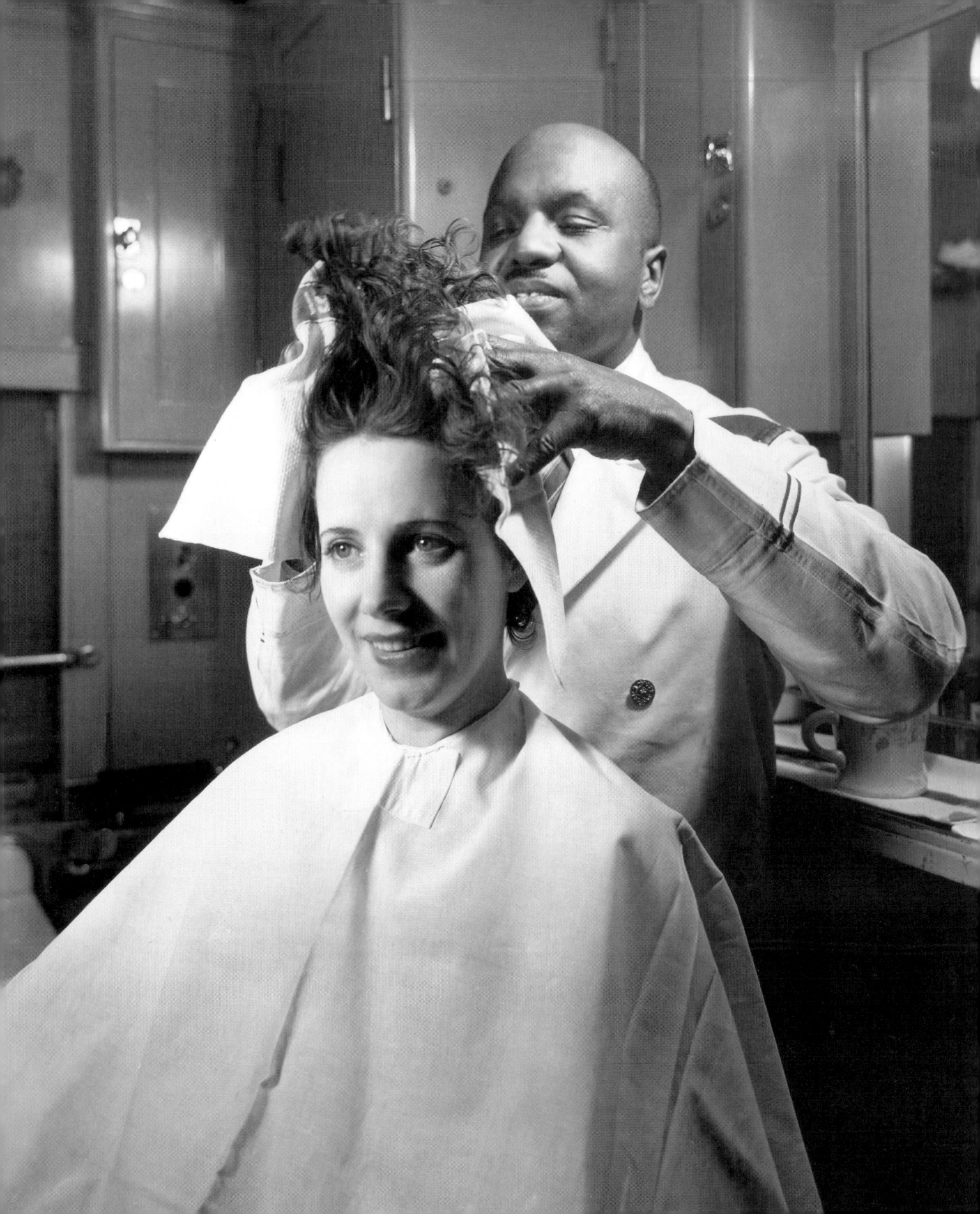

(OPPOSITE) *A few of the most opulent trains had Pullman barbers. Some were African Americans while others were whites. The Milwaukee Road's* Olympian *from Chicago to Seattle–Tacoma, offered a variety of premier services in 1929, the peak decade for luxury travel, including a barbershop and a separate ladies' lounge car. Arthur D. Dubin Collection, Special Collections, Donnelley and Lee Library, Lake Forest College*

Pullman club-car attendants supplemented their incomes by performing valet services. Between serving drinks and food in the lounge and attending to passengers in the compartments, this attendant on the Milwaukee Road's Olympian *presses suits on a portable ironing board in the men's restroom. The photo dates from the later 1920s or 1930s. Arthur D. Dubin Collection, Special Collections, Donnelley and Lee Library, Lake Forest College*

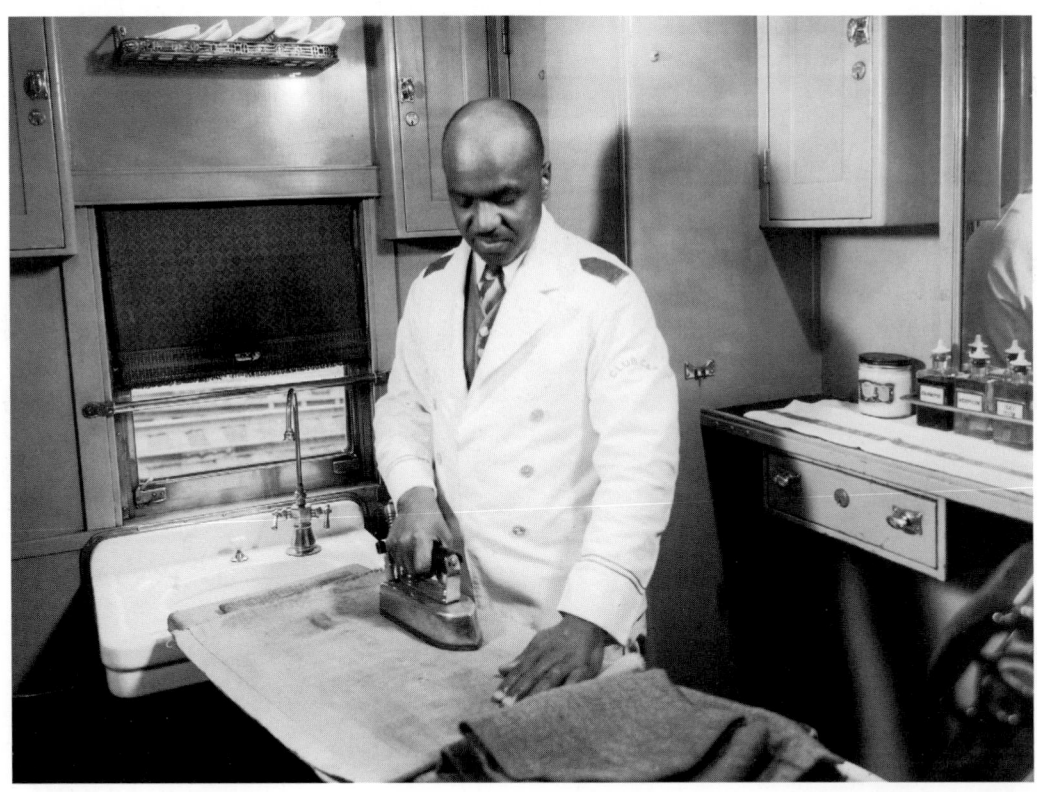

Black laborers were commonplace at southern roundhouses, lending both skill and brawn to routine locomotive maintenance. Many roundhouses, like this Texas & Pacific Railway facility at Texarkana, Texas, in the 1920s, had an "Armstrong" turntable that was not rotated by a motor, but by the efforts of several men with strong arms, pushing on a stout pole. Texas & Pacific Collection, reprinted by permission, Railroad Museum of Pennsylvania

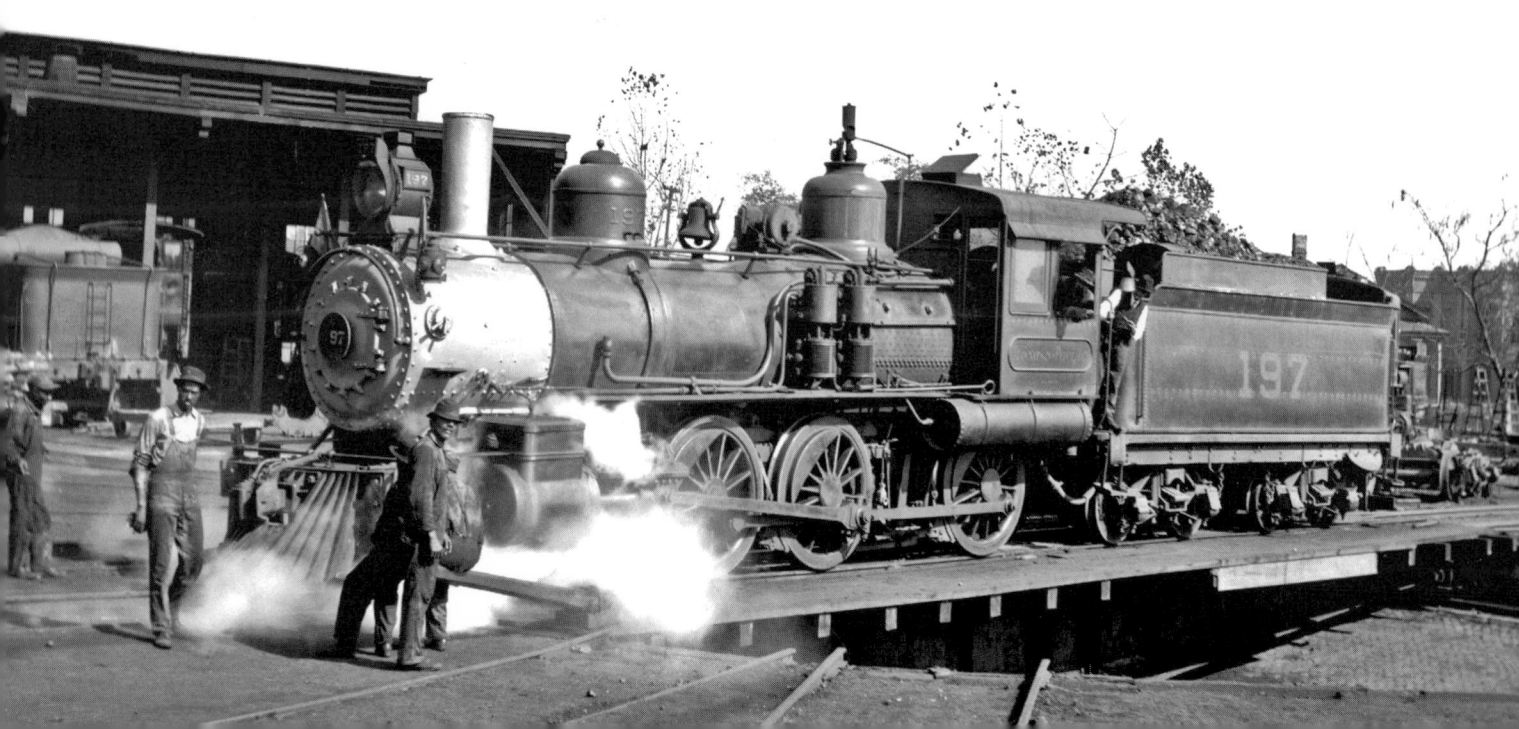

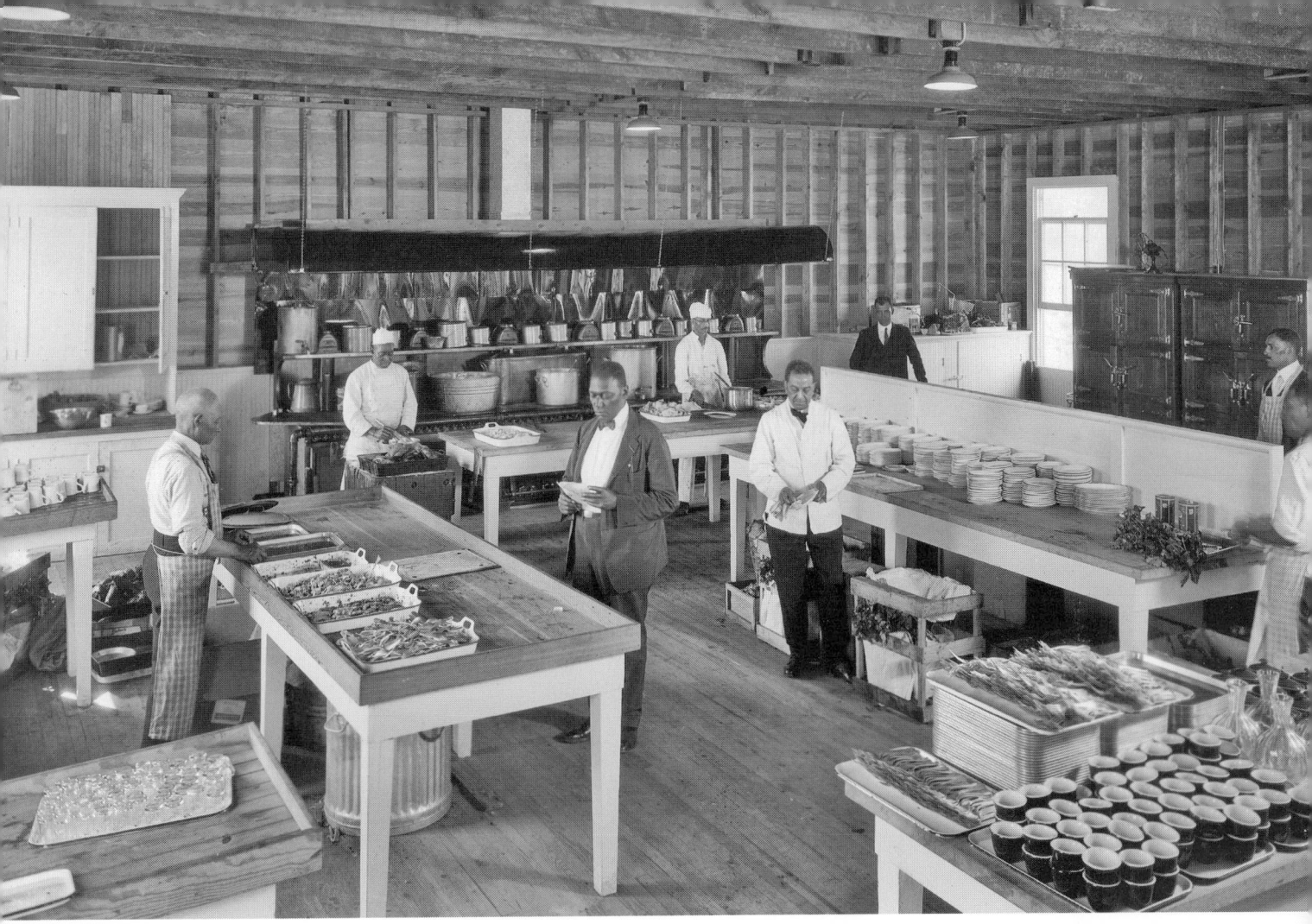

Railroads that operated extensive dining-car fleets, like the Baltimore & Ohio, had large commissary departments where menus were prepared, foodstuffs were stockpiled, some dishes were pre-prepared, and durable supplies like linens, china, and cookware were kept. Here, in a B&O dish and utensil room, African Americans worked as clerks and cart men but not in positions of authority. The photograph dates from the 1920s or 1930s. Courtesy B&O Railroad Museum

Thousands of commuters daily passed through the Central Railroad of New Jersey's terminal in Jersey City, transferring to and from ferries for Manhattan. This station porter, sometime in the 1920s or 1930s, must have had a never-ending job trying to keep the premises clean. No matter how well he performed his job, he could not aspire to become a ticket agent or telegrapher at the station. Reading Railroad Collection, courtesy of Hagley Museum and Library

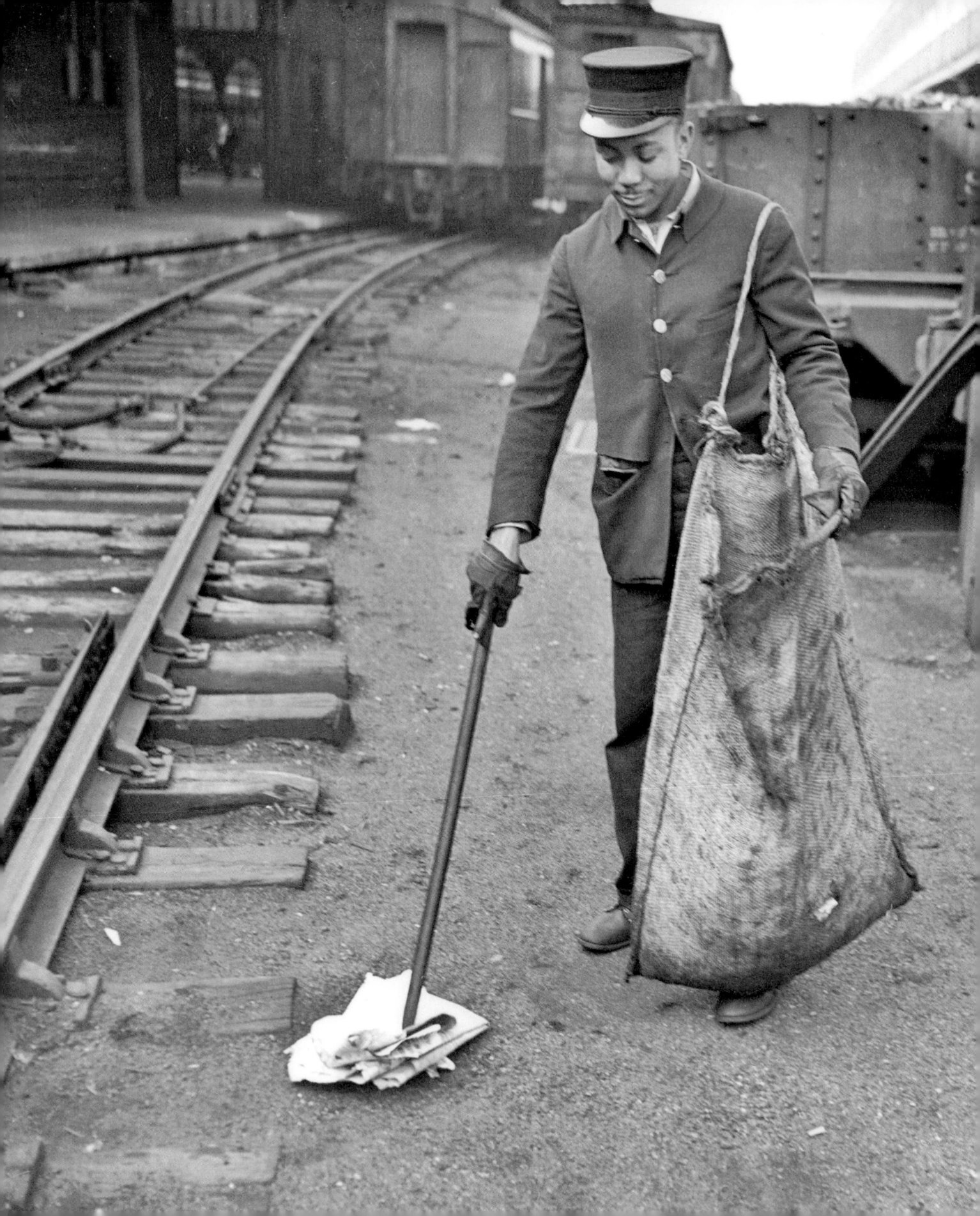

"MARRY A RAILROAD MAN"

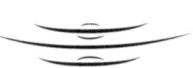

The Communal Life of Black Railroaders

To many African Americans, being a railroader defined one's place in the social order. Railroad employees (of whatever ethnicity) fit into three categories. Some worked for only a short time or occasional periods and did not primarily identify themselves as railroaders. Others were boomers, more or less rootless men who did not work for one line for an extended time. A third category—career railroaders—emerges from the pages of employee magazines. Not only was the longevity of their employment noteworthy, but also the degree to which they were substantial members of their communities. In some towns, a railroad provided nearly the entire industrial employment and its workers (and their pay envelopes) were central to the health of black communities and economies. Such was Bluefield, West Virginia, on the Norfolk & Western Railway's main line from Virginia to Ohio, and site of one of its major shops. Bluefield's black population in 1930 was 3,363. About 30 percent of the total (1,002) were males 21 years of age and over. The N&W was, for many black families, their economic lifeline.[1]

The *Norfolk and Western Magazine* provides rich detail concerning the hopes, dreams, and struggles of the railroad's employees, as do the black workers' news features in many other lines' magazines. Retirements and deaths were noted, often with brief biographies or obituaries. It printed numerous photographs of employees and their family members, although more often whites than blacks. In the early 1930s it added a monthly feature, "News from Our Colored

Employees," which reflected black workers' perspectives, not necessarily those of their employer, and featured news supplied by correspondents from all over the 2,200-mile system. Bluefield had a particularly conscientious correspondent, shop laborer G. R. Watkins, who for several years rarely missed a month in reporting what was significant in the lives of his fellow workers and their kin. Watkins knew best others in the shops, but he also occasionally wrote about brakemen, firemen, and freight-house workers. Over the span of 5 years—from the beginning of 1930 to the end of 1934—Watkins chronicled the activities of about 180 of his fellow railroaders, many repeatedly. These men constituted 18 percent of the adult male African American population of Bluefield.

Missing from Watkins's reports was mention of maintenance of way laborers. Floating (extra) gang members came from all over, and perhaps few if any actually resided in Bluefield, but it is likely that at least some regular section gang men did have roots in town. There is no ready explanation for their absence from Watkins's reports. He also did not mention either train porters or dining-car waiters and cooks, but for a logical reason. Passenger trains did not originate in Bluefield, but passed through on their way between Norfolk, Virginia, and Cincinnati or Columbus, Ohio. Thus, passenger crewmen lived mostly in those terminal cities.

The vast majority of Bluefield's black railroaders were roundhouse and shop laborers, occupying the bottom rank of the industrial order. A minority were helpers who assisted journeymen craftsmen by doing the heavier, dirtier, and less skilled work in the machine, blacksmith, and boiler shops. Only a handful were skilled workers. Although concentrated at the bottom, they generally stressed the value of mutual respect among themselves. In fact, the job ceiling fostered solidarity. On the N&W and every other railroad that profiled workers' lives in its employee magazine, social networks invariably crossed employment categories. An organization of black railroaders, unless it was defined by a specific job category, was just as likely to be led by an office janitor or shop laborer as by a brakeman or fireman.

Quite a few of Bluefield's railroaders were related to one another, either as fathers and sons, as brothers, cousins, and uncles, or by marriage. Other railroads' magazines reveal the same phenomenon. As with white railroaders, many men found their jobs through relatives or friends. The railroads did not commonly need to advertise for black workers, but relied on referrals from their current employees or asked community leaders for recommendations. When black preachers worked for railroads—many ministers' congregations were too poor to support them—they often furnished names of prospective employees.

The life events recorded in the "News From Our Colored Employees" columns, and similar features in other railroads' periodicals, reveal what was important to black communities. Naturally, births and deaths were noted, with appropriate expressions of sympathy for the latter. Railroad employment fostered social bonds, and it was fitting that all celebrate or mourn together. Bluefield's N&W workers maintained a flower fund for condolences. Many entries also noted illness and disability, not just of employees, but of kin as well. Sickness and workplace accidents were common—

railroading was a dangerous occupation—and were part of the shared experience that drew African American communities together.

Another major topic was visitation. Railroad workers were entitled to passes after a minimum period of service (one year on the N&W), essentially a free coach ticket for themselves and their families. This "perk" helped strengthen the kinship bonds that had been essential for survival ever since slavery. Ira Waters, an Asheville, North Carolina roundhouse laborer for the Southern Railway, was able to maintain contact with cousins in distant Cincinnati and Knoxville, Tennessee, because of his pass.[2] On the Norfolk & Western, correspondent Watkins regularly noted visits by employees or their families to other locales as well as pass-holding visitors to Bluefield. By the 1930s, a number of black railroaders owned automobiles, and "motoring" to see friends or relatives was not only worthy of mention but also an indication of one's financial status. Travel outside the segregated South was particularly significant. Railroaders (and more often, their wives) regularly visited relatives or friends in New York and other northern cities.

Watkins's reports reveal other significant aspects of black life. Groups of railroaders took time off to attend Negro League baseball games in distant cities. Others were avid followers of the Bluefield State Teachers College football team. Located on 4 acres adjacent to the N&W's yards, it was the pride of African Americans in West Virginia. Using their passes, N&W employees traveled to Columbus to watch the "Big Blues" play rivals like Kentucky State College. After Jackie Robinson broke the color line in the major leagues, employees traveled on passes to watch him and the Brooklyn Dodgers play the Reds in Cincinnati.[3] And in 1934 numerous N&W black pass riders attended the non-segregated Century of Progress Exposition in Chicago.

Bluefield's black railroaders also shared news of traditional rural southern activities through their column in the *Norfolk and Western Magazine*. Hunting parties—successful or not—were noted. Also newsworthy was the annual hog butchering, with those who raised especially fat hogs receiving particular recognition. Many black southerners clung to their rural roots, even if they lived in towns, so reports of agricultural activities were of interest to many. The *Illinois Central Magazine* often reported that railroaders intended to continue cultivating gardens and raising chickens in their retirement.

Romance found a place in the pages of the *Norfolk and Western Magazine* and other railroads' publications because it, too, knit people and families together. Watkins slyly reported rumors of courtship, and the prospect of wedding bells was always celebrated, particularly if the groom-to-be had theretofore been a confirmed bachelor. The importance of education in African American hopes for the future was also reflected in Watkins's column. High school graduations were always applauded. Even more noteworthy was attendance at one of the historically black colleges. Earning a college degree was a very significant milestone. Photographs of high school and college graduates in academic regalia were regularly included in employee magazines' news columns. And like graduations, the purchases of homes and automobiles were newsworthy because they indicated the progress not only of the individual, but also of the entire race.

The *Missouri Pacific Lines Magazine* also included a regular "Colored Employes" section, which similarly chronicled the rich communal life of its black workers. People wanted to share their experiences with others. Co-workers were interested in their comrades' lives. Visits and travel, illnesses and deaths, births and marriages, all deserved mention because they reinforced the traditional African American notion that "family" included everyone in the community—in this case, a shared workplace—whether or not one was related by biological kinship. And being "family" meant that people honored one another's personal achievements.

Shared railroad employment helped strengthen southern black communities in other ways. Shop and freight house workers formed numerous sports teams. Baseball was not only the "national pastime," it was black employees' favorite sport in the 1920s and 1930s. In the South, they competed in segregated company, industrial, or Negro leagues because white players had to be protected from the humiliation of being beaten by blacks. Sometimes teams were put together with the assistance of a local black entrepreneur who arranged a schedule, furnished uniforms, and took a cut of the gate. Teams were always pictured in snappy uniforms that identified their employer, even though the railroad did not necessarily sponsor them.

On the Missouri Pacific Lines, black "booster clubs" fielded teams that drew players from the entire pool of railroaders in a particular locality, not just a specific shop. Teams traveled considerable distances over the system (on passes) for league play. At least 19 black MoPac nines competed in 1929, 11 playing in a Texas and Louisiana league. Among their number was the Kingsville Black Pioneers, which won 21 of 33 games and also barnstormed with a minstrel troupe in Mississippi and Tennessee. Others were the San Antonio Steers, Houston Texans, Houston Buffalos, Crockett Black Buffs, Palestine Smart Set, Gouldsboro Bears, and Plaquemine Sports. When not meeting league opponents, they played the Little Rock All-Stars, composed of employees of the Chicago, Rock Island & Pacific Railway, the Atchison, Topeka & Santa Fe Railway's Kansas City Scouts, and teams of Southern Pacific Lines' employees from various Texas points. Company baseball was a man's sport, with rare exceptions. During World War II, a Louisville & Nashville Railroad freight house truckers' team included a female player.[4]

Racial barriers were sometimes relaxed in the North. In Chicago, the Illinois Central Railroad (fast-pitch) Softball League comprised six teams, each named for one of the line's crack passenger trains. Five teams were white, but the Seminoles were made up of Red Caps. Capitalizing on the arm of Agis Bray, reputedly one of the best pitchers anywhere, they won the league championship in 1938, for which their name was engraved on a trophy displayed in the Central Station waiting room.[5] Allowing a black team the opportunity to beat white teams would have been impermissible in the Deep South.

Employee baseball was more than recreation: it was a means of knitting together black railroaders and their communities. A ball game was often the most important social event of the week. A trainload of supporters of the visiting team would swell the crowd and expand the social network. At such games, blacks did not have to endure the humiliation of segregated seating. Spectator decorum could reflect black rather than white behaviors. While some concentrated on watching the game, others embarked on courtships or renewed friendships. More or less discreet drinking and gambling took place away from the vigilance of white authorities. A dance sometimes followed the game. So these were not just athletic contests, but larger social occasions.

Wheel rolling was a competitive sport that was unique to African American railroaders. Teams composed of workers in a particular shop competed against others elsewhere on their line. But the most exciting contests involved teams from different railroads. For several years, black shopmen on the Pennsylvania Railroad enjoyed a rivalry with their counterparts on the Norfolk & Western. These friendly competitions brought together teams, families, and fans and built social networks between workers and communities on different lines that otherwise would have no contact.

Inter-railroad wheel-rolling contests rivaled ball games in popularity in the 1930s and 1940s, and they had to be held at venues like Roanoke's City Auditorium, able to accommodate 1,500 spectators. Lengthy programs including invocations, musical numbers by ensembles from both railroads, and remarks by white railroad officials acting as unofficial sponsors preceded the actual contests. The competing 6- or 10-man teams then put 750-pound car wheels through intricate gyrations with judges—one from each team's shop—awarding points. One trick required a man to lie on the stage while others rolled the wheel all around his body. In another, a contestant spun a wheel on edge with one hand while slicing and eating a watermelon with the other. A third stunt featured a man standing atop a car wheel that was balanced on edge. Clinton Scott recalled, "we would line up a row of candles and bounce the wheel over them, kind of make it do a flip-flop, and it would put the candles out." Each competitor had his specialty. As one awed reporter wrote, "the contest held an audience of about 1,500 breathless for about an hour . . . They rolled [a wheel] around like a hoop, flopped it over flange for flange, spun it around like a top . . . made it stand alone, kicked it, put flags on it and rode on top of it."[6]

Black railroaders participated in other competitions, although none was organized as extensively as wheel rolling. Freight-house truckers were men of considerable strength, their iron hand trucks alone weighing as much as 150 pounds. In one Memphis event in 1908, truckers from the Illinois Central; Yazoo & Mississippi Valley; Southern; Chicago, Rock Island & Pacific; Missouri Pacific; and Frisco lines competed to see who could move 60 barrels of flour over a distance of 60 feet in the shortest time. An IC team won with a time of 3 minutes, 57 seconds, 11 seconds faster than its nearest rival. A similar type of event pitted Red Caps against one another to see who could carry 70 pounds of baggage—several suitcases in each hand and under each arm—over a measured distance.[7]

Team competitions, in both traditional sports and unique-to-railroad contests, drew enthusiastic spectators and helped cement relations between railroaders and their surrounding communities. Other events, sponsored by the railroads themselves, solidified employees' own sense of belonging to a particular railroad "family." A number of lines sponsored annual summer employee picnics that were for many decades segregated. The N&W held picnics for each division, or combined two divisions, at rented facilities like "colored" campgrounds, amusement parks, or schools, offering free coach passage on regularly scheduled trains or, when necessary, special trains. These were events for entire families, sometimes even including employees' friends, with attendance numbering in the thousands. All arrived by late morning. Each family brought its own picnic, while a refreshment committee provided cold drinks and watermelons. White guests of honor—railroad officials—were served at separate tables. A variety of competitions followed the meal. The N&W's Scioto Division outing in 1930 included pie-eating, watermelon-eating, and singing contests, as well as a "chicken race" and a "fat ladies' race." Two company teams played a spirited baseball game. A 10-piece orchestra provided music at a dance pavilion. Weary but happy participants boarded trains for home at about five o'clock in the evening. Picnics for other N&W divisions also featured foot races for children and adults, plus crowd-pleasing "skunk races" and chicken-catching contests for children.[8]

The Great Depression did not curtail N&W annual picnics. If anything, they were all the more necessary for maintaining morale. In early September 1933, about 3,000 black employees and family members from the Radford and Pocahontas divisions gathered at the Christiansburg Industrial Institute, an African American agricultural and industrial training school modeled after Tuskegee Institute, located 15 miles west of Roanoke. Radford attendees came by scheduled trains, while the others arrived on three lengthy special trains. While they emptied their food baskets, "members of the picnic committee were spreading a luscious meal for the white folks." The selection of the white guests was strategic. Each division's master mechanic, general foreman, special agent (railroad police), and medical examiner were invited, along with the carmen, electrical workers, machinists, blacksmiths, and electricians unions' shop chairmen, who held the fate of black shop laborers and helpers in their hands.[9]

The N&W recognized the importance of continuing summer employee picnics during the Depression years to cultivate good relations with a workforce that faced layoffs and wage cuts. In 1937 it rented an amusement park for 3,000 guests attending the "colored" Pocahontas–Radford picnic. This time there was more excitement for the children, who flocked to the merry-go-round, roller coaster, Ferris wheel, and airplane swing. Adults mostly entertained themselves with visiting, but for the more introspective, a revival meeting was held, led by a female Holiness preacher who exhorted "wayward picnickers to mend their ways and live better lives."[10]

The Chesapeake & Ohio Railway similarly sought to bolster employee morale and loyalty through annual (segregated) picnics. In 1927 three special trains brought more than 3,000 Richmond MOW and shop employees and their families to a resort at Buckroe Beach, Virginia, where the company treated them to food, merry-go-round rides, an orchestra and dancing, swimming, and a bathing beauty contest. A committee of workers planned the details, under the "general supervision" of the C&O health and recreation department.[11] The Pullman Company's approach was to sponsor "field days" for porters and their families. Such affairs in New York attracted several thousand participants annually in the 1920s who enjoyed parades, baseball games, band, chorus, and quartet performances, track and field competitions, and plenty of food. White officials were in attendance to underscore the company's noblesse oblige.[12]

Another way that railroads tried to encourage loyalty was by sponsoring veteran employees' organizations. The N&W hoped its groups would promote a "Norfolk and Western Family spirit." Because these were social groupings, they were segregated, with the establishment of "colored" associations following the launching of such groups for whites. Although the black groups operated separately from the whites, they were not independent.[13]

The N&W Veterans Association, formed in 1930, required members to have worked at least 20 consecutive years, or 25 years with interruptions. Active workers paid an initial membership fee plus monthly dues. Retired members on the Honor Roll were admitted free. Those who had worked 50 years were awarded a diamond insignia lapel pin. The inaugural meeting of the Colored Division of the N&W Veterans Association was held at St. Paul's Methodist Episcopal Church in Roanoke in late 1930. John Calloway, a yard brakeman with 42 years' service, was elected chairman. His first act was to ask the delegates to rise and give a vote of thanks to the assembled white officials, including N&W president A. C. Needles. This signified the reciprocal obligations between the company and African Americans: it would continue to provide jobs, while expecting black employees to "create among the younger and less experienced men who work with you that same spirit of loyalty and interest in their duties which has been manifested by you." In his address, Needles asserted that "the railway company recognizes and appreciates the valuable contribution made by its colored employees in the progress and development of the railroad. Our company has always had every reason to be proud of its colored employees. No matter how difficult the job, you have always tackled it and conquered it."[14] No mention was made, of course, of its refusal for more than a decade to hire any new black firemen.

The N&W promoted veterans' meetings by furnishing free transportation (including special cars added to regularly scheduled trains) and a meeting place, while the association itself paid for the meal. Company officers were always on hand to give speeches and present diamond pins to new 50-year veterans. The paternalistic dance between black and white was carefully choreographed with company praise for the loyalty and "splendid records" of its workers and the veterans' adoption of resolutions thanking the company and its officers for recognizing them. Such gatherings also featured a black keynote speaker, often an educator of the Booker T. Washington persuasion who lauded manual labor and black economic progress while sidestepping the forbidden subject of political rights. In fact, many southern blacks before World War II still favored Washingtonian strategies for racial amelioration. At the second annual gathering, in 1931, Major Walter R. Brown, dean of men at Hampton Institute (the model for Washington's Tuskegee Institute), intoned that "a man who stays on the job, maintains his home, pays his taxes, settles his bills, cares for his family, supports his church, shares in the community life, is a true citizen in every sense of the word." This was, indeed, a widely accepted catalogue of middle-class virtues, and good relations with the railroad required that citizenship be defined without reference to voting.[15]

Norfolk & Western veterans' meetings were canceled in 1932 and 1933, due to the Depression, so the third meeting, held at a "colored resort" on the Chesapeake Bay near Norfolk, did not occur until 1934. By then, the group's membership numbered 360. Remarkably, about 250 attended, including the sole female member, Sally Craig, who had worked for more than 25 years as a matron at the Roanoke passenger station. The formula was by now familiar: praise for employee loyalty from white officials; thanks to company officials for their "sympathetic cooperation"; presentation of 50-year pins; and an "inspiring" message from a black orator who lauded the Protestant work ethic, interracial harmony, and good will of white railroad executives. As the speaker at the 1936 gathering stated, "the high standard of efficiency insisted upon by the company has given to our community here and elsewhere better citizens, better churches, better schools, and better homes... As our chief benefactor, the N&W Railway has not only been our main source of support, but a substantial torchlight casting its rays upon the path which leads toward real progress."[16] In an era where black firemen were being assassinated in the Deep South, and overall railroad employment was plummeting, many black railroaders saw their best hope for job security in such expressions of cooperation and good will.

Other lines sponsored veterans' organizations. On the Central of Georgia Railway it was known as the Quarter Century Service Club. Yet the much larger Louisville & Nashville did not have such an organization, perhaps because it did not retire workers at the mandatory age of 70, as did the N&W. Track laborers toiled into their 70s and a few L&N employees even kept working into their 80s. Its major employee-relations efforts in the 1930s and 1940s focused instead on motivating workers to avoid accidents and to "sell" the L&N to prospective shippers and passengers.

The first large-scale L&N "Safety-Friendly Service" rallies began in the mid-1930s in rented downtown auditoriums with blacks relegated to the balconies. Perhaps in response to protests, the company began "all-colored" affairs in 1938, although initially the master of ceremonies and two principal speakers were white. In a reversal of southern racial folkways, the 300 white guests occupied the balcony. The purpose of such meetings was undoubtedly to improve efficiency, but for many blacks, the main attraction must have been the dozen music and comedy acts, many of them featuring employees. These rallies soon became community affairs, with employees inviting friends and family to join them. Seizing the opportunity to assert their dignity, ushers wore tuxes, while some female guests came gowned in long evening dresses. Smaller rallies, sometimes held at black churches, were put on for specific groups of employees, like the porters, Red Caps, mail and baggage handlers, maids, and janitors who worked at Nashville Union Station. After World War II, some safety rallies again accommodated both races. Although they were still segregated, some coordination occurred. At a Louisville rally, both black and white usherettes wore long dresses, while in Nashville, the women all wore shorter dresses.[17]

Elsewhere, blacks found safety clubs to be a means not only to address workplace issues, but also to unite socially. Missouri, Kansas & Texas Railway train porters based in Parsons, Kansas, began meeting monthly in 1916 to study the rules and instruct one another (rather than accept

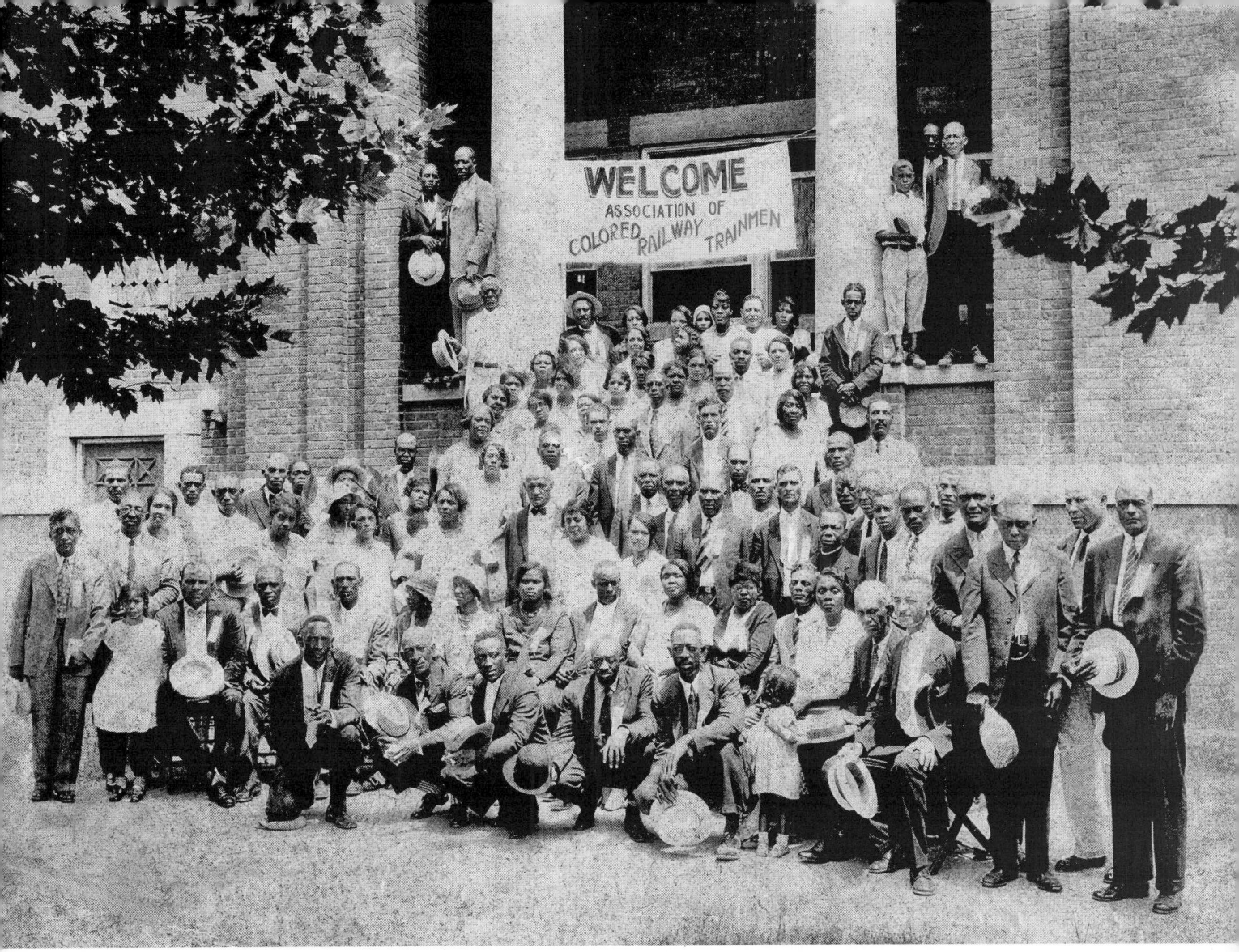

A gathering of the Association of Colored Railway Trainmen, an independent black brakemen's union, sometime in the 1930s. No black railroad union, with the exception of the Brotherhood of Sleeping Car Porters, was able to gain national contracts and significant improvements in pay and working conditions. The ACRT was a valiant but weak voice for its members. By 1942, it had dwindled to a mere 400 paid-up members. Theodore Kornweibel collection

training by a white official) on how to keep cars clean, extend courtesy to passengers, and operate safely. Such groups had consolidated by the 1930s into the Katy Train Porters Association, with annual conventions including activities for entire families. Its ladies' auxiliary was still functioning in the 1950s as the M-K-T Ladies' Safety Council.[18] In fact, many black railroaders' organizations featured female auxiliaries that not only supported the aims of the group but also gave railroaders' wives their own meaningful social outlet.

Similar to safety clubs were company-promoted efficiency organizations. The Central of Georgia, struggling to control costs when passenger revenues declined after World War I, was particularly concerned about the amount of coal burned on its steam engines. Firemen who shoveled the "black diamonds" into locomotives' fireboxes were the key to conservation. The railroad encouraged the formation of Colored Fireman's Fuel Associations at every important terminal. Monthly meetings discussed ways of using less coal. Incentives included annual barbeques for firemen and their families. White officials "showed their appreciation of the colored firemen by attending," although they probably put more significance in their presence than did the firemen.[19]

Whether the railroads sponsored veterans' organizations, safety rallies, or efficiency meetings, they hoped that workers would become "boosters," using their church, fraternal, and other civic connections to drum up new business. This became particularly vital during the Depression. Railroads had begun promoting booster clubs—segregated in the South—in the 1920s to make every employee, not just ticket clerks and freight sales agents, responsible for the lines' profitability. The *Louisville & Nashville Employes' Magazine* printed the name (and sometimes the picture) of every booster who persuaded even one individual to ride the Old Reliable, bestowing particular honor on those who secured whole groups. One outstanding booster (and 60-year veteran) was black fireman Joe Bowles, who was said to have brought in more than $10,000 in passenger fares through soliciting his friends and acquaintances. His crowning achievement was persuading 1,450 delegates to choose the L&N over competing lines for travel to a convention in St. Louis.[20] Although railroad companies obviously wanted boosterism to catch on among their workers, black booster clubs thrived because railroaders transformed them into community institutions providing musical programs, banquets, dances, athletic contests, and excursions not only for themselves but also for their friends and neighbors. And clubs also fed off workers' pride in their companies. A black travel writer observed that "the Negro railroader . . . has always been extremely jealous of the honor and reputation of his own line. There is a friendly but keen rivalry for patronage among employes of different roads traversing the same territory."[21]

The Missouri Pacific encouraged boosterism all over its system. By the end of the 1920s, a "colored booster club" existed everywhere there was a concentration of black employees. In Kansas and Nebraska, where there were relatively fewer black workers, clubs drew membership from entire divisions (e.g., the Northern Kansas Division). Elsewhere clubs were located in cities or towns where hundreds of blacks worked for the railroad. A sampling of their activities in the summer of 1929

Railroads in the African American Experience

is indicative of how important these organizations were, not so much for the railroad's economic fortunes, as in uniting black communities.

The MoPac's Memphis facilities included a roundhouse and shops, freight houses, a passenger terminal, freight yards, and offices. Memphis's black boosters put on an annual evening "frolic" which, in May 1929, was attended by 500 employees and their friends.[22] But booster club events were even more important socially in smaller towns like Gurdon, Arkansas, population about 2,000 in 1930. Many black non-farming males in the county worked for the railroad. In August 1929, the booster club sponsored a picnic that must have been one of the biggest happenings in the black community's experience: 800 boosters and friends spent the day enjoying a barbecue, music, and baseball game, the local shop squad beating a team from the Van Buren, Arkansas shops. The MoPac was similarly the largest industrial employer in Kingsville, Texas (black population of about 500) in 1929. The most important yearly holiday was "Juneteenth," black Texans' emancipation day. Several hundred railroaders and their families took the train 94 miles south to Harlingen (359 black residents) to celebrate with that town's MoPac employees at the local park, where they enjoyed auto races and a baseball game between the MP Kingsville Black Pioneers and a Houston booster team.[23] So while the formation of booster clubs was encouraged by the railroads, black employees maintained them for their own social and recreational purposes.

The Illinois Central, like the MoPac, stretched from the Midwest into the South. It initiated employee clubs in 1929 and by 1936 the number had grown to 73, 15 of which were for "colored boosters." These were mostly clustered along the main stem, running from Chicago and St. Louis down the Mississippi Valley to New Orleans. Women as well as men could be members, although their numbers were small, reflecting the overwhelmingly male nature of the railroad industry. The biggest clubs, in New Orleans and Memphis, had 401 and 550 members, respectively, while the smallest clubs, in Greenville, Mississippi; Jackson, Tennessee; and Cairo and Freeport, Illinois, numbered fewer than 50 participants.

IC booster clubs grew out of "solicitation of business committees" in the late 1920s. Members were encouraged to use their church and fraternal connections to steer freight and passengers—particularly groups traveling to conventions or on excursions—onto IC trains. Recapturing bus passengers was also a priority. Their reward was not only a sense of contributing to the prosperity of their employer, and thus perhaps better assurance of a steady job, but also recognition among their peers and seeing their names mentioned in the *Illinois Central Magazine*. One booster spent his free time at St. Louis's Union Station, which was used by many railroads, to persuade black travelers to ride the IC rather than a competitor's trains.

Like other black organizations, IC booster clubs had an array of offices: a president, as many as three vice presidents, one or two secretaries, and a treasurer. Meetings were held monthly, usually featuring speeches by white officials promoting the company's business, as well as by the club's own officers. Self-interest and community interest could both be served. Clubs organized railroad excursions, open to all community members, and meetings took on a more communal social character with the addition of musical numbers, orations on uplifting topics, and formal addresses by clergymen and school principals. Typical was the May 1930 meeting of the Vicksburg (Mississippi) Negro Booster Club, attended by about 300, including many community residents attracted by the entertainment, not promotion of the railroad. Beginning with "Lift Evr'y Voice and Sing" (the "Negro National Anthem") and an invocation, the program included selections by a church sextet and several vocal and piano solos interspersed by recitations. A banquet concluded the evening. New Orleans boosters put on a "mammoth party" in July 1934 with 1,100 members and friends assembled in an IC warehouse. The highlight was the showing of several "talkies," after which a band played for dancing. Soon the presidents of all the black booster clubs were holding yearly conventions to discuss not only ways to better promote business, but also how to provide more appealing entertainment. Leaders were urged to encourage the formation of ladies' auxiliaries, as "the women are just naturally better boosters."[24]

Illinois Central booster groups evolved in the late 1930s into "colored employes service clubs." Part of their new emphasis was encouraging workplace safety. After World War II the railroad began to use service club meetings for awarding 25-year gold pins and 50-year "Gold Passes" good for free travel anywhere on the system for the remainder of one's life. At the same time clubs became more intentional in their outreach, raising funds for community projects and providing food baskets for the poor at Christmastime.

Railroads had their own self-serving reasons for promoting booster clubs. Of course, they expected them to increase business and efficiency. Obviously they wanted to deflect blacks' unhappiness over the racial job ceiling. And they illogically hoped to quiet discontent over Jim Crow segregation. As one official stated, the IC hoped its clubs would "improve the railroad's reputation for cordial relations with its patrons."[25] To blacks, however, these organizations were social institutions that provided events and programs for their entire communities. Thus, officers had to be persons of sufficient repute and ability to be acceptable to local religious and fraternal leadership. Occupation did not limit civic influence in African American communities. Only three IC booster club officers held jobs that placed them in the top rank of black railroaders, a chief usher (head Red Cap) and two machinists. The other 10 leaders were mostly freight house and roundhouse laborers. (Because they were on the road for long periods, no black firemen, brakemen, porters, cooks, chefs, or waiters held top leadership posts.) In contrast, nearly two-thirds of white club leaders held white-collar jobs, while half of the remainder were conductors and engineers, the prestige operating occupations.[26]

African American railroaders also founded numerous clubs entirely on their own. Following a venerable black tradition, some groups combined social activities with a burial or insurance fund. Such was the L&N Benefit Club, organized by chefs, cooks, and waiters based in Louisville. On one occasion they chartered an entire train of eight coaches, a dining car, and a baggage car in which a band provided music for dancing, for a seven-hour evening excursion. A crowd of 300, including spouses and friends, shared the fun. A similar organization was the Central of Georgia Porters Club, whose membership was initially restricted to porters in the Savannah general offices, but was later opened to other employees. Mutual aid was likewise the objective of IC waiters, cooks, and club-car porters who in 1941 established the Good Fellows Club "to maintain benevolent relationships among the members, especially during illness or misfortune." They paid into a fund from which allotments were disbursed according to need. This type of reciprocal benefit association had been common among blacks for many decades, although such groups were now disappearing with the growth and stability of black insurance companies.[27]

One of the most cherished aspects of black culture was communal singing. No important occasion, whether a safety rally or company picnic, lacked the presence of vocal groups. Spirituals and folksongs were still in fashion into the 1940s, and one of the most popular type of group was the a cappella harmony quartet, which might actually have more than four voices. Numerous ensembles sprang up among black railroaders. In many cases, they were composed of men working at the same job site who began singing for their own pleasure on their lunch breaks, like the Charleston Quartet, four stevedores on the Southern Railway's wharves who sang traditional slave songs of the South Carolina seacoast. The Southern Melody Quintet, C&O section laborers at Parsons Yard, Columbus, Ohio, similarly "specialize[d] in old time melodies." During World War II, 12 N&W Roanoke shop employees calling themselves the Noon-Day Chorus sang at lunchtime every day. Along the L&N in the 1920s and 1930s could be heard a sextet from the South Louisville shops; the Boyles (Alabama) Jubilee Singers (including both shop laborers and switchmen); Nashville freight station employees calling themselves the L&N Four; the Ebony Glee Club, consisting of five freight platform men in Louisville; and the Humming Bird Quartette, four freight platform laborers from East St. Louis, Illinois. Larger ensembles were the Louisville Colored Shopmen's Glee Club, 19 voices strong, and the 50-member Southland Colored Ensemble and Quartet in Birmingham. (The *Humming Bird* and *Southland* were well known L&N passenger trains.) Large events, like the L&N's Safety-Friendly Service rallies, highlighted talented employees and their kin. The first "all colored" rally, in 1938, featured 10 musical acts, including vocal and instrumental solos by a foundry employee, elevator operator, maid, custodian, and the 18-voice Roundhouse Glee Club.[28]

Similar groups performed along the IC. They included the Illinois Central Red Cap Quartet in Chicago; a quartet of shopmen in Jackson, Tennessee; a seven-man gospel ensemble from Paducah, Kentucky; the I. C. Four, from the Paducah shops; the Illinois Central Harmony Boys, all employees of the mechanical department in Memphis; and the Illinois Central Junior Glee Club, six employees from the Nonconnah shops car department in Memphis. Several of these ensembles performed on local radio stations. The most successful was Memphis's Illinois Central Glee Club, later renamed the Humming Birds Quartet, which landed an Okeh Records contract in 1929. Their first appearance on radio station WREC, the "Voice of Memphis," was so well received that they became regular weekly guests. One of their signature numbers, "I'm Goin' Home on the Chickasaw Train," included a whistle and bell plus the "puffing" sound of a locomotive.[29]

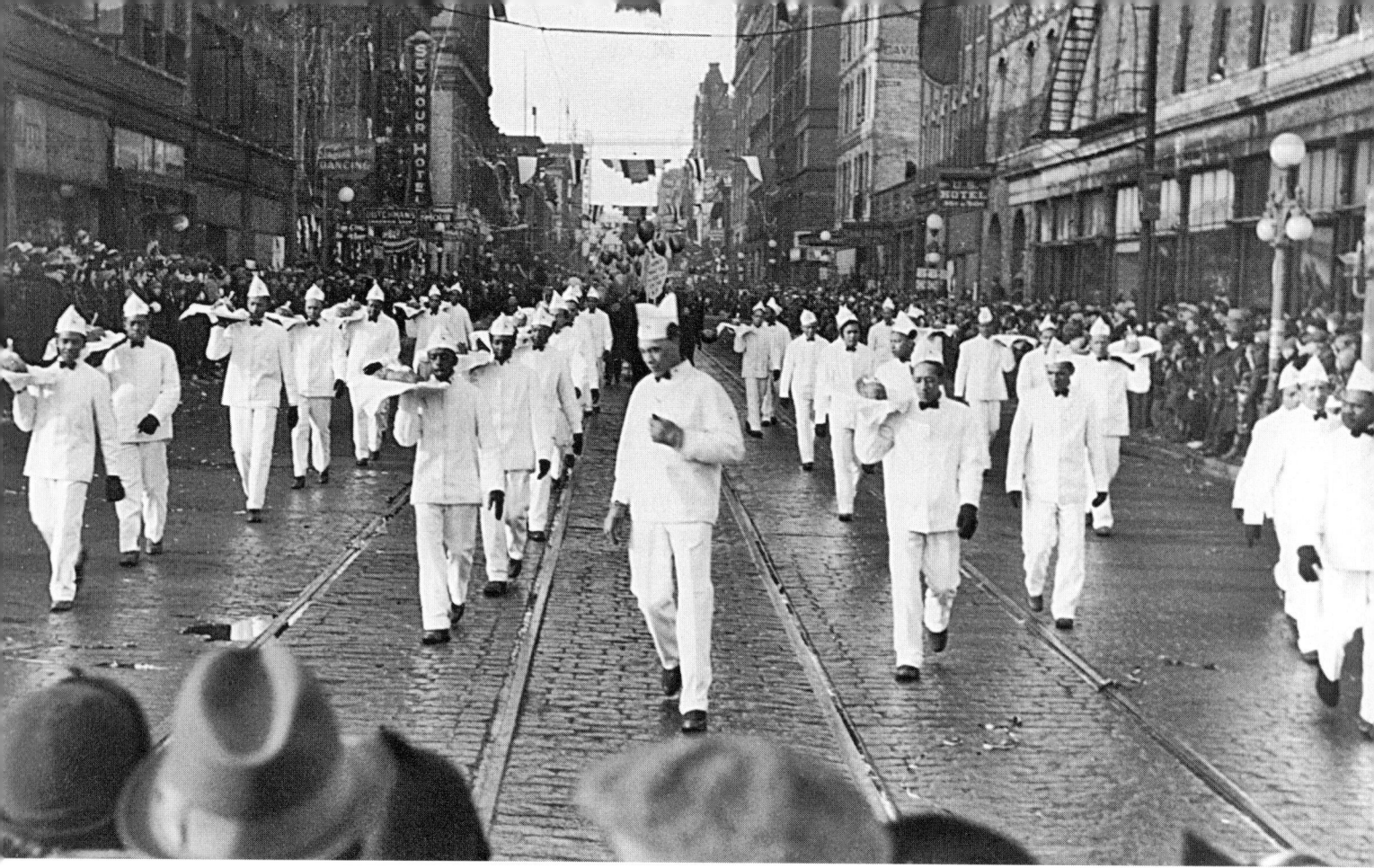

The annual St. Paul (Minnesota) Winter Carnival, featuring a spectacular ice sculpture as well as a parade, offered an opportunity for these Great Northern Railway cooks and waiters, balancing dishes on trays, to strut their stuff before thousands along the 1941 parade route. A smartly uniformed drill team, composed of their daughters, nieces, and younger sisters, also performed. St. Paul Winter Carnival Photograph Collection, Minnesota Historical Society

Black railroaders also formed instrumental ensembles. One of the first actions of the IC's newly established New Orleans booster club was to purchase 32 band instruments. Some members were already accomplished players, but those who were not were invited to take free lessons. Given the prominence of music in the cultural life of black New Orleans, such an initiative is not surprising. IC boosters in Memphis organized a 20-man brass band. As with most formal black organizations, a president, vice president, secretary, and treasurer were chosen. Not to be outdone, local Pullman porters created a nine-piece dance band featuring a Pullman maid as soloist. No location surpassed the Chicago District for Pullman musicality. By 1923, porters there fielded a 50-piece band, a 50-voice chorus, and 10 quartets. Not far behind were the Boston, Philadelphia, Pennsylvania Terminal (New York), and New York districts, each of which also had a band, chorus, and several quartets. And "wearied of the praise showered upon various porter quartets," four Pullman maids running out of Chicago on the *Portland Limited* formed their own ensemble.[30]

The Missouri Pacific's black railroaders similarly knit their communities together through music. The 27-member Kansas City (Missouri) Colored Booster Band played for club events as well as outside dances. Employees in Palestine, Texas, likewise formed a band. When Little Rock boosters organized an excursion to Memphis, their band, resplendent in new uniforms, played en route and then performed two concerts to large crowds. The MoPac workforce in St. Louis included so many talented musicians that two ensembles were formed. And as was the case on many other railroads, workers formed a cappella singing groups, first simply to entertain themselves on work breaks, then to provide inspirational numbers for formal programs. The aptly named Sunshine Quartette, all St. Louis employees, played concerts as far afield as Memphis. (The Missouri Pacific was known as the "Route of the *Sunshine Special*," the name of its premier train.) Even more famous, according to the company magazine, was another St. Louis group, the Diamond Jubilee Quartet, which carried on the tradition of singing spirituals and hymns.[31]

Not all musical groups depended upon a large concentration of workers. Only a modest number of blacks worked at the Santa Fe's shops in Topeka, Kansas, in the early twentieth century but 11 of them formed a Santa Fe Glee Club that for years enjoyed considerable renown. Their repertoire included "all manner of songs from the classics to the latest popular ballads." The group was quite acclaimed at home and, following a performance broadcast on a Kansas City radio station, it laid plans for a 30-city tour all along the line.[32]

Whether they realized it or not, the railroads that most deliberately fostered employee loyalty capitalized on the desire among blacks for identity and community. Certainly the roads were interested mostly in promoting a more stable and conscientious workforce, perhaps with the ancillary effect of retarding independent trade unionism, but their efforts jibed with blacks' need for strong associational ties as a bulwark against the ravages of racism. While railroads encouraged all employees to join booster clubs, black workers used them for purposes beyond those contemplated by whites. No better example of the intersection between corporate and black community interests can be found than the group life of black railroaders on the Missouri Pacific Lines in the 1920s and

1930s. This system included the MoPac itself, plus subsidiaries Texas & Pacific, International–Great Northern, and the Gulf Coast Lines. Its far-flung rail network connected (west to east) Pueblo, Colorado and Omaha, Nebraska with Kansas City, Missouri and St. Louis, while linking the latter two cities with New Orleans and the far corners of Texas: El Paso, Laredo (through San Antonio), and Brownsville (through Houston). It was thus a southern, southwestern, and Great Plains system. Its African American train porters, dining-car waiters and cooks, and section men ranged all over the system, while freight-house truckers could be found in most of the major cities it served. Many black shop workers labored in Texas and Arkansas. Black brakemen and firemen were concentrated on the Gulf Coast Lines (Louisiana and Texas) and on the MoPac's Little Rock Division.

Missouri Pacific Lines' black employees used their strength of numbers to forge formal associational links, based variously on locale and occupation. Men who worked in the South San Antonio (Texas) and McGehee (Arkansas) shops—large complexes, where cars and locomotives were repaired—were divided into many crafts, although most were laborers or helpers to the white craftsmen. This meant they spent nearly all their time in the wheel shop, or boiler shop, or the RIP track, or another specific facility. Their associations allowed them to meet those who worked elsewhere and strengthened the sense of commonality among all black employees at a particular location. The San Antonio shop craft association met in the evenings and on occasion registered a remarkable 80 percent attendance, indicating that such gatherings served important social purposes. At the Little Rock shops, boilermaker helpers, who belonged to an independent black union, held an annual banquet that included their families, friends, and white guests (roundhouse and shop officials). A broader organization was the Missouri Pacific Association, whose various locals brought together power plant employees, coach cleaners, roundhouse laborers, and others. Meetings were important social "glue." After whatever business needed to be transacted, extensive programs included musical numbers, orations by both juveniles and adults, an address by an invited guest, and refreshments (sometimes a supper). Strictly social events also emerged from such workplace associations. Night-shift employees in Little Rock chartered a MoPac bus for a one-day outing. IGN freight-house workers in Houston held annual picnics, one year traveling by train to historic Brazoria on the Brazos River. Gouldsboro's (Louisiana) shop and track workers joined together for similar annual outings. Employees in Monroe and Bastrop, Louisiana, organized several joint outings in 1929 to El Dorado, Arkansas, each group competing to see which could bring the greatest number. Many events included employees and family members as well as friends with no formal connection to the railroad.[33]

Black women railroaders occasionally organized on the basis of their shared workplace. Cleaners and elevator operators in Pennsylvania Railroad offices in Philadelphia organized a Friendly Protective League to enhance fellowship, perform charity, and promote the railroad. During World War II, as African American women were introduced as laborers in the Illinois Central's shops in and around Memphis, they encountered hostility from male workers and social isolation from newly hired white women. Not surprisingly, they formed their own Illinois Central Safety and Social

Club to build bonds of solidarity. Wisely, they met in one another's homes, not the shops, allowing them the freedom to assert their femininity and dignity.[34]

The most prosperous and long-lived of the independent associations among the IC's black railroaders was the Red Caps Club of Chicago, organized in 1922 by men from several railroads who were employed at three of the city's passenger stations. Their purposes were fellowship and encouraging one another to be better workers. The other railroads' Red Caps dropped their memberships during the Depression, but the IC's 125 Red Caps, also known as ushers, held on and even prospered. They were headed by a dynamic leader, chief usher Sandy W. Trice, who was assisted by two vice presidents, financial and corresponding secretaries, a treasurer, a sergeant-at-arms, a chaplain, a reporter, and nine directors. The club took particular satisfaction in the fact that more than 20 former members had completed college and were practicing attorneys, dentists, physicians, and educators. They were equally proud of owning their clubhouse, a three-story stone-faced residence that was remodeled to include reading and card rooms, a pool and billiard room, and a library. The club met its expenses by renting its facilities for lodge meetings and numerous social events. Among the organization's programs was a Sunday Literary Club, which often featured speakers and musicians of national note, and extensive benevolence. During 1934, it distributed $700 to charities and hosted an annual Christmas party with gifts for underprivileged children and food baskets for destitute families. Assisting in these activities was a Ladies Auxiliary.[35]

The most noteworthy female branch of a black railroaders' organization was the Ladies Auxiliary of the Brotherhood of Sleeping Car Porters. First called the Women's Economic Council, it was unique in that its purpose was not benevolence or to promote the business of a railroad, but to help win wage and working improvements for maids and porters from the stubbornly resistant Pullman Company. Naturally, its activities were not featured in the *Pullman News*. In fact, until the BSCP won union recognition and a contract, Auxiliary membership had to be kept secret lest Pullman retaliate against members' husbands, fathers, and brothers. Although they could join the BSCP, Pullman maids were encouraged to become active in the Auxiliary. In addition to supporting the porters, the Ladies Auxiliary advocated for better working conditions and civil rights for all blacks. Members enjoyed a rich social life, visiting one another's homes, holding fund-raising galas, and modeling middle-class female respectability at the same time as they were ardent trade unionists. Historian Melinda Chateauvert writes: "The union wife used her position to expand the power of the trade union movement. She understood that the household budget came from union labor, and returned that money to labor" through purchasing union-made goods, establishing consumer cooperatives, and teaching her children the twin virtues of unionism and civil rights. The two sides of the Auxiliary show remarkable contrasts: tea parties with members attired in formal evening gowns one day, political activism the next. What led them down a more political path than other railroad women's auxiliaries was the unique struggle of the sleeping-car porters union.[36]

Black railroaders and their families found many ways to bond themselves together. As soon as slavery ended, one of the ways former slaves demonstrated their freedom was by traveling. Railroad excursions, blending an attractive destination or program like a county fair with reduced fares, soon became popular. If sufficient numbers were garnered, an entire special train was supplied. The destination might be a picnic ground or amusement park catering to blacks. The prospect of a day's pleasure without the presence of whites or cloud of prejudice was particularly attractive. Other excursions provided group transportation to church or Masonic conventions. Five hundred delegates to the African Methodist Episcopal Zion annual conference in St. Louis in 1904 came in seven chartered trains of Pullman sleepers, thus avoiding Jim Crow cars. One newspaper noted, "as these excursions will start from distant points and be en route for a day or two, the bishops have arranged for religious services to be held on board, a feature of which will be special prayers for the delivery of the negro race from the curse of race prejudice."[37]

The popularity of excursions may be judged from the number of passengers. The annual outing sponsored in 1911 by St. Joseph's African Methodist Episcopal Church, in Durham, North Carolina, attracted 912 participants, surely not only church members, but friends and kinsmen as well. Tragically, their Seaboard Air Line Railway train never reached Charlotte, their destination, because a dispatcher failed to order a freight train traveling in the opposite direction to clear the main at Hamlet. Even though the two trains were traveling slowly, the head-on impact fused both engines together "in a grasp of death." The railroad was negligent in another respect. The special—consisting of seven wooden coaches, each of which could hold no more than 100 passengers, including standees—was greatly overcrowded. It was common practice for railroads to assign their oldest passenger equipment to extras that, in this case, compounded the tragedy. Wooden cars telescoped and splintered easily in collisions. Miraculously, the dead numbered fewer than a dozen, although 60 more were seriously hurt and another 28 suffered minor injuries as 6 of the cars "crumpled like pasteboard." "Great carnage" ensued. A folksong, "The Hamlet Wreck," memorialized the tragedy:

> Now, colored people, I will tell you to your face,
> The train that left Durham was loaded with our race,
> And some did not think of dying
> When they rode on down the line.
> So many have lost their lives.[38]

This event illustrates not only the popularity of excursions, but also the tendency of railroads to assign older, less safe cars for use on black excursions.

The Central of Georgia's Savannah black booster club was particularly successful in sponsoring excursions. In the summer of 1926, 2 special trains took about 2,000 passengers to Augusta to see the C of G All-Star baseball team play the Anderson (South Carolina) Giants. Even during the Depression years, hundreds bought $2 round-trip tickets for the popular 130-mile journeys to Augusta. The 600-member New Orleans IC booster club organized one of the longest excursions, traveling all the way to Chicago in mid-1929 at a special reduced rate.[39] Such an extensive trip held great attraction. Tens of thousands of southern blacks had recently migrated to Chicago, and probably few New Orleaneans did not have a relative or acquaintance that now lived "up South."

A number of other IC booster organizations sponsored popular excursions. The large Memphis club sponsored its own Chicago excursion in 1929, at an affordable $10 fare. More than 600 persons took the trip with railroad officials expressing gratitude for the revenue. Three years before, black employees at Chicago's Burnside shops, with their families and friends, chartered a 15-coach train for a trip to Champaign, Illinois, where more than 1,000 people enjoyed a daylong picnic at the Illinois Central Park. In 1928, an even larger crowd, organized by Paducah, Kentucky shop employees rode 18 coaches on a 32-mile picnic excursion to Kuttawa, on the Cumberland River, a popular resort known for its medicinal mineral springs and summertime evangelistic camp meetings.[40] Water Valley, Mississippi IC boosters celebrated the Fourth of July (and reaffirmed their citizenship) in 1931 with an excursion to Canton, where their special train was met by local boosters and escorted to a restaurant for a "thoroughly satisfying meal." Everyone then watched the Canton and Grenada booster baseball teams battle for the black railroad league championship, followed by a barbecue, dance, and show. Black colleges were important symbols of racial progress, and their special events also drew excursionists. Again in 1931, Water Valley boosters reserved a coach to go to Holly Springs for Rust College's annual intercollegiate debate tournament.[41] Excursions remained attractive in the 1930s, but the renewal of prosperity in the 1940s reduced their appeal. After World War II, more and more blacks could afford automobiles and enjoy "motoring" on their own. Group activities began to decline as all Americans sought—and could afford—more individualistic pleasures.

Black railroaders also expressed their collective identities when opportunities arose to participate in larger community events. For a number of years, Chicago and other cities hosted an annual Railroad Week in June, including parades. In 1935, one contingent in the Chicago festivities was the Illinois Central station usher corps (Red Caps), led by Sandy Trice. Each of the 54 uniformed marchers carried an American flag. Another large group included dining-car stewards, chefs, and waiters whose "immaculate uniforms made them a conspicuous feature of the procession."[42] An even larger civic event was the annual Winter Carnival in St. Paul, Minnesota. In 1941, more than two dozen uniformed Northern Pacific Railway cooks and waiters marched in formation past thousands of spectators, each balancing, on one hand, a tray with serving dishes. The following year featured "the only colored girls' group in the parade," more than 20 young relatives of commissary and dining-car employees. About half were members of a drum and bugle corps, wearing sweaters emblazoned with the NP logo. The others were baton-twirling majorettes in cheerleader outfits, also bearing the railroad's emblem.[43] Massed Pullman porters and maids participated in numerous community parades or those they organized themselves. Such events allowed black railroaders to present themselves to a wider public not in their customary roles, as servants, but as proud, dignified, individuals. This kind of civic participation may not always have been voluntary, however. Black Missouri Pacific employees joined in the 1928 United Confederate Veterans parade in Little Rock, Arkansas, along with white employees.[44] Whether they had a choice in commemorating the Lost Cause is uncertain.

Organizing parade participation, excursions, picnics, ball games, and other recreational activities provided numerous opportunities for black initiative. Such events required extensive planning and those entrusted with leadership took their responsibilities seriously. The 1928 Paducah IC shop employees' excursion to Kuttawa was shepherded by an eight-man committee, including a chairman, a vice chairman, a treasurer, a secretary, chairmen of safety and decorating committees, and two additional committeemen. On the day of the event they were proudly photographed for the *Illinois Central Magazine* wearing summer white trousers and shirts with ties. With 18 coaches full of guests—more than 1,000 riders—theirs was a weighty responsibility that would not go unappreciated by their friends, neighbors, and co-workers, nor by the magazine's black readers. Whites might pay little attention to such efforts, but to Paducah's 6,000 African American residents, this was a demonstration of real community leadership.[45]

Shared employment also created bonds of mutual obligation and support. Black railroaders expected their fellows to care about them. Pullman porters in the New York region used the pages of the *New York Age* to strengthen their "kinship." Two weekly columns reported "family" news, particularly illnesses, retirements, and deaths. Eulogies described the ideal traits of Pullman service, from the porters' point of view. Porters were frequently admonished to visit sick brethren. Duty also included not "laying off" after payday, which burdened more conscientious porters with having to double out. All was not negative, however. Weddings, births, graduations, and promotions were celebrated. Social visits to one another's homes were also noteworthy.[46] Even gossip served to build community. Such news about fellow employees and their families was also a staple of employee magazines. And the most common photographs black railroaders submitted for publication featured their children. Having a snapshot taken in the 1920s and 1930s was a big deal, and it must have been a source of pride to see a son's or daughter's photo in print. One's fellow employees were expected to share that joy.

For more than 100 years, being an African American railroader meant enduring the assaults of racism. Job ceilings were absolute; no matter one's aptitude or ambition, blacks could not become engineers or conductors, freight-house clerks or station agents, telegraphers, or even typists. But these very restrictions threw black railroaders upon themselves, requiring them to develop bonds of mutuality. Facing these impenetrable barriers, they used their occupational identity to build social networks, care for one another, celebrate life's ups and downs, and survive as whole, healthy people. It is ironic that what was intended to limit and circumscribe them certainly did that, but it also drew them together and gave them a collective bulwark that they would not have had as individuals. Just as their slave forebears learned that communal survival strategies were preferable to individualistic efforts, they discovered strength in defining and identifying themselves as communities of railroaders. A demonstration of this phenomenon was the annual Mother's Day service in Washington, D.C., organized by dining-car employees of the several railroads operating into that city. In 1943, more than 700 participants honored the mothers of railroaders, their deceased associates, and comrades serving in the military.[47]

The group life constructed by black railroaders not only enriched their individual lives, but also enriched the broader black communities of which they were a part. During the segregation era, many public entertainments and social occasions were open to whites only. Hence the concerts, excursions, picnics, dances, and ball games sponsored by African American railroaders significantly supplemented the limited commercial entertainments and those sponsored by black schools, churches, and fraternal organizations. Further, the proliferation of railroaders' clubs offered blacks much wider opportunities in which to exercise leadership, hold offices, organize benevolence, and, in general, stand out in one's community. The larger society little appreciated, or even noticed, blacks' achievements, but railroaders' organizations and activities offered important venues for public recognition within the black world. Where numbers of black railroaders were concentrated, leadership emerged, whether in large cities like Memphis and St. Louis or small towns like Water Valley, Mississippi or McGehee, Arkansas. Railroading was an honorable profession, no matter that most were restricted to hard, often dirty, physical labor. Black railroaders were generally respected, not just for their hard work under often-dangerous circumstances, but also for their financial and leadership contributions to racial uplift and progress.

Railroaders' organizational activities also added entertainment and variety to the rhythms of life. All was not toil and hardship and discrimination. Reaching far back into slavery, blacks had always found pleasures in the midst of adversity, refusing to let one's predicament steal all positive meaning from life. Railroaders were more fortunate than many other blacks because they were often employed in large enough numbers to constitute self-conscious and self-identifying social groupings. Section workers and passenger train crews had more difficulty participating in such activities because their work often took them away from home. But they were nonetheless still part of the black railroad fraternity. The railroads insisted, past World War II, in identifying them and separating them as "colored." But this very distinction, meant to reinforce their subordinate positions and roles, knit them together and encouraged them to contribute to and lead their communities.

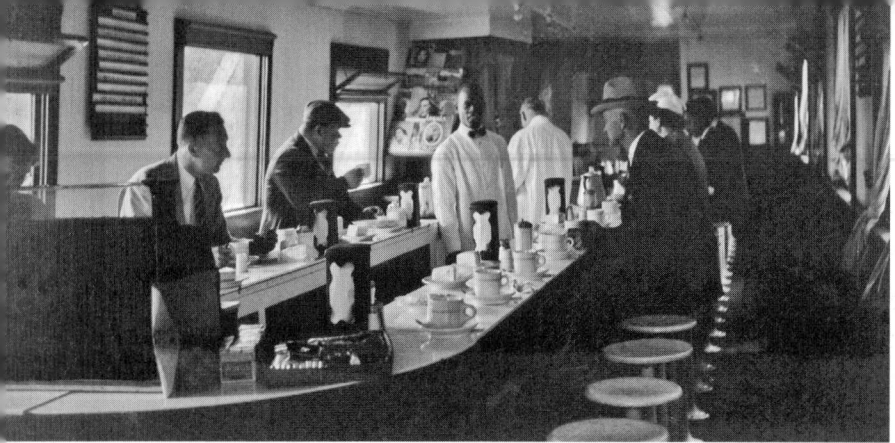

(ABOVE) *Most railroads' passenger ferries had a lunchroom or café, even on a short (1/2 mile) crossing like that made by the Sacramento Northern's* Ramon, *traversing Suisun Bay in the upper reaches of the San Francisco Bay. The cook and waiters were black, like the staff on many other railroad ferries. The photo dates from the 1930s. David Merrill photograph, Western Railway Museum, Bay Area Electric Railroad Association, Suisun City, CA*

(BELOW) *A black fireman, goggles pushed back upon his cap, inspects his Louisville & Nashville Railroad "Mountain"-type fast passenger locomotive while the engineer waits in the cab. Many high-seniority black firemen in the South lost their preferred passenger runs to junior white firemen in the 1930s, when this photograph was probably taken. Hard-fought court victories belatedly preserved the jobs of a dwindling number of them. E. L. DeGolyer, Jr. Photograph Collection, DeGolyer Library, Southern Methodist University*

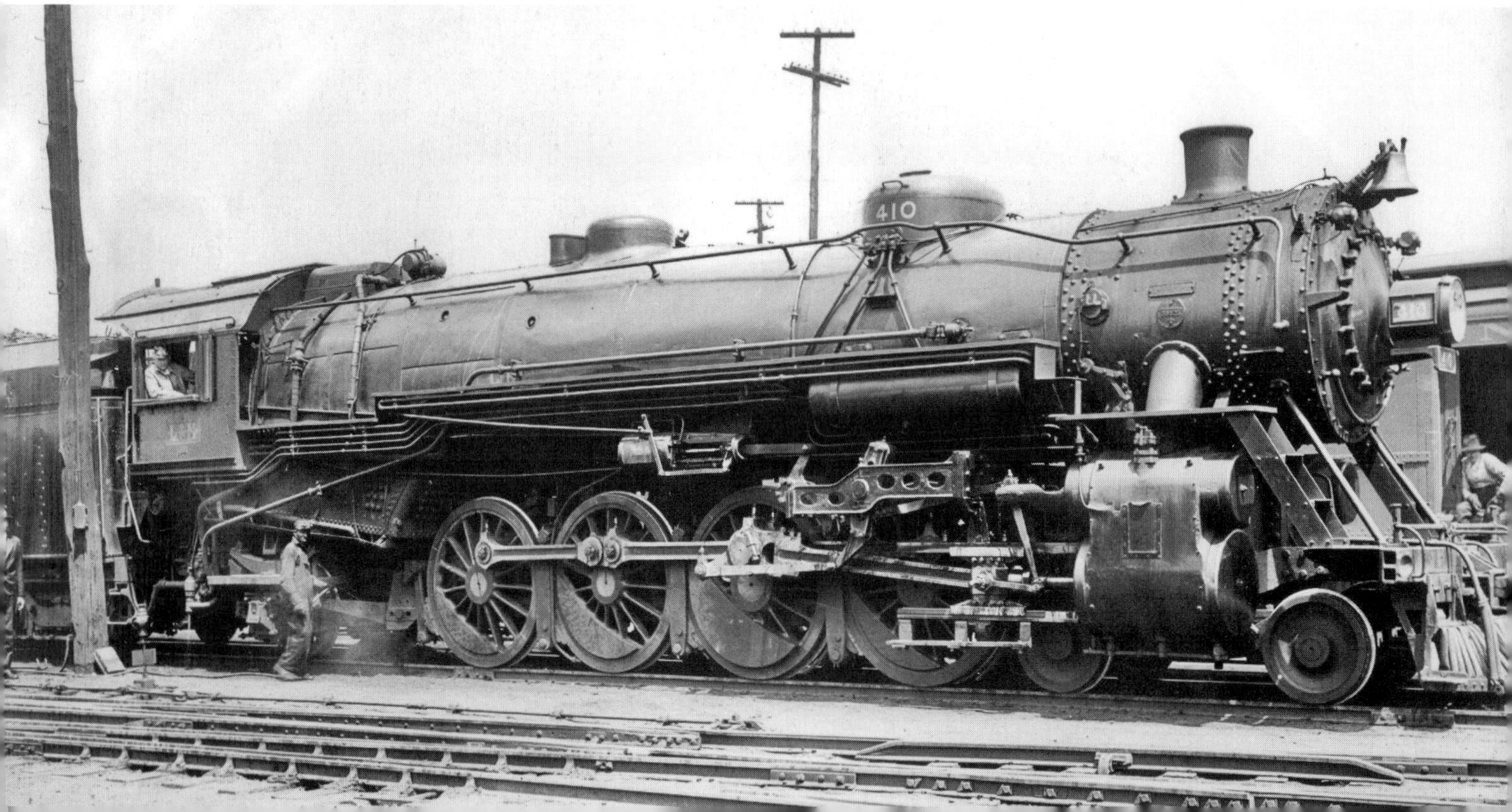

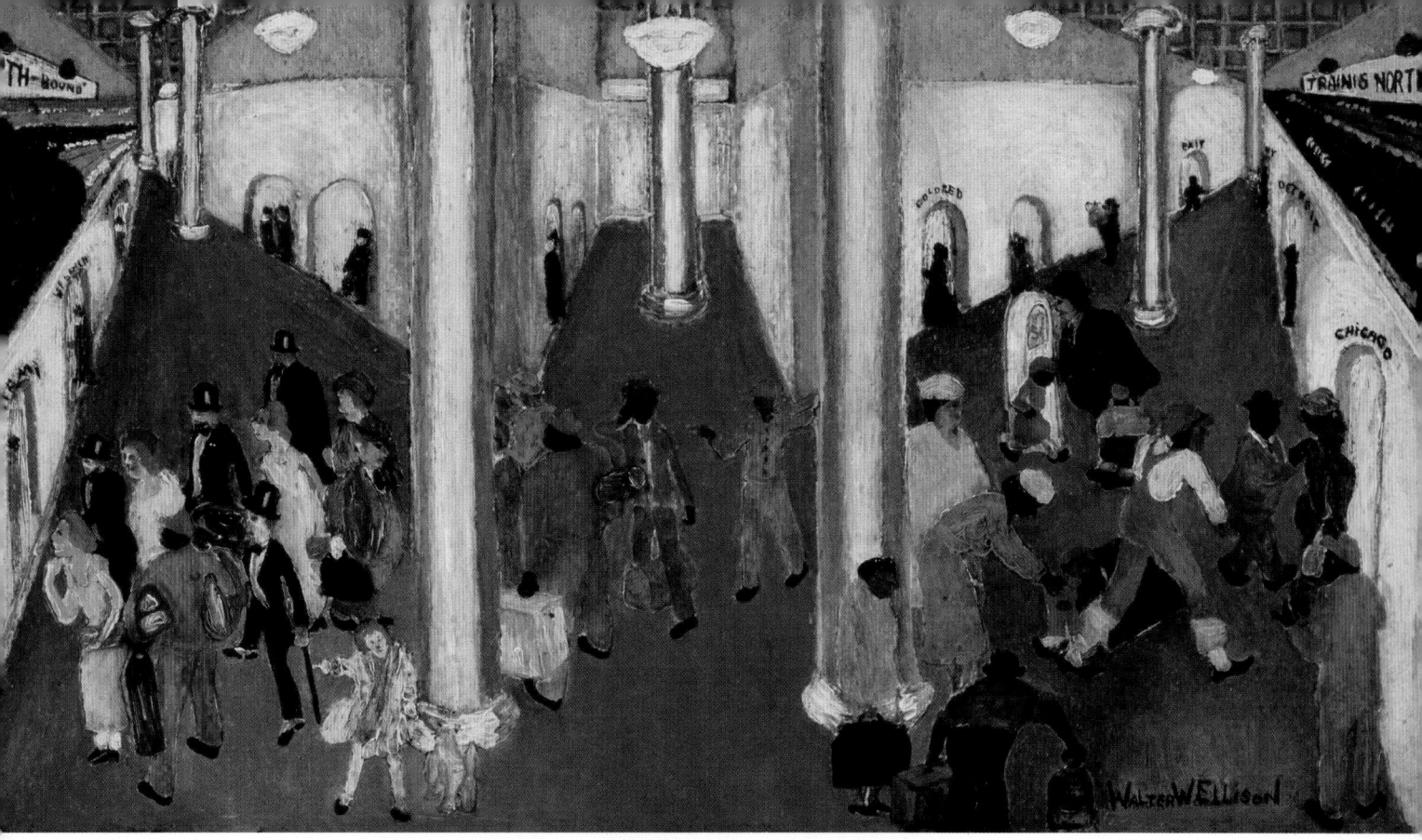

Walter Ellison, Train Station, *1936*. WPA Federal Art Project artist Ellison composed this work in the shape of the letter W after the initial of his first name. It contrasts affluent whites traveling elegantly to Florida vacations with working-class blacks embarking on hopeful Great Migration odysseys to the North and Midwest. Different worlds and destinies continue to separate the races. Charles M. Kurtz Charitable Trust and Barbara Neff Smith and Solomon Byron Smith funds; through the prior gifts of Florence Jane Adams, Mr. and Mrs. Carter H. Harrison, and estate of Celia Schmidt, The Art Institute of Chicago

359

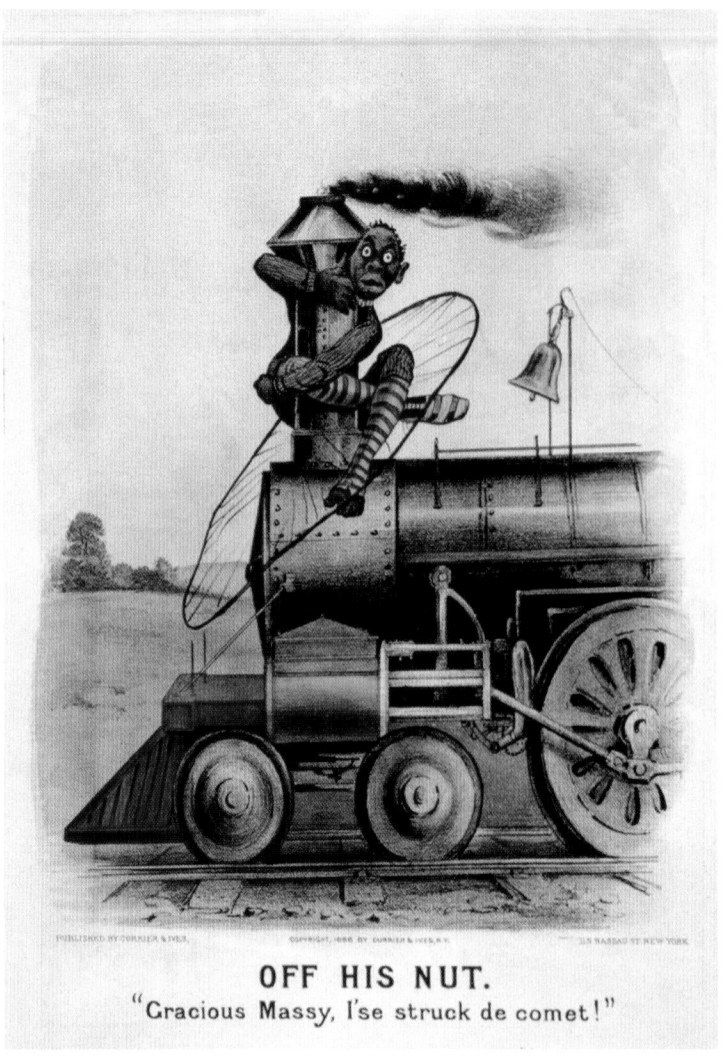

OFF HIS NUT.

"Gracious Massy, I'se struck de comet!"

Many of Currier & Ives's popular nineteenth-century prints featured railroad themes. Some depicted actual railroads, but others were crude caricatures drawing on the popular racism of the day. This typical example, from 1886, portrays a black bicyclist with grotesque features, outlandish dress, and fractured speech, who has paid the price for stupidly ignoring an oncoming locomotive. Prints and Photographs Division, Library of Congress

(OPPOSITE) Atypical for the late nineteenth century, this advertising poster extols the Cincinnati, Hamilton & Dayton Railroad's sleeping- and dining-car services. It portrays a black waiter with rare dignity, not with the exaggerated features and minstrel behavior common in the popular culture of the day. Theodore Kornweibel collection

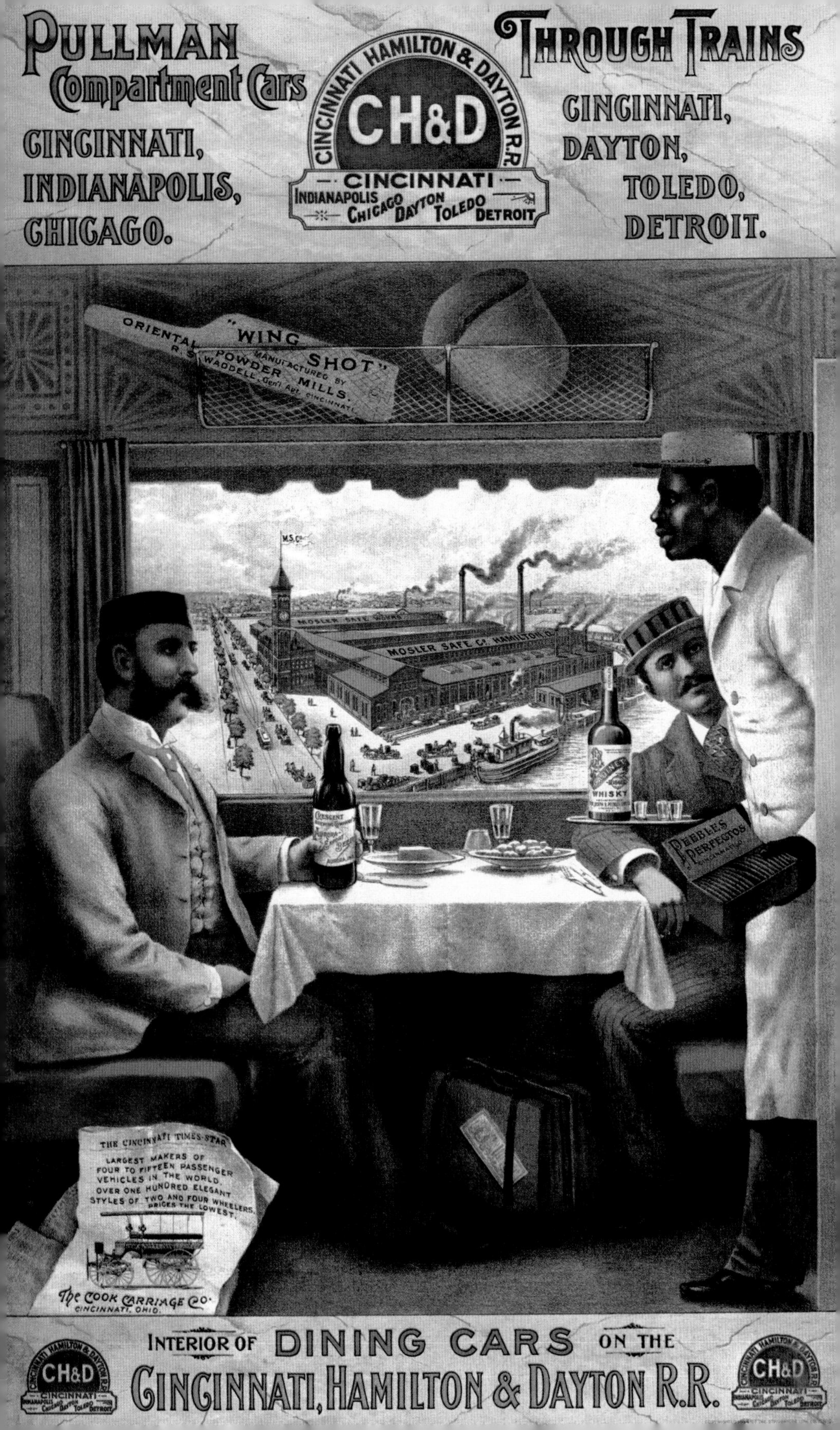

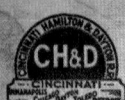
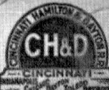

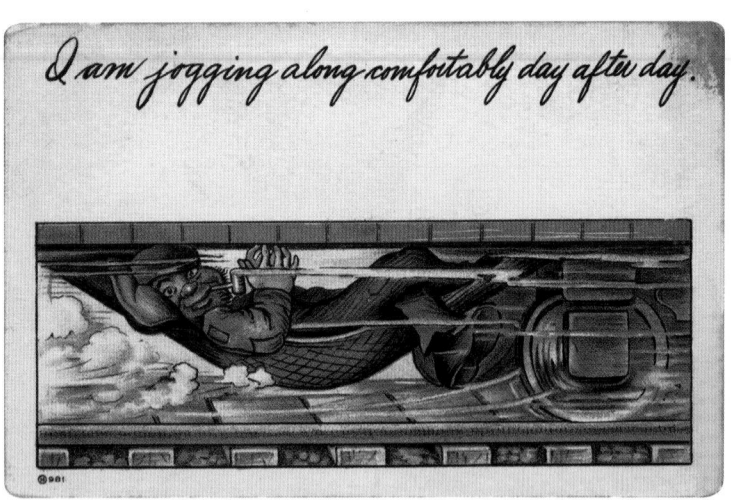

I am jogging along comfortably day after day.

(ABOVE) *Most black hobos were migratory workers, traveling on the cheap in search of jobs. But popular American culture stereotyped black males as lazy, shiftless, footloose, fond of watermelon, and prone to stealing chickens. This postcard from the early twentieth century depicts a happy-go-lucky fellow "riding the rods." Theodore Kornweibel collection*

(BELOW) *Racist postcards have a long pedigree. Some are still produced today. Those employing railroad themes from the early twentieth century caricatured blacks as dim-witted and grotesque in their physical features, as this example from the 1910s shows. Theodore Kornweibel collection*

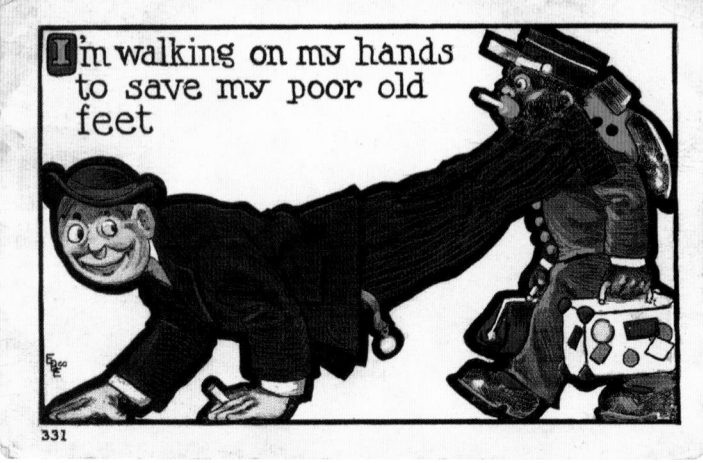

I'm walking on my hands to save my poor old feet

331

(OPPOSITE) *W. C. Handy is often called the "Father of the Blues." Although he did not originate that musical form, he helped popularize it. The sheet music for "The Yellow Dog Rag" was published in 1914. Recorded by Handy's band a few years later, it is considered the first railroad blues recording. Historic American Sheet Music Collection, Rare Book, Manuscript, and Special Collections Library, Duke University*

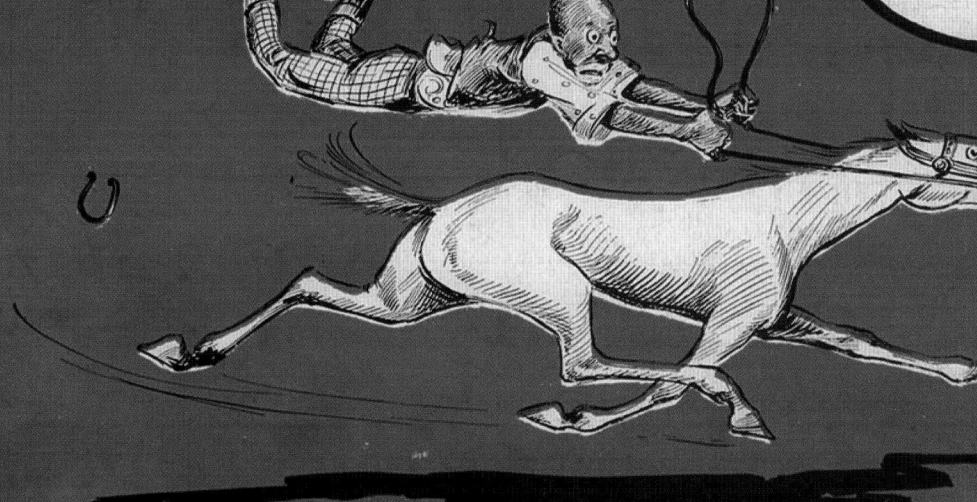

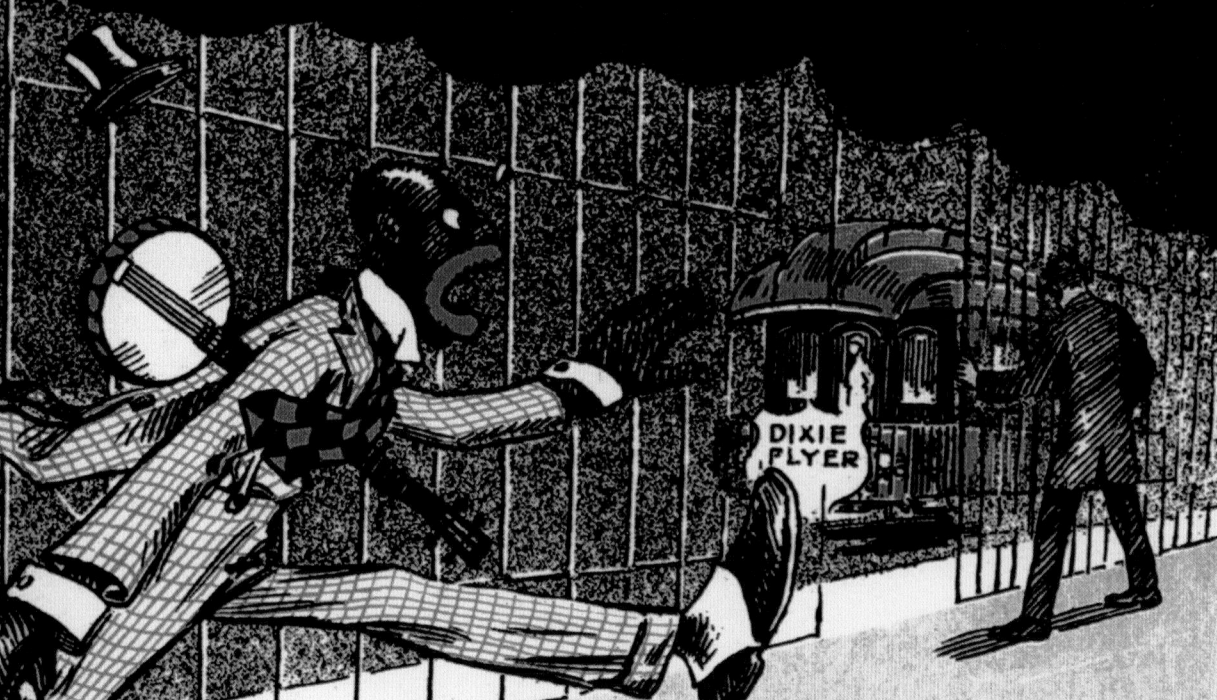

HOLD DAT TRAIN!

WORDS BY
NEILE EDWARDS

MUSIC BY
WALLACE C. CHAMBERS

SOUTHERN MUSIC PUBLISHING CO.

BIRMINGHAM
1814 3rd. Ave.

ATLANTA
·HOME OFFICE·
701-8 Trust Co. of Georgia Bldg.

JACKSONVILLE
28. W. Adams St.

(OPPOSITE) *Every minstrel stereotype appears on the cover of "Hold Dat Train!" from 1919. A gangly black man with huge lips and hands, wearing ridiculously dandified clothes, with banjo in hand and top hat flying, is shown running to catch a train "back home to Dixie Land." Sheet Music Collection, John Hay Library, Brown University*

Sheet music covers and lyrics perpetuated unflattering stereotypes of those black railroaders most familiar to whites, the Pullman porters and Red Caps. The cover of "Pullman Porter Blues," published in 1921, used the familiar caricatures of exaggerated lips and eyes while the lyrics sneeringly ridiculed the porters' aspirations. Theodore Kornweibel collection

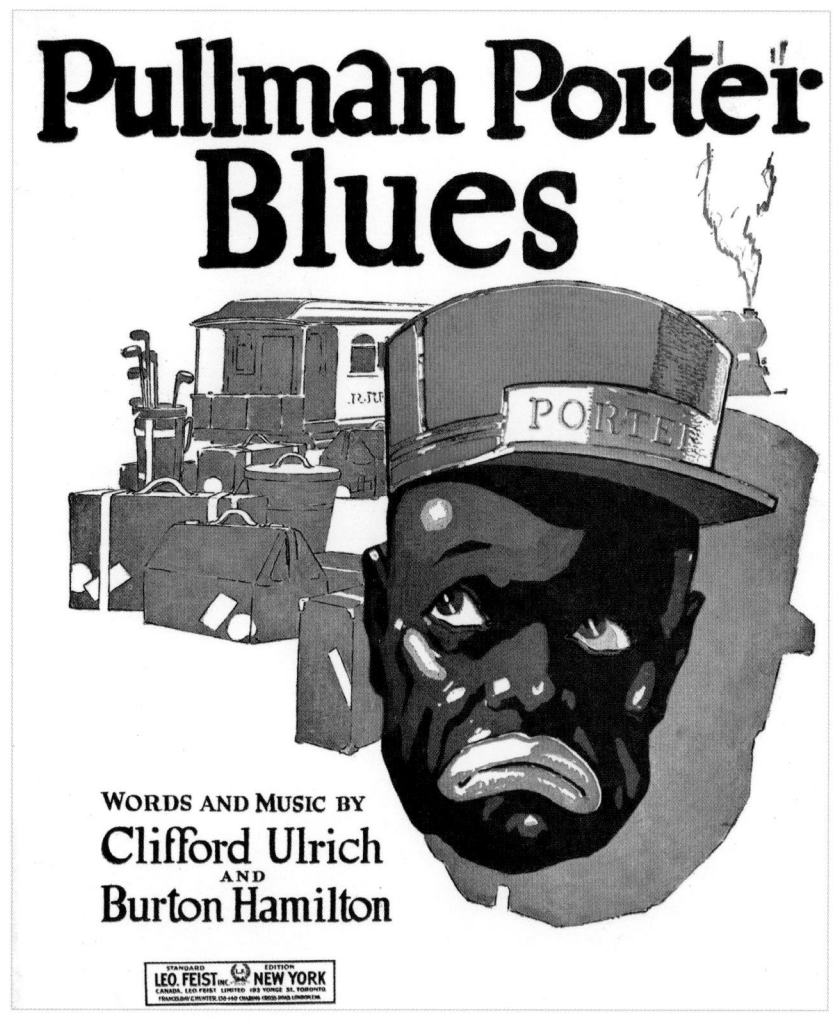

(BELOW) *Pullman porters became stock advertising figures in the first half of the twentieth century, used to promote the sale of many different products. A can of Boyer's Metal Polish marketed in the 1920s—also known as "3B," or "Boyer's Best Brand"—contained the "endorsement" of a cuspidor-cleaning porter speaking in a fractured black lingo. Theodore Kornweibel collection*

(ABOVE) *Passions ran high during the nationwide shop workers' strike in 1922. Black as well as white laborers were urged not to "scab." On many railroads outside the South, where African Americans had never had the opportunity to obtain shop work, many saw no reason to honor picket lines thrown up by white unions that continued to exclude them. Whether this business-card-size flier was effective in persuading blacks to forsake jobs on the Pere Marquette, which crisscrossed Michigan, is unknown. Theodore Kornweibel collection*

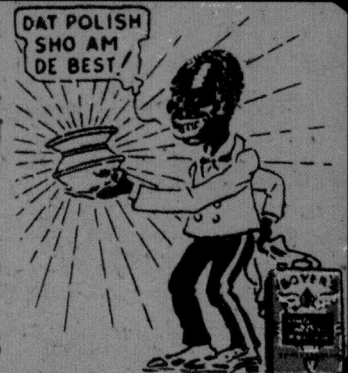

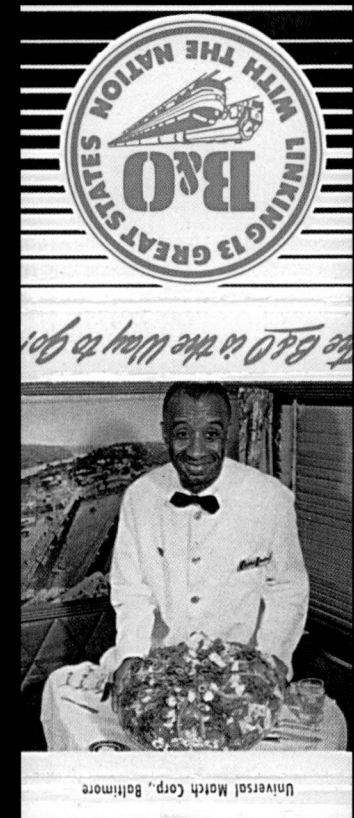

(RIGHT) *A Baltimore & Ohio Railroad matchbook cover from the post–World War II years. By this time some railroads were depicting their black employees in a more dignified manner. This matchbook advertised the B&O's "help yourself salad bowl" offer of unlimited servings. Theodore Kornweibel collection*

Universal Match Corp., Baltimore

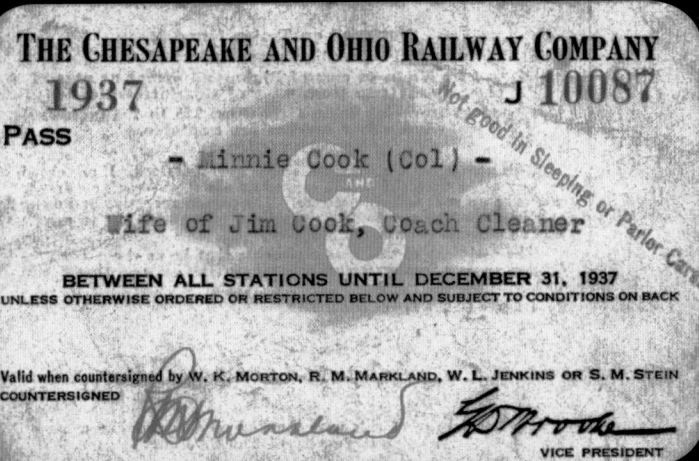

THE CHESAPEAKE AND OHIO RAILWAY COMPANY

1937   J 10087

PASS

– Minnie Cook (Col) –
AND
Wife of Jim Cook, Coach Cleaner

Not good in Sleeping or Parlor Cars

BETWEEN ALL STATIONS UNTIL DECEMBER 31, 1937
UNLESS OTHERWISE ORDERED OR RESTRICTED BELOW AND SUBJECT TO CONDITIONS ON BACK

Valid when countersigned by W. K. MORTON, R. M. MARKLAND, W. L. JENKINS OR S. M. STEIN
COUNTERSIGNED

VICE PRESIDENT

Passes, for oneself and family members, were one of the benefits of railroad employment. Until after World War II, all southern railroads, and many elsewhere, insisted on identifying black employees and their family members by race, with the designations (col) or (c). Annual passes were generally good only for travel in coaches. Black families frequently used passes to visit kinsmen, attend distant athletic events, and go to the North for non-segregated recreation and entertainment. Theodore Kornweibel collection

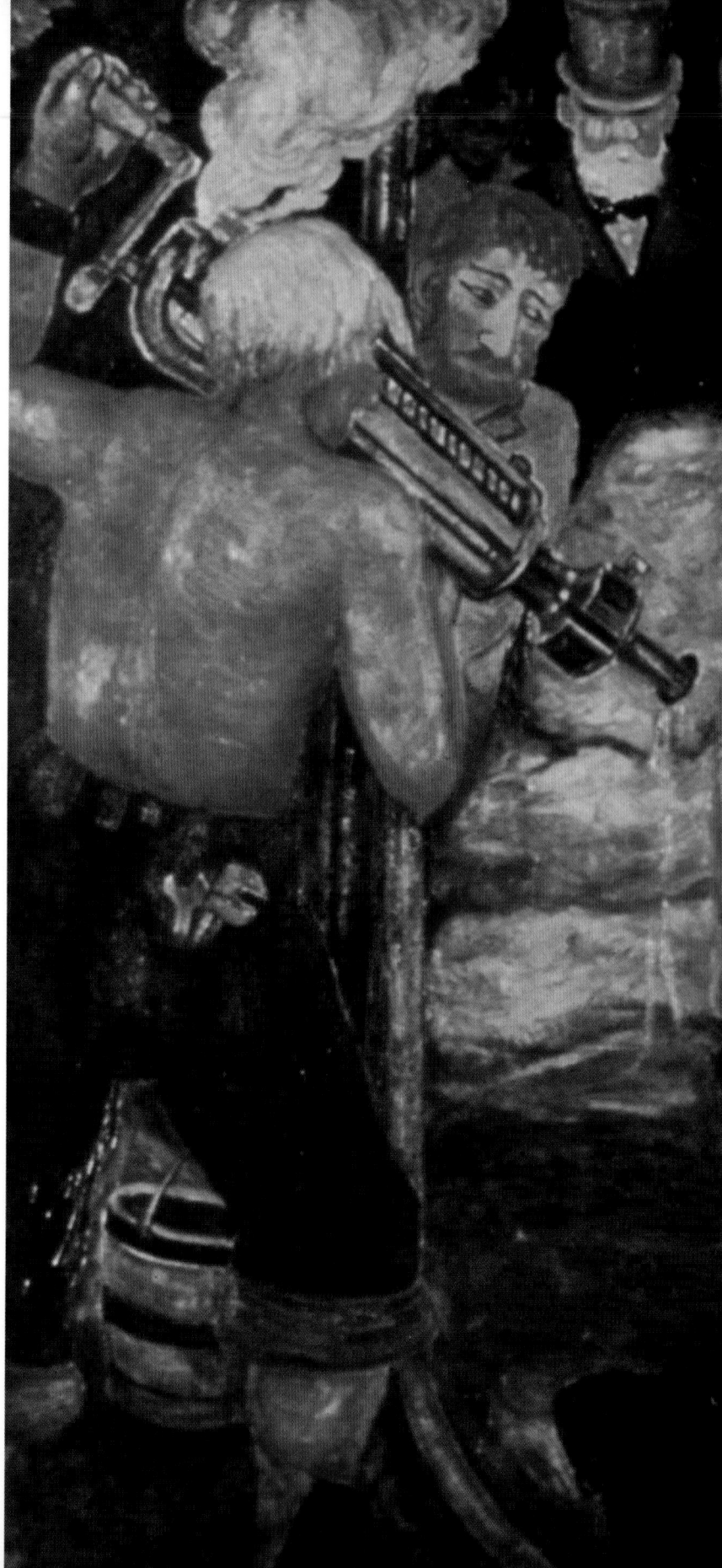

Palmer Hayden, John Henry on the Right, Steam Drill on the Left, *1944–47. The John Henry saga fascinated Hayden for several reasons. His story symbolized African Americans' transformation from agricultural to industrial workers, the strength of black workingmen, and Palmer's belief, now vindicated, that his hero was not merely legendary but also a real historical figure. The contest between steam drill and raw muscle portrays John Henry and his "shaker" gleefully besting the mechanical device and its beleaguered operators. Palmer C. Hayden collection, gift of Miriam A. Hayden, The Museum of African American Art, Los Angeles*

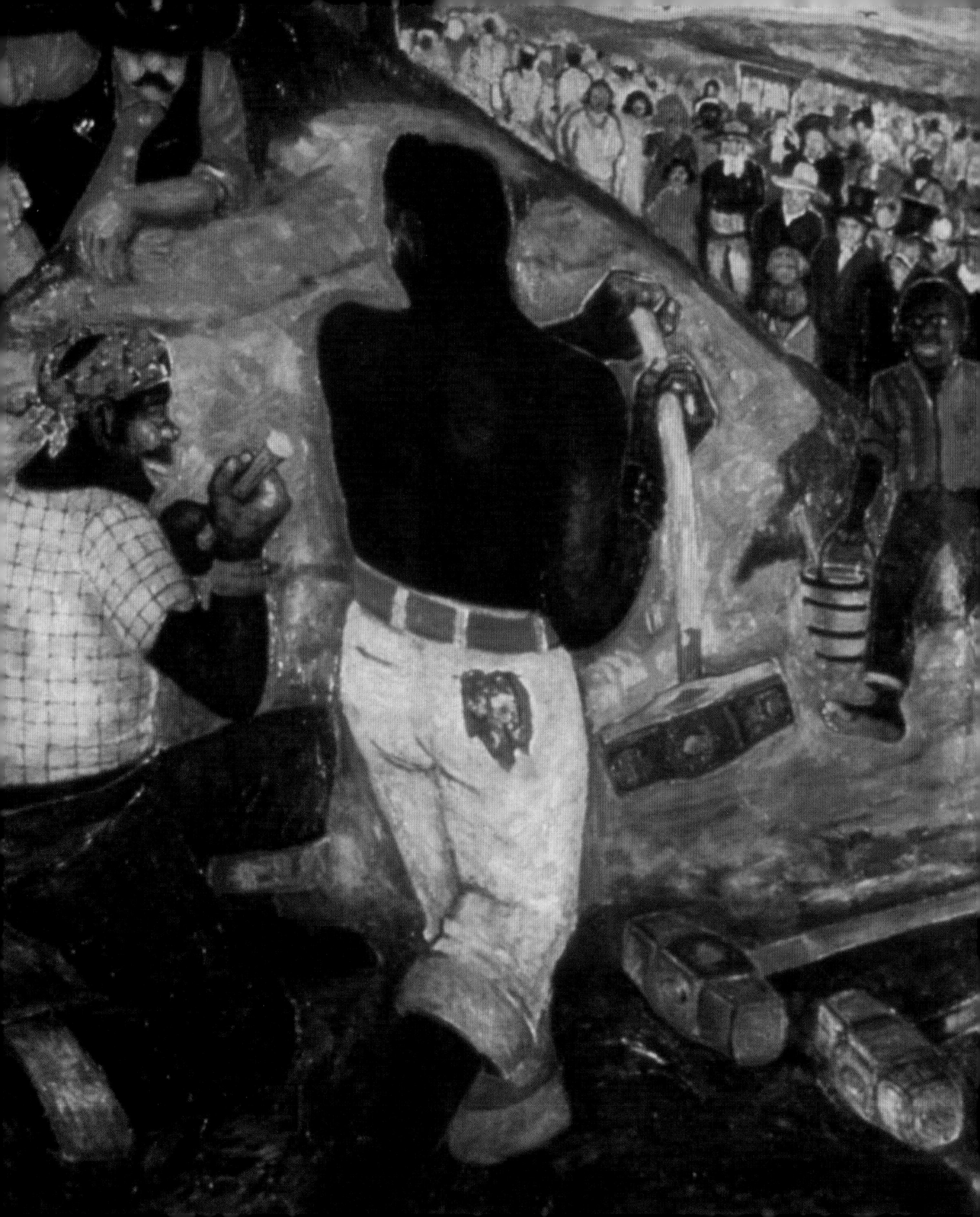

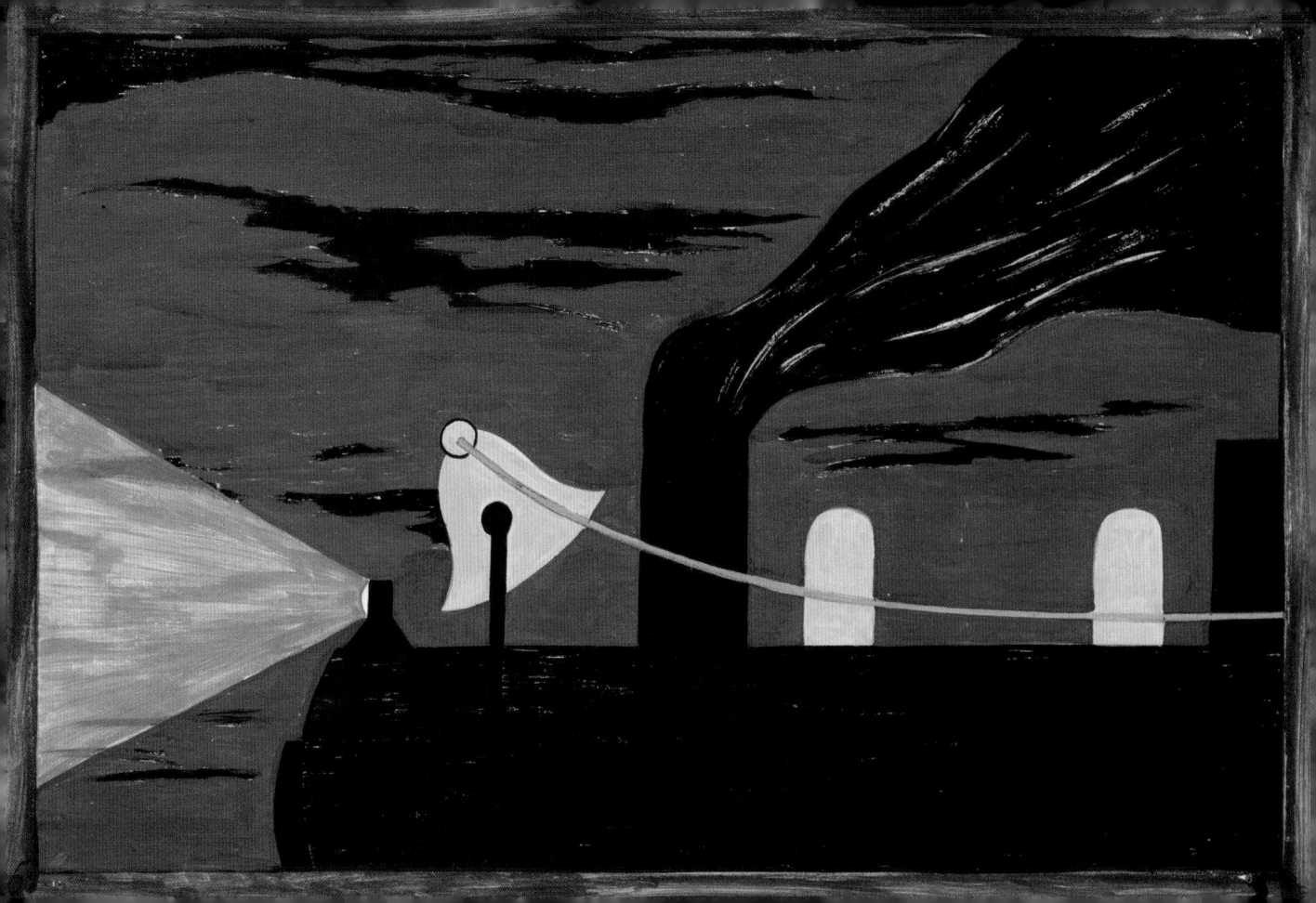

(OPPOSITE) *Jacob Lawrence,* The Migration Series, Panel no. 5: Migrants were advanced passage on the railroads, paid for by northern industry. Northern industry was to be repaid by the migrants out of their future wages, *1940–41. Nearly 20 percent of the 60 paintings in Lawrence's Migration Series employ railroad imagery to convey the yearnings and aspirations of blacks leaving the South for better lives and opportunities in the North. Here a locomotive speeding through the night symbolizes both the urgency of escape from the South and also the desire to quickly reach the hoped-for Promised Land. A piercing headlight leads the way, lending hope in the darkness as migrants press on toward unknown destinies. The Phillips Collection, Washington, DC. © 2009 The Jacob and Gwendolyn Lawrence Foundation, Seattle/Artists Rights Society (ARS), New York*

William H. Johnson, Lunchtime Rest, *c. 1940–41. Johnson, like other artists exploring the African American railroad heritage, focuses on overall-wearing manual laborers, not the Pullman porters and dining-car waiters more familiar to whites. Here exhausted railroad construction workers, having shed their shoes, are trying to recoup their strength in a few minutes' repose. Their elongated bodies, oversize in comparison to the steam shovel and cars, emphasize the continuing reliance on black muscle power despite the advances of mechanization. Gift of the Harmon Foundation, Smithsonian American Art Museum*

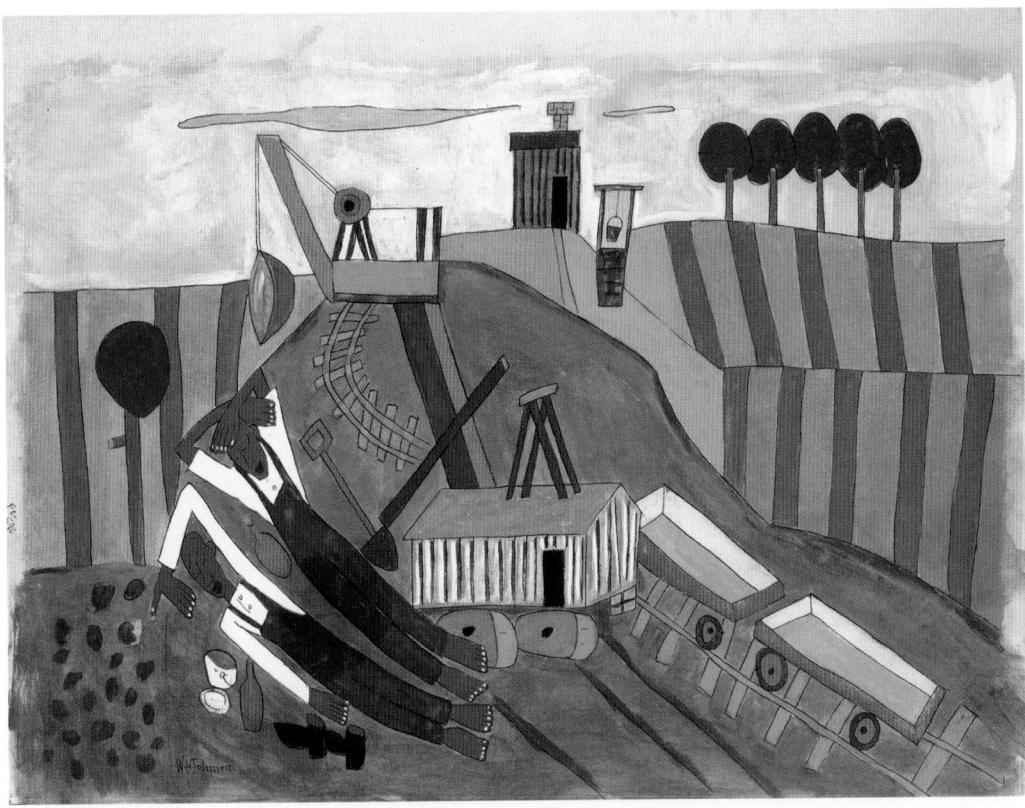

Mark Priest, The Rail Laying, *1998. Priest was a maintenance of way laborer on the Louisville & Nashville Railroad before becoming an artist. His experiences, bad as well as good, inspired dozens of railroad-theme paintings. Human figures dominate his scenes, even though the workers' bosses regarded them as expendable human machines. Women worked alongside men in the post–civil rights era. Like the men, some survived while others quickly quit. No matter one's gender, each had to pull his or her own weight, like this female spike driver. As far back as slavery, black women performed hard manual railroad labor, and that practice has here come full circle, over a century later.*
© *Mark Anthony Priest*

(OPPOSITE) *Romare Bearden,* Pittsburgh Memories, *1984. Dozens of Bearden's collages include steam locomotives interrupting conversations, parting lovers, and, as here, intruding an impersonal industrial order into the intimacies of black families. A stooped workingman leaves the warmth and shelter of home grudgingly, pulled toward the smoking engine and into a cold, geometric world. Nothing is static. Modernity is reshaping traditional black life. Although an oil lamp still provides illumination, a Victrola plays the latest music. Carnegie Museum of Art, Pittsburgh, gift of Mr. and Mrs. Ronald R. Davenport and Mr. and Mrs. Milton A. Washington. Art* © *Romare Bearden Foundation. Licensed by VAGA, New York, NY*

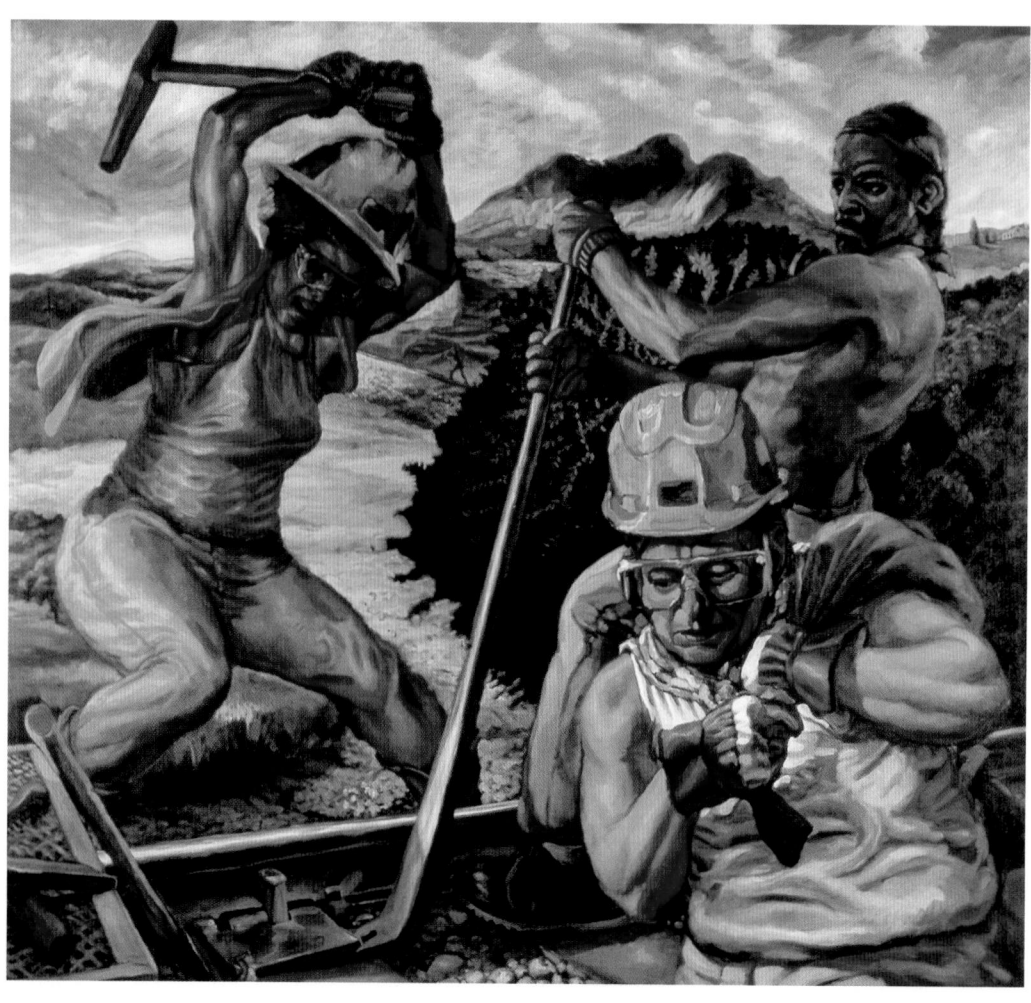

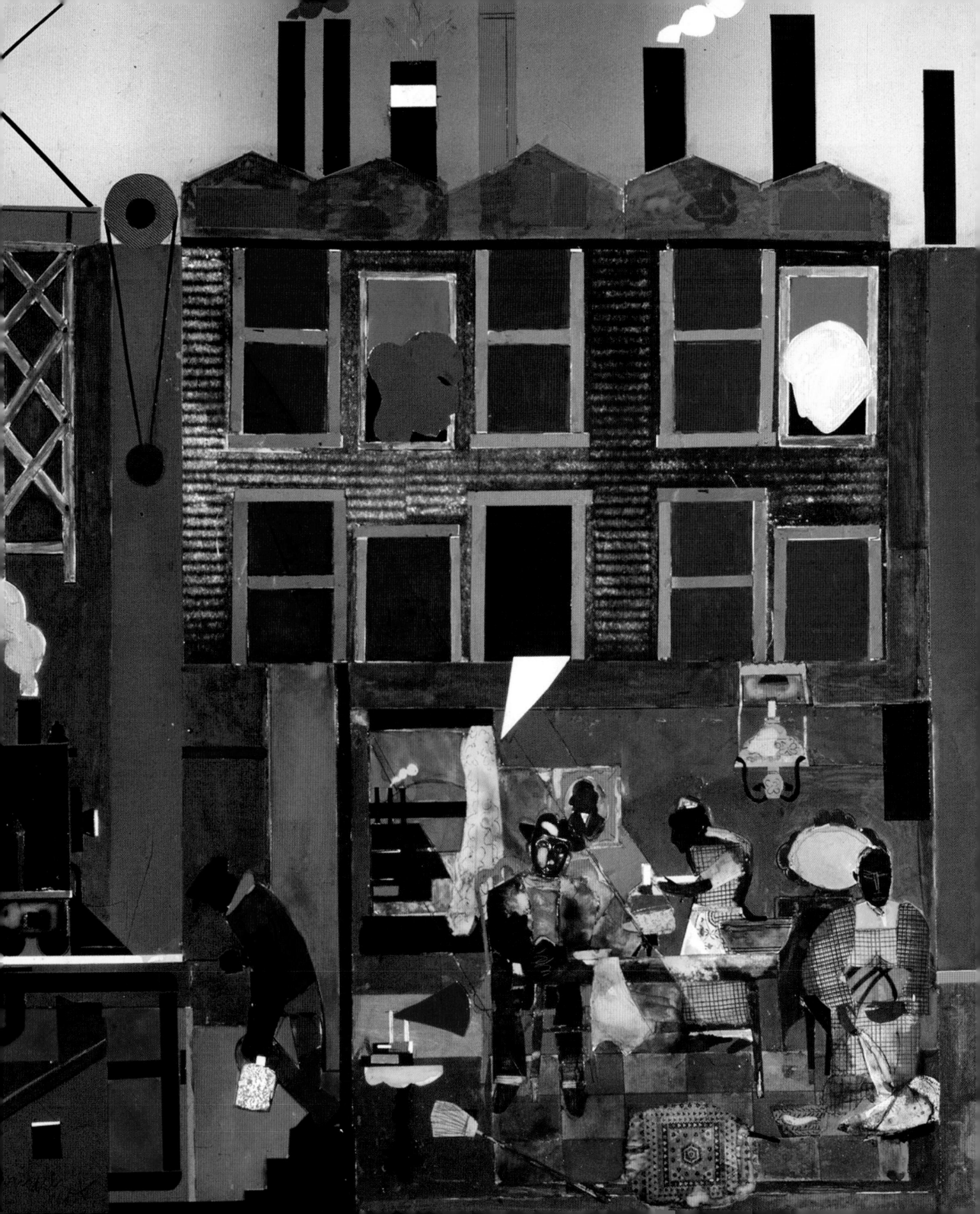

John Biggers, The Gleaners, *1943. Inspired by Millet's* The Gleaners, *Biggers depicts black women gathering coal that has fallen from locomotive tenders alongside the tracks, a venerable survival tactic employed by the poor of all races. The Great Depression has brought upheaval of earthquake magnitude. Men are absent from the painting. Perhaps they have been laid off from the factories, whose smoke-stacks breathe no smoke. The railroad is a thin lifeline, but it, and the rest of industrial America, offers little hope to the scarred land-scape. Art © Estate of John T. Biggers; courtesy of Michael Rosenfeld Gallery, LLC, New York, NY. Licensed by VAGA, New York, NY*

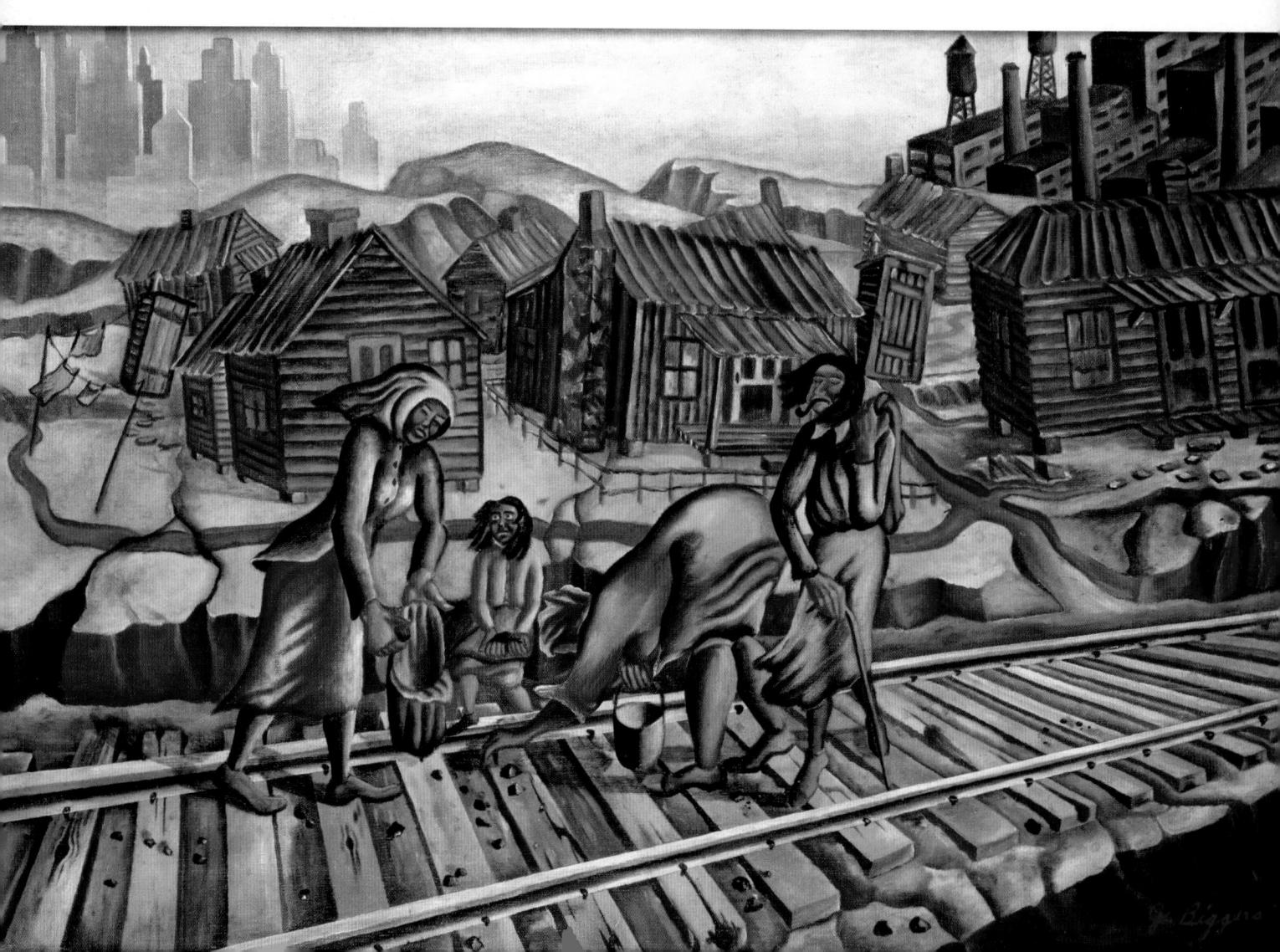

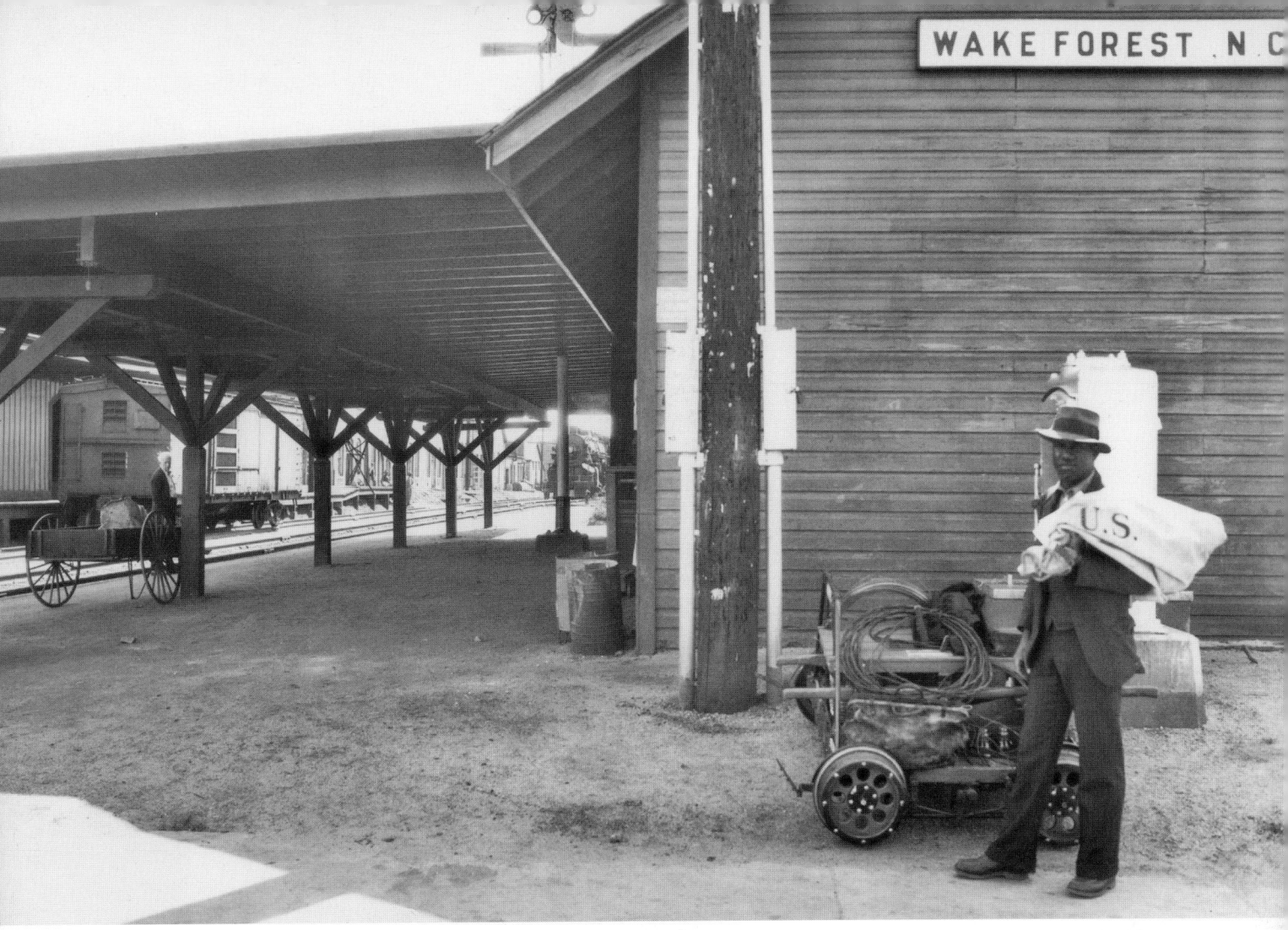

As a Seaboard Air Line Railway train approaches in 1932, a mail courier waits to hand up a sack of first-class mail to a clerk in the railway post office car. If it were a smaller town where the train would not stop, he would mount a catcher pouch on the trackside mail crane for pickup "on the fly." North Carolina Collection, University of North Carolina Library at Chapel Hill

"A GRACIOUS AND OBLIGING GENTLEMAN"

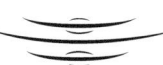

Red Caps and Other Station Personnel

The most familiar African American figure at railroad stations was the Red Cap, who carried departing passengers' luggage from curbside to the baggage room, for later loading on a baggage car, or directly to the train that the passengers were to board. Arriving passengers were met at trackside by Red Caps, who carried their luggage through the station to taxis or to waiting family or friends. If travelers were making connections, Red Caps led them, bags in hand, to the platform where they awaited their next train. The origin of the term, and the distinctive headwear, may be apocryphal, but at least some Red Caps believed that it derived from the free-lance entrepreneur who found female passengers so eager to obtain his help in carrying their luggage that he affixed a piece of red flannel to his cap for easier identification. That enterprising individual who discovered a gold mine at New York's Grand Central Station on Labor Day, 1892, was black teenager James Williams, who persuaded the terminal's managers to hire exclusively blacks for this service. Another version of the story has the same locale, but advances the date to 1900. Travelers were already accustomed to the services of baggage porters who wore dark uniforms. In the midst of a very busy day, Williams attached the red cloth to his hat to attain greater visibility. Whichever creation story is true is less important than the fact that the Red Cap idea spread quickly to other cities. Soon no major terminal was without such a uniformed corps, known in some places as ushers. Williams went on to a 45-year career at Grand Central, eventually overseeing a staff of about

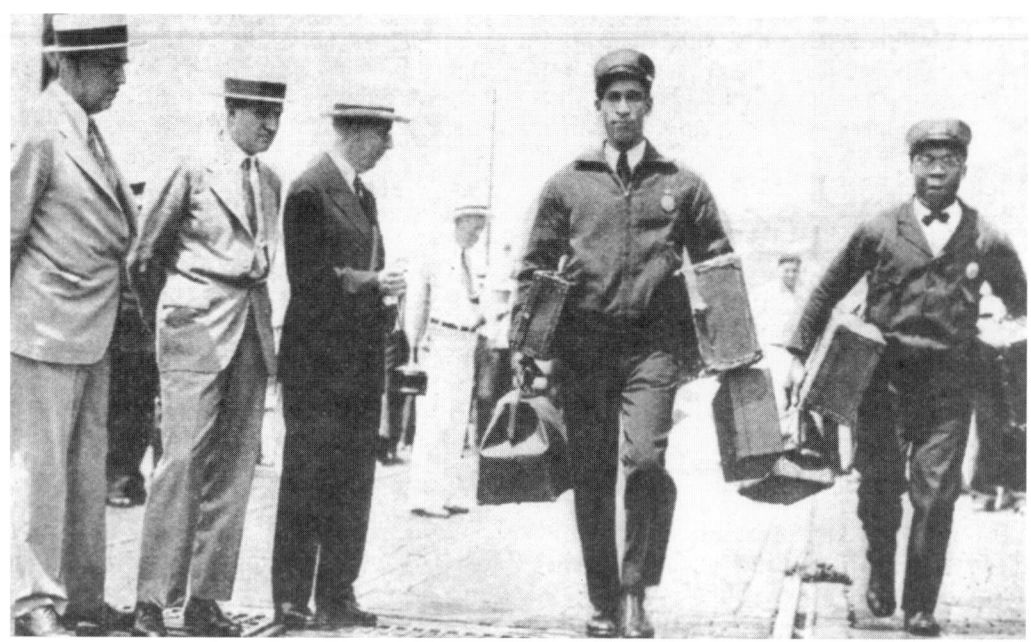

500 Red Caps. He could have retired at 65 but kept working up to his death in 1948 at the age of 69 because pension benefits were too low to support a decent standard of living.[1]

The largest numbers of Red Caps were found at big-city stations where many trains originated or terminated. Far fewer were needed at intermediate stations, even those through which passed many trains. Because most travelers arriving and departing from New Haven, Connecticut, for example, were commuters, its station on the New York, New Haven & Hartford Railroad employed only a dozen men who were more accustomed to serving wealthy young Yalies who could easily have carried their own bags. Finally, many small-town depots had a single "station porter" who more likely wore overalls than a uniform. In addition to assisting passengers, he was janitor, baggage and mail loader, and messenger.

Establishing the number of Red Caps is difficult because the federal census did not include them in a discrete classification. There may have been upwards of 10,000, including college students working during summers, at the peak of passenger travel in the mid-1920s when large "union" stations that served a number of railroads, like that in Washington, D.C., employed hundreds of them. About 600 total worked at Chicago's 6 major terminals at the end of that decade. Although their numbers declined greatly during the Great Depression, nearly 3,800 Red Caps worked nationwide before the outbreak of World War II and resurgence in travel. Even in the mid-1930s, nearly 500 Red Caps worked at New York's Grand Central Terminal, with other hundreds at nearby Pennsylvania Station.[2]

Not all Red Caps were black, but they preponderated, and the job was widely identified with them by the traveling public. Slaves in the South had worked as station porters before the Civil War,

Railroads in the African American Experience

and as free men they continued to ply that trade afterward. In the antebellum North, the first black railroader in any capacity was probably Sam Jones, a baggage man for the Philadelphia & Columbia Railroad in the 1840s. The New York Central Railroad also early employed black baggage men. By the turn of the twentieth century, if not earlier, black luggage carriers were common at northern stations. When the Chicago & North Western Railway moved into a new station in Chicago in 1911, it replaced its white ushers with blacks, explaining that they were easier to recruit and, since travelers were accustomed to African American Pullman porters, it made sense to have uniformity among those serving the public. As the Pennsylvania Railroad saw it, Red Caps were "public relations men," the first railroad representatives that most passengers encountered upon reaching the station, and the last ones with whom they interacted once they arrived at their destination. Whether or not passengers regarded their travel as a pleasurable experience depended at least as much on the courtesy and attentiveness of Red Caps and sleeping-car and coach porters, as on the speed, on-time performance, and comfort of the trains themselves.[3]

Red Caps worked long and hard for their living, sometimes receiving wages, other times none, and always relying on tips. Gratuities ranged from pennies up to, in extraordinary cases, $10. Success generally depended upon serving as many passengers as possible. George Henry Smock, who was a Red Cap at the Atchison, Topeka & Santa Fe Railway station in Los Angeles before becoming a Pullman porter, recalled the day when he found himself frustratingly tied up with just one party of travelers. Hollywood actors (and husband and wife) Franchot Tone and Joan Crawford arrived in a chauffeured limousine and were assisted into the station by another Red Cap. The Red Cap-in-charge directed Smock to get into the limousine and go back to the Ambassador Hotel in

Hollywood to retrieve the couple's 21 pieces of luggage. By the time Smock returned an hour later, swearing under his breath and ruing his misfortune, the couple had already boarded their chartered Pullman. Fortunately, after Smock finished loading the bags onto the car, the actor gave him a $100 bill. "That's the best tip I ever had carrying a bag or any baggage."[4] But Red Caps could just as easily be stiffed, even by the rich and famous. Grand Central Terminal's Ozzie Thorne apparently had a number of unpleasant encounters with Tone, labeling him "the cheapest of them all."[5]

Photos of Red Caps at work typically show them carrying--and often running with--two or three bags under each arm. In Thorne's words, "you had to--excuse the term--'jack-ass' them." Golf bags were particularly bulky and heavy. Sometimes Red Caps were able to transport dozens of items at a time from the curb to the train on a wheeled cart. But during holidays, so great was the crush of humanity at large terminals that it was impossible to maneuver a cart or even a hand truck through the multitudes. Either way, it was hard work. And Red Caps were expected to be more than baggage carriers. The best of them were "a veritable information bureau about schedules, trains and tracks, of arrivals and departures."[6]

While some Red Caps worked only out of necessity, and disliked the menial implications attached to their work, others took pride in serving passengers, especially those having physical limitations or who were unfamiliar with trains or the city. Railroad company magazines printed letters from travelers complimenting the attentiveness of individual Red Caps. Wrote one about North Philadelphia Station's Herman Harvey, a Pennsylvania Railroad employee: "I never met a more gracious and obliging gentleman." Such men took pride in their work, but, as Ozzie Thorne knew, they were also practical psychologists. "The traveling public is our bread and butter. It's up to us to make them feel at home, so the next time they come through the station, they'll look forward to having us serve them." Some Red Caps succeeded so well that passengers might phone in advance or wire from elsewhere in the country to ascertain if their favorite would meet them at their train. Thorne had such a patron, "a big race-horse man from Delaware. He'd always come into Pennsylvania Station, then go over to Grand Central in a couple of cabs. Have a cab just for the bags. He'd call ahead and I'd know when he would be there, and would take his bags and put them away for him until the train left that night. He'd be going up to Montreal to do a little hunting . . . A man like that wanted service and he got it. He paid for it, too."[7]

Red Caps sometimes gave service much beyond carrying luggage. One raced down the platform as a train was pulling out to literally catch in his arms a woman who jumped from the accelerating car, having neglected to get off after seeing her friends on board. Others assisted stranded passengers and unaccompanied children who were lost or had nowhere to go. A woman passing through Pennsylvania Station on the way to her son's wedding had been delayed en route, and a Red Cap not only helped her get quickly to a connecting train, but also phoned ahead to let the wedding party know when she should be met at her destination. Invalids, or those confined to wheelchairs, often received personal attention.[8] The Baltimore & Ohio Railroad believed its Red Caps were the best because they were equally alert to the needs of the humble as to the distinguished. "The poor

Railroads in the African American Experience

woman with babies and baggage, who is making her way with difficulty to the day coach claims his attention to an equal degree with the handsomely gowned woman with her expensive luggage who is on her way to chair car or sleeper."[9]

Railroads were eager to claim that many Red Caps used such work as a stepping-stone to upward mobility. Increased summer travel required additional personnel. The day shift at Grand Central Terminal was known as the "schoolboy tour" because of all the college students working to finance their educations. The same was true elsewhere. Others worked only for short periods, however, because they found the work too hard, physically, or too distasteful. And some, lacking seniority, worked only part-time. But many Red Caps were career men. Sons followed fathers. Ozzie Thorne's father was a Red Cap supervisor at Grand Central Terminal, working until the age of 73. Some racked up impressive statistics. Sandy W. Trice, who worked at the Illinois Central Railroad's Central Station in Chicago, estimated that in his first 36 years on the job he toted 5.4 million pounds of baggage for 135,000 passengers. Trice eventually became the chief usher, or head Red Cap, at that terminal. This was as high as blacks could expect to go among station personnel. Such men were in a position to hire and mentor new employees, and Trice took this role seriously. He was proud of having encouraged many younger men to pursue educations, and nearly two dozen of his protégées went on to become lawyers, ministers, teachers, and physicians. Trice personally modeled the Protestant work ethic. He amassed considerable real property, was active in politics, and held offices in a variety of fraternal organizations.[10]

But there was sometimes another side to big-terminal chief ushers like Trice. He was a thorough company man, opposed to independent unionism. His rise and success cannot be divorced from his unwavering devotion to the Illinois Central. Another mercurial personality was James Williams, chief of Red Caps at Grand Central Terminal. He distinguished himself from the others in wearing a custom-tailored suit, lighter in color than that of the others. "Chief" Williams conducted monthly spit-and-polish inspections, sending anyone home whose grooming or clothing did not meet his high standards (e.g., no worn shoe heels). He was an autocrat who played favorites, hiring and firing at will until the Red Caps unionized and gained an impartial seniority system. Most anyone would be called on the carpet for arriving for work five minutes late, but his favorites could get away with arriving an hour late. Williams even had his stool pigeons who reported what the men did after work up in Harlem. Ozzie Thorne never got along with him: "I could take orders, don't get me wrong, but you had to give me orders that made sense and not just take advantage of me. He and I didn't hit it off."[11]

Specific Red Caps fulfilled additional duties beyond carrying luggage. Often, they were the ones to write on the arrival and departure chalkboard whether a train was expected on time or delayed. Others were gatemen who controlled the flow of passengers, not allowing them onto the platform until their particular train was ready for boarding. (These individuals were sometimes known as train announcers because they proclaimed the first and final calls for boarding.) Gatemen who possessed unusual verbal and musical talents sometimes became renowned train callers, famous for

Passengers on the Southern Pacific's popular Daylights *between San Francisco and Los Angeles brought suitcases on board and also checked luggage for the baggage car. Either the baggage room staff was overburdened or inattentive this day in 1937, necessitating several Red Caps to help unload the baggage car upon arrival at the City of Angels. Courtesy Lucius M. Beebe and Charles M. Clegg, Jr. Collection, California State Railroad Museum*

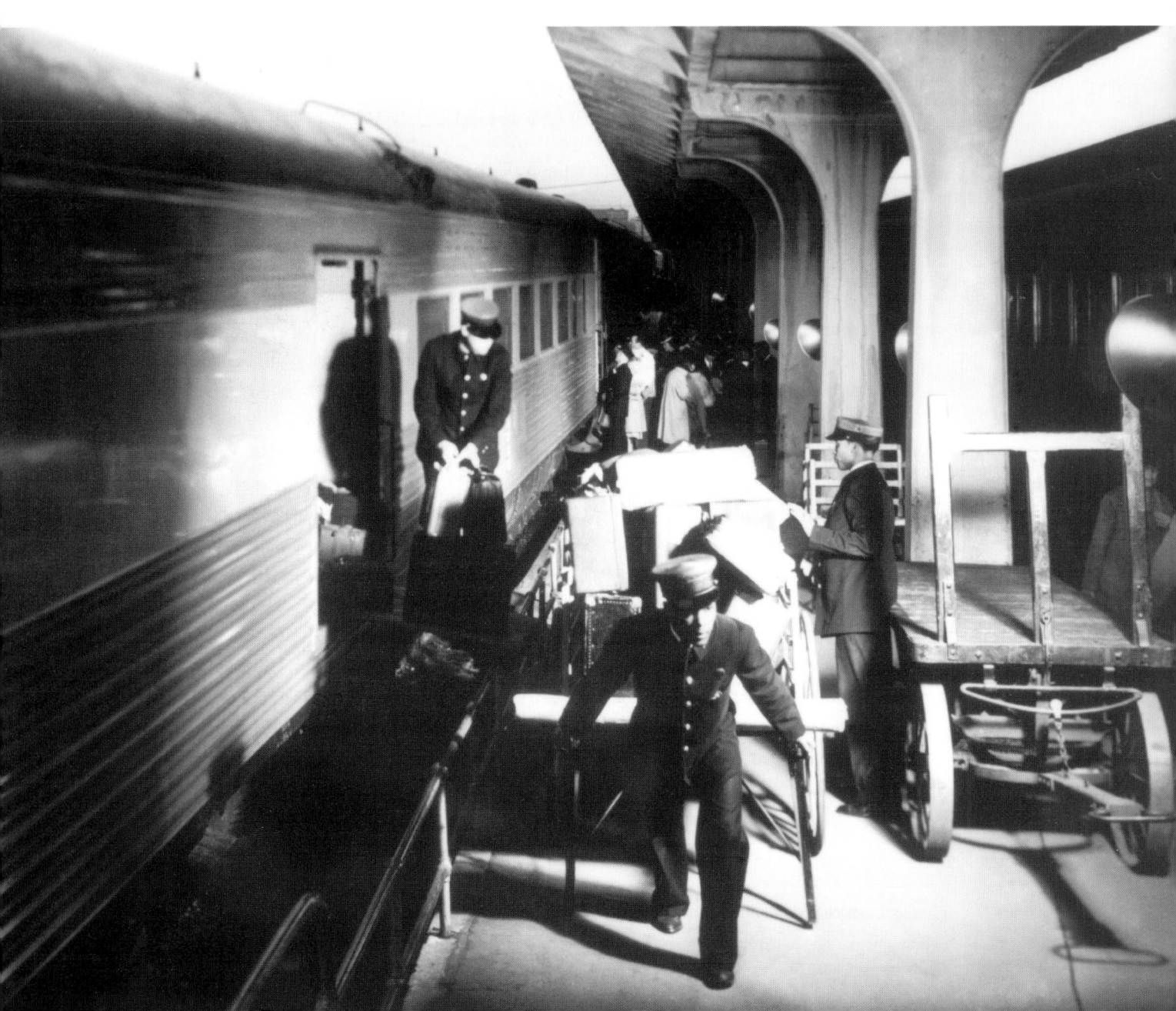

reciting in singsong patter the list of station names at which departing trains would subsequently stop. Red Caps at small town depots doubled as train callers whether or not they had vocal gifts.[12] But at large metropolitan stations, it might take many years to attain this position. Such men bore themselves with dignity. Jim Johnson, head usher at the B&O's Philadelphia station, was a "tall, courteous erect train caller with the neatly trimmed Van Dyke [beard]" who worked for 55 years, to age 76, "never having lost a day's work from illness." According to a company reporter, "his voice is clear and strong without being harsh. His enunciation is perfect, and there is a ringing enthusiasm in the tone which suits admirably the busy, bustling atmosphere of a station." Such men were not idle between arrivals and departures: "He seems always to be busy looking out for the interests of passengers and never to be standing around the station waiting for something to do. One minute he is answering the telephone, giving intelligibly and courteously whatever information the inquirer wants. The next minute he is trying to make clear some point about our service to some one waiting for a train. Then it is calling the dispatcher's office to find out whether a train is on time. Again, we see him shoulder some big valises and put them on the train quickly and courteously for one of our patrons."[13]

One of the last train callers was Daniel Simmons, who achieved celebrity in New York, announcing trains at Pennsylvania Station. A relative latecomer, he began calling trains at the age of 41 and was still working 17 years later, in 1985. His audience was not only the hundreds of employees, but the half million travelers who passed through the station daily. Some came simply to hear Simmons from his broadcast booth in the main waiting room, 10 feet above the floor. "A commuter leaned against a post and waited for Mr. Simmons to bellow his next 'All aboard!', then gave him the thumbs up sign and hustled off to work. An elderly woman waited for an 'All aboard!' then blew Mr. Simmons a kiss and was on her way." Radio stations asked to broadcast his calls. Fans sought his autograph. One of their favorites was calling the *Crescent* to New Orleans, in which he rhythmically sang out the 27 intermediate stations "with the p's popping, the r's trilling, and the t's snapping." "You've got to dress it up. It can get boring for the people waiting for trains and for me," Simmons told an admiring reporter for the *New York Times*. He transported older people back to simpler, happier days, when Mel Blanc, on radio's *Jack Benny Show,* called out "Anaheim, Azusa, and Cucamonga." A waitress in a station restaurant summed up the experience of many: "When he calls out the Rocky Mount, North Carolina, stop, which is near my hometown, I just want to throw down my apron and hop aboard."[14]

Red Caps, despite their smart uniforms, were near the bottom of the railroad hierarchy. The Illinois Central not only sometimes treated them as boys, but even called them such. The entire Red Cap corps at its Central Station in Chicago, including chief usher Sandy Trice, were under the supervision of the lead (white) custodian. The caption for a picture of five dozen Red Caps noted that "these boys . . . are determined to be the neatest group of Red Caps to be found anywhere . . . The boys assembled in the station at 1 o'clock and marched in a column . . . to the terminal superintendent's office on the second floor. Cleanly shaven and with clothes carefully pressed, they presented a splendid appearance, and the only criticisms to be made concerned minor matters

For many decades, the first persons travelers encountered at railroad stations were Red Caps, who assisted them with their baggage. This Southern Pacific Lines' Red Cap, at San Francisco's Third and Townsend Streets Station in 1938, is maximizing his opportunity, carrying as many bags as possible so that he can quickly snag other customers. Courtesy Lucius M. Beebe and Charles M. Clegg, Jr. Collection, California State Railroad Museum

which [the superintendent] was assured would be taken care of before the next [monthly] inspection . . . In the future, there will be four classifications--excellent, good, fair and poor--and the men will be graded according to their appearance. The results will be posted as an incentive to every man to get himself into the top rank."[15] For proud men, who regarded themselves as professionals, this demeaning description must have been disheartening.

No African American railroaders were more exploited, economically, than Red Caps. For years, until they unionized, the railroads (and their corporate kin, the terminal companies) paid them either very little, or nothing at all, on the assumption that they were "independent contractors" and could earn an adequate income on tips. But "you could work all day long and never make a dollar."[16] If they protested working conditions, or tried to organize, management could fire them and easily train replacements. The Red Caps' struggles to unionize and obtain a living wage, which were even more arduous than those of the Pullman porters, have been well described by railroad labor historian Eric Arnesen, so only the highlights need discussion here.

While whites professed to believe that a Red Cap job was "a stepping-stone to other railroad positions," blacks knew that they would not find upward mobility. At best, they hoped for a steady income. But terminal companies and the railroads preferred to let supply and demand determine wages. During World War I, the U.S. Railroad Administration standardized earnings, which reached $45 a month. But wages dropped after federal control ended, and by the early 1920s, Pennsylvania Station (New York) Red Caps received no pay at all, having to rely entirely on tips. Grand Central Terminal employees were in two categories: a few dozen, who worked suburban trains (which carried fewer passengers with luggage) received a paltry $18 monthly, while hundreds of unpaid Red Caps hustled for tips from long-distance travelers. Other stations that continued to pay minimal wages through the 1920s abandoned them when the Depression hit. By then, travelers were not only fewer, but also poorer. Future Red Cap union president Willard Townsend recalled, "there were days when we actually made just about enough to pay our car fare and buy lunch."[17]

Railroads in the African American Experience

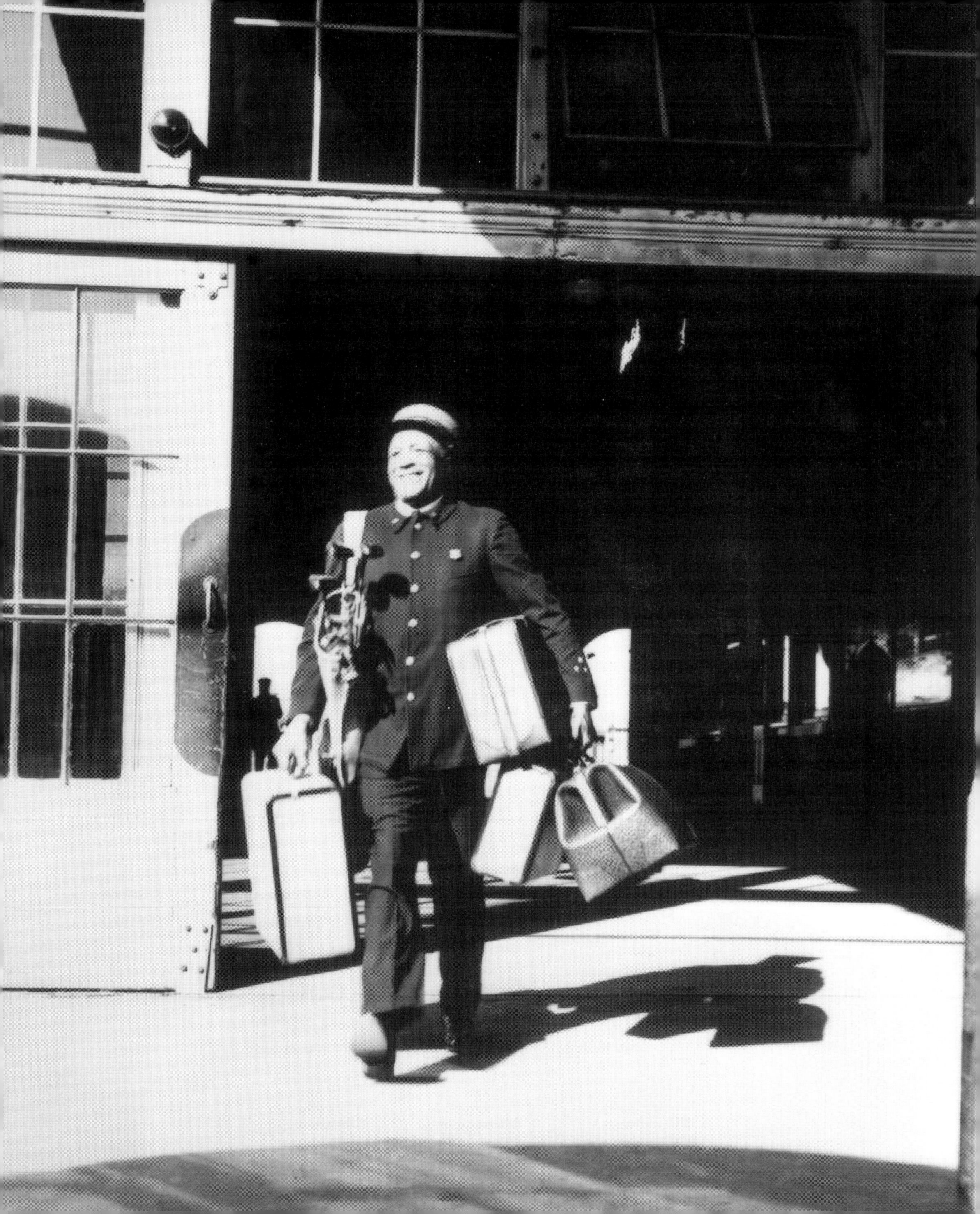

The degree to which Red Caps could be exploited, not only by the railroads but also by one of their own, is seen in the ugly situation that prevailed at the New York Central terminal in Buffalo, New York. Red Caps still received the USRA $45 monthly wage up until 1929, when the railroad canceled all pay. The chief porter (head Red Cap) instituted a 25 cents daily fee for the privilege of working, payable to himself, and at the same time increased the number of Red Caps to 100 men. Although no longer considered railroad employees, the Red Caps remained under the discipline of the NYC, which also continued to assign their hours of work. Appeals to the Railway Labor Board availed nothing. Not until the Red Caps unionized in 1933 did their grievances begin to be addressed.[18]

Early attempts to unionize all ended in failure. The Red Caps had no effective weapon. New recruits readily replaced strikers. A few fraternal and benevolent organizations existed, as well as occasional company-sponsored "booster clubs," but they could not function as bargaining agents for their members. Finally, inspired by the persistence of sleeping-car porters in organizing a union to challenge the Pullman Company, and encouraged by pro-labor New Deal legislation, local Red Caps' unions began to appear in the 1930s. The next step was consolidating them into the new International Brotherhood of Red Caps in 1937, headed by Willard Townsend. For good reasons, it remained suspicious of the American Federation of Labor, whose Brotherhood of Railway and Steamship Clerks claimed jurisdiction over them while barring blacks from membership. Under the Clerks, the Red Caps would only have been admitted to a toothless "federal auxiliary" without the authority to bargain on its own behalf, in its own interests. Ultimately, the IBRC, renamed the United Transport Service Employees of America, affiliated with the AFL's rival, the less-discriminatory Congress of Industrial Organizations.[19]

Organizing a union was one matter; utilizing new labor law was another. New Deal legislation benefited many railroaders, but Red Caps were not deemed to be employees and hence were without access to federal protections and mediation. The first victory was persuading the Interstate Commerce Commission to rule that, since they wore uniforms and were subject to the supervision and discipline of railroad officials, they were, in fact, employees. This opened the door to petitioning the National Mediation Board to hold elections allowing Red Caps working for particular railroads to decide if they wished the IBRC to represent them. When the Chicago & North Western and the Southern Pacific voluntarily agreed in 1937 to recognize the IBRC as the Red Caps' representative and began collective bargaining, other railroads saw that union representation elections were inevitable and followed suit. But union recognition was only a start: contracts still had to be negotiated. Railroad officials "dug in their heels on financial matters." This is not surprising, as 70 percent of Red Caps still received no wages at all. One other avenue remained for the IBRC: the newly enacted Fair Labor Standards Act established a maximum 44-hour work week and a 25 cent minimum wage. The railroads, acting in concert, then declared that tips were wages. Thus, they argued, they shouldn't have to pay any wages so long as the tips earned in a 10-hour day equaled or exceeded $2.50. Within 2 months, by the end of 1938, more than 200 stations had imposed this scheme.[20]

Railroads in the African American Experience

Unfortunately, the Fair Labor Standards Act did not define whether tips were wages. Furthermore, railroad supervisors took advantage of their power to dismiss recalcitrant workers and forced Red Caps to exaggerate the amount of tips on their daily record slips. Thirty-six Grand Central Terminal Red Caps who resisted this coercion were simply fired. Litigation was their only recourse, but the Supreme Court decided against the Red Caps, ruling in 1942 that tips were indeed wages. Justice Hugo Black, in dissent, sarcastically wondered whether "the tip paying public is entitled to know whom it tips, the redcap or the railroad." Even before that decision, however, most stations adopted a new tactic to avoid paying wages. Now, travelers were charged a flat 10 cents rate for each bag carried. Red Caps were thus not simply luggage carriers, but "revenue collectors." If they did not collect the amount necessary to pay their wages, they faced dismissal. Red Caps finally won guaranteed pay in the 1940s, based on a ruling by the Department of Labor's Wage and Hour Division. Their minimum wage rose to 40 cents in 1942, to 57 cents by the end of the war, and to $1.28 in the early 1950s. Compared to the wages of other unionized workers, however, these were very modest gains. And although they finally won eight-hour shifts in the late 1940s, some Red Caps still worked seven days a week, the only time off occurring during one's annual vacation.[21]

The Red Caps' hard-won improvements in wages and working conditions ultimately proved to be hollow victories. Required to pay a set bag fee, more and more travelers elected to tote their own luggage. Particularly serious was the shift to airplanes of more affluent (and more generous) travelers in the 1950s. Revenues from Red Cap services, and the numbers of Red Caps, steadily declined. Pennsylvania Station and Grand Central Terminal employed only 192 and 140 Red Caps, respectively, by 1955. (As late as 1948, Grand Central Terminal had 300 Red Caps.) The introduction of self-service baggage carts at Chicago's LaSalle Street Station (euphemistically called "Red Cap carts") in 1963 dramatically eroded Red Cap service. While a New York Central press release declared that "the new equipment will not replace red caps but will supplement their service," correspondence between the NYC and other lines makes clear that the motive was not traveler convenience but reducing costs and the number of Red Caps. Stations elsewhere introduced self-service carts to similar effect. Los Angeles Union Passenger Terminal reduced the number of Red Caps from 64 to 20, and Dallas Union Terminal from 23 to 15, with 5 of them now working as janitors. Only 42 Red Caps remained at Grand Central Terminal by the early 1960s. "Toward the end it wasn't fun anymore. Sitting around waiting for people wasn't for me," recalled Ozzie Thorne.[22] Like the Pullman porters, Red Caps disappeared into history. A few attendants still ply that trade at the busiest Amtrak terminals, but most who today check luggage for travelers do so at airports.

Career Red Caps may be compared to long-working Pullman and coach porters and dining-car workers. They took pride in serving the public, both the humble and the high-and-mighty. They also took pride in their appearance. A photograph of 40 Chicago & North Western Red Caps, working at its Chicago Passenger Terminal, shows them in polished shoes, trim jackets with badges, and caps squarely on their heads. Grand Central Terminal men looked equally sharp, with uniforms tailored by Brooks Brothers. For many women, marrying a hard-working abstemious Red Cap was a coup.

Although they toiled long hours and for many consecutive days, their labors did not take them out of town. Ozzie Thorne knew "lots of men [who] raised families, bought homes," and educated children on a Red Cap's earnings. Like other black railroaders, they were generally esteemed in their communities and expected to provide leadership and an example to others.[23]

In addition to Red Caps, metropolitan terminals had large baggage room staffs, often entirely black. Ismah Smith logged more than 55 years working for the Baltimore & Ohio, the last 2 decades at Baltimore's Mount Royal station. He and other baggage men handled a huge volume on their hand trucks and heavy steel-wheeled carts, transporting luggage, mail, packages, small crates and boxes, and even coffins to and from train baggage cars. In 1910, they served passengers on 20 Royal Blue Line trains to and from New York and Washington, and many others on at least a dozen through trains en route to Chicago, Louisville, and St. Louis. The company magazine praised Smith's "attention to duty" and "having the good of the Company at heart." He was known for his "reliability, willingness and excellent Christian character," always trying to live out the Golden Rule.[24]

Janitors at large terminals were often called "station porters." One's duties, as outlined by a Santa Fe station inspector, were manifold. Sweeping the floors daily and mopping at least once a week; washing windows monthly; blacking stoves and emptying their ash pans, as well as keeping them lit; dusting and polishing furniture daily; keeping lamps trimmed and polished; cleaning and disinfecting toilets; keeping station exteriors free of rubbish and cinders; and keeping platforms clean, with baggage and express carts out of the way of passengers. In addition to such duties, the B&O's Oliver Cooper, employed at Mount Royal, raised and lowered window shades, depending upon the position of the sun, and ensured that water coolers were replenished and kept clean. On more than one occasion he also swept up rice after the departure of honeymooners. Station porters assisted passengers if Red Caps were not available and helped the baggage room staff if it was overburdened. Harry Smith, working at the Louisville & Nashville Railroad's Birmingham, Alabama passenger station, occupied himself with "loading mail and baggage, sweeping out the concourse, or doing one of the numerous odd jobs to which the stationmaster assigns him."[25] A group photo of the L&N depot force at Pensacola, Florida, shows seven blacks identified as station porters. Most wore work attire, with only one dressed as a Red Cap with tie and vest, indicating that baggage and mail handling, plus janitorial duties, were major parts of their job description, as only 10 passenger trains came through daily. Station porters' photographs in the Reading Railway and Jersey Central Lines employee magazine show them as being fully uniformed, but because many of the stations were commuter stops, with only one porter on duty at a time, they undoubtedly performed janitorial and mail-loading duties in addition to assisting the occasional traveler with luggage. Such was Adrian B. Smith, who retired in 1954 as night porter at the Reading's Manayunk Station, concluding a 47-year career.[26]

Many smaller-town depots also had station porters who performed a variety of duties in addition to directly assisting the traveling public. In the South, such employees were usually African Americans. Some small communities situated on main lines welcomed a steady flow of passenger trains, while in others, only two or four locals might stop. The fewer the trains, the more varied one's duties. Harry Erskine, porter at the Chesapeake & Ohio Railway's St. Albans, West Virginia station in the mid-1920s, wore Red Cap headgear but overalls instead of a uniform. In addition to janitorial work, his duties included loading and unloading baggage cars and managing the baggage room, as well as assisting passengers on and off the 10 mainline trains passing through daily, plus 3 locals on the Coal River branch. Some station porters were also gardeners, responsible for the pleasing appearance of the depot grounds. Scottsville, Kentucky, at the end of a 35-mile L&N branch, saw only one arrival and departure daily. Its "station laborer" was for many years slave-born Henry Hughes, who retired in 1931 at the age of 74. Hughes was a general factotum, doing a variety of tasks in addition to helping passengers.[27]

Older African American men at scores of southern depots were all-purpose workers. A familiar figure at the Norfolk & Western Railway's Bristol, Virginia station in 1942 was 38-year veteran William Norman, the "janitor-messenger, bean-hustler and general handy man." Others were simply identified as "faithful old employees" like Alfred Johnson, a 49-year C&O employee who could always be seen in 1924 "with his broom working away, trying to keep the tracks around Huntington [West Virginia] passenger station clean and sightly." With 16 daily passenger trains spewing smoke and cinders, plus numerous coal drags spreading more dust, keeping the station spic and span would have been a never-ending job. A 1928 photograph of "cinder man" George Wood at the L&N's Paris, Kentucky station, showed him with broom, shovel, and wheelbarrow, which were undoubtedly well used, given that numerous coal trains passed through in addition to the 22 daily passenger trains arriving and departing. Paris also had an unpaid handyman, "Old Charlie." The company reporter apparently saw no need to ascertain his last name, but described him with the racial paternalism typical of employee magazines as "a faithful retainer" for more than 40 years. "He has never been on the payroll, but runs errands for the boys and looks out for their interests there, and is a familiar figure to hundreds of railroaders, past and present. He can be found on hand around the depot in the small hours of the morning and the late hours in the evening. The weather is never too cold nor too hot for him, and his faithfulness, good humor and reliability are a credit to one of his race." It is likely that he exchanged his labor for tips, food, and a warm place to avoid the elements in winter. Those with paid station porter positions undoubtedly earned little, but a steady railroad wage might be enough to put one on the margins of the southern black middle class.[28]

The traveling public encountered African American woman railroaders almost exclusively as station matrons and maids or as waitresses in depot eateries. The introduction of dining cars did not bring an end to station cafés, lunch counters, and restaurants. While white waitresses staffed the Santa Fe's famed Harvey Houses, with the exception of its El Paso establishment and possibly other locations in Texas during World War II, black women food servers were widespread at southern stations and not uncommon elsewhere. Such work had long been identified with African American women who, unlike dining-car waiters, did not have to travel away from home for days at a time. If the railroad operated the restaurants (or track-side canteens, as did the Illinois Central during World War II), such women were railroad employees. Others were in the employ of concessionaires who ran the station eating facilities.

African American station maids or matrons were most common in the South but were also present in some northern terminals. In Chicago, at least, they worked alongside white matrons. The Pennsylvania Railroad employed nearly four dozen black matrons or maids across its vast system in the mid-1920s, with more than half of them working in stations in the New York region. Matrons worked principally in the women's waiting rooms, which were a common feature of large terminals. Their roles ranged from minding babies to informing passengers of departure times, buying tickets, providing change, and furnishing needles and thread to repair a garment. The Illinois Central had a definite image in mind: "The matron at any large railway station is more than merely a hostess to women travelers. She is a motherly person who takes a keen interest in their travels. She greets the young bride and the elderly widow with a sweet smile of welcome. A friend in need to the tired little mother, to the friendless girl, and to the invalid woman . . . The tedium of a long journey is broken by a restful interval in the women's waiting room, where the sympathetic, helpful services of the matron are always available."[29] Not surprisingly, long-serving matrons sometimes got to know personally certain regular travelers. An obituary for Henrietta Banks, matron at the C&O's Main Street Station in Richmond, Virginia, noted, "Aunt Henrietta" was "always pleasant and courteous to our traveling public, and will be missed."[30] Of course, in Richmond as elsewhere in the segregated South, only white females utilized the women's waiting rooms. Some southern stations used the term "ladies waiting room," which underscored both segregation and the ascribed inferiority of African Americans, since no black woman was considered to be a lady.

Because they often had families of their own, black station matrons typically worked their entire careers in one location. It was also not unusual for them to be married to other station employees like porters or elevator operators. It is likely that job vacancies were often filled from "inside," without the need to advertise or recruit. In fact, that was how many blacks all across the job spectrum obtained railroad work.

Matrons at big stations wore distinctive attire. Those working in the IC's Chicago Central Station wore a dark dress that was embellished with a white lace collar. In the South, they were likely to wear a white dress and white cap, or a black dress with white apron and cap, both characteristic servants' attire. And in fact, outside of big southern cities, black station matrons were equally maids. "Aunt" Martha Fife, at the L&N's Richmond, Kentucky depot, was as renowned for her zeal in keeping the station spotless as for her friendliness and courtesy to passengers.[31]

The most unusual black station employees were female train callers, each having her inimitable singsong patter. Train callers were almost always station porters, Red Caps, or gatemen, so the handful of women were notable not just for their vocal brilliance, but on account of their rarity. The Gulf, Mobile & Ohio Railroad's employee magazine celebrated "Susie," the Meridian, Mississippi train announcer and Red Cap, perhaps the only woman to be so designated. That the periodical did not deem it important to record Susie's last name indicates that whites regarded her as a servant.

But the railroad, and, indeed, the city, took pride in her "old time" train calling, singing the stations "much as she does the negro spirituals." The railroad boasted of her being "one of America's best train callers" who had "large crowds on hand to hear her musical negro voice sing the stations from one end of The Rebel Route to the other."[32]

Two other noteworthy female train callers were the Illinois Central's Jenny Pike and Lula Reid. "Aunt Jenny" worked so long at Vicksburg's Cherry Street depot that she was "almost as much of a fixture as the station itself." She was originally a janitress, and became known for "her zeal in seeing that the station and offices are kept clean." Those who heard her call trains never forgot the breadth of her imagination, according to the reporter for the company magazine. "For an eastbound train from Vicksburg, she would call first the nearby stops. Then, she would get into full swing with 'Meridian, Birmingham, Chattanooga, Baltimore, Washington, Philadelphia, and Noo-o-o York.' Having taken the traveler this far, Aunt Jenny would then hold the rest of the world before him with '--and Europe, Asia, Africa and Sha-a-anghai, China' . . . Adding to the distinctive character of her train announcing were certain little trimmings of speech she had contrived by which the announcements were made to rhyme." Aunt Jenny passed the job down to her niece, Lula Reid, but not without merciless instruction and supervision. "Long after the old veteran retired on pension, she used to come down to the station twice a week and scrutinize her niece's work with an eagle eye for shortcomings as a janitress and a critical ear for faults in calling trains. So stern and exacting was the old taskmistress that Lula says she sometimes fairly hated her aunt for 'picking on her.'" Lula Reid perfected her own style, though. Passengers "hear their trains announced in a distinctly unusual way. The voice, clear and reaching everywhere in the vicinity of the station, is feminine, and the stations are called in the softened, ear-pleasing accent of the Southern negro." While perhaps soft and soothing, her "stentorian" voice also carried over the entire station and necessitated a suspension of conversation in its offices, even with the windows closed.[33]

Railroading today reflects only dimly the vast labor force of the past. Where once tens of thousands of stations and depots, large and small, served a majority of American travelers, today Amtrak maintains only about 600 stations, some of which are un-manned "Am-shacks." Most small-town depots closed when the railroads slashed passenger service, especially on branch lines, in the 1950s and 1960s. With them vanished the last non-metropolitan station porters and train callers. In large cities, self-service baggage carts replaced nearly all Red Caps. Today only a few station attendants remain at the largest Amtrak terminals like New York's Penn Station and Chicago, Washington, and Los Angeles Union Stations. For nearly a century, numerous black families survived on tips and (sometimes) a paycheck earned by Red Caps and station porters, who often had to perform a racial dance in which they appeared to be humble, faithful, cheerful, and grateful. Thankfully, their descendants today, who constitute only part of the multiethnic legion of airport baggage checkers, no longer have to put on that mask.

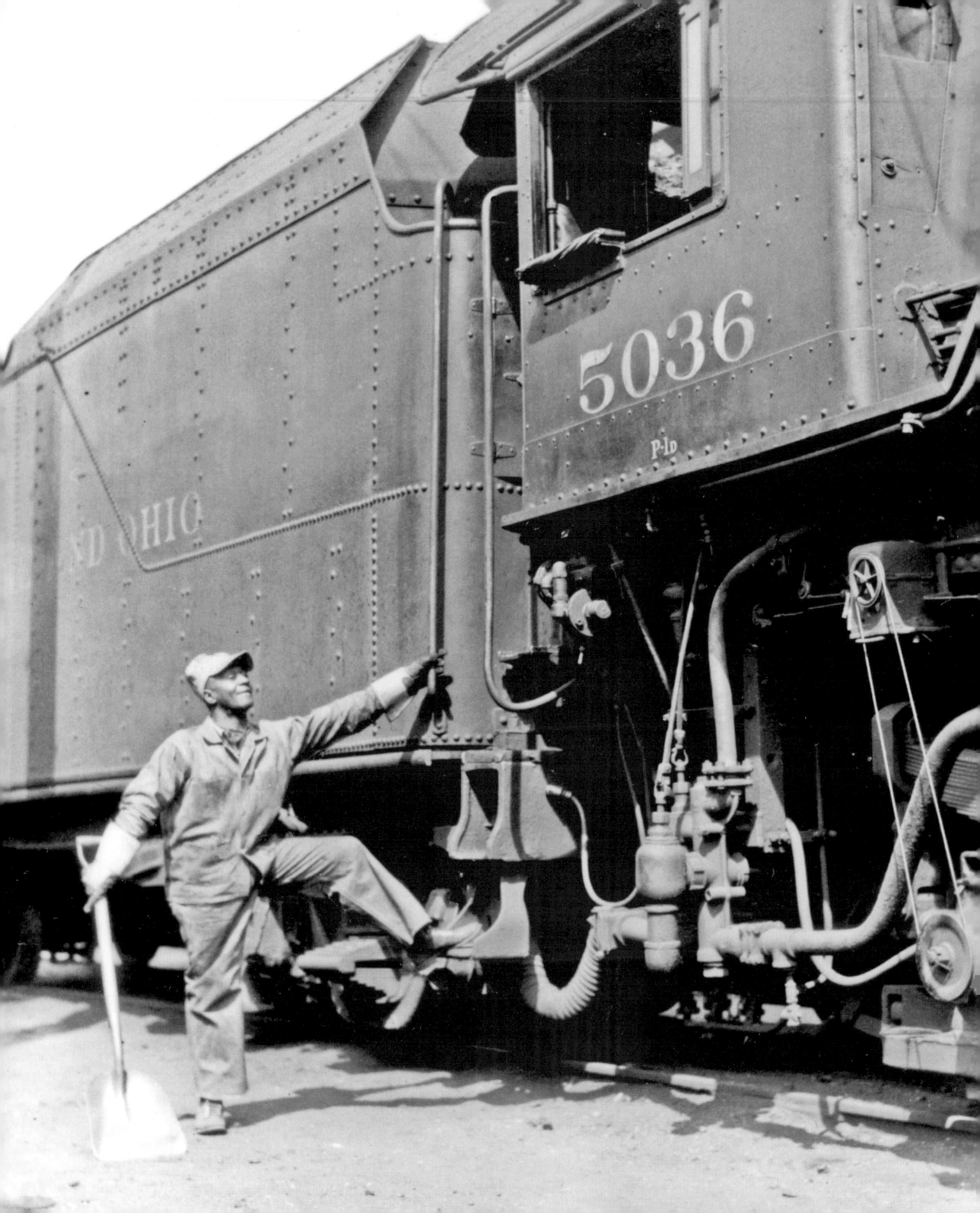

A Baltimore & Ohio Railroad hostler, sometime in the 1930s or 1940s, is boarding a "heavy" Pacific passenger locomotive to tend its fire, his own personal coal scoop in hand. Hostlers prepared locomotives for their runs, moving them from roundhouse to ready track, but that was as close to being an engineer or fireman on the B&O as they could get. On the Chesapeake & Ohio Railway, black hostlers were prohibited from operating labor-saving mechanical stokers, which fed coal into fireboxes via a screw. Instead, they had to shovel coal by hand, the hard, old-fashioned way. Courtesy B&O Railroad Museum

A few Jim Crow cars were quite elaborate. The 68-mile Georgia Northern Railway's center-baggage combination car 15 featured equal appointments for both races, including stained glass panels over the windows and Tiffany lamps on the interior. When photographed at Moultrie, Georgia, in 1940, it was still in good shape. Although the car was spared the scrapper, today it is in derelict condition awaiting possible restoration. Courtesy Paul Darrell Collection, California State Railroad Museum

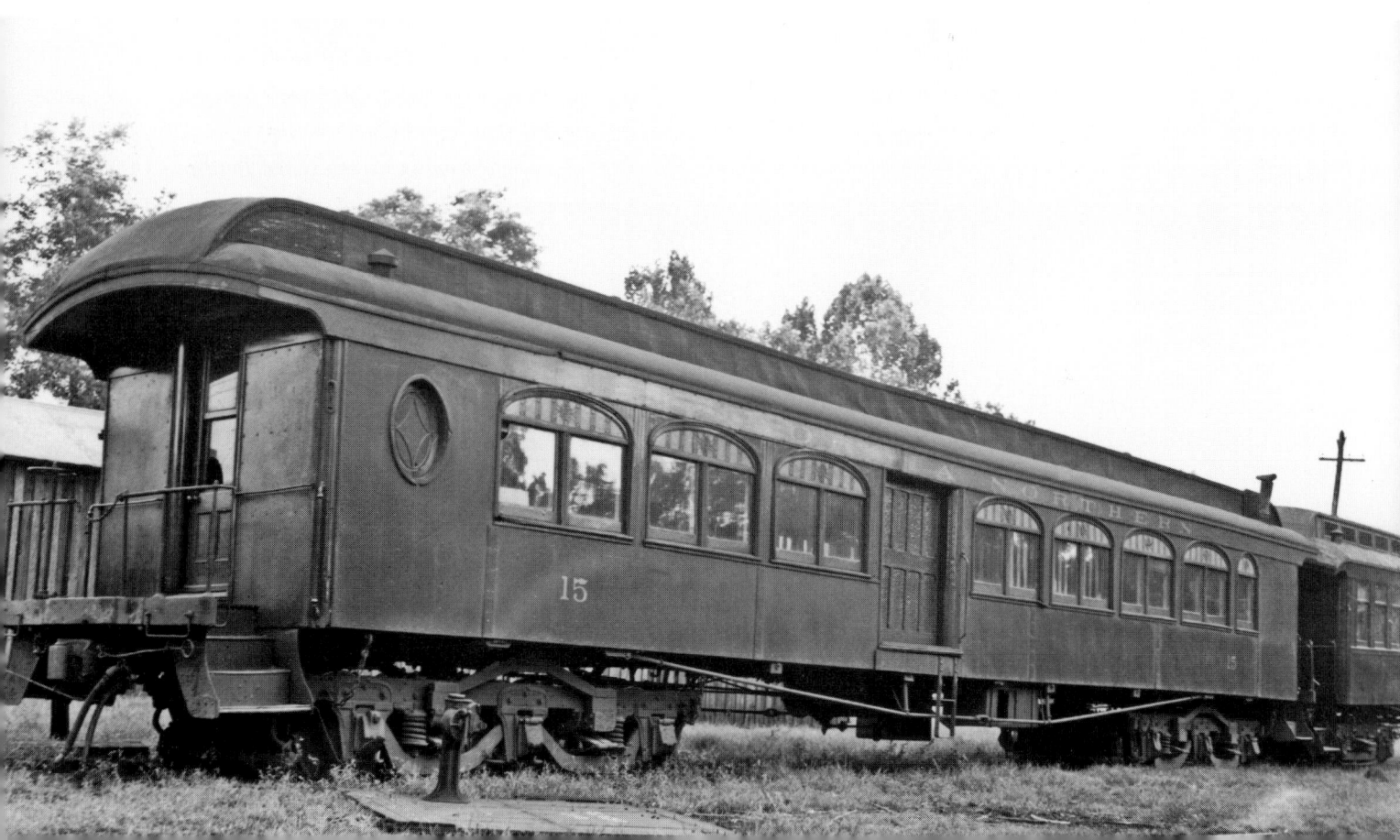

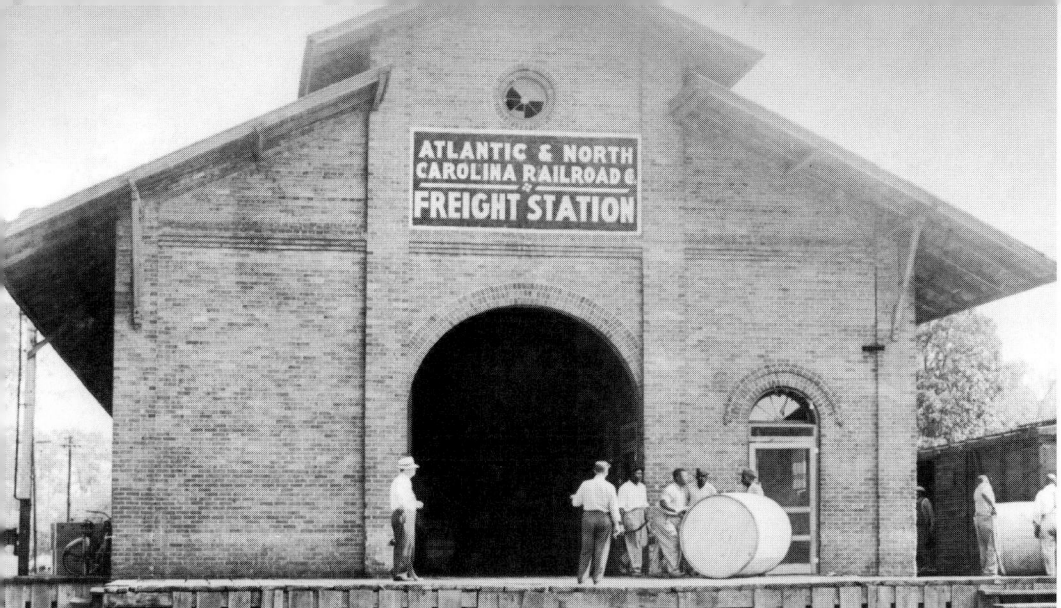

(ABOVE) *Outside an imposing freight house in Kinston, North Carolina, black freight truckers roll hogsheads of tobacco into boxcars sometime in the 1920s or 1930s. At the beginning of southern railroading, enslaved depot hands provided the muscle for loading and unloading freight, and blacks continued to predominate on southern freight docks until package delivery services doomed less-than-carload-lot shipping. Harry P. Edwards Papers, Rare Book, Manuscript, and Special Collections Library, Duke University*

(BELOW) *The black fireman of the Florida East Coast Railway's new* Henry M. Flagler *streamliner, photographed in Miami in 1939, is standing at far right. Only a tiny number of black firemen managed to keep their jobs into the diesel locomotive era. An exception was the FEC, which for decades hired black firemen exclusively. Note how large a crew, including black coach porters, cooks, waiters, lounge-car attendants, and maids, was required for this all-coach Miami–Jacksonville train. State Library and Archives of Florida*

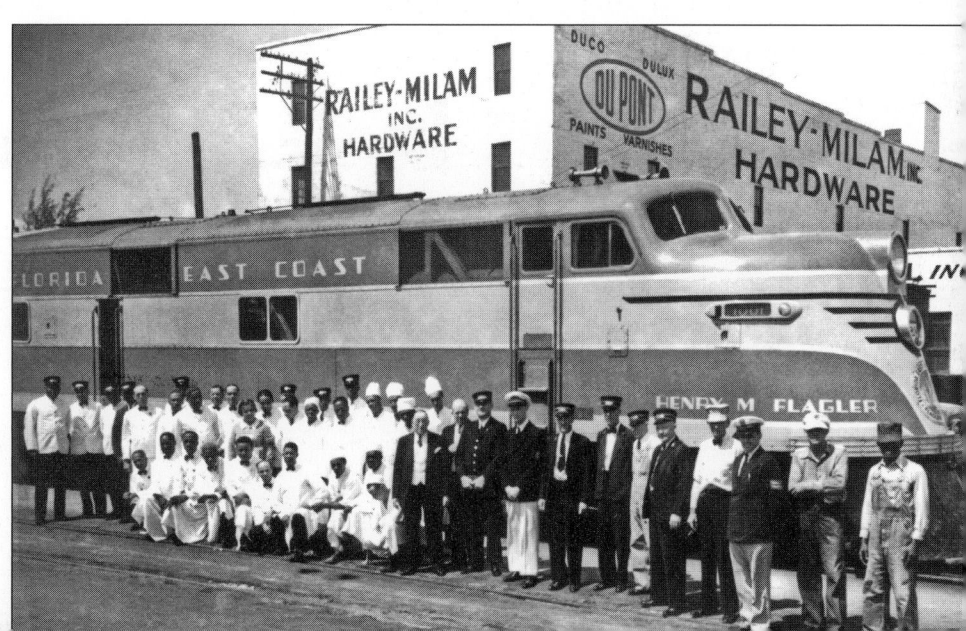

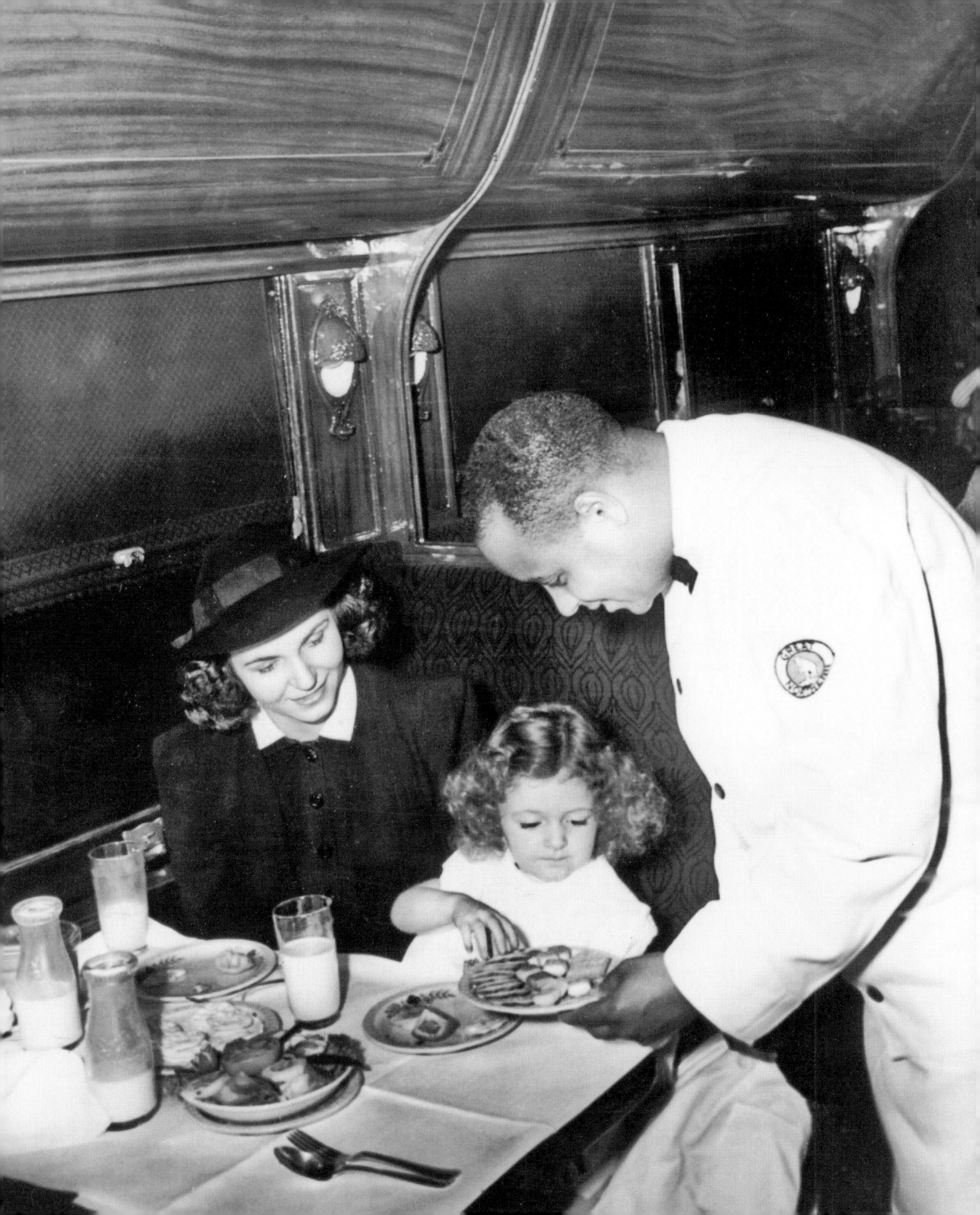

(OPPOSITE) *For the convenience of sleeping-car passengers not wishing to go into the dining car, a Great Northern Railways "upstairs waiter" on the* Empire Builder *has installed a portable table in a Pullman open section, and then delivered the meal. The photo was taken sometime between the train's inauguration in 1929 and its transformation into a stainless-steel streamliner in 1947. Fred Willming photo, Great Northern Railway Records, Minnesota Historical Society*

Whether passengers rode in lower-fare tourist sleepers or the costliest double bedrooms, the Pullman Company expected that porters would not only cheerfully serve them but also anticipate their needs and desires, like offering pillows. Pullman and railroad publicity photographs invariably showed smiling, energetic porters and happy, well-rested travelers, like these Great Northern Railway passengers (or models) in the early 1940s. Great Northern Railway Records, Minnesota Historical Society

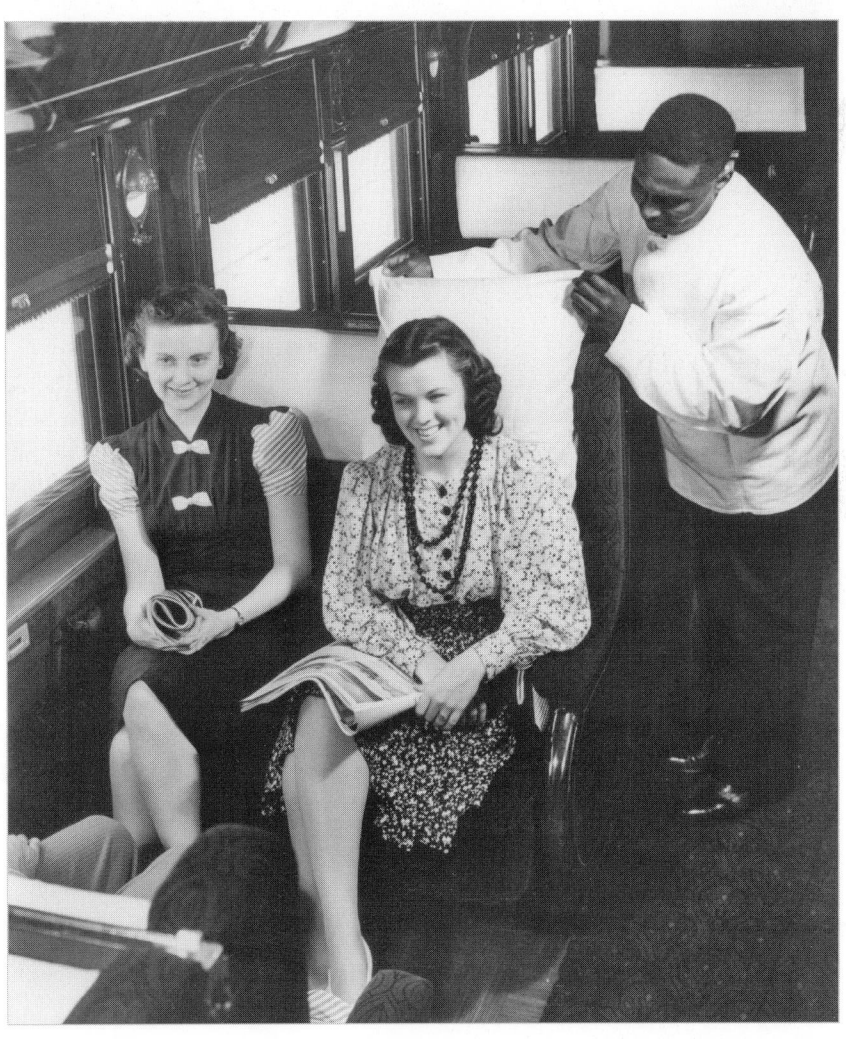

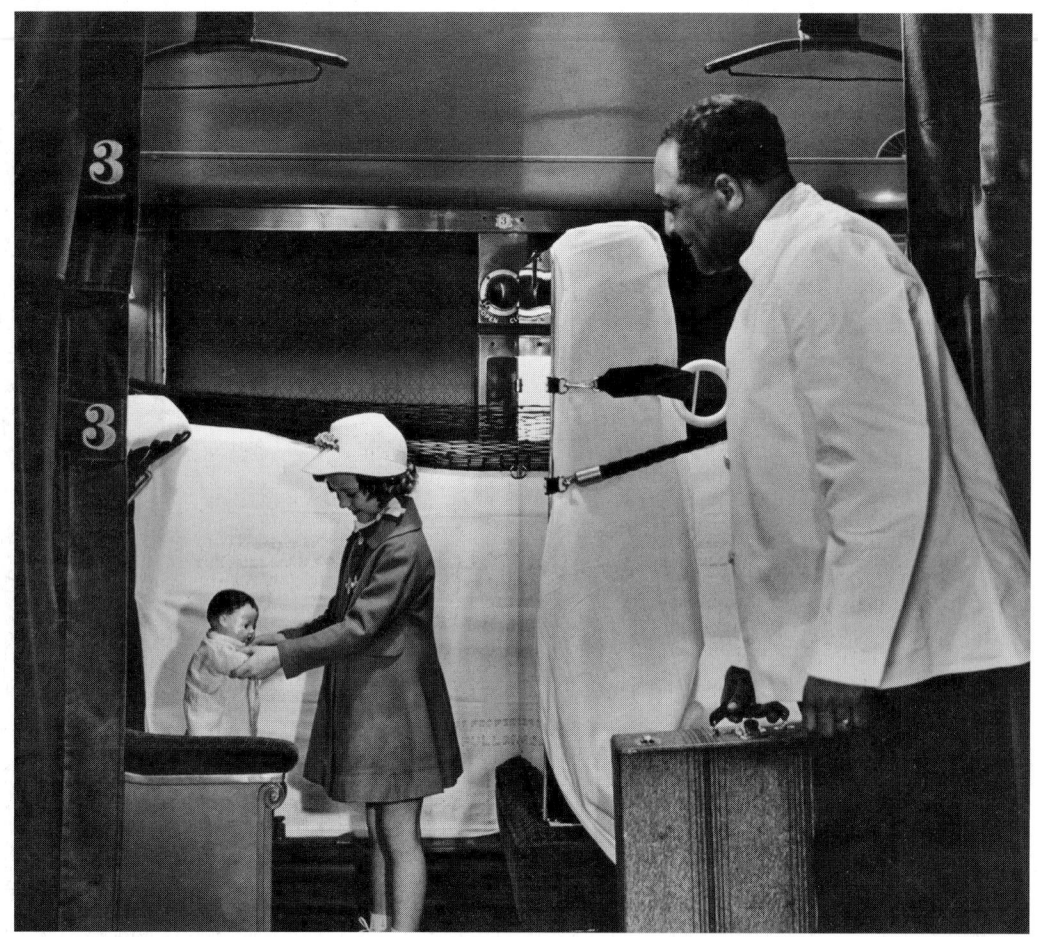

Pullman Company advertising stressed not only the comfort of its accommodations, but also the reliability of its employees. Some advertisements even suggested that porters would baby-sit children while their parents enjoyed a cocktail in the lounge car. The image of trustworthy black males was carefully cultivated, as this photo from the early 1940s shows, and was part of the appeal of Pullman travel. *Theodore Kornweibel collection*

(OPPOSITE) *A Pullman maid dressing a passenger's hair on one of the Baltimore & Ohio Railroad's premier trains in the 1940s. Maids were adept at doing hair and giving manicures. Other duties included assisting female passengers to the bath, keeping the women's restrooms clean, aiding mothers with young children, and helping the elderly and infirm. Because they attended primarily female passengers, they did not earn as much in tips as did the Pullman porters, who served both men and women. Courtesy B&O Railroad Museum*

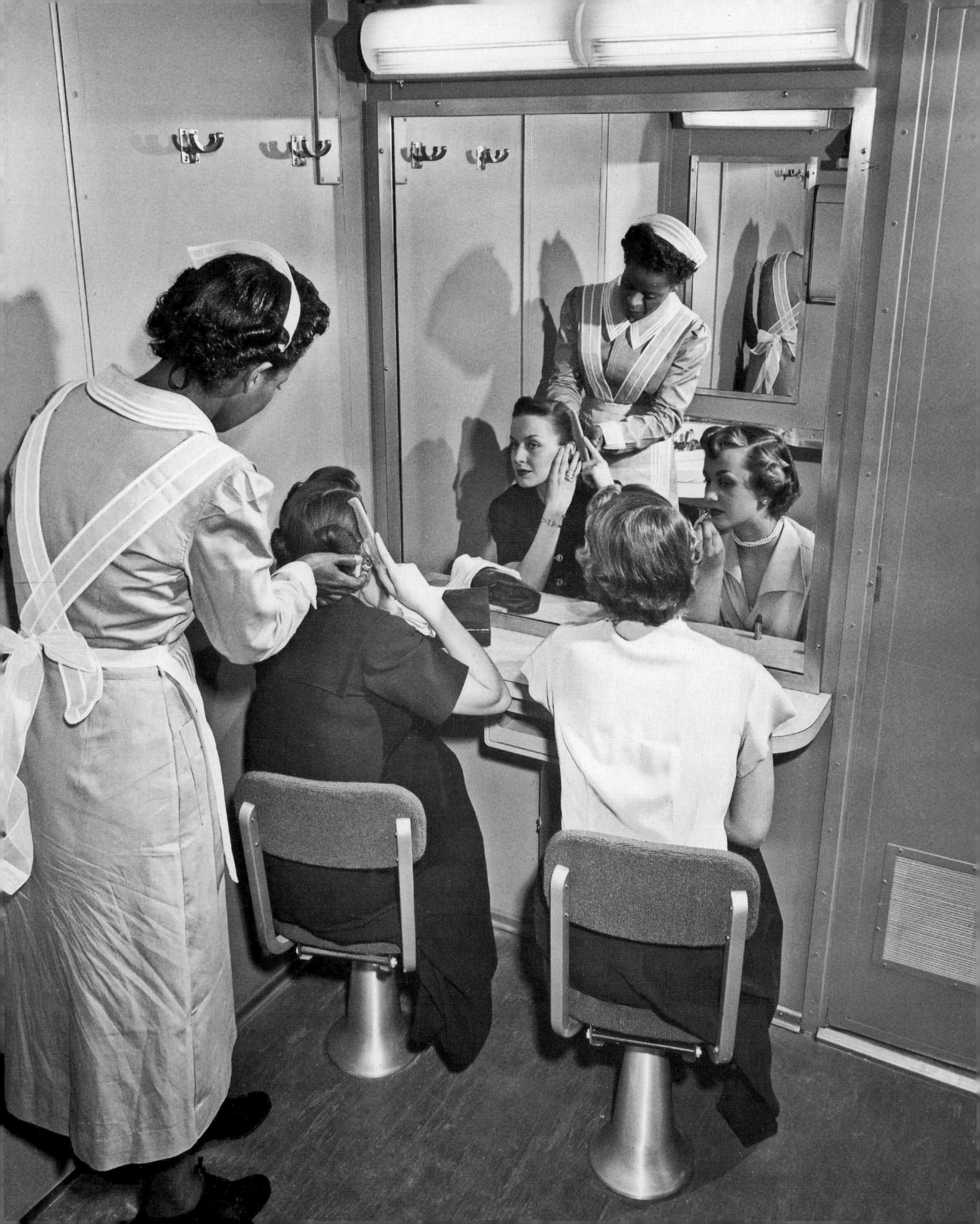

A Reading Company crossing watchman
protects a busy street and rail line in Chester,
Pennsylvania, sometime around 1940, prepared
to warn inattentive motorists and pedestrians
with both paddle sign and whistle. Electric cross-
ing signals and gates would eventually replace
such guards. Reading Company Collection,
courtesy Hagley Museum and Library

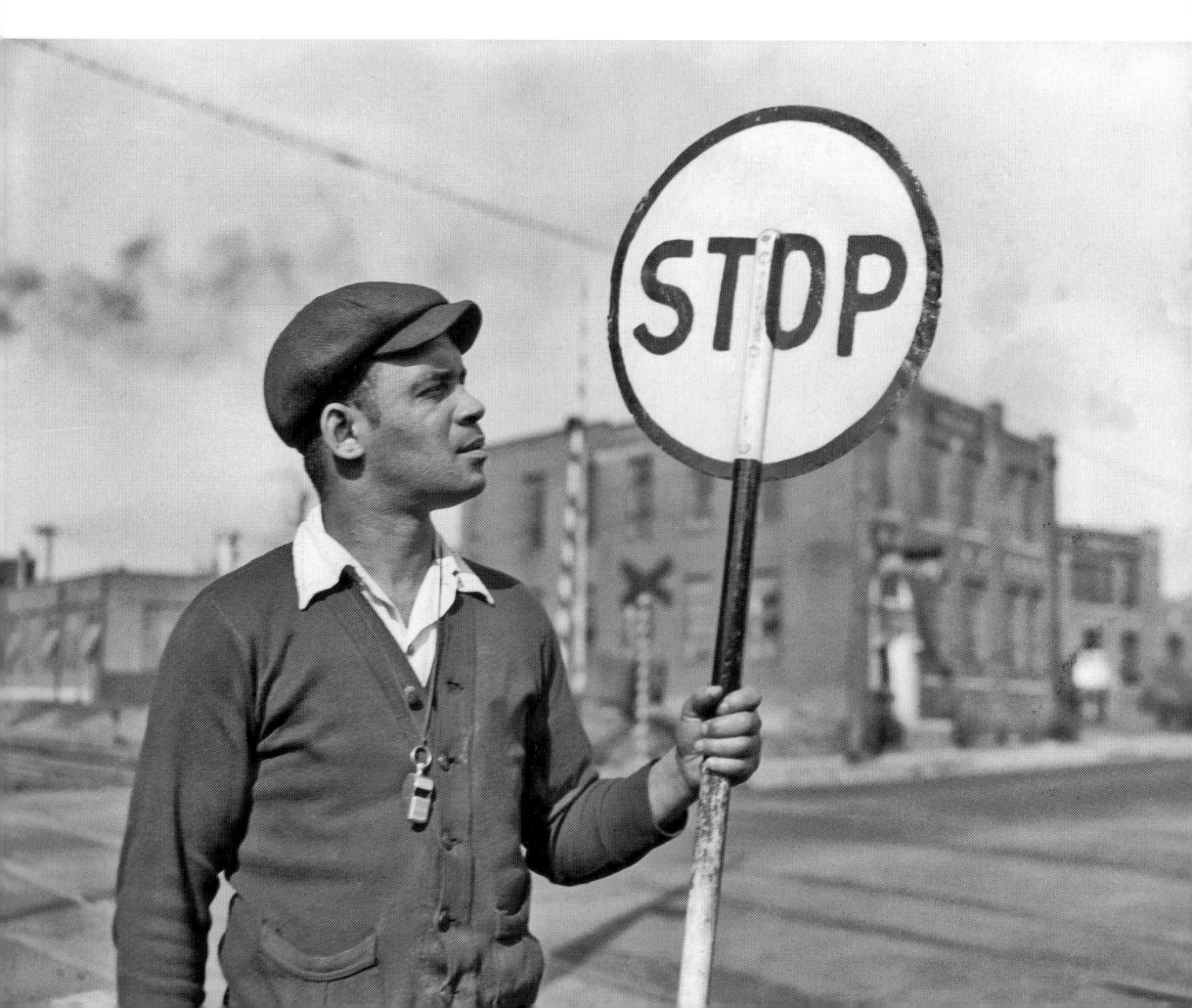

Railroad ferries plied the waters of numerous bays and rivers too wide to be bridged. Their porters performed janitorial duties and sometimes assisted deckhands. The Central Railroad of New Jersey, one of five railroads with vessels crossing the Hudson River, sent the Plainfield *to New York from Jersey City, seen here in 1941, its porter posing just before a departure. Reading Railroad Collection, courtesy of Hagley Museum and Library*

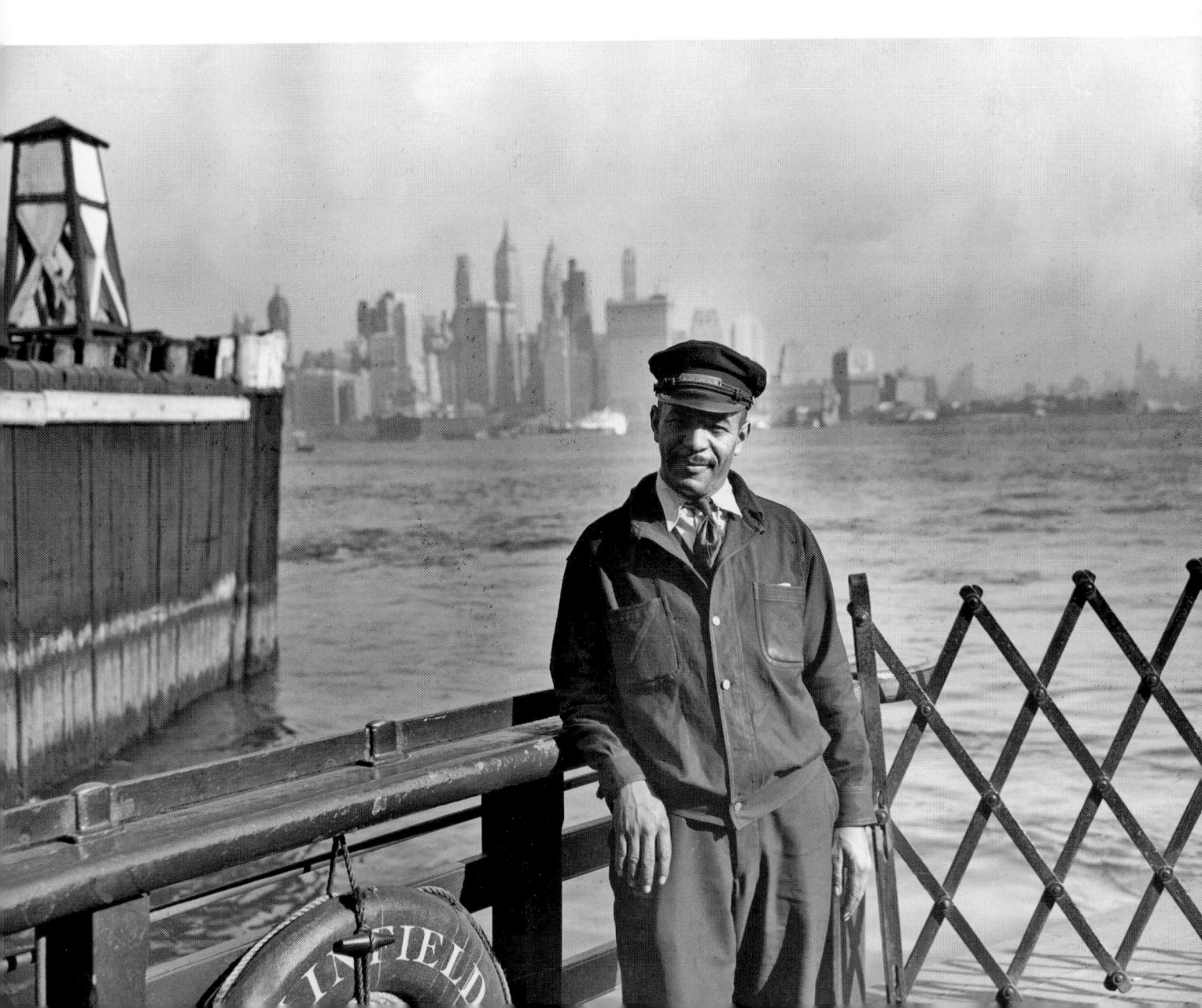

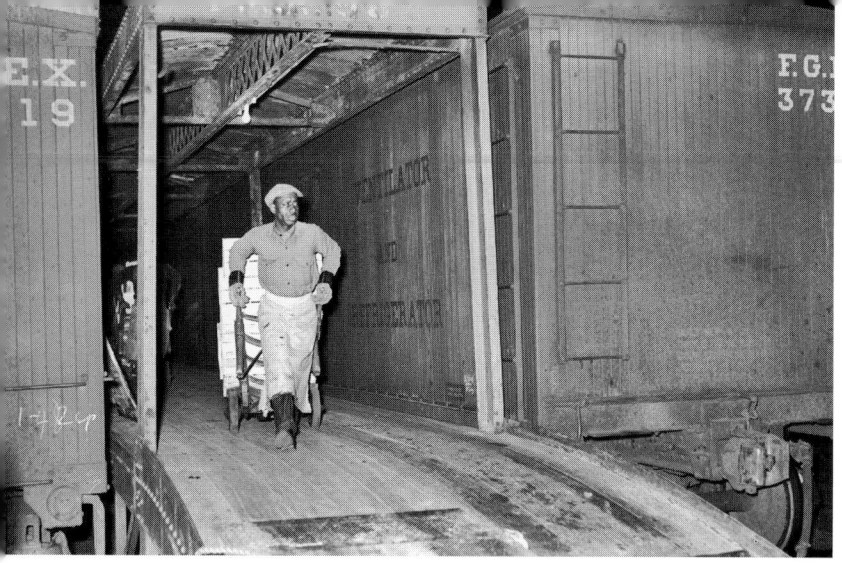

(ABOVE) *A Pennsylvania Railroad freight trucker works at night, unloading oranges from refrigerator cars on a car-float at Pier 29, New York, in 1939. By early morning, the fruit will be sold at a wholesale produce market. Blacks found work as freight truckers in many localities outside of the South, although they did not constitute the majority of such workers there. Arthur Rothstein photo, FSA/OWI Collection, Prints and Photographs Division, Library of Congress*

(BELOW) *The eastbound New Orleans–Florida Limited will depart as soon as the mail and baggage handlers load mail of all classes into a Louisville & Nashville Railroad RPO car at Chattahoochee (River Junction), Florida. The L&N has brought the train this June day in 1940 from the Big Easy; now the Seaboard Air Line Railway will take it on to Jacksonville. All across the South, black station hands muscled baggage and mail at stations large and small, as they had for a century. Marion Post Wolcott photo, FSA/OWI Collection, Prints and Photographs Division, Library of Congress*

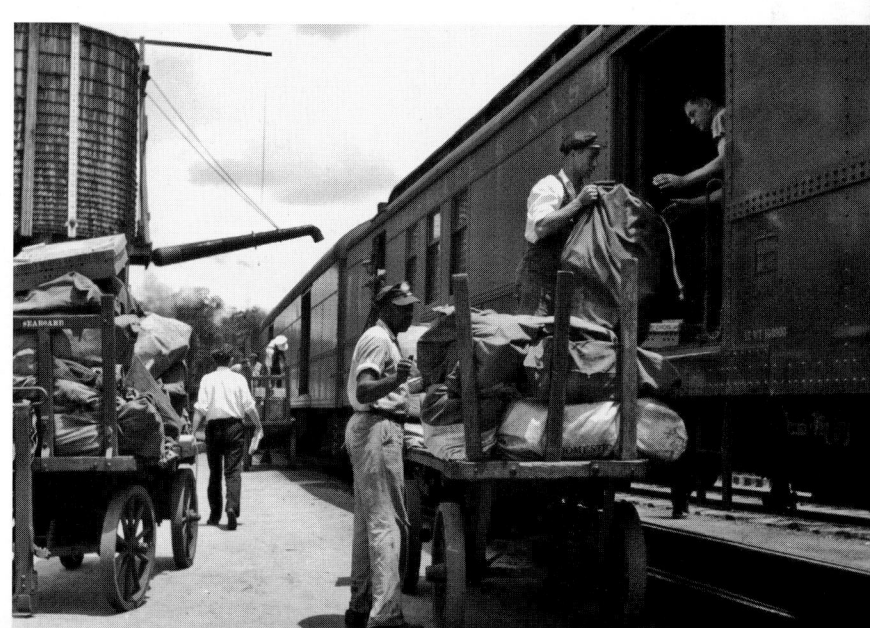

Norfolk & Western Railway helpers work with blacksmiths in the smith shop at Roanoke, Virginia, in 1940. Blacks outnumbered whites as shop helpers and laborers in the South and were concentrated in the hottest, heaviest, and most dangerous trades. Norfolk & Western Historical Photos, Digital Library and Archives, University Libraries, Virginia Polytechnic Institute and University

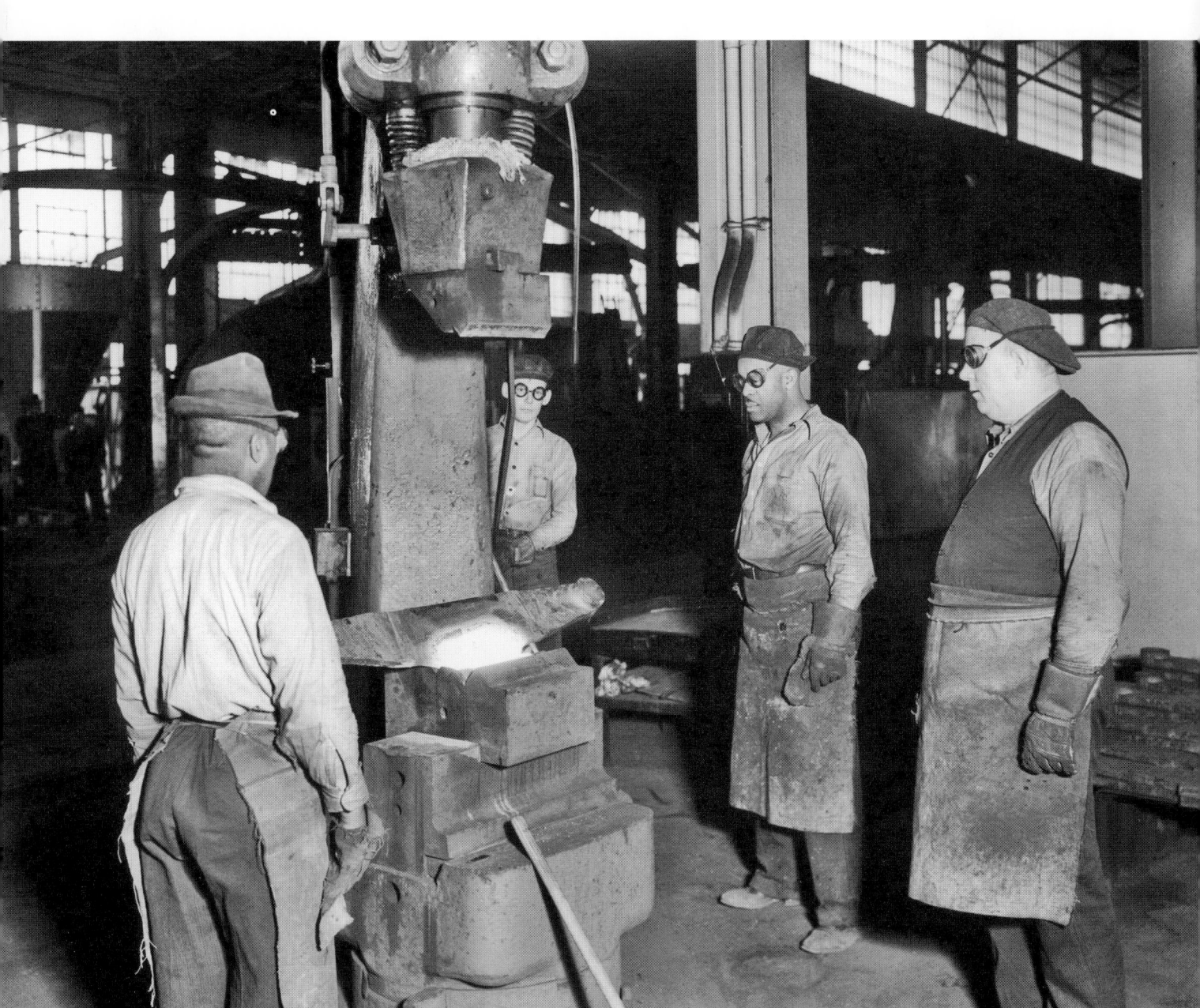

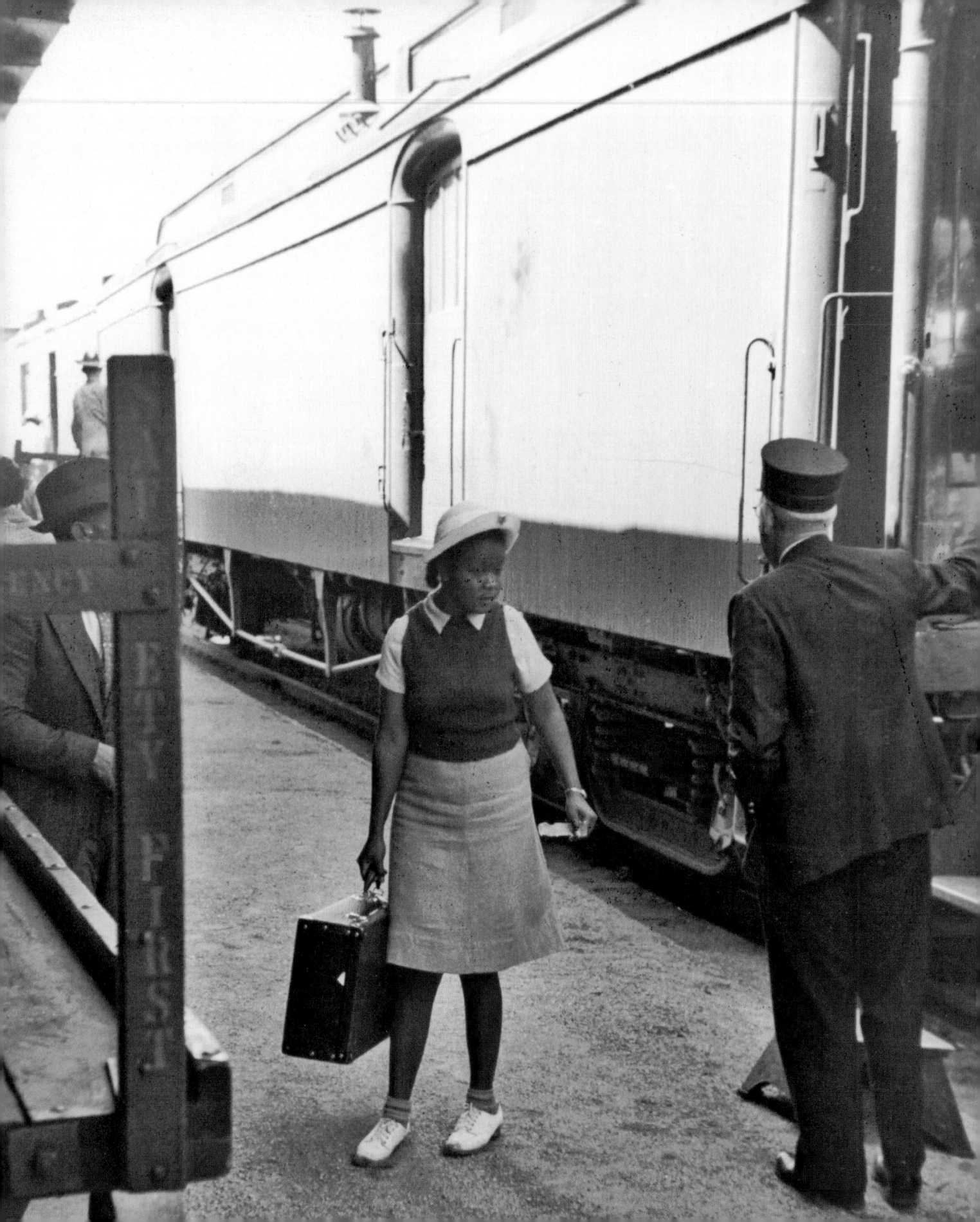

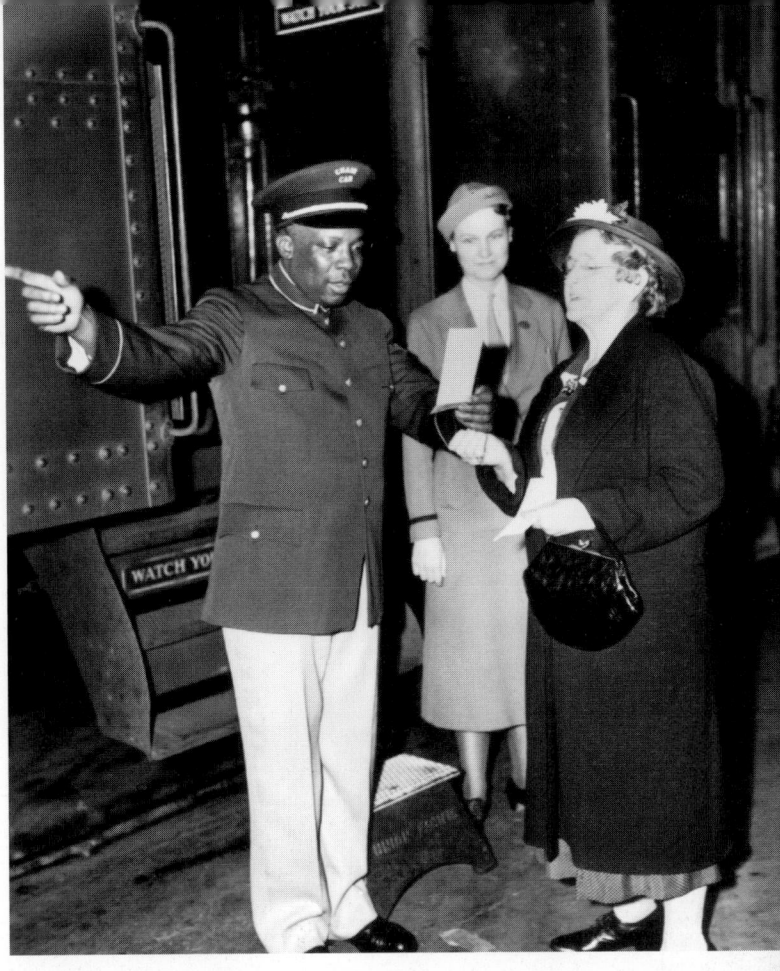

(OPPOSITE) *Train porters were trusted figures within black communities. Parents often committed children traveling alone in coaches to their care, confident that they would see them to their destinations or ensure they made the proper connections. This young lady has just stepped off the Gulf, Colorado & Santa Fe Railway's Jim Crow car at San Augustine, Texas, in August 1939. Russell Lee photo, FSA / OWI Collection, Prints and Photographs Division, Library of Congress*

The number of train porters exceeded that of Pullman porters, because many more passengers rode coaches than sleeping cars. This Union Pacific Railroad train porter helps a passenger board the Los Angeles–Chicago Challenger. *Behind them is a UP nurse-stewardess. This coach and tourist-sleeper train was introduced in the mid-1930s, when this photograph was probably taken, in an effort to win back passengers by offering lower fares and extra personal service. To train porters, nurse-stewardesses represented another level of white authority. Courtesy Lucius M. Beebe and Charles M. Clegg, Jr. Collection, California State Railroad Museum*

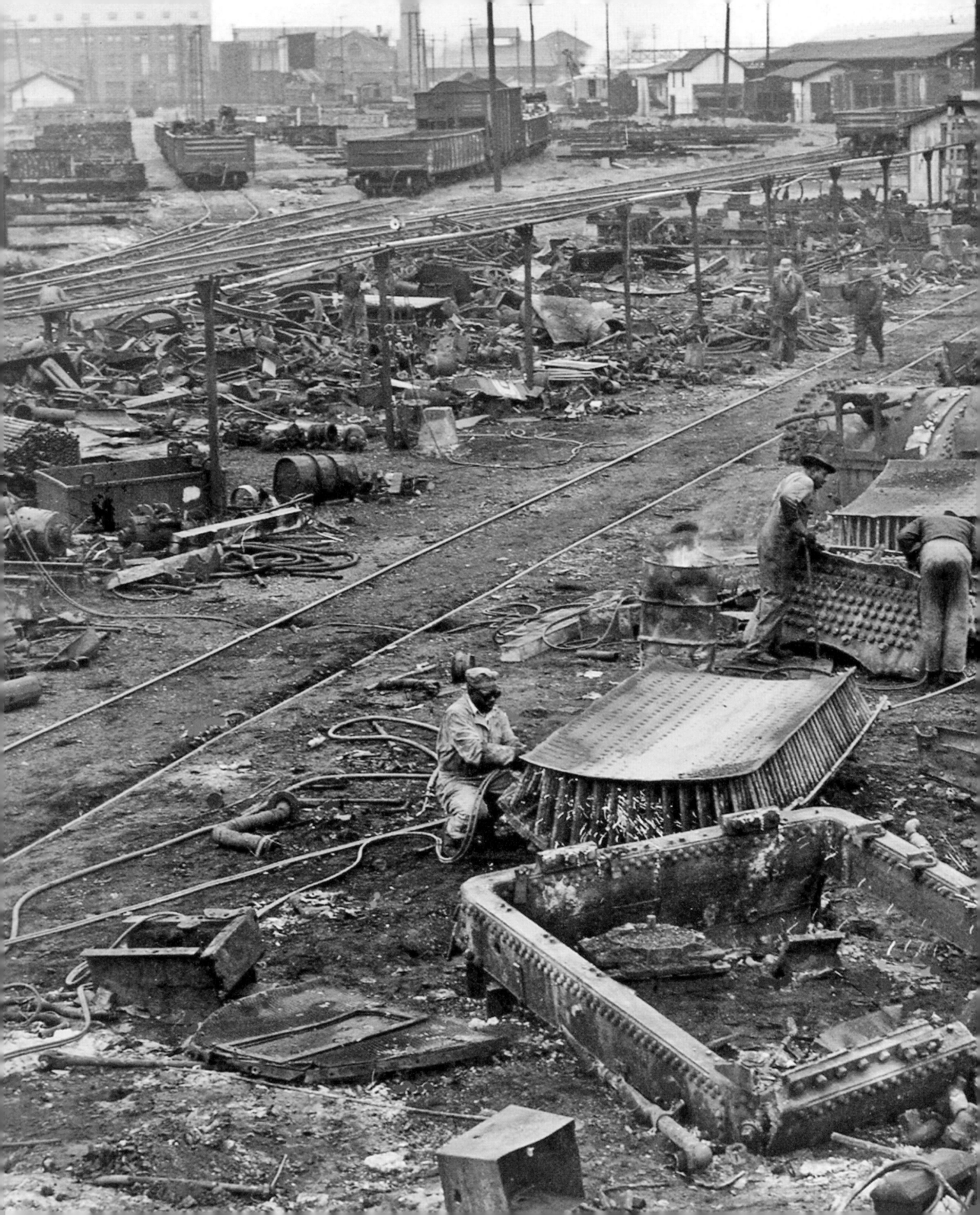

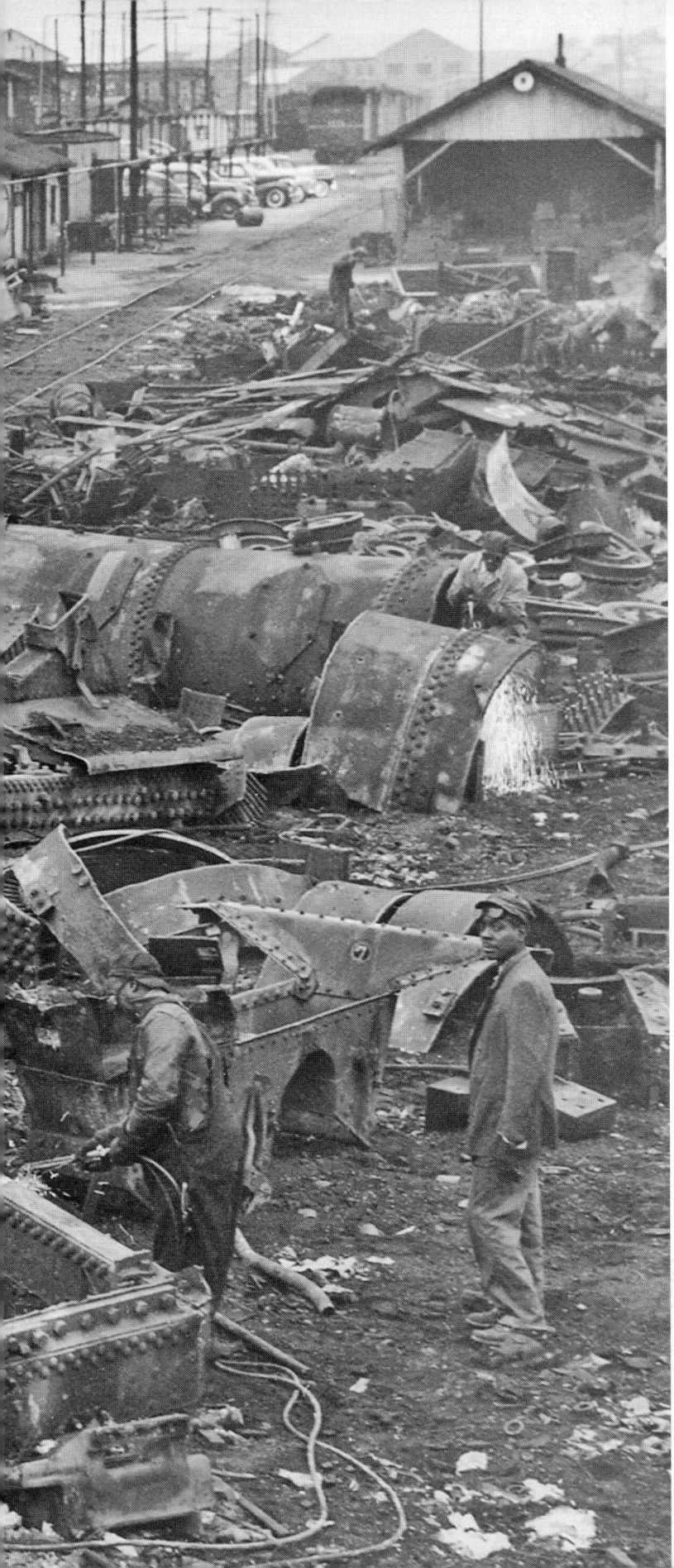

Black laborers swarm over the vast Atlantic Coast Line Railroad "boneyard" (scrap yard) at Emerson Shops, Rocky Mount, North Carolina. Most newly hired black shop workers on the Louisville & Nashville Railroad were first assigned such work in what they called "the penitentiary." Imagine how hot it was in summer, using acetylene cutting torches and sledgehammers to dismantle obsolete locomotives without benefit of shade. This photo shows the end of the steam locomotive era. The ACL's locomotive fleet was completely dieselized by 1958. Courtesy of Wilmington Railroad Museum, Wilmington, NC

407

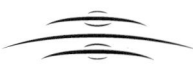

"I PICK UP MY LIFE AND TAKE IT ON THE TRAIN"

Representations of Railroads
in Art and Literature

F rom the earliest railroad days, trains sped into the imaginations of African Americans. In their spirituals, slaves identified the new mode of transportation with freedom. Plantation work songs were adapted for railroad labor. So with railroads an important part of the collective consciousness of black America in the nineteenth century, it is no wonder that they similarly invested twentieth-century African American art and literature. Because black art until relatively recently explored the realities of life, not abstraction, trains, tracks, and workers were treated as recognizable elements of daily life. What is striking, however, is what is missing: when black artists have portrayed railroaders, they have not highlighted the occupations most familiar to whites, like Pullman porters and Red Caps. Instead, they have depicted those who toiled hardest and were exploited most, those in construction and track maintenance.

If any single work is the archetypical African American railroad painting, it might be Walter Ellison's *Train Station*. Ellison grew up in Georgia and boarded a train in Macon for the North, eventually settling in Chicago, where he studied at the Art Institute and participated in the Works Progress Administration's Federal Art Project. *Train Station* could well be Macon's segregated Terminal Station from which Central of Georgia and Southern Railway passenger trains departed for Atlanta and on to cities of the North and Midwest. The walkways between the tracks form a letter *W* (the initial letter of Ellison's first name) and lead the viewer to the two opposite tracks and trains. On the left side of the platform, formally dressed whites leisurely wait for Red Caps to load their suitcases onto a Miami-bound train, en route to their Florida vacations. On the opposite side of the station, a train stands ready to depart for Chicago, Detroit, and New York. Its black passengers, dressed in overalls and other everyday clothing, are in dynamic motion, hurrying to board. Although the trains take one race to leisure, the other to labor, the northbound one represents freedom, opportunity, and hope for a better life elsewhere for African Americans.[1]

The most extensive depiction of the railroads' influence in black life is Jacob Lawrence's suite of paintings depicting the Great Migration. In 1940, when he began work on the series, migrants were again starting to flood northward. The New Deal influenced Lawrence to paint with a political purpose, to portray both the hopes and aspirations of blacks and the obstacles they faced. Enrollment in various WPA arts programs provided the opportunity to paint three historical narrative series, on Toussaint L'Overture, the Haitian liberation leader. and on abolitionists Frederick Douglass and Harriet Tubman. These works brought Lawrence some public attention and a fellowship, allowing him to rent a studio where he laid out pieces of 12-inch by 18-inch Masonite and proceeded to work, in tempera, on all 60 migration paintings at one time. Lawrence composed titles for each one before he began, so in a sense, they are illustrations for a political text. All were finished in 1941, little more than a year after he began.

Eleven of the 60 paintings are railroad scenes. The first and most famous one, *During World War I there was a great migration north by southern African Americans*, depicts a train station where long lines of migrants trade in their life savings for tickets. Other paintings show a waiting room packed with patient travelers and a platform overflowing with boxes, bundles, and suitcases. Coaches are crowded, but that does not deter the migrants, who enter Chicago, Detroit, or Pittsburgh with high expectations. Some newcomers find railroad employment, while others take jobs in industries. *Migrants were advanced passage on the railroad, paid for by northern industry* presents a dramatic contrast, showing no human figures but only the profile of a locomotive speeding into the night, with its headlight peering forward as if entering an uncertain future. The 60th and final painting, *And the migrants kept coming*, depicts yet another crowded station platform and, in its similarity to the first painting, neatly brackets the suite.[2]

Palmer Hayden was a largely self-taught artist who grew up alongside the Richmond, Fredericksburg & Potomac Railroad tracks in Wide Water, Virginia. During his childhood, as he heard his father and others sing the ballad of John Henry, he began to make sketches of this hero. Forty years later, Hayden completed his most famous work, 12 oil paintings called the John Henry series. The canvases narrate scenes from his birth to his death, depicting him as strong and muscular, bigger than others, and wielding an enormous hammer that is much larger than a "nine-pound hammer." In *John Henry on the Right, Steam Drill on the Left*, he has three hammers, presumably wearing them out one by one while triumphing over the white man's machine. Although Hayden's figures are not fully realistic images, they portray ordinary blacks in strong, sympathetic poses and highlight their resilience and ability to enjoy life.[3] His telling of the John Henry legend is as fully realized as the most detailed ballad version.

Romare Bearden, one of the most important twentieth-century African American artists, incorporated trains into dozens of paintings, collages, and prints. His family moved to the North when he was three, but he spent nearly every childhood summer back "home" in Charlotte, North Carolina, within earshot of the busy Southern Railway main line between Washington and Atlanta. His fascination took him to the station to see fast passenger trains, hear the train caller announce their destinations, and fantasize about the exotic places they would go. Years later, Bearden included steam-locomotive-drawn trains in numerous collages with titles like *Southern Limited, The Afternoon Northbound, Sunset Limited,* and *Daybreak Express.* He explained, "a train was one of the most important things in the lives of the African American children in the rural South. Each train had a name that they knew, and as it passed, they could dream about and associate with the image of the cities to which the train was going, cities they had never seen." Bearden wasn't a sentimentalist about the past, but his memories invaded his art.[4]

Multiple meanings inhabit Bearden's train images. "I use the train as a symbol of the other civilization—the white civilization and its encroachment upon the lives of blacks. The train was always something that could take you away and could also bring you to where you were. And in the little towns it's the black people who live near trains." In *The Conversation,* two women are engaged in intense dialogue while a steam locomotive passes behind them, going in an opposite direction. According to Bearden, the train leads to the past, the "homeland of your imagination," but it also represents the ever-present intrusion of racism on the lives of blacks.[5] *Daylight Express,* a collage drawn from Bearden's childhood memories, juxtaposes a sleeping nude facing South with a train charging North, relating the tensions between past and present, home and one's migrant destination, and the soft, warm closeness of rural southern communities with the hard cold steel of modern industrial life. Another dramatic collage, *Work Train,* has two lovers on their bed eying a passing train that is visible through an open window. She remains alluringly nude, while he grudgingly arises to dress and depart for work. Here the juxtaposition of the woman's sensual curves with the hard geometry and inanimate steel of the locomotive again illustrates the pressures of modern life on relationships. Similar themes emerge in *Pittsburgh Memories,* where the impersonal symbols of industrial America—locomotive, steel mill smokestacks—contrast with a tenement room where the intimacy of daily life is enacted. Finally, one of Bearden's simplest, most striking works is *Memories (Mecklenburg County),* a Matisse-like collage with two female figures almost clinging together in private conversation against a backdrop of a landscape dominated by a steam locomotive. It again contrasts the past and future, the bonds of intimacy with the fracture of relationships caused by modern life.

"Naïve" art, because it is largely narrative, readily incorporates railroad imagery. Although not widely recognized during his lifetime, William H. Johnson is today considered one of the most important African American painters in that genre. He grew up in poverty in South Carolina and,

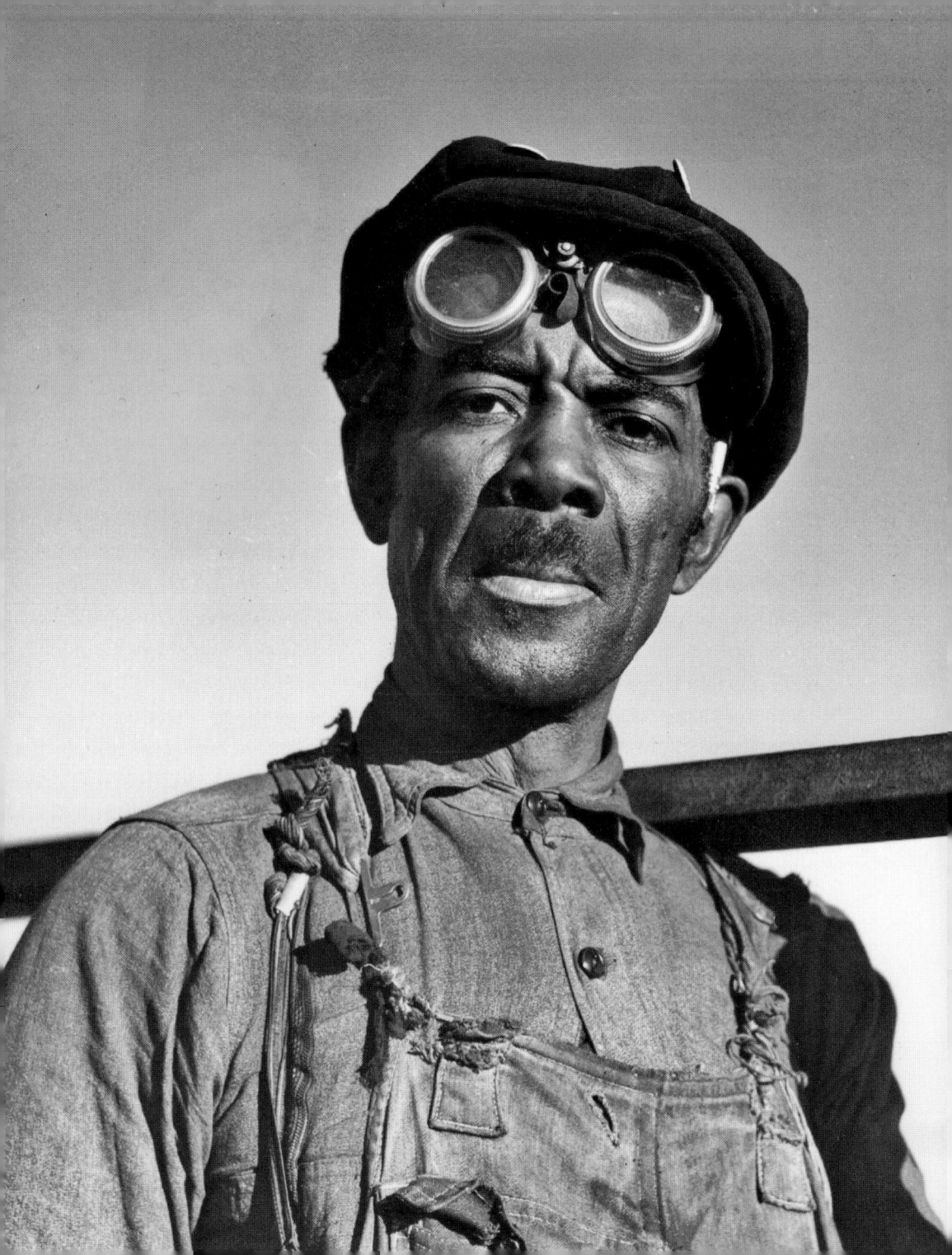

at the age of 17, immigrated to New York in 1918 to seek an art education. In the later 1920s and 1930s he lived in Europe and painted in a variety of modernist styles. But on returning to the United States in 1938, he immersed himself in African American subjects, painting in a consciously folk-art "primitive" style, using only a few basic colors to boldly depict the lives of ordinary people, subjects, and events. "My aim is to express in a natural way what I feel, what is in me, both rhythmically and spiritually, all that which in time has been saved up in my family of primitiveness and tradition, and which is now concentrated in me."[6]

Railroads appear in a number of Johnson's narrative paintings. Daily life on the home front during World War II provided much inspiration, and in *War Voyage*, black soldiers aboard a troop train receive food packages from black female Red Cross volunteers at a station stop. The train and track stretch endlessly into the distance, into the unknown future. As in the works of other black artists, the railroad takes one away from the familiar into new, uncharted, realms. Similar imagery appears in *Farewell*, where a woman and children stand on the platform of a rural station, waving goodbye to a troop train that is receding into the distance. The clash between humanity and modern industrial life is depicted in *Lunchtime Rest*. Two exhausted railroad construction workers, lying in corpse-like poses, catch a nap while steam shovels and ballast cars await their return to work (life). The men dwarf the machines and cars but their bodies are as bent as the curvature of the rails, illustrating the physical toll that railroading took on generations of African Americans. Johnson's life also ended tragically: he spent his last 23 years in a mental hospital, unable to paint.

John Biggers grew up, like Bearden, surrounded by trains. "I went to bed and got up in Gastonia [North Carolina] by train sounds. What we called 'The Bob Train' came in, like clockwork, early every morning on the Southern Line, at 4:12 or 4:15, and woke us up. And we'd play ball with home-plate on the tracks, getting off only to let a train pass through. And we'd swim at Long Creek, north of Gastonia, where the trestle was our diving board. The railroad tracks belonged to us." Biggers painted a number of canvases, including *Shotguns, Shotguns, Third Ward,* and *Shotguns, Fourth Ward,* depicting rows of traditional "shotgun" houses—airy dwellings with porches for socializing—in Houston's black districts. The structures resemble a string of railroad cars riding on tracks in the foreground. The ties are "ballasted" with African textiles, expressing Biggers's interest in African arts and crafts. The roadbed also represents residential segregation, with blacks' neighborhoods lying on the "wrong side of the tracks." In *This Little Light of Mine,* the tracks run from the foreground to the background of the painting, where they disappear into the distance. Rows of shotgun houses and their residents line both sides of the track, illustrating almost literally the intersection of railroads and the lives of blacks.[7]

One of the most striking railroad-theme paintings by any African American artist is an early Biggers canvas, *The Gleaners,* executed in the social realism style of the New Deal period. It depicts an all-too-common Depression-era scene in which desperate folk, including an old woman with a cane, brave a cold wind whipping their flimsy garments to gather lumps of coal spilled from the tenders of passing locomotives. The train track is the focal point, almost cutting the painting in two. An earthquake (the Great Depression) has rent the earth, causing the blacks' rural clapboard cabins to lean precariously. Beyond them, in the distance, loom a huge factory and the silhouette of a big-city skyline. The railroad symbolizes a ray of hope (a tiny bit of warmth at home in the midst of poverty) and, for some, the route to modern industrial life, but the few pieces of coal also tell of how little were the railroads' rewards for hard-working blacks.

Although railroads no longer play the social or economic role in African American communities they once did, Mark Anthony Priest continues to use them to explore, in bold, brilliant colors and forms, the tensions between man and machine. A contemporary African American artist and professor of painting and drawing at the University of Louisville, Priest worked seven years as a laborer and machine operator on a Louisville & Nashville Railroad rail-laying gang. His experiences were little different from those of past generations of gandy dancers. In describing his paintings, Priest explains his interest in the human side of railroading. "In the eyes of the upper echelon, the laborer seemed to function as a mere instrument in the furtherance of a great cause. Individuals appear to count for little." Supervisors regarded them as expendable machines. "The workers developed calluses on their hands; the foremen developed calluses on their hearts." In over 150 paintings and sketches, Priest portrays the humanity of railroad labor, forever "tugging, heaving, hoisting and dragging." Muscles strain heroically, summoning every ounce of mental, emotional, and physical strength. While his art depicts danger, injustice, and exploitation, it is at the same time a celebration of the workers' dignity. Priest writes that "when people think of railroads, they focus on trains, not on . . . [those] who built and maintain the tracks . . . [But] I always will be touched by the people I worked with when laying and repairing rail—they are the crux of my work."[8]

A number of Priest's paintings depict women railroaders who were initially given one of the hardest tasks, "throwing scrap," repeatedly bending over to pick up tie plates, joint bars, spikes, and rail anchors. Few men believed that women could last doing such work, but many did, graduating to other tasks alongside men like the woman driving spikes in *The Rail Laying*. Of course, not all could cut it; Priest recalls that both men and women "buckled under the pressures of the heat, the intensity of the physical labor involved, and the seemingly endless 10 hour days." Priest is a skilled portraitist, reflecting his admiration for Michelangelo's figures, with each worker dramatically "straining, pulling, pushing, running, and falling." Machines or tools are never as important as those who wield them. Yet the paintings are more than portraits; each is a narrative, telling a very real, yet often unrecorded, part of railroading.[9]

Just as black artists located railroads throughout the African American experience, authors have likewise explored railroad themes, symbols, and images. Perhaps the earliest poem of this nature was "Ballade," by the first nationally acclaimed poet of his race, Paul Laurence Dunbar. Writing at the turn of the twentieth century, but expressing a theme more common 50 years before, he wondered if industrialization—here symbolized by a locomotive's "scream" and its "clanging bell"—had forever destroyed the simplicity and peace of rural America. Soon, however, railroads were appearing in poetry as vehicles of white racism. Lizelia Augusta Jenkins Moorer published a volume in 1907 that included the most powerful protest poems by a black woman until the middle of the century. "Jim Crow Cars" was written out of her experiences—as an educated South Carolina college teacher—with the unfairness of segregation on both racial and class grounds:

> If within the cruel Southland you have chanced to take a ride,
> You the Jim Crow cars have noticed, how they crush a Negro's pride,
> How he pays a first class passage and a second class receives,
> Gets the worst accommodations ev'ry friend of truth believes.[10]

No railroad-theme poem written by a career black railroader has been discovered, but at least two came from the daughter of one. Bessie Woodson Yancy (sister of Carter G. Woodson, the "father of black history") knew railroading from her father, who was a construction laborer on the Chesapeake & Ohio in the 1870s and later worked in its Huntington, West Virginia shops. It is ironic that a black person wrote "The Train-Man's Call" celebrating the whistle artistry of locomotive engineers, all of whom were white. Another poem, however, "The Railman's Story," could have been drawn from her father's experiences. It tells of a construction laborer who sustains himself far from home by the love of his sweetheart, only to find that she has not waited for his return and has married another. Yancey's description of labor rings true:

> Just a rough life in the open,
> Taking hardships as they come,
> Little fun we had to cheer us,
> Now and then a word from home.[11]

Railroad life was widely explored in the poetry of the Harlem Renaissance, the explosion of African American creativity in literature, music, and theater in the 1920s and 1930s that brought the black arts into the mainstream of American culture. Some writers wanted to portray the race at its best and eschewed proletarian themes and the common language of the people. Others didn't care whether whites (or other blacks, for that matter) approved of their novels and poems and felt free to write naturalistically and explore themes more relevant to the black masses.[12] Literary criticism and enduring popularity have validated them as the greater artists. Among their number was Jamaican-born Claude McKay. In addition to powerful protest poems, he wrote about the lives of ordinary blacks in his adopted land, offending some readers with themes and dialogue that seemed too pungent. "On the Road" captures the labors and lifestyles of at least some dining-car waiters:

> And worried waiters, some in ugly mood,
> Crowding into the choking pantry hole
> To call out dishes for each angry glutton . . .
> At last the station's reached, the engine stops; . . .
> The waiters pass out weary, listless, glum
> To spend their tips on harlots, cards and rum.[13]

McKay knew whereof he wrote, having worked on dining cars in his earlier years.

Two Renaissance poets, Langston Hughes and Sterling Brown, found particularly rich (and often ironic) meaning in railroads. Like many other youths, Hughes grew up fascinated by trains. He would "walk down to the Santa Fe station [in Lawrence, Kansas] and stare at the railroad tracks . . . The railroad tracks ran to Chicago, and Chicago was the biggest town in the world to me."[14] Hughes spent much of his adult life in Harlem, where he crossed paths with railroaders. He required only

Railroads in the African American Experience

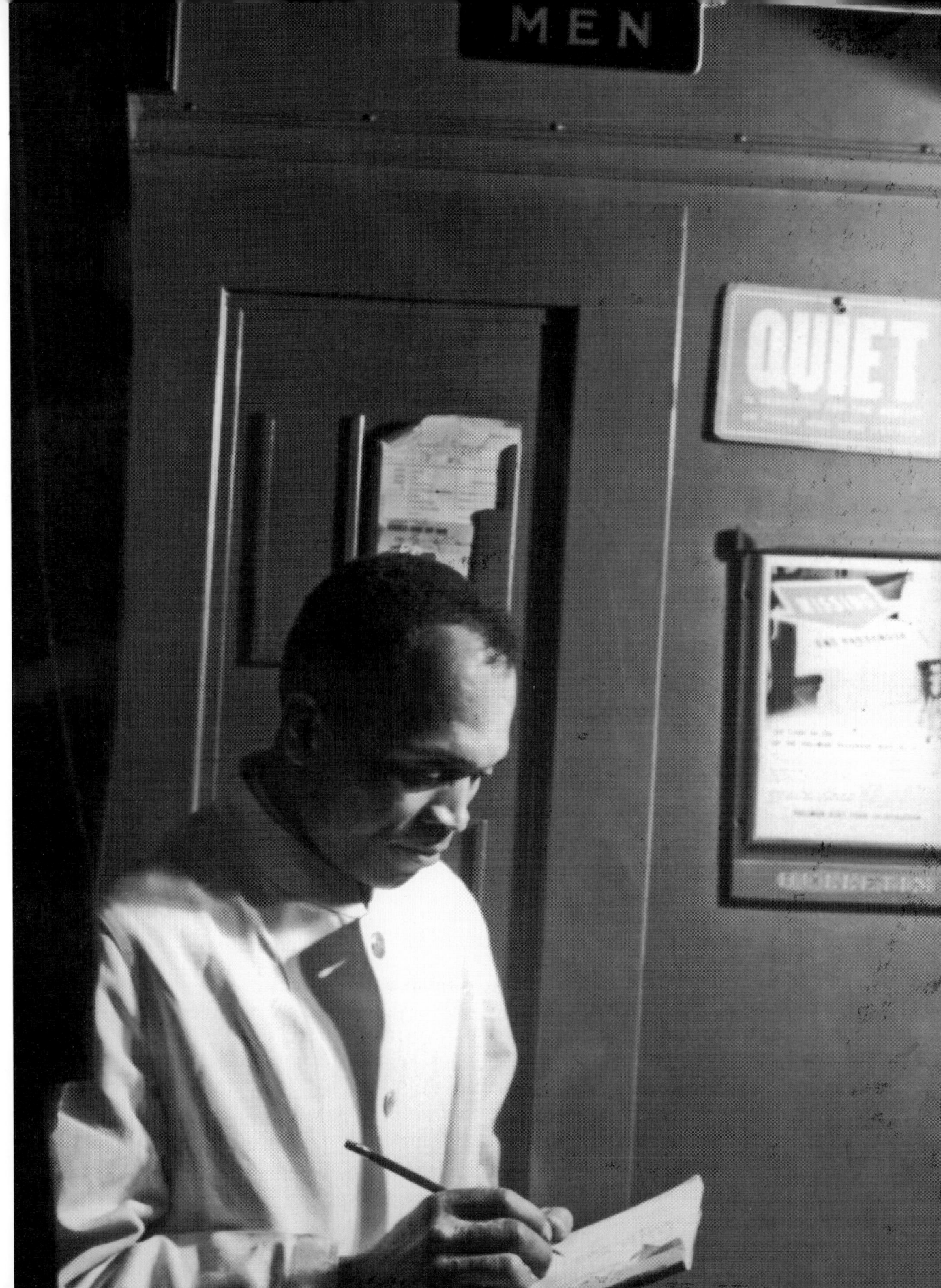

a few cryptic lines to capture how Pullman porters must act if they wanted to earn decent tips, "All my days / Climbing up a great big mountain / Of yes, sirs!"[15] Hughes also had a keen eye for the hopes and dreams of his people. For some would-be migrants, what they most needed was a "One-Way Ticket":

> I pick up my life
> And take it on the train . . .
> Any place that is
> North and West—
> And not South.[16]

Yet, in "Good Morning," Hughes acknowledged that the North (symbolized by New York's Pennsylvania Station) was no Promised Land:

> I've seen them come dar,
>   wondering
>   wide-eyed
>   dreaming
> out of Penn Station—
> but the trains are late.
> The gates open—
>   Yet there're bars
>   At each gate.[17]

Hughes frequently wrote in the blues idiom. The classic blues theme of rambling on a train to escape one's present situation, emerges in "Six-Bits Blues":

> I say six-bits' worth o' ticket
> On a train that runs somewhere.
> I don't care where it's goin'
> Just so it goes far away from here.[18]

Sometimes a train ride was an antidote for the burdens of life, as in "Blues Fantasy":

> Got a railroad ticket,
> Pack my trunk and ride.
> And when I get on the train
> I'll cast my blues aside.[19]

Yet one could just as easily get the "Homesick Blues":

> Went down to de station.
> Ma heart was in ma mouth.
> Lookin' for a box car
> To roll me to de South.[20]

Throughout his publishing career, from 1921 to his death in 1967, Hughes wrote many lines condemning racism. "Jim Crow Car" depicts the spiritual damage done by segregation:

> Get out the lunch-box of your dreams
> And bite into the sandwich of your heart,
> And ride the Jim Crow car until it screams
> And, like an atom bomb, burst apart.[21]

In 1947 and 1948, a "Freedom Train" displaying the Declaration of Independence and other historic documents touting American values toured the country. Blacks were outraged that visitors in the South were segregated. Hughes's "Freedom Train" reached a wide audience, his sarcasm perfectly expressing blacks' dismay at the continual denial of their equality:

> I hope there ain't no Jim Crow on the Freedom Train,
> No back door entrance to the Freedom Train . . .
>
> When it stops in Mississippi will it be made plain
> Everybody's got a right to board the Freedom Train?[22]

Sterling A. Brown also wrote extensively about blacks' railroad experiences. After graduating from Williams College and Harvard University, Brown taught at southern black colleges and went on folklore-collecting expeditions where he gathered raw materials for the social realism and folk idioms with which he would depict the lives and struggles of ordinary blacks. "Tin Roof Blues" expresses the desire to hop a train in search of a more welcoming environment:

> Goin' where de Norfolk Western curves jes' lak de river bends,
> Where de Norfolk Western swing around de river bends,
> Goin' where de people stacks up mo' lak friends.[23]

"Long Gone" is a classic born-to-ramble blues, in which the "railroad man" is a boomer:

I laks yo' kin' of lovin',
     Ain't never caught you wrong,
But it jes' ain' nachal
     Fo' to stay here long;

It jes' ain' nachal
     Fo a railroad man,
With a itch fo' travelin'
     He cain't understan'.[24]

Brown also wrote powerful proletarian verse to expose exploitation of the working class by wealthy capitalists. In "Street Car Gang," blacks toil with jack hammers, shovels, picks, and wheelbarrows "For the bread for the children / The cheap shoes, the overcoat / For the rent, for the number runner / The insurance dues," but also "For the finishing academy / The golf courses, the jodhpurs / The country club soirees."[25] Brown likewise skewered the pretensions of poor whites who claimed to be superior to blacks, even though they lived "Side by Side":

Listen, John Cracker; hear me, Joe Nigg.
You on one side of the railroad, you on the other.
This railroad track is no final separation.
This eighteen foot cut isn't a canyon . . .

Listen, John, does Joe's riding up front in the Jimmy [Jim Crow car]
Sweeten so much the dull grits of your days?[26]

"Break of Day" is a bitter protest poem that only slightly fictionalizes the murders of southern black firemen by white railroaders in the early 1930s, when "crackers craved the job what Jess was holding":

Mob stopped the train crossing Black Bear Mountain
Shot rang out, babe, shot rang out.
They left Big Jess on the Black Bear Mountain,
Break of day, baby, break of day.[27]

Brown's affection for black railroaders, who did much of the heavy, dirty work of the industry, is expressed in "Call Boy." (A call boy woke up railroaders to summon them for their next assignment.) Clearly, the railroad "owned" them more than they owned themselves:

O you shifters and humpers,
You boiler washers,
You oilers and you greasers
Of de drivin' rods,
You switchers and flagmen,
Tie layers and tampers,
You wanted at de Norfolk
And Western yards.[28]

African American poets have also created, re-created, and celebrated black heroes. Some are in the John Henry tradition. Others exalt the indomitable hero/antihero like Railroad Bill. Melvin B. Tolson, influenced by the writers of the Harlem Renaissance, wrote "The Birth of John Henry," supplying "missing" details in that legend:

The night John Henry is born an ax
of lightning splits the sky,
and a hammer of thunder pounds the earth,
and the eagles and panthers cry!

John Henry—he says to his Ma and Pa
"Get a gallon of barleycorn.
I want to start right, like a he-man child,
the night that I am born!"[29]

Plucking another character from the folk memory, Ishmael Reed, poet and novelist of the 1960s Black Arts Movement, made "Railroad Bill, A Conjure Man" immortal, since a sorcerer could change himself into any form he pleased. Whites exulted that Bill was finally dead, but blacks knew differently:

See that livestock grazing there
That Bull is Railroad Bill
The mean one over there near the
Fence, that one is Railroad Bill[30]

Margaret Walker, the first nationally recognized black woman poet, drew on the conventions of folklore to create a new mythic figure in "Two-Gun Buster and Trigger Slim," a poetic ballad about a railroad construction worker who combined John Henry and Stagolee:

> Two-Gun Buster was a railroad han'
> Splittin' ties in the backwoods lan'
> Cuttin' logs and layin' down rails,
> Blazin' out the iron horse trails.

Two-Gun met his fate, however, when he abused a fellow worker who proved to be the faster draw and was rewarded with the moniker "Trigger Slim."[31]

Today's most revered black woman author is Maya Angelou, who overcame an abusive childhood to become a successful singer, a civil rights activist, and then a renowned novelist and poet. In "Worker's Song," she celebrates those blacks, including gandy dancers performing track maintenance, who did the hard manual labor that kept America's economy going, while receiving less than their due:

> Railroads run
> on a twinness track
> > 'cause of my back
> > Whoppa, Whoppa
> > Whoppa, Whoppa[32]

Poet and playwright Amiri Baraka, one of the most influential leaders of the Black Arts Movement, delves deep into the past to evoke the idea of trains as the means to liberation, with whistles being the call to flee. In "History-Wise #22," Baraka calls the Underground Railroad "Ms. 'Moses' Streamliner" (referring to Harriet Tubman, the "Moses" of her people):

> &wayoff
> Like a whistle or a horn
>
> The black night
> fills
> our ears
>
> We gon' go
> has already
>
> gone[33]

Riding trains, especially going "back home," remains an African American tradition. Linda Brown Bragg, whose lyrical poetry began to appear in the 1960s, recalls, in "Between Trains It Rains," the timeless experience of waking up in the middle of the night as one's train pulls away from a station stop:

> The uninterrupted rumble rocks my feet, and
> "Board" is at last heard.
> On the baggage cart, four men sit. Their cigarettes
> become little white blurs,
> As finally we leave the rain between the tracks,
> and trains, and once more
> The gentle sway lulls me to sleep.[34]

Yet some things have changed forever. Carolyn M. Rodgers reminisces in "A Train Ride" about the aging black waiters in the early Amtrak era whose dining cars no longer feature china plates, silver utensils, fresh flowers, and starched linens:

> The curved hands
> that carefully hold the
> sallow paper plates
> held silver rimmed china once,
> and a ghost of the grace remains.[35]

Although not as frequently as poets, black novelists also drew characters, experiences, and events from railroading and train riding. Claude McKay's *Home to Harlem* (1928) is the most detailed and pungent description of railroad work in all of black literature. It was written out of his own experience as a dining-car waiter on the Pennsylvania Railroad in 1917-19. Its two main characters hold down regular jobs on McKay's own New York–Pittsburgh run. Jake, a cook, is footloose, formally uneducated, and always on the lookout for women, a card game, booze, cocaine, or opium. Ray, on the other hand, is a waiter, has a partial college education, and is an avid reader of "race" newspapers and highbrow fiction. He symbolizes the "respectable" ones who don't habitually drink or gamble away their earnings, who don't keep another woman in their "away" city, and who are upstanding middle-class citizens whose lifestyles and achievements are sometimes chronicled in black newspapers. A third figure is a dictatorial chef who showers abuse on the waiters, whom he calls "dime snatchers." Over them all hovers the Irish steward. Waiters and cooks work under pressure, yelling and snarling at one another. Finally, the pantryman (first waiter) exacts his revenge by causing the eggs that the chef has personally loaded onto the car to disappear before breakfast. The

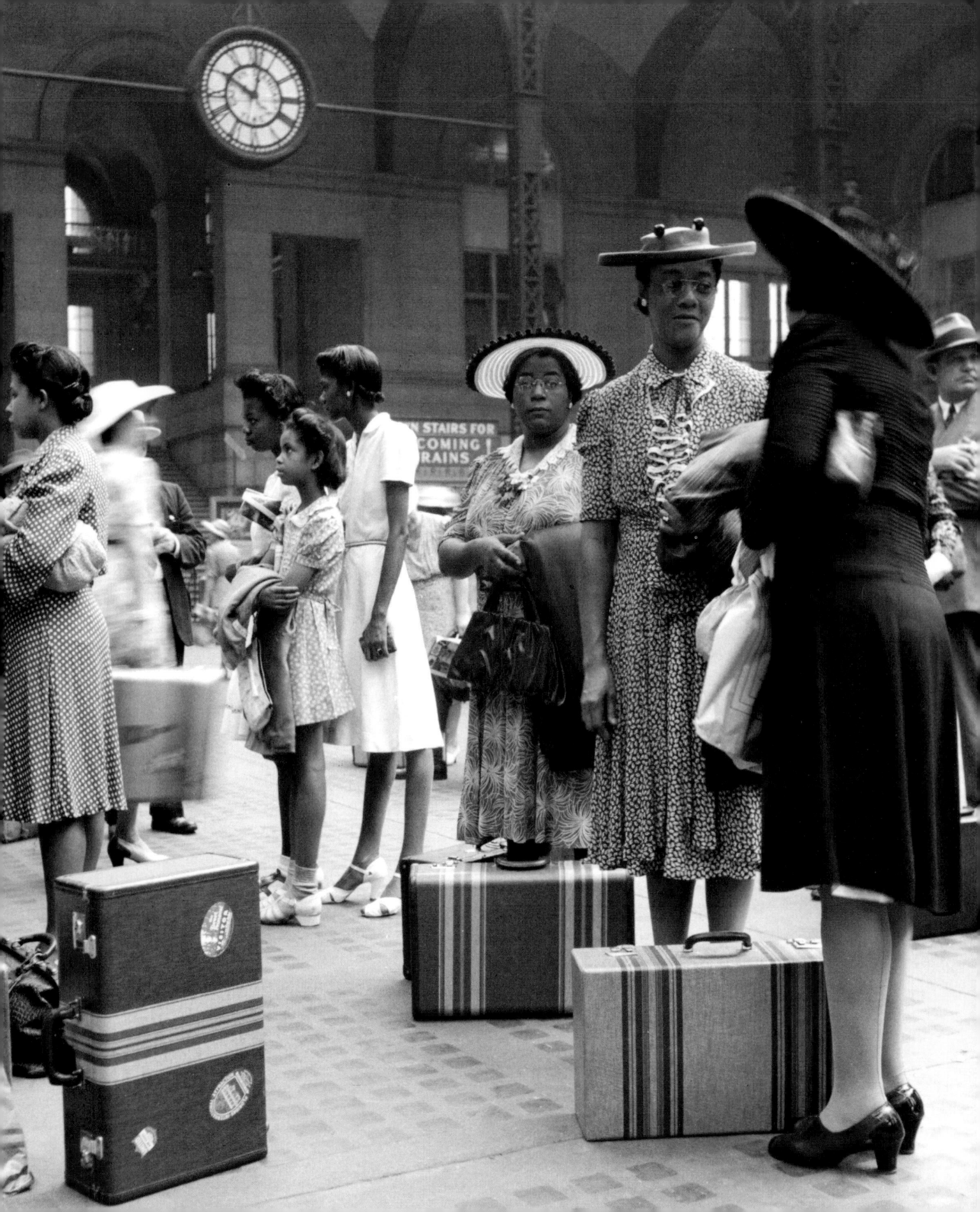

steward, who must scratch egg dishes from the menu, holds the chef responsible and transfers him to another car, where he is demoted to second cook.

McKay's description of the away-from-home quarters arranged for its black employees in Pittsburgh stands in sharp contrast to the Pennsy's own self-congratulation at being a benevolent employer. The lodging was free, but a hellhole of dirty sheets and bedbugs. Sleep came only to those who were utterly exhausted, drunk, or zoned out on "Chinese tobacco." Others, unwilling to keep company with vermin, stayed up to drink and gamble or went out into the city to find speakeasies or brothels. All in all, railroading was hard. According to Ray, work as a waiter was "a crazy, clattering, nerve-shattering life."[36] McKay's dialogue was raw for its day, and most black reviewers of *Home to Harlem* found the book lurid and an embarrassment to the race. It was the only black-authored bestseller in the 1920s, being read by whites more than blacks. Although the conflict between waiters and cooks may be exaggerated, McKay offers vivid descriptions of the close-quarter maneuvering that was required on dining cars, the social distinctions dividing one group from another, and the camaraderie that nonetheless united them, if not always on the cars, then during their layovers.

The other major novelistic description of black railroading is a chapter in Lloyd L. Brown's *Iron City* (1951), a gritty, realistic proletarian novel set in a Pittsburgh prison where several inmates await their fate. Brown was a journalist and communist labor organizer. One of his inmate characters was Isaac Zachary, born in rural Mississippi. Zach's life was transformed at the age of 14, when he first saw the train whose whistle he had heard all his life. He dreamed of becoming an engineer and, leaving home at 16, started working for the "Great Southwestern & Gulf" as a callboy. Two years later, the full-grown Zach was promoted to engine wiper in the roundhouse, where he could be close to the powerful, mysterious machines he revered. Everyone but the roundhouse supervisor was black: hostlers, fire tenders, wipers, even the mechanics, although they were classified as helpers so that they could be paid less than a white craftsman. Out in the yard and on the freight trains, the brakemen were all black, as were a majority of locomotive firemen. But the only blacks to actually "drive" a locomotive were the hostlers, who merely shifted them around the shops. Young Zach was soon familiar with the rigid racial hierarchies but could not shake his dream of being an engineer. The roundhouse and its denizens became his home and family, but he jumped at the chance when he was offered work as a brakeman. He was then able to bid on a fireman's job and eventually became preferred by the white engineers because of his reliability and sobriety.

Life was good for Zach, now a married man, up through the World War I years, although he had gradually to abandon his dream of becoming an engineer. But when the Great Depression hit the railroad and black firemen like Zach kept their jobs while younger white firemen were furloughed, "it became a shooting war." Brown's narrative was written straight out of Mississippi headlines, "when the God-given advantages of being white wasn't worth a damn against the man-made rule of seniority."[37] As Zach returned home late one night, a would-be assassin fired a load of buckshot into his back, nearly killing him. On the first day he could hobble back to work, he found that the deepening Depression had obliterated even more jobs, including his. Zach had little choice but to migrate to the uncertainties of a northern city where he might find a factory job, but where no black man was a locomotive fireman, much less an engineer. His dream died, finally, with the move to Pittsburgh.

One of the most engaging African American works published since the civil rights era is Albert Murray's debut novel, *Train Whistle Guitar* (1974). Murray grew up in Magazine Point, a black community on the outskirts of Mobile, Alabama, which provides the setting for his story of a boy, Scooter, growing into adolescence in the 1920s. The title refers to Scooter's hero, an itinerant musician who could play the guitar "as if he were also an engineer telling tall tales on a train whistle," a man who also had a "notorious holler" that sounded like "a bad express train saying Look out this me and here I come and I'm coming through one more time." Scooter derived his definition of manhood from this musician who played the blues, gambled, hopped freight trains, and occasionally landed in jail.[38]

The geography of Scooter's world was defined by the railroads. "It was as if you had been born hearing and knowing about trains and train whistles," Murray wrote. Young boys' folk hero was Railroad Bill, who was uncatchable "because he worked a mojo on them [whites] that nobody ever heard of before or since." The black settlement of "Gasoline Point" was adjacent to the Louisville & Nashville Railroad's Birmingham–New Orleans main line. Northbound freights often stopped at a siding, providing opportunity for hopping on boxcars. Scooter and his best friend Little Buddy Marshall dreamt of their own someday travels: "We were also reminding ourselves of the inevitability of the day when we too would have to grab ourselves an expert armful of lightning special L & N freight train rolling north by east to the steel blue castles and patent leather avenues of Philamayork, which was the lodestone center of the universe."[39] Even tales of those who had lost limbs or lives in trying to catch moving trains did not scare them for long, because they also dreamed of eventually coming back, all spiffed up and tricked out, on the fabled *Pan-American.*

The first chapter unfolds as Scooter and Little Buddy prepare to catch their first freight. Hiding their schoolbooks, because they are playing hooky, they are about to climb into a boxcar when their blues man hero discovers them. He doesn't administer the expected tongue lashing, but leads them to the hobo jungle where, "like every fireside knee-pony uncle and shade tree uncle and tool shed uncle and barbershop uncle," he tells them "about going to school and learning to use your head like the smart, rich and powerful whitefolks."[40] Murray's rendering of Scooter's railroad-infused childhood is a delightful evocation of the influence of trains on the imaginations of black children and parallels his friend Romare Bearden's own views on the subject.

Railroads also assume major symbolism in the plays of August Wilson, one of America's preeminent playwrights (two Pulitzers, several Tonys) in the last quarter century. Trains represent "freedom and a life's journey . . . cheap and reliable transportation, a ready egress from difficult situations, a source of jobs, and a standard element of storytelling and blues lyrics" as well as the means for migrating back and forth between southern homes and northern employment.[41] The most extensive imagery occurs in *The Piano Lesson* (1990), set in Pittsburgh in 1936. Its main character, and the anchor for an extended family, is Doaker, a widowed railroader who started out on the fabled "Yellow Dog" (Yazoo Delta). The railroad "got yellow boxcars. Sometime the way the whistle blow sound like an old dog howling so the people call it the Yellow Dog." Doaker recalls that "I used to line track. I pieced together the Yellow Dog stitch by stitch. Rail by rail." But for much of the subsequent 27 years, he was a dining-car cook and model to himself, his family, and the black community, of respectability, stability, and economic self-sufficiency. According to his nephew Boy Willie, "every two weeks [when Doaker returns from an extended run] the women all put on their dresses and line up at the railroad station."[42] A bit later Boy Willie sings an old blues, "Berta, Berta":

> When you marry, don't marry no farming man,
> Everyday Monday, hoe handle in your hand.
>
> When you marry, marry a railroad man,
> Everyday Sunday, dollar in your hand.

In fact, life as a dining-car cook is hard. As he irons his uniform, Doaker sings about the peripatetic life of the railroader, as if he were a train caller at a station:

> Gonna leave Jackson Mississippi
> and go to Memphis
> and double back to Jackson
> Come on down to Hattiesburg

Change cars on the Y. D.
Coming through the territory to
Meridian
and Meridian to Greenville
and Greenville to Memphis
I'm on my way and I know where[43]

The folklore of southern railroads is another prominent feature of *The Piano Lesson*, particularly the legend of the Ghosts of the Yellow Dog. A quarter century before, Doaker's brother Boy Charles had caught a freight, fleeing from a lynch mob. But the mob stopped the train, discovered their victim in a boxcar with four hoboes, and shut the door and set the car on fire, incinerating those inside. Soon thereafter, whites started mysteriously dying, events credited to the ghosts. For blacks, however, the ghosts could be benign. "Sometimes you be in trouble they might be around to help you. They say if you go where the Southern cross the Yellow Dog [Moorhead, Mississippi] . . . and call out their names . . . they say they talk back to you."[44] In the play's climactic final scene, the conflict between siblings over whether to sell the family-heirloom piano is resolved as a ghost makes its presence known, to the sound of an approaching train.

Railroad themes also appear in other Wilson plays. Doub, one of the main characters in *Jitney* (1982), was a dining-car cook but now drives an unlicensed cab while waiting to collect his railroad pension. He offers sage advice to younger men, urging them to take advantage of their advantages, get an education, forsake fast living, and make something of themselves. When the jitney business is imperiled, Doub steps in to offer leadership to the company.[45] The main character in *Two Trains Running* (1991) is another strong figure, Memphis Lee, who years before was run out of Mississippi by racists but has made good in Pittsburgh. Prospering from hard work and hitting the numbers, he is now the proprietor of a diner who dresses well and drives a Cadillac. Yet he is determined to ride the train back South to avenge himself on his persecutors. "I'm going back one of these days. I ain't even got to know the way. All I got to do is find my way down to the train depot. They got two trains running every day."[46] Even though, by 1969 (when the play is set), only two railroads still offered passenger service west from Pittsburgh, the Baltimore & Ohio and Penn Central, which connected with the Illinois Central for a trip south to Mississippi, "two trains" continued to make a circuit between old and new homes, past and present, loss and hope.

It's no wonder that painters, poets, novelists, and a playwright found inspiration in railroads. The black arts in the twentieth century repeatedly voiced and reflected the aspirations of working people, many of whom had deep roots in railroading. Peel the bark from most any black family tree today, and one, two, or three generations before, there were railroaders. African Americans were more influenced by railroads than by any other part of the Industrial Revolution. From their earliest acquaintance with railroads, blacks began to identify them as important to their lives, if initially only symbolically (the Underground Railroad). Spirituals, work songs, and the blues embedded railroads in the black folk memory, providing a rich lode from which writers and artists have repeatedly drawn. But as trains receded from public consciousness generally, and from the black imagination specifically, the use of railroad imagery has faded somewhat from the black arts, although individual practitioners, like painter Mark Priest, still find inspiration in today's modern railroading.

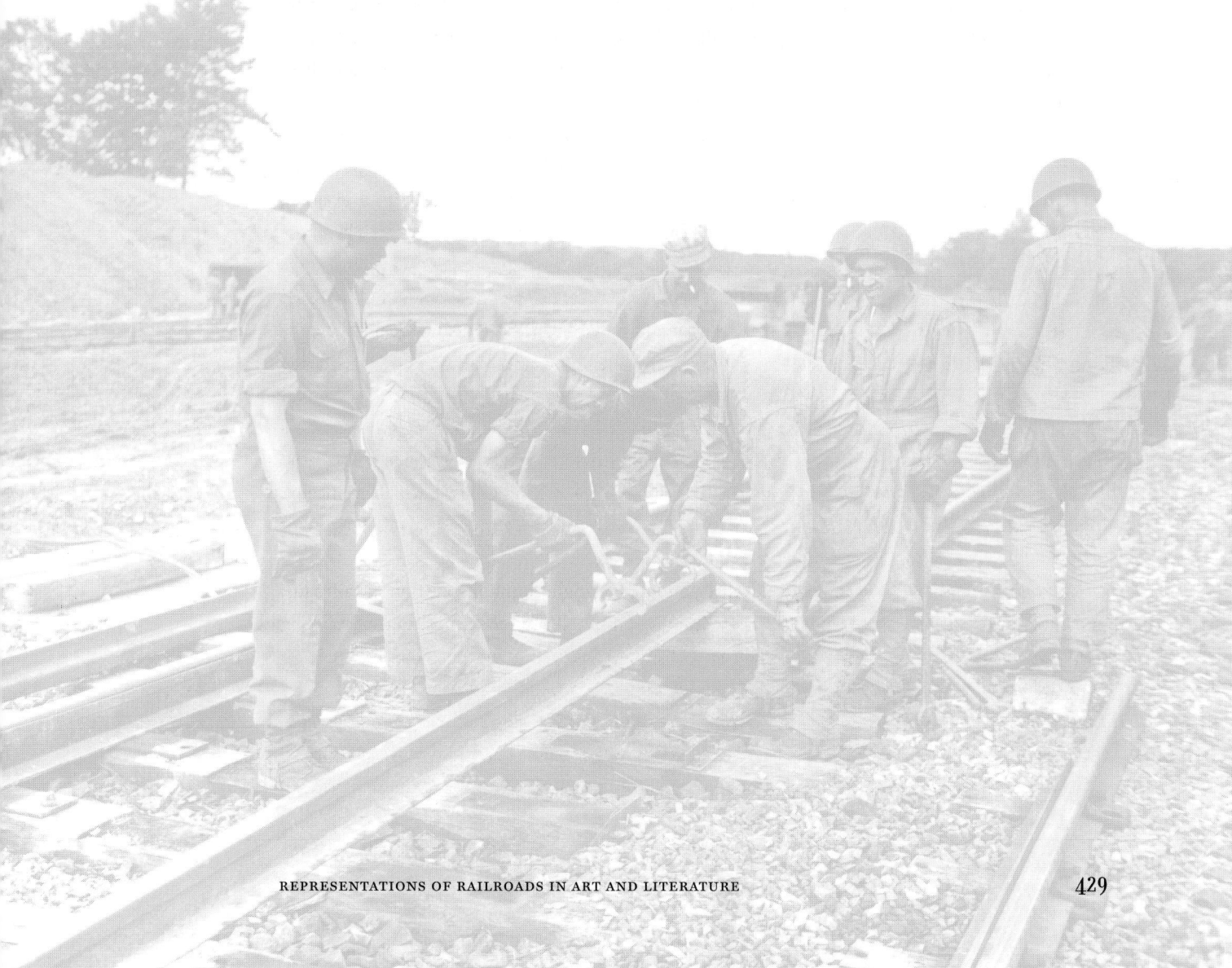

Members of the Black Diamond Diers baseball team worked at the Illinois Central Railroad's Central Station in Memphis, Tennessee, where they were photographed in 1945, proudly wearing uniforms identifying their employer. The front of a locomotive was a favorite place for sports teams and other employee social groups to pose. Theodore Kornweibel collection

430

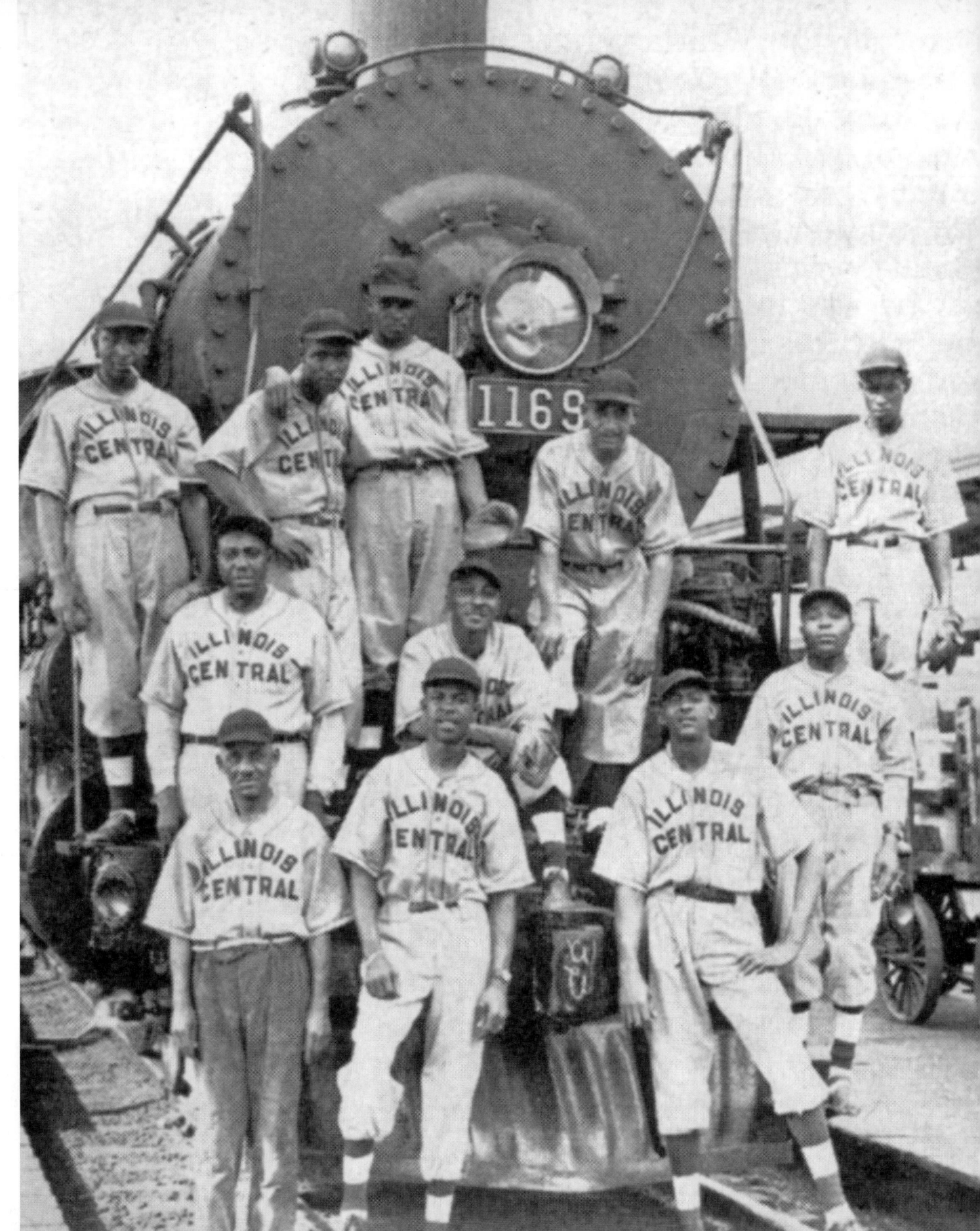

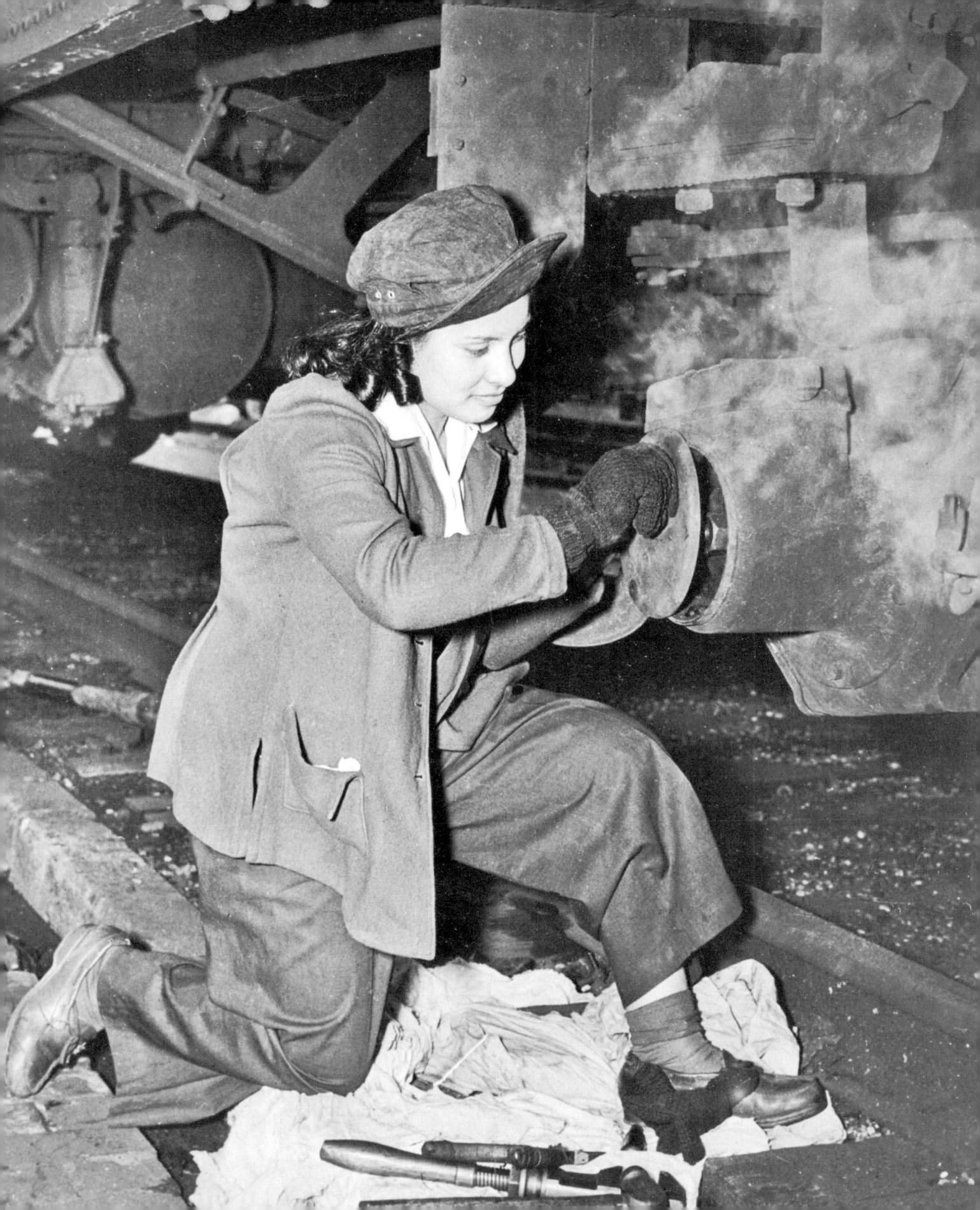

A black woman mechanic, working at the New York Central Railroad's Detroit terminal, repairing a passenger car generator during World War II. She was a rarity. Most skilled railroad jobs were reserved for white women. This young lady has not sacrificed her femininity for shop work: although she wears a man's shoes, cap, and coat, her hair-do is in the latest style. Women's Bureau Records, National Archives

(BELOW) Most black women who found war work in railroad shops and roundhouses during World War II performed unskilled and dirty tasks deemed particularly appropriate to members of their race. One of the dirtiest and noisiest jobs was greasing locomotives. This woman, working for the New York Central Railroad in Buffalo, New York, is performing an essential maintenance function, operating an Alemite gun to grease the moving parts of a steam locomotive's running gear. Women's Bureau Records, National Archives

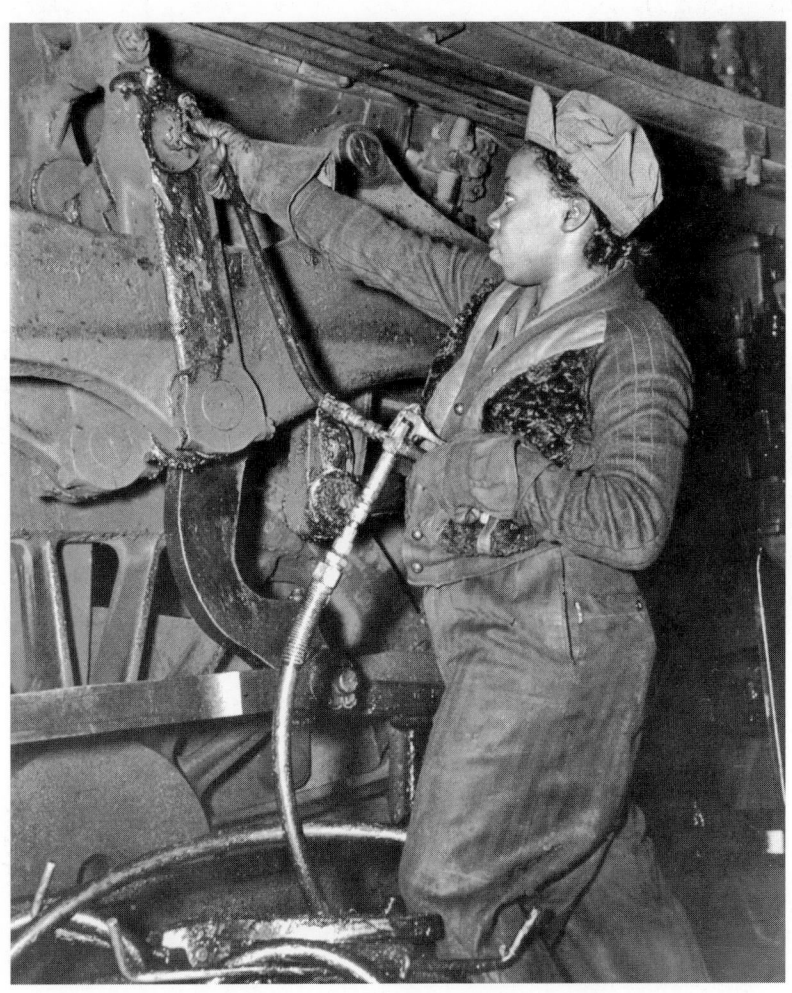

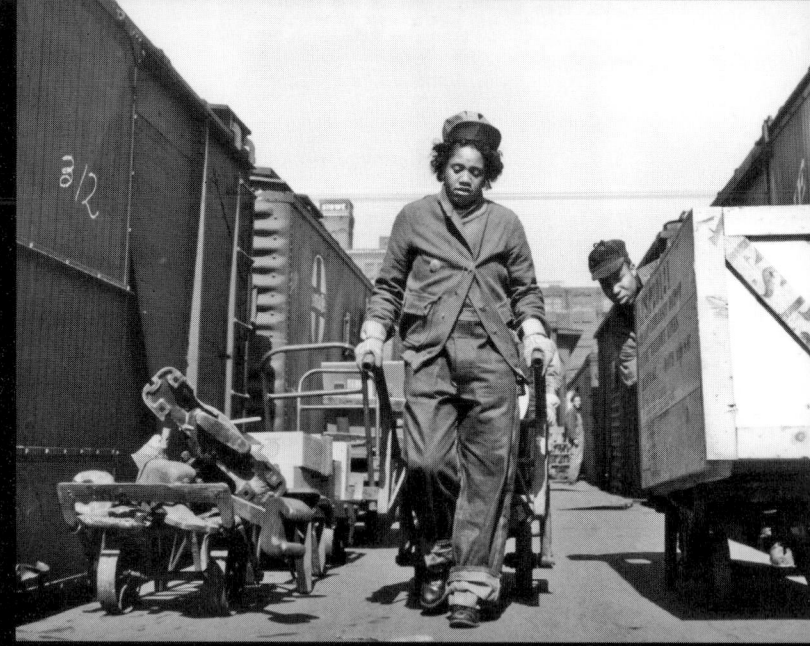

(BELOW) *Elgertha Smith, Beatrice Turner, and Ella Rubardee* (left to right), *inside car cleaners at the Baltimore & Ohio Railroad's Camden Station in Baltimore in 1943. According to B&O's public relations department, they were so highly motivated that they sang constantly while they worked. With crowded wartime travel, cars became dirtier than ever. This was not an employment breakthrough, though. Black women had worked as car cleaners in the North since World War I, and for even longer in the South. Women's Bureau Records, National Archives*

(ABOVE) *Unlike World War I, the federal government did not restrict the type of railroad labor women could perform during World War II. Hence they muscled heavier loads than before. Mildred Williams was one of several female freight truckers working alongside male colleagues at the Santa Fe Railway's Kansas City, Missouri freight depot in early 1943. It must be cold: she is wearing two pairs of pants and several layers under her jacket. Jack Delano photo, FSA / OWI Collection, Prints and Photographs Division, Library of Congress*

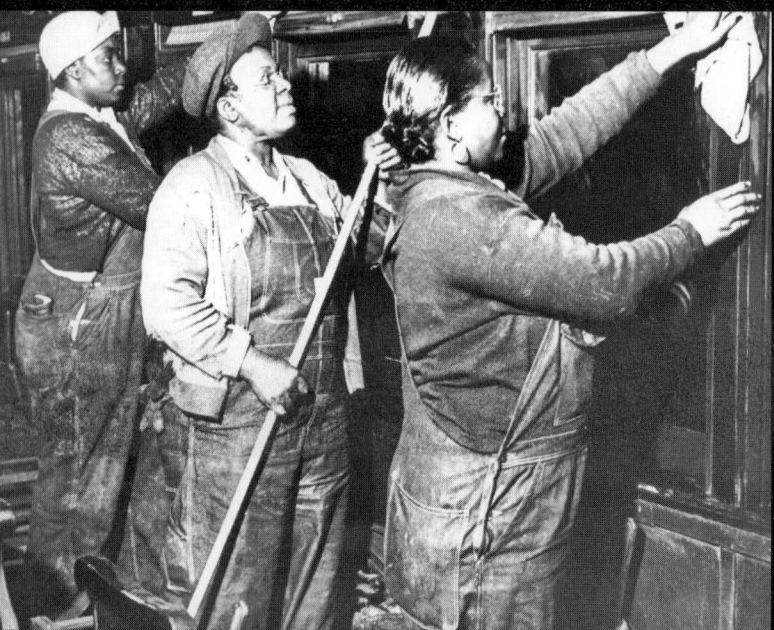

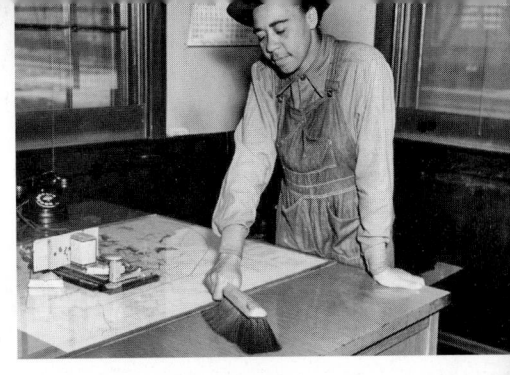

(BELOW) *A Baltimore & Ohio female track crew at Washington, D.C., in 1943, unusual in being supervised by a black foreman, not, as was almost always the case, by a white man. The women are a fascinating group. (Left to right) Marcella Lockhart was the mother of one child while Ida Jackson had 14 children and 36 grandchildren. Catherine Jackson and Lucille Gray were twin sisters. Mildred Johnson, single, worked alongside her mother, Grace Johnson. Eleanor and Mary Naylor were sisters-in-law. And Clarice Cook was single. Grandmother Ida Jackson was said to be as dexterous with a shovel as one a third her age. Were they working out of patriotism, economic necessity, or both? Courtesy B&O Railroad Museum*

(ABOVE) *Black women, no less than black men, found white-collar railroad jobs off-limits. Christine Dobbins, Baltimore & Ohio Railroad office janitress at the Riverside shops in Baltimore in 1944, is keeping things spick and span, but she will have no chance, until at least the 1960s, to trade her overalls for business attire and answer that telephone. Courtesy B&O Railroad Museum*

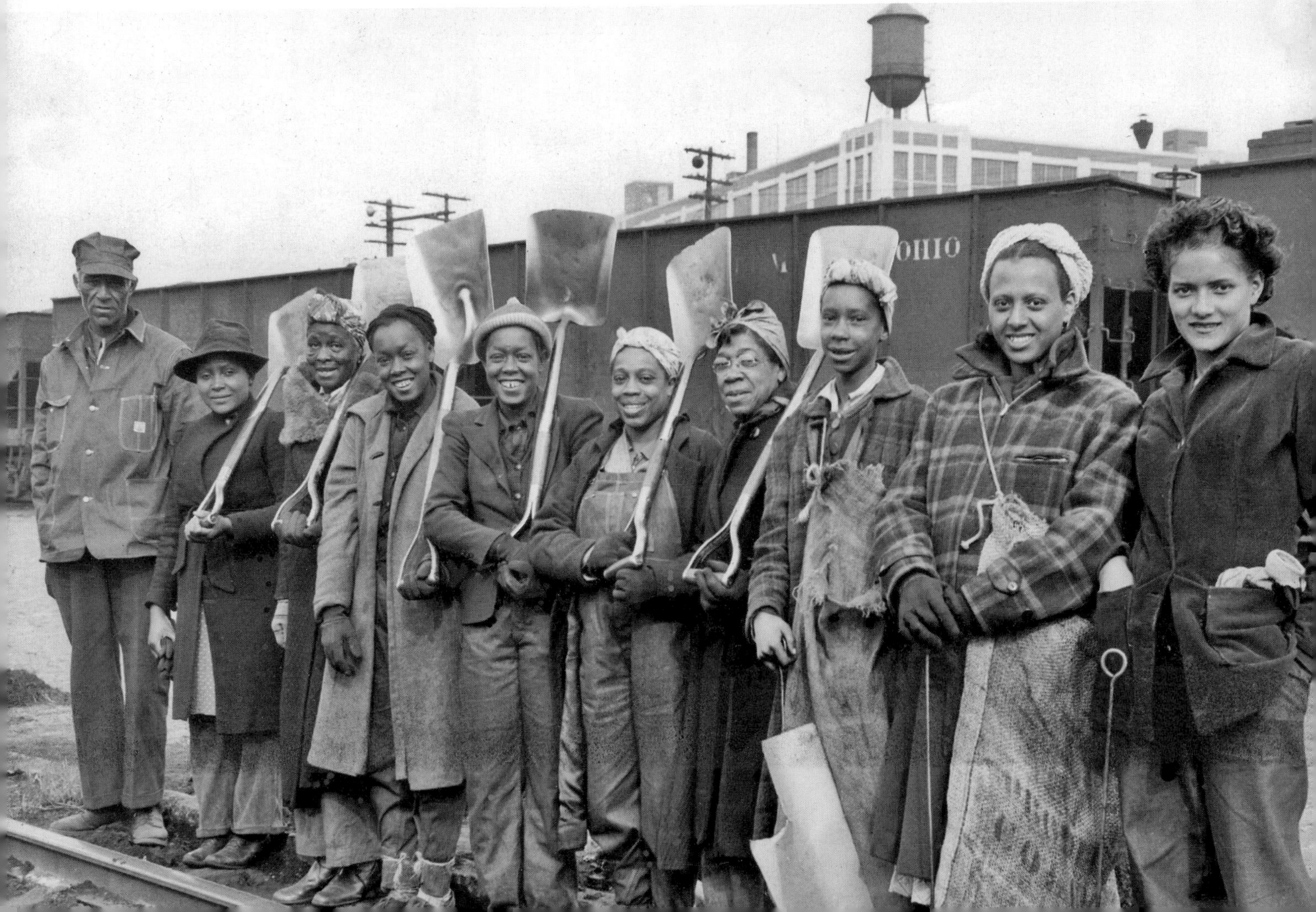

For years before they succeeded in unionizing, Pullman porters were not paid until they actually started their runs. In 1943, however, these porters, receiving reservations diagrams through pneumatic tubes from the reservation room at Chicago Union Station, enjoy better wage and working conditions won for them by the Brotherhood of Sleeping Car Porters. Jack Delano photo, FSA / OWI Collection, Prints and Photographs Division, Library of Congress

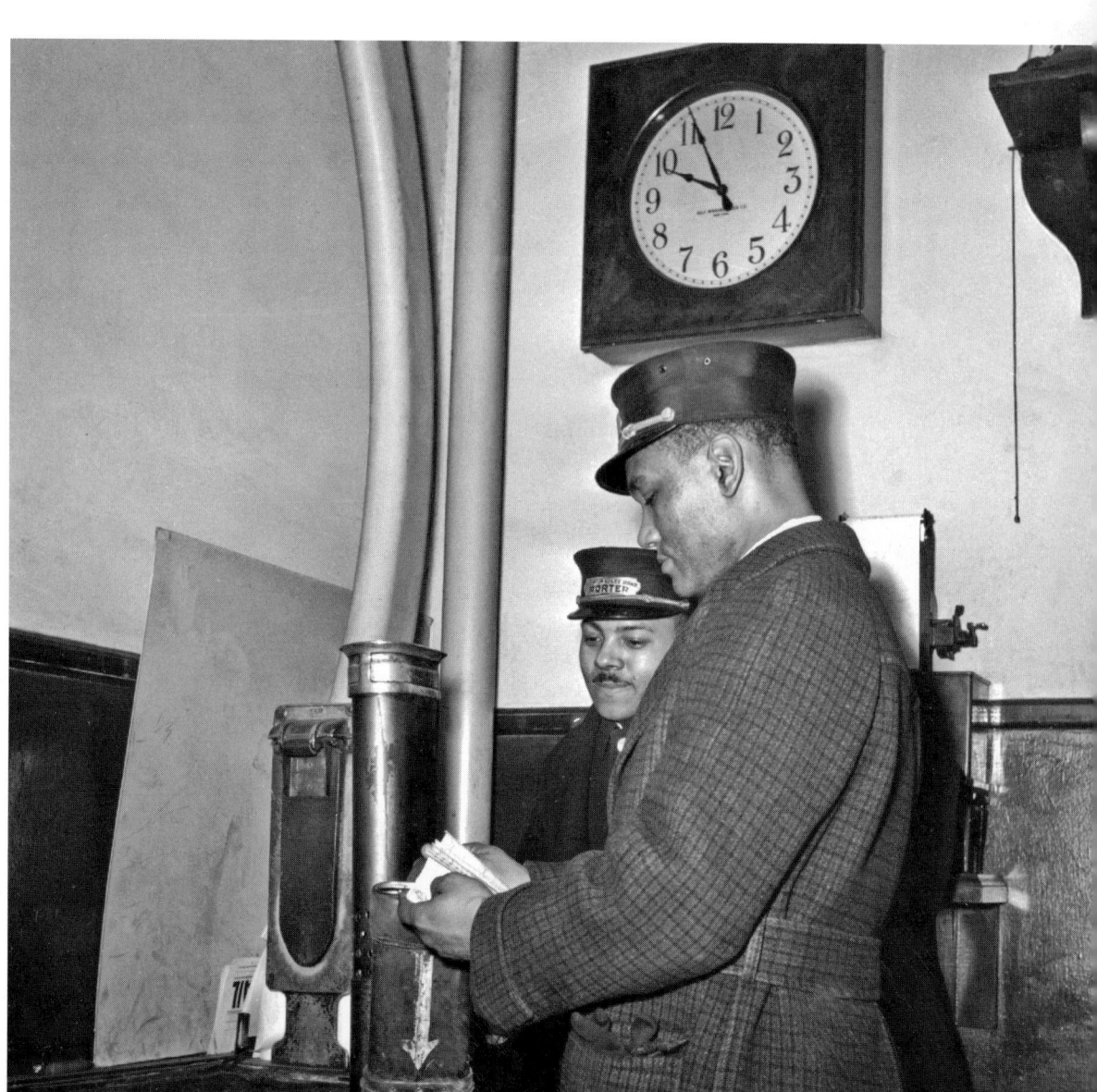

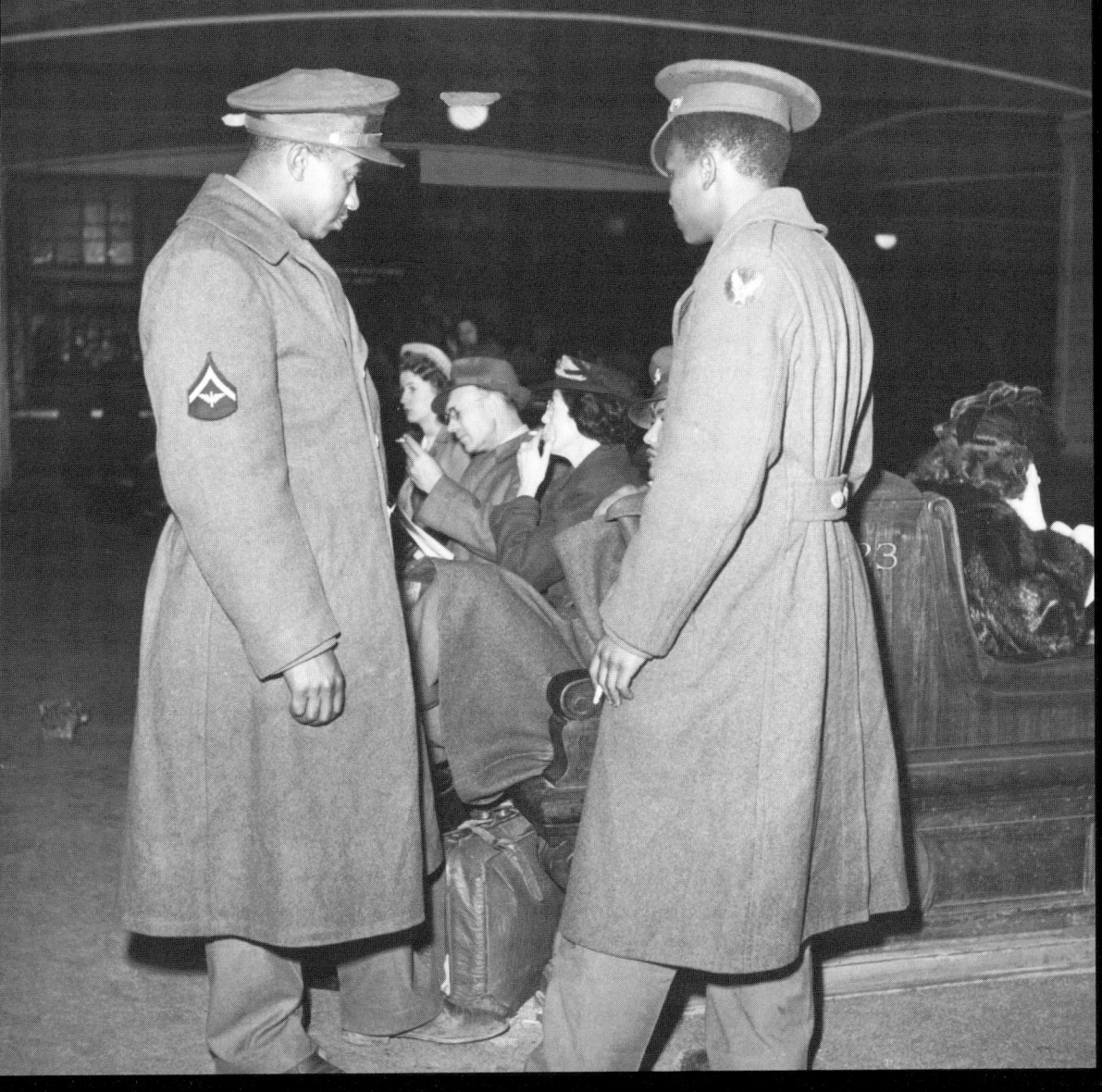

Among World War II travelers were tens of thousands of African American military personnel, some on leave for the last time before going overseas. This scene is at Chicago's Union Station in January 1943. Jack Delano photo, FSA / OWI Collection, Prints and Photographs Division, Library of Congress

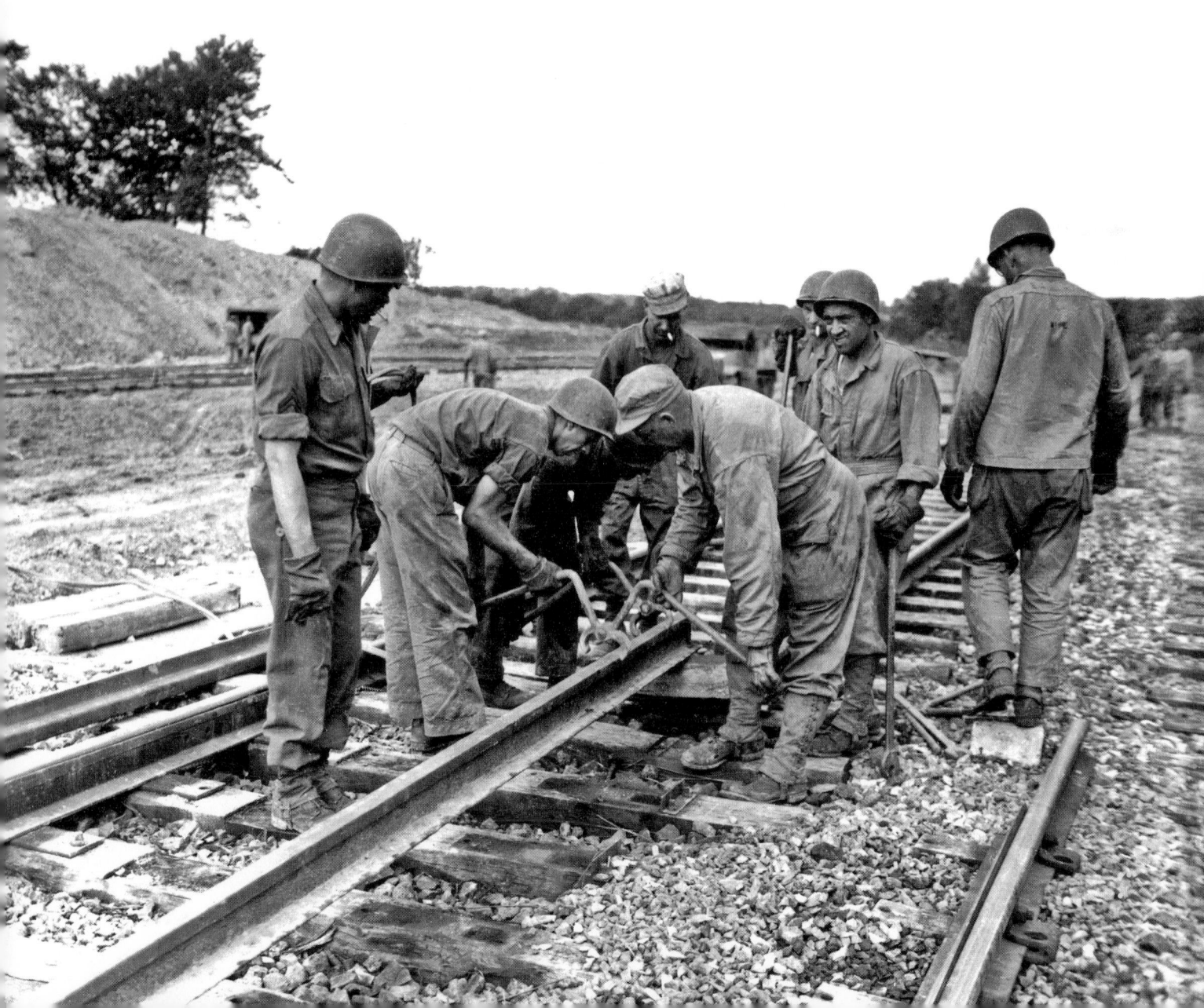

Following its Civil War experience, the army mobilized railroaders during both world wars, using experienced men and training new ones. It followed industry customs in relegating blacks to less-skilled, manual labor jobs, mostly in construction of roadbed, bridges, and other superstructure. These World War II black engineer troops are changing rails in France, Italy, or Germany in 1944 or 1945, using standard American track tools. U.S. Army Transportation Museum, Fort Eustis, VA

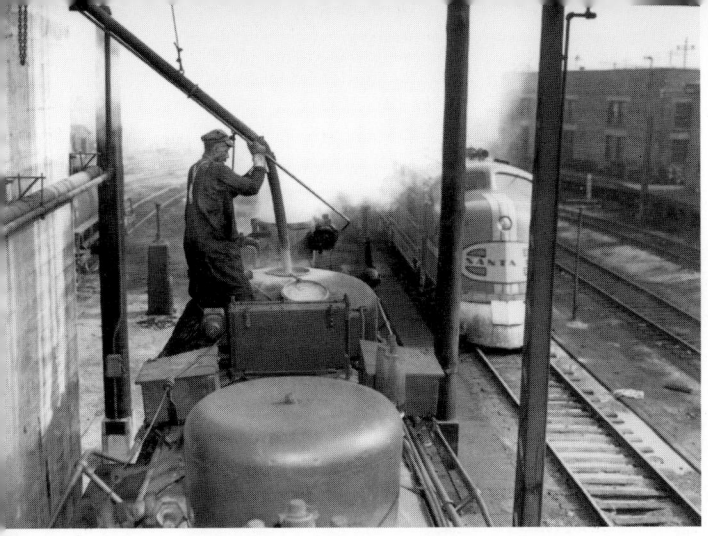

(ABOVE) *A Santa Fe hostler has taken his locomotive from the roundhouse to the sand house to fill its sand dome. To start a train when the rails were wet and slippery, an engineer would sand the rails to gain traction. The time is World War II, and its diesel rival would vanquish this steam engine within a decade. Many a hostler's job would disappear along with it. Atchison, Topeka & Santa Fe Collection, Kansas State Historical Society*

(BELOW) *Lest it be forgotten what it was like to hand-fire a steam locomotive, particularly in the South during the summer, notice the sweat-soaked fireman* (center) *going over train orders or a switch list with the rest of the crew on this August 1942 day on the Gulf, Mobile & Ohio Railroad at New Albany, Mississippi. Gulf, Mobile & Ohio Collection of the John W. Barriger III National Railroad Library, University of Missouri–St. Louis*

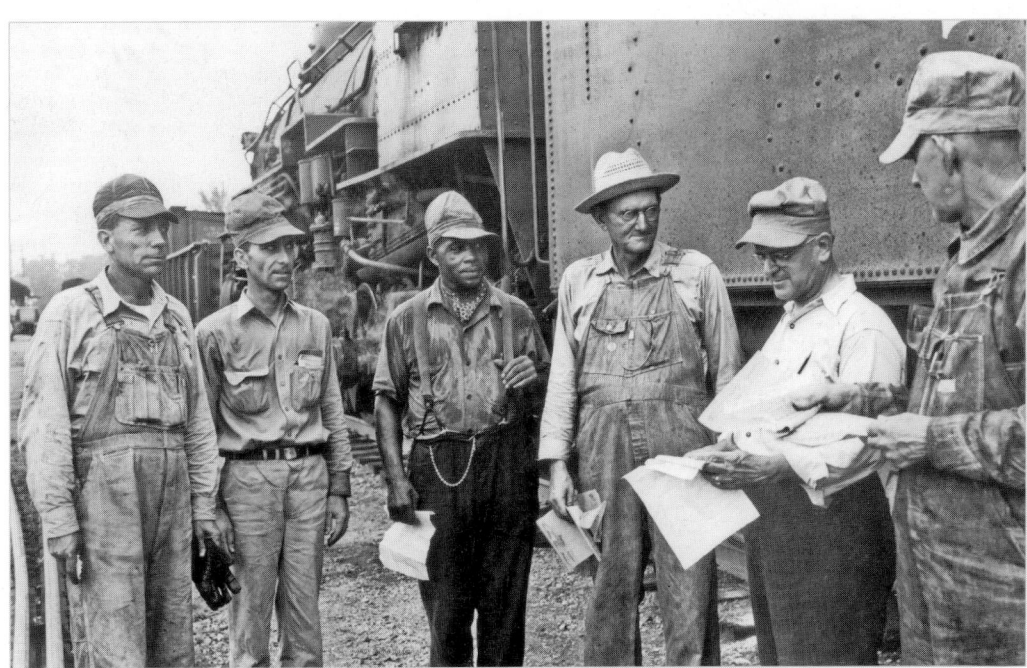

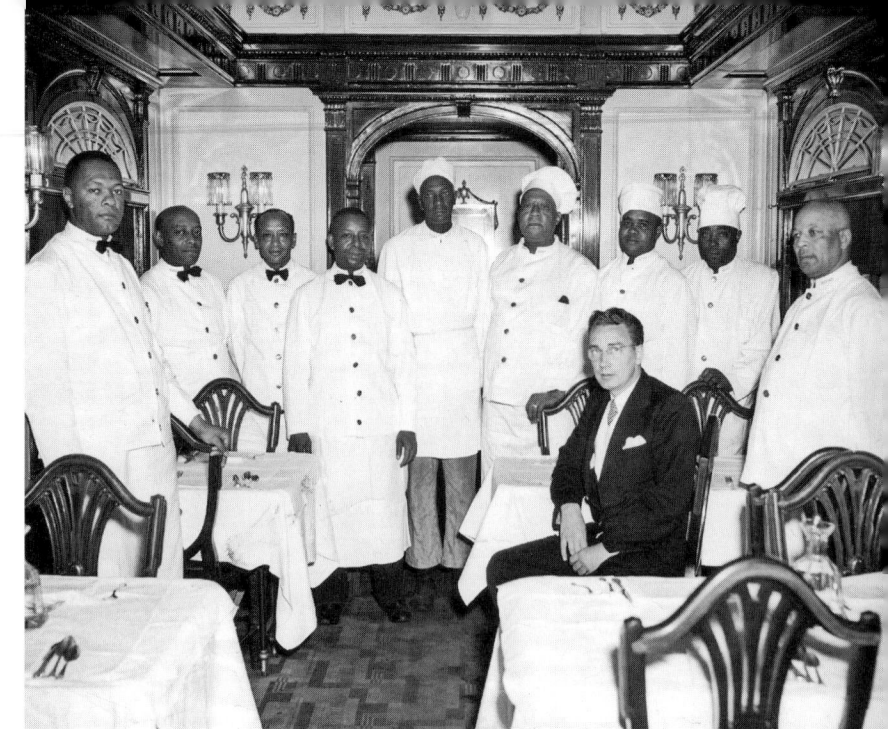

The elite of railroad cooks and waiters were those who worked on private cars, serving the rich and famous, company executives and dignitaries. This crew, normally working the Baltimore & Ohio Railroad's premier Capitol Limited, *was on assignment in late 1944 to President Franklin D. Roosevelt's special trains.* (Left to right) *Nelson Williams, Charles H. Adderley, Percy. V. Mason, Alphonso Lewis, waiters; Fred M. Mitchell, second cook; Clarence W. Queen, chef; Murphy Rolinson, second cook; Peter Moore, chef; Clarence J. Short, waiter. Seated is Edward W. DeGraves, the white steward. Courtesy B&O Railroad Museum*

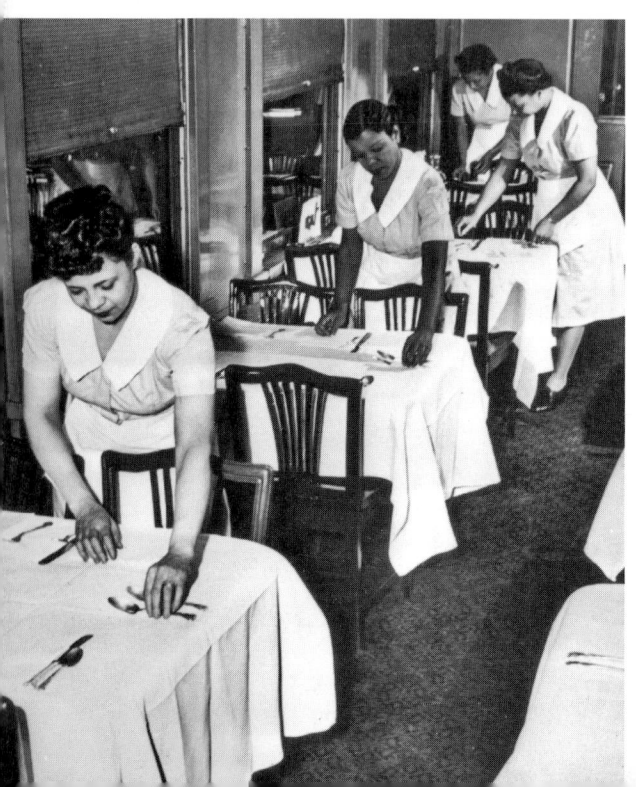

With many railroaders drafted into military service during World War II, women were recruited into previously male-only jobs. But black women, like (front to back) *Marian Turner, Flossie Sawyer, Bessie Carrington, and Gladys Boyd, found work only at tasks previously performed by black men. They are staffing a Pennsylvania Railroad dining car in 1943, operating between Philadelphia and New York, a short run that allowed them to return home at night and avoid having to lay over in accommodations set up to house only men. Women's Bureau Records, National Archives*

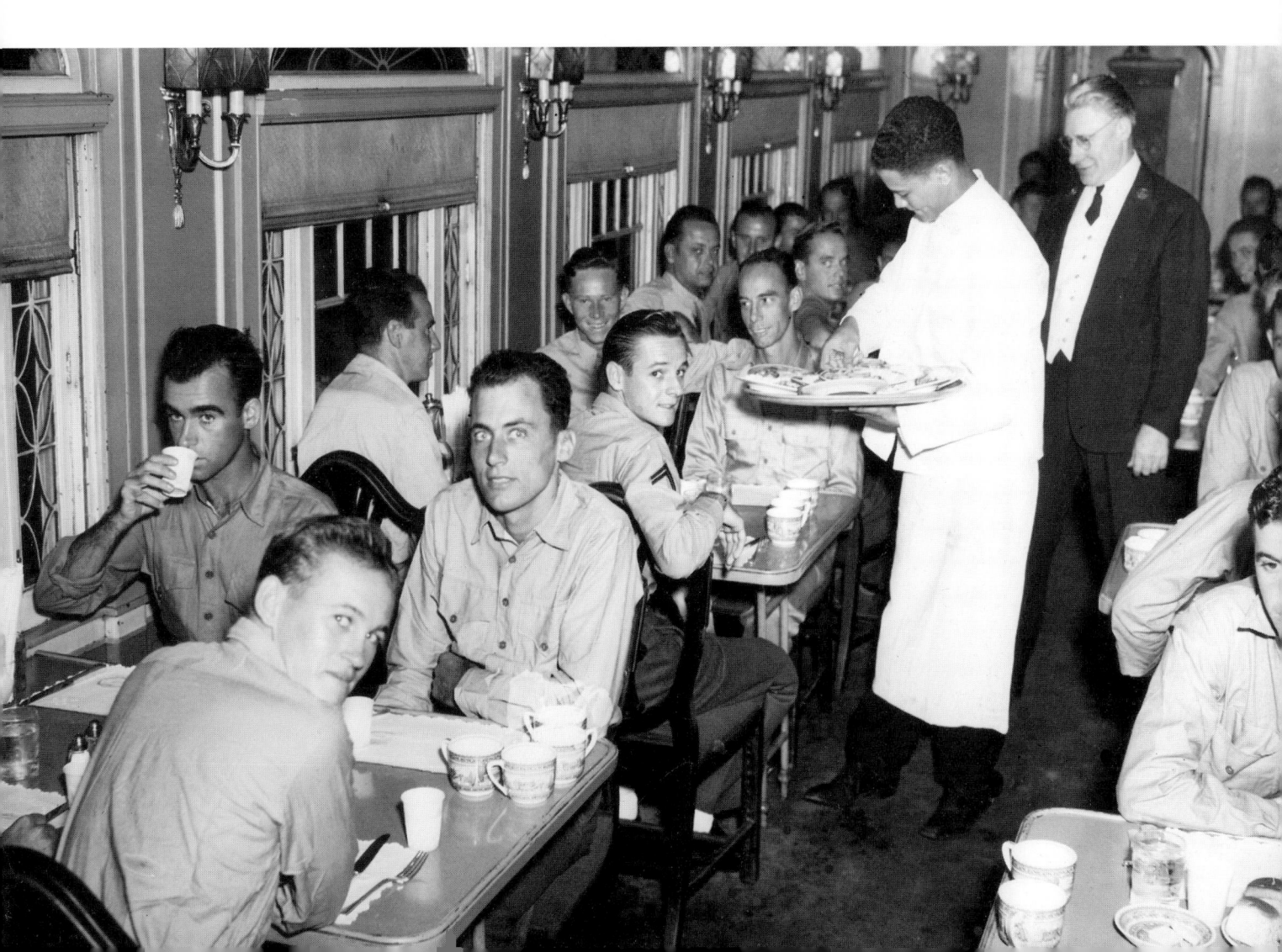

(RIGHT) *Many larger stations employed maids or matrons. In the South, most of them, like Bessie Henderson, working at the Baltimore & Ohio Railroad's bustling Mount Royal Station in Baltimore, were black. Photographed during World War II, she was praised in the company magazine for her diligence in keeping the restrooms "shining." Unlike many other wartime women railroaders, she could expect to keep her job after the war because this was work deemed appropriate for black women. Courtesy B&O Railroad Museum*

(BELOW) *World War II brought crowded dining cars, food shortages, and overworked waiters and cooks. To cut costs and time, this Baltimore & Ohio Railroad dining car has dispensed with linen tablecloths and is using paper placemats, paper cups for water, and coffee mugs rather than cups and saucers. Courtesy B&O Railroad Museum*

One of the hottest and dirtiest railroad jobs
was that of engine wiper, but plenty of women
performed this work during World War II, often
posing for patriotic photos such as this taken in
early 1945 at the Baltimore & Ohio Railroad's
Toledo, Ohio roundhouse. Fannie V. Currel
stands on the ground; the others (left to right)
are Elmanga Hinton, Lilly Belle Gurdan,
and Estella W. Rings. The company magazine
claimed they enjoyed "making the engine shine."
Courtesy B&O Railroad Museum

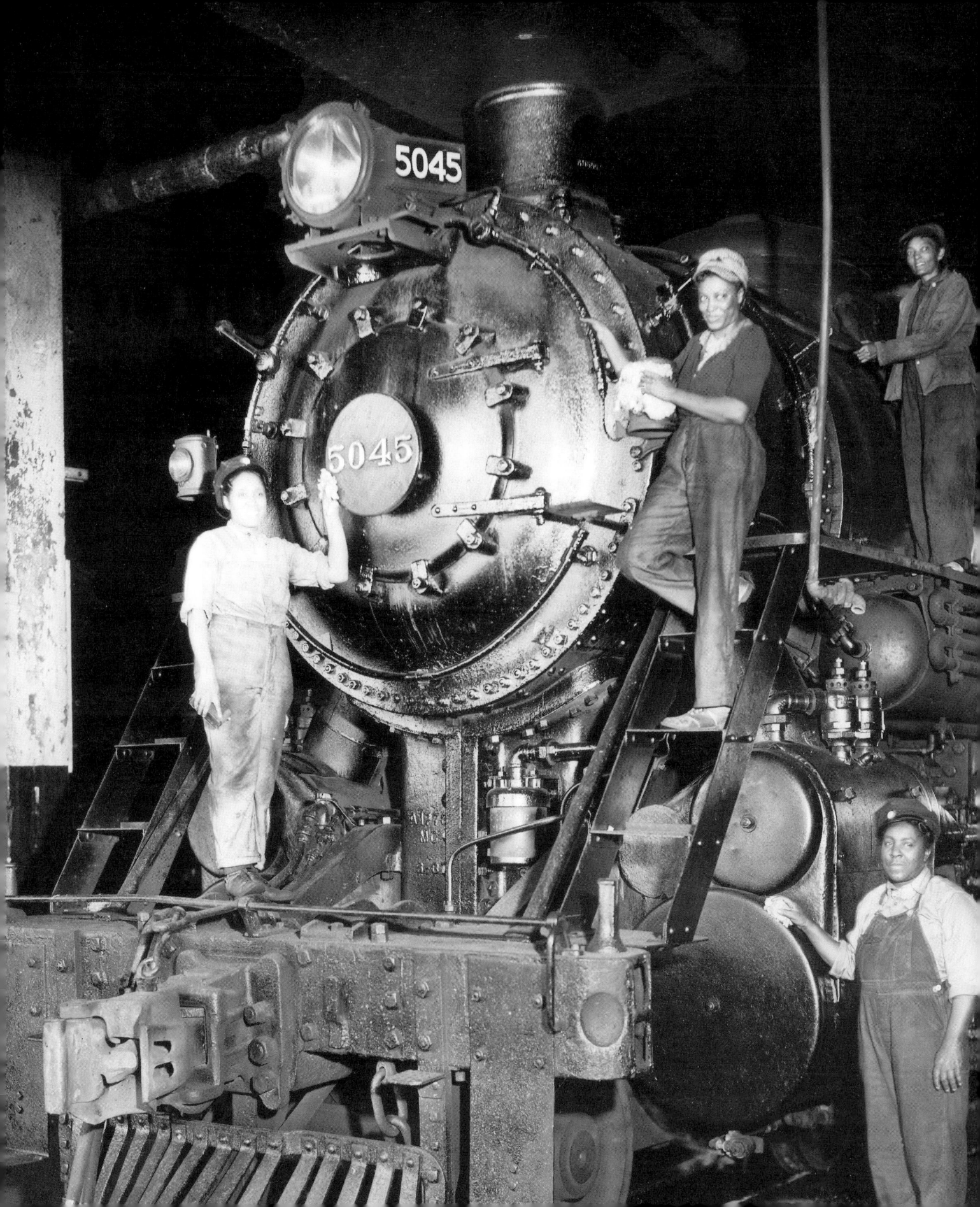

"HE KNOWS HIS PLACE"

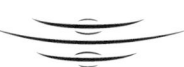

Railroads and Racism

Our examination of blacks' presence in and contributions to railroading has, ironically, been made more thorough because of racism. We know a great deal about African American railroaders because, for a long time, the railroads identified workers by race. For decades, many employee magazines made clear who was black by appending "colored" or "(c)" or "(col)" after their names. For over a century, southern railroads' personnel records likewise used such designations. This was not for statistical purposes. It was to structure a workplace on racial hierarchies. How long did such customs persist? As late as 1958, the Pennsylvania Railroad—*not* a southern carrier kowtowing to Jim Crow pressures—was still marking black employees' passes with the designation "colored." So stubborn was the Pennsy, which had long claimed to be a benevolent employer, that Eleanor Roosevelt urged readers of her nationally syndicated newspaper column to lobby the railroad to scrap this "racially discriminatory practice."[1]

Until recently, the railroad industry, as much as any other business, was permeated by racism. During the slavery era railroad and construction entrepreneurs determined what jobs blacks could and could not do. Officials tailored their practices to the dominant white culture of the day, confining blacks to roles that reflected their low social, economic, and gender position in society. Following the Civil War, fiercely exclusionary railroad labor unions demanded that the most prestigious operating positions—engineers and conductors—be reserved for white men. They also gradually persuaded those railroads that historically employed black firemen, switchmen, and brakemen to reserve these jobs for whites. The unions that represented railroad shop workers likewise drew the color line, succeeding, for the most part, in confining blacks to the lowest job classifications—laborer and helper—while keeping apprenticeships and mobility into the crafts a white monopoly. No other industry had unions capable of imposing such a thoroughly racist order on the entire workplace.

Not all blame rests on the unions. Railroad executives shared with their white employees a racialist view of the capacities and character of black workers, holding that they were suited only for unskilled, menial, and servile roles but not for skilled tasks, exercising supervision or responsibility over others, or white-collar work. Managers also believed the races had to be kept separate on the job. One reason frequently given by railroads outside the South for restricting shop employment was the additional cost of separate toilets and lunchrooms for blacks. And railroads were more than willing to shave costs by paying blacks less than whites for the same work. In short, workplace racism limited the job categories available to blacks, pay, promotion, and interracial contact. Railroads, both North and South, absolved themselves of responsibility for such matters, arguing that they were powerless to change the racial folkways that dictated blacks' inferior position within the industry.[2]

Racism was not confined to the workplace. Until the 1960s, blacks had to endure the humiliations of segregation. Southern railroads operated stations that had separate entrances, waiting rooms, toilets, ticket windows, and lunchrooms. Jim Crow cars tended to be older and more decrepit than those for whites, were frequently less clean, and admitted more smoke and cinders. Blacks either were excluded from dining cars altogether, or were segregated behind curtains. While still a high school student, Martin Luther King, Jr. traveled from Atlanta to Hartford, Connecticut, and back. Seated in the dining car behind the drape, he felt "as if the curtain had been dropped on my selfhood."[3] While it is true that Jim Crow was mandated by state laws, that railroads in the South had no choice in creating and maintaining a segregated environment, the "equal" in "separate but equal" was their responsibility. In that they failed.

The examples of racism summarized thus far resulted from deliberate policies designed to maximize profits or ensure preferential treatment for whites. The railroads also practiced another kind of bigotry that wounded African Americans in particularly personal ways. Their company magazines, published from the early twentieth century onward, included all manner of racist imagery, stereotypes, and language. Such publications were distributed to all employees, including blacks. Covers depicted them eyeing or eating watermelons. Most magazines had a humor page where "Rastus" and "Darkey" jokes about stealing chickens and watermelons abounded. Cartoons depicted grotesque, big-lipped caricatures uttering ignorant, fractured "black" speech. Such jokes and cartoons appeared in southern, northern, and western railroads' publications. For a number of years the *Illinois Central Magazine* featured a monthly cartoon featuring "Ham Hock," a black worker. Real employees were occasionally quoted in "dialect." A caption accompanying the photo-

Railroads in the African American Experience

graph of Central of Georgia Railway engine wiper John McFall had him boasting to be "de champin grease wiper uv de Savannah Shops," proof of which was the fact that "er Mastercanic [master mechanic] give me er Deplooma." Even the *Pullman News* ridiculed its porter employees in printing a shopworn joke and cartoon: "Say, Porter, how come? I've one black shoe and one tan." "Well, dat sure am funny, suh! Dat's the second time dat happened dis mawnin'."[4] And nearly every employee magazine, irrespective of region, highlighted white workers' blackface minstrel shows, even as late as the 1950s.[5]

Company periodicals also validated alleged racial characteristics. Profiles of longtime black workers on southern lines reinforced notions of black inferiority and, by implication, white superiority. Susie, the Gulf, Mobile & Ohio Railroad train caller and baggage handler at Meridian, Mississippi, who was not even dignified with a last name, was called an "Amazon." Slave-born Illinois Central freight trucker "Uncle" Dal Pulley was described as "an old fashioned 'Southern darkey.'" An accompanying photograph showed him eating an enormous slice of watermelon. Magazines spoke fondly of "faithful old darkeys" who were "a credit to their race." Particularly revered were the "old issue" (slave-born) employees. An obituary for IC office porter Victor Jones underscored the behaviors that whites expected of good black employees. It accounted him "one of the old school, a kindly soul who performed his duty well and who gained the esteem of all with whom he came in contact." No higher praise was possible than that bestowed on "Old Ben" Franklin, a slave-born IC office porter and janitor. Franklin was "one of the old-time type of Southern negro, having been brought up under the old regime, which made him courteous and respectful to his superiors." The ultimate accolade was paid to Louisville & Nashville Railroad lamp lighter Jack Anderson: "He knows his place and never presumes to step outside of his limit and as a result is well liked by everyone." Yet these faithful, humble souls were children who on occasion needed to be disciplined as such. Willie Brock was an IC stowman on the Jackson, Mississippi freight platform. He was raised on a farm "where no unusual emphasis was placed on method or system and mistakes were not taken with undue seriousness." In the two years he had worked as a stowman, he made only one mistake, loading a shipment for Oakvale in a boxcar destined for Oakley. "The resemblance between the names . . . caused his confusion, but it did not permit him to escape the consequences of his mistake. His attention was called forcibly to this error. He has never made one since that time." The obedient child had learned his lesson.[6]

Employee magazines further stressed racial hierarchies in photographs, layout, and language. Southern lines' periodicals dignified whites with the courtesy titles "Mr." and "Mrs." while denying blacks such symbols of respect until the 1950s. Photographs of blacks tended to be concentrated together on one page rather than dispersed throughout an issue. In group photos of employees from a particular shop or freight house, blacks were usually clustered together, either behind or to the side of the white workers. When the IC's Baton Rouge car department won an award for going an entire year without injuries, all employees were gathered for a safety meeting and chicken dinner. The 56 white workers posed seated on chairs, while the 32 black employees stood behind them.[7]

Some non-southern railroads' official photographs, too, similarly grouped blacks separately from whites, although others did not.

Railroads also frequently used unflattering racial imagery in promotional materials. The Georgia Southern & Florida Railway issued a souvenir booklet in 1895 with a front cover illustration of a banjo-playing "darkey" caricature. The back cover featured doggerel verses written in a burlesque of black speech:

> Yo' kin tawk erbout yer railroad trains
> Whut runs so pow'ful fas',
> 'Bout yer steamboats and yer lectric kyars
> Dat like shootn' stars go pas'—
> De litnin' flash am pow'ful quick
> As hit busts de lone pine tree,
> But dat GEORGIA SOUTHERN thoo freight
> Am swif' ernuf fur me.[8]

An 1882 L&N advertising folder likewise featured a raggedy black figure exclaiming, "I done tole you bout dat Cannon Ball":

> Dat cannon ball! Dat cannon ball!
> De train dat's fastes' of dem all!
> It leabs at half-past fo' each day
> By Ellen N.—Yes, dat's de way.[9]

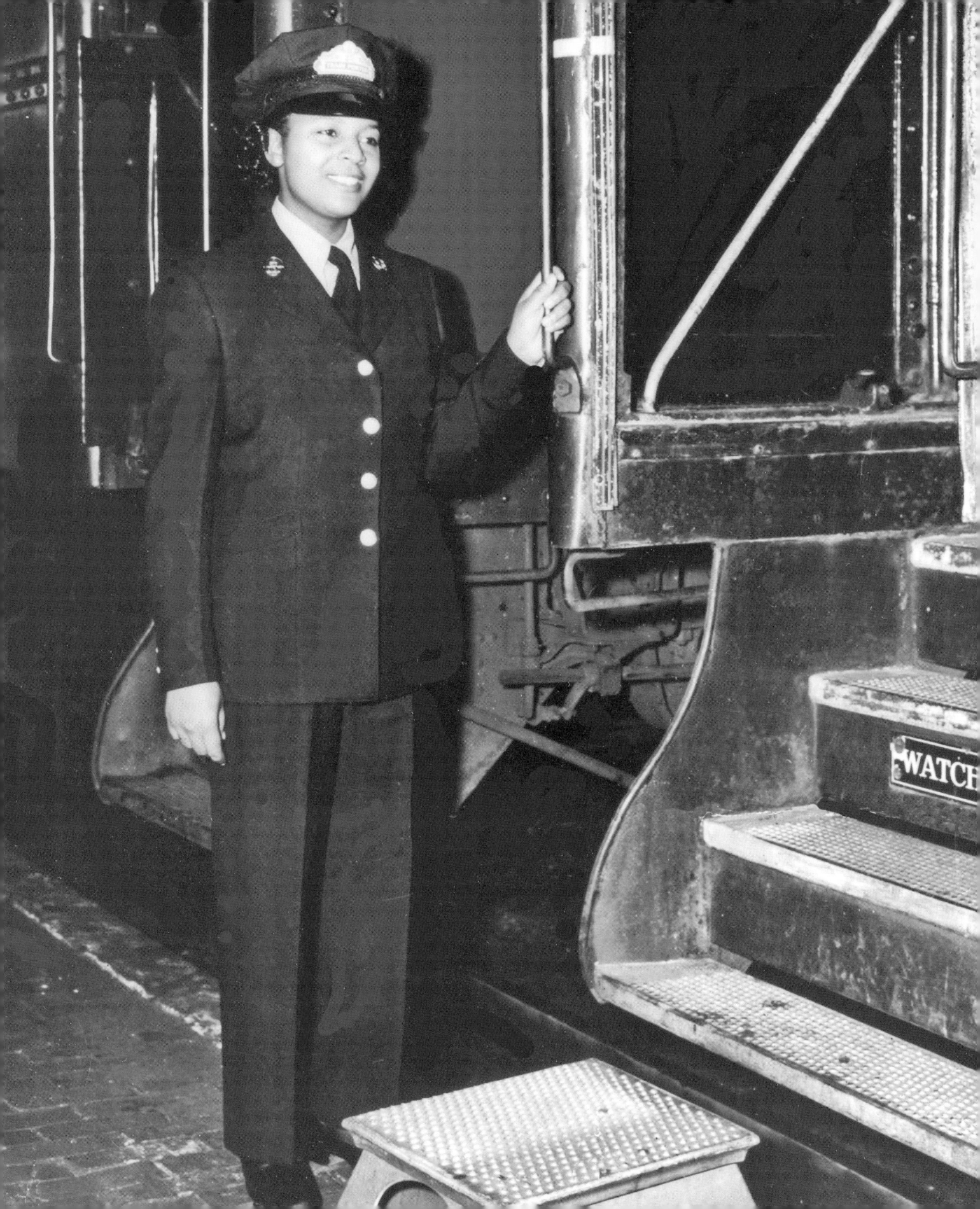

Pullman porters and Red Caps were also caricatured, even as far from the South as California's Mojave Desert, where the Tonopah & Tidewater Railroad's first timetable announcing completion of its connection with the Santa Fe at Ludlow was illustrated with a grotesque big-lipped figure.[10]

When railroads used images of blacks in mass circulation magazine advertisements, at least after 1920, they refrained from grossly offensive stereotypes. Almost invariably, though, blacks were depicted as servants (porters and Red Caps, waiters and cooks), smiling happily while catering to the wishes of whites. So while not overtly demeaning, the railroads' ads reinforced the racial hierarchies of the industry as well as the expectations of many whites as to the appropriate roles for blacks in "their" society and culture.

Some railroad advertisements published during and immediately after World War II departed from the "happy-to-serve-you" theme, developing instead a "we're all doing our part" unity message. A New York Central Railroad ad used cutaway illustrations to show how quickly and efficiently its 800 passenger cars were cleaned and serviced between runs each day. Pictured were a waiter, restocking table linens, as well as black inside and outside car cleaners of both sexes. A 1944 Pennsylvania Railroad ad highlighting women war workers showed a white female boilermaker, brakeman, lathe operator, trucker, engine wiper, and switch-woman. The only blacks were a group of section hands, revealing the railroad's race-based notion of women's roles. After the war, when railroad advertising portrayed black employees, they were almost always passenger service workers. Pullman Company ads, of course, highlighted the traditional attributes of its porters.

By the 1920s, Madison Avenue was using Red Caps and Pullman porters as "humorous" figures in light-hearted illustrations and advertisements for products unrelated to railroads. A *Saturday Evening Post* ad for 1940-model Plymouth automobiles featured a gaping-mouth Red Cap pointing admiringly to the new car. The year before, an advertisement for Roblee shoes depicted a grinning, big-lipped Pullman porter commenting, "Bet ah'll be shining up lots of these shoes 'fore long!" Fruit and vegetable crate labels occasionally used black figures in railroad contexts. The label for "Porter" brand citrus fruit actually depicted, not a sleeping-car attendant, but a bug-eyed dining-car waiter marveling at the size of an orange. At least the label for "Mista Joe" brand vegetables showed a smiling, but not grotesque, black waiter. Railroad and Pullman Company ads, by comparison to non-railroad advertisements, generally depicted blacks with fewer stereotypical features.

When railroad employee magazines and Madison Avenue advertising ridiculed, demeaned, and trivialized blacks, they reflected what was already rampant in American culture. Nineteenth-century popular illustrators Currier and Ives often made sport of blacks, portraying grotesque figures, stupid actions, and butchered language. A two-panel cartoon shows a bicycle-riding dandy approaching a railroad crossing, boasting, "Take a mity smart lokymoky to kotch dis coon!" The second panel has him and the bicycle ensnared on a locomotive's smoke stack, exclaiming, "Gracious Massy, I'se struck de comet!"[11] Another Currier and Ives example is *Crossed By "A Milk Train,"* showing a comically drawn black engineer and fireman on a locomotive whose "boiler" is a tea kettle, futilely waving sticks of firewood at a cow refusing to move off the track. One of the most famous

Currier and Ives prints is *A Kiss in the Dark*. The first panel has the "Mischievous Conductor" announcing "Dark Tunnel, through in half an hour!" It shows a white masher eyeing a comely young woman sitting in the seat behind him. Across the aisle is a black "Mammy" holding a white baby. The second panel is captioned "When the Train struck the light in just 3 minutes," showing the young man caught embracing the black woman, who has traded places with the young lady. Other publishers issued similar pieces ridiculing blacks.

Publishers of "railroad edition" paperback books also propagated cruel racial images. Such volumes, plus magazines and candies, were sold at depot newsstands and by train butchers who walked through the coaches, hawking their wares. One such volume was *Coon Yarns*, a 1903 paperback selling for 10 cents. The full-color cover featured a grotesque black man holding an enormous watermelon.[12] The Thomas W. Jackson Company, in Chicago, was one of a number of cheap joke book publishers. Beginning in 1942, it issued more than a dozen titles, several of which had railroad theme covers. The premier issue was *On a Slow Train Through Arkansaw: Funny Railroad Stories, Sayings of the Southern Darkies, All the Latest and Best Minstrel Jokes of the Day*. While the jokes avoided derogatory terms and referred to blacks as "colored," cartoons depicted porters and Red Caps as less than intelligent.

Racist railroad images can be found in children's literature. One of the most popular books in the 1930s was *Chessie*, the story of a stray kitten found on a train by a cook and a porter. As "invisible men," they have no names. Worse, they speak in fractured "dialect." After discovering Chessie, the passengers are quizzed: "Is dis heah cat any o' you ladies' an' gemmens' cat?" Determining that the stray will need a new home, one admonishes it: "If you gwine live wid de white folks, I got to wash you good." An illustration shows Chessie leaping out of an upper berth, landing on the head of the porter, who has an exaggerated look of panic.[13] Chessie was based on a highly successful advertising campaign by the Chesapeake & Ohio Railway that promised sleeping-car passengers they would "sleep like a kitten."

Two other types of popular culture also made use of racist stereotypes of black railroaders. "Humorous" color postcards made them the butt of crude jokes or depicted them as lazy, watermelon-eating, chicken-stealing, crap-shooting buffoons. Porters and Red Caps were common stock figures with the familiar thick lips and bug-eyes. Sometimes their malapropisms provided the joke; in other cases, maladroit encounters with passengers were the point of the jest.

Before the advent of phonograph recordings, popular songs were marketed through the sale of sheet music. Here, too, Red Caps and porters were familiar characters. The cover of "Pullman Porter Blues" shows a very dark male with exaggerated, thick lips.[14] Some songs play on the stereotype of black males' questionable motives and morals. "Hollyhock" depicts "A Pullman 'Bo' from the B and O" who is rebuffed by the suddenly wealthy young woman he seeks to woo.[15] The "Pullman Porter Man" has wives at each end of his run.[16] "Dapper Dan From Dixie Land," featuring Eddie Cantor in blackface makeup on the cover, is a Pullman porter who has a "girl in every town." In fact, "I won't let no gal run my life, 'cause if I lose them all I still got my wife."[17] The amorous behavior of passengers, a frequent cartoon subject, is the subject of "Don't You Think You'd Like to Fondle Me." Here, the crude temptress who makes an indecent proposal is shown as a repulsive black Jezebel on the cover and described as a "big fat wench."[18] The cover of "Pullman Porters Parade" at least shows dignified individuals, but the lyrics are not:

> Just see those Pullman porters,
> Dolled up with perfumed waters,
> Bought by their dimes and quarters . . .
>
> It's worth a thousand dollars,
> To see those tip collectors,
> Those upper berth inspectors,
> Those Pullman porters on parade.[19]

Such images of black railroaders may have amused whites, but they must have been painful to thousands of Red Caps and porters who lived abstemious lives.

The business chapter of the railroad story illustrates how much blacks were marginalized in the racially skewed American economy. Blacks did not cash in on the investment and entrepreneurial side of the railroad industry. Individuals occasionally purchased stocks in their employing companies—Illinois Central brakeman Thomas Redd voiced his complaints over the mistreatment of black trainmen as both an employee and a stockholder—but their investments were minuscule. In no way could their stock ownership influence corporate policies. Only two railroad lines were started by blacks, with only the second reaching completion. The first was the Wilmington, Wrightsville & Onslow Railroad, begun in 1882 to link that North Carolina seaport city with Onslow County to the north. Two years later, with construction stalled, Thomas Morris Chester, the first black attorney to argue a case before the Pennsylvania Supreme Court, was elected president in an attempt to revive the project. Nevertheless, it died shortly thereafter, never having been completed.[20]

The second black-initiated line, the Dixie Railway, actually got operating. It ran from Benson, Alabama, 15 miles north to a connection with the Central of Georgia at Alexander City. Its founder was William E. Benson, a visionary in the tradition of Booker T. Washington who saw education and economic development as the keys to progress within a segregated society. Besides establishing the Kowaliga School, an important model in rural education, Benson put together the Dixie Industrial Company that owned thousands of acres of land, cotton seed oil and saw mills, a turpentine distillery, a bank, and the railroad. The Dixie Line, as it was locally known, was projected to transport local lumber and cotton to the C of G interchange. Benson had connections to northern white philanthropists through his educational endeavors, and thus entree to investors. Local whites also supported the new road, offering rights of way through their land. A contractor was hired to grade the line, whose largest structure was a 500-foot trestle. Opened in mid-1914, the railroad initially prospered by shipping turpentine and cotton destined for German customers. But soon World War I disrupted Atlantic shipping and the Dixie Line went into receivership and was temporarily shut down. It eventually resumed operation but faced an inevitable death when the Alabama Power Company laid plans to build a hydroelectric dam and flood much of the area. The rails were pulled in the early 1920s. What the *New York Times* reported as the first railroad "conceived, promoted, built and operated by negro people" was in fact the second such line, and although it was financed largely by white investors it stands out as the sole brief success by African Americans seeking to participate in the broader world of American railroading.[21]

While blacks were not successful railroad entrepreneurs, a number of inventors made important contributions to railroad science and engineering, although securing a patent was no guarantee of financial reward. Railroads were the most powerful symbol of the American Industrial Revolution, so it is no wonder that blacks as well as whites were inspired to innovate and improve upon what was, for a season, the archetypical American technology.

Afro-Canadian Elijah McCoy, the son of escaped slaves who took the Underground Railroad to freedom north of America's borders, is the most famous black railroad inventor. At the age of 15, he began an apprenticeship in mechanical engineering in Edinburgh, Scotland, and on returning to the United States in 1870, worked as a fireman on the Michigan Central Railroad. One of his duties was "oiling around," making sure that all moving parts on the engine were well lubricated. This required stopping the locomotive, which was not only time consuming but also increased the danger of a collision, as there was yet no means to communicate messages from one locomotive to another. McCoy designed an automatic lubricator, or oil cup, making it possible to continuously lubricate moving parts while the engine was running. In marketing his device, however, McCoy encountered racism. Some whites, on learning that the inventor was black, canceled orders. But necessity overcame prejudice. Eventually, "no heavy-duty machinery was considered adequate without 'the real McCoy.'" The inventor went on to receive 57 patents, nearly all for lubrication improvements.[22]

Self-taught electrical engineer Granville T. Woods was the most prolific African American railroad inventor. His life story illustrates the obstacles to achieving monetary and professional success as an inventor, no matter the number of patents. Woods was unique in a number of ways. Born in Australia of aboriginal, Malay Indian, and African ancestry, he did not consider himself an African American although he experienced racism in the United States like other blacks. As a young man, Woods worked briefly, in 1880, as a locomotive engineer for the Dayton & Southeastern Railroad in Ohio, a rare position for a black. This experience tutored him in railroading and helped inspire him to invent for that industry. Woods ultimately held 45 patents, over half of which applied to railways. His early years were beset by poverty. Desperately seeking the sum of $15 for each patent application, he became entangled with a swindling backer. It took him several years, and legal actions, to free himself from this exploiter. Woods designed a "synchronous multiplex railway telegraph," applying the science of "telegraphony" to transmit messages to and from trains in motion. Alexander

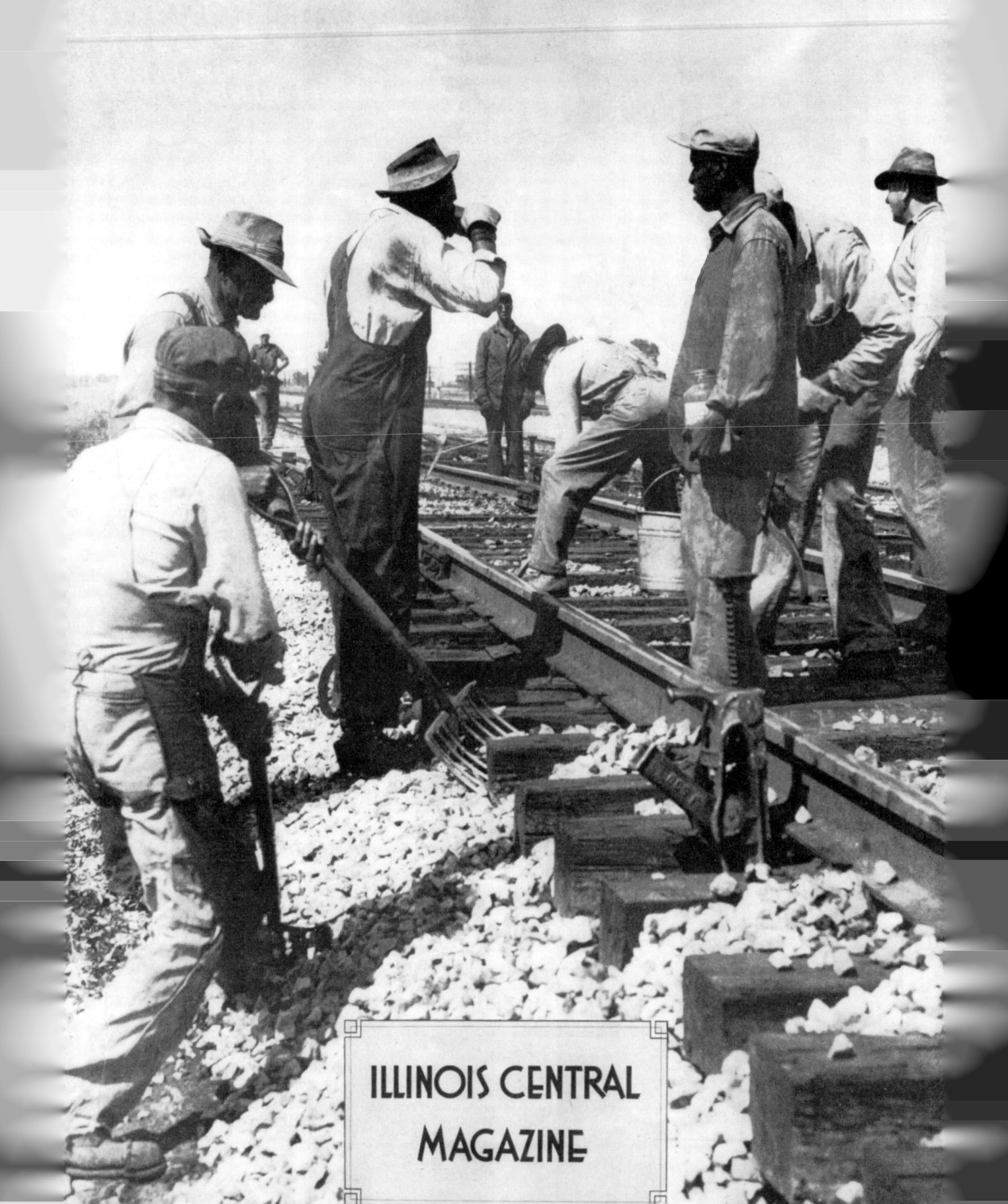

ILLINOIS CENTRAL
MAGAZINE

Soon after slavery ended, black youths began working on track gangs as water boys, often graduating to full section laborers when they gained sufficient stature, muscle, and strength. Many families, out of necessity, valued a wage-paying job more highly than schooling for their sons. This practice of employing water boys persisted well into the twentieth century.
Theodore Kornweibel collection

Graham Bell purchased the rights to produce the device, but Thomas Edison claimed it was his invention and brought suit against Woods. On winning the case, Woods was dubbed "the Black Edison." He prevailed in several other suits initiated by Edison, who finally offered him a job. By this time Woods had started his own company and went on to design a practical overhead power source for streetcars. Woods also invented a third rail electrical pickup to power subways, selling the design to the General Electric Company in 1901. And three other patents, assigned to the Westinghouse Air Brake Company, became part of the technology for automatic air brakes. Although, as his most recent biographer notes, Woods eventually became part of the "dominant electrical culture" as a "knowledgeable independent inventor," he did not, in fact, become a Black Edison. Neither "the dominant late nineteenth-century inventor culture [n]or the dominant American culture [was] ready to accept a Negro system builder shaping the material fabric of America through technology." Despite "the high quality of his inventive ideas," Woods had not achieved true financial success by the time he died in 1910, in his mid-50s.[23]

Protecting one's intellectual property was often difficult. Pullman porter Humphrey H. Reynolds designed a ventilator for passenger cars that admitted air but kept out soot and dust. After Reynolds explained his device, George M. Pullman ordered it installed on all sleeping cars. But when the Pullman Company refused to recognize Reynolds's claim to the design, he had to sue the giant corporation, winning a judgment of $10,000.[24]

Former slave and ex-railroader Andrew Jackson Beard was an unusually successful inventor. After selling two patented plow designs and investing successfully in real estate, he had the wherewithal to pursue an invention to protect the lives and limbs of trainmen, which was of personal concern, as he had lost a leg in a coupling accident. The result was the Jenny coupling device (different from the Janney coupler), which was a major improvement at a time when automatic safety couplers were being widely adopted. He sold the rights to a New York manufacturer for the princely sum of $50,000.[25] A Cleveland streetcar line laborer, James C. Jones, made a valuable contribution to track maintenance, devising a ratchet drill frame that allowed track workers to bore holes through the web of steel rails in 2 minutes rather than the customary 20 minutes. Most black inventors toiled in obscurity, however, getting neither profit nor fame from plans for lanterns, signals, smokestacks, headlights, track maintenance devices, and switches.[26] McCoy's name lives in popular idiom. Woods is remembered, but primarily in association with Thomas Edison. The others have been largely forgotten.

While not denying the weight of racial barriers, it is undeniable that the railroad industry provided the most significant nonagricultural, non-domestic service employment for blacks from the end of slavery to the Great Depression. In 1930, there were more African American laborers on railroads than in any other industry. And when brakemen, firemen, porters, waiters, cooks, and others are added, it is clear that one-third more blacks worked in the railroad field than in the next largest industrial categories, saw and planing mills and building construction.[27]

The economic importance of railroad pay for individual blacks, their families, and their communities cannot be exaggerated. The blues lyric, "When you marry, marry a railroad man / Everyday Sunday, dollar in your hand," was no myth. World War II FEPC director Malcolm Ross wrote that steady railroad employment "made a man a notable in the Negro community, gave him a house with a shaded yard and sent his children to high school and beyond."[28] Numerous profiles of career railroaders in company magazines emphasized their acquisition of homes, farms, and businesses. Property ownership indicated both respectability and upward mobility in the black community. All types of railroaders managed to acquire property: firemen, brakemen, maintenance of way workers, shop laborers, porters, waiters, freight truckers. Because none of these occupations offered a munificent wage, diligence and thrift had to be practiced. When slave-born William Nellons died in 1923, it was learned that the C&O roundhouse sand drier left an estate of $50,000, much of it in real estate. It's no wonder that many sons followed fathers into railroading. Ernest Clark, an IC fireman, was one of 12 children of an IC porter whose tips made it possible to support such a large family. By the time of his own retirement, Ernest Clark owned a home in Canton, Mississippi, plus four other rental houses. Not surprisingly, such a substantial property owner was also a substantial citizen, active in a service club and his church.[29] Others put part of their pay into bank accounts in preparation for retirement. Railroad pension plans became available by the 1920s, further strengthening black communities.

The economic progress of black railroaders was frequently associated with social contributions. Those who owned property were often noted for their civic activities. Some were preachers. Many others were deacons, or simply described as active in their churches. One of the most historic and influential black institutions in Memphis was Salem-Gilfield Baptist Church, many of whose lay leaders and members were IC employees.[30] Active church members were frequently also prominent in fraternal organizations. Profiles in company magazines also noted railroaders' successes in educating their children. Having one's progeny complete high school was no minor achievement, and graduating from college was a source of justifiable pride. There are no statistics indicating the degree of intergenerational mobility in black railroad families, but those with a strong work ethic often passed such habits on to their children. While railroad jobs had the greatest impact in strengthening southern black communities, dining-car personnel and sleeping-car and train porters in other regions were also substantial community members. The existence of a Pullman crew base was always a source of local leadership and civic participation.

Railroads contributed significant incomes and leadership to black communities only so long as black employment remained high. Peaking in the late 1920s, the number of black railroaders dropped significantly in the 1930s. World War II brought a temporary reversal of this trend, but attrition was inexorable thereafter. The postwar replacement of steam locomotives with diesels led, in some cases, to a 70 percent reduction in black shop and roundhouse jobs.[31] At the same time, the decline in passenger traffic progressively reduced the ranks of waiters, cooks, and porters as well as station Red Caps, janitors, and baggage men. Trucking companies and airlines, both significantly (although indirectly) subsidized by the federal government, seriously eroded the railroads' freight and passenger business. Mechanization of track maintenance slashed the number of section hands, long a source of jobs for blacks nationwide. The railroad industry employed 1.5 million workers in 1947, but it lost nearly one-third of that number in the next decade, and another one-third in the decade to follow. Railroad employment increased in only eight years between 1947 and 2004. By the latter date, the number of jobs had shrunk to less than a quarter million.[32]

For almost a century following slavery, railroad jobs were attractive alternatives to sharecropping and domestic service, offering regular cash wages, which agricultural laborers often did not receive, and paying more than a cook or janitor could typically earn. Yet they offered little upward mobility. Only a few section hands were promoted even to assistant foreman. White unions barred the dwindling numbers of black firemen and brakemen from promotion to engineer or conductor. Only a handful of Pullman porters became Pullman conductors in the 1950s and 1960s. Only a few dining-car waiters became stewards after 1940. Shop helpers found advancement into the skilled crafts blocked by unionized white workers. In the North, white railroaders sometimes agitated for a total ban on black railroaders. In mid-1919, as soldiers streamed back from World War I, the Pennsylvania Railroad's Federated Employes' Association went on record as opposing any employment of blacks on that mighty road.[33] Fortunately, the Pennsy, for its own selfish reasons, was not about to abandon use of low-paid black laborers. Lest railroading seem unique, however, one should remember that it was little different from most businesses in the nineteenth and much of the twentieth centuries. Blacks were almost universally confined to low-skilled, low-status blue-collar jobs across the American economy. Yet as labor historian Eric Arnesen has ably demonstrated, "the barriers to black occupational and economic advancement . . . were perhaps most blatant in the railroad industry."[34]

The seeds of change lay within the ranks of black railroaders themselves. Sleeping-car porters waged a long campaign for union recognition that was both a labor and a civil rights crusade. Comparable successes were not achieved by black brakemen and firemen, yet their attempts to preserve their jobs were also civil rights struggles. Long before Martin Luther King, Jr. and Rosa Parks, "black workplace activists pressured their unions, confronted white workers, criticized their employers, pursued legal action, and engaged in shop floor activism." Finally, with passage of the 1964 Civil Rights Act, discrimination by both unions and employers was forbidden. Doors, but not floodgates, began to open. "Some white workers and managers resisted the changes, many others accepted the inevitable, and still others accorded black railroaders a modicum of respect."[35] Change was long overdue.

The Chesapeake & Ohio was neither the worst nor the best employer. It deserves no greater censure than any other southern or multi-regional Class 1 railroad regarding its treatment of black workers. Examination of hiring and promotion practices in the pre–civil rights era shows the railroad world as it appeared to black workers in much of the country for much of the twentieth century. The C&O's roots extended back into slavery and the earliest convict lease, when contractors building the Covington & Ohio Railroad secured black male and female Virginia prisoners in 1860 to build a line from the Shenandoah Valley toward western Virginia. Following the Civil War, former slaves found manual labor work on C&O track gangs and in its shops and freight houses. As railroad jobs drew workers from Virginia's tidewater and Piedmont regions, they birthed black communities along the main line in towns like Clifton Forge, Virginia, and White Sulphur Springs, Ronceverte, and Hinton, West Virginia.

One such transplant drawn to the railroad was Abraham Thompson, born soon after the war on the same Louisa County plantation where his parents had been slaves. He became a farm hand on that plantation, served in the Spanish American War, but around the age of 40 went to Clifton Forge to labor on a C&O section gang. All four of his sons eventually found work in the Clifton Forge shops. Two of them, Isaac and Abraham, ages 91 and 87, respectively, in 1998, recalled with considerable bitterness the lot of black railroaders at Clifton Forge when they began working at the end of the 1920s. Although the railroad had employed quite a few black road brakemen in the link and pin era, only yard brakemen remained: "White men took it over." One black switchman only remained

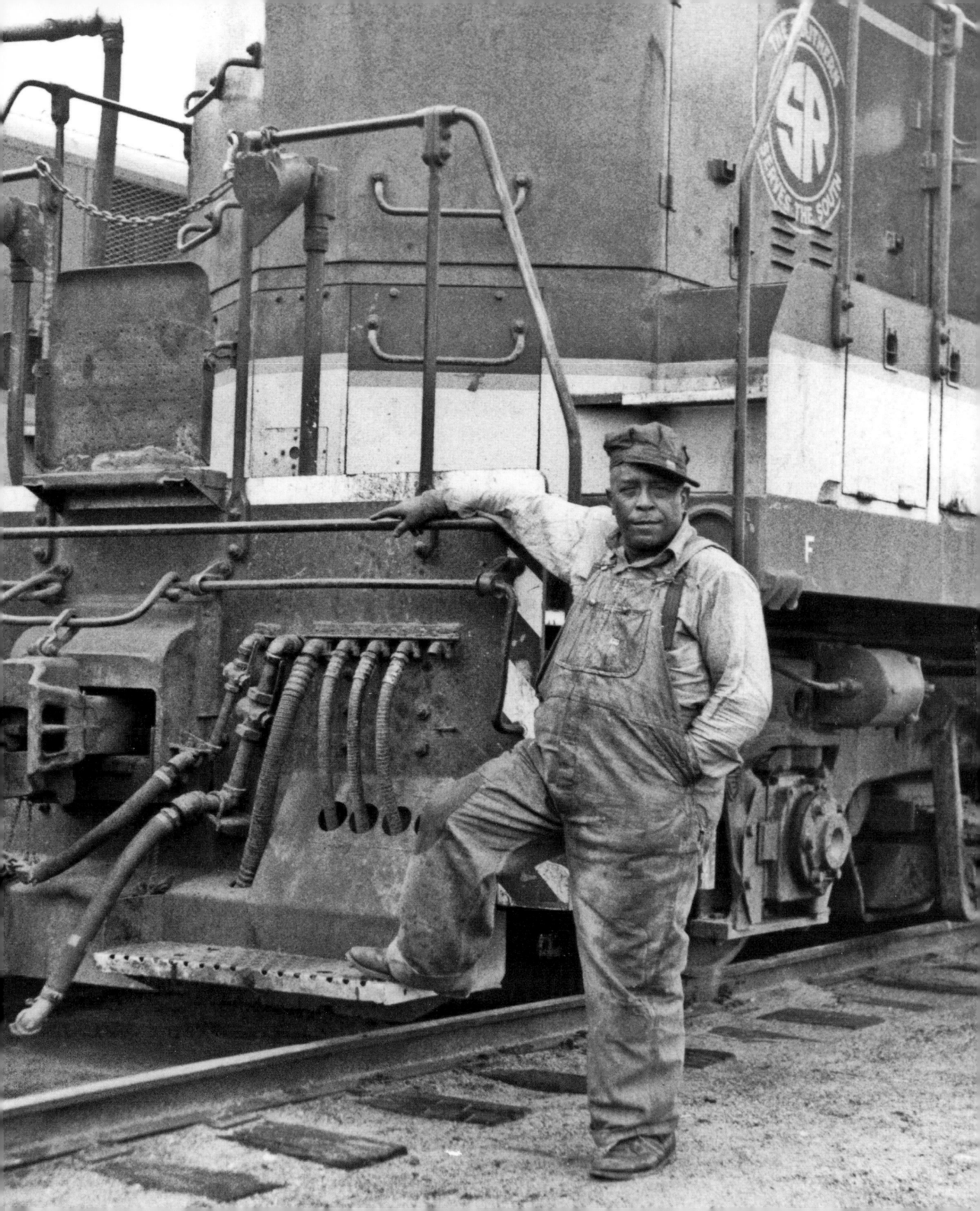

on each shift in the yards. For a while there were two black hostlers at the shops, but they were not allowed to work the yards, and when they died, they were replaced by whites. Most blacks in the shops and roundhouse were laborers, with helpers in smaller numbers. Helpers did the physical jobs for white apprentices and craftsmen like lifting up brake beams so they could put in the pins, and carrying barrels of oil so white carmen could fill the journals. Laborers performed the hard, dirty tasks of steam locomotive maintenance: fueling, sanding, fire cleaning, and lubrication. A few broke the skill barrier during strikes and became machinists, but were never allowed into the union and were quarantined in the third (11:00 p.m. to 7:00 a.m.) trick, doing the roughest jobs. Quite a few blacks were trackwalkers, responsible for inspecting and making minor repairs on 4 to 5 miles of right of way each day. Others were bluff watchmen, alert for landslides, living isolated lives in little shacks along the right of way. A handful worked as station porters at Clifton Forge. Larger numbers were truckers at the freight house. C&O train porters typically did not live in Clifton Forge. Although a conductors' district stretched from Washington to Clifton Forge in 1925, a seven-hour run on a crack passenger train like the *F.F.V.*, a coach porter's run extended from Washington to Hinton, three hours longer.[36]

"I started work as a laborer, and retired as a laborer." Thus Isaac Thompson summed up 43 years dedicated to the C&O, beginning in 1929 at the age of 22 as a Clifton Forge locomotive washer. Actually, he started earlier as a cook at the C&O hospital, although he didn't earn a railroad paycheck. On retirement at 65, he was a box-car cleaner, having recently lost his job as a coach cleaner when Amtrak absorbed the remainder of the C&O's dwindling passenger service. Over the years he did about every manual labor job around a steam locomotive: coaling, watering, sanding, cleaning fires, rebuilding firebrick arches in fireboxes, and high-pressure washing. And there was always work at the coal elevator. Dieselization reduced the need for laborers, but with seniority, he continued fueling and sanding. Cleaning diesel engine compartments was particularly nasty because the engines threw oil. On occasion he was called to cook for crews cleaning up wrecks out on the line. He was known for his bread not having black cinders in it like the loaves baked by another cook, because he closed the cook car's windows when kneading the dough. Isaac was a man of many skills. But he was just a laborer.[37]

Isaac's younger brother Abraham "Abie" Thompson followed his sibling in many respects. He, too, first worked at the C&O hospital as an orderly "wiping a lot of white asses," earning $1 for a 12-hour day. As he was not receiving a railroad paycheck, he accrued no railroad seniority or retirement credit, concerning which he remained bitter. (Like other railroad hospitals of the era, the wards were segregated. And while there were black orderlies, there were no black nurses or doctors.) Abie finally got real railroad work in the early 1940s as a fire watcher, responsible for keeping a number of locomotives steaming, then as a roundhouse laborer. Even though he occasionally "drove" a locomotive, he wasn't formally designated as a hostler. One of his jobs was to push coal hopper cars up an incline at the coal chute, where they were emptied. When white hostlers

Railroads in the African American Experience

complained that he had gotten too good at handling a locomotive, this job was taken from him. Racism took cruel twists. Abie and other blacks weren't allowed to operate the stokers when building or maintaining a locomotive's fire; rather, they had to hand-shovel the coal. He finally got to use a stoker when he became a stationary engineer at the power plant that supplied steam heat for all the buildings in the yards.[38]

Abraham and Isaac Thompson testify from the inside. The C&O's white employees, if they chose to be honest, knew the same things from the outside. A 41-year veteran of the signal department, employed from 1944 to 1985, had a "signal" view of the pre– and post–civil rights eras on the same division as the Thompsons. Blacks were never hired in either the signal or bridge & building departments until after the Civil Rights Act of 1964. Modest numbers had secured jobs in the communications department, mostly as laborers on construction gangs, while a few were linemen (stringing wires on telegraph poles) and radio maintainers. Blacks as well as whites were mixed on section crews, but no blacks were promoted to assistant foremen, much less foremen, until after 1964. Each race bunked in its own camp cars—old Pullman sleepers—but ate in the same commissary car, with a 3-feet-high partition dividing the long tables in two. In the operating department, the C&O hired no black firemen in the modern steam era. The few black hostlers learned their trade as engine watchmen, not as firemen. In the freight houses many, although not all, truckers were black, but all the checkers, who handled the waybills and told the truckers what crates to put in which cars, were white. Blacks readily found work in station restaurants as cooks, waiters, busboys, and dishwashers. Aside from nontraditional roles during World War II, black women before 1964 were confined to jobs in depot restaurants; as maids in railroad YMCAs; as inside passenger-car cleaners; and in C&O laundries where dining-car and "Y" linens were washed.[39] Brawn, not brains, were blacks' main qualifications, across the board.

"Railroad work," observes historian and former railroader John P. Hankey, "is all about two things: making the most money you can, and holding the best job you can." This was a reasonable expectation for all but black railroaders.[40] Until the Civil Rights Act, race (and gender) determined who did what in nearly every corner of railroading save maintenance of way. The railroad industry was a racially structured business. Employment preferences were based on race. Employee-relations efforts privileged Caucasians and often disparaged African Americans. Advertising reflected the same privileging, but was not in this respect unique, simply mirroring the broader culture in which blacks were often comic buffoons. African Americans were so marginalized in the American economy that they could reap almost none of the benefits from railroad prosperity, as either investors, entrepreneurs, inventors, or even well-paid employees. It took almost an entire century, from emancipation to civil rights, to begin to break down institutional and structural racism in the railroad industry. For many, it came too late.

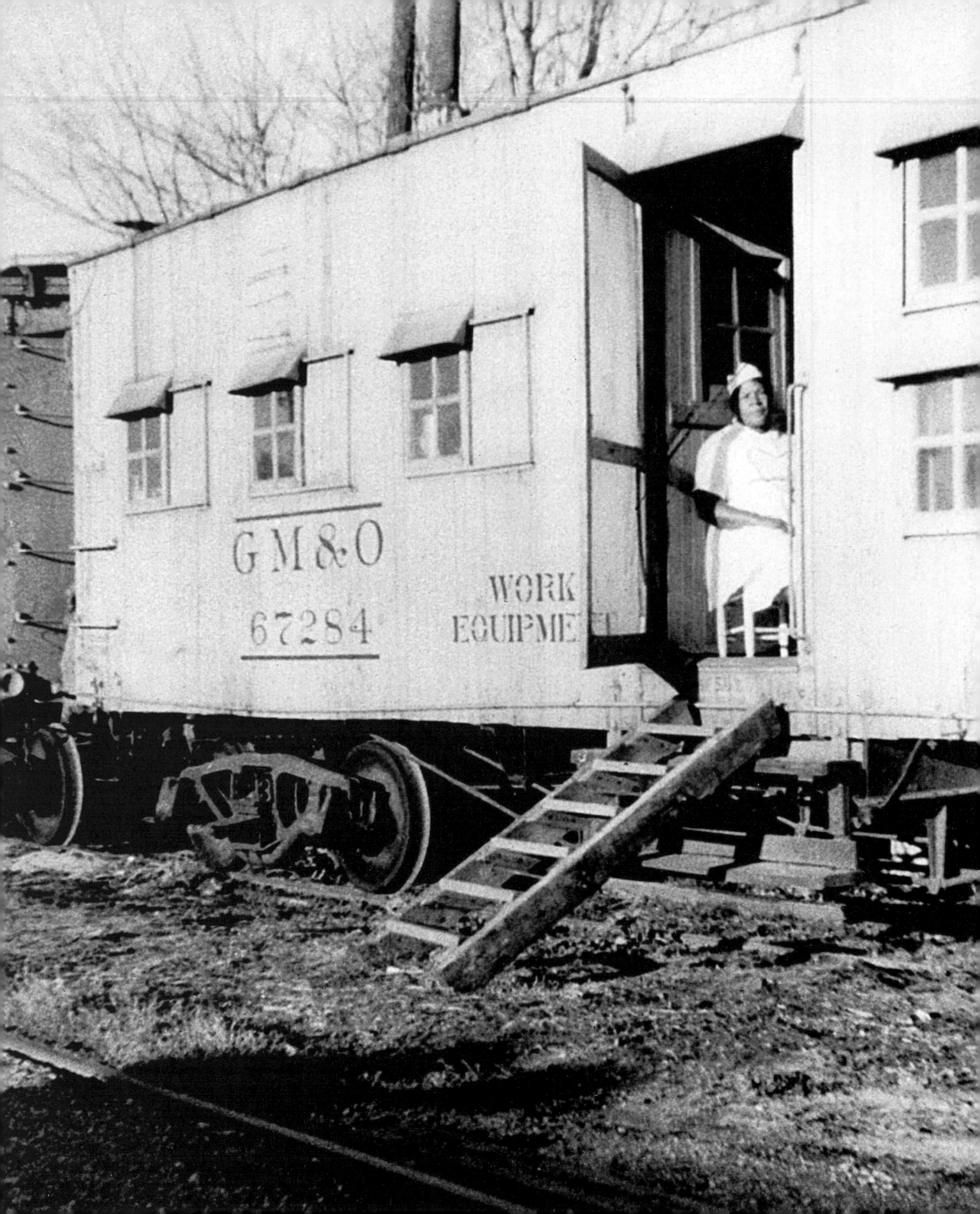

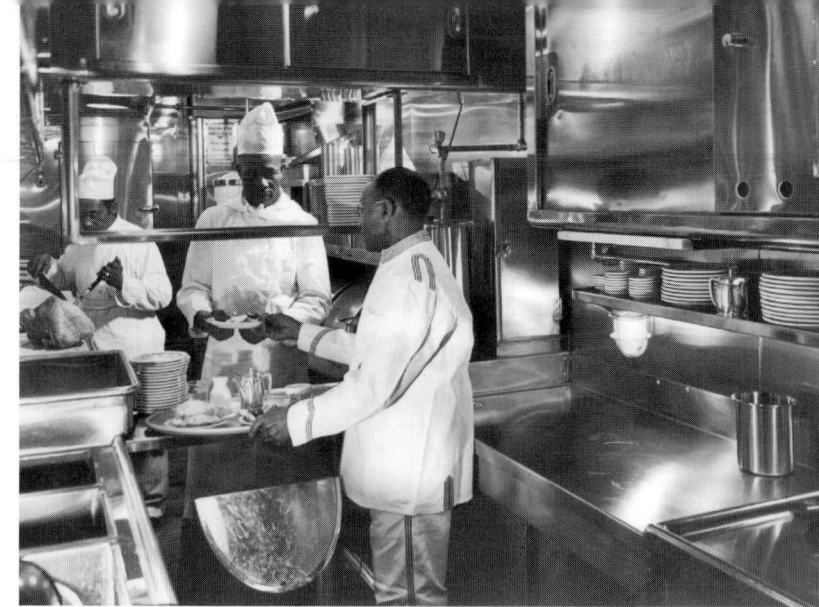

A waiter receives food in the pantry of the "Old Plantation" diner on the Kansas City Southern Railway's streamlined New Orleans–Kansas City Southern Belle *in 1949. Although there was occasional friction, cooks and waiters practiced teamwork in order to efficiently feed a stream of passengers throughout a day that could stretch for 18 hours, with scarcely a break. E. L. DeGolyer, Jr. Photograph Collection, DeGolyer Library, Southern Methodist University*

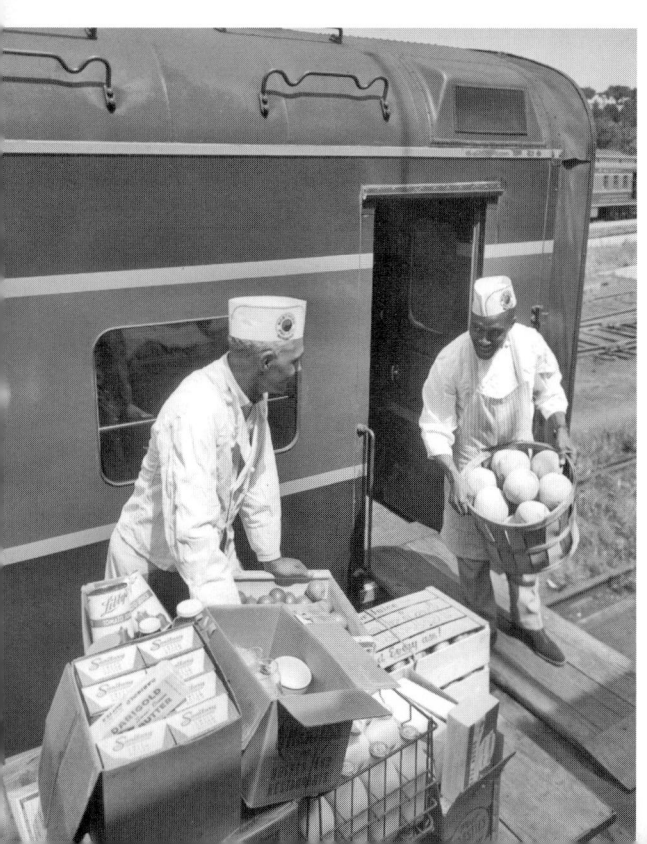

Northern Pacific Railway cooks, loading fresh milk, butter, eggs, and produce onto their dining car in 1954. The car is still in the coach yards, not yet coupled to its train. The crew will have worked for several hours prior to their train's departure and before the first passenger orders a meal. Mallory Hope Ferrell photograph

Much of a railroad's passenger service reputation rested on its dining-car menus and service. Cooks, like these in the stainless-steel kitchen of a Delaware, Lackawanna & Western Railroad lightweight diner in the 1940s or 1950s, prepared fine meals in hot, cramped quarters. A chef presided over the kitchen crew. Some railroads employed only white chefs, while on other lines blacks could work their way up to this eminence. One of the DL&W's signature entrees was beefsteak pie with mushrooms. Delaware, Lackawanna & Western Collection, reprinted by permission, Railroad Museum of Pennsylvania

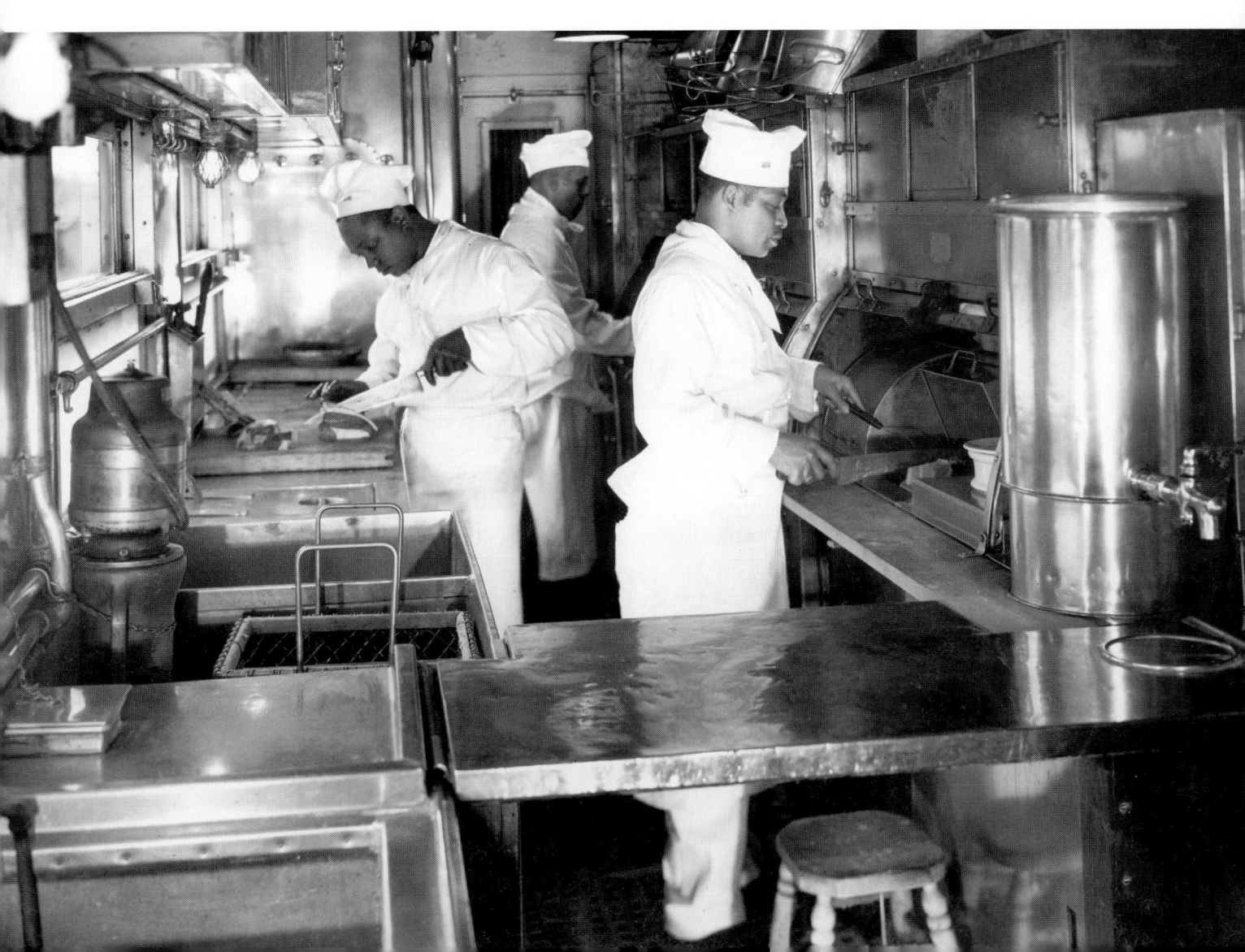

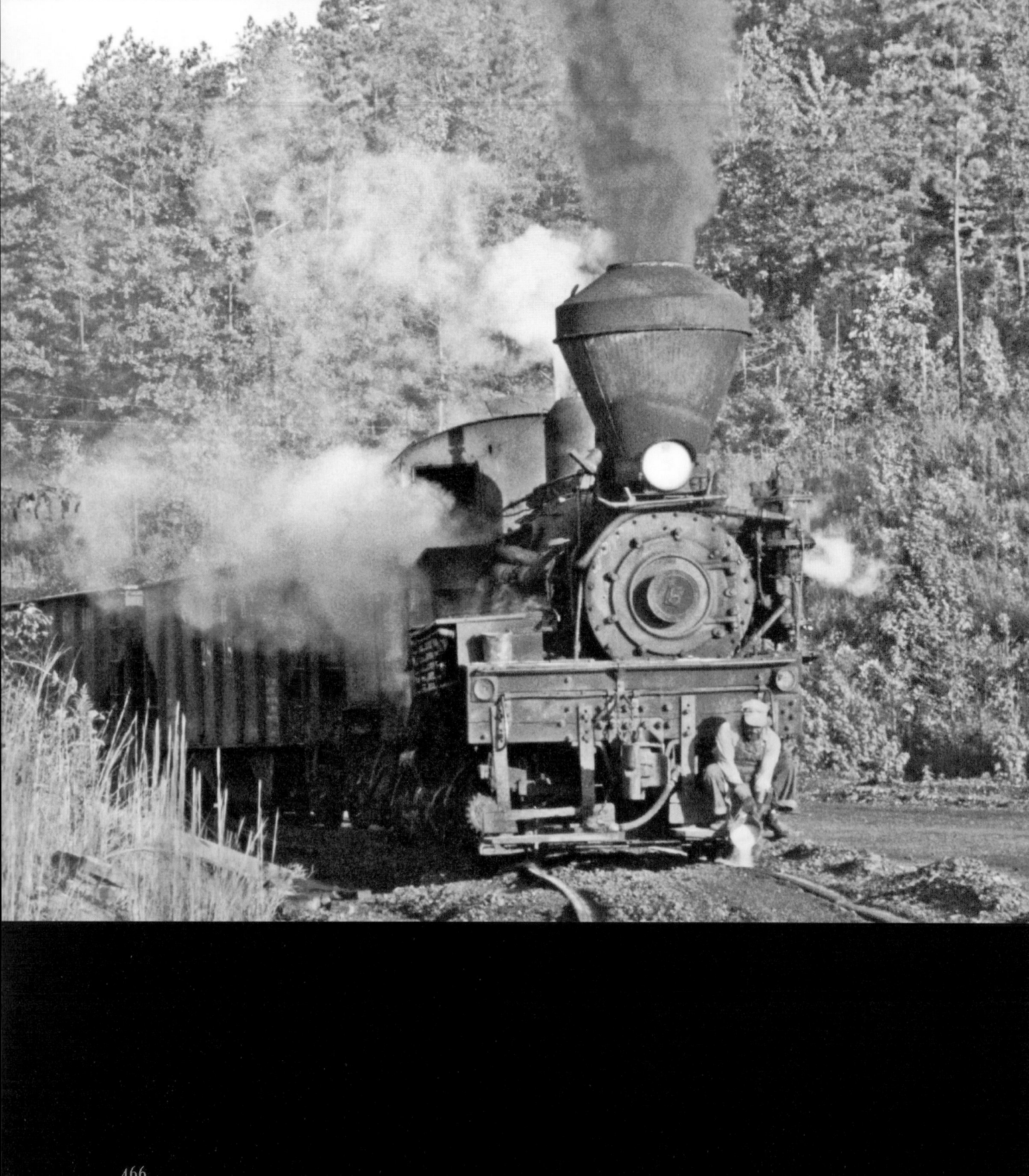

(OPPOSITE) *A Twin Seams Mining Co. brakeman dumps sand on the track so that the ancient Shay geared locomotive's wheels will gain traction to pull eight loaded coal cars from a remote mine between Tuscaloosa and Birmingham, Alabama. When built, the locomotive had sanding pipes, but now, in 1960, they have long ago rusted away. Although the brakeman is perched precariously on the running board, the train is moving little faster than a walk. J. Parker Lamb photograph*

Diesels replaced tens of thousands of steam locomotives in the 1940s and 1950s, but steam lingered on short lines like the Canton & Carthage Railroad in Mississippi, shown here in 1960. The brakeman prepares to couple the caboose to the last freight car of the train. After the engine has pulled back onto the adjacent track, he will throw the switch so that the locomotive may proceed to the front of the train. The white conductor stands ready to board his "office," the caboose. Either he or the brakeman must move the marker lamps to the other end of the caboose before departure. J. Parker Lamb photograph

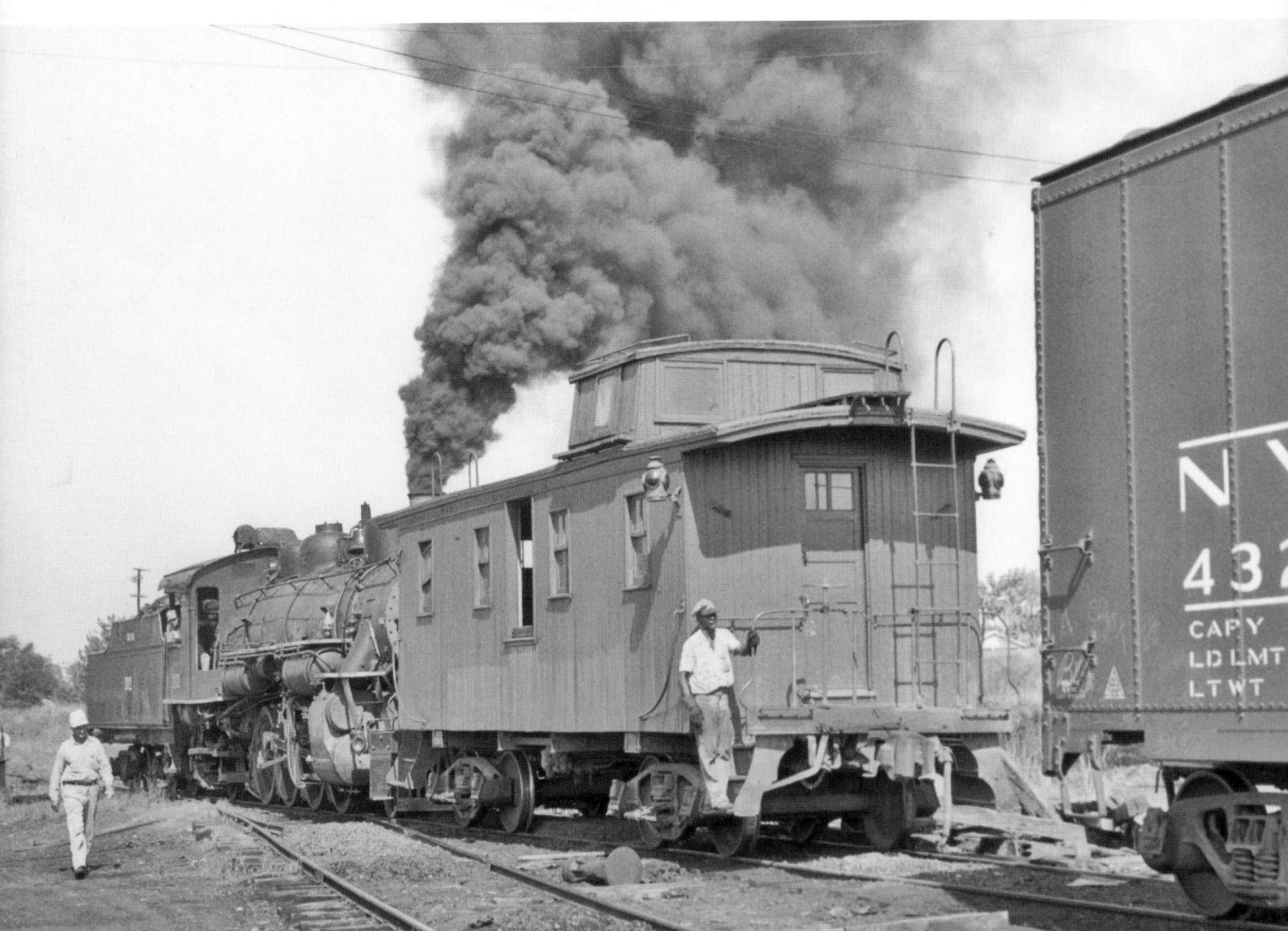

The head brakeman on the 15-mile Sylvania Central Railway's mixed train swings the stop sign and signal protecting the diamond with the Savannah & Atlanta Railway in Sylvania, Georgia, on October 16, 1953. The weed-overgrown line, living on borrowed time, was abandoned five months later. What would be the fate of the non-unionized brakeman? Class 1 railroads were still generally hiring only white brakemen. Gordon S. Crowell photograph

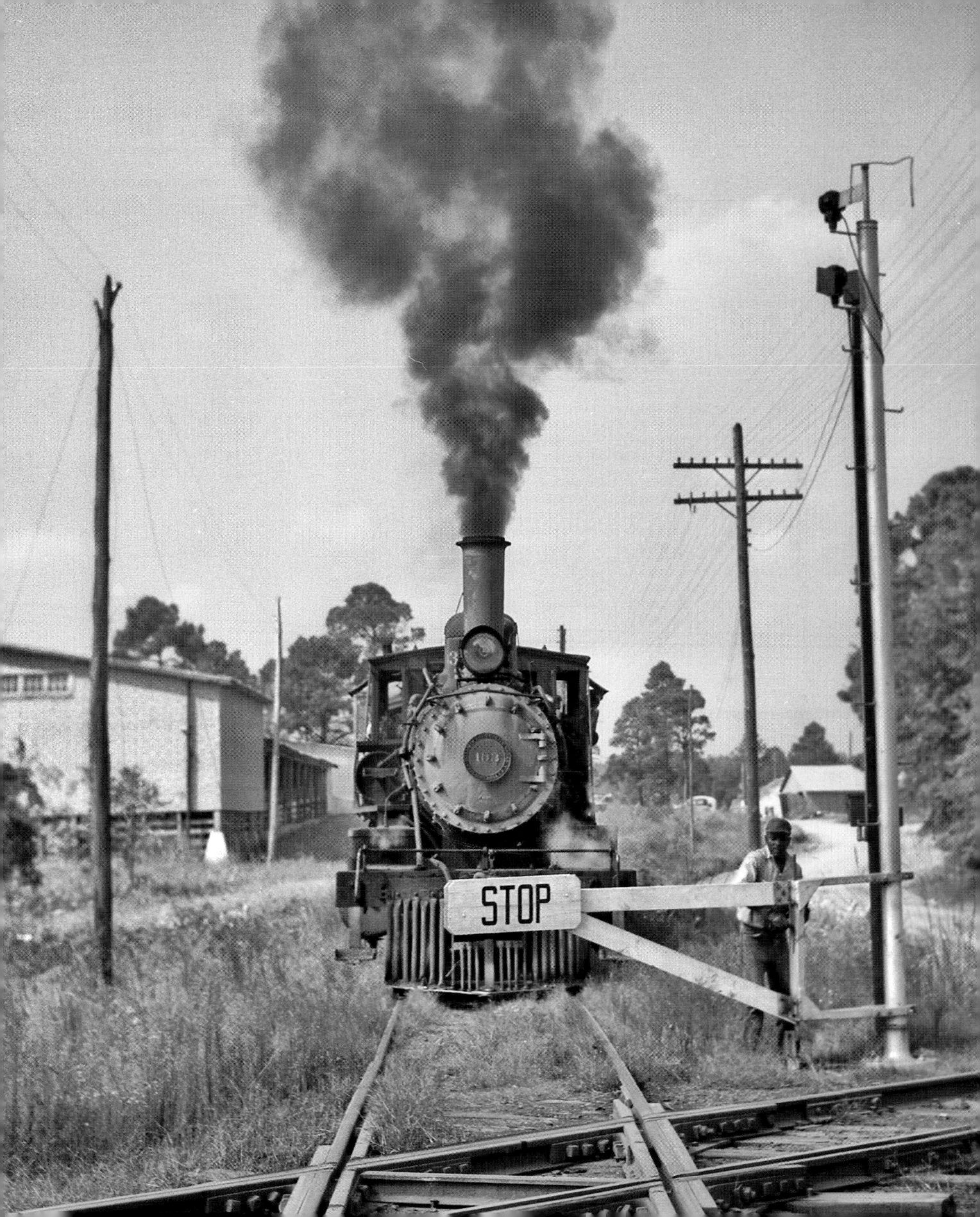

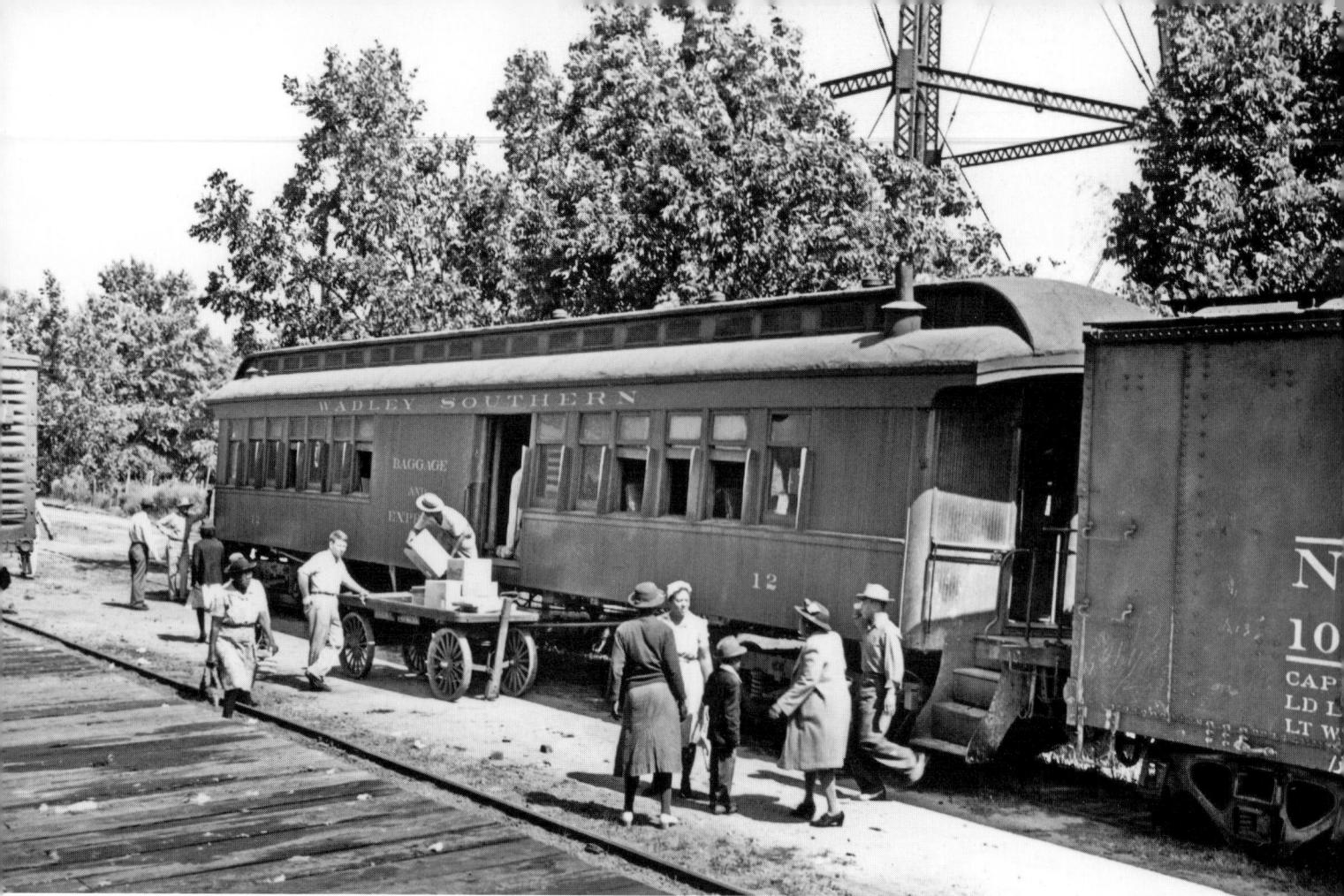

Southern short-line railroads, like Georgia's Wadley Southern Railway, offered at least one "mixed train, daily," a freight train that performed switching along its route, whose tail-end car was a segregated passenger coach. The morning train and its Jim Crow combine have arrived at Swainsboro this September 1946 day, with enough time for passengers to make a connection with the Georgia & Florida Railroad's southbound accommodation from Augusta to Valdosta. Courtesy Lucius M. Beebe and Charles M. Clegg, Jr. Collection, California State Railroad Museum

(OPPOSITE) The Central of Georgia Railway's Nancy Hanks II posing for a photograph before entering regular service in 1947. Blacks, limited to the combine behind the locomotive, would soon complain about overcrowding and the hostile behavior of white trainmen. Because the train traveled exclusively within Georgia, it was not subject to Interstate Commerce Commission rulings banning segregation, but in the end the C of G could not evade the Supreme Court's ruling that segregation even on intrastate trains was illegal. Central of Georgia Collection, reprinted by permission, Railroad Museum of Pennsylvania

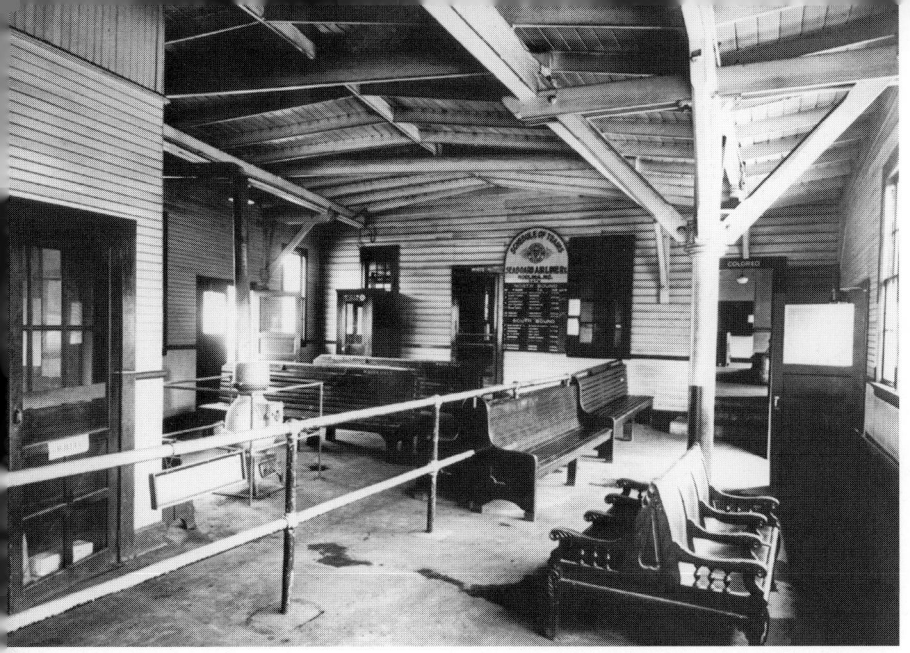

(ABOVE) *Some southern depots segregated the races in entirely separate waiting rooms, but at Norlina, North Carolina, on the Seaboard Air Line Railway's main line, a simple iron railing sufficed. Separate was not fully equal, however. The single stove was in the "white" section, which also had more seats and a pay telephone. The photograph appears to date from the 1940s. Courtesy of the North Carolina State Archives*

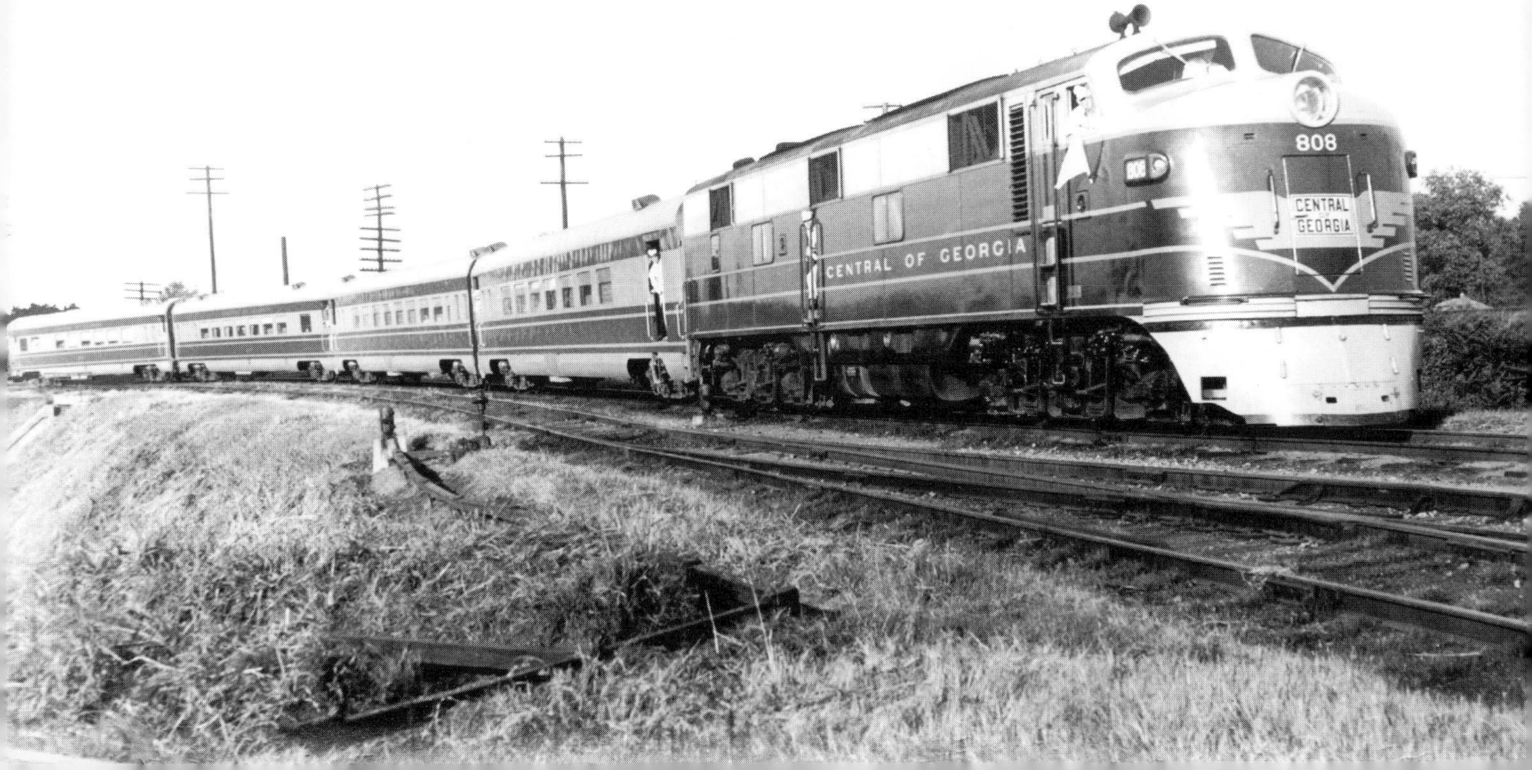

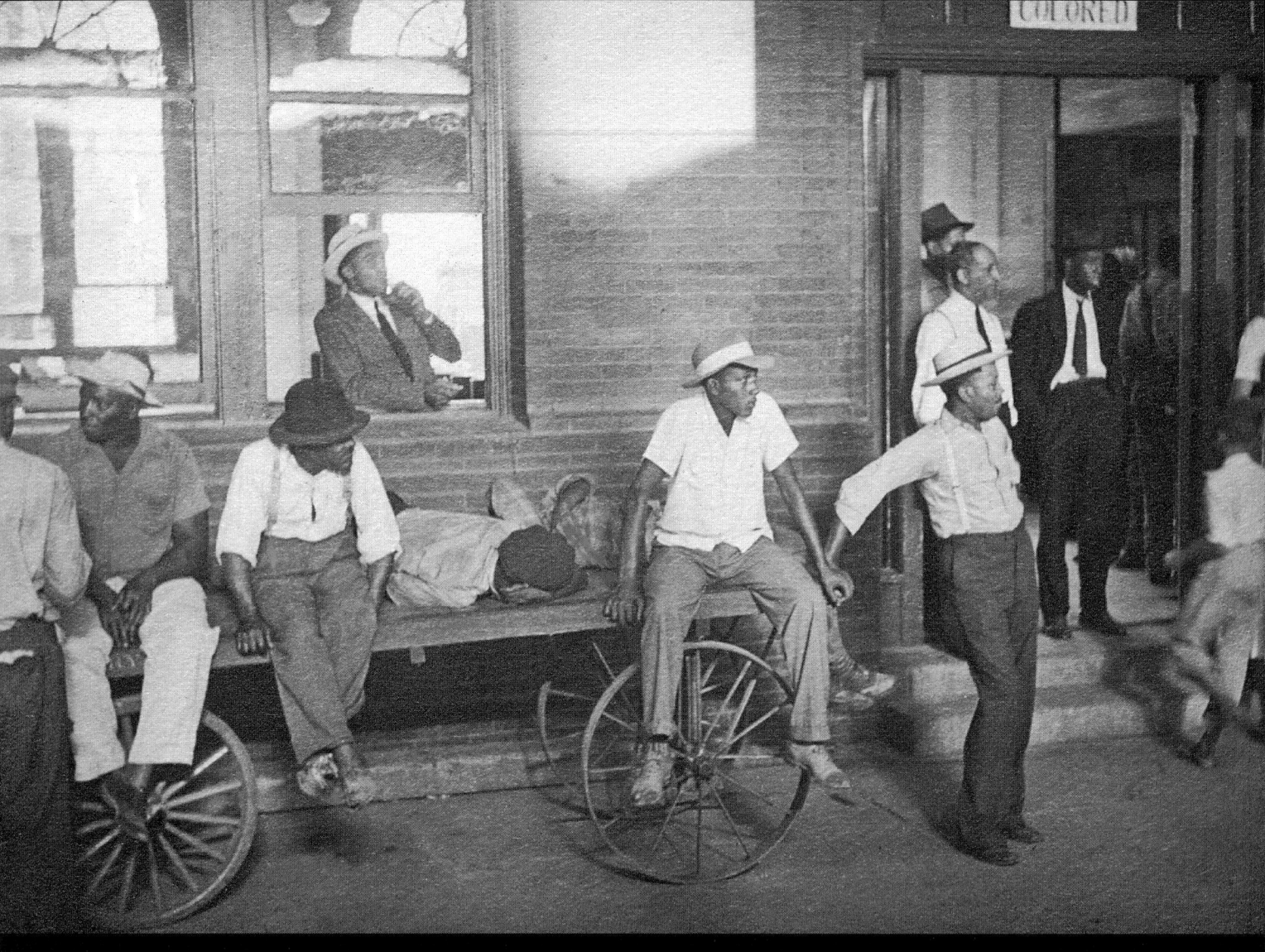

COLORED

Even segregation did not stifle the communal
life that took place at southern railroad depots.
From the absence of luggage, it does not appear
that these individuals are travelers. The fact that
it is a male group indicates a particular social

Railroads played an important role in southern black social life. In many rural localities, farm families flocked into town on Saturday afternoons and evenings to shop and socialize. Those who didn't patronize jook joints or other commercial entertainments often congregated at train stations where friends met, courtships developed, and the cares of daily existence were temporarily forgotten. This scene, on the original Norfolk Southern Railway somewhere in Virginia or North Carolina in the later 1950s, could have taken place almost anywhere in the South. Courtesy Warren Marcus Collection, California State Railroad Museum

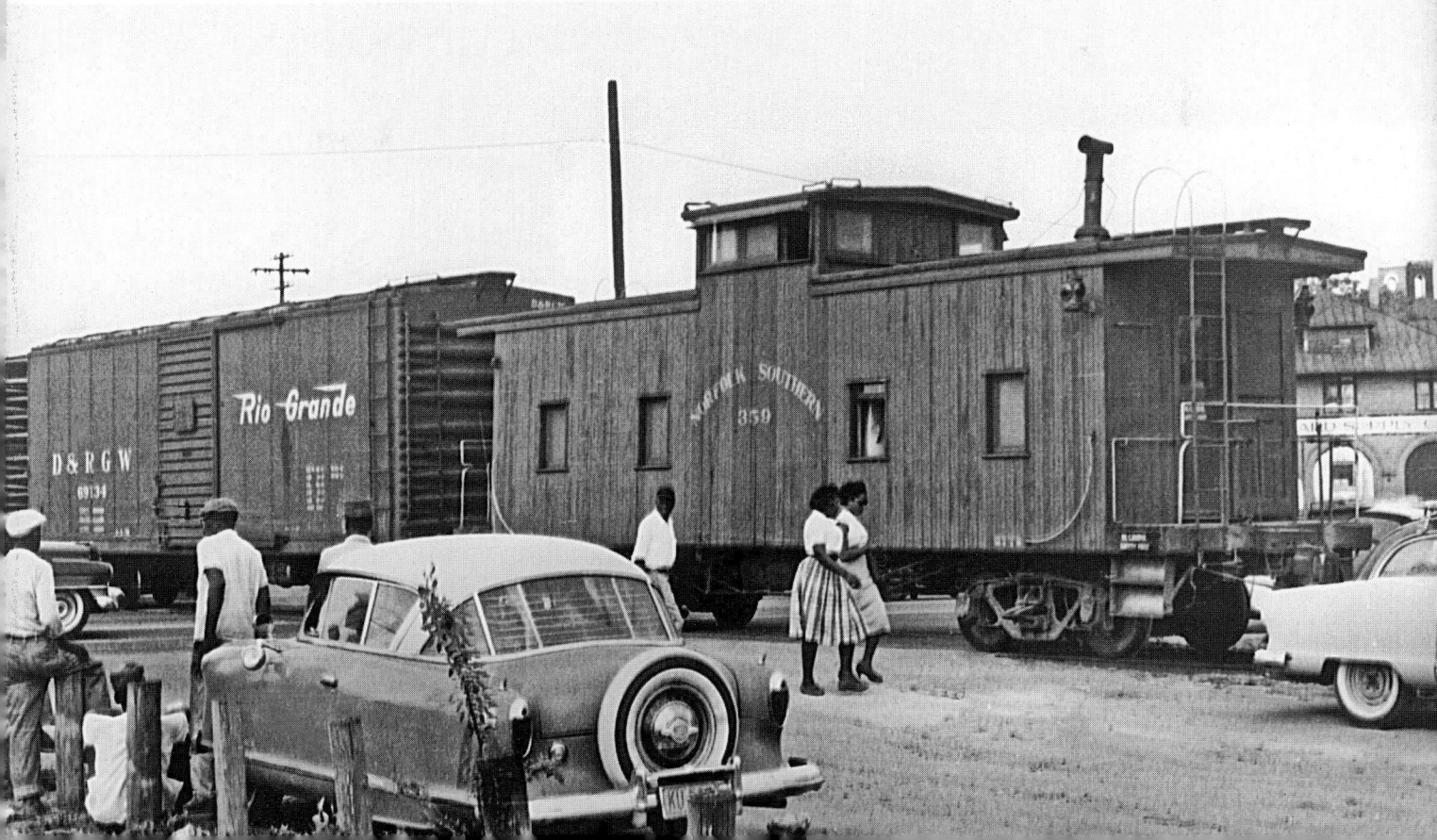

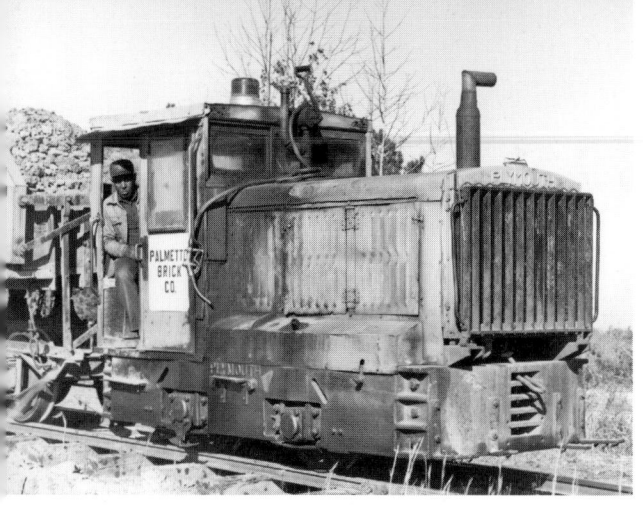

Scattered across the country were black engineers on self-contained industrial lines, like the 36-inch gauge, 1 1/2-mile Palmetto Brick Co. east of Wallace, South Carolina. Two 10-ton gasoline-powered locomotives provided the motive power in 1979. Where else could one find century-old link and pin couplings still in use? Mac Connery photograph

(BELOW) Car oiler O. Stewart squirts oil into the journal box of a wood-body freight car as it nears the top of the "hump" at the Santa Fe's Argentine, Kansas yards. A related but harder and dirtier job was that of box packer, stuffing cotton waste into the journal box around the axle to absorb the oil and keep the bearing lubricated. Sealed roller bearings eliminated these jobs. The photo was probably taken no later than the 1960s, by which time most wood freight cars had been retired. Atchison, Topeka & Santa Fe Collection, Kansas State Historical Society

(OPPOSITE) Machinist Freddie Williams pauses for the photographer in the Durham & Southern Railway's diesel locomotive shop at Dunn, North Carolina, in July 1973. When blacks attained skilled positions in railroad shops, it was more likely on short lines where employees were few and not unionized, as was the case on the 59-mile D&S, all within the Tar Heel state. Mac Connery photograph

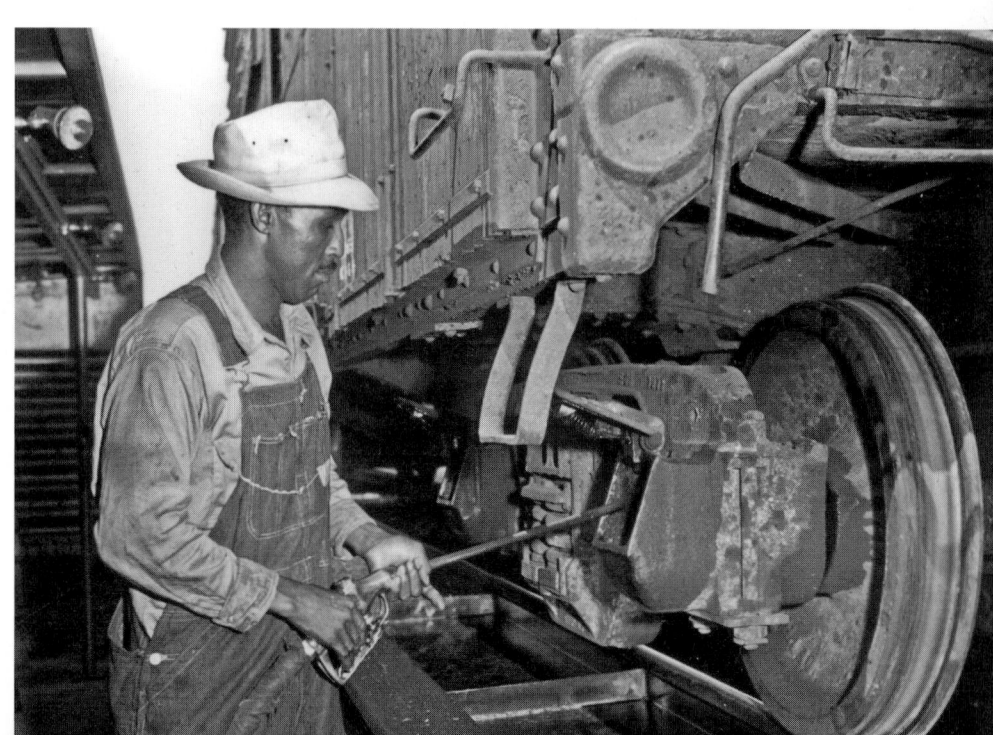

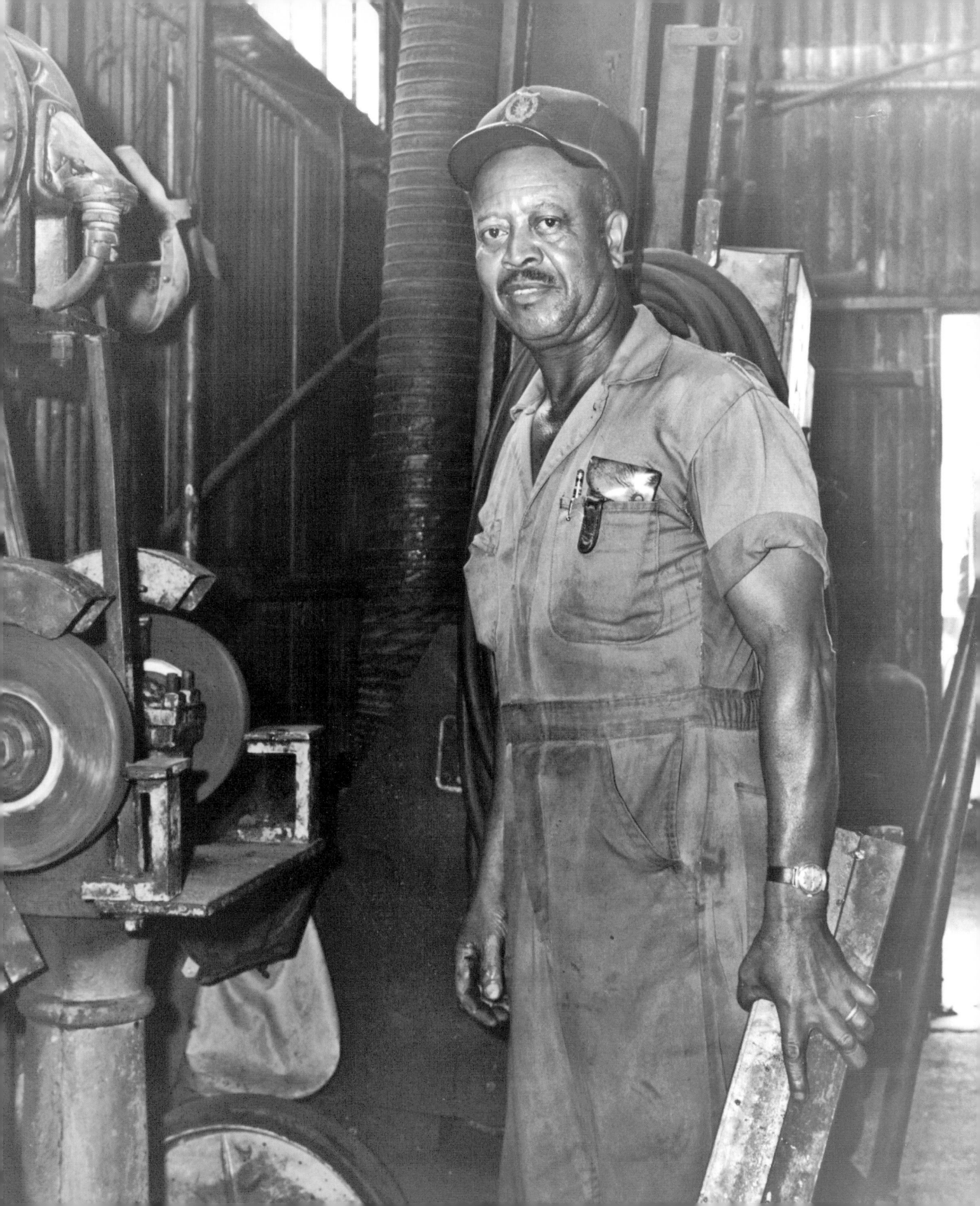

Car riders assembled coal trains at numerous mine sites in Appalachia. This Chesapeake & Ohio Railway car rider (blacks were only called brakemen if they worked in a yard) is posed operating with a safety belt and brake club at the Piney Creek mine in Stanaford, West Virginia, in 1945. Courtesy of the Chesapeake & Ohio Historical Society

(OPPOSITE) *Southern railroads, and those like the Chesapeake & Ohio Railway that linked the South and the North, offered blacks relatively steady employment, but below an impenetrable racial ceiling. An unskilled job usually open to blacks was outside car cleaner, as this one on C&O subsidiary Pere Marquette Railway in 1947. Courtesy of the Chesapeake & Ohio Historical Society*

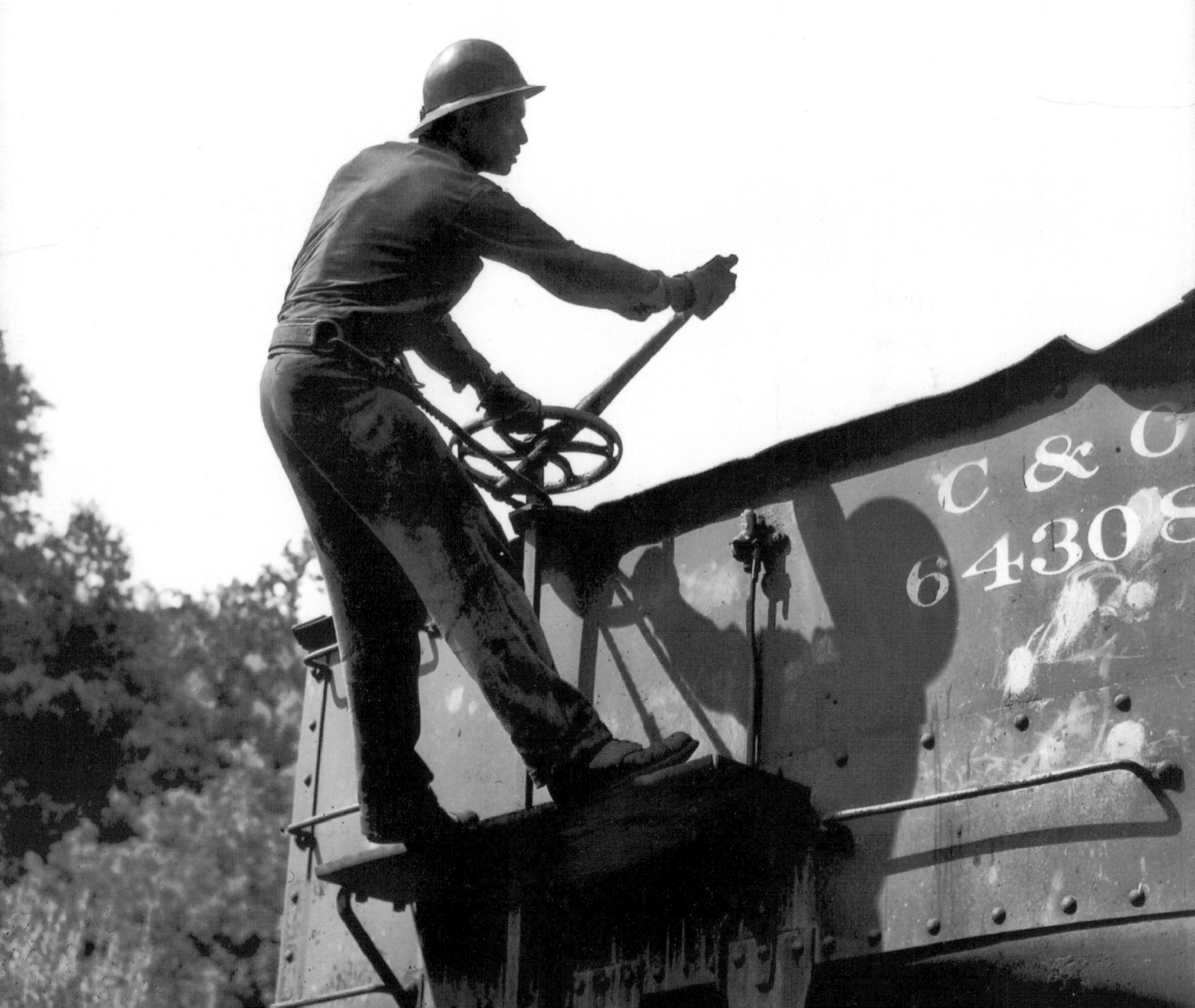

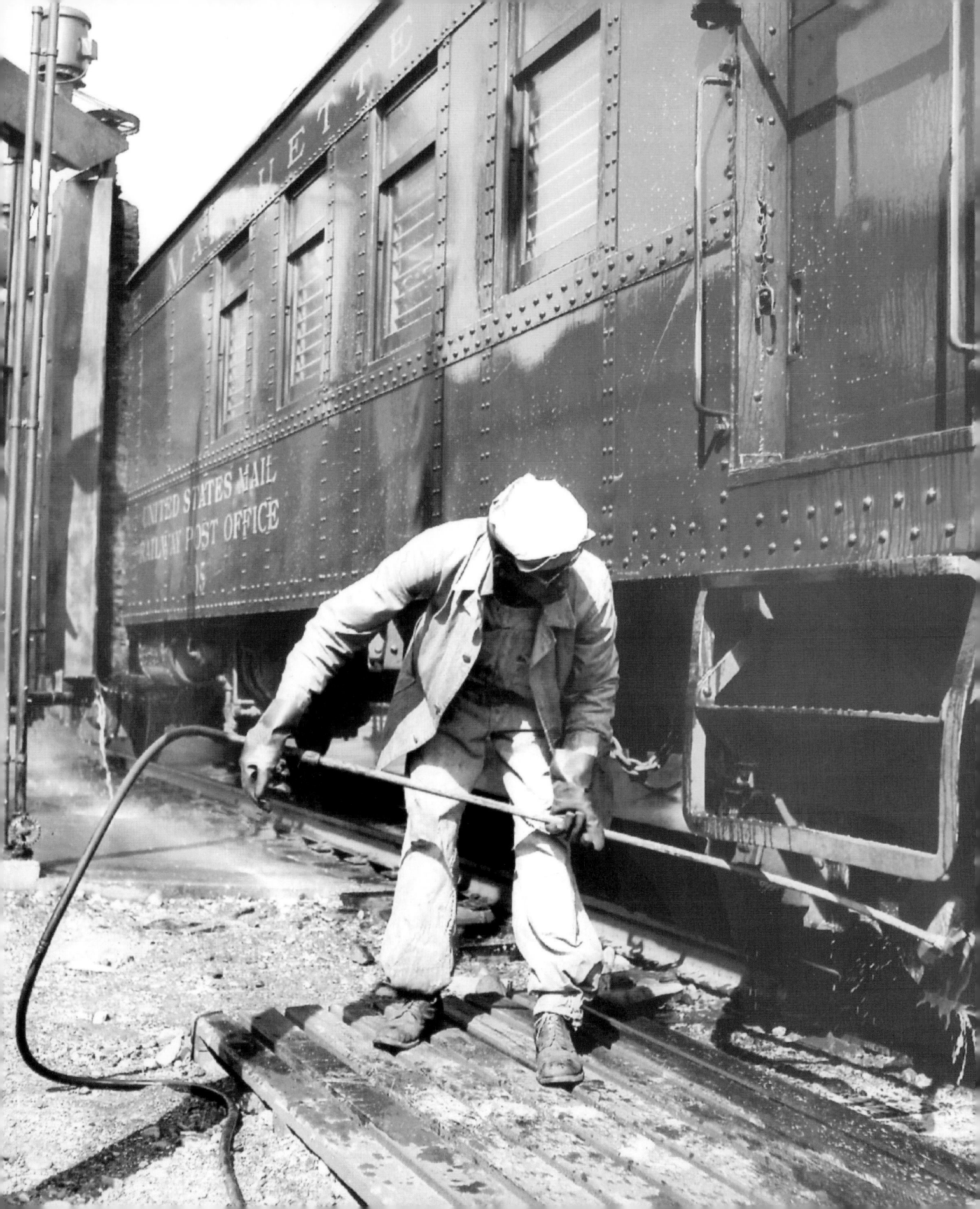

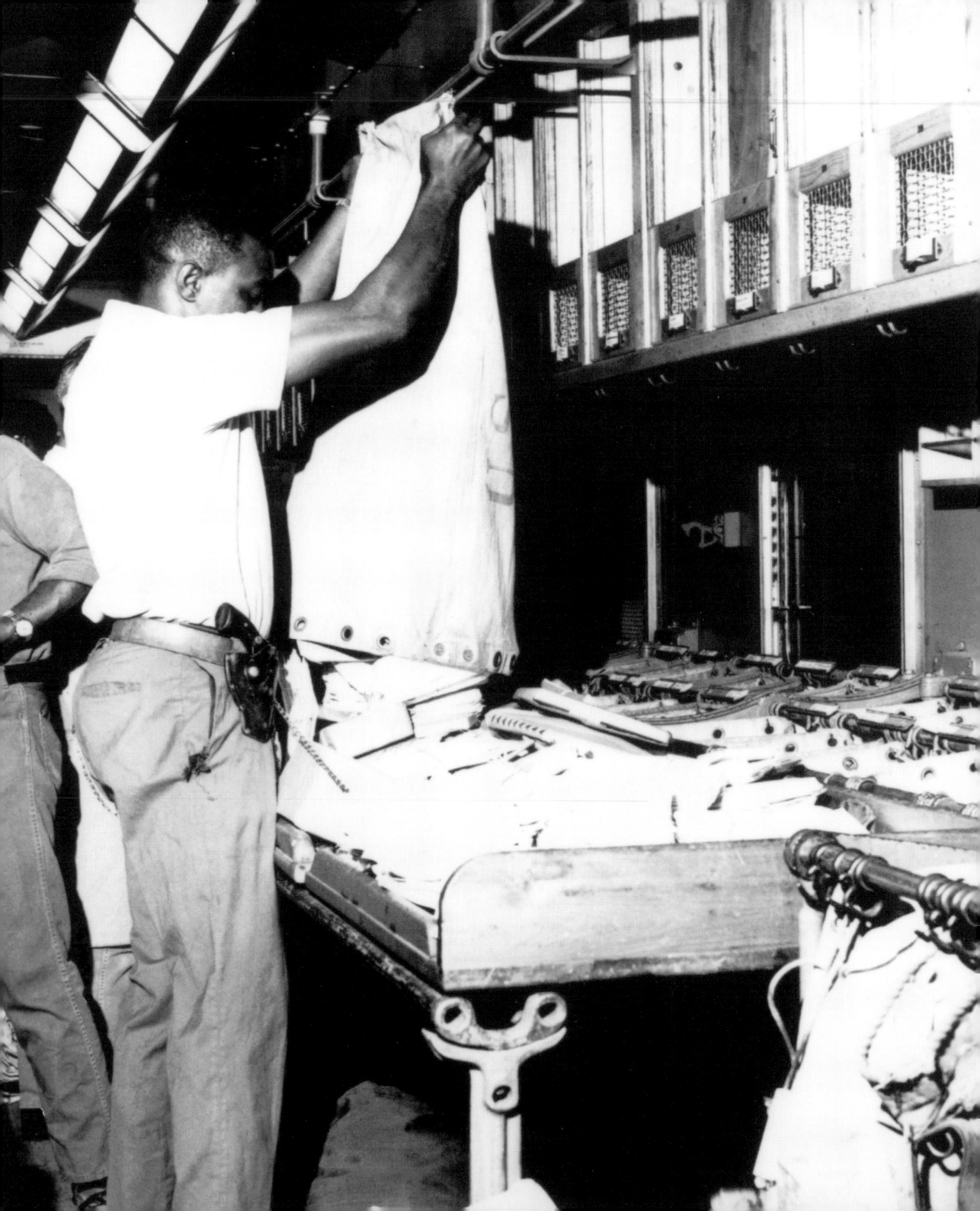

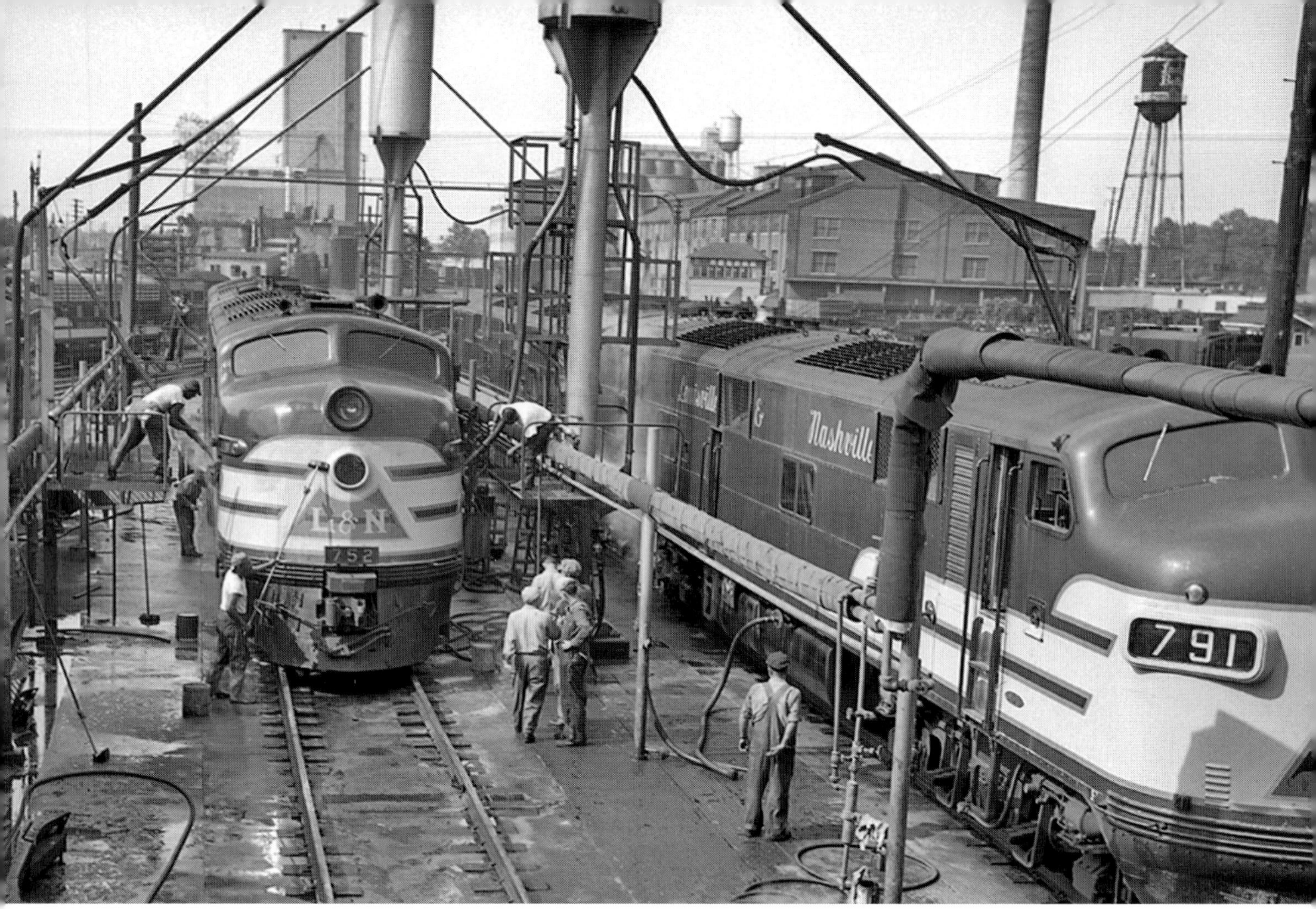

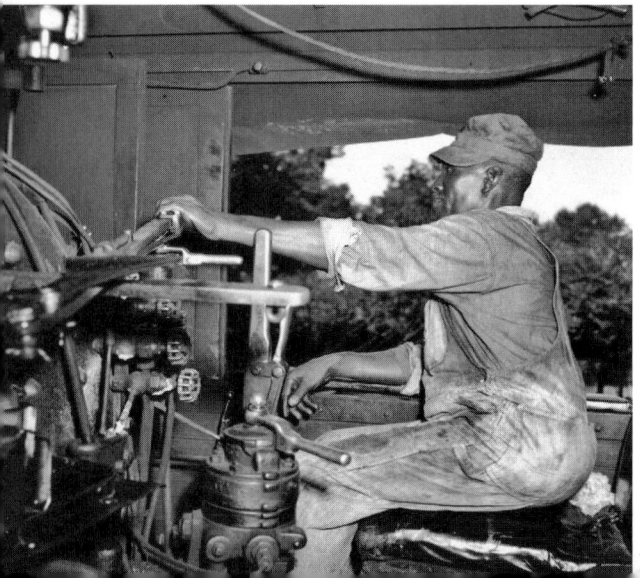

(LEFT) *African Americans lacked the opportunity to become engineers on Class 1 railroads until the post–civil rights era. But some non-unionized southern short lines hired black engineers, free to pay them less than whites would demand. Both engineer and fireman were black on the 17-mile Mississippi & Alabama Railroad linking Vinegar Bend, Alabama, and Leakesville, Mississippi. The pike's last locomotive, 2-6-2 no. 4, was designed to run equally well in both directions, making turning at either end unnecessary. The locomotive and crew were photographed shortly before the line's abandonment in 1950. C. William Witbeck photograph, collection of David S. Price*

(OPPOSITE) *A team of four locomotive washers cleans up a Louisville & Nashville Railroad diesel at the South Louisville shops in 1951. If these men were longtime employees, chances are they had washed many a steam locomotive before this. Jobs as engine wipers and locomotive washers were often reserved for blacks on southern railroads, but with the advent of cleaner diesels, many such jobs were lost. Louisville & Nashville Railroad Records, University of Louisville Archives and Records Center*

Steam railroading provided numerous laborer jobs for blacks that later disappeared with the supremacy of diesel power. Several blacks work on borrowed time at this modest Gulf, Mobile & Ohio Railroad coaling facility in the 1940s. One, on the ground at right, fills the small bottom-dump cart with coal from the hopper car on the trestle. Another spreads the coal evenly in the tender, using a longer-handled shovel than a fireman's coal scoop. The GM&O was one of the first railroads to completely dieselize. The last steam engines dropped their fires forever in 1949. Gulf, Mobile & Ohio Collection of the John W. Barriger III National Railroad Library, University of Missouri—St. Louis

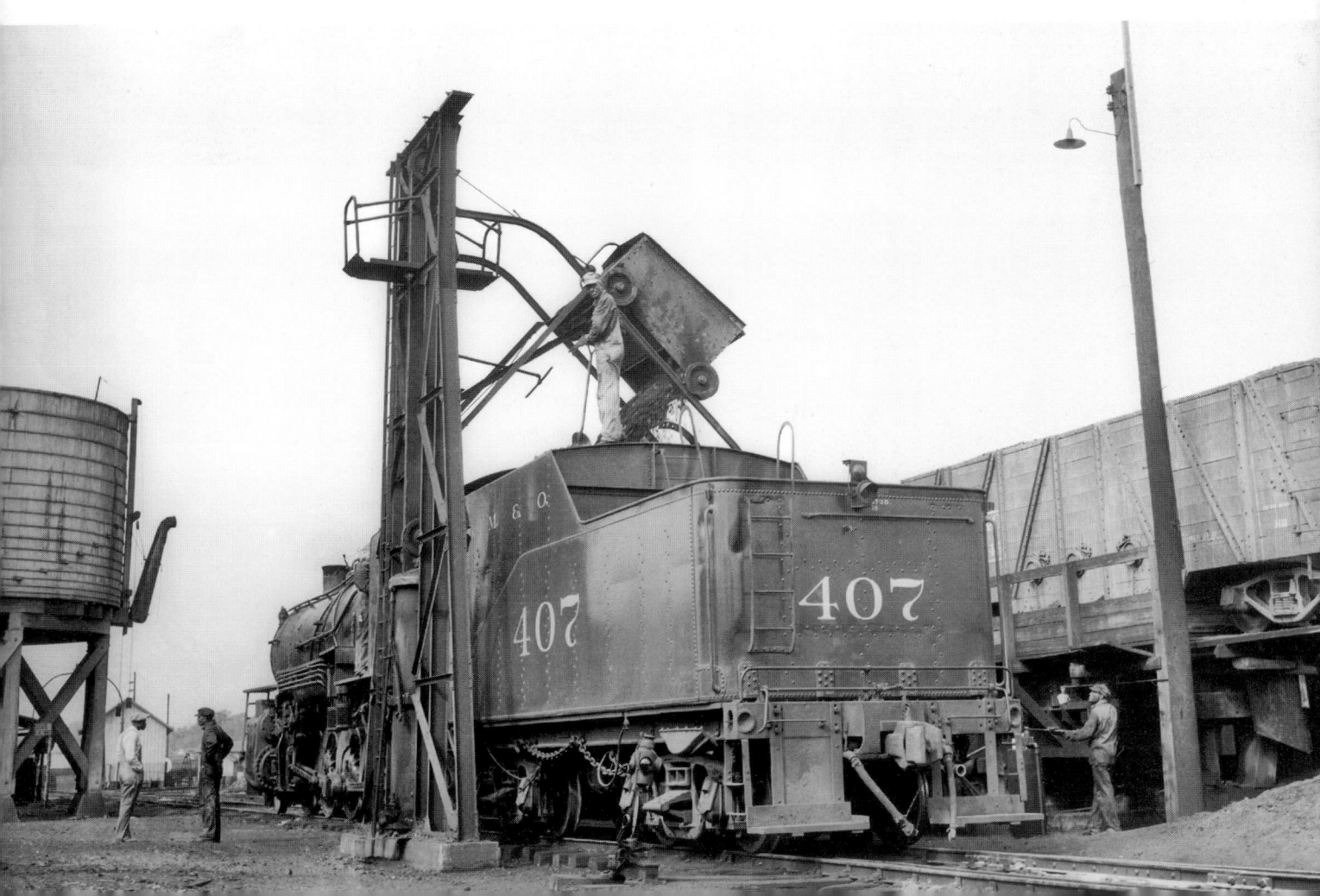

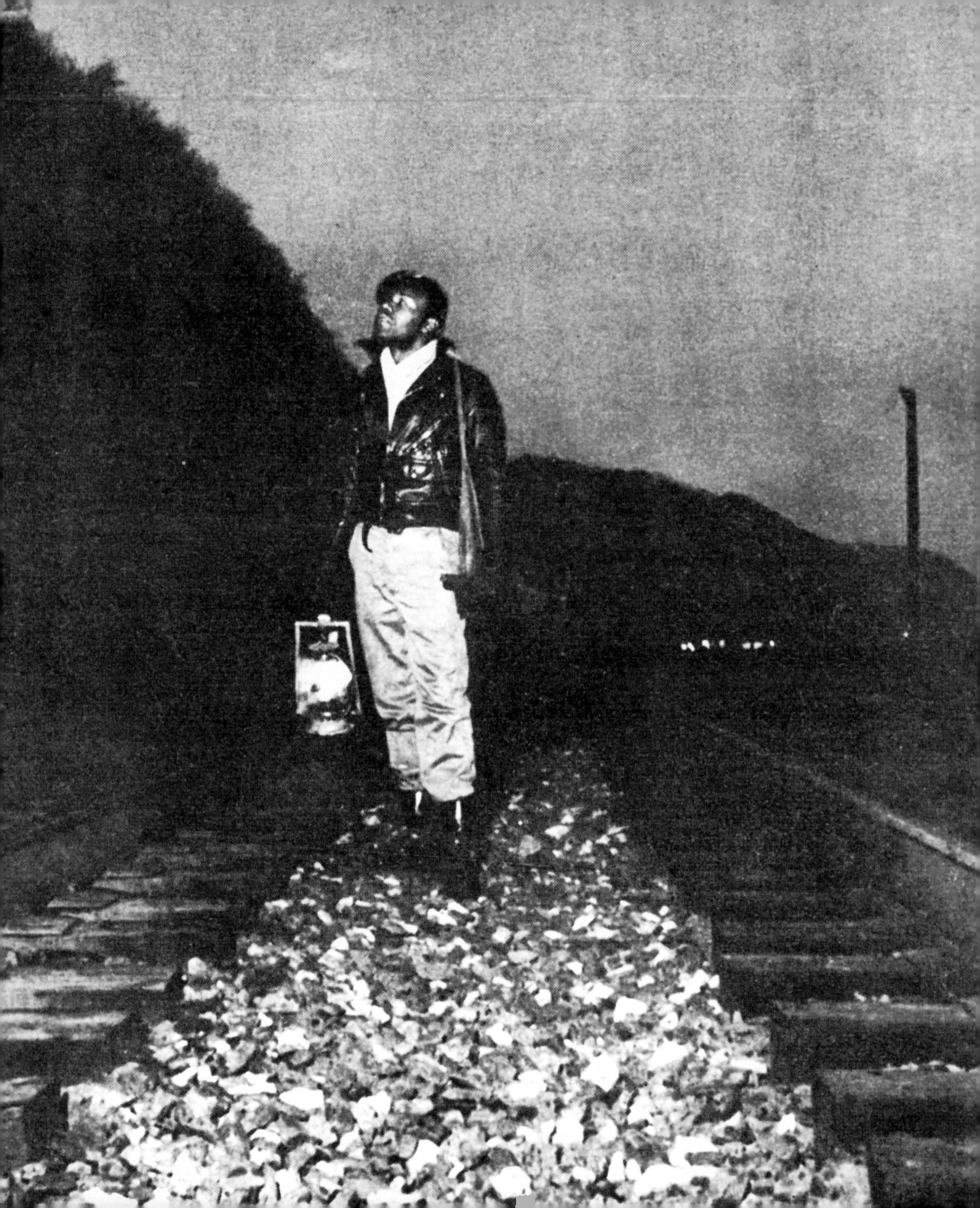

*One of the loneliest railroad jobs was that of cut
or bluff watchman, who nightly patrolled on
foot a section of track particularly prone to rock
slides. The Pennsylvania Railroad's Thomas
Anthony, shown here in 1959, guarded 1 ½
miles of track skirting Mount Washington, near
Pittsburgh. Upon discovering an obstruction,
he would place torpedoes and lighted fusees on
the track on both sides of the slide and close the
circuit between the rails with shunt wires to acti-
vate signals and stop oncoming trains. Today,
electrified fences protect track next to unstable
mountainsides. Theodore Kornweibel collection*

483

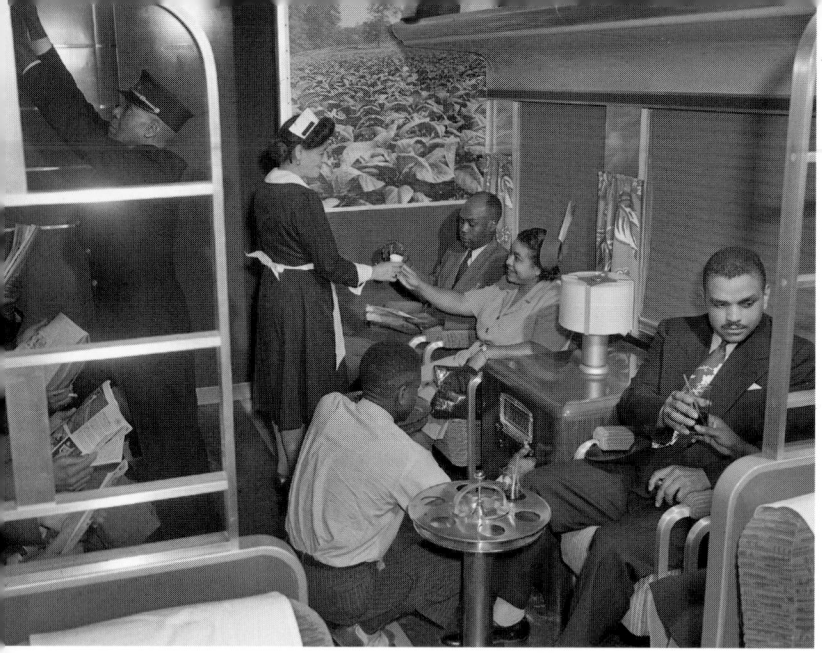

(ABOVE) *When the Louisville & Nashville Railroad inaugurated its streamlined, all-coach* Humming Bird *between Cincinnati and New Orleans in 1946, when this publicity shot with models was taken, it included a separate lounge for African Americans where they could socialize, listen to the radio, and enjoy beverages served by the black train maid. A train porter is stowing luggage. Louisville & Nashville Railroad Records, University of Louisville Archives and Records Center*

(BELOW) *The most odious task for waiters in the South was having to participate in dining-car segregation. Here, on the Missouri–Kansas–Texas Railroad's* Texas Special, *the curtain used to hide black patrons has been pulled back to allow whites to occupy their section. Any blacks now wishing to eat will have to wait until all whites have vacated that area and the curtains can be drawn again. The scene dates from around 1950. Hayes Collection, Texas/Dallas History and Archives Division, Dallas Public Library*

484

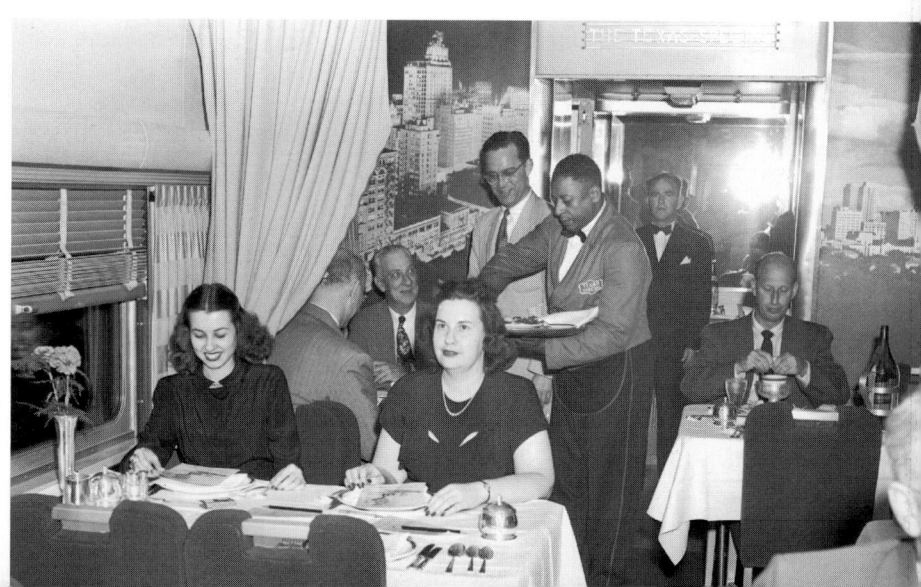

An Atchison, Topeka & Santa Fe Railway chair car porter assists a passenger onto the train with her baggage sometime in the 1960s. The self-service luggage carts indicate that Red Caps have been eliminated at this station. Soon, in 1971, Amtrak will relieve the Santa Fe of the burden of passenger service. Atchison, Topeka & Santa Fe Collection, Kansas State Historical Society

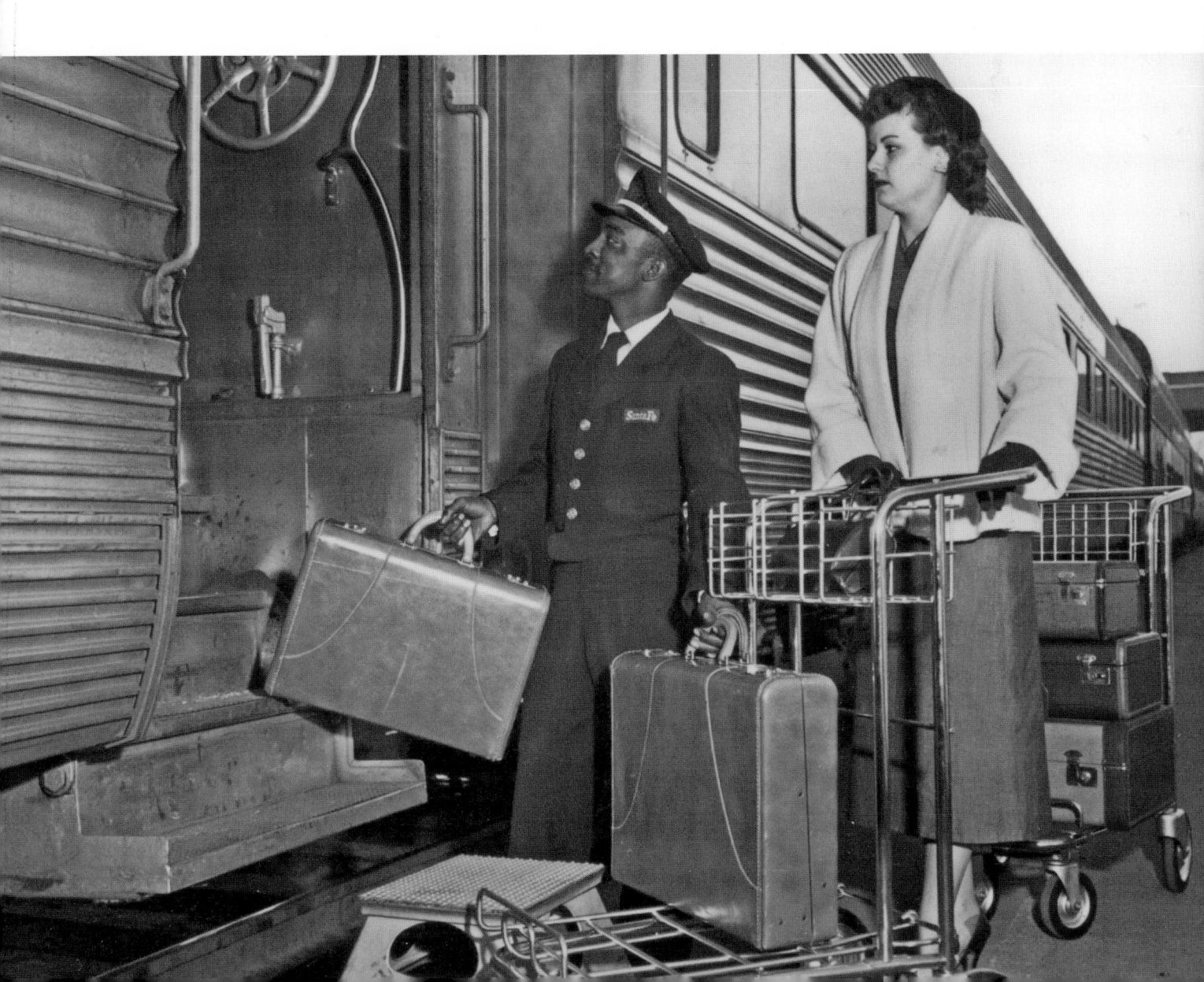

Instructor Elzie E. Currie at the Baltimore & Ohio Railroad's train porter school in 1947, located in a day coach at Washington Union Station. Porters and the B&O's new porterettes received training in safety and operation of a car's heating and air conditioning, how to keep a car clean, and in the psychology of dealing with demanding or troublesome passengers. Courtesy B&O Railroad Museum

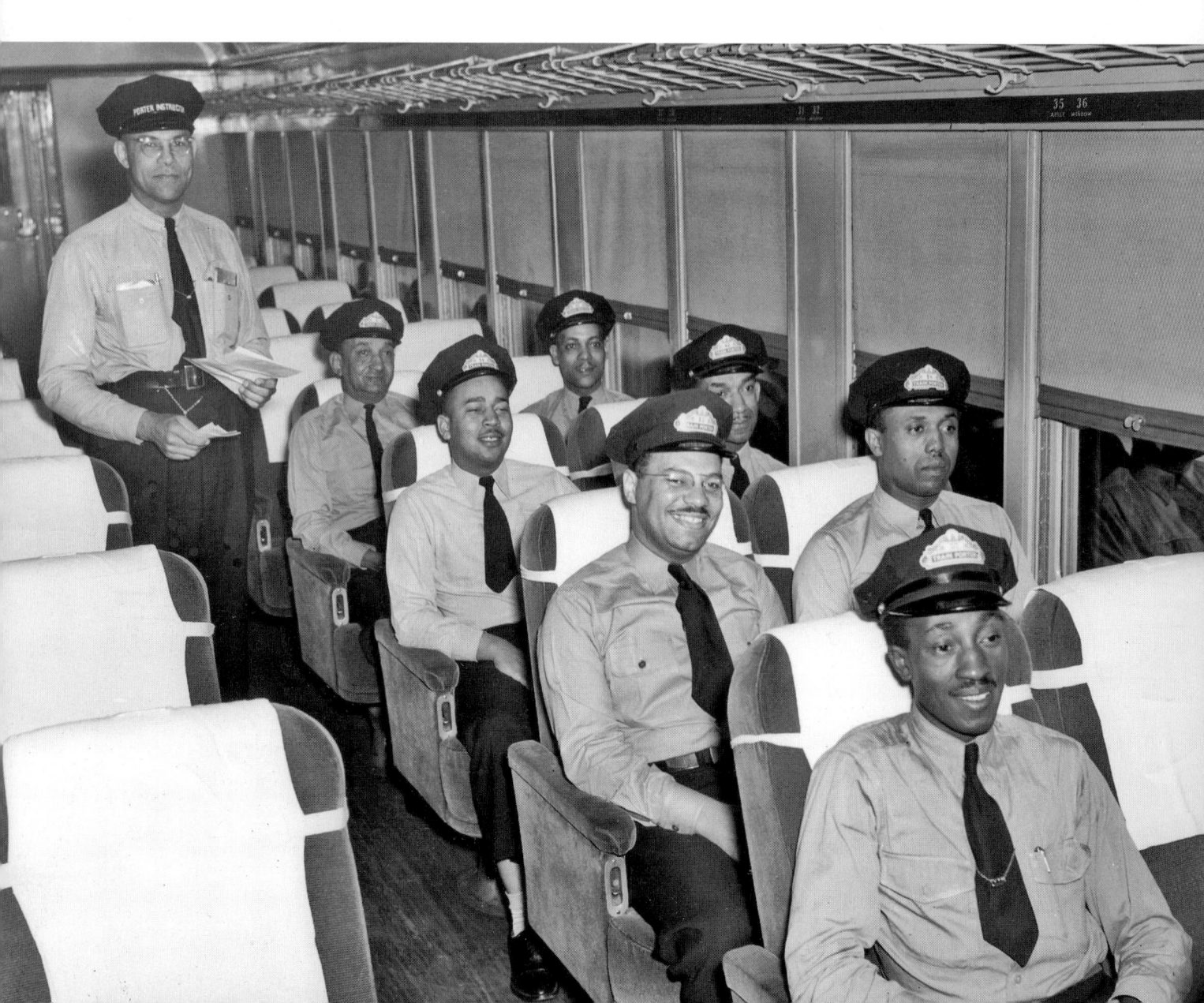

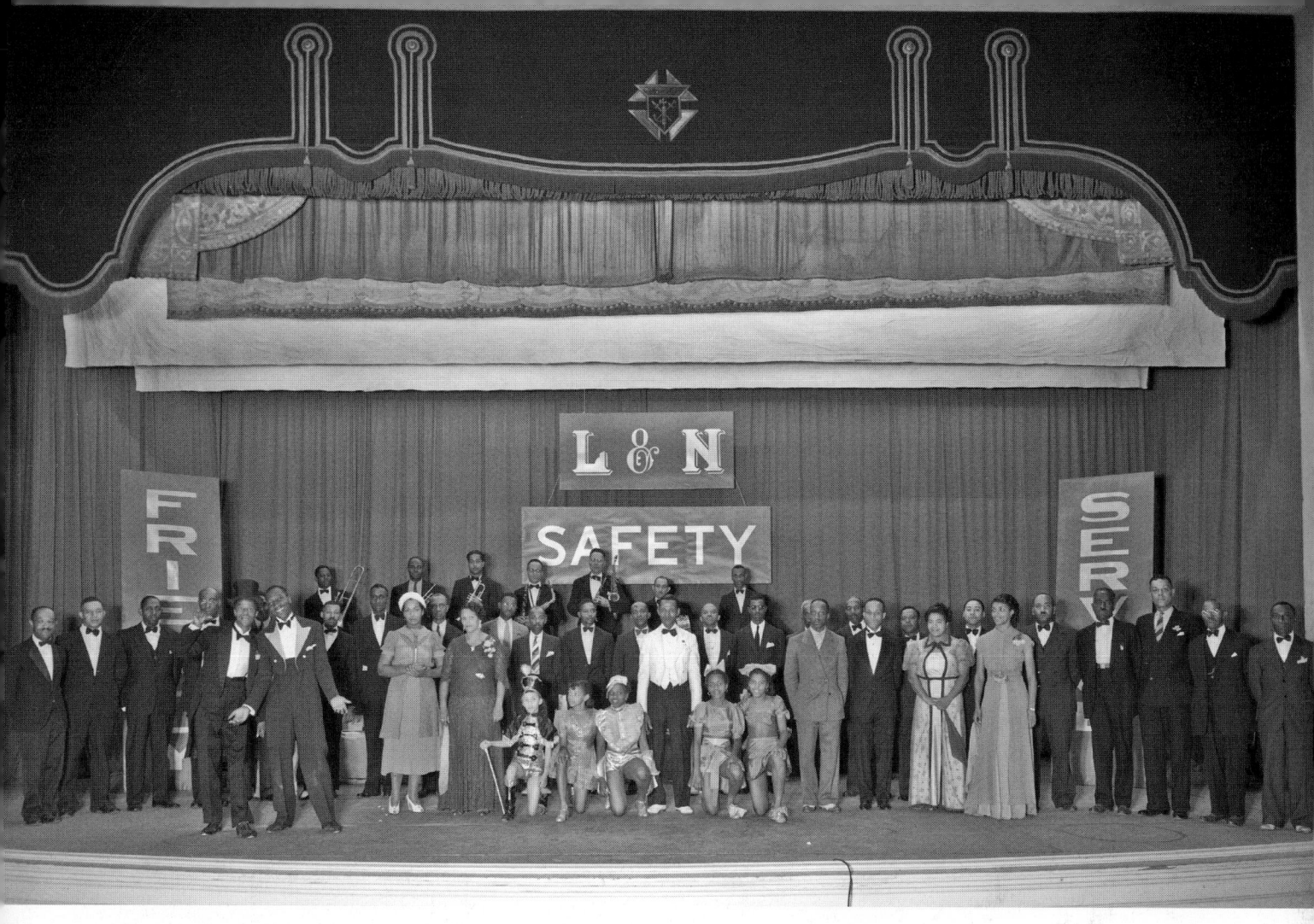

Southern railroads promoted a wide range
of segregated employee organizations like
booster and safety clubs and veteran employees'
associations. Blacks, like these performers at a
Louisville & Nashville Railroad "colored" safety
rally in the later 1940s, regarded such organizations as more than workplace adjuncts. They
provided opportunities for leadership, recreation, civic contributions, and community
entertainment. Courtesy of Caufield & Shook
Collection, Special Collections, University
of Louisville

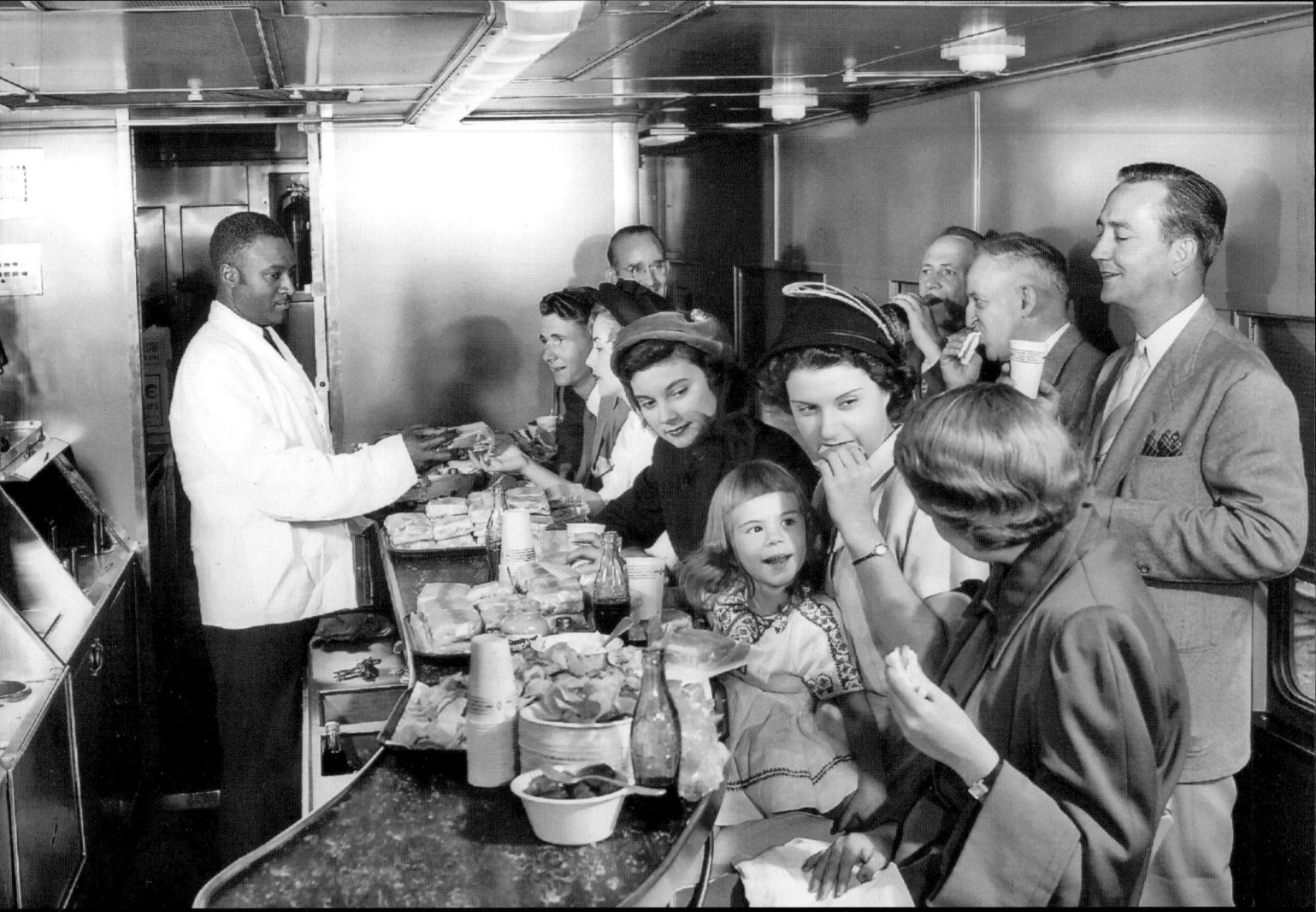

In an effort to make train travel more affordable
in the post–World War II years, railroads
introduced cheaper dining alternatives. The
Chesapeake & Ohio Railway offered a lunch
counter in the tavern-lounge car of its new
"Chessie" streamliner in 1948, depicted in this
publicity shot with models, not actual passengers. But that luxury train was canceled before
its inaugural run and its cars were parceled out
to other trains. Lunch counter service could be
found on many other roads as well. Courtesy
of the Chesapeake & Ohio Historical Society

Hoping to attract passengers after World War II, as more and more people used automobiles for travel, the railroads introduced new equipment like dome cars. Most domes featured coach seating, but this one, on the Union Pacific Railroad's City of Los Angeles *around 1960, offered a scenic dining experience. For waiters, it meant a longer walk from the kitchen and a more difficult balancing act with a tray of food. Arthur D. Dubin Collection, Special Collections, Donnelley and Lee Library, Lake Forest College*

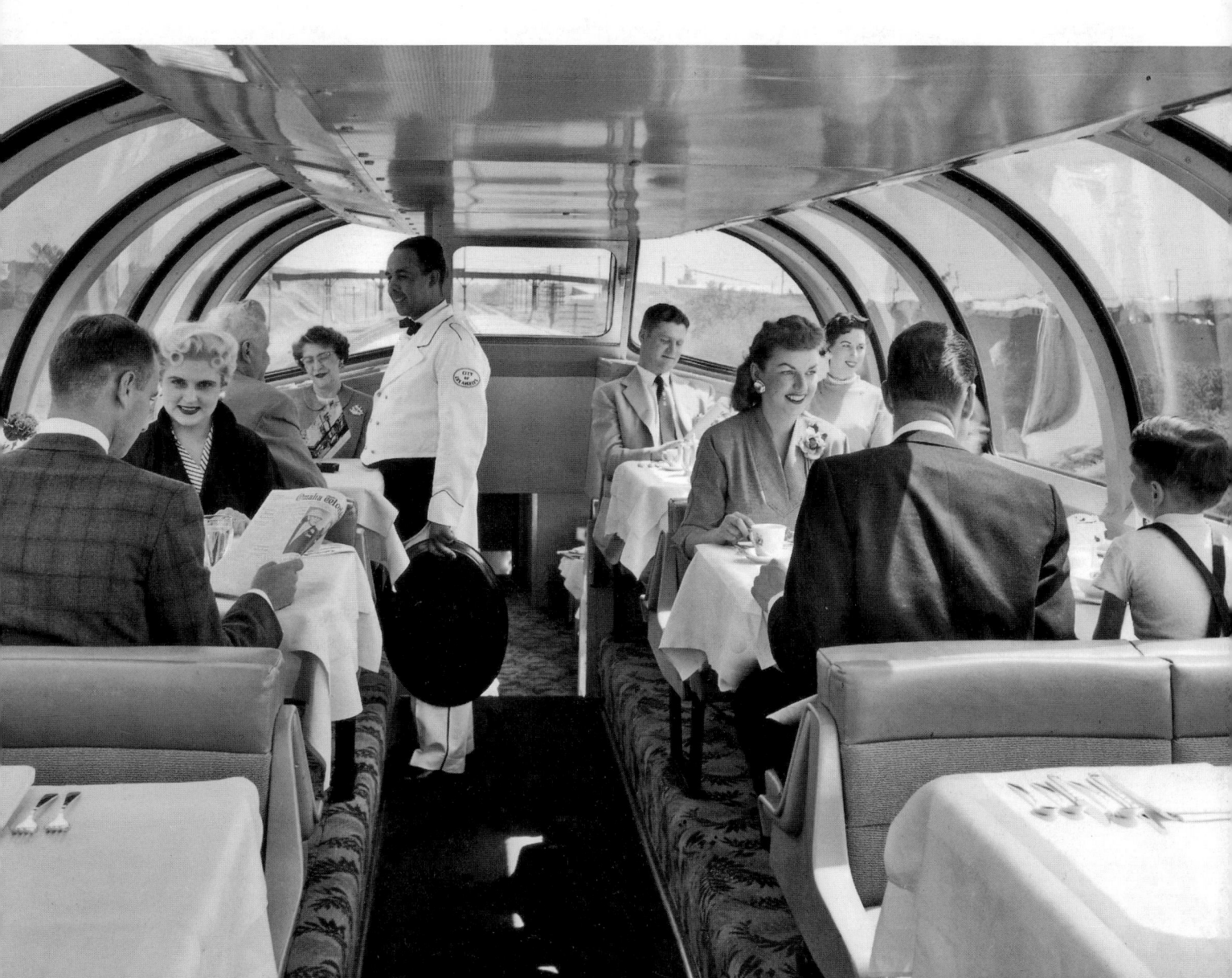

After the Pullman Company lost an antitrust suit in 1944, ownership of its cars passed to the individual railroads while the Pullman Company continued to staff them. By the early 1960s, Pullman was rapidly exiting the business, ceasing all sleeping-car operations in 1968. By then, the individual railroads that still offered sleepers, like the Atchison, Topeka & Santa Fe shown here around 1970, had hired their own porters, usually the same men who had worked many years for Pullman. Atchison, Topeka & Santa Fe Collection, Kansas State Historical Society

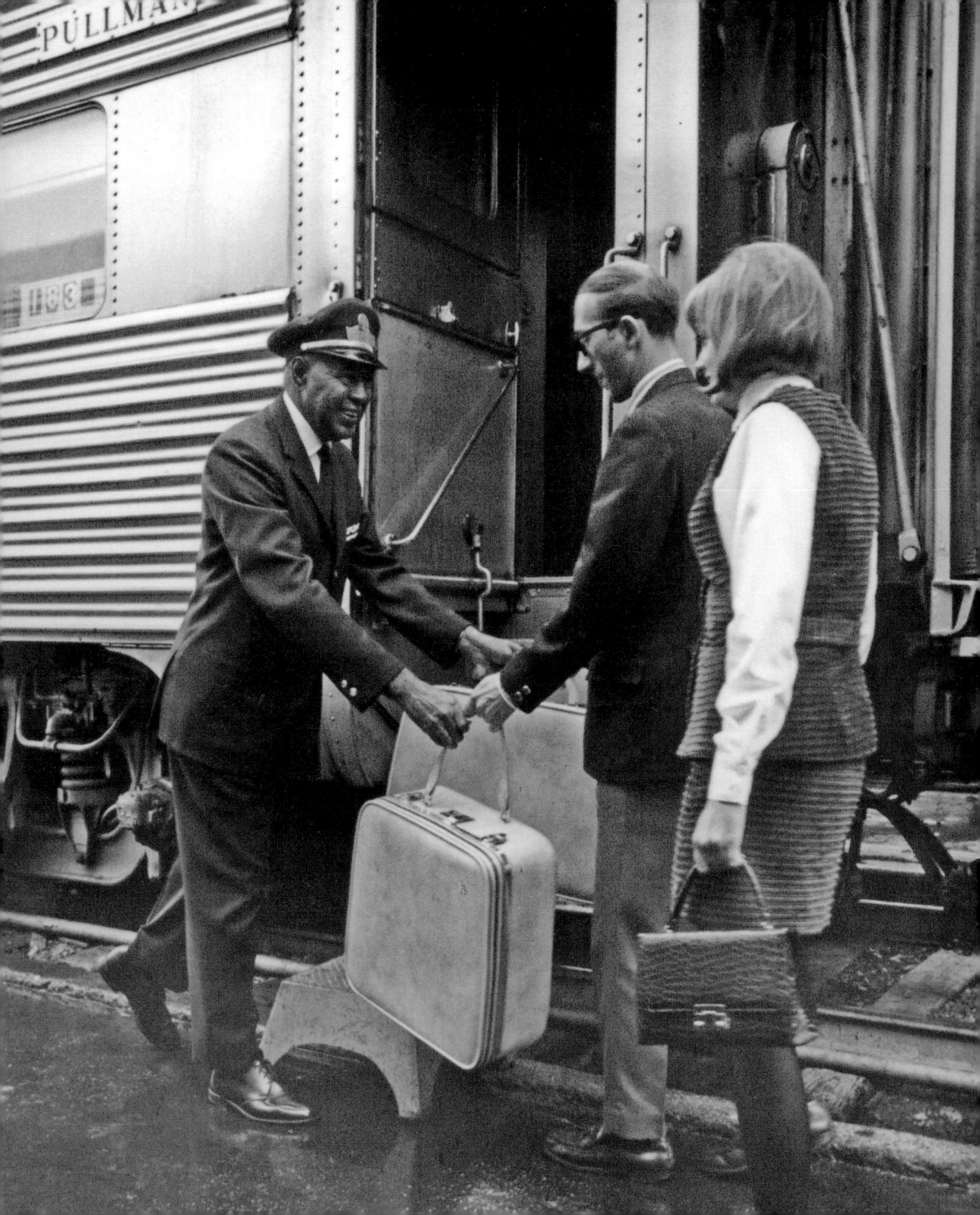

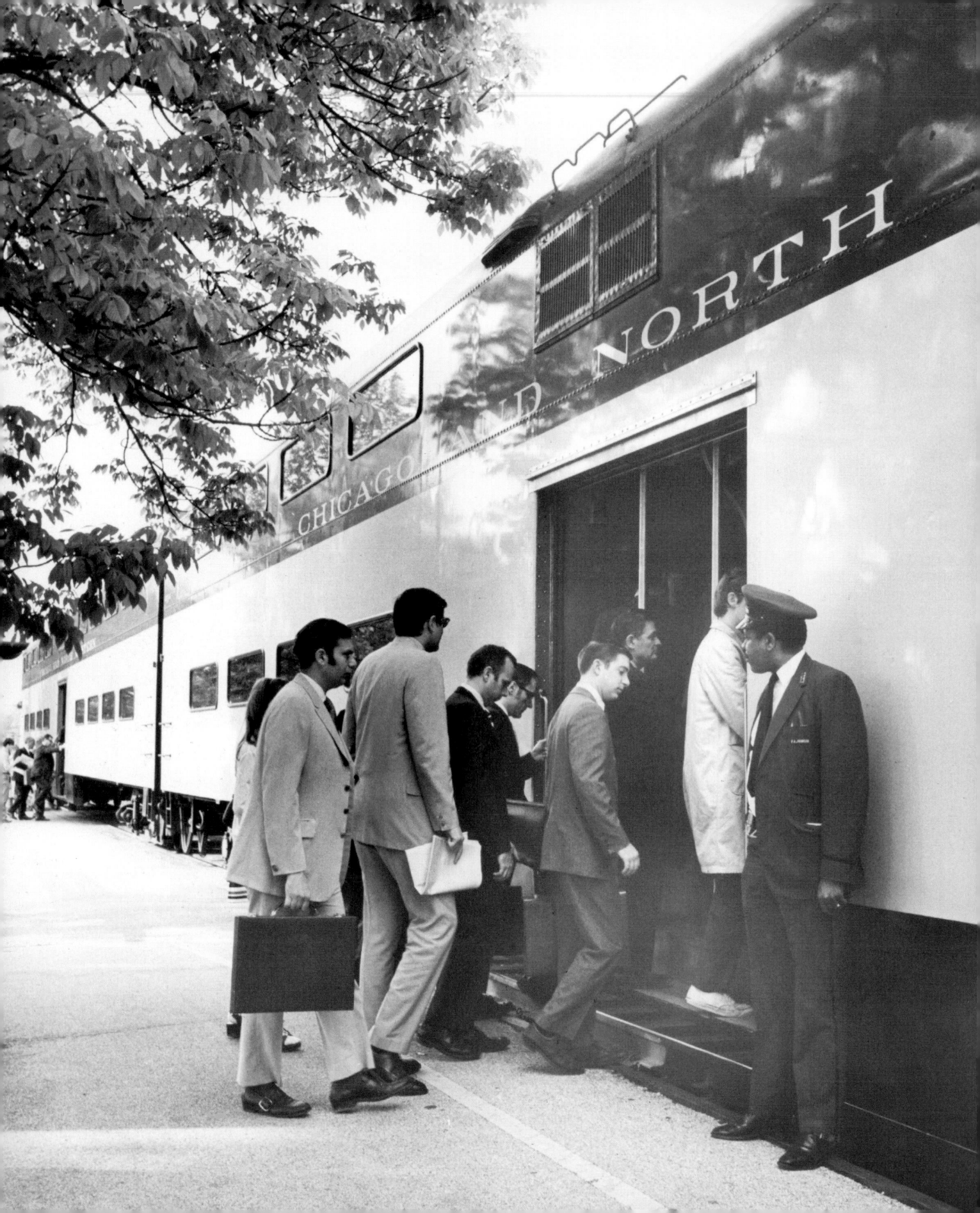

(OPPOSITE) *From the beginning of railroading, with few exceptions, blacks were barred from working as passenger train conductors and brakemen. Not until civil rights legislation did such jobs generally become available. Even then, seniority made it more likely that blacks would work in commuter service than on long-distance trains, as this brakeman on the Chicago & North Western Railway in 1970. But at least he went home after work and didn't have to lay over in a distant location. Theodore Kornweibel collection*

With Amtrak's assumption of nearly all passenger service in 1971, the railroads were finally relieved of money-losing dining- and lounge-car service. Amtrak had no desire to lose money either, so its level of service, from paper cups to soda and beer served in cans, did not aspire to the standards of yore. What old-time waiters would have thought of mini-skirted waitresses can only be conjectured. The photo was taken around 1972. Amtrak Collection, reprinted by permission, Railroad Museum of Pennsylvania

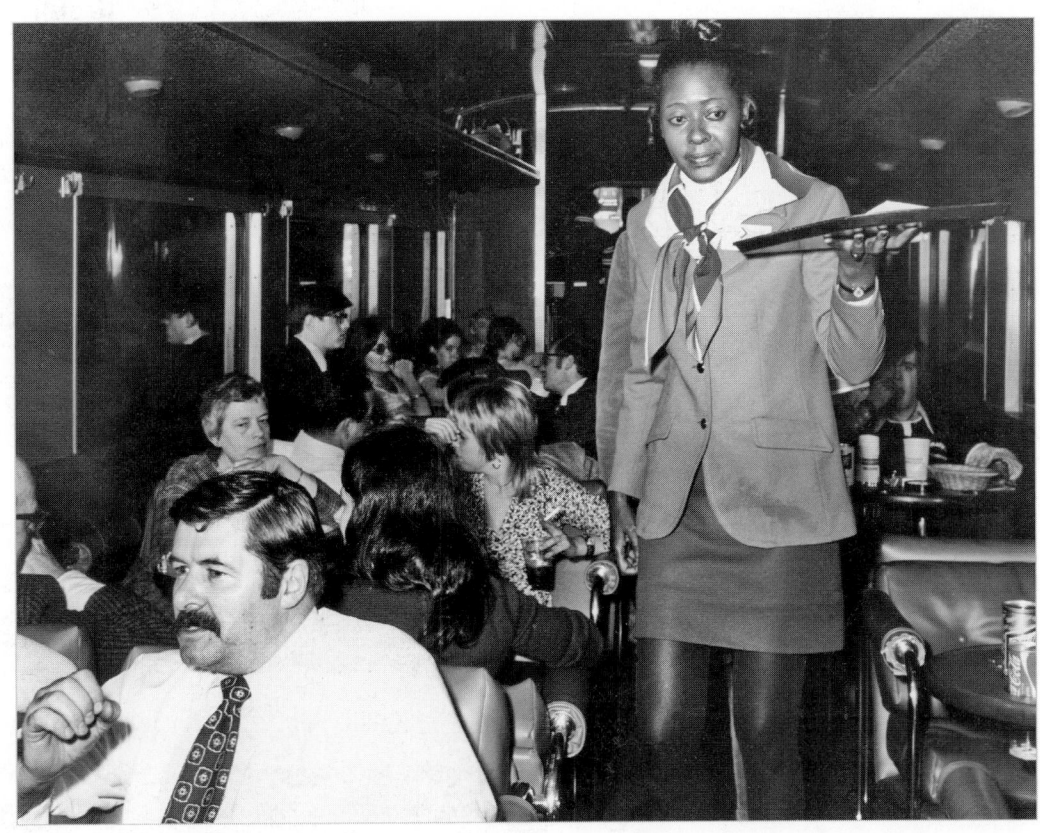

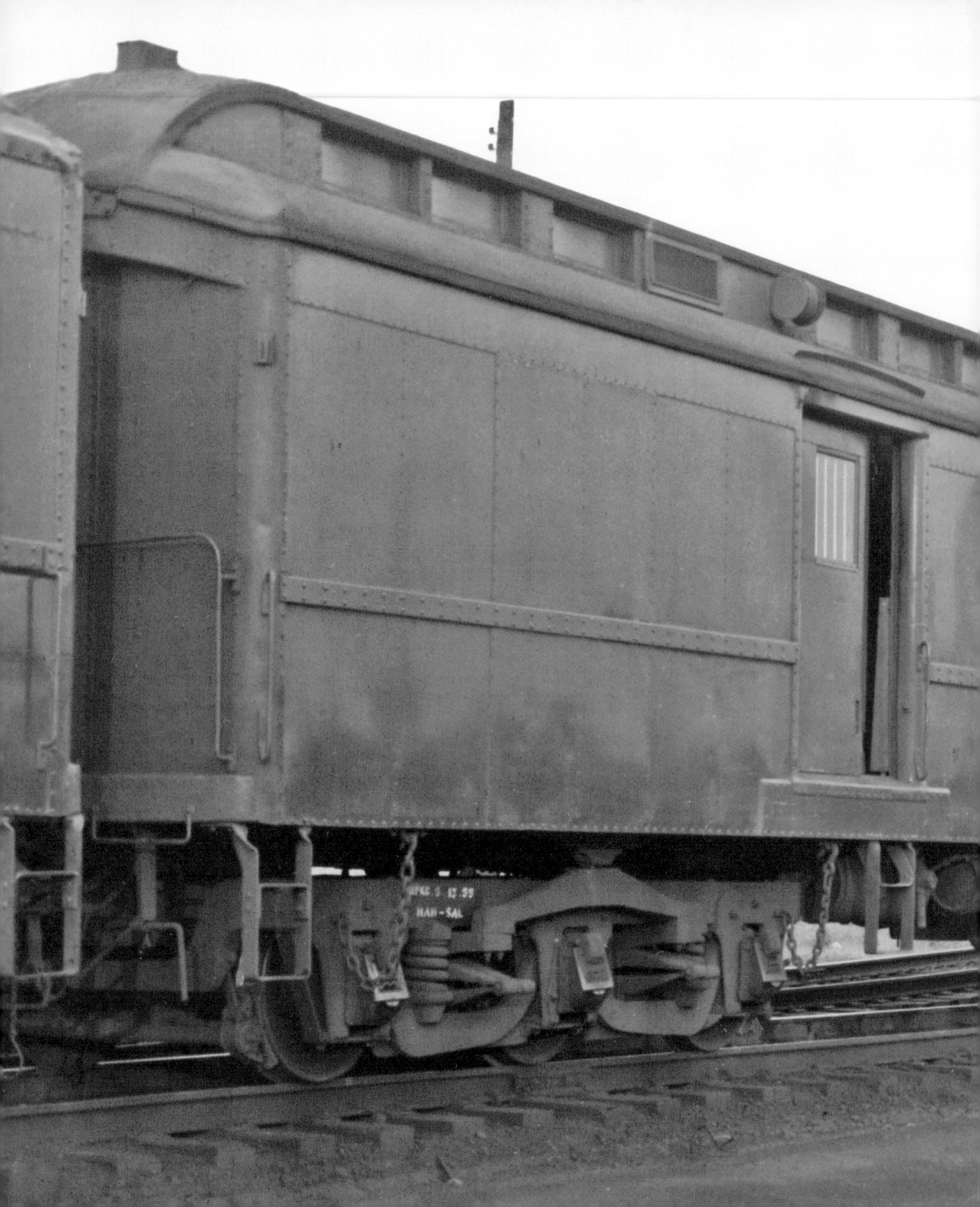

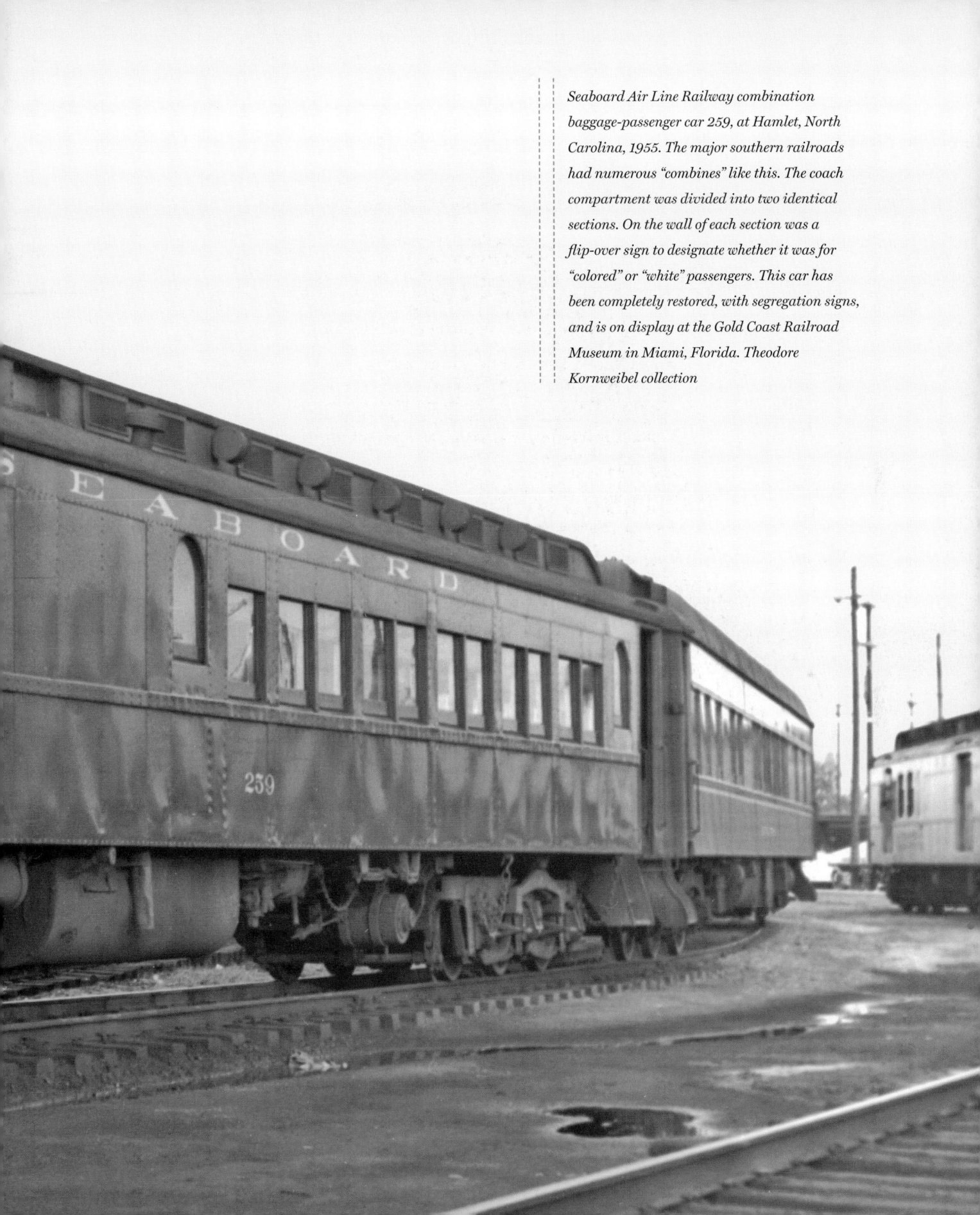

Seaboard Air Line Railway combination baggage-passenger car 259, at Hamlet, North Carolina, 1955. The major southern railroads had numerous "combines" like this. The coach compartment was divided into two identical sections. On the wall of each section was a flip-over sign to designate whether it was for "colored" or "white" passengers. This car has been completely restored, with segregation signs, and is on display at the Gold Coast Railroad Museum in Miami, Florida. Theodore Kornweibel collection

*Modern technology has made a brakeman's job
somewhat easier and less hazardous. Brakeman J. L. Hooker works Durham & Southern
Railway train 45 on July 14, 1974, as it switches
at Apex, North Carolina, shortly after noon.
Gone, thankfully, are the days of directing
switching moves by hand and lantern signals.
Radio is much safer. Mac Connery photograph*

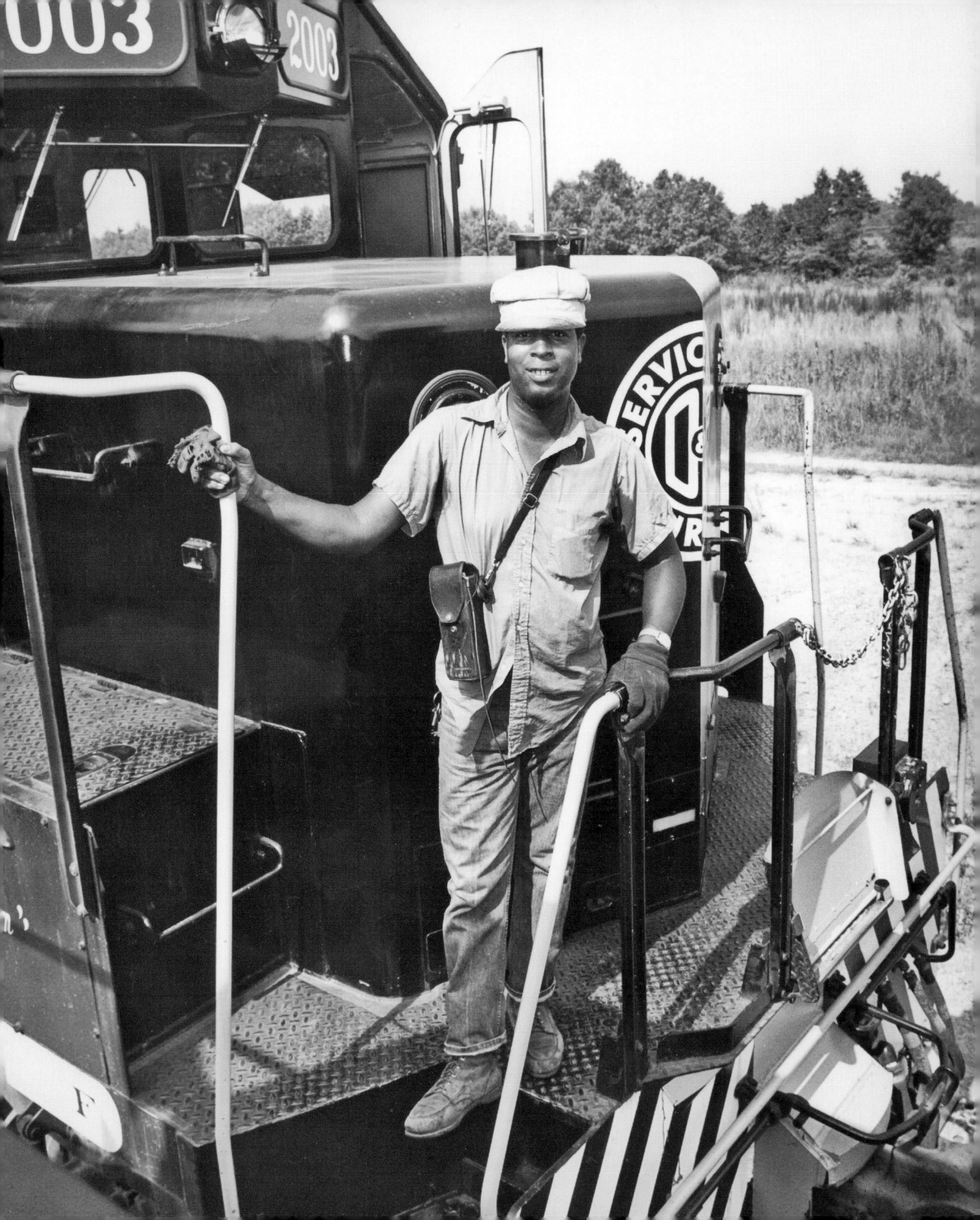

Epilogue

The Civil Rights Act of 1964 did not revolutionize the railroad industry. It only gave black railroaders, and would-be railroaders, new means to redress grievances, open doors, and pursue dreams. It outlawed discrimination in employment on the basis of race, by either employers or labor unions, and established the Equal Employment Opportunity Commission. But making new law was one thing; meaningful implementation was another. It was not an auspicious time for blacks to try to enlarge their presence in the industry. It had been hit hard by recessions in the late 1950s and early 1960s. In response, the carriers aggressively reduced labor costs by curtailing "featherbedding," unproductive work based on antiquated steam-era job descriptions and work rules. Half of all firemen's positions nationwide were eliminated by 1966. Increased mechanization led to major reductions in the number of section workers and shop laborers and helpers. One result was that unionized white workers became all the more protective of their remaining jobs. Overall railroad industry employment fell from 909,000 workers in 1960 to 683,000 by the beginning of 1969.[1]

Remarkably, black railroad employment increased in the 1960s. Although the number of low-skilled workers remained constant, the number of white-collar workers doubled, including males in managerial and sales positions and females in office jobs, although the portion of blacks doing white-collar work was still much lower than their proportion in the total population. And blacks were being gradually upgraded into skilled craft positions in the shops, although their progress was not as rapid because white men with seniority often stood in line before them. Blacks found greater opportunities for advancement on the larger railroads. And, not surprisingly, railroads outside of the South offered better chances for new positions in white-collar work.[2] But such gains were more haphazard than by deliberate intent. By the end of the 1960s, only a few railroads had taken the initiative to seriously recruit new black workers and retrain and upgrade existing employees. Longstanding hiring patterns in which workers recommended family members for job openings were resistant to change. Labor unions had long approved such nepotism and continued to do so. And railroading no longer held the high status within the black community it once had. As other industries began to aggressively recruit blacks for white-collar and professional positions, many blacks now believed that railroading offered only "red, white, and blue jobs," positions with "red caps, white coats, and blue denims." Railroads did not widely engage in college recruiting, and only rarely at black schools.[3] The once-exalted image of railroading was gone.

Railroading has historically been a hidebound industry, learning little from other sectors of the economy and promoting managers and executives up through the ranks rather than recruiting new personnel and adopting new ideas from outside. The symbiotic embrace between management and white unions made it resistant to change on many levels. Not surprisingly, no civil rights law, no EEOC procedures, not even enlightened self-interest on the part of management could immediately overcome the inertia of more than a century. Yet change did occur, sometimes painfully, sometimes not. The employment trajectory of Robert N. Cotton, reputedly the first black engineer on a Class 1 railroad, illustrates the forces at work in the second half of the twentieth century.

Call it serendipity, call it luck. Thirty-year-old Bob Cotton, "fresh out of college," happened to drive by the Louisville & Nashville headquarters in April 1963, just as a line of job applicants scattered for shelter from a rain shower. He ran in the door, took some tests, and was hired as a diesel locomotive fireman. A year later he and many others were furloughed as the railroad attacked featherbedding, but he was willing to work as a switchman, then brakeman, flagman, and baggageman, then back to braking, bidding on jobs others didn't want, until the L&N began to recall firemen because it was running short of engineers. The day he finally "marked up" as an engineer "was the greatest day of my life . . . I was making history." Although some white railroaders had encouraged his progress, others resented him or thought he was an NAACP mole. He endured threatening phone calls, ugly names, snakes and human feces in his bed on layovers, because he was determined that "I was not going to let anyone . . . run me off of a job." Although becoming a "hoghead" fulfilled his dreams, he accepted further promotions to yardmaster, assistant trainmaster, and traveling engineer (training new engineers) because "I've always wanted to make history on the L&N Railroad." Looking back in 1980, he could say with satisfaction, "I started off where they wouldn't allow me to run . . . I'm not through climbing on the L&N Railroad . . . I don't think Black. I don't think White. When I'm on the railroad I think L&N."[4]

Railroads in the African American Experience

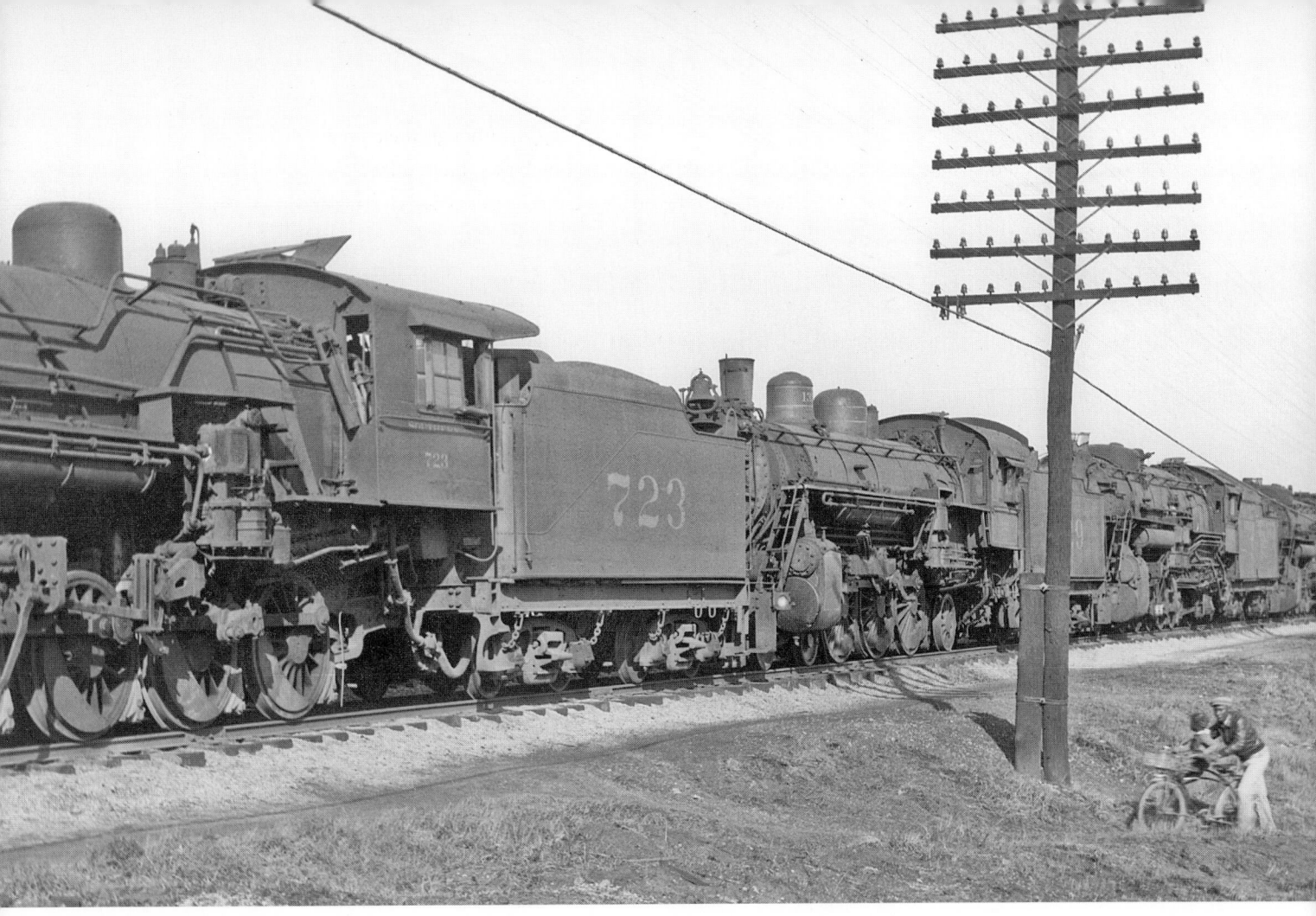

For many blacks, civil rights laws came too late to open doors to higher-status railroad jobs. If this father dreamed of a railroad career for his son riding in the bicycle basket, these obsolete Southern Railway locomotives waiting to be scrapped at Spencer, North Carolina, in 1950 held a grim reality. The end of steam resulted in fewer firemen, fewer shop men, and fewer roundhouse men. Mechanization of MOW cut many more positions. Both races felt the cuts, but blacks disproportionately. R. B. Carneal photograph, collection of C. K. Marsh, Jr.

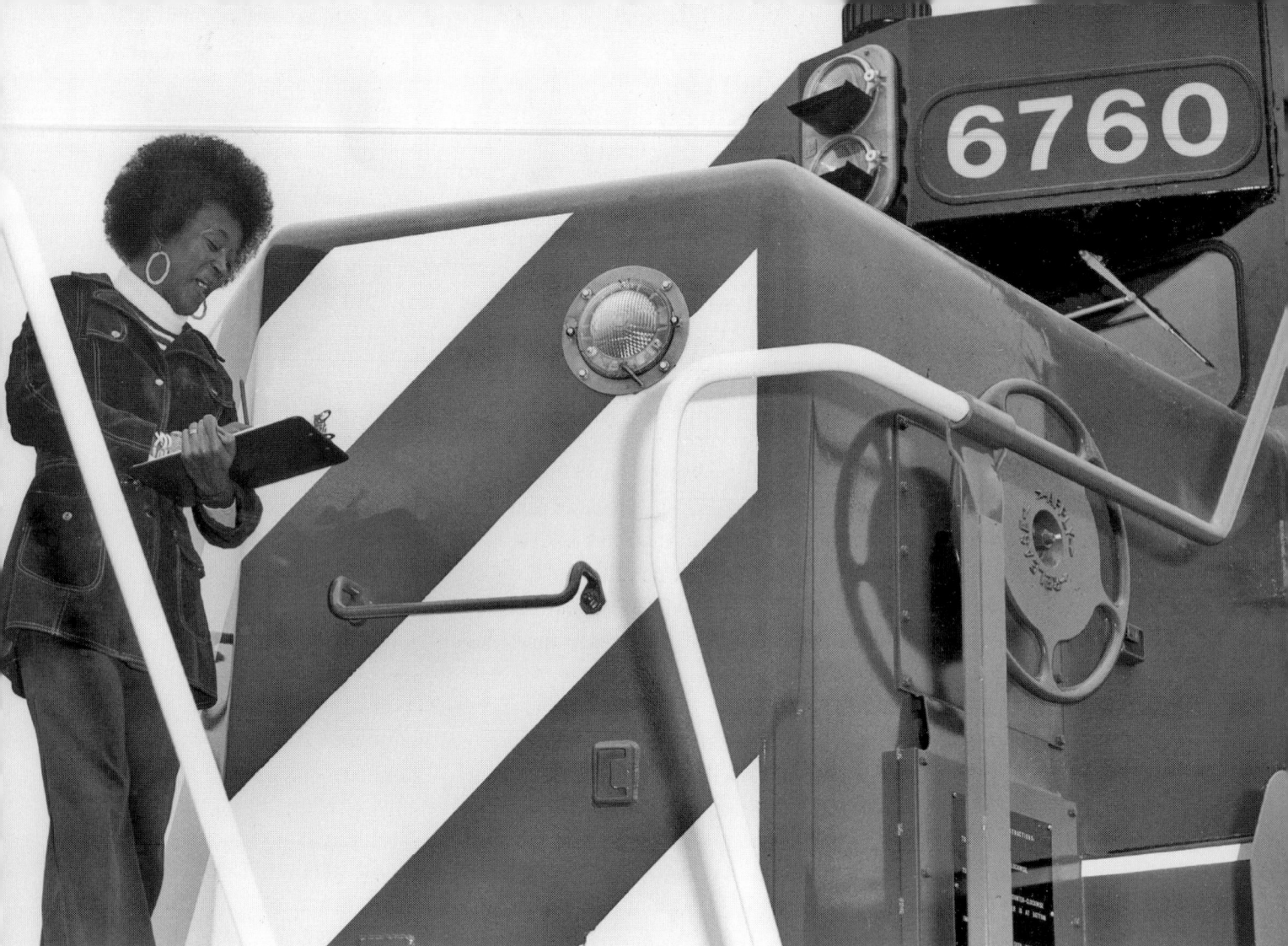

Civil rights legislation began to open unheard of doors. One pioneer was Theola Barrett (Campbell), who became, in 1978, the first black woman to work as a field representative for General Motors' Electro-Motive Division, helping railroads bring their new diesel-electric locomotives on line. EMD photograph, Theola Campbell collection

502

Other pioneers had fewer opportunities. Nelson Wingfield worked for the Southern Railway for 48 years until the opportunity to become an engineer occurred in 1968. Even though he was a veteran railroader, many white hoggers snubbed him until they saw that he was thoroughly qualified, a response that would not have greeted a new white runner.[5] Change came too late for others who had long before abandoned their dreams. As a boy, Edward Blackwell, the son of a Pullman porter, frequently got rides in the cabs of locomotives in Minneapolis. He aspired to being an engineer until the day when a schoolmate shattered his fantasy: "Don't you know there aren't any nigger engineers?" Decades later, the anger still burned.[6]

Not everyone faced nasty barriers in breaking new ground in the railroad industry. Others, younger than Winfield, worked their way up through the ranks, taking advantage of a more open job environment after 1964. Ray Wongus found work as a yard clerk with the Western Maryland Railway in 1968, based on his ability to type. (Old heads in the office could only hunt and peck.) Although he was the first--and only--black in the office, he faced no overt racial hostility, only the traditional hurdle of having to prove oneself. Elsewhere on the WM, black men only worked on section gangs and in the mechanical department, servicing locomotives and cabooses. Wongus really wanted to be an engineer, but when engine service opened up in 1974, he elected to keep his 9-to-5 inside desk job with weekends off. Western Maryland became part of the Chessie System in the mid-1970s, and Wongus moved up to yardmaster, then into the accounting, sales, and pricing departments, and, after another merger, into the CSX marketing department. In 1994, CSX announced that employees could become trainmen and keep their accrued seniority and Wongus finally jumped to the operating department, gaining promotion from trainman to freight conductor to engineer all within two years. Now an "old head," he hopes to serve his remaining days as a hogger. He belongs to the Brotherhood of Locomotive Engineers that today has no hint of its racist past. His path to engineer was paved by the first blacks hired into train service on the Chessie System in the mid-1970s under pressure from the EEOC, which finally broke the lock that white nepotism had on engineer positions.[7]

Black women, too, found a new world opening after passage of the Civil Rights Act. Theola Barrett (Campbell) got her mechanical engineering degree from the General Motors Institute in Flint, Michigan, through a program that alternated six weeks in the classroom with six weeks at one of the GM divisions. She chose GM's Electro-Motive Division, the nation's premier locomotive builder. Upon graduation in 1978, she became EMD's first black female service representative, putting locomotives into service and troubleshooting when things went wrong on the new equipment. Entering roundhouses and shops on the Chicago & North Western, Southern Pacific, Milwaukee Road, Burlington Northern, Union Pacific, Conrail, and Amtrak to diagnose problems on malfunctioning locomotives, she got double-takes when she showed up, a hard hat only partially obscuring her large "Afro" hairstyle. She admits to having had a "demeanor." But she experienced only minor harassment because "people needed me in order to get the equipment running," and she knew her

Today, African Americans may be found working for all the major railroads, at all levels and in all departments. Amtrak's Raleigh, North Carolina station agent has donned gloves to help a male colleague unload checked baggage from the northbound Silver Star in November 2004. Theodore Kornweibel photograph

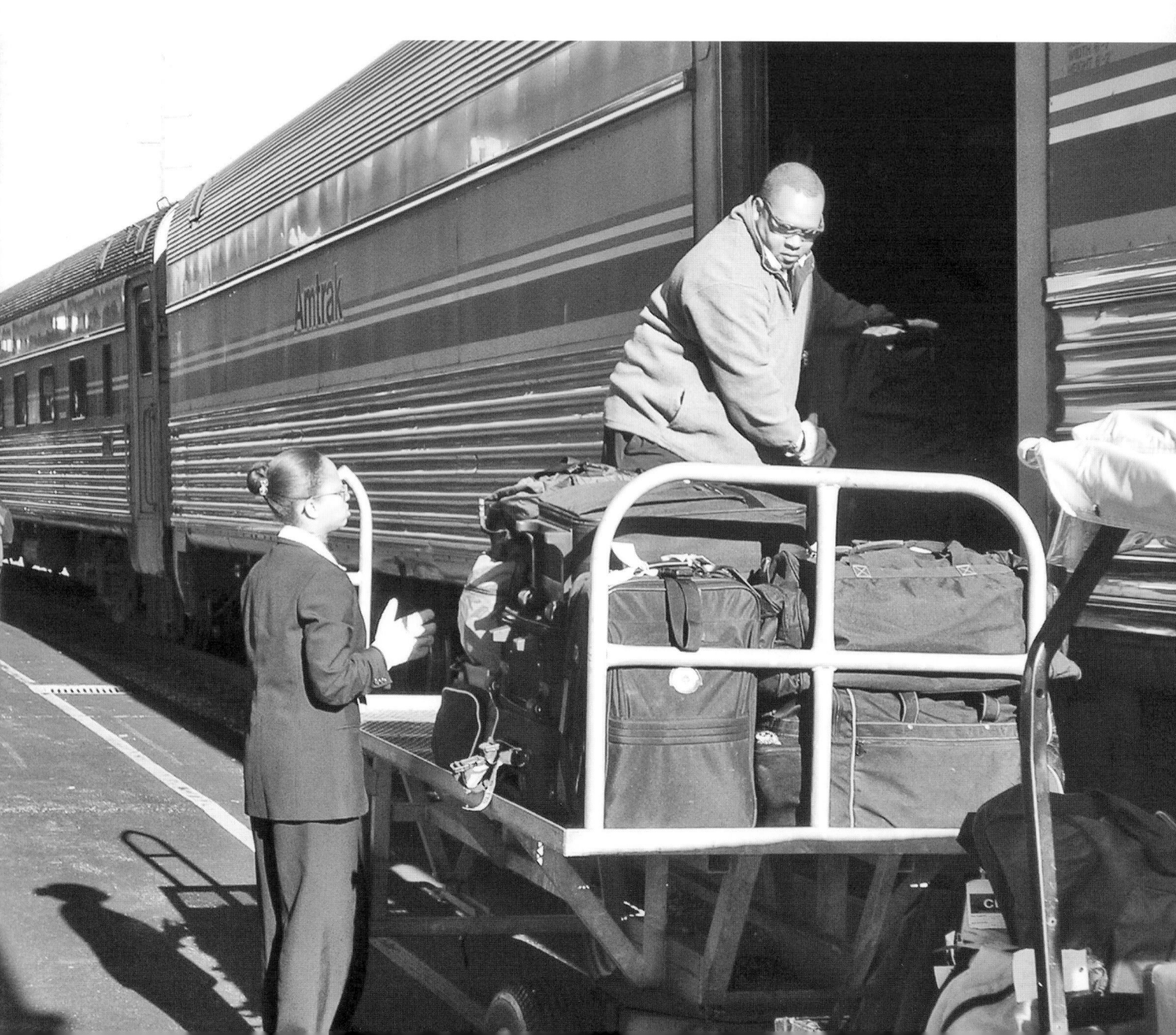

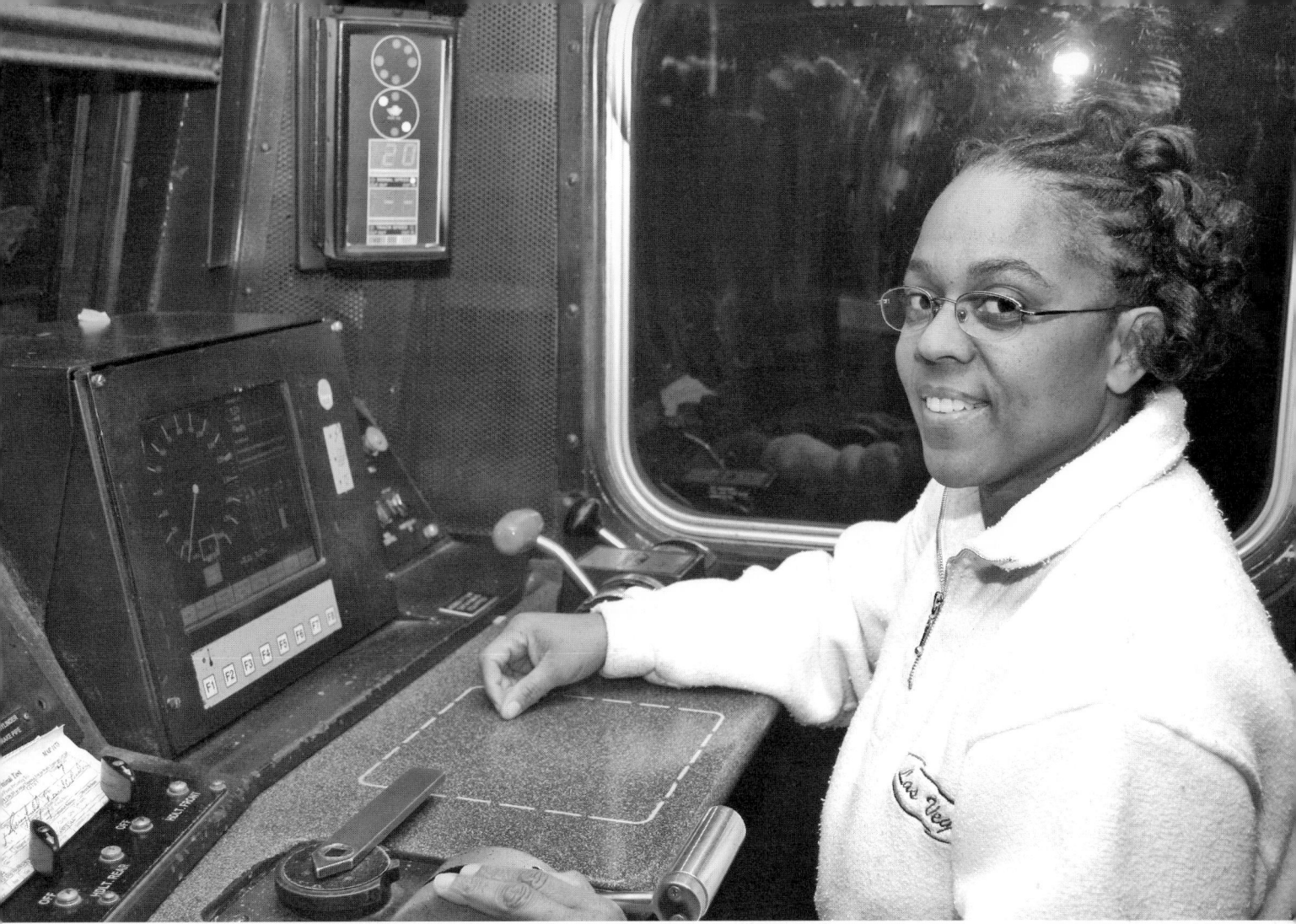

In a scene that no one would have dreamed possible a half-century ago, engineer Lisa Harris sits at the controls of an Amtrak electric locomotive in Washington Union Station in 2007. Her regular assignments include Amtrak's premier Acela Express to New York, America's only high-speed train, which reaches speeds of 150 mph. Doug Riddell photograph

When Macon (Georgia) Terminal Station was built in 1916, it included dual entrances, with "Colored Waiting Room" and "White Waiting Room" chiseled in stone above the porticos. Flash forward to the early twentieth-first century. Passenger trains were a distant memory, but the building was useful as a regional multi-modal transportation center. Some residents urged removing the "Colored Waiting Room" inscription as an unpleasant reminder of an ugly past. More farsighted opinion prevailed, arguing that the offensive text was part of Macon's heritage and that better lessons could be learned by future generations not by burying history, but by remembering it. Today a plaque on the right side states simply that the structure represents the era of forced segregation. Thankfully, at least one southern city had the courage to honestly acknowledge the African American railroad heritage. Courtesy of the Middle Georgia Archives, Washington Memorial Library, Macon, GA

job and did it well. Today, she looks back fondly on her eight years with EMD without regrets, as a time of great personal growth.[8]

Blacks constitute 13.2 percent of the population today and 11.9 percent of all railroad workers. Considerable progress has been made in occupational mobility. As late as 1990, African Americans held fewer than 5 percent of railroad managerial and professional jobs; by 2003, 8.4 percent of railroad managers and officials were black, as were 10.8 percent of professionals. Major gains have also been attained in the two largest job categories, craft workers (almost a half) and operating employees (nearly a quarter of all railroaders). Today, 11.8 percent of engineers, brakemen, and switchmen are black, as are 9.3 percent of those in the skilled trades. The "Obama Express" from Philadelphia to Washington on January 17, 2009, bringing president-elect Barack Obama to his inauguration, was in the hands of Carlyle Smith, an 11-year veteran black Amtrak engineer with 750,000 accident-free miles in his career. At the other end of the spectrum, however, blacks continue to be over-

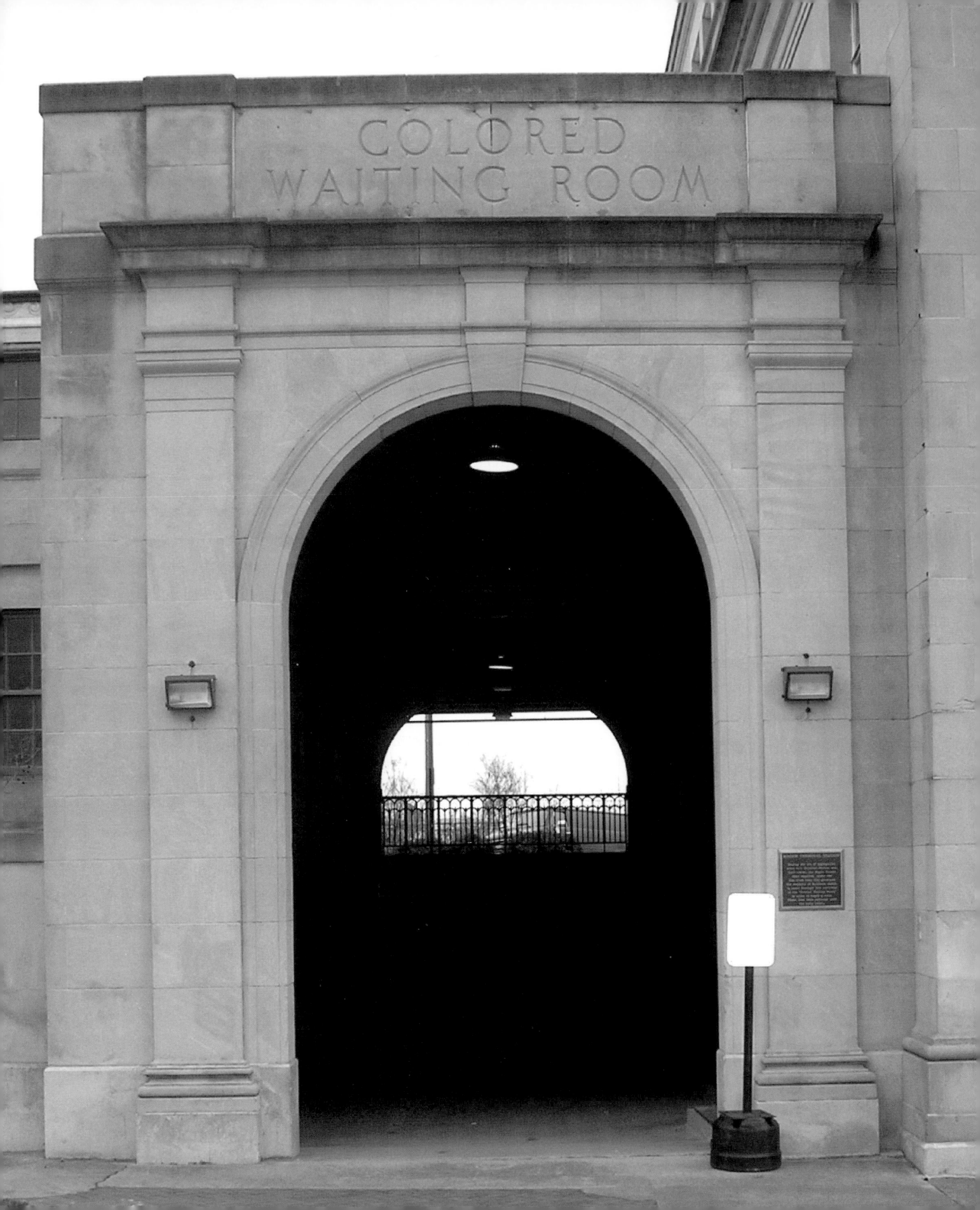

represented in the least-skilled and lower-paid jobs: 19.4 percent of railroad laborers are black, as are a whopping 41.4 percent of service workers.[9]

Progress may be gauged apart from statistics. Today there are no formal barriers to the corporate boardroom. Black men and women hold numerous jobs once reserved for white men: engineers, conductors, dispatchers, yardmasters, foremen, dining-car stewards, supervisors, skilled mechanics, and an array of white-collar positions. Industry giant Norfolk Southern Corporation's website for several years profiled a number of African American pioneers, including a Tuskegee Airman who became the Central of Georgia's first black engineer and later the Southern Railway's first black road foreman of engines; an assistant vice president for information technology who credited Martin Luther King, Jr. with paving the way for blacks' opportunities; and an assistant VP for labor relations descended from "a long line of African American railroaders." Senior general counsel Blair Wimbush, possessing a law degree from the University of Virginia, is the son of sharecroppers. These high achievers' resumes, not surprisingly, all include community service in churches and civic organizations.[10] What NS's website didn't reveal, however, was its foot-dragging that preceded this point. In December 2000, NS settled a $28 million class-action discrimination lawsuit, to be shared by 7,700 current and former black employees who were denied promotion to management positions. As part of the settlement, NS agreed to spend $2.6 million to improve the process for selecting and training future managers from within the corporation.[11] Doors have been pried open, at NS and elsewhere. But railroad employment no longer holds any special significance for African Americans. It's a minor industry. It's just another job.

One thing remains unchanged, though. Railroads still carry black folk to and from ancestral southern homes. Ride Amtrak's long-distance trains into the South, like the *City of New Orleans*, which runs from Chicago to its namesake city. Its coaches were overwhelmingly black, on the author's summer 1994 southbound trip. It discharged half its Chicago coach passengers at nine Mississippi's stops, all small towns except Jackson. Even today, new generations are still traveling from urban homes to their rural roots and back, retracing the steps of their ancestors who rode the old "Chickenbone Specials."

For more than 150 years the railroads were linked to blacks' quest for a better life, a better job, a better status. At times, railroads represented hope. Occasionally they bestowed opportunity. Frequently, they offered only escape. Until recently, they brought exploitation and racism. For many blacks, positive changes and new chances came too late. And now, the African American railroad era is history.

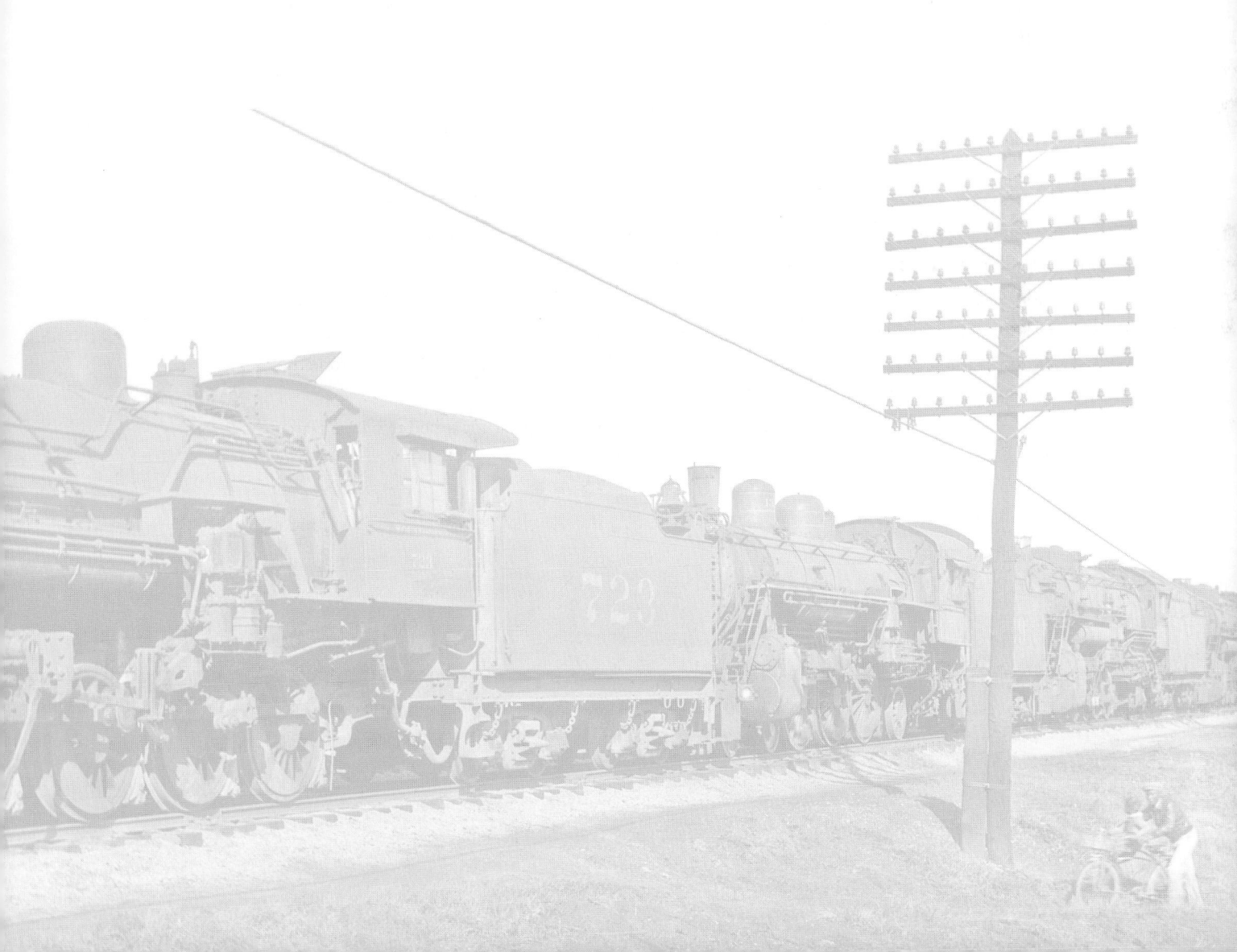

Notes

PREFACE

1. Theodore Kornweibel, Jr., "Jim Crow Cars: A Brief History and Census," *National Railway Bulletin* 62 (1997): 4–21.
2. "Railroads: Slaves 'formed the backbone of the South's railway labor force,'" *USA Today,* February 21, 2002, p. 9A.
3. Theodore Kornweibel, Jr., "Railroads, Race, and Reparations," *Souls: A Critical Journal of Black Politics, Culture, and Society* 5 (Summer 2003): 23–32; Theodore Kornweibel, Jr., "Reparations and Railroads," *Thomas Jefferson Law Review* 29 (Spring 2007): 219–30.
4. Theodore Kornweibel, Jr., "Railroads and Slavery," *Railroad History* 189 (Fall–Winter 2003): 34–59; "Railroads and Slavery: Readers Respond," *Railroad History* 190 (Spring–Summer 2004): 146–52.
5. *Louisville & Nashville Employes' Magazine; Norfolk and Western Magazine; Baltimore and Ohio Magazine; Reading Railroad Magazine; Central of Georgia Magazine; Chesapeake and Ohio Employes' Magazine; Pullman News; Missouri Pacific Lines Magazine; Illinois Central Magazine; The Pennsy* [Pennsylvania Railroad]; *Southern Pacific Bulletin.* Some titles changed slightly over time.

PROLOGUE

1. The 1860 federal census slave schedule shows that Nims owned 16 slaves, in 2 families. Their ages and genders, but not names, are listed. Given the slaves' ages, and the unlikelihood that Nims would have sent a young woman of only 21 or 20 to work as cook for the railroad gang, it is highly likely that Rose was either 42 or 37 years old in 1857, and the mother of several children. Ancestry.com, *1860 U.S. Federal Census—Slave Schedules—County of Gaston, North Carolina* (Provo, Utah, 2004).
2. Frederick Nims to Horace Nims, March 1, 5, 8, 12, 1857, Nims and Rankin Family Papers, Southern Historical Collection, University of North Carolina.
3. Schedules are taken from a slightly later timetable: *Hill & Swayze's Confederate States Rail Road & Steam-Boat Guide* (Griffin, Ga., 1862).
4. Frederick Nims to Horace Nims, March 8, 12, 15, July 3, 9, Dec. 12, 1857, Nims and Rankin Family Papers, Southern Historical Collection, University of North Carolina; "Charleston & Savannah Railroad," *American Railroad Journal,* Jan. 23, 1858, p. 56; Feb. 6, 1858, p. 92; April 10, 1858, p. 237; Oct. 30, 1858, p. 700; H. David Stone, Jr., *Vital Rails: The Charleston & Savannah Railroad and the Civil War in Coastal South Carolina* (Columbia, S.C., 2008), pp. 24–25.
5. Frederick Nims to Horace Nims, June 20, 27, July 3, Aug. 30, Oct. 24, 1858, H. Fox to Horace Nims, July 12, 1858, Nims and Rankin Family Papers, Southern Historical Collection, University of North Carolina. See Todd Savitt, *Medicine and Slavery: The Diseases and Health Care of Blacks in Antebellum Virginia* (Urbana, Ill., 1978), pp. 17–35, for the incidence and consequences of malaria.

CHAPTER 1. "NEGROES WILL DO MORE WORK"

1. *The American Beacon and Norfolk and Portsmouth Daily Advertiser,* Aug. 27, 1836, p. 4.
2. Allen W. Trelease, *The North Carolina Railroad, 1849-1871, and the Modernization of North Carolina* (Chapel Hill, 1991), p. 35.
3. *Report of the President, Directors, &c., of the Milledgeville R. Road Co.* (Aug. 1862), pp. 9–10.
4. Robert S. Starobin, *Industrial Slavery in the Old South* (New York, 1970), pp. 12–30; Jonathan D. Martin, *Divided Mastery: Slave Hiring in the American South* (Cambridge, Mass., 2004), pp. 1–9.
5. Starobin, *Industrial Slavery,* pp. 165–67; Peter Way, *Common Labour Workers and the Digging of North American Canals, 1780-1860* (Cambridge, U.K., 1993), pp. 13, 26, 84, 87–89, 125–26, 137.
6. Austrian traveler Franz Anton von Gerstner noted only two southern railroads using steam pile drivers in 1838–39, the Pontchartrain and the New Orleans & Nashville railroads, both out of the Crescent City. Frederick C. Gamst, *Early American Railroads: Franz Anton Ritter von Gerstner's Die innern Communicationen (1842-1843)* (Stanford, Calif., 1997), pp. 748, 751. I am indebted to John H. White for pointing this out to me.

7. Trelease, *The North Carolina Railroad*, p. 34; David E. Paterson, *Frontier Link With the World: The Upson County Railroad* (Macon, Ga., 1998), p. 42; H. David Stone, Jr., *Vital Rails: The Charleston & Savannah Railroad and the Civil War in Coastal South Carolina* (Columbia, S.C., 2008), p. 25.

8. F. H. King to Horace Nims, June 23, 1850, Nims and Rankin Family Papers, Southern Historical Collection, University of North Carolina. I am indebted to David Bright for furnishing information on rails and ties.

9. Unhealthy living conditions are described in *Lane v. Washington*, 8 Jones N. C. 248, Dec. 1860. See also Aaron W. Marrs, *Railroads in the Old South: Pursuing Progress in a Slave Society* (Baltimore, 2009), pp. 69, 71–72.

10. See, for example, "List of Negroes to be hired out by W. C. Pittman, 1855," in Craven County, Slaves and Free Negroes, bonds-petitions, 1775–1861 (broken series), North Carolina State Archives.

11. "List of Negroes to be hired out by W. C. Pittman, 1855," in Craven County, Slaves and Free Negroes, bonds-petitions, 1775–1861 (broken series), North Carolina State Archives; *Memphis & Charleston Railroad Co. v. Jones*, 2 Head 517, April 1859 [Tennessee]; *Duncan v. South Carolina Railroad Co.*, 2 Richardson 613, May 1846 [South Carolina]; *Harvey v. Skipworth*, 57 Virginia 393, May 1863; *Butler v. Wallace*, Rice 182, Feb. 1839 [South Carolina]. For an example of the danger of constructing bridges over large or rapid rivers, see the *Report of the President of the Charleston & Savannah Rail-Road Company, to the Stockholders* (Charleston, 1861), p. 21. Only a few corporate reports acknowledged the hazards of mid-nineteenth-century railroading.

12. Martin, *Divided Mastery*, p. 103.

13. Quoted in Stephen G. Collins, "Progress and Slavery on the South's Railroads," *Railroad History* (Autumn 1999): 20.

14. Joseph Hicks to Samuel Downey, Feb. 27, 1836, Samuel Smith Downey Papers, Manuscript Department, Duke University.

15. Joseph Hicks to Downey, March 28, May 14, 1836, Samuel Smith Downey Papers, Manuscript Department, Duke University.

16. Joseph Hicks to Downey, May 14, June 30, July 14, 1836, Samuel Smith Downey Papers, Manuscript Department, Duke University.

17. Hiring contract, E. W. Wall to Joseph Hicks (for Downey), Jan. 21, 1836; Joseph Hicks to Downey, June 30, July 14, 1836, Samuel Smith Downey Papers, Manuscript Department, Duke University.

18. Joseph Hicks to Downey, Aug. 25, 1836, Samuel Smith Downey Papers, Manuscript Department, Duke University.

19. Joseph Hicks to John Hicks, Sept. 8, 1836, Joseph Hicks to Downey, July 14, Aug. 25, Sept. 8, Oct. 29, 1836, Samuel Smith Downey Papers, Manuscript Department, Duke University.

20. Collins, "Progress and Slavery," p. 20; Todd Savitt, *Medicine and Slavery: The Diseases and Health Care of Blacks in Antebellum Virginia* (Urbana, Ill., 1978), pp. 81–82.

21. Joseph Hicks to John Hicks, Jan. 23, 1837, Joseph Amis to Downey, May 5, 1837, Samuel Smith Downey Papers, Manuscript Department, Duke University.

22. Joseph Hicks to Downey, Feb. 13, March 28, 1838, Joseph Hicks to Amis, June 20, 1838, Samuel Smith Downey Papers, Manuscript Department, Duke University. See Deborah Gray White, *Ar'n't I a Woman: Female Slaves in the Plantation South*, rev. ed. (New York, 1999), pp. 79–84, for a thorough discussion of feigning illness as an act of resistance.

23. Joseph Hicks to Downey, June 30, 1836, Samuel Smith Downey Papers, Manuscript Department, Duke University.

24. "Slave Labor Upon Public Works at the South," *DeBow's Review,* July 1854, p. 80.

25. Joseph Hicks to Downey, Feb. 13, 1838, Samuel Smith Downey Papers, Manuscript Department, Duke University.

26. Thomas D. Clark, *A Pioneer Southern Railroad from New Orleans to Cairo* (Chapel Hill, 1936), pp. 30–37; Hicks to President and Directors of the Bank of Mississippi Rail Road Company, March 2, 6, 10, 1840, A. Arnold to Hicks (?), March 11, 1840, Samuel Smith Downey Papers, Manuscript Department, Duke University.

27. Scott R. Nelson, *Iron Confederacies: Southern Railways, Klan Violence, and Reconstruction* (Chapel Hill, 1999), p. 17; Trelease, *The North Carolina Railroad*, p. 79.

28. Trelease, *The North Carolina Railroad*, pp. 31–35; Paterson, *Frontier Link*, pp. 40–42; "The Riot," *Sumter* (S.C.) *Banner*, March 14, 1855, "The Late Rioters on the North E. R. Road," *Sumter Banner*, March 28, 1855; Marrs, *Railroads in the Old South*, pp. 69, 81–82.

29. Quoted in Richard C. Wade, *Slavery in the Cities: The South, 1820–1860* (New York, 1964), p. 37; "Slave Labor Upon Public Works at the South," *DeBow's Review*, July 1854, p. 17; Ira Berlin, *Slaves Without Masters: The Free Negro in the Antebellum South* (New York, 1975), p. 227; Frederick Law Olmstead, *The Cotton Kingdom: A Traveller's Observations on Cotton and Slavery in the American Slave States* (New York, 1953 [1861]), p. 65; Nelson, *Iron Confederacies*, p. 17.

30. *Annual Report to the Stockholders of the Montgomery & West Point Rail Road Company, for the year ending First March, 1850* (Montgomery, 1850), pp. 6–7.

31. *Report of the President and Directors to the Second Annual Meeting of the Stockholders of the Mobile and Gt. Northern R. R. Co.* (Mobile, 1861), pp. 10, 14–15, 17–18, 20–22.

32. Eric Arnesen, "'Like Banquo's Ghost, It Will Not Down': The Race Question and the American Railroad Brotherhoods, 1880–1920," *American Historical Review* 99 (1994): 1607.

33. Gamst, *Early American Railroads*, p. 696; Eugene Alvarez, *Travels on Southern Antebellum Railroads, 1828–1860* (University, Ala., 1974), pp. 146, 161; Trelease, *The North Carolina Railroad*, p. 61.

34. Nelson, *Iron Confederacies*, p. 89.

35. James H. Brewer, *The Confederate Negro: Virginia's Craftsmen and Military Laborers, 1861–1865* (Durham, N.C., 1969), p. 86; Alvarez, *Travels on Southern Antebellum Railroads*, p. 161; Olmstead, *The Cotton Kingdom*, p. 167.

36. Paterson, *Frontier Link*, pp. 91–92.

37. Trelease, *The North Carolina Railroad*, pp. 52, 59–60; Gamst, *Early American Railroads*, pp. 714–15; *Henry v. Graham*, 9 Richardson Equities 346, May 1857 [South Carolina].

38. Martin, *Divided Mastery*, p. 82.

39. *Proceedings of the Stockholders of the South-Carolina Rail-Road Company, and of the South-Western Rail-Road Bank, at their Annual Meeting* (Charleston, 1847), pp. 9–10; *Annual Reports of the President and Directors and the General Superintendent of the South Carolina Railroad Company, for the year ending Dec. 31, 1857* (Charleston, 1858), pp. 18–19.

40. *Proceedings of the Seventh Annual Meeting of the Stockholders of the Raleigh & Gaston Rail Road Company* (Raleigh, 1857), pp. 11–12; *Proceedings of the Thirteenth Annual Meeting . . .* (Raleigh, 1863), p. 7.

41. *Fifth Annual Report of the President and Directors of the Savannah, Albany and Gulf Rail Road Company* (Savannah, 1861), p. 17.

42. *Georgia Journal and Messenger*, Jan. 29, 1851, p. 4; Dec. 22, 1852, p. 1; Paterson, *Frontier Link*, pp. 64, 92.

43. Quoted in Richard E. Prince, *The Seaboard Air Line Railway* (Green River, Wyo., 1969), pp. 71–72.

44. Quoted in Richard Reinhardt, *Workin' on the Railroad: Reminiscences from the Age of Steam* (Palo Alto, 1970), p. 230.

45. *Wilmington & Weldon R. R. Company. Time Table No. 5* (Wilmington, 1859), instructions paragraphs 13, 16.

46. Clark, *A Pioneer Southern Railroad*, pp. 61–62; "Texas and New Orleans Railroad," *American Railroad Journal*, Nov. 24, 1860, pp. 1037–38.

47. W. G. Bonner, chief engineer, VS&T Railroad, to L. P. Grant, Sept. 1, 1856, folder 1, box 6, Lemuel Pratt Grant Papers, Atlanta History Center.

48. Gamst, *Early American Railroads*, pp. 675, 715; *Dr. Peake v. Scaife*, 11 Richardson 672, Nov. 1858 [South Carolina].

49. Ulrich B. Phillips, *A History of Transportation of the Eastern Cotton Belt to 1860* (New York, 1968 [c. 1908]), p. 157; Prince, *The Seaboard Air Line Railway*, p. 72; *James v. Wilmington & Manchester Railroad Co.*, 9 Richardson 416, May 1856 [South Carolina].

50. Quoted in Nelson, *Iron Confederacies*, p. 18.

51. Hiring bonds, binders 170, 184, 191, 198, 202, Richmond, Fredericksburg & Potomac Railroad Papers, Virginia Historical Society.

52. North Carolina Railroad records, Correspondence, 1851–1867: bound volume, "Hand hire bonds Jan. 1st 1862 to Jan. 1st 1864 N. c. r. r."; bound volume, "North Carolina Railroad Slave Book"; Box 22, "Hire of Slaves 1864–1865," five undated lists [1864], "Bills of sale for slaves bought by NCR, 1864," North Carolina State Archives.

53. Nelson, *Iron Confederacies*, pp. 39–40, 45, 117.

54. A graphic study of the convict lease in Georgia after slavery is Alex Lichtenstein's *Twice the Work of Free Labor: The Political Economy of Convict Labor in the New South* (New York, 1996).

55. Proposed contract for hiring free Negro and slave convicts, signed by Robert F. and David G. Bibb, Nov. 30, 1860, Executive Papers, Gov. John Letcher, letters rec'd, Nov. 1860, Library of Virginia; contract with Gov. John Letcher for hire of free Negro and slave convicts, signed by Bibb and Bibb, Dec. 31, 1861, list of free Negro and slave convicts in custody of Bibb and Bibb, [Dec. 1861], Executive Papers, Gov. Letcher, letters rec'd, Dec. 1860, Library of Virginia. Grown women who were healthy and not pregnant were customarily considered three-quarter hands; see White, *Ar'n't I a Woman*, p. 121.

56. Contract with Gov. John Letcher for hire of free Negro and slave convicts, signed by Thomas Roper, [Dec. 1861], Executive Papers, Gov. Letcher, letters rec'd, Dec. 1860, Library of Virginia.

57. Philip J. Schwarz, *Slave Laws in Virginia* (Athens, Ga., 1996), pp. 114–15.

58. *Mann v. Macon & Western Railroad Co.*, 32 Georgia 345, March 1861; *Henry v. Graham*; *The American Beacon and Norfolk and Portsmouth Daily Advertiser*, Aug. 27, 1836, p. 4.

59. J. N. Horne to L. P. Grant, May 28, 1851, Grant Papers, Atlanta History Center; Kenneth W. Noe, *Southwest Virginia's Railroad: Modernization and the Sectional Crisis* (Urbana, Ill., 1994), p. 83; Alvarez, *Travels on Southern Antebellum Railroads*, p. 134; Clark, *A Pioneer Southern Railroad*, p. 20; Olmstead, *The Cotton Kingdom*, pp. 45, 87, 126, 155.

60. Jacob Stroyer, *My Life in the South*, 3rd ed. (Salem, 1889), pp. 39–42.

61. Paterson, *Frontier Link*, pp. 103–4. See also numerous entries in the RF&P papers, Virginia Historical Society. For an extensive discussion of extra work, see Marrs, *Railroads in the Old South*, pp. 79–80.

62. Olmstead, *The Cotton Kingdom*, p. 45.

63. Quoted in Starobin, *Industrial Slavery*, pp. 78, 79–80.

64. Starobin, *Industrial Slavery*, p. 87.

65. *Harley v. De Witt*, 2 Hill Equities 367, Dec. 1835 [South Carolina]; *Henry v. Graham*.

66. An excellent analysis of female networks is in White, *Ar'n't I a Woman*, chap. 4.

67. White, *Ar'n't I a Woman*, pp. 95–96, 152–53, 187.

68. In re African-Am. Slave Descendants Litig., 375 F. Supp. 2d 721 (N.D. Ill. 2005), *affirmed as modified in*, 471 F.3d 754 (7th Cir. 2006). The cases were dismissed with prejudice for lack of standing. However, the Seventh Circuit remanded several consumer protection claims.

CHAPTER 2. "WASN'T NO EQUIPMENT—IT WAS MANUAL LABOR"

1. "Veterans—Colored Division," *Norfolk and Western Magazine*, March 1930, pp. 166–67.

2. James Hutton Lemly, *The Gulf, Mobile and Ohio: A Railroad That Had to Expand or Expire* (Homewood, Ill., 1953), p. 39; "Berta, Berta," quoted in August Wilson, *The Piano Lesson* (New York, 1990), p. 40.

3. George B. Abdill, *Civil War Railroads* (New York, 1961), pp. 15, 31, 57, 82, 99.

4. Scott R. Nelson, *Iron Confederacies: Southern Railways, Klan Violence, and Reconstruction* (Chapel Hill, 1999), pp. 34, 39–41, 89.

5. Nelson, *Iron Confederacies*, p. 89; Alex Lichtenstein, *Twice the Work of Free Labor: The Political Economy of Convict Labor in the New South* (New York, 1996), p. 44.

6. For a detailed discussion of the freedmen's attitudes toward work, see Daniel Letwin, *The Challenge of Interracial Unionism: Alabama Coal Miners, 1878-1921* (Chapel Hill, 1998), pp. 25, 27–28.

7. *Annual Report of the President and Directors of the Muscogee Railroad Co. for the year ending July 31, 1867* (n.p.), p. 10; John F. Stover, *The Railroads of the South, 1865-1900: A Study in Finance and Control* (Chapel Hill, 1955), pp. 42, 57.

8. Eric Arnesen, "'Like Banquo's Ghost, It Will Not Down': The Race Question and the American Railroad Brotherhoods, 1880-1920," *American Historical Review* 99 (1994): 1607.

9. Lorenzo J. Greene and Carter G. Woodson, *The Negro Wage Earner* (Washington, 1930), p. 33; C. Vann Woodward, *Origins of the New South, 1877-1913* (Baton Rouge, La., 1951), pp. 120–21; Gerald D. Jaynes, *Branches Without Roots: Genesis of the Black Working Class in the American South, 1862-1882* (New York, 1986), p. 272.

10. Greene and Woodson, *The Negro Wage Earner*, p. 21; James McCague, *Moguls and Iron Men: The Story of the First Transcontinental Railroad* (New York, 1964), p. 117; Stephen E. Ambrose, *Nothing Like It In the World: The Men Who Built the Transcontinental Railroad, 1863-1869* (New York, 2003), pp. 177, 274.

11. Kyle K. Wyatt to author, Jan. 3, 2007.

12. Bureau of the Census, *Negroes in the United States: 1920-32* (Washington, 1935), pp. 303–9.

13. Nell Irvin Painter, *Exodusters: Black Migration to Kansas After Reconstruction* (New York, 1977); Robert G. Athearn, *In Search of Canaan: Black Migration to Kansas, 1879-80* (Lawrence, Kans., 1978).

14. Bureau of the Census, *Negroes in the United States: 1920–32*, p. 305.

15. Clare V. McKanna, Jr., "Black Enclaves of Violence: Race and Homicide in Great Plains Cities, 1890–1920," *Great Plains Quarterly* 23 (2003): 147–59; James H. Ducker, *Men of the Steel Rails: Workers on the Atchison, Topeka & Santa Fe Railroad, 1869–1900* (Lincoln, Neb., 1983), p. 74.

16. Ducker, *Men of the Steel Rails*, pp. 57–59.

17. John F. Stover, *The Routledge Historical Atlas of the American Railroads* (New York, 1999), p. 41; Savannah, Florida and Western Railway Company and Charleston and Savannah Railway Company, Order No. 117 (May ? 1886), Savannah, Florida & Western Railway, Series IV, Box 25, Norfolk Southern Railway Co., Atlanta History Center. Within a few years the gauge throughout the South was narrowed another half inch to today's 4 feet 8 1/2 inches standard. The southern gauge change also included broadening 3-foot narrow gauge trackage to the new standard.

18. David E. Peterson, *Frontier Link With the World: The Upson County Railroad* (Macon, Ga., 1998), p. 184.

19. *Cleveland Gazette*, Aug. 22, 1896, p. 2.

20. Lists of men sent to Western North Carolina Railroad, Jan. 6, Aug. 28, 1879, Box 43, 1879 pay for guards, Box 45, Western North Carolina Railroad, in Office of State Treasurer, Treasurer's and Comptrollers' Papers, Internal Improvements, Railroads, North Carolina State Archives; Lichtenstein, *Twice the Work of Free Labor*, p. 29. Karin A. Shapiro, *A New South Rebellion: The Battle Against Convict Labor in the Tennessee Coalfields, 1871–1896* (Chapel Hill, 1998), p. 253, likewise shows the large percentage of Tennessee's black prison laborers convicted of larceny.

21. Jaynes, *Branches Without Roots*, p. 272; Edward L. Ayers, *Vengeance and Justice: Crime and Punishment in the 19th Century American South* (New York, 1984), p. 192; Shapiro, *A New South Rebellion*, pp. 6–7; Lichtenstein, *Twice the Work of Free Labor*, p. xv.

22. Mark Colvin, *Penitentiaries, Reformatories, and Chain Gangs: Social Theory and the History of Punishment in Nineteenth-Century America* (New York, 1997), pp. 243–46.

23. Matthew J. Mancini, "Race, Economics, and the Abandonment of Convict Leasing," *Journal of Negro History* 63 (1978): 341; A. Elizabeth Taylor, "The Origin and Development of the Convict Lease System in Georgia," in *Black Southerners and the Law, 1865–1900*, ed. Donald G. Nieman (New York, 1994), p. 334; Lichtenstein, *Twice the Work of Free Labor*, pp. 47–51, 56–57. For a comprehensive discussion, see Matthew J. Mancini, *One Dies, Get Another: Convict Leasing in the American South, 1866–1928* (Columbia, S.C., 1996), and Milfred C. Fierce, *Slavery Revisited: Blacks and the Southern Convict Lease System, 1865–1933* (Brooklyn, N.Y., 1994).

24. Lichtenstein, *Twice the Work of Free Labor*, p. 54; Colvin, *Penitentiaries*, pp. 246–49; Department of Corrections, *Biennial Report of Inspectors of the Alabama Penitentiary* (Montgomery, 1884), pp. 40–41.

25. Colvin, *Penitentiaries*, p. 248.

26. Albert D. Oliphant, *The Evolution of the Penal System of South Carolina From 1866 to 1916* (Columbia, S.C., 1916), pp. 5–7; Taylor, "Origin and Development of the Convict Lease," pp. 333–38; Albert M. Langley, Jr., *Charleston & Western Carolina Railway Album* (North Augusta, S.C., 2000), p. 3; contract with Georgia & North Carolina Railroad, Oct. 2, 1876, Prison Department: Central (State) Prison, contracts for prison labor, list of prisoners, report on prisoners, etc., 1877–1928, North Carolina State Archives.

27. J. C. Powell, *The American Siberia, or Fourteen Years' Experience in a Southern Convict Camp* (Chicago, 1891), pp. 11–13.

28. Powell, *The American Siberia*, pp. 21–22.

29. Powell, *The American Siberia*, pp. 144–51.

30. Gordon B. McKinney, "Zeb Vance and the Construction of the Western North Carolina Railroad," *Appalachian Journal* 29 (2001–2): 62–66.

31. Scott Nelson, "Who Was John Henry? Railroad Construction, Southern Folklore, and the Birth of Rock and Roll," *Labor: Studies in Working-Class History of the Americas* 2 (2005): 53–79. For a more comprehensive discussion, see Scott R. Nelson, *Steel Drivin' Man: John Henry, the Untold Story of an American Legend* (New York, 2006).

32. Quoted in Lemly, *The Gulf, Mobile and Ohio*, p. 290.

33. Interview with Owen White, Jan. 22, 1980, L&N Oral History Project, University of Louisville Archives and Records Center, pp. 1–2, 9, 11.

34. *Gandy Dancers*, film by Barry Dornfeld and Maggie Holtzberg-Call (Cinema Guild, 1994).

35. H. Reid, *The Virginian Railway* (Milwaukee, 1961), pp. 74–75.

36. Reid, *The Virginian Railway*, pp. 74–75; interview, Owen White, pp. 9–10.

37. Peterson, *Frontier Link*, p. 179.

38. *Gandy Dancers.*

39. Interview, Owen White, pp. 10–11; Neil R. McMillan, *Dark Journey: Black Mississippians in the Age of Jim Crow* (Urbana, Ill., 1990), pp. 202–4.

40. Eric Arnesen, *Brotherhoods of Color: Black Railroad Workers and the Struggle for Equality* (Cambridge, Mass., 2001), pp. 6–7; Ducker, *Men of the Steel Rails*, pp. 27–28.

41. Greene and Woodson, *The Negro Wage Earner*, p. 266; Emmett J. Scott, *Negro Migration During the War* (n.p., 1920), pp. 38–39, 55, 69, 120–21. For an example of strikebreaking for the PRR, see "Strike-Breakers Desert Railroad," Trenton (N.J.) *Evening Times*, March 13, 1913, p. 1.

42. Scott, *Negro Migration*, pp. 55, 100, 120–21, 135.

43. Bureau of the Census, *Negro Population, 1790–1915* (Washington, 1918), pp. 517–20; Bureau of the Census, *Negroes in the United States*, pp. 303–9.

44. Statement showing number of Negro employees by occupations, their household conditions, and status in community, as of Jan. 16, 1924, Employment of Blacks and Race Relations, 1920–1925, Personnel Department, General Office Files, Box 818, Pennsylvania Railroad Collection, MSS 1810, Hagley Museum and Library.

45. Greene and Woodson, *The Negro Wage Earner*, pp. 270–71; file 011.124, Mexican Laborers, Misc., 1920–1945, Superintendent Labor & Wage Bureau—Western Region, Pennsylvania Railroad Collection, Hagley Museum and Library.

46. Charles S. Johnson, "Negroes in the Railway Industry," *Phylon* 3 (1942): 5–13; Howard W. Risher, Jr., *The Negro in the Railroad Industry* (Philadelphia, 1971), pp. 47–48.

47. Risher, *Negro in the Railroad Industry*, pp. 48–49.

48. Interview, Allen Brown, Nov. 6, 1980, West Virginia and Regional History Collection, West Virginia University Libraries.

49. *Louisville & Nashville Employes' Magazine*, Dec. 1931, p. 42; April 1943, p. 36; Nov. 1949, p. 25.

50. *Gandy Dancers.*

51. "Occupational Status of Negro Railroad Employees," *Monthly Labor Review* 56 (March 1943): 484–85; PRR employment ad in Zanesville (Ohio) *Times-Recorder*, March 2, 1943, p. 8.

52. L. W. Horning, NYC Manager, Personnel, to Lawrence W. Cramer, Executive Secretary, President's Committee on Fair Employment Practice, Jan. 10, 1943, in Employment, Railroads, Agreements, Legal Division Hearings, 1941–1946, FEPC, RG228, National Archives.

53. Risher, *Negro in the Railroad Industry*, pp. 80–83.

54. Risher, *Negro in the Railroad Industry*, pp. 68–69.

55. *Gandy Dancers.*

56. Interview, Allen Brown.

CHAPTER 3. "WITH HIS STRONG ARM AND A SHOVEL"

1. Katie Letcher Lyle, *Scalded to Death By the Steam: Authentic Stories of Railroad Disasters and the Ballads That Were Written About Them* (Chapel Hill, 1983), p. 28.

2. Eric Arnesen, "'Like Banquo's Ghost, It Will Not Down': The Race Question and the American Railroad Brotherhoods, 1880–1920," *American Historical Review* 99 (December 1994): 1608.

3. Deborah C. Malamud, "The Story of *Steele v. Louisville & Nashville Railroad*: White Unions, Black Unions, and the Struggle for Racial Justice on the Rails," in *Labor Law Stories*, ed. Laura J. Cooper and Catherine L. Fisk (New York, 2005), p. 57.

4. John H. White, Jr., "Oh, To Be a Locomotive Engineer," *Railroad History* 189 (Fall–Winter 2003): 28–33; 190 (Spring–Summer 2004): 58; Mark Aldrich, *Death Rode the Rails: American Railroad Accidents and Safety, 1828–1965* (Baltimore, 2006), pp. 98–99; Malamud, "The Story of *Steele v. Louisville & Nashville Railroad*," p. 57.

5. White, "Oh, To Be a Locomotive Engineer," *Railroad History* 189 (Fall–Winter 2003): 16. Even after the end of the steam era, the "tradition" of abusing firemen did not entirely disappear. On the author's first run as a volunteer apprentice fireman on the steam-powered tourist New Hope & Ivyland Railroad, the crusty engineer explained little, criticized much, and cut his unpracticed assistant no slack. Seeing no reason why a volunteer should have to suffer abuse, the author became a conductor instead.

6. Recollections of Robert L. Thomas, in Stuart Leuthner, *The Railroaders* (New York, 1983), pp. 45–46.

7. Malamud, "The Story of *Steele v. Louisville & Nashville Railroad*," pp. 57–58; Eric Arnesen, *Brotherhoods of Color: Black Railroad Workers and the Struggle for Equality* (Cambridge, Mass., 2001), p. 24.

8. Theodore Kornweibel, Jr., "Railroads and Slavery," *Railroad History* 189 (Fall–Winter 2003): 47, 50.

9. Quoted in Mark Aldrich, "Safe and Suitable Boilers: The Railroads, the Interstate Commerce Commission, and Locomotive Safety, 1900–1945," *Railroad History* 171 (Autumn 1994): 23. See also recollection of the engineer in B. A. Botkin and Alvin F. Harlow, eds., *A Treasury of Railroad Folklore* (New York, 1953), pp. 72–73.

10. Ulrich B. Phillips, *A History of Transportation of the Eastern Cotton Belt to 1860* (New York, 1968 [c. 1908]), p. 143.

11. Kornweibel, "Railroads and Slavery," pp. 34–37; Allen W. Trelease, *The North Carolina Railroad, 1849-1871, and the Modernization of North Carolina* (Chapel Hill, 1991), p. 352; Phillips, *A History of Transportation*, p. 157.

12. Virginia Central Railroad annual reports, 1860–67.

13. Richmond & Petersburg Railroad, annual reports, 1860–67.

14. Virginia & Tennessee Railroad, annual reports, 1856–65.

15. Trelease, *The North Carolina Railroad*, p. 252.

16. Arnesen, "Like Banquo's Ghost," pp. 1619–21; William H. Harris, *The Harder We Run: Black Workers since the Civil War* (New York, 1982), pp. 39, 45–46.

17. Quoted in Arnesen, *Brotherhoods of Color*, p. 25.

18. Arnesen, *Brotherhoods of Color*, pp. 27–28, 33.

19. Sterling D. Spero and Abram L. Harris, *The Black Worker* (New York, 1968 [c. 1931]), pp. 284–85, 287; Lorenzo J. Greene and Carter G. Woodson, *The Negro Wage Earner* (Washington, 1930), p. 269; Arnesen, *Brotherhoods of Color*, pp. 24–25; Arnesen, "Like Banquo's Ghost," p. 1622.

20. Quoted in Arnesen, "Like Banquo's Ghost," p. 1629; Paul Worthman, "Black Workers and Labor Unions in Birmingham, Alabama, 1897-1904," *Labor History* 10 (Summer 1969): 380.

21. John M. Matthews, "The Georgia Race Strike of 1909," *Journal of Southern History* 40 (1974): 613–30; Hugh B. Hammett, "Labor and Race: The Georgia Railroad Strike of 1909," *Labor History* 16 (1975): 470–84; Harris, *The Harder We Run*, p. 46; Spero and Harris, *The Black Worker*, p. 289; Arnesen, *Brotherhoods of Color*, p. 36.

22. Spero and Harris, *The Black Worker*, pp. 290–91; Harris, *The Harder We Run*, pp. 46–48; Hammett, "Labor and Race," pp. 470–84; Matthews, "The Georgia Race Strike of 1909," pp. 613–30; David E. Bernstein, *Only One Place of Redress: African Americans, Labor Regulations, and the Courts from Reconstruction to the New Deal* (Durham, N.C., 2001), p. 51.

23. *Crisis*, April 1911, pp. 7–8; Spero and Harris, *The Black Worker*, pp. 286, 291–93; Arnesen, *Brotherhoods of Color*, pp. 37–38. Black scholar and editor W. E. B. DuBois viewed the settlement as "on the whole a victory for the colored workers." *Crisis*, May 1911, p. 9.

24. Melvyn Dubofsky, *Hard Work: The Making of Labor History* (Urbana, Ill., 2000), pp. 107–8; Melvyn Dubofsky, *Industrialism and the American Worker, 1865-1920* (Arlington Heights, Ill., 1975), p. 110; Joseph A. McCartin, *Labor's Great War: The Struggle for Industrial Democracy and the Origins of Modern American Labor Relations, 1912-1921* (Chapel Hill, 1997), pp. 2–3; Colin J. Davis, *Power at Odds: The 1922 National Railroad Shopmen's Strike* (Urbana, Ill., 1997), pp. 1–2.

25. Theodore Kornweibel, Jr., *"Investigate Everything": Federal Efforts to Compel Black Loyalty During World War I* (Bloomington, Ind., 2002); Theodore Kornweibel, Jr., *"Seeing Red": Federal Campaigns Against Black Militancy, 1919-1925* (Bloomington, Ind., 1998).

26. Arnesen, *Brotherhoods of Color*, p. 67.

27. Arnesen, *Brotherhoods of Color*, pp. 48–49, 52, 54–55; Bernstein, *Only One Place of Redress*, p. 52; McCartin, *Labor's Great War*, pp. 116–17.

28. Arnesen, *Brotherhoods of Color*, pp. 58–62; *Agreement between the Colored Firemen and the Management of the New Orleans, Texas & Mexico Railway Company, the Beaumont, Sour Lake & Western Railway Company, and the New Iberia & Northern Railroad Company* (1925), copy courtesy of Seth Bramson.

29. Spero and Harris, *The Black Worker*, pp. 294–99; Arnesen, *Brotherhoods of Color*, pp. 65–66, 70-71, 81; Bernstein, *Only One Place of Redress*, p. 53.

30. Memorandum, Francis X. Riley to Lawrence W. Cramer, Nov. 16, 1942, Misc. letters, telegrams, reports, Legal Division Hearings, 1941-1946, FEPC, RG228, National Archives.

31. Spero and Harris, *The Black Worker,* pp. 306-7; Bernstein, *Only One Place of Redress,* pp. 57–58; memorandum, Riley to Cramer, Nov. 27, 1942, Misc. correspondence, Legal Division Hearings, 1941–1946, FEPC, RG228, National Archives.

32. Hilton Butler, "Murder for the Job," *Nation,* July 12, 1933, 44; Arnesen, *Brotherhoods of Color,* pp. 120–21; Horace R. Cayton and George S. Mitchell, *Black Workers and the New Unions* (Chapel Hill, 1939), pp. 439–43.

33. Michael K. Honey, *Southern Labor and Black Civil Rights: Organizing Memphis Workers* (Urbana, Ill., 1993), p. 59; Harris, *The Harder We Run,* p. 48; Herbert R. Northup, *Organized Labor and the Negro* (New York, 1944), p. 52; Howard W. Risher, Jr., *The Negro in the Railroad Industry* (Philadelphia, 1971), pp. 40–42; Charles H. Houston, "Foul Employment Practice on the Rails," *Crisis,* Oct. 1949, p. 269; Walter White, secretary, NAACP, to Frank M. Parrish, Dept. of Justice, April 5, 1932, Asst. Attny. Gen. Nugent Dodds to White, April 7, 1932, Straight Numerical Files 158260-47, RG60, National Archives; Riley to Cramer re interview with G. P. Brock, VP, GM&O RR, Nov. 11, 1942, Misc. railroads, Legal Division Hearings, 1941–1946, FEPC, RG228, National Archives; Arnesen, *Brotherhoods of Color,* pp. 123–25; Cayton and Mitchell, *Black Workers and the New Unions,* pp. 443–44.

34. Arnesen, *Brotherhoods of Color,* pp. 118–20, 126–31; Railroads, discrimination, employment questionnaire, B. H. Green, Aug. 30, 1943, Negro hostler upgrading, L&N Sibert Shops, Legal Division Hearings, 1941–1946, FEPC, RG228, National Archives; Bernstein, *Only One Place of Redress,* pp. 59–61.

35. Arnesen, *Brotherhoods of Color,* pp. 184, 196.

36. W. Don Ellinger to Louis Wise, Dec. 18, 1944, file 13-UR-435, Railroad Trainmen, Brotherhood of, FEPC, RG228, National Archives; Beth Tompkins Bates, *Pullman Porters and the Rise of Protest Politics in Black America, 1925–1945* (Chapel Hill, 2001), pp. 148–74; Andrew E. Kersten, *Race, Jobs, and the War: The FEPC in the Midwest, 1941–46* (Urbana, Ill., 2000), pp. 2–3, 14–20; Merl E. Reed, *Seedtime for the Modern Civil Rights Movement: The President's Committee on Fair Employment Practice, 1941–1946* (Baton Rouge, La., 1991), pp. 13–17; Arnesen, *Brotherhoods of Color,* pp. 189–95; Harris, *The Harder We Run,* pp. 117–18. An older but still useful history of FEPC is Herbert Garfinkel, *When Negroes March: The March on Washington Movement in the Organizational Politics for FEPC* (Glencoe, Ill., 1959).

37. Arnesen, *Brotherhoods of Color,* pp. 181–82, 195–97; *Negro Railway Labor News,* June–July 1949, p. 2; Harris, *The Harder We Run,* pp. 118–19; Bernstein, *Only One Place of Redress,* pp. 61–62; Malamud, "The Story of *Steele v. Louisville & Nashville Railroad,*" pp. 65–66. The Central of Georgia Railway's president was a racial paternalist and disagreed with the Washington Agreement because it required that long-employed, loyal black firemen be laid off so as to maintain the quota of white firemen. Memorandum, Riley to Cramer, Nov. 12, 1942, Misc. correspondence, Legal Division Hearings, 1941–1946, FEPC, RG228, National Archives.

38. Arnesen, *Brotherhoods of Color,* pp. 200–202.

39. Arnesen, *Brotherhoods of Color,* p. 205.

40. Railroad discrimination employment questionnaire, Bester Steele?, Aug. 1943, L&N Birmingham Terminal, Negro Fireman, Legal Division Hearings, 1941–1946, FEPC, RG228, National Archives.

41. Malamud, "The Story of *Steele v. Louisville & Nashville Railroad,*" pp. 59, 80–95; Bernstein, *Only One Place of Redress,* pp. 62–64; Arnesen, *Brotherhoods of Color,* pp. 196, 203–9.

42. Arnesen, *Brotherhoods of Color,* pp. 211–15; Malamud, "The Story of *Steele v. Louisville & Nashville Railroad,*" pp. 98–100; *Negro Railway Labor News,* Jan.–Feb. 1950, p. 3.

43. Arnesen, *Brotherhoods of Color,* pp. 217–19; Charleston (W.V.) *Gazette,* March 10, 1959, p. 17; Zanesville (Ohio) *Times-Recorder,* Sept. 24, 1959, p. 1.

44. Leuthner, *The Railroaders,* p. 47.

45. Memorandum, James C. Evans to Robert C. Weaver, June 12, 1943, Misc. railroads, Legal Division Hearings, 1941–1946, FEPC, RG228, National Archives; memorandum, Maceo W. Hubbard to Milton P. Webster, Employment hearings, Legal Division Hearings, 1941–1946, FEPC, RG228, National Archives; Seth Bramson to author, July 18, 2004; interview, Charlie Castner, May 8, 1999.

46. White, "Oh, To Be a Locomotive Engineer," *Railroad History* 190 (Spring–Summer 2004): 74 (overall statistics); Bernstein, *Only One Place of Redress,* p. 64 (percentage of black firemen in the South).

47. Summary of the Hearings of the President's Committee on Fair Employment Practice held at Washington, D.C., Sept. 15-18, 1943; Findings and Directions Against Norfolk and Western Railway Company, Brotherhood of Locomotive Firemen and Enginemen and Brotherhood of Railroad Trainmen, Legal Division Hearings, 1941–1946, FEPC, RG228, National Archives.

48. *Railroad Gazette,* Feb. 23, 1883.

49. *Railroad Stories*, Nov. 1935, p. 132.

50. *Crisis*, April 1917, p. 296; *Railroad Magazine*, April 1945, p. 128.

51. Arnesen, *Brotherhoods of Color*, p. 238; Hugh Davis Graham, *The Civil Rights Era: Origins and Development of National Policy, 1960–1972* (New York, 1990), pp. 146–52, 186–89; Borgna Brunner, "Timeline of Affirmative Action Milestones" (2007), http://www.infoplease.com/spot/affirmativetimeline1.html.

52. Arnesen, *Brotherhoods of Color*, pp. 230–31.

53. www.nscorp.com/nscorphtml/aarm/whitaker.html.

54. On the L&N, J. G. Lachaussee to author, Dec. 30, 2002; on the FEC, Seth Bramson to author, July 18, 2004.

CHAPTER 4. "WARY FEET, AN ALERT MIND, AND CHILLED NERVES"

1. John Cohen and Mike Seeger, eds., *Old-Time String Band Songbook* (New York, 1964), p. 92.

2. Fred Gamst to author, Jan. 16, 2006.

3. Quotation courtesy of Herb Harwood, to author, Nov. 22, 2004.

4. Richard Reinhardt, ed., *Workin' on the Railroad: Reminiscences from the Age of Steam* (Palo Alto, 1970), pp. 274–75; Mark Aldrich, *Death Rode the Rails: American Railroad Accidents and Safety, 1828–1965* (Baltimore, 2006), pp. 104–9.

5. Virginia Central Railroad, 25th–29th annual reports, 1860–64.

6. Virginia & Tennessee Railroad, 9th–18th annual reports, 1856–65.

7. S. B. Rice, "Some Recollections of the RF&P When It Was Only About 31 Years Old," Folder 417, Series 13, Richmond, Fredericksburg & Potomac Collection, Virginia Historical Society.

8. Allen W. Trelease, *The North Carolina Railroad, 1849–1871, and the Modernization of North Carolina* (Chapel Hill, 1991), p. 352.

9. *Railroad Stories*, Nov. 1935, p. 132.

10. Box 3, Railroad Annual Reports, 1889, Secretary of State, North Carolina State Archives.

11. Accident reports, 1898–1933, Corporation Commission, Chief Clerk's Office, North Carolina State Archives. Among the other half of injuries and fatalities, many were convicts constructing the rugged mountain line in the western part of the state, including the Swanannoa Tunnel, where numerous prisoners lost their lives.

12. Typescript injury reports, 9/25/1905 through 9/26/1907, Mississippi Central Railroad Collection, University of Southern Mississippi.

13. *Illinois Central Magazine*, April 1919, pp. 27–28. Statistics cited here reflect subtracting passenger and trespasser accidents from the total.

14. *Illinois Central Magazine*, Dec. 1943, p. 47; July 1926, p. 58; Nov. 1943, p. 48; Aug. 1943, p. 9.

15. Disciplinary records of brakemen, Folder 285, 1906–1907, Folder 286, 1907–1910, Employee Records, RF&P Collection, Virginia Historical Society.

16. Sterling D. Spero and Abram L. Harris, *The Black Worker* (New York, 1931), p. 315.

17. Memorandum, Francis X. Riley to Lawrence W. Cramer, Nov. 13, 1942, Misc. letters, telegrams, reports, Legal Division Hearings, 1941–1946, FEPC, RG228, National Archives.

18. James H. Ducker, *Men of the Steel Rails: Workers on the Atchison, Topeka & Santa Fe Railroad, 1869–1900* (Lincoln, Neb., 1983), pp. 120–21; Eric Arnesen, *Brotherhoods of Color: Black Railroad Workers and the Struggle for Equality* (Cambridge, Mass., 2001), pp. 24–25, 34–35; *Cleveland Gazette*, Oct. 11, 25, 1890; *The Locomotive Engineer*, Nov. 1890, p. 214.

19. New Orleans & North-eastern Railroad time book, 1900–1903, Box 23, Predecessor and Subsidiary Roads, Norfolk Southern Railway Collection, Atlanta History Center.

20. David A. Gerber, *Black Ohio and the Color Line, 1860–1915* (Urbana, Ill., 1976), pp. 73–75; *Cleveland Gazette*, July 21, 1894.

21. *Railroad Magazine*, Jan. 1945, p. 112; March 1945, p. 130; April 1945, p. 128; Aug. 1945, pp. 110–11. The NAACP's monthly magazine noted a black brakeman on the Rock Island (in Chicago) and Union Pacific (in Denver). *Crisis*, Jan. 1921, p. 131; March 1921, p. 224.

22. Spero and Harris, *The Black Worker*, p. 288.

23. David E. Peterson, *Frontier Link With the World: The Upson County Railroad* (Macon, Ga., 1998), pp. 180–82; Spero and Harris, *The Black Worker*, p. 293; undated memorandum concerning attacks on black trainmen, File 134, Subject 8/Spl, Assassination of black trainmen, Yazoo & Mississippi Valley, 1931, Box 8, Discrimination, General, Illinois Central Gulf Railroad Papers, Cornell University Library; *Illinois Central Magazine*, June 1918, p. 68.

24. File E38-30, Employes: Wages: Instructions Governing Wages and Employment of Negroes as Firemen, Hostlers, Switchmen, Etc., Subject Classified General File of the Division of Labor, U.S. Railroad Administration, RG14, National Archives; Spero and Harris, *The Black Worker*, pp. 296–98; Arnesen, *Brotherhoods of Color*, pp. 65–70, quote p. 70.

25. Spero and Harris, *The Black Worker*, pp. 298–99; Arnesen, *Brotherhoods of Color*, pp. 80–81; undated memorandum concerning attacks on black trainmen, File 134, Subject 8/Spl, Assassination of black trainmen, Yazoo & Mississippi Valley, 1931, Box 8, Discrimination, General, Illinois Central Gulf Railroad Papers, Cornell University; Michael K. Honey, *Southern Labor and Black Civil Rights: Organizing Memphis Workers* (Urbana, Ill., 1993), p. 19.

26. By southern custom, blacks were not to be rear brakemen or flagmen, because that person gave signals to the engineer when the train was backing up, and that would be construed as the black flagman giving "orders" to the white engineer.

27. Files 2-3-25, 5-12-25, 11-4-21-1, Docketed Case Files, 1920–1926, U.S. Railroad Labor Board, National Mediation Board, RG13, National Archives; Spero and Harris, *The Black Worker*, pp. 299–302; Arnesen, *Brotherhoods of Color*, pp. 70–71.

28. Arnesen, *Brotherhoods of Color*, pp. 75–77.

29. Arnesen, *Brotherhoods of Color*, p. 79; Lorenzo J. Greene and Carter G. Woodson, *The Negro Wage Earner* (Washington, 1930), pp. 103, 269.

30. Arnesen, *Brotherhoods of Color*, pp. 127–29.

31. Howard W. Risher, Jr., *The Negro in the Railroad Industry* (Philadelphia, 1971), pp. 43–44.

32. File 134, Subject 8/Spl, Colored Employes Train and Engine Service–Kentucky Division–Thomas D. Redd, Office of Operating Department, Box 8, Discrimination, General, Illinois Central Gulf Railroad Papers, Cornell University.

33. Thomas D. Redd to General Manager J. J. Pelley, Feb. 22, 1924, File 134, Subject 8/Spl, Colored Employes Train and Engine Service–Kentucky Division–Thomas D. Redd, Office of Operating Department, Box 8, Discrimination, General, Illinois Central Gulf Railroad Papers, Cornell University.

34. Memorandum for files, July 15, 1924, File 134, Subject 8/Spl, Colored Employes Train and Engine Service–Kentucky Division–Thomas D. Redd, Office of Operating Department, Box 8, Discrimination, General, Illinois Central Gulf Railroad Papers, Cornell University.

35. J. M. Egan to A. E. Clift, Oct. 8, 1922, Thomas D. Redd to C. O. Cecil, Jan. 24, 1924, File 134, Subject 8/Spl, Colored Employes Train and Engine Service–Kentucky Division–Thomas D. Redd, Office of Operating Department, Box 8, Discrimination, General, Illinois Central Gulf Railroad Papers, Cornell University.

36. T. S. Jackson to Redd, July 27, 1933, File 134, Subject 8/Spl, Colored Trainmen on Kentucky Division filing petition, Illinois Central Gulf Railroad Papers, Cornell University.

37. Arnesen, *Brotherhoods of Color*, pp. 119, 131–39.

38. Undated memorandum concerning attacks on black trainmen, File 134, Subject 8/Spl, Assassination of black trainmen, Yazoo & Mississippi Valley, 1931, Box 8, Discrimination, General, Illinois Central Gulf Railroad Papers, Cornell University.

39. "N&W Railway Employees Director: Seniority Roster and Reference Guide, 1937–1938," Virginia Museum of Transportation; memorandum, Francis X. Riley to Lawrence W. Cramer, Nov. 27, 1942, Misc. correspondence, Legal Division Hearings, 1941–1946, FEPC, RG228, National Archives.

40. 1931 Standard Railway Employees Seniority List and Time Book, Southern Railway, Danville and Winston–Salem Divisions, Marvin Black collection.

41. 1943 Standard Railway Employees Seniority List and Time Book, Southern Railway, Asheville Division, Marvin Black collection.

42. 1953 Standard Railway Employees Seniority List and Time Book, Southern Railway. Asheville Division, Marvin Black collection.

43. Atlantic & North Carolina Railroad seniority list, Sept. 1, 1939, Marvin Black collection.

44. File 1948, Durham & Southern Railroad Co. Collection, Special Collections Library, Duke University.

45. Charles H. Houston, "Foul Employment Practice on the Rails," *Crisis*, Oct. 1949, pp. 269–71, 284; *Illinois Central Magazine*, Oct. 1943, back cover.

46. File 10-BR-406, Missouri Pacific Railroad, Committee on Fair Employment Practice, Regional Files, Region X, closed cases, RG228, National Archives.

47. File 13-BR-261, Southern Pacific Lines, file 13-UR-435, Railroad Trainmen, Brotherhood of, Active Cases, Committee on Fair Employment Practice, Regions X and XIII, RG228, National Archives.

48. "Summary, findings and directions in re New York Central Railroad Company, Brotherhood of Railroad Trainmen, Brotherhood of Railway Carmen of America, International Association of Machinists, International Brotherhood of Boilermakers, Iron Ship Builders and Helpers of America," "Summary, findings and directions in re Pennsylvania Railroad Company, the Brotherhood of Railway Shop Crafts of America, the Brotherhood of Railroad Trainmen, and the Brotherhood of Railway and Steamship Clerks, Freight Handlers, Express and Station Employees," n.d. [1943], Railroad Cases, Legal Division Hearings, 1941–1946, FEPC, RG228, National Archives.

49. *New York Herald Tribune,* Jan. 8, 1953.

50. "Jimcrow Trains Are Still Running on America's Railroads," *The Worker,* Sept. 1, 1957.

51. Folder 14, Louisville & Nashville Railroad, 1959–1971, Casework, Discrimination in Employment, Supplement, Non-Partisan Voters League Papers, University of Southern Alabama; *Louisville & Nashville Magazine,* Jan. 1970, pp. 14–15.

52. *Railroad Stories,* Nov. 1935, p. 132.

53. "Conditions changed fast for African-American railroad men," *Asheville Citizen-Times,* March 16, 2002; "A friendship chronicles integration on the railway," *Ashville Citizen-Times,* June 1, 2002.

54. U.S. Equal Employment Opportunity Commission, 2003 EEO-1 Aggregate Report, NAICS Code 482: Rail Transportation, available online.

55. Federal Railroad Administration, Worker Safety Report—Reportable Conditions, January 2004–December 2004, available online.

CHAPTER 5. "THE WORLD'S MOST PERFECT SERVANT"

1. *Pullman News,* Aug. 1922, p. 101; William H. Harris, *The Harder We Run: Black Workers Since the Civil War* (New York, 1982), p. 78.

2. Numerous antebellum southern railroads' annual reports; Eugene Alvarez, *Travels on Southern Antebellum Railroads, 1828–1860* (University, Ala., 1974), p. 161; John H. White, Jr., *The American Railroad Passenger Car* (Baltimore, 1978), p. 232.

3. Beth Tomkins Bates, *Pullman Porters and the Rise of Protest Politics in Black America, 1925–1945* (Chapel Hill, 2001), p. 17; Jack Santino, *Miles of Smiles, Years of Struggle: Stories of Black Pullman Porters* (Urbana, Ill., 1989), p. 7.

4. Kyle Wyatt to author, June 24, 2004.

5. *Pullman News,* July 1922, p. 90, and Nov. 1922, p. 218 [re: Wagner Palace Car Co.]; Nov. 1922, p. 226 [re: Southern Palace Car Co.]; Oct. 1923, p. 186 [re: Rip Van Winkle Sleeping Car Co.].

6. *Pullman News,* June 1922, p. 43; July 1922, pp. 73, 90; May 1923, p. 11.

7. William H. Harris, *Keeping the Faith: A Philip Randolph, Milton P. Webster, and the Brotherhood of Sleeping Car Porters, 1925–37* (Urbana, Ill., 1977), pp. 2, 16; Santino, *Miles of Smiles,* pp. 6, 9–10; George Pullman quoted in Jervis Anderson, *A Philip Randolph: A Biographical Portrait* (New York, 1973), p. 159; Bates, *Pullman Porters,* pp. 18–19.

8. David D. Perata, *Those Pullman Blues: An Oral History of the African American Railroad Attendant* (Lanham, Md., 1996), pp. xiv, xix; *Pullman News,* May 1922, p. 11; June 1922, p. 36. Bates (*Pullman Porters,* p. 18) states that about 12,000 porters worked in the early 1920s, and inexplicably cites Perata, who in fact agrees with the Pullman Company's figure of 9,000.

9. Joe Welsh and Bill Howes, *Travel by Pullman: A Century of Service* (St. Paul, 2004), pp. 50–51.

10. *Pullman News,* Jan. 1950, pp. 30–33; advertisement in *National Geographic,* Jan. 1942, p. 4; The Pullman Company, "Instructions to Porters," Jan. 1, 1925, in folder 33, file 05/01/06, Employee Instruction Books, Pullman Collection, Newberry Library; Stuart Leuthner, *The Railroaders* (New York, 1983), pp. 16–17; Stanley G. Grizzle, *My Name's Not George: The Story of the Brotherhood of Sleeping-car Porters in Canada* (Toronto, 1998), pp. 40–41; Santino, *Miles of Smiles,* pp. 19–23.

11. Harris, *Keeping the Faith,* pp. 15–17; Harris, *The Harder We Run,* p. 78; Patricia and Fredrick McKissack, *A Long Hard Journey: The Story of the Pullman Porter* (New York, 1989), p. 33.

12. Bates, *Pullman Porters,* p. 31.

13. Andrew E. Kersten, *A. Philip Randolph: A Life in the Vanguard* (Lanham, Md., 2007), pp. 30, 32; Bates, *Pullman Porters,* pp. 50–51.

14. Bates, *Pullman Porters*, pp. 30–31, 40–55; Harris, *Keeping the Faith*, pp. 17–18.

15. Black meat packinghouse workers in Chicago in the 1920s earned more than porters, and worked fewer hours, although their work was "dirty, smelly, and dangerous." Bates, *Pullman Porters*, p. 26.

16. Theodore Kornweibel, Jr., *"No Crystal Stair": Black Life and the Messenger, 1917–1928* (Westport, Conn., 1975), chaps. 6–7, epilogue; Kornweibel, *"Seeing Red": Federal Campaigns Against Black Militancy, 1919–1925* (Bloomington, Ind., 1998), chap. 5, quote p. 77.

17. Barbara M. Posadas, "The Hierarchy of Color and Psychological Adjustment in an Industrial Environment: Filipinos, the Pullman Company, and the Brotherhood of Sleeping Car Porters," *Labor History* 23 (Summer 1982): 355–56.

18. Harris, *The Harder We Run*, pp. 82–88.

19. A. Philip Randolph related this statement by Pullman vice president Champ Carry to historian William H. Harris in an interview nearly 40 years after the event. The protagonists are both long since deceased. The accuracy of the quote can neither be proved nor disproved. Harris, *Keeping the Faith*, p. 208.

20. See the numerous weekly columns by porter J. T. Reid, clinging to the Pullman Porters and Maids Protective Association, in the *New York Age* following the new contract. E.g., "The New Agreement," Sept. 25, 1937, p. 11.

21. Harris, *Keeping the Faith*; Harris, *The Harder We Run*, chap. 4; Anderson, *A. Philip Randolph*, chaps. 12–14; Larry Tye, *Rising From the Rails: Pullman Porters and the Making of the Black Middle Class* (New York, 2004), chap. 4; Bates, *Pullman Porters*, p. 126; Melinda Chateauvert, *Marching Together: Women of the Brotherhood of Sleeping-Car Porters* (Urbana, Ill., 1998).

22. The earliest black Canadian railroaders were escaped slaves who found work on the Great Western Railway, guarding and clearing tracks of stray animals. After the Civil War a small number of black Canadians helped lay tracks on transcontinental lines while others found employment as dining car cooks and waiters. But the number of black railroaders increased sharply when the Pullman Company introduced sleeping cars—and black porters—to Canada. Some held runs on "international" (cross-border) trains. Others worked solely on Canadian roads. The Canadian Pacific Railway built and operated its own sleeping and dining cars, staffed with its own employees, many recruited from the South (particularly black colleges) and the Caribbean. White railroaders tried to halt the importation of blacks, but the CPR wielded extraordinary political muscle. It openly flouted the Alien Labour Act, which banned recruitment of foreign workers or paying their travel expenses. The mere possession of a CPR sleeping and dining car department business card was sufficient for African Americans to pass Canadian border guards without trouble. Porters on the Canadian National Railway and the CPR founded their own Order of Sleeping Car Porters nearly a decade before Pullman employees in the United States organized the BSCP. The OSCP continued to represent CNR porters, while those on the CPR eventually affiliated with the BSCP. Sarah-Jane Mathieu, "North of the Colour Line: Sleeping-Car Porters and the Battle Against Jim Crow on Canadian Rails, 1880–1920," *Labour/Le Travail* 47 (2001): 9–41; Jonathan Hanna, Corporate Historian, Canadian Pacific Railway, to author, Sept. 21, 2004; Grizzle, *My Name's Not George*, pp. 14–19.

23. *Pullman News*, May 1922, 11; June 1922, back cover.

24. *Pullman News*, Dec. 1922, p. 233.

25. *Pullman News*, Oct. 1923, p. 164; July 1939, p. 11; Oct. 1940, p. 42; July 1941, p. 5.

26. See, for example, Aug. 1922, p. 101; Nov. 1922, p. 208; Oct. 1923, pp. 195–96; Jan. 1924, p. 274; July 1925, p. 79; Oct. 1938, p. 42; Oct. 1939, p. 45; July 1940, p. 9.

27. *Pullman News*, April 1946, p. 5.

28. *Pullman News*, Oct. 1923, p. 186.

29. Employment of Filipinos as Pullman Porters—comparisons to blacks, file 541.3, Chief of Passenger Transportation, Box 395, Pennsylvania Railroad Collection, Hagley Museum and Library.

30. *Pullman News*, Sept. 1922, p. 152.

31. *Pullman News*, Dec. 1924, p. 237.

32. *Pullman News*, July 1924, p. 70.

33. *Pullman News*, July 1929, p. 75.

34. *Pullman News*, March 1926, p. 357.

35. Perata, *Those Pullman Blues*, pp. 21ff.

36. Perata, *Those Pullman Blues*, p. xxv.

37. Leuthner, *The Railroaders*, p. 15.

38. Santino, *Miles of Smiles*, pp. 19–23.

39. Perata, *Those Pullman Blues*, p. 78.

40. Perata, *Those Pullman Blues,* pp. 55, 78–79.
41. Perata, *Those Pullman Blues,* pp. xix, 54–55.
42. Perata, *Those Pullman Blues,* pp. 8–9.
43. *Pullman News,* July 1933, p. 16; May 1931, p. 12; Perata, *Those Pullman Blues,* pp. 19, 141–42; obituary, Garrard Smock, Jr., *Los Angeles Times,* Jan. 14, 2005.
44. *Cleveland Gazette,* July 7, 1894, p. 2.
45. "In the matter of the Pullman Porters and Maids Protective Association concerning Upgrading and the Hiring of Negroes as Pullman Conductors. (A Report to the President's Committee on Fair Employment Practice.)," Legal Division Hearings, 1941–1946, FEPC, RG228, National Archives; "'In-Charge' Porters Prove That Salesmanship Pays Off," *Pullman News,* April 1950, p. 28.
46. Santino, *Miles of Smiles,* pp. 89–90; *New York Age,* April 18, 1931, p. 9.
47. Santino, *Miles of Smiles,* pp. 23, 25, 89.
48. Santino, *Miles of Smiles,* pp. 17, 30, 92.
49. Perata, *Those Pullman Blues,* p. xxv.
50. Perata, *Those Pullman Blues,* p. 76.
51. Perata, *Those Pullman Blues,* pp. 2–3, 9.
52. Perata, *Those Pullman Blues,* p. 36.
53. Santino, *Miles of Smiles,* p. 28.
54. Perata, *Those Pullman Blues,* pp. 35–36.
55. Santino, *Miles of Smiles,* p. 100.
56. *Pullman News,* March 1926, p. 360.
57. Perata, *Those Pullman Blues,* p. 77.
58. Leuthner, *The Railroaders,* p. 14; Santino, *Miles of Smiles,* pp. 31, 126; obituary, Garrard Smock, Jr.
59. Santino, *Miles of Smiles,* p. 94.
60. Santino, *Miles of Smiles,* pp. 98–99.
61. Santino, *Miles of Smiles,* pp. 98–99.
62. Tye, *Rising from the Rails,* p. 45; Santino, *Miles of Smiles,* pp. 31, 95; Perata, *Those Pullman Blues,* p. 59.
63. Tye, *Rising from the Rails,* p. 46.
64. Santino, *Miles of Smiles,* pp. 71–74.
65. Tye, *Rising from the Rails,* p. 47; obituary, Garrard Smock, Jr. A detailed chart comparing Pullman's monthly pay rates from 1915 to 1947 for service on tourist cars, standard cars, parlor cars, and private cars, plus rates for porters-in-charge, attendants, bus boys, and maids, is in folder 315, file 06/01/03, General Labor Files, Pullman Collection, Newberry Library.
66. Santino, *Miles of Smiles,* p. 79.
67. *Pullman News,* Sept. 1922, p. 154.
68. Perata, *Those Pullman Blues,* pp. 17–18, 70–71.
69. Perata, *Those Pullman Blues,* p. 24.
70. *Pullman News,* Dec. 1922, p. 257.
71. Grizzle, *My Name's Not George,* p. 37.
72. Santino, *Miles of Smiles,* pp. 14–17.
73. *Pullman News,* Feb. 1923, pp. 297–98.
74. "Porter," in *The Collected Poems of Langston Hughes,* ed. Arnold Rampersad (New York, 1995), p. 169.
75. *Pullman News,* May 1924, p. 5.
76. *Pullman News,* July 1922, pp. 73–74; Oct. 1940, p. 46; Jan. 1945, p. 101; April 1952, p. 10.
77. Bates, *Pullman Porters,* p. 126.
78. *Pullman News,* Oct. 1944, p. 62; April 1946, p. 7.
79. *Pullman News,* Oct. 1922, p. 179; Leuthner, *The Railroaders,* p. 17.
80. Santino, *Miles of Smiles,* pp. 131, 135–36.
81. *New York Age,* various issues, 1931–37.
82. Eric Arnesen, *Brotherhoods of Color: Black Railroad Workers and the Struggle for Equality* (Cambridge, Mass., 2001), pp. 240–41.
83. Perata, *Those Pullman Blues,* p. 159.

CHAPTER 6. "CAPABLE OF WORKING IN ANY FINE RESTAURANT"

1. John H. White, Jr., *The American Railroad Passenger Car* (Baltimore, 1978), pp. 311–19.
2. "Railroads Serve 25,000,000 Meals Annually in Dining Cars," *The Rail* [Chesapeake & Ohio and Pere Marquette Railroads], April 1937, p. 12; Michael E. Zega, "The Best on Wheels," *Trains*, April 2006, pp. 66–69.
3. Other significant employment was as coal miners, longshoremen, and sawmill workers.
4. Lillian Serece Williams, *Strangers in the Land of Paradise: The Creation of an African American Community, Buffalo, New York, 1900–1940* (Bloomington, Ind., 1999), p. 67.
5. David D. Perata, *Those Pullman Blues: An Oral History of the African American Railroad Attendant* (Lanham, Md., 1996), pp. 124–27.
6. Perata, *Those Pullman Blues,* pp. 104–5; *The Rail,* April 1937, p. 12.
7. Thomas Fleming, "Cooking on the Southern Pacific," *Classic Trains,* Fall 2002, pp. 42–43; Stuart Leuthner, *The Railroaders* (New York, 1983), p. 100.
8. Perata, *Those Pullman Blues,* pp. 85, 107–8; Fleming, "Cooking on the Southern Pacific," pp. 39–40; Leuthner, *The Railroaders,* p. 100.
9. Perata, *Those Pullman Blues,* pp. 94, 108; Leuthner, *The Railroaders,* p. 100; *Negro Railway Labor News,* June–July 1949, pp. 2, 4; Jan.–Feb. 1950, p. 1.
10. Perata, *Those Pullman Blues,* pp. 85–86; Fleming, "Cooking on the Southern Pacific," p. 43.
11. Fleming, "Cooking on the Southern Pacific," pp. 39, 41.
12. Perata, *Those Pullman Blues,* pp. 87, 110–11; Leuthner, *The Railroaders,* p. 101.
13. Perata, *Those Pullman Blues,* pp. 110–11, 136.
14. White, *The American Railroad Passenger Car,* pp. 327–28; Perata, *Those Pullman Blues,* p. 136.
15. Perata, *Those Pullman Blues,* pp. 88, 111; Leuthner, *The Railroaders,* p. 101.
16. Fleming, "Cooking on the Southern Pacific," p. 42; Leuthner, *The Railroaders,* p. 99.
17. Fleming, "Cooking on the Southern Pacific," p. 41; Perata, *Those Pullman Blues,* pp. 88, 91, 111–12.
18. John Gruber, "Memories of a Chef for the Chicago & North Western," *Trains,* April 2006, pp. 81–84; Perata, *Those Pullman Blues,* pp. 95–96.
19. Fleming, "Cooking on the Southern Pacific," p. 42.
20. Perata, *Those Pullman Blues,* pp. 107–9, 117–19.
21. Perata, *Those Pullman Blues,* pp. 112–13.
22. Perata, *Those Pullman Blues,* pp. 93–94.
23. Perata, *Those Pullman Blues,* p. 18.
24. Perata, *Those Pullman Blues,* pp. 132–33.
25. Perata, *Those Pullman Blues,* pp. 128–29, 133–34.
26. Fleming, "Cooking on the Southern Pacific," p. 44; Leuthner, *The Railroaders,* p. 100; Agreement between the colored brakemen and the management of the Gulf Coast Lines, Jan. 1, 1929, Box 20, Colored Trainmen of America Papers, Houston Public Library; Perata, *Those Pullman Blues,* p. 131.
27. Louie Stewart, L&N Oral History Project, March 4, 1980, University of Louisville, pp. 23–24.
28. Perata, *Those Pullman Blues,* pp. 31–32.
29. Perata, *Those Pullman Blues,* pp. 141–42.
30. Perata, *Those Pullman Blues,* p. 130.
31. Perata, *Those Pullman Blues,* p. 134; Southern Pacific Condensed Timetable, Dec. 31, 1944, p. 6.
32. Perata, *Those Pullman Blues,* pp. 88, 135, 140–41.
33. Perata, *Those Pullman Blues,* pp. 140–41; *Central of Georgia Magazine,* Feb. 1932, p. 22; *Louisville & Nashville Employes' Magazine,* Dec. 1944, p. 17; *Chesapeake and Ohio and Hocking Valley Employes' Magazine,* Feb. 1928, p. 15; *Santa Fe Employes' Magazine,* Jan. 1911, p. 60.
34. White, *The American Railroad Passenger Car,* p. 658.
35. Gruber, "Memories of a Chef," pp. 82–83.
36. Blacks did not have an absolute monopoly outside of the South. In mid-1929, the Great Northern Railway experimented with replacing black waiters, pantrymen, and cooks with white men, giving as a reason the theory that whites were more "expert" concerning food. Lorenzo J. Greene and Carter G. Woodson, *The Negro Wage Earner* (Washington, 1930), pp. 232–33.
37. James D. Porterfield, *Dining by Rail* (New York, 1993), pp. 114–15.
38. Joseph M. Welsh, *By Streamliner: New York to Florida* (Andover, N.J., 1994), p. 84.
39. Louie Stewart oral history, p. 22.

40. Porterfield, *Dining by Rail*, pp. 126–27.

41. Perata, *Those Pullman Blues*, p. xx.

42. *Baltimore and Ohio Magazine*, Nov. 1941, p. 13.

43. Seaboard Railway, *Rules Governing Employees of Dining Car Department*, April 1, 1944, pp. 16–17.

44. Louie Stewart oral history, pp. 25–27; Jack Santino, *Miles of Smiles, Years of Struggle: Stories of Black Pullman Porters* (Urbana, Ill., 1989), p. 30; SAL instructions quoted in Welsh, *By Streamliner*, p. 83.

45. Louie Stewart oral history, pp. 10–11.

46. *Altoona* (Pa.) *Mirror*, Feb. 14, 1993.

47. *Altoona Mirror*, Feb. 14, 1993; Louie Stewart oral history, p. 29.

48. *Altoona Mirror*, Feb. 14, 1993.

49. Malcolm X, *The Autobiography of Malcolm X* (New York, 1965), pp. 71–79.

50. *Baltimore and Ohio Employes Magazine*, May 1916, p. 58.

51. Perata, *Those Pullman Blues*, pp. xxi, xxxiii–xxiv.

52. Many waiters found employment through friends and family members. Even though Louie Stewart's brother told an L&N commissary official, "they don't come any greener," he was willing to hire Stewart because his brother was a former waiter. Louie Stewart oral history, pp. 4–5.

53. Perata, *Those Pullman Blues*, p. 24. A lounge-car waiter also performed valet service. Tipping Pullman porters 25 cents for every suit they brought from their passengers, he could earn $1.25 for pressing a suit, $1.50 for an overcoat. Starting at ten or eleven in the evening, as the crowd in his car thinned, he might iron a dozen suits by four or five in the morning. Like the Pullman porters, they also brushed their own passengers' clothes and hats and shined their shoes. Perata, *Those Pullman Blues*, pp. 25–26.

54. Perata, *Those Pullman Blues*, pp. 5–6.

55. Perata, *Those Pullman Blues*, pp. 27–29.

56. Perata, *Those Pullman Blues*, p. 43.

57. Perata, *Those Pullman Blues*, pp. 43, 71.

58. Perata, *Those Pullman Blues*, p. 25.

59. Malcolm X, *The Autobiography*, p. 76.

60. Perata, *Those Pullman Blues*, pp. 7, 29–30, 44.

61. Perata, *Those Pullman Blues*, p. 30.

62. Perata, *Those Pullman Blues*, pp. 75, 77.

63. Perata, *Those Pullman Blues*, pp. 25, 30.

64. Perata, *Those Pullman Blues*, p. 27.

65. *Negro Railway Labor News*, June–July 1949, pp. 3, 4.

66. Eric Arnesen, *Brotherhoods of Color: Black Railroad Workers and the Struggle for Equality* (Cambridge, Mass., 2001), pp. 59, 96.

67. Arnesen, *Brotherhoods of Color*, pp. 97–101; *Negro Railway Labor News*, June–July 1948, p. 1; Jan.–Feb. 1950, p. 3.

68. Chicago Commission on Race Relations, *The Negro in Chicago: A Study of Race Relations and a Race Riot* (Chicago, 1921), pp. 390–91.

69. Railroads operating café cars had been using black waiters-in-charge long before World War II. The Big Four (New York Central System) had four such employees in 1916. *Crisis*, May 1916, pp. 10–11.

70. Herbert R. Northrup, *Organized Labor and the Negro* (New York, 1944), pp. 96–97; *The Negro in Chicago*, pp. 390–91; Arnesen, *Brotherhoods of Color*, p. 106; Leuthner, *The Railroaders*, p. 100; *Chicago Defender*, undated 1944 clipping, author's collection; R. N. Thompson to T. A. Jackson, Sept. 14, 1943, "Summary, Findings and Directions in re New York Central Railroad Company, Brotherhood of Railroad Trainmen, Brotherhood of Railway Carmen of America, International Association of Machinists, International Brotherhood of Boilermakers, Iron Ship Builders and Helpers of America," memorandum, Edward Lawson to John Beecher, Jan. 6, 1943, memorandum, G. James Fleming to Will Maslow, Nov. 20, 1944, "Answer of Louisville & Nashville Railroad to Summary of Complaints Submitted with the Committee's Letter of August 30, 1943," "Summary findings and directions in re Missouri–Kansas–Texas Railroad of Texas," press release, March 1, 1944, "Crack Railroad Discrimination. Negro Stewards on Northwestern Railroad," Dining Car Employees Union and Joint Council Dining Car Employees, Headquarters Records, Legal Division Hearings, 1941–1946, FEPC, RG228, National Archives; Oklahoma City *Daily Oklahoman*, June 19, 1957, p. 26.

71. Perata, *Those Pullman Blues*, p. 86.

72. Louie Stewart oral history, pp. 36–37.

1. James R. Grossman, *Land of Hope: Chicago, Black Southerners, and the Great Migration* (Chicago, 1989), p. 66.
2. Their daring escape is narrated in *Running a Thousand Miles for Freedom* (1860).
3. William McFeely, *Frederick Douglass* (New York, 1991), pp. 70–71.
4. Christopher Phillips, *Freedom's Port: The African American Community of Baltimore, 1790–1860* (Urbana, Ill., 1997), p. 194.
5. William J. Switala, *The Underground Railroad in Pennsylvania* (Mechanicsburg, Pa., 2001), pp. 59, 146–47; J. Blaine Hudson, *Fugitive Slaves and the Underground Railroad in the Kentucky Borderland* (Jefferson, N.C., 2002), p. 68.
6. Arna Bontemps and Jack Conroy, *Anyplace But Here* (New York, 1966), p. 43.
7. Glennette T. Turner, *The Underground Railroad in Illinois* (Glen Ellyn, Ill., 2001), p. 6.
8. See, for example, correspondence of a Missouri slave-owning family whose "property" rode trains to abscond to the Union army, in the Kennett Family Papers, Missouri Historical Society.
9. David E. Paterson, *Frontier Link With the World: The Upson County Railroad* (Macon, Ga., 1998), p. 57.
10. Harriet C. Frazier, *Runaway and Freed Missouri Slaves and Those Who Helped Them, 1763–1865* (Jefferson, N.C., 2004), p. 93.
11. *Regulations and Instructions for the Government of the Transportation Department and the Running of Trains, etc., on the North Carolina Railroad, to go into effect on the first Monday in October, 1854* (Raleigh, 1854), p. 17, copy in Norfolk Southern Railway Collection, Atlanta History Center.
12. *O'Neall v. South Carolina Railroad Co.*, 9 Richardson 465 (1856); *Wallace and Wallace v. Spollock*, 32 Georgia 488 (1861); *Southwestern Railroad Company v. Pickett*, 36 Georgia 85 (1867); *Western & Atlantic Railroad Co. v. Fulton*, 4 Sneed 589 (1857).
13. Edward King, *The Great South* (Hartford, 1875), pp. 113, 123, 650.
14. Lorenzo J. Greene and Carter G. Woodson, *The Negro Wage Earner* (Washington, 1930), p. 33; Neil R. McMillen, *Dark Journey: Black Mississippians in the Age of Jim Crow* (Urbana, Ill., 1989), pp. 259–60; letter, Susan Gillis, Fort Lauderdale Historical Society, to author, May 29, 1998; "The Negro Exodus," *Frank Leslie's Illustrated Newspaper*, Feb. 15, 1890, p. 35.
15. Scholars and hoboes alike disagree on terminology. Some insist that a hobo is a migratory worker, traveling by train, while a tramp is a migratory, walking, non-worker. Others use "tramp," "vagabond," and "hobo" interchangeably.
16. Nine black teenagers riding on a Southern Railway freight train were falsely accused of raping two white prostitutes, riding as hoboes. All but one were sentenced to death after sham trials in Scottsboro, Alabama. The Supreme Court overturned their convictions, ruling that they had been denied adequate legal counsel guaranteed by the Fourteenth Amendment's due process clause. New trials resulted in new death sentences that were again voided by the Supreme Court on the grounds that blacks were systematically excluded from the jury pool. Although none of the Scottsboro boys was guilty, they spent many years in horrid prison conditions in a case that revealed to the world the injustices of the southern legal system. See Dan T. Carter, *Scottsboro: A Tragedy of the American South*, 2nd ed. (Baton Rouge, La., 1984).
17. Gypsy Moon, *Done and Been: Steel Rail Chronicles of American Hobos* (Bloomington, Ind., 1996), pp. 4–6, 35–37, 40; Kenneth L. Kusmer, *Down & Out, On the Road: The Homeless in American History* (New York, 2002), pp. 138–40; narrative of New York Slim, in Cliff Williams, *One More Train to Ride: The Underground World of Modern American Hoboes* (Bloomington, Ind., 2003), pp. 18–27; Frank Tobias Higbie, *Indispensable Outcasts: Hobo Workers and Community in the American Midwest, 1880–1930* (Urbana, Ill., 2003), pp. 109–10; Paul Garon and Gene Tomko, *What's the Use of Walking if There's a Freight Train Going Your Way? Black Hoboes & their Songs* (Chicago, 2006), pp. 129–33, 239.
18. U.S. Department of Commerce, Bureau of the Census, *Negroes in the United States: 1920–32* (Washington, 1935), p. 55.
19. Division of Negro Economics, U.S. Department of Labor, *Negro Migration in 1916–17* (Washington, 1919), pp. 12, 19–21, 86, 100, 122; Grossman, *Land of Hope*, pp. 47, 96, 103.
20. Theodore Kornweibel, "'The most dangerous of all Negro journals': Federal Efforts to Suppress the *Chicago Defender* during World War I," *American Journalism* 11 (Spring 1994): 154–68; Bontemps and Conroy, *Anyplace But Here*, pp. 158, 163; Florette Henri, *Black Migration: Movement North, 1900–1920* (Garden City, N.Y., 1976), p. 65; Grossman, *Land of Hope*, p. 78.
21. Bontemps and Conroy, *Anyplace But Here*, pp. 161–62; Grossman, *Land of Hope*, p. 87.

22. *Negro Migration in 1916–17*, p. 119.
23. *Negro Migration in 1916–17*, pp. 118–22.
24. Emmett J. Scott, *Negro Migration During the War* (New York, 1969 [c. 1920]), pp. 38–39, 55; John Dittmer, *Black Georgia in the Progressive Era, 1900–1920* (Urbana, Ill., 1977), pp. 186–87; *Negro Migration in 1916–17*, p. 28; James W. Johnson, *Black Manhattan* (New York, 1968 [1930]), p 151.
25. *Negro Migration in 1916–17*, pp. 66, 118; Dittmer, *Black Georgia*, pp. 186–87.
26. Jacksonville *Florida Times-Union*, Oct. 28, 29, Nov. 4, 1916, all p. 1 articles.
27. *Negro Migration in 1916–17*, pp. 53, 81, 121–22; Eric Arnesen, *Black Protest and the Great Migration: A Brief History with Documents* (Boston, 2003), pp. 58–59; Chief A. B. Bielaski to Bureau of Investigation agent F. L. Garbarino, Philadelphia, Oct. 26, 1916, agent H. R. McClintock, Dothan, Ala., to Bureau, Nov. 1, 1916, Miscellaneous file 10015, Federal Bureau of Investigation, RG65, National Archives.
28. Agent Todd Daniel, Philadelphia, to Bureau, Oct. 26, 1916, clerk Joseph Polen, Norfolk, to Bielaski, Oct. 25, 1916, Miscellaneous file 10015, Federal Bureau of Investigation, RG65, National Archives; *Negro Migration in 1916–17*, pp. 53, 109, 123–24, 144–46, 157–58.
29. Agent William B. Matthews, Pittsburgh, to Bureau, Oct. 25, 1916, Miscellaneous file 10015, Federal Bureau of Investigation, RG65, National Archives; *Negro Migration in 1916–17*, pp. 123–24, 145–46, 157–58.
30. *Negro Migration in 1916–17*, pp. 122, 123, 146; agent A. J. Devlin, Memphis, to Bureau, Oct. 19, 1916, agent E. S. Underhill, NYC, to Bureau, Oct. 23, 1916, agent L. D. Strickland, Buffalo, to Bureau, Oct. 31, 1916, Matthews to Bureau, Nov. 3, 1916, agent Leverett F. Englesby to Bureau, Nov. 7, 1916, Miscellaneous file 10015, Federal Bureau of Investigation, RG65, National Archives.
31. Louis F. Post, Asst. Sec., Dept. of Labor, to Attny. Gen. Thomas W. Gregory, Oct. 16, 1916, Miscellaneous file 10015, Federal Bureau of Investigation, RG65, National Archives; *Negro Migration in 1916–17*, pp. 122–23, 146.
32. *Negro Migration in 1916–17*, pp. 122–23, 146, 157–58.
33. Robert Gregg, *Sparks From the Anvil of Oppression: Philadelphia's African Methodists and Southern Migrants, 1890–1940* (Philadelphia, 1993), p. 35; *Negro Migration in 1916–17*, pp. 122–23, 146, 157–58; Devlin to Bureau, Oct. 19, 1916, Post to Gregory, Oct. 16, 1916, Bielaski to Div. Supt. William M. Offley, NYC, Oct. 21, 1916, Miscellaneous file 10015, Federal Bureau of Investigation, RG65, National Archives.
34. Greene and Woodson, *Negro Wage Earner*, p. 266; Elliott M. Rudwick, *Race Riot at East St. Louis, July 2, 1917* (Cleveland, 1966), pp. 161, 169; Scott, *Negro Migration*, pp. 102, 108.
35. Eric Arnesen, *Brotherhoods of Color: Black Railroad Workers and the Struggle for Equality* (Cambridge, Mass., 2001), p. 45; *Crisis*, May 1917, p. 36; June 1917, p. 86; Scott, *Negro Migration*, p. 71; Higbie, *Indispensable Outcasts*, pp. 108–9; Charles E. Hall, *Negroes in the United States, 1920–1932* (Washington, 1935), p. 309.
36. *Negro Migration in 1916–17*, p. 109; Division of Negro Economics, U.S. Department of Labor, *The Negro at Work During the World War and During Reconstruction* (Washington, 1921), p. 117; Greene and Woodson, *Negro Wage Earner*, pp. 266–69; Scott, *Negro Migration*, pp. 38–39, 47–48, 69, 102, 103, 120–21, 122, 135.
37. *Negro Migration in 1916–17*, pp. 119–21; Devlin to Bureau, Oct. 19, 1916, Miscellaneous file 10015, Federal Bureau of Investigation, RG65, National Archives.
38. Scott, *Negro Migration*, pp. 61–62; Henri, *Black Migration*, p. 61.
39. Bontemps and Conroy, *Anyplace But Here*, p. 163; Scott, *Negro Migration*, pp. 44–46.
40. Scott, *Negro Migration*, pp. 47–48; *Negro Migration in 1916–17*, p. 150.
41. Alferdteen Harrison, ed., *Black Exodus: The Great Migration from the American South* (Jackson, Miss., 1991), p. 45; Henri, *Black Migration*, p. 66; Bontemps and Conroy, *Anyplace But Here*, pp. 160, 162; Grossman, *Land of Hope*, pp. 103–4.
42. Scott, *Negro Migration*, pp. 63–64; *Negro Migration in 1916–17*, pp. 53, 55–56.
43. *Negro Migration in 1916–17*, pp. 84–85; Bontemps and Conroy, *Anyplace But Here*, p. 164; Grossman, *Land of Hope*, p. 103; McMillan, *Dark Journey*, pp. 262–63.
44. Agent George G. Calmes, Tampa, to Bureau, Aug. 26, Englesby to Bureau, Oct. 31, 1916, Miscellaneous file 10015, Federal Bureau of Investigation, RG65, National Archives; Henri, *Black Migration*, pp. 67–68; Lawrence R. Rodgers, *Canaan Bound: The African-American Great Migration Novel* (Chicago, 1997), p. 15; Grossman, *Land of Hope*, pp. 48, 108, 109; Scott, *Negro Migration*, pp. 66, 78; Bontemps and Conroy, *Anyplace But Here*, p. 164.
45. Quoted in McMillan, *Dark Journey*, p. 273.
46. Dittmer, *Black Georgia*, pp. 188–91; Arnesen, *Brotherhoods of Color*, p. 44; Grossman, *Land of Hope*, pp. 48, 109; Scott, *Negro Migration*, pp. 73–76; *Negro Migration in 1916–17*, p. 110.

47. Calmes to Bureau, Oct. 14, Polen to Bielaski, Oct. 25, Englesby to Bureau, Oct. 30, agent Ralph H. Daughton, Norfolk, to Bureau, Oct. 31, 1916, Miscellaneous file 10015, Federal Bureau of Investigation, RG65, National Archives; *Negro Migration in 1916–17*, pp. 57, 97; Grossman, *Land of Hope*, p. 48.

48. Greene and Woodson, *Negro Wage Earner*, pp. 266–69; Theodore Kornweibel, Jr., "An Economic Profile of Black Life in the Twenties," *Journal of Black Studies* 6 (June 1976): 307–20.

49. Gregg, *Sparks from the Anvil*, pp. 200–201; Arnesen, *Brotherhoods of Color*, p. 45.

50. Carey McWilliams, "Report on Importation of Negro Labor to California," Aug. 10, 1942, Misc., Southern Pacific Railroad, Headquarters Records, Legal Division Hearings, 1941–1946, FEPC, RG228, National Archives; Arnesen, *Brotherhoods of Color*, pp. 183–84.

51. Arnesen, *Brotherhoods of Color*, p. 184.

52. Barbara A. Driscoll, *The Tracks North: The Railroad Bracero Program of World War II* (Austin, Tex., 1999).

53. Leon R. Harris, "The Railroads are Losing Negro Patronage," *Railway Progress,* Nov. 1950, p. 20.

54. Clifton L. Taulbert, *When We Were Colored* (New York, 1995), pp. 142–43.

55. Taulbert, *When We Were Colored*, pp. 140–41, 143.

56. Dwayne E. Walls, *The Chickenbone Special* (New York, 1971), pp. 78–79.

57. Clifton L. Taulbert, *Last Train North* (New York, 1995), pp. i–ii, 3–4.

58. Taulbert, *Last Train North*, p. 24; Walls, *Chickenbone Special*, p. 15.

59. Walls, *Chickenbone Special*, pp. 73–75, 77.

60. Walls, *Chickenbone Special*, p. 69.

61. Grossman, *Land of Hope*, p. 113; Taulbert, *Last Train North*, p. 14.

CHAPTER 8. "REPRESENT THE BEST IN COLORED"

1. David D. Perata, *Those Pullman Blues: An Oral History of the African American Railroad Attendant* (Lanham, Md., 1996), p. xix.

2. *Pullman News*, April 1948, p. 32.

3. James H. Ducker, *Men of Steel: Workers on the Atchison, Topeka & Santa Fe Railroad, 1869–1900* (Lincoln, Neb., 1983), p. 121.

4. Quoted in *Ties Magazine*, Nov.–Dec. 1992, p. 12.

5. Chesapeake & Ohio Railway Company Specifications for Uniforms, Misc. circulars & instructions, Martin Collection, C&O Historical Society.

6. Subject file 1.97, comparison of wages, Norfolk & Western Railroad Company Collection, Virginia Polytechnic Institute and State University.

7. Charles Watts to A. M. Schoyer, Dec. 17, 1910, in Porters—rates of pay, 1908–1915, Box 1313, General Superintendent Southwest System, Lines West, Pennsylvania Railroad Collection, Hagley Museum and Library.

8. Sterling D. Spero and Abram L. Harris, *The Black Worker* (New York, 1931), pp. 303–5.

9. W. A. Winburn to Winchell, Oct. 7, 1918, File 4931; protest letter, M. Griffin and others to USRA Director General William Gibbs McAdoo, Nov. 24, 1918, File 4931; W. A. Winburn to E. H. Lamb, Oct. 21, 1919, Statement of L. F. Glenn, white porter on train no. 2 of Sept. 14, 1919, Central of Georgia Railway Collection, Georgia Historical Society.

10. Cyrus Campfield to L. A. Downs, Jan. 17, 26, 1925; Downs to Campfield, Jan. 19, 1925; W. H. Wright to Campfield, Jan. 21, 23, 1925; *Savannah Journal*, Jan. 31, 1925; President to Rev. A. C. Danforth, March 23, 1927; Charles W. Washington to A. E. Clift, Jan. 13, 1930; A. E. Clift to Charles W. Washington, Jan. 14, 1930; Clift to E. I. Robinson, May 13, 1930, File 4931, Central of Georgia Railway Collection, Georgia Historical Society.

11. "Portering," Educational Guidelines in Personal Service Occupations, Company 4735, CCC, Charlotte, Arkansas, 1938, copy in author's possession.

12. Agreement between Gulf, Mobile and Ohio Railroad Company and the Brotherhood of Trainmen, Brakemen, Porters, Switchmen, Firemen and Railway Employees, Incorporated, governing rates of pay, rules, and working conditions, effective April 7, 1942, Glen P. Brock Collection, University of South Alabama.

13. *Baltimore and Ohio Magazine*, Sept. 1947, pp. 12–13; Memorandums of agreement by various carriers with the BSCP, Sept. and Oct. 1949, Employee and Labor Relations, General Labor File, 06/01/03, Pullman Company Records, Newberry Library.

14. R. G. McGehee to R. Vawtor, July 25, 1952, "Misc. Old Material—Working," Martin Collection, C&O Historical Society; Committee of train porters to C. McD. Davis, April 27, 1954, file 64, salaries and payrolls, Atlantic Coast Line Railroad Papers, Southern Historical Collection, University of North Carolina Library.

15. Eric Arnesen, *Brotherhoods of Color: Black Railroad Workers and the Struggle for Equality* (Cambridge, Mass., 2001), p. 222. For the Southern, see "Agreement between Southern Railway Company . . . and Train Porters as represented by Association of Train Porters, Brakemen and Switchmen. Rules Revised as of January 9, 1942," in Railroad Union Agreements, Railroads, Discrimination, Legal Division Hearings, 1941-1946, FEPC, RG228, National Archives.

16. Ducker, *Men of Steel*, p. 121.

17. H. C. Brady to R. E. McCarty, Nov. 12, 1919, file 011.124, Superintendent of Labor and Wage Bureau, Pennsylvania Railroad Collection, Hagley Museum and Library; Arnesen, *Brotherhoods of Color*, pp. 38-39; "Menace to Colored Man!" and "To the Colored Voters of Missouri," broadsides, Charles H. Turner scrapbook, vol. 1, Missouri Historical Society.

18. Quotation: General Manager to Jno. G. Walber, Oct. 29, 1914; many other documents in Porters—rates of pay, 1908-1915, General Superintendent Southwest System, Lines West, file 011.124, Superintendent of Wage and Labor Bureau, Pennsylvania Railroad Collection, Hagley Museum and Library; Newark (Ohio) *Daily Advocate*, Aug. 3, 1911, p. 6.

19. Correspondence in: Porters—rates of pay, 1908-1915, file 001.124, Pennsylvania Railroad Collection, Hagley Museum and Library.

20. Porters—rates of pay, 1908-1915, file 011.124, Pennsylvania Railroad Collection, Hagley Museum and Library.

21. Blacks—employed as trainmen and porters, 1919-1925, General Manager, Southwestern Region, Pennsylvania Railroad Collection, Hagley Museum and Library. Pennsylvania Railroad historian Chris Baer points out that "in the period immediately after World War I, the economy went from hot inflation caused by the war, to sharp deflation and depression, and back to recovery in the space of a few years, thus making real wage comparisons difficult. The PRR imposed wage cuts across the board of about 20 percent in 1921, along with layoffs, and then increases in late 1922 after conditions improved. It would seem, however, that both the cut and restoration endured by 'colored trainmen' (porters) exceeded the norm, and the restoration came earlier, meaning that the factors cited were operating above the regular wage cycle." Chris Baer to author, Dec. 27, 2006.

22. Six brakemen porters to W. G. McAdoo, May 24, 1918, T. A. Keith to Walter D. Hines, June 16, 1919, Subject Classified File of the Division of Labor, RG14, United States Railroad Administration, National Archives. The requirement for SRR brakemen-porters to water locomotives lasted at least to the beginning of World War II. See "Agreement between Southern Railway Company . . . and Train Porters as represented by Association of Train Porters, Brakemen and Switchmen. Rules Revised as of January 9, 1942," in Railroad Union Agreements, Railroads, Discrimination, Legal Division Hearings, 1941-1946, FEPC, RG228, National Archives.

23. Spero and Harris, *The Black Worker*, p. 303; Arnesen, *Brotherhoods of Color*, pp. 75-77.

24. Gulf Coast Lines, rules and rates of pay for train porters, effective July 1, 1921; rates of pay and working conditions governing colored Brakemen, Jan. 1, 1925, agreement between the colored brakemen and the management of the Gulf Coast Lines effective Jan. 1, 1929, Box 20, Colored Trainmen of America Papers, Houston Public Library; Herbert R. Northrup, *Organized Labor and the Negro* (New York, 1944), p. 266n4.

25. Arnesen, *Brotherhoods of Color*, pp. 221-22.

26. *Negro Railway Labor News*, June–July 1948, p. 3; Northrup, *Organized Labor*, pp. 69-70.

27. *Negro Railway Labor News*, June–July 1948, p. 3; Arnesen, *Brotherhoods of Color*, pp. 221-26.

28. Folder 290, Employee Records, train porter Littleton Hughes, Jr., Richmond, Fredericksburg & Potomac Railroad Collection, Virginia Historical Society.

29. Arnesen, *Brotherhoods of Color*, pp. 239-40.

30. Clifton L. Taulbert, *When We Were Colored* (New York, 1995), p. 142.

31. Taulbert, *When We Were Colored*, p. 142.

32. "Berta, Berta," quoted in August Wilson, *The Piano Lesson* (New York, 1990), p. 40.

33. Raymond J. Baxter and Arthur G. Adams, *Railroad Ferries of the Hudson* (New York, 1999), pp. 200-201, 226-28.

34. *Reading Railroad Magazine*, July 1929, p. 27; May 1931, p. 27; March 1931, p. 25; *Reading-Jersey Central Magazine*, Oct. 1937, p. 19; April 1940, p. 29; Sept. 1938, p. 31; Nov. 1937, p. 9.

35. *Reading Railroad Magazine*, April 1926, p. 31; Aug. 1928, p. 13.

36. *Reading-Jersey Central Magazine*, Oct. 1937, p. 27; Dec. 1942, p. 21.

37. Thomas C. Fleming, "Cooking on the Southern Pacific," *Classic Trains*, Fall 2002, p. 41.

38. *Chesapeake and Ohio Employes Magazine*, Sept. 1916, pp. 25-26; *Chesapeake and Ohio and Hocking Valley Employes' Magazine*, Jan. 1924, p. 59; Aug. 1925, p. 39; http://schoonervirginia.org/virginias_history.php.

39. Michael Krieger, *Where Rails Meet the Sea* (New York, 1998), pp. 66–67.

40. *The Official Guide of the Railways*, Feb. 1901, p. 819.

41. Krieger, *Where Rails Meet the Sea*, pp. 91–93; *Central of Georgia Magazine*, Feb. 1942, p. 12.

42. "Mail by Rail: Not Always a Smooth Ride," *The American Postal Worker*, Sept.–Oct. 2005, p. 20; "The Post Office Department and Jim Crow," *The American Postal Worker*, Jan.–Feb. 2006, p. 18; *Crisis*, May 1915, p. 10; Frank R. Scheer to author, Feb. 19, 2007. Porters' income is reported in *Crisis*, June 1915, p. 62.

43. "Mail by Rail," p. 20; *Crisis*, July 1912, p. 116; March 1914, p. 221.

44. "The Post Office Department and Jim Crow," p. 18; Fred J. Romanski, "The 'Fast Mail': A History of the U.S. Railway Mail Service," *Prologue* 37 (Fall 2005): 19–20.

45. "Post Office Department and Jim Crow," pp. 18–19; National Alliance of Postal and Federal Employees web page: www.napfe.com.

46. Spero and Harris, *The Black Worker*, pp. 67–69; *Crisis*, Nov. 1913, p. 323; 10-GR-15, Railway Mail Service, Closed Cases, Region X, Regional Files, FEPC, RG228, National Archives.

47. Frank R. Scheer to author, Feb. 19, 2007.

CHAPTER 9. "NOT AT ALL PROPER FOR WOMEN"

1. James W. Holden, "Railroad Women," *Railroad Magazine*, April 1942, p. 77; Chester W. Gregory, *Women in Defense Work During World War II: An Analysis of the Labor Problem and Women's Rights* (New York, 1974), p. 131.

2. Deborah Gray White, *Ar'n't I a Woman? Female Slaves in the Plantation South*, rev. ed. (New York, 1999), pp. 5, 12, 15.

3. James H. Brewer, *The Confederate Negro: Virginia Craftsmen and Military Laborers, 1861–1865* (Durham, N.C., 1969), p. 86; John H. White, Jr., "Oh, To Be a Locomotive Engineer," *Railroad History* 190 (Spring–Summer 2004): 73.

4. Eric Arnesen, *Brotherhoods of Color: Black Railroad Workers and the Struggle for Equality* (Cambridge, Mass., 2001), p. 15; Allen W. Trelease, *The North Carolina Railroad, 1849–1871, and the Modernization of North Carolina* (Chapel Hill, 1991), p. 165.

5. Southern Railway Company, "The Honor Roll of those who have been in the service twenty-five years or more to March, 1916" (n.d., n.p.; in Marvin Black collection), pp. 23, 33, 38; Abstract of Rolls, North Carolina R.R. (Raleigh Sub-Division), North Western North Carolina, and State University R.R., as of September 1886; List of Employees of RF&PRR Co. 1885, Section 7: employees of Milford Hotel, Richmond, Fredericksburg & Potomac Railroad Collection, Virginia Historical Society.

6. Manager, Women's Service Section, to Georgia Baxter, Nov. 17, 1919, file 97-28-262, Record Group 14, U.S. Railroad Administration, National Archives. I wish to thank Jan Davidson for giving me this document.

7. Mark Colvin, *Penitentiaries, Reformatories, and Chain Gangs: Social Theory and the History of Punishment in Nineteenth-Century America* (New York, 1997), pp. 246–49. For a number of years, every Georgia convict, male and female, was leased out for railroad construction. Annual reports listed convicts of both sexes in a single list, and used male-gendered language to refer to all of them. *Report of the Principal Keeper of the Georgia Penitentiary, For the Year 1869* (Atlanta, 1870), pp. 6, 14–19; *Report of the Principal Keeper of the Georgia Penitentiary, for the year ending December 31, 1870* (Atlanta, 1871), pp. 6, 16–21; *Reports of the Principal Keeper of the Georgia Penitentiary, from the first day of April, 1872, to the 31st December, 1873* (Atlanta, 1873), pp. 4–5, 28–36.

8. *Biennial Report of the Principal Keeper of the Georgia Penitentiary from the 20th of October, 1880, to 20th of October, 1882* (Atlanta, 1882), pp. 1, 11, 51ff.

9. A rare exception: "The president of the Erie railroad has appointed the daughter of a colored steward on his road, George C. Burke, as stenographer in the Erie office at Jersey City." *Crisis*, July 1916, p. 117.

10. Maurine Weiner Greenwald, *Women, War, and Work: The Impact of World War I on Women Workers in the United States* (Westport, Conn., 1980), pp. 25–26, 87, 106–7, 116.

11. Information for the National Industrial Conference Board, Boston, Massachusetts, Regarding the Employment of Females, June 5, 1918, in Women—employment, 1918–1922, general files, Superintendent of Labor and Wage Bureau, Eastern Region, Pennsylvania Railroad Collection, Hagley Museum and Library; Greenwald, *Women, War, and Work*, pp. 92–93.

12. Arnesen, *Brotherhoods of Color*, p. 46; Division of Negro Economics, *The Negro at Work During the World War and During Reconstruction* (Washington, 1921), pp. 125–27; Inspections Sheets, Santa Fe Railroad, Kansas City freight house, Oct. 1917, Women's Service Section, U.S. Railroad Administration, National Archives; undated,

unsigned report on female labor, in Women—employment, 1918–1922, general files, Superintendent of Labor and Wage Bureau, Eastern Region, Pennsylvania Railroad Collection, Hagley Museum and Library; *Crisis*, Dec. 1917, p. 87; Jan. 1918, p. 142; Sept. 1918, p. 288.

13. "Used Women in Gangs," *The Right Way Magazine* [Central of Georgia] (April 1918): 18. Black women section hands were reported on the Baltimore & Ohio in St. Louis and East St. Louis, but it is unknown whether they did the full range of tasks normally assigned to men. *Crisis*, Sept. 1917, p. 260.

14. Arnesen, *Brotherhoods of Color*, p. 46; memorandum, G. M. Kittle, Federal Manager, USRA, October 2, 1918, file 600–56, USRA Subject Files, Mississippi Central Railroad Papers, University of Southern Mississippi; Greenwald, *Women, War, and Work*, p. 107.

15. Mary E. Jackson, "The Colored Woman in Industry, *Crisis*, Nov. 1918, p. 15.

16. *Baltimore and Ohio Magazine*, Sept. 1924, pp. 27–30; Kimberley L. Phillips, *AlabamaNorth: African-American Migrants, Community, and Working-Class Activism in Cleveland, 1915–45* (Urbana, Ill., 1999), p. 74.

17. Inspection sheets, Southern Railway, Jan.–Feb. 1920, Women's Service Section, U.S. Railroad Administration, National Archives; Illustrative Statement of Change in Rates Paid by the Pullman Co. To its car cleaners from June 1st 1913 through December 1932, folder 315, file 06/01/03, Pullman Collection, Newberry Library.

18. Based on compilations from inspection sheets nationwide, Women's Service Section, U.S. Railroad Administration, National Archives; Arnesen, *Brotherhoods of Color*, p. 46; Greenwald, *Women, War, and Work*, pp. 114–15; Phillips, *AlabamaNorth*, p. 74.

19. Inspection sheets, Morris & Essex Series, Delaware, Lackawanna & Western Railroad, May–June 1919, Women's Service Section, U.S. Railroad Administration, National Archives.

20. Inspection sheets, Washington Terminal, Oct. 1918, Women's Service Section, U.S. Railroad Administration, National Archives.

21. Jackson, "The Colored Woman," p. 12; *Crisis*, July 1917, p. 143; Nov. 1917, p. 86; Phillips, *AlabamaNorth*, pp. 72–73.

22. Theodore Kornweibel, Jr., *"Investigate Everything": Federal Efforts to Compel Black Loyalty during World War I* (Bloomington, Ind., 2002), chaps. 2–3.

23. Jacqueline Jones, *Labor of Love, Labor of Sorrow: Black Women, Work, and the Family from Slavery to the Present* (New York, 1985), p. 167; Phillips, *AlabamaNorth*, p. 72.

24. "Women Start Well in Railroad Work," *Santa Fe Magazine*, Aug. 1917, p. 69; "A Woman Section Gang at Work in Pennsylvania," *Santa Fe Magazine*, Dec. 1917, p. 55; Jackson, "The Colored Woman," p. 16; Inspection sheets, Eastern Series, October 1918, Illinois Series, Nov. 1918, Santa Fe Railroad, Women's Service Section, U.S. Railroad Administration, National Archives.

25. Greenwald, *Women, War, and Work*, pp. 107, 113.

26. Greenwald, *Women, War, and Work*, pp. 128–29, 134.

27. Inspection sheets, Cleveland Series 88, Women's Service Section, New York Central, U.S. Railroad Administration, National Archives; Statement Showing Number of Negro Employes by Occupations, Their Housing Conditions and Status in Community as of January 15, 1924, Employment of Blacks and Race Relations, 1920–1925, Personnel Department, General Office Files, box 818; Statement Showing Number of Negro Employes by Occupation, Their Housing Conditions and Status in Community, Oct. 5, 1925, in folder 1, Blacks—Employment of, 1923–1924, General Manager, Southwestern Region, box 760, Pennsylvania Railroad Collection, Hagley Museum and Library; Lorenzo J. Greene and Carter G. Woodson, *The Negro Wage Earner* (Washington, 1930), p. 268.

28. *Pullman News*, Jan. 1923, p. 291.

29. Employee service records, 1890–1969, Maids, file 06/02/03, Pullman Collection, Newberry Library; Melinda Chateauvert, *Marching Together: Women of the Brotherhood of Sleeping Car Porters* (Urbana, Ill., 1998), pp. 21–24, 28.

30. Number of Full Time Maids and Average Earnings, folder 511, box 19, file 06/01/04, Pullman Collection, Newberry Library; Chateauvert, *Marching Together*, pp. 42, 188–89.

31. Employee service records, 1890–1969, Maids, file 06/02/03, Pullman Collection, Newberry Library; *Pullman News*, Oct. 1943, p. 72.

32. Employee service records, 1890–1969, Maids, file 06/02/03, Pullman Collection, Newberry Library; *Southern Pacific Bulletin*, July 1928, p. 18; Chateauvert, *Marching Together*, p. 42.

33. "Instructions for Maids," April 15, 1925, Employee instruction books, folder 28, box 5, file 05/01/02, Pullman Collection, Newberry Library; Chateauvert, *Marching Together*, pp. 23–24, 83; *Pullman News*, Jan. 1923, p. 291.

34. Chateauvert, *Marching Together,* pp. 3, 15, 39, 60–61. See also Paula F. Pfeffer, "The Women Behind the Union: Halena Wilson, Rosina Tucker, and the Ladies' Auxiliary to the Brotherhood of Sleeping Car Porters," *Labor History* 36 (Fall 1995): 557–78.

35. *Pullman News,* Feb. 1929, pp. 330–32; April 1931, pp. 474–75; *Illinois Central Magazine,* Oct. 1927, pp. 40–41.

36. *Pullman News,* Feb. 1928, p. 330; April 1931, pp. 474–75; July 1946, pp. 5–6; Oct. 1953, pp. 2–7.

37. Photo 6-83, Series 1, AT&SF Collection, Kansas State Historical Society; Lesley Poling-Kempes, *The Harvey Girls: Women Who Opened the West* (New York, 1991), p. 40, asserts that black women were never true Harvey Girls.

38. "Negro Women in Transportation," *The Negro Traveler,* March 1945, p. 7; "Sandwich Wagons Meet Trains at Three Stations," *Illinois Central Magazine,* Dec. 1943, pp. 3–4.

39. Basic Wage Rates, Dec. 11, 1933, General Labor Files, folder 134, box 6, file 06/01/03, Average Monthly Wage Per Man, June 24, 1938, Laundry and Barbers, folder 400, box 15, file 06/01/04, Pullman Collection, Newberry Library; "Rail Workers' Pay 93% of 1929 Level," *New York Times,* Dec. 26, 1935.

40. *Southern Pacific Bulletin (Pacific Lines),* Nov. 1942, pp. 3–7.

41. *Central of Georgia Magazine,* May 1943, p. 2; *Illinois Central Magazine,* Feb. 1944, p. 4; "Railroad Women," *Railroad Magazine,* April 1942, p. 77.

42. Statements of numbers of black female employees, as of Aug. 15, 1943, May 15, 1944, June 15, 1945, Jan. 15, 1946, in file 100.08, Employment of Blacks, 1943–1945, Personnel Department, General Office Files, Pennsylvania Railroad Collection, Hagley Museum and Library; undated advertisement in Pennsylvania Railroad, Legal Division Hearings, 1941–1946, FEPC, RG228, National Archives.

43 Based on photographs in the *Reading Railroad Magazine,* 1941–45.

44. "Hire Women Section Hands," Zanesville (Ohio) *Signal,* Nov. 25, 1942, p. 2.

45. Patricia Cooper and Ruth Oldenziel, "'Cherished Classifications': Bathrooms and the Construction of Gender/Race on the Pennsylvania Railroad during World War II," *Feminist Studies* 25 (Spring 1999): 7–43.

46. *The People's Voice,* Sept. 2, 1944; Chateauvert, *Marching Together,* pp. 134–35.

47. C. H. Matthews to C. E. Musser, Nov. 30, 1943, in file 100.08, Employment of Blacks, 1943–1945, Personnel Department, General Office Files, Pennsylvania Railroad Collection, Hagley Museum and Library; "Mrs. Casey Jones Takes Over," *Click,* Oct. 1943, pp. 10–13.

48. "The Wartime Problem of Railroad 'Housekeeping,'" undated Association of American Railroads advertisement, Publicity materials, V.P. Public Affairs, Pennsylvania Railroad Company, Pennsylvania Historical and Museum Commission, Pennsylvania State Archives; *Southern Pacific Bulletin (Pacific Lines),* Dec. 1943, p. 10; C&NW seniority list, July 1, 1943, Employment, railroads, agreements, Legal Division Hearings, 1941–1946, FEPC, RG228, National Archives.

49. *Southern Pacific Bulletin (Pacific Lines),* Nov. 1942, p. 6.

50. Quoted in Arnesen, *Brotherhoods of Color,* p. 186.

51. *Southern Pacific Bulletin (Texas-Louisiana Lines),* April 1944, p. 9; "Negro Women in Transportation," *The Negro Traveler,* Nov. 1944; Arnesen, *Brotherhoods of Color,* p. 186.

52. "Women of the Shops," *Louisville & Nashville Employes' Magazine,* Oct. 1943, pp. 6–8; oral history of Rebecca Jane Smith, L&N Project, University of Louisville, p. 37.

53. Rebecca Jane Smith oral history, pp. 40–42.

54. Duane Galloway and Jim Wrinn, *Southern Railway's Spencer Shops: 1896-1996* (Lynchburg, Va., 1996), pp. 34–35, 75.

55. "Mrs. Casey Jones Takes Over," pp. 10–13; *Baltimore and Ohio Magazine,* May 1943, p. 34, June 1945, 34; D. E. R. to A. J. C., June 8, 1944, Pitcairn, Pennsylvania, file 350; L. E. G. to D. E. R. et al., Aug. 20, 1945, labor camps, file 350, Box 365, Superintendent Pittsburgh Division, Pennsylvania Railroad Collection, Pennsylvania State University; Cooper and Oldenziel, "Cherished Classifications," pp. 7–43.

56. Cooper and Oldenziel, "Cherished Classifications," pp. 7–43.

57. Chateauvert, *Marching Together,* pp. 125–28.

58. Chateauvert, *Marching Together,* pp. 128–30.

59. An exception was female laborers photographed mixing concrete on SP Extra Gang No. 1 at Houston. *Southern Pacific Bulletin (Texas and Louisiana Lines),* March 1946, p. 11.

60. Rebecca Jane Smith oral history, pp. 1–14.

61. Statement of Number of Colored Employes as of Feb. 14, 1953, in file 100.08, Employment of Blacks, 1945–1955, Personnel Department, General Office Files, Pennsylvania Railroad Collection, Hagley Museum and Library.

62. John F. Stover, *The Routledge Historical Atlas of the American Railroads* (New York, 1999), pp. 120–23.

63. File 70, Gulf, Mobile & Ohio Railroad, Casework: Employment Discrimination, Non-Partisan Voters League Collection, University of South Alabama.

64. U.S. Equal Employment Opportunity Commission, 2001 EEO-1 Aggregate Report, SIC 40: Railroad Transportation (www.eeoc.gov/stats/jobpat/2001/sic2/40.html).

65. For a vivid story of male prejudice against female railroaders (in this case, a white woman), see Linda Niemann, "The Hospital Yard," *Trains*, Jan. 2003, pp. 42–49.

CHAPTER 10. "NOBODY RIDE BUT DE CHOCOLATE TO DE BONE"

1. John H. White, Jr., *The American Railroad Passenger Car* (Baltimore, 1978), pp. 14–15; Louis Ruchames, "Jim Crow Railroads in Massachusetts," *American Quarterly* 8 (Spring 1956): 61–75.

2. White, *The American Railroad Passenger Car*, p. 463.

3. Alan Trelease, *The North Carolina Railroad, 1849–1871, and the Modernization of North Carolina* (Chapel Hill, 1991), pp. 56–57, 83; Frederick Law Olmstead, *The Cotton Kingdom: A Traveller's Observations on Cotton and Slavery in the American Slave States* (New York, 1953 [1861]), pp. 45, 126.

4. Leonard P. Curry, *The Free Black in Urban America, 1800–1850* (Chicago, 1981), p. 90; Ira Berlin, *Slaves Without Masters: The Free Negro in the Antebellum South* (New York, 1974), p. 323.

5. Quoted in Ulrich B. Phillips, *A History of Transportation of the Eastern Cotton Belt to 1860* (New York, 1968 [c. 1908]), p. 165.

6. Ruchames, "Jim Crow Railroads in Massachusetts," pp. 61–75; Leon F. Litwack, *North of Slavery: The Negro in the Free States, 1790–1860* (Chicago, 1961), pp. 106–8.

7. Ruchames, "Jim Crow Railroads in Massachusetts," pp. 61–75; Litwack, *North of Slavery*, pp. 106–8.

8. "Railroad Intelligence," *American Railroad Journal*, March 20, 1847, p. 186; Litwack, *North of Slavery*, pp. 108–9.

9. Trempealeau (Wis.) *Representative*, June 16, 1860, p. 2; Curry, *The Free Black*, p. 90.

10. Quoted in John F. Stover, *The Railroads of the South, 1865–1900* (Chapel Hill, 1955), p. 46n51.

11. Catherine A. Barnes, *Journey from Jim Crow: The Desegregation of Southern Transit* (New York, 1983), pp. 2–4.

12. Barnes, *Journey from Jim Crow*, pp. 2–4.

13. Barnes, *Journey from Jim Crow*, pp. 4–5; Edward L. Ayers, *The Promise of the New South: Life After Reconstruction* (New York, 1992), p. 137.

14. *Memphis Daily Appeal*, Dec. 25, 1884; James W. Davidson, *"They Say": Ida B. Wells and the Reconstruction of Race* (New York, 2007), pp. 64–75, 109.

15. Iowa City *Iowa State Press*, Dec. 14, 1901, p. 2.

16. Quoted in Ayers, *Promise of the New South*, p. 141.

17. William S. Osborn, "Curtains for Jim Crow: Law, Race, and the Texas Railroads," *Southwestern Historical Quarterly* 105 (Jan. 2002): 393–94.

18. *Ithaca* (N.Y.) *Daily News*, Feb. 24, 1903.

19. Ayers, *Promise of the New South*, pp. 138–40, newspaper quote p. 139; *Acts of Alabama, 1890–91* (Montgomery, 1891), pp. 412–13; Osborn, "Curtains for Jim Crow," p. 398.

20. John Oldfield, "State Politics, Railroads, and Civil Rights in South Carolina, 1883–89," *American Nineteenth Century History* 5 (Summer 2004): 86–88; Ayers, *Promise of the New South*, pp. 140–43.

21. *Report and Order of the Interstate Commerce Commission*, No. 1001. Nashville, Chattanooga & St. Louis Railway Company, decided June 24, 1907.

22. Ayers, *Promise of the New South*, pp. 137–46; Barnes, *Journey from Jim Crow*, pp. 5–10; *Plessy v. Ferguson* (163 U.S. 537). A good summary of state laws is R. H. Boyd, *The Separate or "Jim Crow" Car Laws or Legislative Enactments of the Fourteen Southern States* (Nashville, 1909).

23. Statesville (N.C.) *Landmark*, July 31, 1900, p. 2.

24. Frederick (Md.) *News*, July 11, 1900, p. 3.

25. Osborn, "Curtains for Jim Crow," p. 401.

26. Case file 2261, Chief Clerk's Office, Utilities Commission, North Carolina Archives.

27. Case file 3194, Chief Clerk's Office, Utilities Commission, North Carolina Archives.

28. Case file 3509, Chief Clerk's Office, Utilities Commission, North Carolina Archives.

29. Case file 4205, Chief Clerk's Office, Utilities Commission, North Carolina Archives; *Crisis*, Dec. 1915, pp. 87–98. Short-line railroads were also guilty of giving inferior treatment. See complaints against the Atlantic & Western

Railroad and the Carolina Railroad: Case files 3481, 5101, 4627, Chief Clerk's Office, Utilities Commission, North Carolina Archives.

30. Case file 4845, Chief Clerk's Office, Utilities Commission, North Carolina Archives.

31. Two years later, a real tragedy occurred on the Nashville, Chattanooga & St. Louis Railway in Tennessee when 13 blacks, riding in an antiquated Jim Crow car, were killed in a collision. *Crisis,* Feb. 1916, p. 168.

32. Complaint of E. A. Johnson et al. vs. The Seaboard Air Line and Southern Railroads [1895], case file 609, Chief Clerk's Office, Utilities Commission, North Carolina Archives.

33. Case file 609, Chief Clerk's Office, Utilities Commission, North Carolina Archives. A blueprint from 1909 shows the correction of the toilet problem: Raleigh, N.C., Union Passenger Station as rearranged, April 14, 1909, in Maps, Utilities Commission, North Carolina Archives.

34. Case files 3077, 4241, 5162, 5317, Chief Clerk's Office, Utilities Commission, North Carolina Archives. Railroads, including the SAL and N&W, did, on occasion, persuade the Commission to disregard the separate waiting room rule.

35. Salisbury station plan in *Ties Magazine,* Nov.–Dec. 1992, p. 13; Richmond plan in *Railway Age,* Feb. 14, 1919, p. 403, also, in greater detail, in folder 337, Sec. 12, Equipment/Construction, Richmond, Fredericksburg & Potomac Railroad Collection, Virginia Historical Society.

36. File 272, Office of Vice President & General Manager, Mississippi Central Railroad Collection, University of Southern Mississippi; Missouri–Kansas–Texas Lines standard combination stations, May 1925, Katy Railroad Historical Society; folder 30, Authority for Expenditure, Southern Railway Co. in Mississippi. Columbus & Greenville Railway Collection, Mississippi Archives; John A. Droege, *Passenger Terminals and Trains* (New York, 1916), p. 268 (Virginian Rwy.).

37. Frederick *News,* May 25, 1904, p. 4; June 14, 1904, p. 3.

38. Frederick *News,* July 14, 1904, p. 3; Aug. 10, 1904, p. 3.

39. "A Northern Railroad Meets Jim Crow," *National Railway Bulletin* 62 (1997): 22–23.

40. *Crisis,* Jan. 1914, p. 117; March 1914, p. 221.

41. *Crisis,* July 1913, p. 120; July 1914, p. 116; Feb. 1916, p. 197; George Shaw Cook to William Gibbs McAdoo, Oct. 28, 1918, file P19–3, Passengers: Protest Against Discrimination Against Colored Passengers, United States Railroad Administration, RG14, National Archives.

42. Statesville (N.C.) *Landmark,* June 23, 1899, p. 2.

43. Rev. H. J. Peeples to Hon. Charles H. Markham, July 30, 1912, File 4931 (Negro Complaints), Executive Correspondence Files, Executive Department, Central of Georgia Railway Collection, Georgia Historical Society.

44. J. C. Haile to W. A. Winburn, Aug. 19, 1912, T. Moise to Winburn, Nov. 15, 1912, File 4931, Central of Georgia Railway Collection, Georgia Historical Society.

45. Theodore H. Price to B. L. Winchell, Sept. 13, 1918, File 4931, Central of Georgia Railway Collection, Georgia Historical Society; memorandum, McAdoo to Walter D. Hines, Oct. 25, 1918, P19–3, USRA, RG14, National Archives. Hines took over leadership of the USRA after the Armistice and continued McAdoo's policy, stressing that black passengers should be "given the consideration [in passenger coach and station facilities] to which they are justly entitled." Hines to Regional Directors, Sept. 15, 1919, P19–3, USRA, RG14, National Archives.

46. W. A. Winburn to Winchell, Oct. 7, 1918, File 4931, Central of Georgia Railway Collection, Georgia Historical Society.

47. See protest letter, M. Griffin and others to William Gibbs McAdoo, Nov. 24, 1918, File 4931, Central of Georgia Railway Collection, Georgia Historical Society.

48. On trains southbound out of Washington during the war, Jim Crow cracked but did not disappear. When their cars filled, whites took seats in blacks' coaches, and vice versa. But these were "accidental happenings," not policy changes. *New York Evening Post,* quoted in Bridgeport (Conn.) *Telegram,* May 2, 1918, p. 7.

49. See following complaints: A. A. Burns to McAdoo, Sept. 24, 1918, unsigned to McAdoo, Oct. 19, 1918, File 4931, Central of Georgia Railway Collection, Georgia Historical Society.

50. Benjamin J. Davis to McAdoo, Nov. 30, 1918, File 4931, Central of Georgia Railway Collection, Georgia Historical Society.

51. Winburn to A. R. Lawton, Jan. 24, 1919, H. D. Pollard to Winburn, Jan. 28, 1919, Winburn to E. H. Lamb, May 24, 1919, Winchell to Winburn, Sept. 19, 1919, F. J. Robinson to Winburn, Sept. 22, 1919, Winburn to Winchell, Sept. 24, 1919, File 4931, Central of Georgia Railway Collection, Georgia Historical Society.

52. See, for example, J. L. Butler to Walter D. Hines, Oct. 3, 1919, File 4931, Central of Georgia Railway Collection, Georgia Historical Society.

53. H. D. Pollard to Superintendents, Oct. 13, 1919, R. W. Brimmer to M. B. Smith, Oct. 14, 1919, File 4931, Central of Georgia Railway Collection, Georgia Historical Society.

54. W. A. Winburn to E. H. Lamb, Oct. 21, 1919, Statement of L. F. Glenn, white porter on train no. 2 of Sept. 14, 1919, File 4931, Central of Georgia Railway Collection, Georgia Historical Society.

55. Cyrus Campfield to L. A. Downs, Jan. 17, Jan. 26, 1925, Downs to Campfield, Jan. 19, 1925, W. H. Wright to Campfield, Jan. 21, Jan. 23, 1925, *Savannah Journal*, Jan. 31, 1925, File 4931, Central of Georgia Railway Collection, Georgia Historical Society.

56. President to Rev. A. C. Danforth, March 23, 1927, File 4931, Central of Georgia Railway Collection, Georgia Historical Society.

57. Interview, porter E. Davis, Dec. 30, 1975, aboard Southern Railway's *Southern Crescent*; Osborn, "Curtains for Jim Crow," p. 398.

58. T. M. Campbell to L. A. Downs, Oct. 6, 1925, Downs to Campbell, Oct. 8, 1925, File 4931, Central of Georgia Railway Collection, Georgia Historical Society.

59. H. R. Butler to President, Feb. 4, 1927, President to Butler, Feb. 7, 1927, File 4931, Central of Georgia Railway Collection, Georgia Historical Society.

60. Commission on Negro Legislation to Corporation Commission of North Carolina, Dec. 14, 1920, and rest of file 5605, Utilities Commission, Chief Clerk's Office, North Carolina State Archives.

61. T. M. Curry to A. T. Stovall, Feb. 9, Stovall to Curry, Feb. 12, and J. H. Rigby to Stovall, Feb. 23, 1929, file C83:48, correspondence, Office of President, Columbus & Greenville Railway Company, Mississippi Archives.

62. Charles W. Washington to A. E. Clift, Jan. 13, 1930, Clift to Washington, Jan. 14, 1930, Clift to E. I. Robinson, May 13, 1930, File 4931, Central of Georgia Railway Collection, Georgia Historical Society.

63. Barnes, *Journey from Jim Crow*, pp. 1–2.

64. Quoted in Athens (Ala.) *Limestone Democrat*, May 8, 1941, p. 7.

65. Obituary, Irene Morgan Kirkaldy, *San Diego Union-Tribune*, Aug. 19, 2007, p. H8; Bayard Rustin, *Down the Line: The Collected Writings of Bayard Rustin* (Chicago, 1971), pp. 14–25.

66. For representative comment and analysis of the *Henderson* decision, see Sheboygan (Wis.) *Press*, June 5, 1950, p. 12; Florence (S.C.) *Morning News*, June 7, 1950, pp. 1, 4; Oakland (Calif.) *Tribune*, June 6, 1950, p. 6; Dothan (Ala.) *Eagle*, June 7, 1950, p. 4; "Negro Charges Southern Rwy. Still Discriminates in Diner," *New York Post*, Dec. 17, 1950.

67. Osborn, "Curtains for Jim Crow," pp. 413–17.

68. Osborn, "Curtains for Jim Crow," pp. 395, 404–21.

69. Wisconsin Rapids (Wis.) *Daily Tribune*, June 7, 1944, p. 3.

70. "How a Negro Travels Into the Southland," *PM*, March 7, 1948; W. H. Jernagin, Fraternal Council of Negro Churches in America, to W. W. Clement, Oct. 20, 1944, V.P. Operations, file 011.11, Employment, Blacks, 1944–53, Pennsylvania Railroad Collection, Hagley Museum and Library. The PRR maintained similar practices on the *Southland* and *South Wind* from Chicago to Miami, handing them off to the L&N at, respectively, Cincinnati and Louisville.

71. Monessen (Pa.) *Daily Independent*, Oct. 20, 1949, p. 2; Pittsfield (Mass.) *Berkshire Evening Eagle*, Oct. 21, 1949, p. 17.

72. Herman H. Long, "Segregation in Interstate Railway Coach Travel," A field research project of the Race Relations Department, American Missionary Association, Fisk University, 1952, pp. 81–86.

73. Joint Memorandum, American Jewish Committee, Anti Defamation League of B'nai B'rith, from Frances Levenson and Sol Rabkin, June 22, 1951, author's collection.

74. "SP Railroad Sued by Victims of Jimcrow," *Daily Worker*, June 16, 1954.

75. E. E. Schlottman to Mr. Davis, April 30, 1947, file I-5-49, Illinois Central Railroad Papers, University of Southern Mississippi Library.

76. Long, "Segregation," pp. 17–35, 73.

77. *The Official Guide of the Railways*, June 1950, p. 543; Long, "Segregation," pp. 42–46.

78. Long, "Segregation," pp. 37–41; Leon R. Harris, "The Railroads are Losing Negro Patronage," *Railway Progress*, Nov. 1950, pp. 21–22.

79. Long, "Segregation," pp. 57–67, quote p. 60.

80. A. R. Lawton to T. J. Stewart, July 13, 1950, File 4931, Central of Georgia Railway Collection, Georgia Historical Society.

81. [unsigned] to A. W. Benkert, June 20, 1950; car diagrams; both in Passenger Equipment files, Engineering Department, Central of Georgia Railway Collection, Georgia Historical Society.

82. C. L. Harper and R. E. Thomas, Jr., to M. P. Callaway, March 9, 1951, R. R. Cummins to Callaway, March 19, 1951, Callaway to Harper and Thomas, April 13, 1951, File 4931, Central of Georgia Railway Collection, Georgia Historical Society.

83. Edward McGlockton to J. Monroe Johnson, Jan. 5, Feb. 26, 1951, M. P. Callaway to Johnson, Jan. 31, 1951, File 4931, Central of Georgia Railway Collection, Georgia Historical Society.

84. J. M. Johnson to E. McGlockton, March 2, 1951, W. P. Bartel to M. P. Callaway, April 9, 1951, Callaway to Bartel, May 7, 1951, File 4931, Central of Georgia Railway Collection, Georgia Historical Society.

85. A. R. Lawton to E. F. Bidez, May 24, 1951, File 4931, Central of Georgia Railway Collection, Georgia Historical Society.

86. A. R. Lawton to M. P. Callaway, Nov. 12, 1952, File 4931, Central of Georgia Railway Collection, Georgia Historical Society.

87. Passenger Traffic Department circulars no. S-573, 587, "Instructions Regarding Passenger Train Accommodations for Different Races," Nov. 20, 1952, File 4931, Central of Georgia Railway Collection, Georgia Historical Society.

88. Passenger Traffic Department circulars no. S-573, 587, "Instructions Regarding Passenger Train Accommodations for Different Races," Nov. 20, 1952, File 4931, Central of Georgia Railway Collection, Georgia Historical Society.

89. E. McGlockton to J. M. Johnson, Jan. 7, 1953, File 4931, Central of Georgia Railway Collection, Georgia Historical Society.

90. E. McGlockton to Hon. Adam Clayton Powell, Jr., July 27, 1953; McGlockton to J. M. Johnson, Oct. 12, 1953, File 4931, Central of Georgia Railway Collection, Georgia Historical Society.

91. President, Central of Georgia Railway, to J. M. Johnson, Oct. 22, 1953, W. E. Dillard to B. J. Tarbutton, Nov. 6, 1953, File 4931, Central of Georgia Railway Collection, Georgia Historical Society.

92. Barnes, *Journey from Jim Crow*, pp. 86–99.

93. Barnes, *Journey from Jim Crow*, pp. 103–4.

94. Barnes, *Journey from Jim Crow*, pp. 120–22, 129–30. It is difficult to tell whether continued segregation was authorized by the railroads, or was the personal resistance of stubborn white conductors. Clearly, some trainmen attempted to maintain a Jim Crow car, but could no longer physically prevent blacks from entering other cars. See, for example, folders 6A–6C, L&N RR, 1956–63, Casework: Discrimination in Public Accommodations, Supplement, Non-Partisan Voters League Collection, University of South Alabama.

95. Southern; L&N; IC; ACL; SAL; SP; CRI&P; C of G; C&O; N&W; MoPac; St. Louis-San Francisco; Kansas City Southern; Louisiana & Arkansas; Florida East Coast; Western of Alabama; Nashville, Chattanooga & St. Louis; and Gulf, Mobile & Ohio; Barnes, *Journey from Jim Crow*, p. 265n3.

96. Barnes, *Journey from Jim Crow*, pp. 177–78, 182, 265n3; folder 6A–6C, L&N RR, Non-Partisan Voters League Collection, University of South Alabama; Clayborne Carson, *In Struggle: SNCC and the Black Awakening of the 1960s* (Cambridge, Mass., 1981), pp. 37, 59.

97. Commonwealth of Virginia, Department of the State Corporation Commission, *Constitutional Provisions, Statutes and Public Regulations Governing Railroads and Other Common Carriers in the State of Virginia, Revised to July 1, 1966* (Charlottesville, Va., 1966).

98. *Washington Post*, Sept. 12, 1906, p. 4; Gettysburg (Pa.) *Star and Sentinel*, Dec. 3, 1902, p. 1; Holland (Mich.) *Evening Sentinel*, Jan. 29, 1949, p. 5.

99. Douglas Wornom to author, Jan. 2, 1998.

100. Quoted in John A. Lomax, "Self Pity in Negro Folk Songs," *The Nation*, Aug. 9, 1917, p. 144.

CHAPTER 11. "LITTLE BLACK TRAIN A-COMIN'"

1. Harold Courlander, *Negro Folk Music, U.S.A.* (New York, 1963), p. 72.

2. Norm Cohen, *Long Steel Rail: The Railroad in American Folksong* (Urbana, Ill, 1981), pp. 619–22.

3. Cohen, *Long Steel Rail*, pp. 601–2.

4. Dorothy Scarborough, *On the Trail of Negro Folk-Songs* (Hatboro, Pa., 1963), pp. 253–54.

5. Courlander, *Negro Folk Music*, p. 41.

6. E. A. McIlhenny, *Befo' De War Spirituals* (Boston, 1933), pp. 79–80.

7. Scarborough, *On the Trail*, p. 255.

8. E. C. Perrow, "Songs and Rhymes from the South," *Journal of American Folklore* 26 (April–June 1913): 162.

9. Cohen, *Long Steel Rail*, pp. 621–22.

10. Mary Allen Grissom, *The Negro Sings a New Heaven* (Chapel Hill, 1930), pp. 48–49.
11. Grissom, *The Negro Sings*, pp. 82–83.
12. Scarborough, *On the Trail*, pp. 257–58.
13. Cohen, *Long Steel Rail*, pp. 619–20.
14. Cohen, *Long Steel Rail*, pp. 629–30.
15. Folkways Records FG3586 (1956).
16. Vocalion Records 1098 (1927), advertisement reprinted in Cohen, *Long Steel Rail*, p. 603.
17. Columbia Records 14145-D (1926).
18. Cohen, *Long Steel Rail*, p. 645.
19. Quoted in Courlander, *Negro Folk Music*, pp. 81–82.
20. Courlander, *Negro Folk Music*, pp. 90–91.
21. Courlander, *Negro Folk Music*, pp. 95–96.
22. Barry Dornfeld and Maggie Holtzberg-Call, *Gandy Dancers*, Cinema Guild, Inc., 1994; *The Pennsy*, Nov. 1957, p. 17.
23. Courlander, *Negro Folk Music*, pp. 96–97.
24. *Gandy Dancers.*
25. *Gandy Dancers.*
26. *Gandy Dancers.*
27. *Gandy Dancers.*
28. Paramount Records 12478 (1927), transcribed in Cohen, *Long Steel Rail*, p. 646.
29. Paramount Records 12478 (1927), transcribed in Cohen, *Long Steel Rail*, p. 647.
30. *Gandy Dancers.*
31. Scarborough, *On the Trail*, p. 219.
32. Paul Oliver, *Blues Fell this Morning: Meaning in the Blues* (New York, 1990), pp. 25–26.
33. Scott R. Nelson, "Who Was John Henry?" *Labor: Studies in Working-Class History of the Americas* 2 (2005): 53–79. For a complete discussion, see Scott R. Nelson, *Steel Drivin' Man: John Henry, the Untold Story of an American Legend* (New York, 2006). The C&O *Railroad* went into receivership in 1875 and reorganized in 1878 as the C&O *Railway*.
34. Cohen, *Long Steel Rail*, pp. 70–72.
35. http://www.ibiblio.org/john_henry/prison.html.
36. Cohen, *Long Steel Rail*, pp. 124–26.
37. Carl Sandburg, *American Songbag* (New York, 1955), p. 384.
38. Cohen, *Long Steel Rail*, p. 134.
39. Columbia Records 14095-D (1925).
40. Cohen, *Long Steel Rail*, pp. 441–42; Max Haymes, "'This Cat's Got the Yellow Dog Blues': Origins of the Term Yellow Dog," http://www.earlyblues.com/Yellow%20Dog.htm.
41. Columbia Records 14000-D (1923).
42. Okeh Records 8345 (1926).
43. Columbia Records 14079-D (1925).
44. Paramount Records 12262 (1925).
45. Ada Brown's version: Vocalion Records 1009 (1926).
46. Decca Records 7019 (1934).
47. Paramount Records 12697 (1928).
48. Hazel V. Carby, "'It Just Be's Dat Way Sometime': The Sexual Politics of Women's Blues," *Radical America* 20 (1986): 15–16.
49. Columbia Records 14041-D (1924).
50. Columbia Records 14196-D (1927).
51. "'Katy's At the Station, Santa Fe Is In the Yard': On the Rail Trail of Bessie Tucker—Queen of the Texas Moaners," www.earlyblues.com.
52. Okeh Records 06410 (1941).
53. "Berta, Berta," quoted in August Wilson, *The Piano Lesson* (New York, 1990), p. 40.
54. Columbia Records 14053-D (1924).
55. Brunswick Records 7051 (1928).
56. Paramount Records 12558 (1927).

57. Cohen, *Long Steel Rail*, p. 437.
58. Okeh Records 8863 (1931).
59. Bluebird Records B-5916 (1935).
60. Flair Records 1057 (1954).
61. Columbia Records 14145 (1929).
62. Paramount Records 12877 (1929).
63. Bluebird Records B-7315 (1937).
64. Chess Records 1469 (1962).
65. Victor Records 23333 (1932).
66. "Mean Old Frisco Blues," RCA Bluebird Records 34-0704 (1942).
67. RPM Records 398 (1949).
68. Columbia Records 14400-D (1929).
69. Victor Records 20-2733 (1947).
70. Paramount Records 12347 (1926).
71. Decca Records 7307 (1937).
72. A.R.C. 7-05-81 (1936); reissue Vocalion 03519 (1936).
73. Checker Records 1043 (1963).
74. Folkways Records FS2326 (1957).
75. RCA Bluebird Records B-5998 (1935).
76. Vocalion Records 02568 (1933).
77. Decca Records 7558 (1938).
78. Paramount Records 13065 (1931).
79. Vee Jay Records 1071 (1959).
80. Vocalion Records 1700 (1932).
81. Decca Records 7211 (1936).
82. Victor Records 21279 (1928).
83. Paramount Records 13129 (1932).
84. Decca Records 7491 (1938).
85. Vocalion Records 02651 (1934).
86. Vocalion Records 04618 (1938).
87. Paramount Records 12325 (1925).
88. Columbia Records 14632 (1931).
89. Crown Records 5188 (1961).
90. "We Want Some Pussy," recorded 1986; reissue Little Joe Records.
91. Elektra Records 301/2 (1962).
92. Biograph Records BLP12013 (1969).
93. Cohen, *Long Steel Rail*, pp. 472–74.
94. Joel Dinerstein, *Swinging the Machine: Modernity, Technology, and African American Culture between the World Wars* (Amherst, Mass., 2003), p. 74.
95. Dinerstein, *Swinging the Machine*, pp. 77–79.
96. Dinerstein, *Swinging the Machine*, pp. 69–71.
97. Decca Records 23610 (1946). I wish to thank Neill Herring for letting me read his unpublished "Railroads on Record" with its artful discussion of this song.
98. United Records 110 (1952).
99. Cavalier Records 5006 (1955).
100. Chess Records 1620 (1956).
101. Parker's recording: Sun Records 192 (1953).
102. Neill Herring to author, April 30, 2007.
103. Chess 1615 (1955). I am indebted to Neill Herring for calling this song to my attention.
104. Chess 1714 (1960).
105. Columbia Records CK 36430 (1980).
106. ABC-Paramount Records 10622 (1965).
107. Buddah Records 383 (1973).
108. Bluebird Records B-7126 (1937).

1. Herbert R. Northrup, *Organized Labor and the Negro* (New York, 1944), pp. 78–81; Howard W. Risher, Jr., *The Negro in the Railroad Industry* (Philadelphia, 1971), pp. 45–46; Charles E. Hall, *Negroes in the United States, 1920–1930* (Washington, 1935), tables 23, 24. Compiling data from both tables, 144,244 African Americans were listed as holding railroad occupations, including over 25,000 sleeping-car and coach porters. The tables also include figures for cooks and waiters, but do not distinguish which ones worked on railroad dining cars, so estimates must be hazarded. On long-distance trains, the number of dining-car workers usually exceeded the number of porters, so it is likely that the railroads employed at least 20,000 of the former. Thus probably 165,000 blacks made their living on railroads in 1930, near the peak of overall railroad employment.

2. Horace R. Cayton and George S. Mitchell, *Black Workers and the New Unions* (Chapel Hill, 1939), pp. 284–86.

3. *Classic Trains*, Winter 2004, pp. 64–67; Duane Galloway and Jim Wrinn, *Southern Railway's Spencer Shops, 1896–1966* (Lynchburg, Va., 1996), pp. 74–75.

4. R. C. Goebel to J. W. Devins, Feb. 1, 1945, Authorization for Expenditure, March 29, 1945, Minneapolis & St. Louis Railway, author's collection, copies courtesy of Gene Green, Chicago & North Western Historical Society.

5. *Louisville & Nashville Employes' Magazine*, Aug. 1945, pp. 4–9; Galloway and Wrinn, *Southern Railways' Spencer Shops*, p. 75.

6. Cayton and Mitchell, *Black Workers*, pp. 285–86; *Louisville & Nashville Employes' Magazine*, Feb. 1929, several photos.

7. *Louisville & Nashville Employes' Magazine*, April 1929, p. 91; April 1948, p. 58.

8. *Constitution of the United Brotherhood of Maintenance-of-Way Employes and Railway Shop Laborers* (Detroit, 1918), pp. 20–21; Sterling D. Spero and Abram L. Harris, *The Black Worker* (New York, 1931), pp. 57–58; Joseph A. McCartin, *Labor's Great War: The Struggle for Industrial Democracy and the Origins of Modern American Labor Relations, 1912–1921* (Chapel Hill, 1997), p. 116.

9. Rules, rev. May 1, 1925, Chicago & Alton Railroad, folder B5-4-1-27.1, Gulf, Mobile & Ohio Collection, St. Louis Mercantile Library; William H. Harris, *The Harder We Run: Black Workers Since the Civil War* (New York, 1982), p. vii.

10. Colin J. Davis, *Power at Odds: The 1922 National Railroad Shopmen's Strike* (Urbana, Ill., 1997), pp. 27–30; Cayton and Mitchell, *Black Workers*, pp. 291, 293; Spero and Harris, *The Black Worker*, p. 308.

11. Davis, *Power at Odds*, pp. 68–69, 118–19; Cayton and Mitchell, *Black Workers*, pp. 290–91; Spero and Harris, *The Black Worker*, p. 308.

12. Spero and Harris, *The Black Worker*, pp. 308–9.

13. *Louisville & Nashville Employes' Magazine*, April 1931, p. 26.

14. *Louisville & Nashville Employes' Magazine*, March 1931, p. 30; July 1941, p. 30; May 1926, p. 45; Aug. 1935, p. 12.

15. Cayton and Mitchell, *Black Workers*, p. 284.

16. Statistics compiled from the *Norfolk and Western Magazine*'s monthly "News from Our Colored Employees" column, 1931–34.

17. *Louisville & Nashville Employes' Magazine*, Aug. 1945, pp. 4–9.

18. *Illinois Central Magazine*, Sept. 1919, p. 62.

19. *Central of Georgia Magazine*, Aug. 1936, p. 6.

20. *Norfolk and Western Magazine*, Nov. 1924, p. 41.

21. *Southern News Bulletin*, Oct. 1928, p. 5.

22. Kimberley L. Phillips, *AlabamaNorth: African-American Migrants, Community, and Working-Class Activism in Cleveland, 1915–45* (Urbana, Ill., 1999), p. 64; Division of Negro Economics, U.S. Department of Labor, *Negro Migration in 1916–17* (Washington, 1919), p. 109; Division of Negro Economics, U.S. Department of Labor, *The Negro at Work During the World War and During Reconstruction* (Washington, 1921), p. 117; Lorenzo J. Greene and Carter G. Woodson, *The Negro Wage Earner* (Washington, 1930), pp. 266–69; Special Agent L. D. Strickland to Bureau of Investigation headquarters, Oct. 28, 30, 1916, Special Agent Wm. B. Matthews to BI HQ, Nov. 1, 1916, Miscellaneous file 10015, RG65, Federal Bureau of Investigation, National Archives; Fort Wayne (Ind.) *Daily News*, March 14, 1917, p. 7; May 23, 1917, p. 5.

23. R. B. White, Supt., B&O System, Philadelphia, to Lt. D. C. Elphinstone, Aug. 8, 1918, file 10218-223-2, RG165, Military Intelligence Division, National Archives.

24. *Santa Fe Magazine*, Nov. 15, 1915, p. 96; Letter Authority Number CD-247 [to move car body], Oct. 5, 1923, Colorado Division, Union Pacific Railroad, Union Pacific Museum, copy furnished to author by K. Forrest.

25. Pennsylvania Railroad, *Seventy-Eighth Annual Report for the year 1924*, p. 59; Statement showing number of Negro employes by occupations, their housing conditions and status in community as of January 16, 1924, Box 818, Personnel Dept., General Office Files, Pennsylvania Railroad Collection, Hagley Museum and Library. Railroad historian Dan Cupper points out that "the Pennsylvania Railroad's hiring and promotion practices were complex, rigid, and ritualized." In addition to ethnicity, "religion played a major factor. Advancement went to Presbyterians and Episcopalians, and even more so to those who also belonged to Masonic organizations. Those who generally did not climb far or fast—or at all—were Jews and Baptists. On other railroads, the situation as regards religion was flipped, though, of course, never in favor of blacks. The New York Central, Central of New Jersey, and Milwaukee Road were known as Catholic railroads, on which promotion and advancement went to adherents of that faith." Cupper to author, Feb. 2, 2007.

26. Statement showing number of Negro employes by occupations . . . as of January 16, 1924, Pennsylvania Railroad Collection, Hagley Museum and Library.

27. *Santa Fe Magazine*, July 1916, p. 62.

28. Risher, *Negro in the Railroad Industry*, p. 46; Northrup, *Organized Labor*, p. 79; McCartin, *Labor's Great War*, p. 116.

29. Cayton and Mitchell, *Black Workers*, pp. 286–91, 295.

30. Cayton and Mitchell, *Black Workers*, pp. 286–89.

31. "Statement of Number of Negro Employes in All Departments of the Pennsylvania Railroad System as of July 15, 1943," file 100.08, Employment of Blacks, 1945–1955, Personnel Department, General Office Files, Pennsylvania Railroad Collection, Hagley Museum and Library; "Creating a Racial Issue Where None Now Exists," wartime advertising scrapbooks, 1942–1945, vol. 2, 1943—newspaper advertising, 1943, MG 286, Pennsylvania Railroad Collection, Pennsylvania Historical and Museum Commission, State Archives; "Summary, Findings and Directions in re Pennsylvania Railroad Company, the Brotherhood of Railway Shop Crafts of America, the Brotherhood of Railroad Trainmen, and the Brotherhood of Railway and Steamship Clerks, Freight Handlers, Express and Station Employees," Railroad Cases, Legal Division Hearings, 1941–1946, FEPC, RG228, National Archives.

32. "Summary, Findings and Directions in re Union Pacific Railroad Company, International Brotherhood of Firemen and Oilers and International Brotherhood of Boilermakers, Iron Ship Builders and Helpers [1943], Union Pacific, Jesse J. Gonzalez to Franklin D. Roosevelt, March 12, 1943 [2 letters], Shopworkers of Mexican descent—upgrading, UPRR, railroads, discrimination, employment, Legal Division Hearings, 1941–1946, FEPC, RG228, National Archives.

33. "Summary, Findings and Directions in re Chesapeake and Ohio Railway Company, International Association of Machinists, International Brotherhood of Boilermakers, Iron Ship Builders and Helpers of America," 1943, Legal Division Hearings, 1941–1946, FEPC, RG228, National Archives.

34. "Summary, Findings and Directives in re Baltimore and Ohio Chicago Terminal Railroad Company and the Brotherhood of Railway Carmen of America," 1943, Legal Division Hearings, 1941–1946, FEPC, RG228, National Archives.

35. "Summary, Findings and Directives in re New York Central Railroad Company, Brotherhood of Railroad Trainmen, Brotherhood of Railway Carmen of America, International Association of Machinists, International Brotherhood of Boilermakers, Iron Ship Builders and Helpers of America," 1943, NYC Div. Gen. Car Foreman G. A. Miller to F. S. Haylett, Local Chrm., Lily of the Valley Lodge No. 309, Brotherhood Railway Carmen of America, Aug. 11, 1942, Agreements, Railroad Employment, Legal Division Hearings, 1941–1946, FEPC, RG228, National Archives.

36. "History of the Railroad Cases referred to President Roosevelt by the Committee on Fair Employment Practice on or about December 27, 1943," Malcolm Ross to Samuel I. Rosenman, July 24, 1945, Stacy Committee, Richard W. Smith to Ross, Dec. 21, 1943, Miscellaneous, "Chicago and North Western Railway Company Motive Power and Car Departments Seniority Roster of Employees Coming Within the Scope of Federated Crafts' Agreement," July 1, 1943, Agreements, Railroads, Legal Division Hearings, 1941–1946, FEPC, RG228, National Archives.

37. "History of the Railroad Cases referred to President Roosevelt by the Committee on Fair Employment Practice on or about December 27, 1943," from Malcolm Ross to Samuel I. Rosenman, July 24, 1945, Stacy Committee, Legal Division Hearings, 1941–1946, FEPC, RG228, National Archives.

38. *Illinois Central Magazine*, March 1934, p. 13; *Chesapeake and Ohio and Hocking Valley Employes' Magazine*, Jan. 1928, p. 21.

39. James H. Ducker, *Men of the Steel Rails: Workers on the Atchison, Topeka & Santa Fe Railroad, 1869–1900* (Lincoln, Neb., 1983), p. 44; *Illinois Central Magazine*, July 1928, p. 8; July 1946, p. 47.

40. Statement showing number of Negro employes by occupations . . . as of January 16, 1924, Pennsylvania Railroad Collection, Hagley Museum and Library.
41. *Louisville & Nashville Employes' Magazine,* Sept. 1949, p. 18; Aug. 1928, p. 82; Feb. 1928, p. 85.
42. *Illinois Central Magazine,* April–May 1948, p. 42; July 1949, p. 3; Feb. 1946, p. 44; *Louisville & Nashville Employes' Magazine,* Oct. 1933, p. 9; Feb. 1935, p. 17.
43. Statement showing number of Negro employes by occupations . . . as of January 16, 1924, Pennsylvania Railroad Collection, Hagley Museum and Library.
44. Northrup, *Organized Labor,* pp. 82–85; Risher, *Negro in the Railroad Industry,* pp. 50–52.
45. Office of Emergency Management memorandum, Olcott R. Abbott to files, Sept. 18, 1944, file 5-BR-115, Cleveland, NYC RR, memorandum, Elmer W. Henderson to Clarence M. Mitchell, March 7, 1945, file 6-BR-671, Big Four Lines (NYC), Headquarters Records, Legal Division, Anderson H. Thomas to Malcolm S. McLean, Dec. 22, 1942, Union Pacific, Misc., Legal Division Hearings, 1941–1946, FEPC, RG228, National Archives.
46. *J. D. Conley et al. v. Pat J. Gibson,* 355 U.S. 41, 78 S. Ct. 99.
47. Mark V. Wetherington, "The Savannah Negro Laborers' Strike of 1891," in *Southern Workers and Their Unions, 1880-1975: Selected Papers, The Second Southern Labor History Conference, 1978,* ed. Merl E. Reed et al. (Westport, Conn., 1981), pp. 4–16.
48. Eric Arnesen, "Biracial Waterfront Unionism in the Age of Segregation," in *Waterfront Workers: New Perspectives on Race and Class ,* ed. Calvin Winslow (Urbana, Ill., 1998), pp. 30–35, 38; Eric Arnesen, *Waterfront Workers of New Orleans: Race, Class, and Politics, 1863-1923* (New York, 1991), pp. 40, 99–103.
49. *Norfolk and Western Magazine,* May 1934, p. 166.
50. *Louisville & Nashville Employes' Magazine,* Nov. 1941, pp. 4–7.
51. *Baltimore and Ohio Magazine,* Feb. 1922, p. 31.
52. *Baltimore and Ohio Magazine,* Feb. 1922, p. 31.
53. *Louisville & Nashville Employes' Magazine,* July 1926, p. 22.
54. *Baltimore and Ohio Magazine,* Jan. 1924, p. 61.
55. *Louisville & Nashville Employes' Magazine,* April 1938, p. 18.
56. Statement showing number of Negro employes by occupations . . . as of January 16, 1924, Pennsylvania Railroad Collection, Hagley Museum and Library.
57. *Reading Railroad Magazine,* Jan. 1928, p. 20.
58. *The Right Way Magazine,* June 1928, p. 25; June 1920, p. 18.
59. *The Pennsy,* Jan.–Feb. 1958, p. 13.
60. *The Pennsy,* Nov. 1955, p. 24.
61. *Louisville & Nashville Employes' Magazine,* Dec. 1928, p. 67.
62. *North Western Newsliner,* Sept. 1954, p. 19.

CHAPTER 13. "MARRY A RAILROAD MAN"
1. U.S. Department of Commerce, Bureau of the Census, *Negroes in the United States, 1920-32* (Washington, 1935), pp. 65–66, 839.
2. "Conditions changed fast for African-American railroad men," *Asheville Citizen-Times,* March 16, 2002.
3. Clinton D. Scott, "We did all kinds of tricks and nicks and nacks," *Paces,* Jan.–Feb. 2000.
4. *Louisville & Nashville Employes' Magazine,* July 1944, p. 21.
5. *Illinois Central Magazine,* Nov. 1938, p. 14.
6. *Norfolk and Western Magazine,* Dec. 1931, pp. 743–44; Oct. 1933, pp. 390–91; Dec. 1937, p. 609; Dec. 1938, p. 570; Scott, "We did all kinds of tricks."
7. *Illinois Central Magazine,* March 1929, p. 44.
8. *Norfolk and Western Magazine,* Sept. 1930, pp. 587–88, 643.
9. *Norfolk and Western Magazine,* Oct. 1933, p. 391.
10. *Norfolk and Western Magazine,* Oct. 1937, p. 441.
11. *Chesapeake and Ohio and Hocking Valley Employes' Magazine,* Oct. 1927, p. 8.
12. *Pullman News,* Oct. 1922, p. 172; Sept. 1924, p. 147; Sept. 1928, p. 157; Sept. 1929, p. 159.
13. *Norfolk and Western Magazine,* Dec. 1930, pp. 793–94.
14. *Norfolk and Western Magazine,* Dec. 1930, pp. 793–95, 814–15; Alfreda M. Duster, ed., *Crusade for Justice: The Autobiography of Ida B. Wells* (Chicago, 1970), pp. 18–20.
15. *Norfolk and Western Magazine,* Oct. 1931, pp. 570–74.

16. *Norfolk and Western Magazine*, Aug. 1934, pp. 275–77, 299–300; Oct. 1935, pp. 359–61; Sept. 1936, pp. 306–9, 344; Dec. 1938, pp. 546–47, 569–70. At least into the mid-1950s, the Veterans Association was still segregated. *Norfolk and Western Magazine*, Oct. 1956, pp. 604–7, 640.

17. *Louisville & Nashville Employes' Magazine*, Aug. 1935, pp. 2–4; Oct. 1935, pp. 9–11; July 1938, pp. 10–11; April 1941, pp. 10–11; Jan. 1946, p. 25; July 1946, pp. 10–11; Aug. 1947, p. 28.

18. *Missouri, Kansas & Texas Employes' Magazine*, Jan. 1916, p. 14; Oct. 1931, p. 35; *M-K-T Employees' Magazine*, Oct. 1954, p. 12; May 1956, p. 12.

19. Jackson McQuigg et al., *Central of Georgia Railway* (Mount Pleasant, S.C., 2004), p. 47.

20. *Louisville & Nashville Employes' Magazine*, July 1930, p. 58; Nov. 1925, p. 24; July 1938, p. 11.

21. Leon R. Harris, "The Railroads are Losing Negro Patronage," *Railway Progress*, Nov. 1950, p. 19.

22. *Missouri Pacific Lines Magazine*, July 1929, p. 75.

23. *Missouri Pacific Lines Magazine*, Aug. 1929, pp. 68–69.

24. *Illinois Central Magazine*, June 1930, p. 42; Aug. 1934, p. 10; March 1936, p. 15.

25. *Illinois Central Magazine*, March 1936, p. 15.

26. *Illinois Central Magazine*, April 1934, p. 6; Nov. 1936, p. 19.

27. *Louisville & Nashville Employes' Magazine*, Oct. 1949, p. 32; *Right Way Magazine*, Feb. 1925, p. 33; April 1928, p. 42; *Illinois Central Magazine*, July 1942, p. 40.

28. *Southern News Bulletin*, Oct. 1931, p. 6; *Chesapeake and Ohio and Hocking Valley Employes' Magazine*, Jan. 1928, p. 67; *Norfolk and Western Magazine*, July 1942, p. 364; *Louisville & Nashville Employes' Magazine*, July 1938, pp. 10–11.

29. *Illinois Central Magazine*, March 1929, p. 49; Oct. 1929, p. 38.

30. *Illinois Central Magazine*, April 1929, p. 11; July 1929, p. 24; Sept. 1933, p. 10; *Pullman News*, Oct. 1923, p. 166; Dec. 1929, p. 284.

31. *Missouri Pacific Lines Magazine*, Aug. 1929, p. 68; Sept. 1929, p. 71; Oct. 1929, pp. 78–79; Nov. 1929, pp. 80–81; Feb. 1930, p. 19.

32. *Santa Fe Magazine*, May 1924, p. 40; see Aug. 1920, p. 67, for a Topeka office porters' glee club.

33. *Missouri Pacific Lines Magazine*, 1920s–30s.

34. *The Pennsy*, Nov. 1955, p. 24; *Illinois Central Magazine*, Aug. 1943, p. 30.

35. *Illinois Central Magazine*, Feb. 1931, p. 25; July 1934, p. 18.

36. Melinda Chateauvert, *Marching Together: Women of the Brotherhood of Sleeping Car Porters* (Urbana, Ill., 1998), quote p. 138; Paula F. Pfeffer, "The Women Behind the Union: Halena Wilson, Rosina Tucker, and the Ladies' Auxiliary to the Brotherhood of Sleeping Car Porters," *Labor History* 36 (Fall 1995): 557–78.

37. *Decatur* (Ill.) *Daily Review*, April 25 1904, p. 5.

38. Katie Letcher Lyle, *Scalded to Death By the Steam: Authentic Stories of Railroad Disasters and the Ballads That Were Written About Them* (Chapel Hill, 1991), pp. 77–82.

39. *Right Way Magazine*, Sept. 1926, p. 42; June 1930, p. 18; *Illinois Central Magazine*, April 1929, p. 11.

40. *Illinois Central Magazine*, Oct. 1929, pp. 37–38; Sept. 1926, p. 20; Sept. 1928, p. 75.

41. *Illinois Central Magazine*, Aug. 1931, pp. 23–24; June 1931, p. 15.

42. *Illinois Central Magazine*, July 1935, p. 5.

43. Photographs MR2.9/SP9.1/1941/p10; MR2.9/SP9.1/1942/pp6–8, Minnesota Historical Society.

44. Photographs, author's collection.

45. *Illinois Central Magazine*, Sept. 1928, p. 75.

46. Based on *New York Age*, 1931–37.

47. *Atlantic Coast Line News*, June 1943, p. 5.

CHAPTER 14. "A GRACIOUS AND OBLIGING GENTLEMAN"

1. Eric Arnesen, *Brotherhoods of Color: Black Railroad Workers and the Struggle for Equality* (Cambridge, Mass., 2001), pp. 153–54; Stuart Leuthner, *The Railroaders* (New York, 1983), p. 53; *Negro Railway Labor News*, June–July 1948, p. 2.

2. Arnesen, *Brotherhoods of Color*, pp. 154–55.

3. Walter Licht, *Working For the Railroad: The Organization of Work in the Nineteenth Century* (Princeton, N.J., 1983), pp. 223–24; *Crisis*, July 1911, p. 98; *The Pennsy*, April 1954, pp. 1–3.

4. David D. Perata, *Those Pullman Blues: An Oral History of the African American Railroad Attendant* (Lanham, Md., 1996), p. 16.

5. Leuthner, *The Railroaders*, p. 54.
6. *Illinois Central Magazine*, Sept. 1946, pp. 6–7.
7. *The Pennsy*, April 1954, p. 3; Leuthner, *The Railroaders*, p. 54.
8. *The Pennsy*, April 1954, pp. 1–3.
9. *Baltimore and Ohio Employes Magazine*, Dec. 1916, p. 124.
10. Leuthner, *The Railroaders*, pp. 53, 55; *Illinois Central Magazine*, May 1940, pp. 11–12.
11. Leuthner, *The Railroaders*, p. 53.
12. *Illinois Central Magazine*, June 1930, p. 70; *Baltimore and Ohio Employes Magazine*, April 1937, p. 42.
13. *Baltimore and Ohio Employes Magazine*, Dec. 1916, pp. 124, 126.
14. *New York Times*, Jan. 5, 1985, p. 23.
15. *Illinois Central Magazine*, March 1931, p. 30.
16. Leuthner, *The Railroaders*, pp. 53–54.
17. Arnesen, *Brotherhoods of Color*, pp. 156–58.
18. Lillian Serece Williams, *Strangers in the Land of Paradise: The Creation of an African American Community, Buffalo, New York, 1900–1940* (Bloomington, Ind., 1999), p. 138.
19. Herbert R. Northrup, *Organized Labor and the Negro* (New York, 1944), pp. 82–87; Howard W. Risher, Jr., *The Negro in the Railroad Industry* (Philadelphia, 1971), pp. 52–53; Arnesen, *Brotherhoods of Color*, pp. 160–63.
20. Arnesen, *Brotherhoods of Color*, pp. 168–72.
21. Arnesen, *Brotherhoods of Color*, pp. 172–74; *Illinois Central Magazine*, Sept. 1946, pp. 6–7; H. E. Jones, Bureau of Information of the Eastern Railways, Circular Letter no. 2097-2(a), March 29, 1949, Red Cap agreement, Box 4, New York Central Papers, Syracuse University Library; Black quoted in Northrup, *Organized Labor*, p. 87.
22. Arnesen, *Brotherhoods of Color*, p. 175; *Negro Railway Labor News*, June–July 1948, p. 2; E. C. Johnson to J. F. Nash, April 24, 1963, NYC Press release, New York, April 18, 1963, R. D. Workman, LAUPT, to R. E. Dean, LaSalle Street Station, March 28, 1963, G. F. Ahrens, Union Terminal Co. [Dallas], March 21, 1963, C. J. Wallace, NOUPT, to R. E. Dean, March 21, 1963, file 543-2, New York Central Papers, Syracuse University Library; Leuthner, *The Railroaders*, p. 55.
23. *North Western Railway Magazine*, Feb. 1923, p. 14; Leuthner, *The Railroaders*, p. 53.
24. *Baltimore and Ohio Employes Magazine*, July 1916, pp. 83–84.
25. *Santa Fe Magazine*, July 1916, p. 77; *Baltimore and Ohio Employes Magazine*, July 1923, p. 13; *Louisville & Nashville Employes' Magazine*, Dec. 1937, p. 26.
26. *Louisville & Nashville Employes' Magazine*, March 1928, p. 88; *Reading Railroad Magazine*, Feb. 1954, p. 27.
27. *Chesapeake and Ohio and Hocking Valley Employes' Magazine*, June 1926, p. 38; *Louisville & Nashville Employes' Magazine*, March 1932, p. 24.
28. *Chesapeake and Ohio and Hocking Valley Employes' Magazine*, Sept. 1924, p. 50; *Norfolk and Western Magazine*, July 1942, p. 364; *Louisville & Nashville Employes' Magazine*, May 1928, p. 70; Oct. 1941, p. 35.
29. *Illinois Central Magazine*, Aug. 1926, p. 45.
30. *Chesapeake and Ohio and Hocking Valley Employes' Magazine*, April 1927, p. 50.
31. *Louisville & Nashville Employes' Magazine*, July 1930, p. 71; May 1936, p. 12.
32. *Rebel Route News*, March 15, 1941, p. 8.
33. *Illinois Central Magazine*, Feb. 1931, p. 8.

CHAPTER 15. "I PICK UP MY LIFE AND TAKE IT ON THE TRAIN"
1. http://www.artic.edu/artaccess/AA_AfAm/pages/AfAm_4.shtml#.
2. Elizabeth Hutton Turner, ed., *Jacob Lawrence: The Migration Series* (Washington, 1993).
3. Allan M. Gordon, *Echoes of Our Past: The Narrative Artistry of Palmer C. Hayden* (Los Angeles, 1988); Mary Schmidt Campbell, *Harlem Renaissance: Art of Black America* (New York, 1987); Samella Lewis, *Art: African American*, rev. ed. (Los Angeles, 1990).
4. Gail Gelburd, *A Graphic Odyssey: Romare Bearden as Printmaker* (Philadelphia, 1992), p. 12; Myron Schwartzman, *Romare Bearden: His Life and Art* (New York, 1990), pp. 20–24.
5. Gelburd, *A Graphic Odyssey*, pp. 79–80.
6. Richard J. Powell, "In My Family of Primitiveness and Tradition: William H. Johnson's *Jesus and the Three Marys*," *American Art* 5 (Fall 1991): 21.
7. *Black Art: Ancestral Legacy* (Dallas, 1989), pp. 122–23; Alvia J. Wardlaw, *The Art of John Biggers: View from the Upper Room* (New York, 1995), pp. 63, 108–11.

8. "Mark Anthony Priest: Artist's Statement," Looking At Painting (Kentucky Educational Television), www.ket.org/painting/priest.htm; "Women on the Railroad: Paintings by Mark Priest," press release and exhibition pamphlet, George Meany Center for Labor Studies, 1998.

9. "Steel-Drivin' Women," *Washington Post*, Aug. 13, 1998; "Women on the Railroad: Paintings by Mark Priest"; Mark Priest, "Memories on Track: Paintings of a Railway Artist," *Labor's Heritage* 6, no. 2 (Fall 1994): 32.

10. Joan R. Sherman, ed., *Collected Black Women's Poetry*, vol. 3 (New York, 1988), pp. 14–15.

11. Bessie Woodson Yancey, *Echoes from the Hills* (Washington, 1939), pp. 42–43.

12. Langston Hughes, "The Negro Artist and the Racial Mountain," *The Nation*, June 23, 1926, pp. 692–94.

13. Claude McKay, *Selected Poems of Claude McKay* (New York, 1953), p. 64.

14. Langston Hughes, *The Big Sea, An Autobiography* (New York, 1940), p. 23.

15. "Porter," in *The Collected Poems of Langston Hughes*, ed. Arnold Rampersad (New York, 1995), p. 169.

16. Langston Hughes, *One-Way Ticket* (New York, 1949), pp. 61–62.

17. Rampersad, *Collected Poems*, pp. 426–27.

18. Langston Hughes, *Shakespeare in Harlem* (New York, 1942), p. 37.

19. Langston Hughes, *The Weary Blues* (New York, 1926), p. 37.

20. Rampersad, *Collected Poems*, p. 72.

21. Rampersad, *Collected Poems*, p. 467.

22. Rampersad, *Collected Poems*, pp. 323–25.

23. Michael S. Harper, ed., *The Collected Poems of Sterling A. Brown* (New York, 1980), p. 92.

24. Sterling A. Brown, ed., *The Negro Caravan* (New York, 1941), pp. 381–82.

25. Harper, *Collected Poems*, pp. 206–7.

26. Harper, *Collected Poems*, pp. 208–12.

27. Harper, *Collected Poems*, p. 146.

28. Harper, *Collected Poems*, pp. 225–26.

29. Keith Gilyard and Anissa Janine Wardi, eds., *African American Literature* (New York, 2004), pp. 382–83.

30. Gilyard and Wardi, *African American Literature*, pp. 360–65.

31. Margaret Walker, *This is My Century: New and Collected Poems* (Athens, Ga., 1989), pp. 35–36.

32. Maya Angelou, *The Complete Collected Poems of Maya Angelou* (New York, 1994), p. 223.

33. Paul Vangelisti, ed., *Transbluesency: The Selected Poems of Amiri Baraka/LeRoi Jones, 1961-1995* (New York, 1995), pp. 235–37.

34. Linda Brown Bragg, *A Love Song to Black Men* (Detroit, 1974), p. 7.

35. Carolyn M. Rodgers, *how I got ovah: New and Selected Poems* (Garden City, N.Y., 1976), p. 32.

36. Claude McKay, *Home to Harlem* (New York, 1928), p. 239.

37. Lloyd L. Brown, *Iron City* (Boston, 1994 [c. 1951]), p. 161.

38. Albert Murray, *Train Whistle Guitar* (New York, 1974), pp. 8, 10.

39. Murray, *Train Whistle Guitar*, pp. 15–16, 20, 50, 64.

40. Murray, *Train Whistle Guitar*, p. 29.

41. Mary Ellen Snodgrass, *August Wilson: A Literary Companion* (Jefferson, N.C., 2004), pp. 164–65.

42. August Wilson, *The Piano Lesson* (New York, 1990), pp. 17–18, 85.

43. Wilson, *The Piano Lesson*, pp. 40, 55.

44. Wilson, *The Piano Lesson*, p. 86.

45. August Wilson, *Jitney* (Woodstock, N.Y., 2001).

46. August Wilson, *Two Trains Running* (New York, 1992), p 31.

CHAPTER 16. "HE KNOWS HIS PLACE"

1. "My Day," (Reno) *Nevada State Journal*, April 29, 1958, p. 4.

2. "Answer of Louisville & Nashville Railroad to Summary of Complaints Submitted with the Committee's Letter of August 30, 1943," attached to E. F. Jouett to President's Committee on Fair Employment Practice, Sept. 13, 1943, Louisville & Nashville Railroad, Legal Division Hearings, 1941–1946, FEPC, RG228, National Archives.

3. Quoted in David L. Lewis, *King: A Critical Biography* (New York, 1970), pp. 16–17.

4. *Central of Georgia Magazine*, June 1937, p. 6; *Pullman News*, Dec. 1924, p. 237.

5. For example, Pennsylvania Railroad employees: *The Pennsy*, July–Aug. 1955, p. 8.

6. *Rebel Route News*, March 15, 1941, p. 8; *Illinois Central Magazine*, Oct. 1931, p. 4; Oct. 1929, p. 66; April 1926, p. 20; Sept. 1928, p. 15; *Louisville & Nashville Employes' Magazine*, Nov. 1931, p. 45.

7. *Illinois Central Magazine*, May 1945, p. 4.

8. Series IV, Box 20, Predecessor and Subsidiary Railroads, Georgia Southern & Florida Railway, Norfolk Southern Railway Co. Papers, Atlanta History Center.

9. Reproduced in the *Louisville & Nashville Employes' Magazine*, Dec. 1927, p. 28.

10. Doug Wornom collection.

11. Entitled "On His Style" and "Off His Nut" (1888).

12. *Coon Yarns* (New York, 1903).

13. Ruth Carroll, *Chessie* (n.p., 1936).

14. New York, 1921.

15. New York, 1904.

16. New York, 1911.

17. New York, 1921.

18. New York, 1900.

19. New York, 1913.

20. William J. Simmons, *Men of Mark: Eminent, Progressive and Rising* (New York, 1968 [1887]), pp. 463–66; (Winnipeg) *Manitoba Daily Free Press*, Nov. 8, 1882, p. 6.

21. Michael Sznajderman and Leah Rawls Atkins, "William Benson and the Kowaliga School," *Alabama Heritage* (Spring 2005); *Railway Age Gazette*, June 13, 1913, p. 1342; Aug. 1, 1913, p. 211; Jan. 9, 1914, p. 102; *New York Times*, June 15, 1914.

22. James M. Brodie, *Created Equal: The Lives and Ideas of Black American Innovators* (New York, 1993), pp. 62–65, 103, 108; "Elijah McCoy," Norfolk Southern Corporation African American Railroader Month web page, www.nscorp.com/nscorphtml/aarm/mccoy.html.

23. Rayvon Fouche, *Black Inventors in the Age of Segregation* (Baltimore, 2003), pp. 27–81, 186–89, quotation on p. 78. See also Brodie, *Created Equal*, pp. 58–61; "Granville T. Woods," www.nscorp.com/nscorphtml/aarm/woods.html.

24. Portia James, *The Real McCoy: African American Invention 1619–1930* (Washington, 1989), p. 72.

25. Brodie, *Created Equal*, pp. 47–48; http://inventors.about.com/library/inventors/blbeard.htm.

26. African-American Inventors–Railroad/Transportation Industry, www.nscorp.com/nscorphtml/aarm/inventors/html.

27. Sterling D. Spero and Abram L. Harris, *The Black Worker* (New York, 1931), p. 285; Bureau of the Census, *Negroes in the United States: 1920–32* (Washington, 1935), Table 23, p. 303.

28. Malcolm Ross, *All Manner of Men* (New York, 1948), p. 122.

29. *Chesapeake and Ohio Employes' Magazine*, June 1923, p. 54; *Illinois Central Magazine*, June–July 1948, p. 8.

30. *Illinois Central Magazine*, March 1941, p. 48.

31. *Negro Railway Labor News*, Jan.–Feb. 1950, p. 4.

32. U.S. Department of Labor, Bureau of Labor Statistics, quoted in www.railserve.com/employment.html.

33. *Cleveland Advocate*, July 26, 1919, p. 8.

34. Eric Arnesen, *Brotherhoods of Color: Black Railroad Workers and the Struggle for Equality* (Cambridge, Mass., 2001), p. 248.

35. Arnesen, *Brotherhoods of Color*, pp. 249–50.

36. Isaac Thompson, interview, Nov. 24, 1998.

37. Isaac Thompson, interview, Nov. 24, 1998.

38. Abraham Thompson, interview, Nov. 24, 1998.

39. Stewart H. Bostic, interview, Nov. 23, 1998.

40. John P. Hankey, "Thinking Local," Trains, July 2007, p. 34.

EPILOGUE

1. Howard W. Risher, Jr., *The Negro in the Railroad Industry* (Philadelphia, 1971), pp. 85–86.

2. Risher, *Negro in the Railroad Industry*, pp. 96–97, 111–13.

3. Risher, *Negro in the Railroad Industry*, pp. 114–21.

4. Robert N. Cotton, L&N Oral History Project, University of Louisville, May 10, 1980, pp. 1–26.

5. John H. White, Jr., "Oh, To Be a Locomotive Engineer," Part 2, *Railroad History* 190 (Spring–Summer 2004): 73, 76.

6. Edward H. Blackwell, "There Aren't Any Nigger Engineers," *Trains*, Jan. 1971, p. 58.

7.   Interview, Ray Wongus, Oct. 7, 1998.

8.   Interview, Theola Barrett Campbell, Oct. 5, 2006.

9.   U.S. Equal Employment Opportunity Commission, 2003 EEO-1 Aggregate Report, NAICS Code 482–Rail Transportation, www.eeoc.gov/stats/jobpat/2003/naics3/482.html; "Meet Carlyle Smith, the Engineer Who Drove the President's Train, *Baltimore Sun*, Feb. 22, 2009.

10.   www.nscorp.com/nscorphtml/aarm.

11.   Associated Press report, furnished courtesy of John P. Hankey.

musical groups (employees), 349–51
Muscogee Railroad, 40–41

Nancy Hanks II, 260, 261, 262–63, 470–71
Nash, Rosetta, 226
Nashville, Chattanooga & St. Louis Railway, 305
National Alliance of Postal Employees, 205
National Association for the Advancement of Colored People, 245, 259–60, 263
National Railroad Adjustment Board, 150, 195, 200
National Railway Labor Relations Board, 202
Naylor, Eleanor, 435
Naylor, Mary, 435
Negro Railway Labor Executive Committee, 76
Nellons, William, 456
New Deal legislation, 75, 96, 194
New Orleans & Jackson Railroad, 22
New Orleans & North-eastern Railroad, 92–93
Newsome, James B., 124, 128
Newton, Eddie, 282
New York Central Railroad, 52, 55–56, 75, 101, 119, 123, 142–44, 146, 149, 157, 177, 202, 217, 218, 219, 220, 226, 291, 307, 311, 314–15, 318, 325, 386, 387, 433
New York & New England Railroad, 79
New York, New Haven & Hartford Railroad, 101, 153, 157, 178, 378
Nims, Frederick, 1–4, 7
Nix, A. W., 275–76
Nixon, Richard, 79, 153
Norfolk Southern Railway, 28, 34, 77, 208, 473
Norfolk & Western Magazine, 337–39
Norfolk & Western Railway, 39, 73, 79, 95, 97, 99, 161, 193, 255, 306, 308–10, 329, 337–39, 340, 341–44, 403
Norman, William, 389
North Carolina Corporation Commission, 244–46
North Carolina Railroad, 12, 23, 67, 68, 90, 171, 212
Northern Pacific Railway, 53, 358, 464

office porters, 132, 319–20
Olmsted, Frederick Law, 25, 26, 276
Olympian, 331
Oriental Limited, 220, 300–301, 324
Orleanean, 72

Osborne, Jim, 91
Owens, James, 113

Pacific Railway, 191–92
Parker, Little Junior, 294
Parker, Mitchell, 108
Patton, Charlie, 287, 291
Peeples, H. J., 250
Penniman, "Little Richard," 294
Pennsylvania Railroad (Pennsy), 52–53, 55, 101, 119, 123, 132–33, 152, 157, 158–59, 174, 175–77, 178, 182, 183, 192, 196–97, 202, 204, 214, 215, 218, 219, 220, 224–25, 226, 227, 229, 232, 247, 249, 256–57, 277, 304, 311, 313, 314, 317, 320, 322, 329, 341, 379, 380, 402, 425, 440, 445, 450, 457, 483, 539n25
Pensacola & Georgia Railroad, 21
Pere Marquette Railway, 477
Peters, James H. "Jim," 148
Philadelphia & Columbia Railroad, 379
Philadelphia & Reading Railway, 113, 170
Philadelphia, Wilmington & Baltimore Railroad, 14, 15, 138, 170, 212
Piedmont Railroad, 23
Pike, Jennie, 391
Pinkerton, Alan, 170–71
pioneers, 30–31, 40
Pittsburgh, Cincinnati, Chicago & St. Louis Railway, 196
Plessy v. Ferguson (1896), 242, 260, 263–64, 265
porter brakemen, 137, 195–96, 197–98, 200, 201, 209, 520n26; unions, 196–98, 200–201; wages, 195–98, 200–201
porterettes, 225, 448–49
porters. *See* business car porters; coach (train) porters; ferry porters; office porters; porter brakemen; Pullman porters; station porters; steamship porters
Portland Limited, 351
Powell, Adam Clayton, Jr., 262
Presley, Elvis, 294
Priest, Mark Anthony, 372, 414–15
Provisional Committee to Organize Colored Locomotive Firemen, 78
Pryor, Sandy, 39
Pulley, "Uncle" Dal, 447
Pullman, George Mortimer, 32, 114–15, 139–40. *See also* Pullman Company
Pullman barbers, 300

Pullman cars, 33, 152, 398. *See also* sleeping cars

Pullman Company, 93, 113, 114–17, 119–20, 128–30, 140, 153, 155–57, 241, 296, 307–8, 315, 342–43, 353, 450, 455, 490, 523n65; women, 212, 213, 216, 219–20, 222, 223, 229. *See also* Pullman porters

Pullman Employee Representation Plan, 116–17

Pullman News, 117, 120, 447

Pullman porters, 32, 113–30, 162, 163, 191, 192, 194–95, 324, 326–27, 329, 364–65, 366, 397, 398, 404–5, 416–17, 436, 449–52, 457–58; duties, 115–16; "George," 124–25; "ideal porters," 117–20; non-Pullman sleeping car porters, 490–91; passenger abuse, 124–25; physical labor, 128–29; tips, 126–27

Pullman valets, 331, 525n52

Queen, Clarence W., 440

racism, 4, 28, 60, 64, 167, 205–6, 367, 392–93, 445–61; advertising, 361, 366–67, 450–51; civil rights, 181–82, 457–58; convict lease, 43–48, 213; entrepreneurial barriers, 452–53; inventors, 453, 455–56; job ceilings, 69, 79, 122, 141–42, 158, 224, 229, 266, 305, 310–11, 333, 356, 392–93, 425–26, 435, 457, 458, 460–61; popular white culture, 360, 362, 364–65, 450–52; railroad employment practices, 40, 55, 69, 73–75, 92–94, 96–101, 114–15, 149, 156, 193–201, 217, 277, 314, 317, 320, 383–84, 387, 439, 487, 500, 508; railroad publications, 117, 120, 232, 233, 235, 313, 446–49; segregation, 237–65, 296, 299, 419, 470–71, 484, 494–95; unions, 303, 445–46

Railroad Bill (Morris Slater), 280–81

Railroad Labor Board, 96, 386

Railroad Safety Appliance Act, 88

Railway Labor Act, 73, 75, 96–97, 157

Railway Mail Association, 205–6

Railway Mail Service, 205

Railway Men's International Benevolent Industrial Association, 72–73

Railway Post Office clerks, 83, 191, 205–6, 375, 478–79

Raleigh & Gaston Railroad, 20–21, 61

Randolph, A. Philip, 75–76, 78, 117, 200, 228. *See also* Brotherhood of Sleeping Car Porters

Reading Railroad, 53, 55, 177–78, 202, 224, 316, 388, 400

Rebel, 194–95

Reconstruction, 32, 34, 35, 41, 42, 43, 44, 68, 171–72, 239–40

Red, Tampa, 289

Red Caps, 353, 377–91, 449–52, 485; advertisements, 449–52; duties, 381, 383; tips, 379–80, 387; uniforms, 387–88; unionization, 384, 385–87; wages, 384, 385–87

Redd, Thomas, 97–99

Reed, Ishmael, 421

Reed, James, 79–80

Reid, Lula, 391

Reparations lawsuits, x, 28

Reynolds, Humphrey H., 455

Richie, L. C., 125

Richmond & Danville Railroad, 23, 212, 310

Richmond, Fredericksburg & Potomac Railroad, 12, 23, 89–90, 212, 410–11

Richmond & Petersburg Railroad, 7, 26, 67

Rings, Estella, 442–43

Rivers, "Coffee," 78

Rockton & Rion Railway, 79

Rodgers, Carolyn M., 423

Rolinson, Murphy, 440

Roosevelt, Eleanor, 445

Roosevelt, Franklin D., 75, 76, 148, 440

Roper, Thomas, 24

Rose (slave of Frederick Nims), 1–4

Ross, "Aunt" Nettie, 322

roundhouse workers, 304–5, 309–15, 322, 338, 481

Rubardee, Ella, 434

Ruggles, David, 238

Rutland, Laura, 212

Sacramento Northern Railway, 203, 358

St. Louis–San Francisco Railway, 73, 100, 179, 198, 200, 206, 299, 241

Samuels, Les, 320

San Joaquin, 144

Sanders, John, 148

Saunders, Wallace "Wash," 281–82

Savannah, Albany & Gulf Railroad, 21

Savannah & Atlanta Railway, 468–69

Savannah, Florida & Western Railway, 83

Sawyer, Flossie, 440